Business Law Today: The Essentials

Selected Chapters for Los Angeles Pierce College

7th Edition

Roger LeRoy Miller
Gaylord A. Jentz

CENGAGE Learning™

Australia • Brazil • Japan • Korea • Mexico • Singapore • Spain • United Kingdom • United States

CENGAGE
Learning™

Business Law Today: The Essentials : Selected Chapters for Los Angeles Pierce College, 7th Edition

Miller/ Jentz

Executive Editors:
Michele Baird
Maureen Staudt
Michael Stranz

Project Development Manager:
Linda deStefano

Senior Marketing Coordinators:
Sara Mercurio
Lindsay Shapiro

Production/Manufacturing Manager:
Donna M. Brown

PreMedia Services Supervisor:
Rebecca A. Walker

Rights & Permissions Specialist:
Kalina Hintz

Cover Image:
Getty Images*

ISBN-13: 978-0-324-35508-6

ISBN-10: 0-324-35508-4

Cengage Learning
5191 Natorp Boulevard
Mason, Ohio 45040
USA

Cengage Learning is a leading provider of customized learning solutions with office locations around the globe, including Singapore, the United Kingdom, Australia, Mexico, Brazil, and Japan. Locate your local office at:
international.cengage.com/region

Cengage Learning products are represented in Canada by Nelson Education, Ltd.

For your lifelong learning solutions, visit **custom.cengage.com**

Visit our corporate website at **cengage.com**

Printed in the United States of America

Custom Contents

Part I

CHAPTER 1

The Historical and Constitutional Foundations

"The law is of as much interest
to the layman as it is to the lawyer."
Lord Balfour, 1848–1930
(British prime minister, 1902–1905)

CHAPTER OUTLINE

- SOURCES OF AMERICAN LAW
- THE COMMON LAW TRADITION
- CLASSIFICATIONS OF LAW
- THE CONSTITUTIONAL POWERS OF GOVERNMENT
- BUSINESS AND THE BILL OF RIGHTS
- DUE PROCESS AND EQUAL PROTECTION
- PRIVACY RIGHTS

LEARNING OBJECTIVES

After reading this chapter, you should be able to answer the following questions:

1. What is the common law tradition?
2. What is a precedent? When might a court depart from precedent?
3. What is the difference between remedies at law and remedies in equity?
4. What constitutional clause gives the federal government the power to regulate commercial activities among the various states?
5. What is the Bill of Rights? What freedoms are guaranteed by the First Amendment?

Lord Balfour's assertion in the quotation above emphasizes the underlying theme of every page in this book—that law is of interest to all persons, not just to lawyers. Those entering the world of business will find themselves subject to numerous laws and government regulations. A basic knowledge of these laws and regulations is beneficial—if not essential—to anyone contemplating a successful career in the business world of today.

There have been and will continue to be different definitions of law. Although the definitions vary in their particulars, they all are based on the general observation that, at a minimum, **law** consists of *enforceable rules governing relationships among individuals and between individuals and their society.* These "enforceable rules" may consist of unwritten principles of behavior established by a nomadic tribe. They may be set forth in an ancient or a contemporary law code. They may consist of

LAW
A body of enforceable rules governing relationships among individuals and between individuals and their society.

written laws and court decisions created by modern legislative and judicial bodies, as in the United States. Regardless of how such rules are created, they all have one thing in common: they establish rights, duties, and privileges that are consistent with the values and beliefs of their society or its ruling group. In the study of law, often referred to as **jurisprudence**, these broad statements provide a point of departure for all legal scholars and philosophers.

JURISPRUDENCE The science or philosophy of law.

In this introductory chapter, we first look at the basic sources of American law, the common law tradition, and some general classifications of law. We then examine some important constitutional concepts and clauses and their significance for business. The chapter concludes with a discussion of how fundamental freedoms guaranteed by the Constitution affect businesspersons and the workplace.

Sources of American Law

PRIMARY SOURCE OF LAW A document that establishes the law on a particular issue, such as a constitution, a statute, an administrative rule, or a court decision.

There are numerous sources of American law. **Primary sources of law,** or sources that establish the law, include the following:

1. The U.S. Constitution and the constitutions of the various states.
2. Statutes, or laws, passed by Congress and by state legislatures.
3. Regulations created by administrative agencies, such as the federal Food and Drug Administration.
4. Case law (court decisions).

We describe each of these important primary sources of law in the following pages. (See the appendix at the end of this chapter for a discussion of how to find statutes, regulations, and case law.)

SECONDARY SOURCE OF LAW A publication that summarizes or interprets the law, such as a legal encyclopedia, a legal treatise, or an article in a law review.

Secondary sources of law are books and articles that summarize and clarify the primary sources of law. Legal encyclopedias, compilations (such as *Restatements of the Law*, which summarize court decisions on a particular topic), official comments to statutes, treatises, articles in law reviews published by law schools, and articles in other legal journals are examples of secondary sources of law. Courts often refer to secondary sources of law for guidance in interpreting and applying the primary sources of law discussed here.

CONSTITUTIONAL LAW

The federal government and the states have separate written constitutions that set forth the general organization, powers, and limits of their respective governments. **Constitutional law** is the law as expressed in these constitutions.

CONSTITUTIONAL LAW The body of law derived from the U.S. Constitution and the constitutions of the various states.

The U.S. Constitution is the supreme law of the land. As such, it is the basis of all law in the United States. A law in violation of the Constitution, if challenged, will be declared unconstitutional and will not be enforced no matter what its source. Because of its paramount importance in the American legal system, we discuss the U.S. Constitution later in this chapter and present the complete text of the Constitution in Appendix A.

The Tenth Amendment to the U.S. Constitution reserves to the states all powers not granted to the federal government. Each state in the union has its own constitution. Unless it conflicts with the U.S. Constitution or a federal law, a state constitution is supreme within the state's borders.

Young students view the U.S. Constitution on display in Washington, D.C. Can a law be in violation of the Constitution and still be enforced? Why or why not? (Michael Evans/ Corbis Sygma)

Statutory Law

Statutes enacted by legislative bodies at any level of government make up another source of law, which is generally referred to as **statutory law.**

Federal Statutes Federal statutes are laws that are enacted by the U.S. Congress. Any federal statute that violates the U.S. Constitution will be held unconstitutional if it is challenged.

Federal statutes that affect business operations include laws regulating the purchase and sale of securities (corporate stocks and bonds—discussed in Chapter 21), consumer protection statutes (discussed in Chapter 13), and statutes prohibiting employment discrimination (discussed in Chapter 18). Whenever a particular statute is mentioned in this text, we usually provide a footnote showing its **citation** (a reference to a publication in which a legal authority—such as a statute or a court decision—or other source can be found). In the appendix following this chapter, we explain how you can use these citations to find statutory law.

State and Local Statutes and Ordinances State statutes are laws enacted by state legislatures. Any state law that is found to conflict with the U.S. Constitution, with federal laws enacted by Congress, or with the state's constitution will be declared invalid if challenged. Statutory law also includes the **ordinances** passed by cities and counties, none of which can violate the U.S. Constitution, the relevant state constitution, or federal or state laws.

State statutes include state criminal statutes (discussed in Chapter 6), state corporation statutes (discussed in Chapter 20), and state versions of the Uniform Commercial Code (to be discussed shortly). Local ordinances include zoning ordinances and local laws regulating housing construction and such things as the overall appearance of a community.

A federal statute, of course, applies to all states. A state statute, in contrast, applies only within the state's borders. State laws thus vary from state to state.

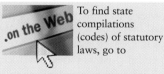

.on the Web To find state compilations (codes) of statutory laws, go to

http://findlaw.com/casecode/state.html.

STATUTORY LAW
The body of law enacted by legislative bodies (as opposed to constitutional law, administrative law, or case law).

CITATION
A reference to a publication in which a legal authority–such as a statute or a court decision–or other source can be found.

ORDINANCE
A regulation enacted by a city or county legislative body that becomes part of that state's statutory law.

Uniform Laws The differences among state laws were particularly notable in the 1800s, when conflicting state statutes frequently created problems for the rapidly developing trade and commerce among the states. To counter these problems, a group of legal scholars and lawyers formed the National Conference of Commissioners on Uniform State Laws (NCCUSL) in 1892 to draft uniform ("model") statutes for adoption by the states. The NCCUSL still exists today and continues to issue uniform statutes.

Each state has the option of adopting or rejecting a uniform law. *Only if a state legislature adopts a uniform law does that law become part of the statutory law of that state.* Note that a state legislature may adopt all or part of a uniform law as it is written, or the legislature may rewrite the law however the legislature wishes. Hence, even when a uniform law is said to have been adopted in many states, those states' laws may not be entirely "uniform."

The earliest uniform law, the Uniform Negotiable Instruments Law, was completed by 1896 and was adopted in every state by the early 1920s (although not all states used exactly the same wording). Over the following decades, other acts were drawn up in a similar manner. In all, over two hundred uniform acts have been on the Web You can find links to most uniform laws online at the Web site of the National Conference of Commissioners on Uniform State Laws. Go to

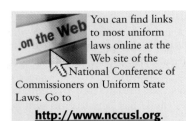

http://www.nccusl.org.

issued by the NCCUSL since its inception. The most ambitious uniform act of all, however, was the Uniform Commercial Code.

The Uniform Commercial Code (UCC) The Uniform Commercial Code (UCC), which was created through the joint efforts of the NCCUSL and the American Law Institute,[1] was first issued in 1952. The UCC has been adopted in all fifty states,[2] the District of Columbia, and the Virgin Islands. The UCC facilitates commerce among the states by providing a uniform, yet flexible, set of rules governing commercial transactions. The UCC assures businesspersons that their contracts, if validly entered into, normally will be enforced.

Because of its importance in the area of commercial law, we cite the UCC frequently in this text. We also present excerpts from the version of the UCC that is currently in effect in most states in Appendix B. (For a discussion of the creation of the UCC, see the *Landmark in the Law* in Chapter 11.)

ADMINISTRATIVE LAW

ADMINISTRATIVE LAW
The body of law created by administrative agencies (in the form of rules, regulations, orders, and decisions) in order to carry out their duties and responsibilities.

ADMINISTRATIVE AGENCY
A federal or state government agency established to perform a specific function. Administrative agencies are authorized by legislative acts to make and enforce rules to administer and enforce the acts.

EXECUTIVE AGENCY
An administrative agency within the executive branch of government. At the federal level, executive agencies are those within the cabinet departments.

INDEPENDENT REGULATORY AGENCY
An administrative agency that is not considered part of the government's executive branch and is not subject to the authority of the president. Independent agency officials cannot be removed without cause.

Another important source of American law is **administrative law,** which consists of the rules, orders, and decisions of administrative agencies. An **administrative agency** is a federal, state, or local government agency established to perform a specific function. Rules issued by various administrative agencies now affect virtually every aspect of a business's operation, including the firm's capital structure and financing, its hiring and firing procedures, its relations with employees and unions, and the way it manufactures and markets its products.

At the national level, numerous **executive agencies** exist within the cabinet departments of the executive branch. For example, the Food and Drug Administration is within the Department of Health and Human Services. Executive agencies are subject to the authority of the president, who has the power to appoint and remove officers of federal agencies. There are also major **independent regulatory agencies** at the federal level, including the Federal Trade Commission, the Securities and Exchange Commission, and the Federal Communications Commission. The president's power is less pronounced in regard to independent agencies, whose officers serve for fixed terms and cannot be removed without just cause.

There are administrative agencies at the state and local levels as well. Commonly, a state agency (such as a state pollution-control agency) is created as a parallel to a federal agency (such as the Environmental Protection Agency). Just as federal statutes take precedence over conflicting state statutes, so do federal agency regulations take precedence over conflicting state regulations. Because the rules of state and local agencies vary widely, we focus here exclusively on federal administrative law.

ENABLING LEGISLATION
A statute enacted by Congress that authorizes the creation of an administrative agency and specifies the name, composition, purpose, and powers of the agency being created.

Agency Creation Because Congress cannot possibly oversee the actual implementation of all the laws it enacts, it must delegate such tasks to others, particularly when the issues relate to highly technical areas, such as air and water pollution. Congress creates an administrative agency by enacting **enabling legislation,** which specifies the name, composition, purpose, and powers of the agency being created.

---

1. This institute was formed in the 1920s and consists of practicing attorneys, legal scholars, and judges.
2. Louisiana has adopted only Articles 1, 3, 4, 5, 7, 8, and 9.

ADJUDICATE
To render a judicial decision. In the administrative process, the proceeding in which an administrative law judge hears and decides issues that arise when an administrative agency charges a person or a firm with violating a law or regulation enforced by the agency.

ADMINISTRATIVE PROCESS
The procedure used by administrative agencies in the administration of law.

RULEMAKING
The process undertaken by an administrative agency when formally adopting a new regulation or amending an old one. Rulemaking involves notifying the public of a proposed rule or change and receiving and considering the public's comments.

.on the Web You can find proposed and final rules issued by administrative agencies by accessing the *Federal Register* online at **http://www.gpoaccess.gov/fr/index.html**.

■ EXAMPLE 1.1 The Federal Trade Commission (FTC) was created in 1914 by the Federal Trade Commission Act.[3] This act prohibits unfair and deceptive trade practices. It also describes the procedures the agency must follow to charge persons or organizations with violations of the act, and it provides for judicial review (review by the courts) of agency orders. Other portions of the act grant the agency powers to "make rules and regulations for the purpose of carrying out the Act," to conduct investigations of business practices, to obtain reports from interstate corporations concerning their business practices, to investigate possible violations of the act, to publish findings of its investigations, and to recommend new legislation. The act also empowers the FTC to hold trial-like hearings and to **adjudicate** (resolve judicially) certain kinds of trade disputes that involve FTC regulations. ■

Note that the FTC's grant of power incorporates functions associated with the legislative branch of government (rulemaking), the executive branch (investigation and enforcement), and the judicial branch (adjudication). Taken together, these functions constitute **administrative process,** which is the administration of law by administrative agencies.

Rulemaking One of the major functions of an administrative agency is **rulemaking**—creating or modifying rules, or regulations, pursuant to its enabling legislation. The Administrative Procedure Act[4] of 1946 imposes strict procedural requirements that agencies must follow in their rulemaking and other functions.

The most common rulemaking procedure involves three steps. First, the agency must give public notice of the proposed rulemaking proceedings, where and when the proceedings will be held, the agency's legal authority for the proceedings, and the terms or subject matter of the proposed rule. The notice must be published in the *Federal Register,* a daily publication of the U.S. government. Second, following this notice, the agency must allow ample time for interested parties to comment in writing on the proposed rule. After the comments have been received and reviewed, the agency takes them into consideration when drafting the final version of the regulation. The third and last step is the drafting of the final rule and its publication in the *Federal Register.* (See the appendix following this chapter for an explanation of how to find agency regulations.)

A suspicious stock transaction brought Martha Stewart to the attention of the Securities and Exchange Commission and resulted in criminal charges and sanctions, illustrating the investigation and enforcement powers of agencies. Should agencies have this much power? Why or why not? (EPA/Peter Foley)

Investigation and Enforcement Agencies have both investigatory and prosecutorial powers. An agency can request that individuals or organizations hand over specified books, papers, records, or other documents. In addition, agencies may conduct on-site inspections, although a search warrant is normally required for such inspections. Sometimes, a search of a home, an office, or a factory is the only means of obtaining evidence needed to prove a regulatory violation. Agencies investigate a wide range of activities, including coal mining, automobile manufacturing, and the industrial discharge of pollutants into the environment.

Adjudication After conducting its own investigation of a suspected rule violation, an agency may decide to take action against a specific party. The action may involve

3. 15 U.S.C. Sections 45–58.
4. 5 U.S.C. Sections 551–706.

ADMINISTRATIVE LAW JUDGE (ALJ) One who presides over an administrative agency hearing and has the power to administer oaths, take testimony, rule on questions of evidence, and make determinations of fact.

a trial-like hearing before an **administrative law judge (ALJ)**. The ALJ may compel the charged party to pay a fine or may prohibit the party from carrying on some specified activity. Either side may appeal the ALJ's decision to the commission or board that governs the agency. If the party fails to get relief there, appeal can be made to a federal court.

Case Law and Common Law Doctrines

CASE LAW The rules of law announced in court decisions. Case law includes the aggregate of reported cases that interpret judicial precedents, statutes, regulations, and constitutional provisions.

The rules of law announced in court decisions constitute another basic source of American law. These rules of law include interpretations of constitutional provisions, of statutes enacted by legislatures, and of regulations created by administrative agencies. Today, this body of judge-made law is referred to as **case law,** or the *common law.* The common law—the doctrines and principles embodied in case law—governs all areas not covered by statutory law or administrative law. Because of the importance of the common law in our legal system, we look at the origins and characteristics of the common law tradition in some detail in the pages that follow.

The Common Law Tradition

Because of our colonial heritage, much of American law is based on the English legal system. A knowledge of this tradition is crucial to understanding our legal system today because judges in the United States still apply common law principles when deciding cases.

Early English Courts

COMMON LAW That body of law developed from custom or judicial decisions in English and U.S. courts, not attributable to a legislature.

After the Normans conquered England in 1066, William the Conqueror and his successors began the process of unifying the country under their rule. One of the means they used to do this was the establishment of the king's courts, or *curiae regis.* Before the Norman Conquest, disputes had been settled according to the local legal customs and traditions in various regions of the country. The king's courts sought to establish a uniform set of rules for the country as a whole. What evolved in these courts was the beginning of the **common law**—a body of general rules that applied throughout the entire English realm. Eventually, the common law tradition became part of the heritage of all nations that were once British colonies, including the United States.

PRECEDENT A court decision that furnishes an example or authority for deciding subsequent cases involving identical or similar facts.

Courts developed the common law rules from the principles underlying judges' decisions in actual legal controversies. Judges attempted to be consistent, and whenever possible, they based their decisions on the principles suggested by earlier cases. They sought to decide similar cases in a similar way and considered new cases with care, because they knew that their decisions would make new law. Each interpretation became part of the law on the subject and served as a legal **precedent**—that is, a decision that furnished an example or authority for deciding subsequent cases involving similar legal principles or facts.

In the early years of the common law, there was no single place or publication where court opinions, or written decisions, could be found. Beginning in the late thirteenth and early fourteenth centuries, however, each year portions of significant decisions of that year were gathered together and recorded in *Year Books.* The *Year Books* were useful references for lawyers and judges. In the sixteenth century, the *Year Books* were discontinued, and other reports of cases became available. (See the

The court of chancery in the reign of King George I. Early English court decisions formed the basis of what type of law? (From a painting by Benjamin Ferrers in the National Portrait Gallery, Photo Corbis Bettmann)

appendix following this chapter for a discussion of how cases are reported, or published, in the United States today.)

STARE DECISIS

The practice of deciding new cases with reference to former decisions, or precedents, eventually became a cornerstone of the English and American judicial systems. The practice forms a doctrine called ***stare decisis***[5] ("to stand on decided cases").

The Importance of Precedents in Judicial Decision Making The doctrine of *stare decisis* means that once a court has set forth a principle of law as being applicable to a certain set of facts, that court and courts of lower rank must adhere to that principle and apply it in future cases involving similar fact patterns.

■ EXAMPLE 1.2 Suppose that the lower state courts in California have reached conflicting conclusions on whether drivers are liable for accidents they cause while merging into freeway traffic, even though the drivers looked and did not see any oncoming traffic and even though witnesses (passengers in their cars) testified to that effect. To settle the law on this issue, the California Supreme Court decides to review a case involving this fact pattern. The court rules that in such a situation, the driver who is merging into traffic is liable for any accidents caused by the driver's failure to yield to freeway traffic—even if the driver looked carefully and did not see an approaching vehicle. The California Supreme Court's decision on the matter will influence the outcome of all future cases on this issue brought before the California state courts. ■ Similarly, a decision on a given issue by the United States Supreme Court (the nation's highest court) is binding on all other courts.

STARE DECISIS
A common law doctrine under which judges are obligated to follow the precedents established in prior decisions.

BINDING AUTHORITY
Any source of law that a court must follow when deciding a case. Binding authorities include constitutions, statutes, and regulations that govern the issue being decided, as well as court decisions that are controlling precedents within the jurisdiction.

Controlling precedents in a *jurisdiction* (an area in which a court or courts have the power to apply the law—see Chapter 3) are referred to as binding authorities. A **binding authority** is any source of law that a court must follow when deciding a case. Binding authorities include constitutions, statutes, and regulations that govern the issue being decided, as well as court decisions that are controlling precedents within the jurisdiction. Is a case precedent decided in 1875 still binding? For the answer to this question, see this chapter's *Letter of the Law* feature on the following page.

***Stare Decisis* and Legal Stability** The doctrine of *stare decisis* helps the courts to be more efficient, because if other courts have carefully reasoned through a similar case, their legal reasoning and opinions can serve as guides. *Stare decisis* also makes the law more stable and predictable. If the law on a given subject is well settled, someone bringing a case to court can usually rely on the court to make a decision based on what the law has been.

Departures from Precedent Although courts are obligated to follow precedents, sometimes a court will depart from the rule of precedent if it decides that a given precedent should no longer be followed. If a court decides that a precedent is simply incorrect or that technological or social changes have rendered the precedent inapplicable, the court might rule contrary to the precedent. Cases that overturn precedent often receive a great deal of publicity.

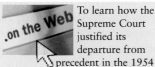

.on the Web To learn how the Supreme Court justified its departure from precedent in the 1954 *Brown* decision, you can access the Court's opinion online by going to

http://findlaw.com/casecode/supreme.html

and entering "347 U.S. 483" in the "Citation Search" box.

5. Pronounced *ster*-ay dih-*si*-ses.

LETTER OF THE LAW Is an 1875 Case Precedent Still Binding?

In a suit against the U.S. government for breach of contract, Boris Korczak sought compensation for services that he had allegedly performed for the Central Intelligence Agency (CIA) from 1973 to 1980. Korczak claimed that the government had failed to pay him an annuity and other compensation required by a secret *oral* agreement he had made with the CIA. The federal trial court dismissed Korczak's claim, and Korczak appealed the decision to the U.S. Court of Appeals for the Federal Circuit.

At issue on appeal was whether a Supreme Court case decided in 1875, *Totten v. United States,*[a] remained the controlling precedent in this area. In the *Totten* case, the plaintiff alleged that he had formed a secret contract with President Lincoln to collect information on the Confederate army during the Civil War. When the plaintiff sued the government for compensation for his services, the Supreme Court held that the agreement was unenforceable. According to the Court, to enforce such agreements could result in the disclosure of information that "might compromise or embarrass our government" or cause other "serious detriment" to the public. In Korczak's case, the federal appellate court held that the *Totten* case precedent was still "good law," and therefore Korczak, like the plaintiff in *Totten,* could not recover compensation for his services. Said the court, "*Totten,* despite its age, is the last pronouncement on this issue by the Supreme Court. . . . We are duty bound to follow the law given us by the Supreme Court unless and until it is changed."[b]

THE BOTTOM LINE

Supreme Court precedents, no matter how old, remain controlling until they are overruled by a subsequent decision of the Supreme Court, by a constitutional amendment, or by congressional legislation.

a. 92 U.S. 105 (1875).

b. *Korczak v. United States,* 124 F.3d 227 (Fed.Cir. 1997).

■ EXAMPLE 1.3 In *Brown v. Board of Education of Topeka,*[6] the United States Supreme Court expressly overturned precedent when it concluded that separate educational facilities for whites and blacks, which had been upheld as constitutional in numerous previous cases,[7] were inherently unequal. The Supreme Court's departure from precedent in *Brown* received a tremendous amount of publicity as people began to realize the ramifications of this change in the law. ■

When There Is No Precedent At times, courts hear cases for which there are no precedents within their jurisdictions on which to base their decisions. When hearing such cases, called "cases of first impression," courts often look to precedents set in other jurisdictions for guidance. Precedents from other jurisdictions, because they are not binding on the court, are referred to as **persuasive authorities.** A court may also consider a number of factors, including legal principles and policies underlying previous court decisions or existing statutes, fairness, social values and customs, public policy, and data and concepts drawn from the social sciences.

PERSUASIVE AUTHORITY
Any legal authority or source of law that a court may look to for guidance but on which it need not rely in making its decision. Persuasive authorities include cases from other jurisdictions and secondary sources of law.

ETHICAL ISSUE 1.1

Should the Supreme Court look to other nations' laws for guidance? Over the last several years, justices on the United States Supreme Court have exhibited an increasing tendency to consider foreign law when deciding issues of national importance. For example, in 2003—for the first time ever—a majority opinion of the Supreme

6. 347 U.S. 483, 74 S.Ct. 686, 98 L.Ed. 873 (1954). See the appendix following this chapter for an explanation of how to read legal citations.

7. See *Plessy v. Ferguson,* 163 U.S. 537, 16 S.Ct. 1138, 41 L.Ed. 256 (1896).

Court cited foreign law (references to foreign law have appeared in footnotes and dissents on a few occasions in the past). The citation occurred in a controversial case in which the Court struck down laws that prohibit oral and anal sex between consenting adults of the same gender. In the majority opinion (an opinion that the majority of justices have signed), Justice Anthony Kennedy mentioned that the European Court of Human Rights and other foreign courts have consistently acknowledged that homosexuals have a right "to engage in intimate, consensual conduct."[8] This comment sparked debate in legal circles over whether the Supreme Court, or other U.S. courts, should ever consider world opinion or cite foreign law as persuasive authority. The practice has many critics, including Justice Antonin Scalia, who believes that foreign views are irrelevant to rulings on U.S. law. Several of the Supreme Court justices, however, believe that in our increasingly global community we should not ignore the opinions of courts in the rest of the world. ■

EQUITABLE REMEDIES AND COURTS OF EQUITY

REMEDY
The relief given to an innocent party to enforce a right or compensate for the violation of a right.

A **remedy** is the means given to a party to enforce a right or to compensate for the violation of a right. ■ EXAMPLE 1.4 Suppose that Shem is injured because of Rowan's wrongdoing. A court may order Rowan to compensate Shem for the harm by paying Shem a certain amount of money. ■

In the early king's courts of England, the kinds of remedies that could be granted were severely restricted. If one person wronged another, the king's courts could award as compensation either money or property, including land. These courts became known as *courts of law,* and the remedies were called *remedies at law.* Even though this system introduced uniformity in the settling of disputes, when plaintiffs wanted a remedy other than economic compensation, the courts of law could do nothing, so "no remedy, no right."

Remedies in Equity *Equity* refers to a branch of the law, founded in justice and fair dealing, that seeks to supply a fair and adequate remedy when no remedy is available at law. In medieval England, when individuals could not obtain an adequate remedy in a court of law, they petitioned the king for relief. Most of these petitions were decided by an adviser to the king called the *chancellor.* The chancellor was said to be the "keeper of the king's conscience." When the chancellor thought that the claim was a fair one, new and unique remedies were granted. In this way, a new body of rules and remedies came into being, and eventually formal *chancery courts,* or *courts of equity,* were established. The remedies granted by these courts were called *remedies in equity.* Thus, two distinct court systems were created, each having a different set of judges and a different set of remedies.

PLAINTIFF
One who initiates a lawsuit.

DEFENDANT
One against whom a lawsuit is brought; the accused person in a criminal proceeding.

Plaintiffs (those bringing lawsuits) had to specify whether they were bringing an "action at law" or an "action in equity," and they chose their courts accordingly. ■ EXAMPLE 1.5 A plaintiff might ask a court of equity to order a **defendant** (a person against whom a lawsuit is brought) to perform within the terms of a contract. A court of law could not issue such an order, because its remedies were limited to payment of money or property as compensation for damages. A court of equity, however, could issue a decree for *specific performance*—an order to perform what was

8. *Lawrence v. Texas,* 539 U.S. 558, 123 S.Ct. 2472, 156 L.Ed.2d 508 (2003). Other cases in which the Supreme Court has referenced foreign law include *Grutter v. Bollinger,* 539 U.S. 306, 123 S.Ct. 2325, 156 L.Ed.2d 304 (2003), in the dissent; and *Atkins v. Virginia,* 536 U.S. 304, 122 S.Ct. 2242, 153 L.Ed.2d 335 (2002), in footnote 21 to the majority opinion.

promised. A court of equity could also issue an *injunction,* directing a party to do or refrain from doing a particular act. In certain cases, a court of equity could allow for the *rescission* (cancellation) of the contract so that the parties would be returned to the positions that they held prior to the contract's formation. ■ Equitable remedies will be discussed in greater detail in Chapter 9.

REMEMBER Even though, in most states, courts of law and equity have merged, the principles of equity still apply.

The Merging of Law and Equity Today, in most states the courts of law and equity have merged, and thus the distinction between the two courts has largely disappeared. A plaintiff may now request both legal and equitable remedies in the same action, and the trial court judge may grant either form—or both forms—of relief. The merging of law and equity, however, does not diminish the importance of distinguishing legal remedies from equitable remedies. To request the proper remedy, a businessperson (or her or his attorney) must know what remedies are available for the specific kinds of harms suffered. Today, as a rule, courts will grant an equitable remedy only when the remedy at law (money damages) is inadequate. Exhibit 1–1 summarizes the procedural differences (applicable in most states) between an action at law and an action in equity.

EQUITABLE PRINCIPLES AND MAXIMS General propositions or principles of law that have to do with fairness (equity).

Equitable Principles and Maxims Over time, a number of **equitable principles and maxims** evolved that have since guided the courts in deciding whether plaintiffs should be granted equitable relief. Because of their importance, both historically and in our judicial system today, these principles and maxims are set forth in this chapter's *Landmark in the Law* feature.

Classifications of Law

SUBSTANTIVE LAW Law that defines, describes, regulates, and creates legal rights and obligations.

PROCEDURAL LAW Law that establishes the methods of enforcing the rights established by substantive law.

CYBERLAW An informal term used to refer to all laws governing electronic communications and transactions, particularly those conducted via the Internet.

The huge body of the law may be broken down according to several classification systems. For example, one classification system divides law into **substantive law** (all laws that define, describe, regulate, and create legal rights and obligations) and **procedural law** (all laws that establish the methods of enforcing the rights established by substantive law). Other classification systems divide law into federal law and state law or private law (dealing with relationships between persons) and public law (addressing the relationship between persons and their governments).

Frequently, people use the term **cyberlaw** to refer to the emerging body of law that governs transactions conducted via the Internet. Cyberlaw is not really a classification of law, nor is it a new *type* of law. Rather, it is an informal term used to describe traditional legal principles that have been modified and adapted to fit situations that are unique to the online world. Of course, in some areas new statutes have been

EXHIBIT 1–1 PROCEDURAL DIFFERENCES BETWEEN AN ACTION AT LAW AND AN ACTION IN EQUITY

PROCEDURE	ACTION AT LAW	ACTION IN EQUITY
Initiation of lawsuit	By filing a complaint	By filing a petition
Decision	By jury or judge	By judge (no jury)
Result	Judgment	Decree
Remedy	Monetary damages	Injunction, specific performance, or rescission

LANDMARK IN THE LAW

Equitable Principles and Maxims

In medieval England, courts of equity had the responsibility of using discretion in supplementing the common law. Even today, when the same court can award both legal and equitable remedies, it must exercise discretion. Courts often invoke equitable principles and maxims when making their decisions. Here are some of the most significant equitable principles and maxims:

1. *Whoever seeks equity must do equity.* (Anyone who wishes to be treated fairly must treat others fairly.)
2. *Where there is equal equity, the law must prevail.* (The law will determine the outcome of a controversy in which the merits of both sides are equal.)
3. *One seeking the aid of an equity court must come to the court with clean hands.* (Plaintiffs must have acted fairly and honestly.)
4. *Equity will not suffer a wrong to be without a remedy.* (Equitable relief will be awarded when there is a right to relief and there is no adequate remedy at law.)
5. *Equity regards substance rather than form.* (Equity is more concerned with fairness and justice than with legal technicalities.)
6. *Equity aids the vigilant, not those who rest on their rights.* (Equity will not help those who neglect their rights for an unreasonable period of time.)

The last maxim has become known as the *equitable doctrine of laches.* The doctrine arose to encourage people to bring lawsuits while the evidence was fresh; if they failed to do so, they would not be allowed to bring a lawsuit. What constitutes a reasonable time, of course, varies according to the circumstances of the case. Time periods for different types of cases are now usually fixed by **statutes of limitations.** After the time allowed under a statute of limitations has expired, no action can be brought, no matter how strong the case was originally.

STATUTE OF LIMITATIONS
A federal or state statute setting the maximum time period during which a certain action can be brought or certain rights enforced.

APPLICATION TO TODAY'S WORLD

The equitable maxims listed above underlie many of the legal rules and principles that are commonly applied by the courts today—and that you will read about in this book. For example, in Chapter 7 you will read about the doctrine of promissory estoppel. *Under this doctrine, a person who has reasonably and substantially relied on the promise of another may be able to obtain some measure of recovery, even though no enforceable contract, or agreement, exists. The court will* estop *(bar, or impede) the one making the promise from asserting the lack of a valid contract as a defense. The rationale underlying the doctrine of promissory estoppel is similar to that expressed in the fourth and fifth maxims above.*

RELEVANT WEB SITES

To locate information on the Web concerning equitable principles, *go to this text's Web site at* **http://blt.westbuslaw.com**, *select "Chapter 1," and click on "URLs for Landmarks."*

enacted, at both the federal and state levels, to cover specific types of problems stemming from online communications. Throughout this book, you will read how the law in a given area is evolving to govern specific legal issues that arise in the online context.

Civil Law and Criminal Law

CIVIL LAW
The branch of law dealing with the definition and enforcement of all private or public rights, as opposed to criminal matters.

Civil law spells out the rights and duties that exist between persons and between persons and their governments, and the relief available when a person's rights are violated. Typically, in a civil case, a private party sues another private party (although the government can also sue a party for a civil law violation) to make that other party comply with a duty or pay for the damage caused by the failure to comply with a duty. Much of the law that we discuss in this text is civil law. Contract law, for example, which we discuss in Chapters 7 through 10, is civil law. The whole body of tort law (see Chapter 4) is civil law.

CRIMINAL LAW
Law that defines and governs actions that constitute crimes. Generally, criminal law has to do with wrongful actions committed against society for which society demands redress.

Criminal law has to do with wrongs committed against society for which society demands redress. Criminal acts are proscribed by local, state, or federal government statutes. Thus, criminal defendants are prosecuted by public officials, such as a district attorney (D.A.), on behalf of the state, not by their victims or other private parties. Whereas in a civil case the object is to obtain remedies (such as money damages) to compensate the injured party, in a criminal case the object is to punish the wrongdoer and to deter others from similar actions. Penalties for violations of criminal statutes consist of fines and/or imprisonment—and, in some cases, death. We will discuss the differences between civil and criminal law in greater detail in Chapter 6.

National and International Law

.on the Web The Library of Congress offers extensive information on national and international law at **http://www.loc.gov**.

NATIONAL LAW
Law that pertains to a particular nation (as opposed to international law).

INTERNATIONAL LAW
The law that governs relations among nations. National laws, customs, treaties, and international conferences and organizations are generally considered to be the most important sources of international law.

The law of a particular nation, such as the United States or Sweden, is **national law.** National law, of course, varies from country to country because each country's law reflects the interests, customs, activities, and values that are unique to that nation's culture. Even though the laws and legal systems of various countries differ substantially, broad similarities do exist.

In contrast to national law, international law applies to more than one nation. **International law** can be defined as a body of written and unwritten laws observed by independent nations and governing the acts of individuals as well as governments. International law is an intermingling of rules and constraints derived from a variety of sources, including the laws of individual nations, the customs that have evolved among nations in their relations with one another, and treaties and international organizations. In essence, international law is the result of centuries-old attempts to reconcile the traditional need of each nation to be the final authority over its own affairs with the desire of nations to benefit economically from trade and harmonious relations with one another.

The key difference between national law and international law is that national law can be enforced by government authorities. If a nation violates an international law, however, the most that other countries or international organizations can do (if persuasive tactics fail) is to resort to coercive actions against the violating nation. Coercive actions range from the severance of diplomatic relations and boycotts to, at the last resort, war. We examine the laws governing international business transactions in Chapter 25.

The Constitutional Powers of Government

Laws that govern business have their origin in the lawmaking authority granted by the U.S. Constitution, which is the supreme law in this country. As mentioned earlier in this chapter, neither Congress nor any state can enact a law that is in conflict with the Constitution.

FEDERAL FORM OF GOVERNMENT
A system of government in which the states form a union and the sovereign power is divided between the central government and the member states.

The U.S. Constitution created a **federal form of government** in which the national government and the states *share* sovereign power. The Constitution sets forth specific powers that can be exercised by the national government and provides that the national government has the implied power to undertake actions necessary to carry out its expressly designated powers. All other powers are "reserved" to the states. The broad language of the Constitution, though, has left much room for debate over the specific nature and scope of these powers. Generally, it has been the task of the courts to determine where the boundary line between state and national powers should lie—and that line changes over time.

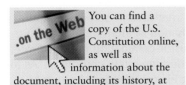

.on the Web You can find a copy of the U.S. Constitution online, as well as information about the document, including its history, at **http://www.constitutioncenter.org**.

THE COMMERCE CLAUSE

To prevent states from establishing laws and regulations that would interfere with trade and commerce among the states, the Constitution expressly delegated to the national government the power to regulate interstate commerce. Article I, Section 8, of the U.S. Constitution expressly permits Congress "[t]o regulate Commerce with foreign Nations, and among the several States, and with the Indian Tribes." This clause, referred to as the **commerce clause,** has had a greater impact on business than any other provision in the Constitution.

COMMERCE CLAUSE
The provision in Article I, Section 8, of the U.S. Constitution that gives Congress the power to regulate interstate commerce.

For some time, the commerce power was interpreted as being limited to *interstate* commerce (commerce among the states) and not applicable to *intrastate* commerce (commerce within a state). In 1824, however, in *Gibbons v. Ogden*,[9] the United States Supreme Court held that commerce within a state could also be regulated by the national government as long as the commerce *substantially affected* commerce involving more than one state.

The Commerce Clause and the Expansion of National Powers As the nation grew and faced new kinds of problems, the commerce clause became a vehicle for the additional expansion of the national government's regulatory powers. Even activities that seemed purely local came under the regulatory reach of the national government if those activities were deemed to substantially affect interstate commerce. ■ **EXAMPLE 1.6** In 1942, in *Wickard v. Filburn*,[10] the Supreme Court held that wheat production by an individual farmer intended wholly for consumption on his own farm was subject to federal regulation. The Court reasoned that the home consumption of wheat reduced the demand for wheat and thus could have a substantial effect on interstate commerce. ■

The landmark case on the next page involved a challenge to the scope of the national government's constitutional authority to regulate local activities.

---

9. 22 U.S. (9 Wheat.) 1, 6 L.Ed. 23 (1824).
10. 317 U.S. 111, 63 S.Ct. 82, 87 L.Ed. 122 (1942).

LANDMARK AND CLASSIC CASES

CASE 1.1 Heart of Atlanta Motel v. United States

Supreme Court of the United States, 1964.
379 U.S. 241,
85 S.Ct. 348,
13 L.Ed.2d 258.
http://supct.law.cornell.edu/supct/cases/name.htm[a]

HISTORICAL AND SOCIAL SETTING *In the first half of the twentieth century, state governments sanctioned segregation on the basis of race. In 1954, the United States Supreme Court decided that racially segregated school systems violated the Constitution. In the following decade, the Court ordered an end to racial segregation imposed by the states in other public facilities, such as beaches, golf courses, buses, parks, auditoriums, and courtroom seating. Privately owned facilities that excluded or segregated African Americans and others on the basis of race were not subject to the same constitutional restrictions, however. Congress passed the Civil Rights Act of 1964 to prohibit racial discrimination in "establishments affecting interstate commerce." These facilities included "places of public accommodation."*

FACTS The owner of the Heart of Atlanta Motel, in violation of the Civil Rights Act of 1964, refused to rent rooms to African Americans. The motel owner brought an action in a federal district court to have the Civil Rights Act declared unconstitutional, alleging that Congress had exceeded its constitutional authority to regulate commerce by enacting the act. The owner argued that his motel was not engaged in interstate commerce but was "of a purely local character." The motel, however, was accessible to state and interstate highways. The owner advertised nationally, maintained billboards throughout the state, and accepted convention trade from outside the state (75 percent of the guests were residents of other states). The court ruled that the act did not violate the Constitution and enjoined (prohibited) the owner from discriminating on the basis of race. The owner appealed. The case ultimately went to the United States Supreme Court.

a. This is the "Historic Supreme Court Decisions—by Party Name" page within the "Caselists" collection of the Legal Information Institute available at its site on the Web. Click on the "H" link or scroll down the list of cases to the entry for the *Heart of Atlanta* case. Click on the case name. When the link opens, click on one of the choices to read the "Syllabus," the "Full Decision," or the "Edited Decision."

ISSUE Did Congress exceed its constitutional power to regulate interstate commerce by enacting the Civil Rights Act of 1964?

DECISION No. The United States Supreme Court upheld the constitutionality of the act.

REASON The Court noted that the act was passed to correct "the deprivation of personal dignity" accompanying the denial of equal access to "public establishments." Testimony before Congress leading to the passage of the act indicated that African Americans in particular experienced substantial discrimination in attempting to secure lodging while traveling. This discrimination impeded interstate travel and thus impeded interstate commerce. As for the owner's argument that his motel was "of a purely local character," the Court said that even if this was true, the motel affected interstate commerce. According to the Court, "if it is interstate commerce that feels the pinch, it does not matter how local the operation that applies the squeeze." Therefore, under the commerce clause, "the power of Congress to promote interstate commerce also includes the power to regulate the local incidents thereof, including local activities."

COMMENTS *If the United States Supreme Court had invalidated the Civil Rights Act of 1964, the legal landscape of the United States would be much different today. The act prohibits discrimination based on race, color, national origin, religion, or gender in all "public accommodations," including hotels and restaurants. The act also prohibits discrimination in employment based on these criteria. Although state laws now prohibit many of these forms of discrimination as well, the protections available vary from state to state—and it is not certain when (and if) such laws would have been passed had the 1964 federal Civil Rights Act been deemed unconstitutional.*

RELEVANT WEB SITES *To locate information on the Web concerning the* Heart of Atlanta Motel *case, go to this text's Web site at* **http://blt.westbuslaw.com**, *select "Chapter 1," and click on "URLs for Landmarks."*

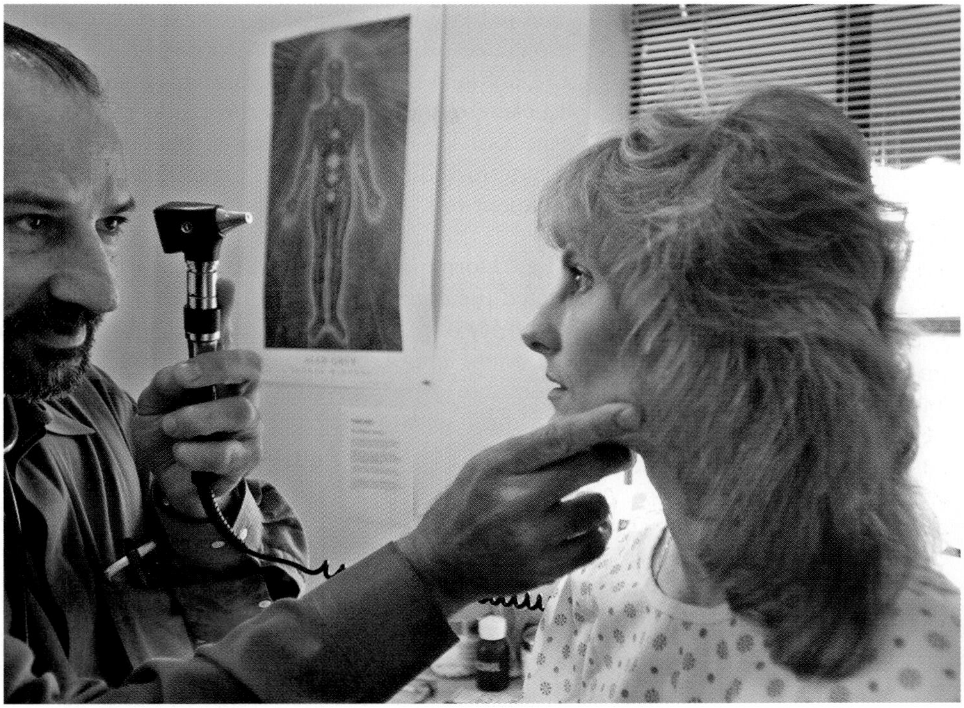

A physician examines the eyes of a woman who suffers from a brain tumor. The woman was partially paralyzed on the right side of her body until she started smoking marijuana. A significant issue today is whether the federal government can use its power under the commerce clause to prohibit the use of medical marijuana within a state's borders. Should the legality of using marijuana for medical purposes be determined by the federal government or by individual states? (AP Photo/Ben Margot)

The Commerce Power Today Today, at least theoretically, the power over commerce authorizes the national government to regulate every commercial enterprise in the United States. Federal (national) legislation governs virtually every major activity conducted by businesses—from hiring and firing decisions to workplace safety, competitive practices, and financing.

In the last decade or so, however, the Supreme Court has begun to curb somewhat the national government's regulatory authority under the commerce clause. In 1995, the Court held—for the first time in sixty years—that Congress had exceeded its regulatory authority under the commerce clause. The Court struck down an act that banned the possession of guns within one thousand feet of any school because the act attempted to regulate an area that had "nothing to do with commerce."[11] Subsequently, the Court invalidated other federal laws on the ground that they exceeded Congress's commerce clause authority.[12]

POLICE POWERS
Powers possessed by the states as part of their inherent sovereignty. These powers may be exercised to protect or promote the public order, health, safety, morals, and general welfare.

The Regulatory Powers of the States As part of their inherent sovereignty, state governments have the authority to regulate affairs within their borders. This authority stems in part from the Tenth Amendment to the Constitution, which reserves all powers not delegated to the national government to the states. State regulatory powers are often referred to as **police powers.** The term encompasses not only the enforcement of

---

11. The United States Supreme Court held the Gun-Free School Zones Act of 1990 to be unconstitutional in *United States v. Lopez,* 514 U.S. 549, 115 S.Ct. 1624, 131 L.Ed.2d 626 (1995).

12. See, for example, *Printz v. United States,* 521 U.S. 898, 117 S.Ct. 2365, 138 L.Ed.2d 914 (1997), involving the Brady Handgun Violence Prevention Act of 1993; and *United States v. Morrison,* 529 U.S. 598, 120 S.Ct. 1740, 146 L.Ed.2d 658 (2000), concerning the federal Violence Against Women Act of 1994.

criminal law but also the right of state governments to regulate private activities to protect or promote the public order, health, safety, morals, and general welfare. Fire and building codes, antidiscrimination laws, parking regulations, zoning restrictions, licensing requirements, and thousands of other state statutes covering virtually every aspect of life have been enacted pursuant to a state's police powers. Local governments, including cities, also exercise police powers.[13] Generally, state laws enacted pursuant to a state's police powers carry a strong presumption of validity.

The "Dormant" Commerce Clause The United States Supreme Court has interpreted the commerce clause to mean that the national government has the *exclusive* authority to regulate commerce that substantially affects trade and commerce among the states. This express grant of authority to the national government, which is often referred to as the "positive" aspect of the commerce clause, implies a negative aspect—that the states do *not* have the authority to regulate interstate commerce. This negative aspect of the commerce clause is often referred to as the "dormant" (implied) commerce clause.

The dormant commerce clause comes into play when state regulations affect interstate commerce. In this situation, the courts normally weigh the state's interest in regulating a certain matter against the burden that the state's regulation places on interstate commerce. Because courts balance the interests involved, it can be extremely difficult to predict the outcome in a particular case.

■ EXAMPLE 1.7 A Michigan statute prohibited out-of-state wineries from shipping wine directly to Michigan residents but allowed in-state wineries to do so. The U.S. Court of Appeals for the Sixth Circuit ruled that the statute violated the dormant commerce clause. The court concluded that the regulations benefited in-state wineries and burdened out-of-state wineries, while failing to promote any legitimate local purpose.[14] Other appellate courts, however, have taken different positions on cases involving direct wine shipments. For instance, in 2004, the U.S. Court of Appeals for the Second Circuit upheld a similar statute on the ground that the state had a legitimate interest in monitoring the flow of alcohol into the state.[15] ■

What if a state law attempts to regulate the types of materials that may be distributed to state residents via the Internet? Would such a law violate the dormant commerce clause? See this chapter's *Adapting the Law to the Online Environment* feature for a discussion of that question.

THE SUPREMACY CLAUSE

SUPREMACY CLAUSE
The provision in Article VI of the Constitution that provides that the Constitution, laws, and treaties of the United States are "the supreme Law of the Land." Under this clause, state and local laws that directly conflict with federal law will be rendered invalid.

PREEMPTION
A doctrine under which certain federal laws preempt, or take precedence over, conflicting state or local laws.

Article VI of the Constitution provides that the Constitution, laws, and treaties of the United States are "the supreme Law of the Land." This article, commonly referred to as the **supremacy clause,** is important in the ordering of state and federal relationships. When there is a direct conflict between a federal law and a state law, the state law is rendered invalid. Because some powers are *concurrent* (shared by the federal government and the states), however, it is necessary to determine which law governs in a particular circumstance.

Preemption occurs when Congress chooses to act exclusively in a concurrent area. In this circumstance, a valid federal statute or regulation will take precedence over a conflicting state or local law or regulation on the same general subject. Often,

13. Local governments derive their authority to regulate their communities from the state, because they are creatures of the state. In other words, they cannot come into existence unless authorized by the state to do so.
14. *Heald v. Engler,* 342 F.3d 517 (6th Cir. 2003).
15. *Swedenburg v. Kelly,* 358 F.3d 223 (2d Cir. 2004).

ADAPTING THE LAW TO THE ONLINE ENVIRONMENT

Can States Regulate Internet Commerce?

The Constitution's commerce clause—and most of the United States Supreme Court's decisions interpreting that clause—were created long before the Internet became a reality. Prior to the advent of the Internet, "interstate commerce" typically meant commerce in goods or services that extended beyond a particular state's borders. In the online environment, however, physical boundaries do not exist. Thus, one of the difficulties facing the courts in the last several years has been how to apply this traditional body of law to online transactions.

TRADITIONAL COMMERCE CLAUSE ANALYSIS

The Constitution's commerce clause, as interpreted by the United States Supreme Court, gives the national government the *exclusive* power to regulate interstate commerce. That means, in effect, that states *cannot* regulate interstate commerce. As noted elsewhere in this chapter, this limitation on state powers is referred to as the negative, or "dormant," commerce clause. If a court finds that a state law places too great a burden on interstate commerce, the law will be deemed unconstitutional on the ground that it violates the dormant commerce clause.

By and large, the courts have applied traditional commerce clause analysis in cases challenging the constitutionality of state laws regulating the Internet. As in traditional commerce clause cases, the courts tend to invalidate state laws regulating the Internet if those laws extend to activities beyond their borders and place too great a burden on interstate commerce.

CAN VERMONT LIMIT MINORS' ACCESS TO WEB MATERIAL?

Consider a case that came before a federal appellate court in *American Booksellers Foundation v. Dean.*[a] The case challenged the constitutionality of a Vermont law that prohibited the Internet distribution to minors of sexually explicit materials that are "harmful to minors."

The effect of this law on out-of-state residents was made clear in the argument put forth by one of the plaintiffs (those who brought the lawsuit), Sexual Health Network, Inc. (SHN). SHN, which was located in Connecticut, operated a Web site on which it posted information concerning a range of sex-related topics. SHN's aim was to provide access to sexuality-related information designed to assist persons with disabilities, illnesses, and changes in their lifestyles. Clearly, SHN could not prevent minors living in Vermont (or any other state—or nation) from accessing its Web site. To avoid possible prosecution for violating Vermont's law, SHN would virtually have to shut down its Web site. SHN and the other plaintiffs, including the American Civil Liberties Union, thus sought a court order barring the enforcement of the Vermont statute on the ground that, among other things, it violated the dormant commerce clause.

The court agreed with the plaintiffs. The court held that the Vermont law violated the dormant commerce clause because it "regulates Internet commerce occurring wholly outside Vermont's borders." The court noted that although Vermont aimed to protect only Vermont minors, in effect the rest of the nation was forced to comply with its regulation or risk prosecution under Vermont's law.

FOR CRITICAL ANALYSIS

In its opinion, the court pointed out that "at the same time that the Internet's geographic reach increases Vermont's interest in regulating out-of-state conduct, it makes state regulation impracticable." Analyze this statement.

a. 342 F.3d 96 (2d Cir. 2003).

it is not clear whether Congress, in passing a law, intended to preempt an entire subject area against state regulation. In these situations, it is left to the courts to determine whether Congress intended to exercise exclusive power over a given area. No single factor is decisive as to whether a court will find preemption. Generally, congressional intent to preempt will be found if a federal law regulating an activity is so pervasive, comprehensive, or detailed that the states have little or no room to regulate in that area. Also, when a federal statute creates an agency—such as the National Labor Relations Board—to enforce the law, matters that may come within the agency's jurisdiction will likely preempt state laws.

Business and the Bill of Rights

BILL OF RIGHTS The first ten amendments to the U.S. Constitution.

The importance of a written declaration of the rights of individuals eventually caused the first Congress of the United States to submit twelve amendments to the Constitution to the states for approval. The first ten of these amendments, commonly known as the **Bill of Rights,** were adopted in 1791 and embody a series of protections for the individual against various types of interference by the federal government.[16] Some constitutional protections apply to business entities as well. For example, corporations exist as separate legal entities, or legal persons, and enjoy many of the same rights and privileges as natural persons do. Summarized here are the protections guaranteed by these ten amendments (see the Constitution in Appendix A for the complete text of each amendment):

BE CAREFUL Although most of these rights apply to actions of the states, some of them apply only to actions of the federal government.

1. The First Amendment guarantees the freedoms of religion, speech, and the press and the rights to assemble peaceably and to petition the government.
2. The Second Amendment guarantees the right to keep and bear arms.
3. The Third Amendment prohibits, in peacetime, the lodging of soldiers in any house without the owner's consent.
4. The Fourth Amendment prohibits unreasonable searches and seizures of persons or property.
5. The Fifth Amendment guarantees the rights to *indictment* (formal accusation—see Chapter 6) by grand jury, to due process of law, and to fair payment when private property is taken for public use. The Fifth Amendment also prohibits compulsory self-incrimination and double jeopardy (trial for the same crime twice).
6. The Sixth Amendment guarantees the accused in a criminal case the right to a speedy and public trial by an impartial jury and with counsel. The accused has the right to cross-examine witnesses against him or her and to solicit testimony from witnesses in his or her favor.
7. The Seventh Amendment guarantees the right to a trial by jury in a civil (noncriminal) case involving at least twenty dollars.[17]
8. The Eighth Amendment prohibits excessive bail and fines, as well as cruel and unusual punishment.
9. The Ninth Amendment establishes that the people have rights in addition to those specified in the Constitution.
10. The Tenth Amendment establishes that those powers neither delegated to the federal government nor denied to the states are reserved for the states.

As originally intended, the Bill of Rights limited only the powers of the national government. Over time, however, the Supreme Court "incorporated" most of these

16. One of these proposed amendments was ratified 203 years later (in 1992) and became the Twenty-seventh Amendment to the Constitution. See Appendix A.
17. Twenty dollars was forty days' pay for the average person when the Bill of Rights was written.

Police searching a crack house in Florida. Should the owners and occupants of such houses receive protection from unreasonable searches and seizures under the U.S. Constitution? Why or why not? (© Corbis. All rights reserved.)

rights into the protections against state actions afforded by the Fourteenth Amendment to the Constitution. That amendment, passed in 1868 after the Civil War, provides in part that "[n]o State shall . . . deprive any person of life, liberty, or property, without due process of law." Starting in 1925, the Supreme Court began to define various rights and liberties guaranteed in the national Constitution as constituting "due process of law," which was required of state governments under the Fourteenth Amendment. Today, most of the rights and liberties set forth in the Bill of Rights apply to state governments as well as the national government.

REMEMBER The First Amendment guarantee of freedom of speech applies only to *government* restrictions on speech.

We will look closely at several of the amendments included in the Bill of Rights in Chapter 6, in the context of criminal law and procedures. Here we examine two important guarantees of the First Amendment—freedom of speech and freedom of religion. These and other First Amendment freedoms (of the press, assembly, and petition) have all been applied to the states through the due process clause of the Fourteenth Amendment. As you read through the following pages, keep in mind that none of these (or other) constitutional freedoms confers an absolute right. Ultimately, it is the United States Supreme Court, as the final interpreter of the Constitution, that gives meaning to these rights and determines their boundaries.

The First Amendment—Freedom of Speech

Freedom of speech is the most prized freedom that Americans have. Indeed, it forms the basis for our democratic form of government, which could not exist if people were not allowed to express their political opinions freely and criticize government actions or policies. Because of its importance, the courts traditionally have protected this right to the fullest extent possible.

SYMBOLIC SPEECH
Nonverbal expressions of beliefs. Symbolic speech, which includes gestures, movements, and articles of clothing, is given substantial protection by the courts.

Speech often includes not only what we say but also what we do to express our political, social, and religious views. The courts generally protect **symbolic speech**—gestures, movements, articles of clothing, and other forms of nonverbal expressive conduct. ■ EXAMPLE 1.8 In 1989, the Supreme Court held that the burning of the American flag to protest government policies is a constitutionally protected form of expression.[18] Similarly, participating in a hunger strike or wearing a black armband would be protected as symbolic speech. ■

Expression—oral, written, or symbolized by conduct—is subject to reasonable restrictions. For example, on the campus of a public high school, certain rights may be circumscribed or denied, in part to protect minors from predatory adults and to protect adults and others from predatory minors. A balance must be struck, however, between a government's obligation to protect its citizens and those citizens' exercise of their rights. These competing interests were at issue in the following case.

18. See *Texas v. Johnson,* 491 U.S. 397, 109 S.Ct. 2533, 105 L.Ed.2d 342 (1989).

CASE 1.2 Hodgkins v. Peterson

United States Court of Appeals,
Seventh Circuit, 2004.
355 F.3d 1048.

FACTS Shortly after 11 P.M. on August 26, 1999, sixteen-year-old Colin Hodgkins and three friends left a Steak 'n Shake restaurant in Indianapolis, Indiana, where they had stopped to eat after a school soccer game. At the time, an Indiana statute made it illegal for minors between fifteen and seventeen years old to be in a public place after 11 P.M. on weeknights unless accompanied by a parent or guardian, with a few exceptions. As Colin and his friends left the restaurant, police arrested and handcuffed them for violating this statute. Colin's mother, Nancy Hodgkins, and others filed a suit in a federal district court against Bart Peterson, the mayor of Indianapolis, and other local government officials, asking the court to order the defendants to stop enforcing the curfew on the ground that it violated the First Amendment. The court ruled in the defendants' favor, and the plaintiffs appealed to the U.S. Court of Appeals for the Seventh Circuit.

ISSUE Did the curfew violate the First Amendment rights of the minors?

DECISION Yes. The U.S. Court of Appeals for the Seventh Circuit reversed the lower court's judgment and ordered a permanent injunction against the enforcement of the curfew.

REASON The appellate court stated, "The strength of our democracy depends on a citizenry that knows and understands its freedoms, exercises them responsibly, and guards them vigilantly. Young adults are not suddenly granted the full panoply of constitutional rights on the day they attain the age of majority. We not only permit but expect youths to exercise those liberties–to learn to think for themselves, to give voice to their opinions, to hear and evaluate competing points of view–so that they might attain the right to vote at age eighteen with the tools to exercise that right. A juvenile's ability to worship, associate, and speak freely is therefore not simply a privilege that benefits her as an individual, but a necessary means of allowing her to become a fully enfranchised member of a democratic society." Many First Amendment activities can occur during curfew hours. The statute threatened the arrest of minors who were participating in these activities. "The chill that the prospect of arrest imposes on a minor's exercise of his or her First Amendment rights is patent [obvious]."

FOR CRITICAL ANALYSIS—Political Consideration
Can a curfew law be written to protect both the fundamental constitutional rights of minors and the safety of all citizens?

Corporate Political Speech Political speech by corporations also falls within the protection of the First Amendment. ■ EXAMPLE 1.9 In *First National Bank of Boston v. Bellotti*,[19] national banking associations and business corporations sought United States Supreme Court review of a Massachusetts statute that prohibited corporations from making political contributions or expenditures that individuals were permitted to make. The Court ruled that the Massachusetts law was unconstitutional because it violated the right of corporations to freedom of speech. ■ Similarly, the Court has held that a law prohibiting a corporation from using bill inserts to express its views on controversial issues violates the First Amendment.[20] Although a more conservative Supreme Court subsequently reversed this trend somewhat,[21] corporate political speech continues to be given significant protection under the First Amendment.

Commercial Speech The courts also give substantial protection to "commercial" speech, which consists of communications—primarily advertising and marketing—made by business firms that involve only their commercial interests. The protection given to commercial speech under the First Amendment is not as extensive as that afforded to noncommercial speech, however. A state may restrict certain kinds of advertising, for example, in the interest of protecting consumers from being misled by the advertising practices. States also have a legitimate interest in the beautification of roadsides, and this interest allows states to place restraints on billboard advertising.

.on the Web The law firm of Arent Fox offers extensive information relating to advertising law at **http://www.advertisinglaw.com**.

Generally, a restriction on commercial speech will be considered valid as long as it meets the following three criteria: (1) it must seek to implement a substantial government interest, (2) it must directly advance that interest, and (3) it must go no further than necessary to accomplish its objective. ■ EXAMPLE 1.10 The South Carolina Supreme Court held that a state statute banning ads for video gambling violated the First Amendment because the statute did not directly advance a substantial government interest. Although the court acknowledged that the state had a substantial interest in minimizing gambling, there was no evidence that a reduction in video gambling ads would result in a reduction in gambling.[22] ■

The court in the following case applied these principles to determine the constitutionality of a county ordinance that regulated video games based on their content—the ordinance applied only to "graphically violent" video games.

19. 435 U.S. 765, 98 S.Ct. 1407, 55 L.Ed.2d 707 (1978).
20. *Consolidated Edison Co. v. Public Service Commission,* 447 U.S. 530, 100 S.Ct. 2326, 65 L.Ed.2d 319 (1980).
21. See *Austin v. Michigan Chamber of Commerce,* 494 U.S. 652, 110 S.Ct. 1391, 108 L.Ed.2d 652 (1990), in which the Court upheld a state law prohibiting corporations from using general corporate funds for independent expenditures in state political campaigns.
22. *Evans v. State,* 344 S.C. 60, 543 S.E.2d 547 (2001).

CASE 1.3 Interactive Digital Software Association v. St. Louis County, Missouri

United States Court of Appeals,
Eighth Circuit, 2003.
329 F.3d 954.

FACTS St. Louis County, Missouri, passed an ordinance that made it unlawful for any person knowingly to sell, rent, or make available "graphically violent" video games

(Continued)

CASE 1.3—Continued

to minors or to "permit the free play of" such games by minors, without a parent or guardian's consent.[a] Interactive Digital Software Association, and others that create or provide the public with video games and related software, filed a suit against the county in a federal district court. The plaintiffs asserted that the ordinance violated the First Amendment. The county argued that the ordinance promoted the compelling state interest of protecting the "psychological well-being of minors" by reducing the harm suffered by children who play violent video games. A psychologist, a high school principal, and other experts offered their conclusions that playing violent video games leads to aggressive behavior, but the county did not provide proof of a link between the games and any psychological harm. The court dismissed the case. The plaintiffs appealed to the U.S. Court of Appeals for the Eighth Circuit.

ISSUE Are video games entitled to the same First Amendment protection as other types of speech?

DECISION Yes. The U.S. Court of Appeals for the Eighth Circuit reversed the judgment of the lower court and remanded the case for the entry of an injunction against the county's enforcement of its ordinance. The defendants failed to present the evidence of harm required to uphold a law threatening protected speech.

a. St. Louis County Revised Ordinances Sections 602.425 through 602.460.

REASON The appellate court reasoned that "[i]f the first amendment is versatile enough to shield the painting of Jackson Pollock, music of Arnold Schoenberg, or Jabberwocky verse of Lewis Carroll, we see no reason why the pictures, graphic design, concept art, sounds, music, stories, and narrative present in video games are not entitled to a similar protection." The court noted that video games contain stories, imagery, age-old themes of literature, and messages, even ideologies, similar to books and movies. With video games, players may skip the expressive parts of the game and proceed straight to the player-controlled action. But the same could be said of action-packed movies, the court explained. There is no justification for disqualifying video games as speech simply because they are constructed to be interactive. The court also noted that some books, "in which the reader makes choices that determine the plot of the story, * * * can be every bit as interactive." Because video games are entitled to protection, the court held that the county must provide some objective evidence that violent video games cause psychological harm to minors. In this case, the county failed to present the substantial supporting evidence of harm as is required to uphold the ordinance.

WHY IS THIS CASE IMPORTANT? *Even though the courts allow more regulation of commercial speech than other types of speech, the state's power to regulate the speech is still limited. Proof that the message is violent or objectionable in some way does not justify regulating commercial speech. The government must establish that it has a substantial interest in regulating the speech and that the proposed regulation advances that interest.*

Unprotected Speech The United States Supreme Court has made it clear that certain types of speech will not be given any protection under the First Amendment. Speech that harms the good reputation of another, or defamatory speech (see Chapter 4), will not be protected. Speech that violates criminal laws (such as threatening speech) is not constitutionally protected. Other unprotected speech includes "fighting words," or words that are likely to incite others to respond violently.

The Supreme Court has also held that obscene speech is not protected by the First Amendment. The Court has grappled from time to time with the problem of trying to establish an objective definition of obscene speech. In a 1973 case, *Miller v. California*,[23] the Supreme Court created a test for legal obscenity, which involved a set of requirements that must be met for material to be legally obscene. Under this

23. 413 U.S. 15, 93 S.Ct. 2607, 37 L.Ed.2d 419 (1973).

test, material is obscene if (1) the average person finds that it violates contemporary community standards; (2) the work taken as a whole appeals to a prurient (arousing or obsessive) interest in sex; (3) the work shows patently offensive sexual conduct; and (4) the work lacks serious redeeming literary, artistic, political, or scientific merit.

Because community standards vary widely, the *Miller* test has had inconsistent applications, and obscenity remains a constitutionally unsettled issue. Numerous state and federal statutes make it a crime to disseminate obscene materials, however, and the Supreme Court has often upheld such laws, including laws prohibiting the sale and possession of child pornography.[24]

.on the Web To learn about issues involving free speech and cyberspace, go to the Web site of the American Civil Liberties Union at

http://www.aclu.org.

Click on one of the issues listed on the right side of the screen for links to ACLU articles on that issue.

Online Obscenity Congress first attempted to protect minors from pornographic materials on the Internet by passing the Communications Decency Act (CDA) of 1996. The CDA made it a crime to make available to minors online any "obscene or indecent" message that "depicts or describes, in terms patently offensive as measured by contemporary community standards, sexual or excretory activities or organs."[25] The act was challenged as an unconstitutional restraint on speech, and ultimately the United States Supreme Court ruled that portions of the act were unconstitutional. The Court held that the terms *indecent* and *patently offensive* covered large amounts of nonpornographic material with serious educational or other value.[26]

The Child Online Protection Act (COPA)[27] of 1998, which banned material "harmful to minors" distributed without some kind of age-verification system to separate adult and minor users, also encountered constitutional stumbling blocks. The act has largely been tied up in the courts since its passage.[28] Another controversial act was the Children's Internet Protection Act (CIPA) of 2000,[29] which requires public schools and libraries to block adult content from access by children by installing **filtering software.** Such software is designed to prevent persons from viewing certain Web sites by responding to a site's Internet address or its key words. In 2003, however, the Supreme Court held that the act did not violate the First Amendment.[30]

FILTERING SOFTWARE
A computer program that includes a pattern through which data are passed. When designed to block access to certain Web sites, the pattern blocks the retrieval of a site whose URL or key words are on a list within the program.

ESTABLISHMENT CLAUSE
The provision in the First Amendment to the Constitution that prohibits the government from establishing any state-sponsored religion or enacting any law that promotes religion or favors one religion over another.

FREE EXERCISE CLAUSE
The provision in the First Amendment to the Constitution that prohibits the government from interfering with people's religious practices or forms of worship.

THE FIRST AMENDMENT—FREEDOM OF RELIGION

The First Amendment states that the government may neither establish any religion nor prohibit the free exercise of religious practices. The first part of this constitutional provision is referred to as the **establishment clause,** and the second part is known as the **free exercise clause.** Government action, both federal and state, must be consistent with this constitutional mandate.

The Establishment Clause The establishment clause prohibits the government from establishing a state-sponsored religion, as well as from passing laws that promote

24. For example, see *Osborne v. Ohio,* 495 U.S. 103, 110 S.Ct. 1691, 109 L.Ed.2d 98 (1990).
25. 47 U.S.C. Section 223(a)(1)(B)(ii).
26. *Reno v. American Civil Liberties Union,* 521 U.S. 844, 117 S.Ct. 2329, 138 L.Ed.2d 874 (1997).
27. 47 U.S.C. Section 231.
28. For the most recent court decision concerning the constitutionality of this act, see *American Civil Liberties Union v. Ashcroft,* ___ U.S. ___, 124 S.Ct. 2783, 159 L.Ed.2d 690 (2003).
29. 17 U.S.C. Sections 1701–1741.
30. *United States v. American Library Association,* 539 U.S. 194, 123 S.Ct. 2297, 156 L.Ed.2d 221 (2003).

(aid or endorse) religion or that show a preference for one religion over another. The establishment clause does not require a complete separation of church and state, though. On the contrary, it requires the government to accommodate religions.[31]

The establishment clause covers all conflicts about such matters as the legality of state and local government support for a particular religion, government aid to religious organizations and schools, the government's allowing or requiring school prayers, and the teaching of evolution versus fundamentalist theories of creation. The Supreme Court has held that for a government law or policy to be constitutional, it must be secular in aim, must not have the primary effect of advancing or inhibiting religions, and must not create "an excessive government entanglement with religion."[32] Generally, federal or state regulation that does not promote religion or place a significant burden on religion is constitutional even if it has some impact on religion.

■ EXAMPLE 1.11 "Sunday closing laws" make the performance of some commercial activities on Sunday illegal. These statutes, also known as "blue laws" (from the color of the paper on which an early Sunday law was written), have been upheld on the ground that it is a legitimate function of government to provide a day of rest. The United States Supreme Court has held that the closing laws, although originally of a religious character, have taken on the secular purpose of promoting the health and welfare of workers.[33] Even though Sunday closing laws admittedly make it easier for Christians to attend religious services, the Court has viewed this effect as an incidental, not a primary, purpose of Sunday closing laws. ■

ETHICAL ISSUE 1.2

Do religious displays on public property violate the establishment clause? The thorny issue of whether religious displays on public property violate the establishment clause often arises during the holiday season. Time and again, the courts have wrestled with this issue, but it has never been resolved in a way that satisfies everyone. In a 1984 case, the United States Supreme Court decided that a city's official Christmas display, which included a crèche (Nativity scene), did not violate the establishment clause because it was just one part of a larger holiday display that featured secular symbols, such as reindeer and candy canes.[34] In a later case, the Court held that the presence of a crèche within a county courthouse violated the establishment clause because it was not in close proximity to nonreligious symbols, including a Christmas tree, which were located outside, on the building's steps. The presence of a menorah (a nine-branched candelabrum used in celebrating Hanukkah) on the building's steps, however, did not violate the establishment clause because the menorah was situated in close proximity to the Christmas tree.[35] The courts continue to apply this reasoning in cases involving similar issues. For example, in 2004 a federal appellate court ruled that displaying a monument of the Ten Commandments in a city park in Nebraska violated the establishment clause.[36] ■

The Free Exercise Clause The free exercise clause guarantees that a person can hold any religious belief that she or he wants; or a person can have no religious belief. When religious *practices* work against public policy and the public welfare, however,

31. *Zorach v. Clauson,* 343 U.S. 306, 72 S.Ct. 679, 96 L.Ed. 954 (1952).
32. *Lemon v. Kurtzman,* 403 U.S. 602, 91 S.Ct. 2105, 29 L.Ed.2d 745 (1971).
33. *McGowan v. Maryland,* 366 U.S. 420, 81 S.Ct. 1101, 6 L.Ed.2d 393 (1961).
34. *Lynch v. Donnelly,* 465 U.S. 668, 104 S.Ct. 1355, 79 L.Ed.2d 604 (1984).
35. See, for example, *County of Allegheny v. American Civil Liberties Union,* 492 U.S. 573, 109 S.Ct. 3086, 106 L.Ed.2d 472 (1989).
36. *ACLU Nebraska Foundation v. City of Plattsmouth,* 358 F.3d 1020 (8th Cir. 2004). This issue is now before the Supreme Court.

Sultana Freeman reads from the Qur'an, the holy book of the Islamic religion, to illustrate that her religious beliefs require her to keep her head and face covered. The woman is testifying that it is unconstitutional for the government to force her to remove her veil and be photographed to get a driver's license in Florida. By taking a photo of an Islamic woman without her face covered, does the state violate the woman's religious freedom? Why or why not? What state interests might justify such an intrusion? (Library of Congress)

DUE PROCESS CLAUSE
The provisions in the Fifth and Fourteenth Amendments to the Constitution that guarantee that no person shall be deprived of life, liberty, or property without due process of law. Similar clauses are found in most state constitutions.

the government can act. For example, regardless of a child's or parent's religious beliefs, the government can require certain types of vaccinations. Similarly, although children of Jehovah's Witnesses are not required to say the Pledge of Allegiance at school, their parents cannot prevent them from accepting medical treatment (such as blood transfusions) if in fact their lives are in danger. Additionally, public school students can be required to study from textbooks chosen by school authorities.

For business firms, an important issue involves the accommodation that businesses must make for the religious beliefs of their employees. For example, if an employee's religion prohibits him or her from working on a certain day of the week or at a certain type of job, the employer must make a reasonable attempt to accommodate these religious requirements. Employers must reasonably accommodate an employee's religious beliefs even if the beliefs are not based on the tenets or dogma of a particular church, sect, or denomination. The only requirement is that the belief be religious in nature and sincerely held by the employee. (We will look further at this issue in Chapter 18, in the context of employment discrimination.)

Due Process and Equal Protection

Two other constitutional guarantees of great significance to Americans are mandated by the due process clauses of the Fifth and Fourteenth Amendments and the equal protection clause of the Fourteenth Amendment.

DUE PROCESS

Both the Fifth and the Fourteenth Amendments provide that no person shall be deprived "of life, liberty, or property, without due process of law." The **due process clause** of each of these constitutional amendments has two aspects—procedural and substantive.

Procedural Due Process Procedural due process requires that any government decision to take life, liberty, or property must be made fairly. For example, fair procedures must be used in determining whether a person will be subjected to punishment or have some burden imposed on him or her. Fair procedure has been interpreted as requiring that the person have at least an opportunity to object to a proposed action before a fair, neutral decision maker (which need not be a judge). Thus, for example, if a driver's license is construed as a property interest, some sort of opportunity to object to its suspension or termination by the state must be provided.

Substantive Due Process Substantive due process focuses on the content, or substance, of legislation. If a law or other governmental action limits a *fundamental right,* it will be held to violate substantive due process unless it promotes a compelling or overriding state interest. Fundamental rights include interstate travel, privacy, voting, and all First Amendment rights. Compelling state interests could include, for example, the public's safety. ■ **EXAMPLE 1.12** Laws setting speed limits may be upheld even though they affect interstate travel, if they are shown to reduce highway fatalities. The courts uphold these laws because the state has a compelling interest in protecting the lives of its citizens. ■

In situations not involving fundamental rights, a law or action does not violate substantive due process if it rationally relates to any legitimate governmental end. It is almost impossible for a law or action to fail the "rationality" test. Under this test, virtually any business regulation will be upheld as reasonable—the United States Supreme Court has sustained insurance regulations, price and wage controls, banking limitations, and restrictions of unfair competition and trade practices against substantive due process challenges.

■ EXAMPLE 1.13 If a state legislature enacted a law imposing a fifteen-year term of imprisonment without a trial on all businesspersons who appeared in their own television commercials, the law would be unconstitutional on both substantive and procedural grounds. Substantive review would invalidate the legislation because it abridges freedom of speech. Procedurally, the law is unfair because it imposes the penalty without giving the accused a chance to defend her or his actions. ■ The lack of procedural due process will cause a court to invalidate any statute or prior court decision. Similarly, the courts will overrule any state or federal law that violates the Constitution by denying substantive due process.

EQUAL PROTECTION

EQUAL PROTECTION CLAUSE
The provision in the Fourteenth Amendment to the Constitution that guarantees that no state will "deny to any person within its jurisdiction the equal protection of the laws." This clause mandates that the state governments treat similarly situated individuals in a similar manner.

Under the Fourteenth Amendment, a state may not "deny to any person within its jurisdiction the equal protection of the laws." The United States Supreme Court has used the due process clause of the Fifth Amendment to make the **equal protection clause** applicable to the federal government as well. Equal protection means that the government must treat similarly situated individuals in a similar manner.

Both substantive due process and equal protection require review of the substance of the law or other governmental action rather than review of the procedures used. When a law or action limits the liberty of all persons to do something, it may violate substantive due process; when a law or action limits the liberty of some persons but not others, it may violate the equal protection clause. ■ EXAMPLE 1.14 If a law prohibits all persons from buying contraceptive devices, it raises a substantive due process question. If a law prohibits only unmarried persons from buying the same devices, it raises an equal protection issue. ■

Basically, in determining whether a law or action violates the equal protection clause, a court will consider questions similar to those previously noted as applicable in a substantive due process review. Under an equal protection inquiry, when a law or action distinguishes between or among individuals, the basis for the distinction—that is, the classification—is examined. Depending on the classification, the courts apply one of the following three levels of scrutiny, or "tests," to determine whether the law or action violates the equal protection clause:

1. *Minimal Scrutiny—The "Rational Basis" Test.* Generally, laws regulating economic and social matters are presumed to be valid and are subject to only minimal scrutiny. A classification will be considered valid if there is any conceivable "rational basis" on which the classification might relate to any *legitimate government interest.* It is almost impossible for a law or action to fail the rational basis test.
2. *Intermediate Scrutiny.* This is a harder standard to meet and is applied in cases involving discrimination based on gender or legitimacy. Laws using these classifications must be substantially related to *important government objectives.*
3. *Strict Scrutiny.* This is the most difficult standard to meet. Very few cases survive strict-scrutiny analysis, which is applied when a law or action inhibits some persons' exercise of a fundamental right or is based on a suspect trait (such as race, national origin, or citizenship status). Strict scrutiny means that the court will examine the law or action involved very closely, and the law or action will

be allowed to stand only if it is necessary to promote a *compelling government interest.*

Privacy Rights

In the past, privacy issues typically related to personal information that government agencies, including the Federal Bureau of Investigation, might obtain and keep about an individual. Since the 1990s, one of the major concerns of individuals has been how to protect privacy rights in cyberspace and to safeguard private information that may be revealed online (including credit-card numbers and financial information).

Today, individuals face additional concerns about government intrusions into their privacy. Legislation passed by Congress in the wake of the terrorist attacks of September 11, 2001, gave increased authority to government officials to monitor Internet activities (such as e-mail and Web site visits) and to gain access to personal financial data and student information.[37] The government must certify that the information likely to be obtained is relevant to an ongoing criminal investigation, but it does not need to provide proof of any wrongdoing to gain access to this information. Privacy advocates argue that this law has adversely affected the constitutional rights of all Americans, and it has been widely criticized in the media, fueling the public debate over how to secure privacy rights in an electronic age.

In this section, we look at the protection of privacy rights under the U.S. Constitution and various federal statutes. Note that state constitutions and statutes also protect individuals' privacy rights, often to a significant degree. Privacy rights are also protected under tort law (see Chapter 4). Additionally, the Federal Trade Commission has played an active role in protecting the privacy rights of online consumers (see Chapter 13). The protection of employees' privacy rights, particularly with respect to electronic monitoring practices, is another area of growing concern (see Chapter 18).

Constitutional Protection of Privacy Rights

The U.S. Constitution does not explicitly mention a general right to privacy, and only relatively recently have the courts regarded the right to privacy as a constitutional right. In a landmark 1965 case, *Griswold v. Connecticut,*[38] the Supreme Court invalidated a Connecticut law that effectively prohibited the use of contraceptives. The Court held that the law violated the right to privacy. Justice William O. Douglas formulated a unique way of reading this right into the Bill of Rights. He claimed that "emanations" from the rights guaranteed by the First, Third, Fourth, Fifth, and Ninth Amendments formed and gave "life and substance" to "penumbras" (partial shadows) around these guaranteed rights. These penumbras included an implied constitutional right to privacy.

When we read these amendments, we can see the foundation for Justice Douglas's reasoning. Consider the Fourth Amendment. By prohibiting unreasonable searches and seizures, the amendment effectively protects individuals' privacy. Consider also the words of the Ninth Amendment: "The enumeration in the Constitution of certain rights, shall not be construed to deny or disparage others retained by the people." In other words, although neither the Constitution nor its amendments mentions the right to privacy, this right does exist.

---

37. Uniting and Strengthening America by Providing Appropriate Tools Required to Intercept and Obstruct Terrorism Act of 2001, also known as the USA Patriot Act, was enacted as Pub. L. No. 107-56 (2001).
38. 381 U.S. 479, 85 S.Ct. 1678, 14 L.Ed.2d 510 (1965).

FEDERAL STATUTES PROTECTING PRIVACY RIGHTS

In the last several decades, Congress has enacted a number of statutes that protect the privacy of individuals in various areas of concern. In 1966, Congress enacted the Freedom of Information Act, which allows any person to request copies of any information on her or him contained in federal government files. The Privacy Act of 1974 also gives persons the right to access such information. These and other major federal laws protecting privacy rights are listed and described in Exhibit 1–2.

Responding to the growing need to protect the privacy of individuals' health records—particularly computerized records—Congress passed the Health Insurance Portability and Accountability Act (HIPAA)[39] of 1996. This act, which took effect on April 14, 2003, defines and limits the circumstances in which an individual's "protected health information" may be used or disclosed.

39. The HIPAA was enacted as Pub. L. No. 104-191 (1996) and is codified in 29 U.S.C.A. Sections 1181 *et seq.*

EXHIBIT 1–2 FEDERAL LEGISLATION RELATING TO PRIVACY

TITLE	PROVISIONS CONCERNING PRIVACY
Freedom of Information Act (1966)	Provides that individuals have a right to obtain access to information about them collected in government files.
Family and Educational Rights and Privacy Act (1974)	Limits access to computer-stored records of education-related evaluations and grades in private and public colleges and universities.
Privacy Act (1974)	Protects the privacy of individuals about whom the federal government has information. Under this act, agencies that use or disclose personal information must make sure that the information is reliable and guard against its misuse. Individuals must be able to find out what data concerning them the agency is compiling and how the data will be used. In addition, the agency must give individuals a means to correct inaccurate data and must obtain their consent before using the data for any other purpose.
Tax Reform Act (1976)	Preserves the privacy of personal financial information.
Right to Financial Privacy Act (1978)	Prohibits financial institutions from providing the federal government with access to customers' records unless a customer authorizes the disclosure.
Electronic Communications Privacy Act (1986)	Prohibits the interception of information communicated by electronic means.
Driver's Privacy Protection Act (1994)	Prevents states from disclosing or selling a driver's personal information without the driver's consent.
Health Insurance Portability and Accountability Act (1996)	Prohibits the use of a consumer's medical information for any purpose other than that for which such information was provided, unless the consumer expressly consents to the use. Final rules became effective on April 14, 2003.
Financial Services Modernization Act (Gramm-Leach-Bliley Act) (1999)	Prohibits the disclosure of nonpublic personal information about a consumer to an unaffiliated third party unless strict disclosure and opt-out requirements are met. Final rules became mandatory on July 1, 2001.

APPLICATION How Can You Choose and Use a Lawyer?*

If you are contemplating a career in the business world, sooner or later you will probably face the question, "Do I need a lawyer?" The answer to this question will likely be "Yes," at least at some time during your career. Even businesspersons who have gone to law school often hire an outside lawyer to help them with their legal problems. Today, it is virtually impossible for nonexperts to keep up with the myriad rules and regulations that govern the conduct of business in the United States. It is also increasingly possible for businesspersons to incur penalties for violating laws or regulations of which they are totally unaware.

Although lawyers may seem expensive—anywhere from $100 to $500 or more per hour—cautious businesspersons will make sure that they are not "penny wise and pound foolish." The consultation fee paid to an attorney may be insignificant compared with the potential liability facing a businessperson.

SELECTING AN ATTORNEY

In selecting an attorney, you can ask friends, relatives, or business associates to recommend someone. Alternatively, you can call the local or state bar association to obtain the names of several lawyers. West Group has an online database containing biographies of attorneys throughout the country, listed by area of specialty and by state. You can find attorneys in your area by accessing West's Legal Directory online at http://directory.findlaw.com. Some legal aid programs have staff attorneys, and others may refer you to volunteers. You might also investigate legal clinics and prepaid legal service plans.

For your initial meeting with the attorney you have selected, you should prepare a written list of your questions and perhaps a summary of the problem for which you need legal advice. Attach to your list copies of any relevant documents that you can leave with the lawyer. While at the meeting, ask about legal fees, discuss the legal problem you are facing (remember that virtually everything you say to your attorney is protected by the attorney-client privilege of confidentiality), and clarify the scope of what you want the lawyer to do for you.

EVALUATING YOUR ATTORNEY

Ask yourself the following questions after your first meeting: Did the attorney seem knowledgeable about what is needed to address your concerns? Did he or she seem willing to investigate the law and the facts further to ensure an accurate understanding of your legal situation? Did you communicate well with each other? Did the attorney perceive what issues were of foremost concern to you and address those issues to your satisfaction? Did the attorney "speak your language" when explaining the legal implications of those issues?

Continue to evaluate the relationship over time. For many businesspersons, relationships with attorneys last for decades. Make sure that your relationship with your attorney will be a fruitful one.

CHECKLIST FOR CHOOSING AND USING A LAWYER

1. If you ever think that you need legal advice, you probably do.
2. When choosing an attorney, try to get recommendations from friends, relatives, or business associates who have had long-standing relationships with their attorneys. If that fails, check with your local or state bar association or check West Group's online directory.
3. When you initially consult with an attorney, bring a written list of questions to which you want answers, perhaps a summary of your problem, and copies of relevant documents.
4. Do not hesitate to ask about the legal fees that your attorney will charge, and be sure to clarify the scope of the work to be undertaken by the attorney. Ask whatever questions are necessary to ensure that you understand what your legal options are. Do not worry about appearing foolish.

* With appreciation to James D. Van Tassel at Mission College, California, for his helpful suggestions on this topic.

KEY TERMS

CHAPTER SUMMARY The Historical and Constitutional Foundations

Sources of American Law (See pages 2–6.)	1. *Constitutional law*—The law as expressed in the U.S. Constitution and the various state constitutions. The U.S. Constitution is the supreme law of the land. State constitutions are supreme within state borders to the extent that they do not violate the U.S. Constitution or a federal law. 2. *Statutory law*—Laws or ordinances created by federal, state, and local legislatures and governing bodies. None of these laws can violate the U.S. Constitution or the relevant state constitutions. Uniform laws, when adopted by a state legislature, become statutory law in that state. 3. *Administrative law*—The rules, orders, and decisions of federal or state government administrative agencies. Federal administrative agencies are created by enabling legislation enacted by the U.S. Congress. Agency functions include rulemaking, investigation and enforcement, and adjudication. 4. *Case law and common law doctrines*—Judge-made law, including interpretations of constitutional provisions, of statutes enacted by legislatures, and of regulations created by administrative agencies. The common law—the doctrines and principles embodied in case law—governs all areas not covered by statutory law (or agency regulations issued to implement various statutes).
The Common Law Tradition (See pages 6–10.)	1. *Common law*—Law that originated in medieval England with the creation of the king's courts, or *curiae regis,* and the development of a body of rules that were common to (or applied throughout) the land. 2. *Stare decisis*—A doctrine under which judges "stand on decided cases"—or follow the rule of precedent—in deciding cases. *Stare decisis* is the cornerstone of the common law tradition. 3. *Remedies*— a. Remedies at law—Money or something else of value.

CHAPTER SUMMARY The Historical and Constitutional Foundations—Continued

The Common Law Tradition—Continued	b. Remedies in equity—Remedies that are granted when the remedies at law are unavailable or inadequate. Equitable remedies include specific performance, an injunction, and contract rescission (cancellation).
Classifications of Law (See pages 10–12.)	The law may be broken down according to several classification systems, such as substantive or procedural law, federal or state law, and private or public law. Two broad classifications are civil and criminal law, and national and international law. Cyberlaw is not really a classification of law but a term that is applied to the growing body of case law and statutory law that applies to Internet transactions.
The Constitutional Powers of Government (See page 13.)	The U.S. Constitution established a federal form of government, in which government powers are shared by the national government and the state governments. At the national level, government powers are divided among the legislative, executive, and judicial branches.
The Commerce Clause (See pages 13–16.)	1. *The expansion of national powers*—The commerce clause expressly permits Congress to regulate commerce. Over time, courts expansively interpreted this clause, thereby enabling the national government to wield extensive powers over the economic life of the nation. 2. *The commerce power today*—Today, the commerce power authorizes the national government, at least theoretically, to regulate every commercial enterprise in the United States. In recent years, the Supreme Court has reined in somewhat the national government's regulatory powers under the commerce clause. 3. *The regulatory powers of the states*—The Tenth Amendment reserves all powers not expressly delegated to the national government to the states. Under their police powers, state governments may regulate private activities to protect or promote the public order, health, safety, morals, and general welfare. 4. *The "dormant" commerce clause*—If state regulations substantially interfere with interstate commerce, they will be held to violate the "dormant" commerce clause of the U.S. Constitution. The positive aspect of the commerce clause, which gives the national government the exclusive authority to regulate interstate commerce, implies a "dormant" aspect—that the states do *not* have this power.
The Supremacy Clause (See pages 16–18.)	The U.S. Constitution provides that the Constitution, laws, and treaties of the United States are "the supreme Law of the Land." Whenever a state law directly conflicts with a federal law, the state law is rendered invalid.
Business and the Bill of Rights (See pages 18–25.)	The Bill of Rights, which consists of the first ten amendments to the U.S. Constitution, was adopted in 1791 and embodies a series of protections for individuals—and, in some instances, business entities—against various types of interference by the federal government. Freedoms guaranteed by the First Amendment that affect businesses include the following: 1. *Freedom of speech*—Speech, including symbolic speech, is given the fullest possible protection by the courts. Corporate political speech and commercial speech also receive substantial protection under the First Amendment. Certain types of speech, such as defamatory speech and lewd or obscene speech, are not protected under the First Amendment. Government attempts to regulate unprotected forms of speech in the online environment have, to date, met with numerous challenges. 2. *Freedom of religion*—Under the First Amendment, the government may neither establish any religion (the establishment clause) nor prohibit the free exercise of religion (the free exercise clause).

(Continued)

CHAPTER SUMMARY The Historical and Constitutional Foundations—Continued

Due Process and Equal Protection (See pages 25–27.)	1. *Due process*—Both the Fifth and the Fourteenth Amendments provide that no person shall be deprived of "life, liberty, or property, without due process of law." Procedural due process requires that any government decision to take life, liberty, or property must be made fairly, using fair procedures. Substantive due process focuses on the content of legislation. Generally, a law that is not compatible with the Constitution violates substantive due process unless the law promotes a compelling state interest, such as public safety. 2. *Equal protection*—Under the Fourteenth Amendment, a state may not "deny to any person within its jurisdiction the equal protection of the laws." A law or action that limits the liberty of some persons but not others may violate the equal protection clause. Such a law may be deemed valid, however, if there is a rational basis for the discriminatory treatment of a given group or if the law substantially relates to an important government objective.
Privacy Rights (See pages 27–28.)	Americans are increasingly becoming concerned over privacy issues raised by Internet-related technology. The Constitution does not contain a specific guarantee of a right to privacy, but such a right has been derived from guarantees found in several constitutional amendments. A number of federal statutes protect privacy rights. Privacy rights are also protected by many state constitutions and statutes, as well as under tort law.

FOR REVIEW

Answers for the even-numbered questions in this For Review *section can be found in Appendix I at the end of this text.*

1. What is the common law tradition?
2. What is a precedent? When might a court depart from precedent?
3. What is the difference between remedies at law and remedies in equity?
4. What constitutional clause gives the federal government the power to regulate commercial activities among the various states?
5. What is the Bill of Rights? What freedoms are guaranteed by the First Amendment?

QUESTIONS AND CASE PROBLEMS

1–1. Reading Citations. Assume that you want to read the entire court opinion in the case of *Thompson v. Altheimer & Gray*, 248 F.3d 621 (7th Cir. 2001). The case deals with whether an attorney may dismiss "for cause" a prospective juror in a case involving racial discrimination. Read the section entitled "Finding Case Law" in the appendix that follows this chapter, and then explain specifically where you would find the court's opinion.

1–2. Sources of American Law. This chapter discussed a number of sources of American law. Which source of law takes priority in each of the following situations, and why?

(a) A federal statute conflicts with the U.S. Constitution.
(b) A federal statute conflicts with a state constitution.
(c) A state statute conflicts with the common law of that state.
(d) A state constitutional amendment conflicts with the U.S. Constitution.
(e) A federal administrative regulation conflicts with a state constitution.

1–3. *Stare Decisis*. In the text of this chapter, we stated that the doctrine of *stare decisis* "became a cornerstone of the English and American judicial systems." What does *stare decisis* mean, and why has this doctrine been so fundamental to the development of our legal tradition?

1–4. Commercial Speech. A mayoral election is about to be held in a large U.S. city. One of the candidates is Luis Delgado, and his campaign supporters wish to post campaign signs on lampposts and utility posts throughout the city. A city ordinance, however, prohibits the posting of any signs on public property. Delgado's supporters contend that the city ordinance is unconstitutional because it violates their rights to free speech. What factors might a court consider in determining the constitutionality of this ordinance?

1–5. **Commerce Clause.** Suppose that Georgia enacts a law requiring the use of contoured rear-fender mudguards on trucks and trailers operating within its state lines. The statute further makes it illegal for trucks and trailers to use straight mudguards. In thirty-five other states, straight mudguards are legal. Moreover, in the neighboring state of Florida, straight mudguards are explicitly required by law. There is some evidence suggesting that contoured mudguards might be a little safer than straight mudguards. Discuss whether this Georgia statute would violate the commerce clause of the U.S. Constitution.

CASE PROBLEM WITH SAMPLE ANSWER

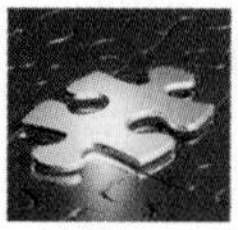

1–6. In February 1999, Carl Adler mailed a driver's license renewal application form and a check for $28 to the New York Department of Motor Vehicles (DMV). The form required Adler's Social Security number, which he intentionally omitted. The DMV returned the application and check and told Adler to supply his Social Security number or send proof that the Social Security Administration could not give him a number. Claiming a right to privacy, Adler refused to comply. The DMV responded that federal law authorizes the states to obtain Social Security numbers from individuals in the context of administering certain state programs, including driver's license programs, and that Adler's application would not be processed until he supplied the number. Adler filed a suit in a New York state court against the DMV, asserting in part that it was in violation of the federal Privacy Act of 1974. Adler asked the court to, among other things, order the DMV to renew his license. Should the court grant Adler's request? Why or why not? [*Adler v. Jackson,* 712 N.Y.S.2d 240 (Sup. 2000)]

After you have answered this problem, compare your answer with the sample answer given on the Web site that accompanies this text. Go to <u>http://blt.westbuslaw.com</u>, select "Chapter 1," and click on "Case Problem with Sample Answer."

1–7. **Free Speech.** Henry Mishkoff is a Web designer whose firm does business as "Webfeats." When Taubman Co. began building a mall called "The Shops at Willow Bend" near Mishkoff's home, Mishkoff registered the domain name "shopsatwillowbend.com" and created a Web site with that address. The site featured information about the mall, a disclaimer indicating that Mishkoff's site was unofficial, and a link to the mall's official site. Taubman discovered Mishkoff's site and filed a suit in a federal district court against him. Mishkoff then registered other names, including "taubmansucks.com," with links to a site documenting his battle with Taubman. (A Web name with a "sucks.com" moniker attached to it is known as a "complaint name," and the process of registering and using such names is known as "cybergriping.") Taubman asked the court to order Mishkoff to stop using all of these names. Should the court grant Taubman's request? On what basis might the court protect Mishkoff's use of the names? [*Taubman Co. v. Webfeats,* 319 F.3d 770 (6th Cir. 2003)]

1–8. **Due Process.** In 1994, the Board of County Commissioners of Yellowstone County, Montana, created Zoning District 17 in a rural area of the county and a Planning and Zoning Commission for the district. The commission adopted zoning regulations, which provided, among other things, that "dwelling units" could be built only through "on-site construction." Later, county officials could not identify any health or safety concerns that the on-site construction provision addressed, and there was no indication that homes built off-site would affect property values or any other general welfare interest of the community. In December 1999, Francis and Anita Yurczyk bought two forty-acre tracts in District 17. The Yurczyks also bought a modular home and moved it onto the property the following spring. Within days, the county advised the Yurczyks that the home violated the on-site construction regulation and would have to be removed. The Yurczyks filed a suit in a Montana state court against the county, alleging in part that the regulation violated the Yurczyks' due process rights. Should the court rule in the plaintiffs' favor? Explain. [*Yurczyk v. Yellowstone County,* 2004 MT 3, 319 Mont. 169, 83 P.3d 266 (2004)]

A QUESTION OF ETHICS

1–9. In 1999, in an effort to reduce smoking by children, the attorney general of Massachusetts issued comprehensive regulations governing the advertising and sale of tobacco products. Among other things, the regulations banned cigarette advertisements within one thousand feet of any elementary school, secondary school, or public playground and required retailers to post any advertising in their stores at least five feet off the floor, out of the immediate sight of young children. A group of tobacco manufacturers and retailers filed suit against the state, claiming that the regulations were preempted by the federal Cigarette Labeling and Advertising Act of 1965, as amended. That act sets uniform labeling requirements and bans broadcast advertising for cigarettes. Ultimately, the case reached the United States Supreme Court, which held that the federal law on cigarette ads preempted the cigarette advertising restrictions adopted by Massachusetts. The only portion of the Massachusetts regulatory package to survive was the requirement that retailers had to place tobacco products in an area accessible only by the sales staff. In view of these facts, consider the following questions.

[*Lorillard Tobacco Co. v. Reilly,* 533 U.S. 525, 121 S.Ct. 2404, 69 L.Ed.2d 532 (2001)]

1. Some argue that having a national standard for tobacco regulation is more important than allowing states to set their own standards for tobacco regulation. Do you agree? Why or why not?
2. According to the Court in this case, the federal law does not restrict the ability of state and local governments to adopt general zoning restrictions that apply to cigarettes, so long as those restrictions are "on equal terms with other products." How would you argue in support of this reasoning? How would you argue against it?

FOR CRITICAL ANALYSIS

1–10. In recent years, many people have criticized the film and entertainment industries for promoting violence by exposing the American public, and particularly American youth, to extremely violent films and song lyrics. Do you think that the right to free speech can (or should) be traded off in an attempt to reduce violence in the United States? Generally, in the wake of the September 11, 2001, terrorist attack on the World Trade Center towers and the Pentagon, should Americans trade off some of their civil liberties for (possibly) more protection against violence and terrorism?

INTERNET EXERCISES

Go to the *Business Law Today: The Essentials* home page at **http://blt.westbuslaw.com,** select "Chapter 1," and click on "Internet Exercises." There you will find the following Internet research exercises that you can perform to learn more about topics covered in this chapter.

Activity 1–1: LEGAL PERSPECTIVE—Commercial Speech

Activity 1–2: MANAGEMENT PERSPECTIVE—Privacy Rights in Cyberspace

Activity 1–3: SOCIAL PERSPECTIVE—The Case of the Speluncean Explorers

BEFORE THE TEST

Go to the *Business Law Today: The Essentials* home page at **http://blt.westbuslaw.com,** select "Chapter 1," and click on "Interactive Quizzes." You will find at least twenty interactive questions relating to this chapter.

CHAPTER 1

Appendix

The statutes, agency regulations, and case law referred to in this text establish the rights and duties of businesspersons engaged in various types of activities. The cases presented in the following chapters provide you with concise, real-life illustrations of how the courts interpret and apply these laws. Because of the importance of knowing how to find statutory, administrative, and case law, this appendix offers a brief introduction to how these laws are published and to the legal "shorthand" employed in referencing these legal sources.

Finding Statutory and Administrative Law

When Congress passes laws, they are collected in a publication titled *United States Statutes at Large.* When state legislatures pass laws, they are collected in similar state publications. Most frequently, however, laws are referred to in their codified form—that is, the form in which they appear in the federal and state codes. In these codes, laws are compiled by subject.

UNITED STATES CODE

.on the Web If you are interested in searching the *United States Code,* you can do so online at **http://www4.law.cornell.edu/uscode**.

The *United States Code* (U.S.C.) arranges all existing federal laws of a public and permanent nature by subject. Each of the fifty subjects into which the U.S.C. arranges the laws is given a title and a title number. For example, laws relating to commerce and trade are collected in "Title 15, Commerce and Trade." Titles are subdivided by sections. A citation to the U.S.C. includes title and section numbers. Thus, a reference to "15 U.S.C. Section 1" means that the statute can be found in Section 1 of Title 15. ("Section" may also be designated by the symbol §, and "Sections" by §§.)

Sometimes a citation includes the abbreviation *et seq.*—as in "15 U.S.C. Sections 1 *et seq.*" The term is an abbreviated form of *et sequitur,* which in Latin means "and the following"; when used in a citation, it refers to sections that concern the same subject as the numbered section and follow it in sequence.

Commercial publications of these laws and regulations are available and are widely used. For example, West Group publishes the *United States Code Annotated* (U.S.C.A.). The U.S.C.A. contains the complete text of laws included in the U.S.C., as well as notes of court decisions that interpret and apply specific sections of the statutes, plus the text of presidential proclamations and executive orders. The U.S.C.A. also includes research aids, such as cross-references to related statutes, historical notes, and library references. A citation to the U.S.C.A. is similar to a citation to the U.S.C.: "15 U.S.C.A. Section 1."

STATE CODES

State codes follow the U.S.C. pattern of arranging law by subject. The state codes may be called codes, revisions, compilations, consolidations, general statutes, or statutes, depending on the preferences of the states. In some codes, subjects are designated by number. In others, they are designated by name. For example, "13 Pennsylvania Consolidated Statutes Section 1101" means that the statute can be found in Title 13, Section 1101, of the Pennsylvania code. "California Commercial Code Section 1101" means the statute can be found under the subject heading "Commercial Code" of the California code in Section 1101. Abbreviations may be used. For example, "13 Pennsylvania Consolidated Statutes Section 1101" may be abbreviated "13 Pa. C.S. § 1101," and "California Commercial Code Section 1101" may be abbreviated "Cal. Com. Code § 1101."

ADMINISTRATIVE RULES

.on the Web The *Code of Federal Regulations* is online at **http://www.gpoaccess.gov/cfr/index.html**.

Rules and regulations adopted by federal administrative agencies are compiled in the *Code of Federal Regulations* (C.F.R.). Like the U.S.C., the C.F.R. is divided into fifty titles. Rules within each title are assigned section numbers. A full citation to the C.F.R. includes title and section numbers. For example, a reference to "17 C.F.R. Section 230.504" means that the rule can be found in Section 230.504 of Title 17.

Finding Case Law

Before discussing the case reporting system, we need to look briefly at the court system (which will be discussed in detail in Chapter 3). There are two types of courts in the United States, federal courts and state courts. Both the federal and state court systems consist of several levels, or tiers, of courts. *Trial courts,* in which evidence is presented and testimony given, are on the bottom tier (which also includes lower courts handling specialized issues). Decisions from a trial court can be appealed to a higher court, which commonly would be an intermediate *court of appeals,* or an *appellate court.* Decisions from these intermediate courts of appeals may be appealed to an even higher court, such as a state supreme court or the United States Supreme Court.

STATE COURT DECISIONS

Most state trial court decisions are not published. Except in New York and a few other states that publish selected opinions of their trial courts, decisions from state trial courts are merely filed in the office of the clerk of the court, where the decisions are available for public inspection. (Sometimes, they can be found online as well.) Written decisions of the appellate, or reviewing, courts, however, are published and distributed. As you will note, most of the state court cases presented in this book are from state appellate courts. The reported appellate decisions are published in volumes called *reports* or *reporters,* which are numbered consecutively. State appellate court decisions are found in the state reporters of that particular state.

Additionally, state court opinions appear in regional units of the *National Reporter System,* published by West Group. Most lawyers and libraries have the West reporters because they report cases more quickly and are distributed more widely than the state-published reports. In fact, many states have eliminated their own reporters in favor of West's National Reporter System. The National Reporter System divides the states into the following geographic areas: *Atlantic* (A. or A.2d), *South Eastern* (S.E. or S.E.2d), *South Western* (S.W., S.W.2d, or S.W.3d), *North Western* (N.W. or N.W.2d), *North Eastern* (N.E. or N.E.2d), *Southern* (So. or So.2d), and *Pacific* (P., P.2d, or P.3d). (The *2d* and *3d* in the abbreviations refer to *Second Series* and *Third Series,* respectively.) The states included in each of these regional divisions are indicated in Exhibit 1A–1, which illustrates West's National Reporter System.

EXHIBIT 1A–1 NATIONAL REPORTER SYSTEM—REGIONAL/FEDERAL

Regional Reporters	Coverage Beginning	Coverage
Atlantic Reporter (A. or A.2d)	1885	Connecticut, Delaware, Maine, Maryland, New Hampshire, New Jersey, Pennsylvania, Rhode Island, Vermont, and District of Columbia.
North Eastern Reporter (N.E. or N.E.2d)	1885	Illinois, Indiana, Massachusetts, New York, and Ohio.
North Western Reporter (N.W. or N.W.2d)	1879	Iowa, Michigan, Minnesota, Nebraska, North Dakota, South Dakota, and Wisconsin.
Pacific Reporter (P., P.2d, or P.3d)	1883	Alaska, Arizona, California, Colorado, Hawaii, Idaho, Kansas, Montana, Nevada, New Mexico, Oklahoma, Oregon, Utah, Washington, and Wyoming.
South Eastern Reporter (S.E. or S.E.2d)	1887	Georgia, North Carolina, South Carolina, Virginia, and West Virginia.
South Western Reporter (S.W., S.W.2d, or S.W.3d)	1886	Arkansas, Kentucky, Missouri, Tennessee, and Texas.
Southern Reporter (So. or So.2d)	1887	Alabama, Florida, Louisiana, and Mississippi.
Federal Reporters		
Federal Reporter (F., F.2d, or F.3d)	1880	U.S. Circuit Courts from 1880 to 1912; U.S. Commerce Court from 1911 to 1913; U.S. District Courts from 1880 to 1932; U.S. Court of Claims (now called U.S. Court of Federal Claims) from 1929 to 1932 and since 1960; U.S. Courts of Appeals since 1891; U.S. Court of Customs and Patent Appeals since 1929; U.S. Emergency Court of Appeals since 1943.
Federal Supplement (F.Supp. or F.Supp.2d)	1932	U.S. Court of Claims from 1932 to 1960; U.S. District Courts since 1932; and U.S. Customs Court since 1956.
Federal Rules Decisions (F.R.D.)	1939	U.S. District Courts involving the Federal Rules of Civil Procedure since 1939 and Federal Rules of Criminal Procedure since 1946.
Supreme Court Reporter (S.Ct.)	1882	U.S. Supreme Court since the October term of 1882.
Bankruptcy Reporter (Bankr.)	1980	Bankruptcy decisions of U.S. Bankruptcy Courts, U.S. District Courts, U.S. Courts of Appeals, and U.S. Supreme Court.
Military Justice Reporter (M.J.)	1978	U.S. Court of Military Appeals and Courts of Military Review for the Army, Navy, Air Force, and Coast Guard.

NATIONAL REPORTER SYSTEM MAP

After appellate decisions have been published, they are normally referred to (cited) by the name of the case; the volume, name, and page number of the state's official reporter (if different from West's National Reporter System); the volume, name, and page number of the *National Reporter;* and the volume, name, and page number of any other selected reporter. This information is included in the *citation.* (Citing a reporter by volume number, name, and page number, in that order, is common to all citations.) When more than one reporter is cited for the same case, each reference is called a *parallel citation.* For example, consider the following case: *Yale Diagnostic Radiology v. Estate of Harun Foundation,* 267 Conn. 351, 838 A.2d 179 (2004). We see that the opinion in this case may be found in Volume 267 of the official *Connecticut Reports,* on page 351. The parallel citation is to Volume 838 of the *Atlantic Reporter, Second Series,* page 179. In presenting appellate opinions in this text, in addition to the reporter, we give the name of the court hearing the case and the year of the court's decision.

A few states—including those with intermediate appellate courts, such as California, Illinois, and New York—have more than one reporter for opinions issued by their courts. Sample citations from these courts, as well as others, are listed and explained in Exhibit 1A–2.

FEDERAL COURT DECISIONS

Federal district court decisions are published unofficially in West's *Federal Supplement* (F.Supp. or F.Supp.2d), and opinions from the circuit courts of appeals (federal reviewing courts) are reported unofficially in West's *Federal Reporter* (F., F.2d, or F.3d). Cases concerning federal bankruptcy law are published unofficially in West's *Bankruptcy Reporter* (Bankr.). The official edition of United States Supreme Court decisions is the *United States Reports* (U.S.), which is published by the federal government. Unofficial editions of Supreme Court cases include West's *Supreme Court Reporter* (S.Ct.) and the *Lawyers' Edition of the Supreme Court Reports* (L.Ed. or L.Ed.2d). Sample citations for federal court decisions are also listed and explained in Exhibit 1A–2.

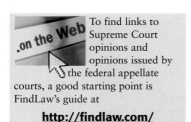

.on the Web To find links to Supreme Court opinions and opinions issued by the federal appellate courts, a good starting point is FindLaw's guide at **http://findlaw.com/10fedgov/judicial**.

UNPUBLISHED OPINIONS AND OLD CASES

Many court opinions that are not yet published or that are not intended for publication can be accessed through Westlaw® (abbreviated in citations as "WL"), an online legal database maintained by West Group. When no citation to a published reporter is available for cases cited in this text, we give the WL citation (see Exhibit 1A–2 for an example).

On a few occasions, this text cites opinions from old, classic cases dating to the nineteenth century or earlier; some of these are from the English courts. The citations to these cases may not conform to the descriptions given above because the reporters in which they were published have since been replaced.

Reading and Understanding Case Law

The cases in this text have been condensed from the full text of the courts' opinions and paraphrased by the authors. For those wishing to review court cases for future research projects or to gain additional legal information, the following sections will provide useful insights into how to read and understand case law.

EXHIBIT 1A–2 HOW TO READ CITATIONS

State Courts

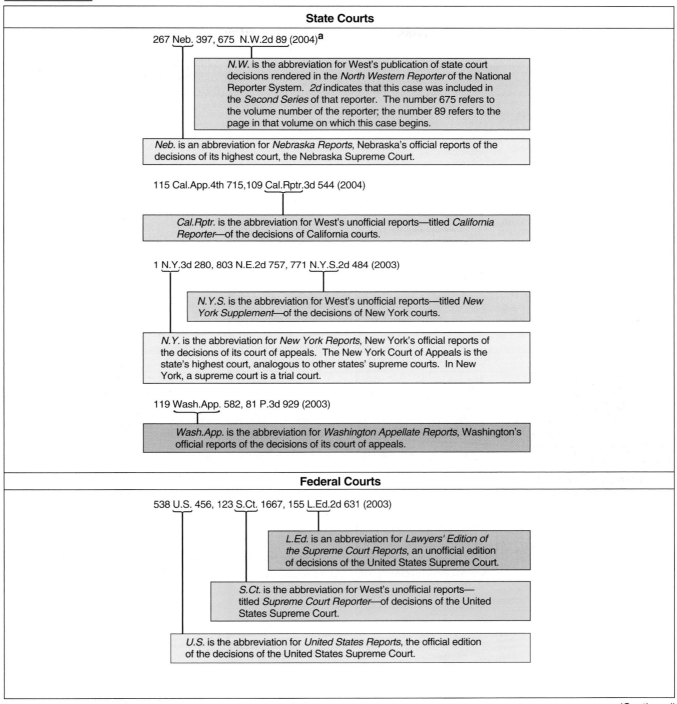

267 Neb. 397, 675 N.W.2d 89 (2004)[a]

N.W. is the abbreviation for West's publication of state court decisions rendered in the *North Western Reporter* of the National Reporter System. *2d* indicates that this case was included in the *Second Series* of that reporter. The number 675 refers to the volume number of the reporter; the number 89 refers to the page in that volume on which this case begins.

Neb. is an abbreviation for *Nebraska Reports*, Nebraska's official reports of the decisions of its highest court, the Nebraska Supreme Court.

115 Cal.App.4th 715,109 Cal.Rptr.3d 544 (2004)

Cal.Rptr. is the abbreviation for West's unofficial reports—titled *California Reporter*—of the decisions of California courts.

1 N.Y.3d 280, 803 N.E.2d 757, 771 N.Y.S.2d 484 (2003)

N.Y.S. is the abbreviation for West's unofficial reports—titled *New York Supplement*—of the decisions of New York courts.

N.Y. is the abbreviation for *New York Reports*, New York's official reports of the decisions of its court of appeals. The New York Court of Appeals is the state's highest court, analogous to other states' supreme courts. In New York, a supreme court is a trial court.

119 Wash.App. 582, 81 P.3d 929 (2003)

Wash.App. is the abbreviation for *Washington Appellate Reports*, Washington's official reports of the decisions of its court of appeals.

Federal Courts

538 U.S. 456, 123 S.Ct. 1667, 155 L.Ed.2d 631 (2003)

L.Ed. is an abbreviation for *Lawyers' Edition of the Supreme Court Reports*, an unofficial edition of decisions of the United States Supreme Court.

S.Ct. is the abbreviation for West's unofficial reports—titled *Supreme Court Reporter*—of decisions of the United States Supreme Court.

U.S. is the abbreviation for *United States Reports*, the official edition of the decisions of the United States Supreme Court.

(Continued)

a. The case names have been deleted from these citations to emphasize the publications. It should be kept in mind, however, that the name of a case is as important as the specific page numbers in the volumes in which it is found. If a citation is incorrect, the correct citation may be found in a publication's index of case names. In addition to providing a check on errors in citations, the date of a case is important because the value of a recent case as an authority is likely to be greater than that of older cases.

EXHIBIT 1A–2 HOW TO READ CITATIONS—CONTINUED

Federal Courts (Continued)

354 F.3d 508 (5th Cir. 2004)

5th Cir. is an abbreviation denoting that this case was decided in the United States Court of Appeals for the Fifth Circuit.

298 F.Supp. 2d 276 (D. Conn. 2004)

D. Conn. is an abbreviation indicating that the United States District Court for the District of Connecticut decided this case.

English Courts

9 Exch. 341, 156 Eng.Rep. 145 (1854)

Eng.Rep. is an abbreviation for *English Reports, Full Reprint,* a series of reports containing selected decisions made in English courts between 1378 and 1865.

Exch. is an abbreviation for *English Exchequer Reports*, which included the original reports of cases decided in England's Court of Exchequer.

Statutory and Other Citations

18 U.S.C. Section 1961(1)(A)

U.S.C. denotes *United States Code*, the codification of *United States Statutes at Large*. The number 18 refers to the statute's U.S.C. title number and 1961 to its section number within that title. The number 1 refers to a subsection within the section and the letter A to a subdivision within the subsection.

UCC 2–206(1)(b)

UCC is an abbreviation for *Uniform Commercial Code*. The first number 2 is a reference to an article of the UCC and 206 to a section within that article. The number 1 refers to a subsection within the section and the letter b to a subdivision within the subsection.

Restatement (Second) of Torts, Section 568

Restatement (Second) of Torts refers to the second edition of the American Law Institute's *Restatement of the Law of Torts.* The number 568 refers to a specific section.

17 C.F.R. Section 230.505

C.F.R. is an abbreviation for *Code of Federal Regulations*, a compilation of federal administrative regulations. The number 17 designates the regulation's title number, and 230.505 designates a specific section within that title.

EXHIBIT 1A–2 HOW TO READ CITATIONS—CONTINUED

Westlaw® Citations

2005 WL 405961

WL is an abbreviation for Westlaw®. The number 2005 is the year of the document that can be found with this citation in the Westlaw® database. The number 405961 is a number assigned to a specific document. A higher number indicates that a document was added to the Westlaw® database later in the year.

Uniform Resource Locators[b]

www.westlaw.com

The suffix *com* is the top level domain (TLD) for this Web site. The TLD *com* is an abbreviation for "commercial," which usually means that a for-profit entity hosts (maintains) this Web site.

westlaw is the host name—the part of the domain name selected by the organization that registered the name. In this case, West Group registered the name. This Internet site is the Westlaw database on the Web.

www is an abbreviation for "World Wide Web." The Web is a system of Internet servers[c] that support documents formatted in *HTML* (hypertext markup language). HTML supports links to text, graphics, and audio and video files.

www.uscourts.gov

This is "The Federal Judiciary Home Page." The host is the Administrative Office of the U.S. Courts. The TLD *gov* is an abbreviation for "government." This Web site includes information and links from, and about, the federal courts.

www.law.cornell.edu/index.html

This part of a URL points to a Web page or file at a specific location within the host's domain. This page, at this Web site, is a menu with links to documents within the domain and to other Internet resources.

This is the host name for a Web site that contains the Internet publications of the Legal Information Institute (LII), which is a part of Cornell Law School. The LII site includes a variety of legal materials and links to other legal resources on the Internet. The TLD *edu* is an abbreviation for "educational institution" (a school or a university).

www.ipl.org.ref/RR

RR is an abbreviation for this Web site's "Ready Reference Collection," which contains links to a variety of Internet resources.

ref is an abbreviation for "Internet Public Library Reference Center," which is a map of the topics into which the links at this Web site have been categorized.

ipl is an abbreviation for Internet Public Library, which is an online service that provides reference resources and links to other information services on the Web. The IPL is supported chiefly by the School of Information at the University of Michigan. The TLD *org* is an abbreviation for "organization" (usually nonprofit).

b. The basic form for a URL is "service://hostname/path." The Internet service for all of the URLs in this text is *http* (hypertext transfer protocol). Most Web browsers will add this prefix automatically when a user enters a host name or a hostname/path.
c. A *server* is hardware that manages the resources on a network. For example, a network server is a computer that manages the traffic on the network, and a print server is a computer that manages several printers.

CASE TITLES AND TERMINOLOGY

The title of a case, such as *Adams v. Jones,* indicates the names of the parties to the lawsuit. The *v.* in the case title stands for *versus,* which means "against." In the trial court, Adams was the plaintiff—the person who filed the suit. Jones was the defendant. If the case is appealed, however, the appellate court will sometimes place the name of the party appealing the decision first, so the case may be called *Jones v. Adams.* Because some reviewing courts retain the trial court order of names, it is often impossible to distinguish the plaintiff from the defendant in the title of a reported appellate court decision. You must carefully read the facts of each case to identify the parties.

The following terms and phrases are frequently encountered in court opinions and legal publications. Because it is important to understand what these terms and phrases mean, we define and discuss them here.

Plaintiffs and Defendants As mentioned in Chapter 1, the plaintiff in a lawsuit is the party that initiates the action. The defendant is the party against which a lawsuit is brought. Lawsuits frequently involve more than one plaintiff and/or defendant.

Appellants and Appellees The *appellant* is the party that appeals a case to another court or jurisdiction from the court or jurisdiction in which the case was originally brought. Sometimes, an appellant is referred to as the *petitioner.* The *appellee* is the party against which the appeal is taken. Sometimes, the appellee is referred to as the *respondent.*

Judges and Justices The terms *judge* and *justice* are usually synonymous and represent two designations given to judges in various courts. All members of the United States Supreme Court, for example, are referred to as justices. And justice is the formal title usually given to judges of appellate courts, although this is not always the case. In New York, a justice is a judge of the trial court (which is called the Supreme Court), and a member of the Court of Appeals (the state's highest court) is called a judge. The term *justice* is commonly abbreviated to J., and *justices* to JJ. A Supreme Court case might refer to Justice O'Connor as O'Connor, J., or to Chief Justice Rehnquist as Rehnquist, C.J.

Decisions and Opinions Most decisions reached by reviewing, or appellate, courts are explained in written *opinions.* The opinion contains the court's reasons for its decision, the rules of law that apply, and the judgment. When all judges or justices unanimously agree on an opinion, the opinion is written for the entire court and can be deemed a *unanimous opinion.* When there is not unanimous agreement, a *majority opinion* is written, outlining the views of the majority of the judges or justices deciding the case.

Often, a judge or justice who feels strongly about making or emphasizing a point that was not made or emphasized in the unanimous or majority opinion will write a *concurring opinion.* That means the judge or justice agrees (concurs) with the judgment given in the unanimous or majority opinion but for different reasons. When there is not a unanimous opinion, a *dissenting opinion* is usually written by a judge or justice who does not agree with the majority. The dissenting opinion is important because it may form the basis of the arguments used years later in overruling the precedential majority opinion. Occasionally, a court issues a *per curiam*

(Latin for "of the court") opinion, which does not indicate which judge or justice authored the opinion.

A Sample Court Case

Knowing how to read and analyze a court opinion is an essential step in undertaking accurate legal research. A further step involves "briefing" the case. Legal researchers routinely brief cases by summarizing and reducing the texts of the opinions to their essential elements. The cases contained within the chapters of this text have already been analyzed and briefed by the authors, and the essential aspects of each case are presented in a convenient format consisting of four basic sections: *Facts, Issue, Decision,* and *Reason,* as shown in Exhibit 1A–3 on the following page, which has also been annotated to illustrate the kind of information that is contained in each section.

Throughout this text, in addition to this basic format, we sometimes include a special introductory section entitled *Historical and Social [Economic, Technological, Political, or other] Setting.* In some instances, a *Company Profile* is included in place of the introductory setting. These profiles provide a background on one of the parties to the lawsuit. Each case is followed by either a brief *For Critical Analysis* section, which, as in Exhibit 1A–3, presents a question regarding some issue raised by the case, or a *Why Is This Case Important?* section, which explains the significance of the case.

The Supreme Court building in Washington, D.C. In what reporters are Supreme Court opinions published? (PhotoDisc)

EXHIBIT 1A–3 A SAMPLE COURT CASE

1 UMG RECORDINGS, INC. v. SINNOTT

2 United States District Court,
Eastern District of California, 2004.

3 300 F.Supp.2d 993.

4 FACTS Richard Sinnott owns and operates the Marysville Flea Market (MFM) in Marysville, California. The MFM is open every Sunday and has the capacity to accommodate about two hundred vendor booths. Each vendor, or seller, pays Sinnott a fee to rent a booth to sell merchandise. Sinnott provides security personnel, utilities, restrooms, and other amenities. On September 3, 2000, investigators with the Recording Industry Association of America (RIAA) found MFM vendors offering counterfeit CDs and cassettes for sale and asked Sinnott to help stop the illegal activity. The investigators told Sinnott that he could be liable for the sales and offered to train MFM employees to detect counterfeit recordings. Sinnott refused and ordered the investigators out of his office. Over the next two years, the investigators visited six more times and found vendors offering as many as 20,000 counterfeit items for sale. The RIAA wrote Sinnott four letters, repeatedly advising him of the illegal activity, his potential liability, and their offer to train MFM employees. When Sinnott failed to cooperate, UMG Recordings, Inc., and other owners of the rights to the pirated music filed a suit in a federal district court against Sinnott, seeking to hold him responsible. The plaintiffs filed a motion for summary judgment.

5 ISSUE Can a flea market owner be held liable for a vendor's infringement of another's copyright?

6 DECISION Yes. In the first federal court decision on the issue, the court held a flea market owner contributorily liable for the copyright infringement by the owner's vendors. The court granted a summary judgment in the plaintiffs' favor.

7 REASON The court explained that the Copyright Act does not impose secondary liability for copyright infringement, but "courts have long recognized that in certain circumstances, vicarious or contributory liability will be imposed. * * * To hold Sinnott liable for contributory infringement, Plaintiffs must show that Sinnott knew or had reason to know of direct infringement" and that he materially contributed to that infringement. "RIAA investigators personally told him of the infringement * * *. Sinnott claims this is insufficient to establish actual knowledge because he did not know who or what RIAA was, and claims to have felt threatened by the investigators. What he does not claim, however, is that he did not receive and understand the message the investigators delivered. * * * The fact that he was not personally acquainted with the messenger does not mean that he can ignore the message and claim ignorance of its contents." Finally, "[o]perating a flea market or swap meet involves providing vendors with support services such as the provision of space, utilities, parking, advertising, plumbing, and customers. This is all that is required to satisfy the requirement of material contribution."

8 FOR CRITICAL ANALYSIS—Social Consideration *What should flea market owners, and others similarly situated, do to prevent sales of pirated music on their property?*

REVIEW OF SAMPLE COURT CASE

1 The name of the case is *UMG Recordings, Inc. v. Sinnott.* One of the owners of the copyrighted music at the center of this case is the identified plaintiff; the owner of the flea market is the defendant.

2 The court deciding this case is the U.S. District Court for the Eastern District of California.

3 The case citation includes a citation to the official *Federal Supplement, Second Series.* The case can be found in Volume 300 of this reporter, on page 993.

4 The *Facts* section identifies the plaintiff and the defendant, describes the events leading up to this suit, and explains what the plaintiff sought to obtain by bringing this action. If this were a case before an appellate court, the rulings of the lower court and the appellant's contention on appeal would also be included here.

5 The *Issue* section presents the central issue (or issues) to be decided by the court. This case involves copyright infringement. Under the Copyright Act, persons who author original works in music or literature, for example, can bring a copyright infringement action against anyone who makes unauthorized copies (see Chapter 5). In this case, the issue is whether to extend that liability to other persons who indirectly but knowingly contribute to that infringement. Most cases concern more than one issue, but the authors of this textbook have edited each case to focus on just one issue.

6 The *Decision* section, as the name indicates, contains the court's decision on the issue or issues before the court. The decision reflects the opinion of the judge, or the majority of the judges or justices, hearing the case. In this particular case, the court granted the plaintiffs' motion for summary judgment (a summary judgment for one party can be entered by the judge before the case proceeds to trial—see Chapter 3). In other words, the court decided that the flea market owner was liable because he knew about the infringing activities of the vendors and did nothing to stop them, thereby contributing to the infringement. Decisions by appellate courts are frequently phrased in reference to the lower court's decision; that is, the appellate court may "affirm" the lower court's ruling or "reverse" it. In either situation, the appellate court may "remand," or send back, the case for further proceedings.

7 The *Reason* section indicates what relevant laws and judicial principles were applied in forming the particular conclusion arrived at in the case at bar ("before the court"). In this case, the relevant statute was the Copyright Act, which governs the rights of authors and others to certain literary or artistic productions. The court determined that a flea market owner who had reason to know about a vendor's infringement of another's copyright may be held liable under the Copyright Act when the vendor offers for sale counterfeit CDs or cassettes.

8 The *For Critical Analysis—Social Consideration* section raises a question to be considered in relation to the case just presented. Here the question involves a "social" consideration. In other cases presented in this text, the "consideration" may involve a cultural, economic, environmental, ethical, international, political, social, or technological consideration.

CHAPTER 2

Ethics and Professional Responsibility

"New occasions teach new duties."
James Russell Lowell, 1819–1891
(American editor, poet, and diplomat)

CHAPTER OUTLINE

- BUSINESS ETHICS
- SETTING THE RIGHT ETHICAL TONE
- BUSINESS ETHICS AND THE LAW
- APPROACHES TO ETHICAL REASONING
- PROFESSIONAL RESPONSIBILITY
- DEFYING THE RULES: THE ENRON CASE
- THE SARBANES-OXLEY ACT OF 2002
- BUSINESS ETHICS ON A GLOBAL LEVEL

LEARNING OBJECTIVES

After reading this chapter, you should be able to answer the following questions:

1. What is ethics? What is business ethics? Why is business ethics important?
2. How can business leaders encourage their companies to act ethically?
3. How do duty-based ethical standards differ from outcome-based ethical standards?
4. What duties do professionals owe to those who rely on their services?
5. What types of ethical issues might arise in the context of international business transactions?

During the early part of the 2000s, the American public was shocked as one business ethics scandal after another became headline news. Each scandal involved serious consequences. Certainly, those responsible for grossly inflating the reported profits at WorldCom, Inc., ended up not only destroying shareholder value in a great company but also facing possible prison terms. Those officers and directors at Enron Corporation who utilized a system of complicated off-the-books transactions to inflate current earnings saw their company go bankrupt—one of the largest bankruptcies in U.S. history. They harmed not only their employees and shareholders but also the communities in which they worked—and themselves (some of them have since received prison sentences, and others have been indicted). The officers and directors of Tyco International who used corporate funds to pay for lavish personal lifestyles also ended up in court. The shareholders of that company suffered dearly, too.

In response to the public's outrage over these scandals, Congress passed the Sarbanes-Oxley Act of 2002. This act imposed requirements on corporations that are designed to deter similar unethical and illegal business behavior in the future. As the chapter-opening quotation states, "New occasions teach new duties." Indeed, the ethics scandals of the early 2000s taught businesses throughout the country that corporate governance is not to be taken lightly.

Business ethics, the focus of this chapter, is not just theory. It is practical, useful, and essential. Although a good understanding of business law and the legal environment is critical, it is not enough. Understanding how one should act in her or his business dealings is equally—if not more—important in today's business arena.

Business Ethics

ETHICS
Moral principles and values applied to social behavior.

Before we look at business ethics, we need to discuss what is meant by ethics generally. **Ethics** can be defined as the study of what constitutes right or wrong behavior. It is the branch of philosophy that focuses on morality and the way in which moral principles are derived or the way in which a given set of moral principles applies to one's conduct in daily life. Ethics has to do with questions relating to the fairness, justness, rightness, or wrongness of an action. What is fair? What is just? What is the right thing to do in this situation? These are essentially ethical questions.

WHAT IS BUSINESS ETHICS?

BUSINESS ETHICS
Ethics in a business context; a consensus of what constitutes right or wrong behavior in the world of business and the application of moral principles to situations that arise in a business setting.

Business ethics focuses on what constitutes right or wrong behavior in the business world and on how moral and ethical principles are applied by businesspersons to situations that arise in their daily activities in the workplace. Note that business ethics is not a separate *kind* of ethics. The ethical standards that guide our behavior as, say, mothers, fathers, or students apply equally well to our activities as businesspersons. Business decision makers, though, must often address more complex ethical issues and conflicts in the workplace than they face in their personal lives.

WHY IS BUSINESS ETHICS IMPORTANT?

Why is business ethics important? The answer to this question is clear from this chapter's introduction. A keen and in-depth understanding of business ethics is important to the long-run viability of a corporation. A thorough knowledge of business ethics is also important to the well-being of the individual officers and directors of the corporation, as well as to the welfare of the firm's employees and various "stakeholders" in the entity's well-being. Certainly, corporate decisions and activities can significantly affect not only those who own, operate, or work for the company but also such groups as suppliers, the community, and society as a whole.

Note that questions concerning ethical and responsible behavior are not confined to the corporate context. Business ethics applies to *all* businesses, regardless of their organizational forms. In a business partnership, for example, partners owe a *fiduciary duty* (a duty of trust and loyalty) to each other and to their firm. This duty can sometimes conflict with what a partner sees as his or her own best interest. Partners who act solely in their own interests may violate their duties to the other partners and the firm, however. By violating this duty, they may end up paying steep penalties—as the following case illustrates.

CASE 2.1 Time Warner Entertainment Co. v. Six Flags Over Georgia, L.L.C.

Georgia Court of Appeals, 2002.
254 Ga.App. 598,
563 S.E.2d 178.
http://www.ganet.org/appeals/opinions/index.cgi[a]

FACTS The Six Flags Over Georgia theme park in Atlanta, Georgia, was developed in 1967 as a limited partnership known as Six Flags Over Georgia, L.L.C. (Flags). The sole limited partner was Six Flags Fund, Limited (Fund). The general partner was Six Flags Over Georgia, Inc. (SFOG). In 1991, Time Warner Entertainment Company (TWE) became the majority shareholder of SFOG. The next year, TWE secretly bought 13.7 acres of land next to the park, limiting the park's expansion opportunities. Over the next couple of years, using confidential business information from the park, TWE began plans to develop a competing park. Meanwhile, TWE installed no major new attractions at the park, deferred basic maintenance, withheld financial information from Fund (the limited partner), and began signing future employment contracts with SFOG officers. TWE also charged Flags for unrelated expenses, including over $4 million for lunches in New York City and luxury automobiles for TWE officers. Flags and Fund filed a suit in a Georgia state court against TWE and SFOG, alleging, among other things, breach of fiduciary duty. A jury awarded the plaintiffs $197,296,000 in compensatory damages and $257,000,000 in punitive damages. TWE appealed to a state intermediate appellate court, alleging in part that the amount of the punitive damages was excessive.

a. This Web site is sponsored by the state of Georgia. At the search screen, click on "Search Court of Appeals Opinions." On the appellate court's screen, set the search year to "all." You can go to a case most directly if you use as key words the full name of a party—for example, "Time Warner Entertainment Co."

ISSUE Was the amount of punitive damages excessive?

DECISION No. The state intermediate appellate court affirmed the judgment of the lower court.

REASON The appellate court held that the award of punitive damages was not excessive, considering the amount of compensatory damages ("the ratio of compensatory to punitive damages is 1 to 1.3"), the defendants' financial status "with collective assets measured in billions of dollars," and their "reprehensible" (blameworthy) conduct toward the plaintiffs. The appellate court stated, "In examining the degree of reprehensibility of a defendant's conduct, [there are] a number of aggravating factors [to consider], including whether the harm was more than purely economic in nature, and whether the defendant's behavior evinced [showed] indifference to or reckless disregard for the health and safety of others. Here, although the harm to Flags and Fund was primarily economic, it was caused by conduct we find especially reprehensible. Appellants' intentional breach of its fiduciary duty revealed a callous indifference to the financial well-being of its limited partners and their individual investors." The court concluded that "[a]ppellants' conduct was, in short, the kind of behavior we find deserving of reproof, rebuke, or censure; blameworthy—the very definition of reprehensible.
* * * Trickery and deceit are reprehensible wrongs, especially when done intentionally through affirmative acts of misconduct."

FOR CRITICAL ANALYSIS—Ethical Consideration
If TWE had proceeded with its plans to build a competing park but had not otherwise acted "reprehensibly" toward Flags and Fund, how might the decision in this case have been different?

Setting the Right Ethical Tone

Many unethical business decisions are made simply because they *can* be made. In other words, the decision makers not only have the opportunity to make such decisions but also are not too concerned about being seriously sanctioned for their unethical actions. Perhaps one of the most difficult challenges for business leaders today is to create the right "ethical tone" in their workplaces so as to deter unethical conduct.

THE IMPORTANCE OF ETHICAL LEADERSHIP

Talking about ethical business decision making means nothing if management does not set standards. Moreover, managers must apply those standards to themselves and to the employees in the company. The *Application* feature at the end of this chapter provides additional suggestions on how management can create an ethical workplace.

Attitude of Top Management One of the most important factors in creating and maintaining an ethical workplace is the attitude of top management. Managers who are not totally committed to maintaining an ethical workplace will rarely succeed in creating one. Surveys of business executives indicate that management's behavior, more than anything else, sets the ethical tone of a firm. In other words, employees take their cue from management. If a firm's managers adhere to obvious ethical norms in their business dealings, employees will likely follow their example. In contrast, if managers act unethically, employees will see no reason not to do so themselves. ■ **EXAMPLE 2.1** An employee observes a manager cheating on her expense account. That employee quickly understands that such behavior is acceptable. ■

Looking the Other Way A manager who looks the other way when he knows about an employee's unethical behavior also sets an example—one indicating that ethical transgressions will be accepted. Managers must show that they will not tolerate unethical business behavior. Although this may seem harsh, managers have found that discharging even one employee for ethical reasons has a tremendous impact as a deterrent to unethical behavior in the workplace. The following case illustrates what can happen when managers look the other way.

CASE 2.2 In re the *Exxon Valdez*

United States District Court,
District of Alaska, 2004.
296 F.Supp.2d 1071.

FACTS Exxon Shipping Company owned the *Exxon Valdez,* an oil supertanker as long as three football fields with the capacity to hold 53 million gallons of crude oil. The captain of the *Valdez* was Joseph Hazelwood, an alcoholic, who had sought treatment in 1985 but had relapsed before the next spring. Exxon knew that Hazelwood had relapsed and that he drank while onboard ship, but nevertheless allowed him to command the *Valdez.* On March 24, 1989, the *Valdez* ran aground on Bligh Reef in Prince William Sound, Alaska. About 11 million gallons of crude oil leaked from the ship and spread around the sound. Commercial fisheries closed for the rest of the year. Subsistence fishing and shore-based businesses dependent on the fishing industry were disrupted. Exxon spent $2.1 billion to clean up the spilled oil and paid $303 million to those whose livelihoods were disrupted. Thousands of claims were consolidated into a single case tried in a federal district court. The jury awarded, in part, $5 billion in punitive damages against Exxon. Exxon appealed to the U.S. Court of Appeals for the Ninth Circuit, which remanded the case for reconsideration of this award, according to the reprehensibility of the defendant's conduct and other factors. The court also instructed the lower court to reduce the amount if the award was upheld.

ISSUE Did the $5 billion punitive damages award against Exxon constitute grossly excessive or arbitrary punishment?

DECISION No. The court determined that Exxon's conduct was "intentionally malicious" and "highly reprehensible." Concluding that "[p]unitive damages should reflect the enormity of the defendant's offense," the court upheld the award but reduced the amount to $4.5 billion "as the means of resolving the conflict between its conclusion and the directions of the court of appeals."

REASON The court pointed out that "Exxon's conduct did not simply cause economic harm to the plaintiffs. Exxon's decision to leave Captain Hazelwood in command

(Continued)

CASE 2.2—Continued

of the *Exxon Valdez* demonstrated reckless disregard for a broad range of legitimate Alaska concerns: the livelihood, health, and safety of the residents of Prince William Sound, the crew of the *Exxon Valdez,* and others. Exxon's conduct targeted some financially vulnerable individuals, namely subsistence fishermen [those who make their living by fishing]. Plaintiffs' harm was not the result of an isolated incident but was the result of Exxon's repeated decisions, over a period of approximately three years, to allow Captain Hazelwood to remain in command despite Exxon's knowledge that he was drinking and driving again." The court compared Exxon's conduct to other cases in which punitive damages were awarded and concluded that "Exxon's conduct was many degrees of magnitude more egregious [conspicuously wrongful]. For approximately three years, Exxon management, with knowledge that Captain Hazelwood had fallen off the wagon, willfully permitted him to operate a fully loaded, crude oil tanker in and out of Prince William Sound—a body of water which Exxon knew to be highly valuable for its fisheries resources. Exxon's argument that its conduct in permitting a relapsed alcoholic to operate an oil tanker should be characterized as less reprehensible * * * suggests that Exxon, even today, has not come to grips with the opprobrium [disgrace, contempt] which society rightly attaches to drunk driving."

WHY IS THIS CASE IMPORTANT? *This case is an excellent illustration of the consequences that a business may face when it ignores a serious risk that has been created by its action (or inaction). By allowing Captain Hazelwood, a relapsed alcoholic, to remain in charge of the* Exxon Valdez, *Exxon created serious risks to the environment and the residents of Prince William Sound. These risks led to severe harms. The consequences for Exxon—$4.5 billion in punitive damages—were also severe.*

Setting Realistic Goals Helps Managers can reduce the probability that employees will act unethically by setting realistic production or sales goals. ■ EXAMPLE 2.2 Suppose that a sales quota can be met only through high-pressure and unethical sales tactics. Employees trying to act "in the best interests of the firm" may think that management is implicitly asking them to behave unethically. ■

Periodic Evaluation Some companies require their managers to meet individually with employees and to grade them on their ethical (or unethical) behavior. ■ EXAMPLE 2.3 One company asks its employees to fill out ethical checklists each month and return them to their supervisors. This practice serves two purposes: First, it demonstrates to employees that ethics matters. Second, employees have an opportunity to reflect on how well they have measured up in terms of ethical performance. ■

CREATING ETHICAL CODES OF CONDUCT

One of the most effective ways of setting a tone of ethical behavior within an organization is to create an ethical code of conduct. A well-written code of ethics explicitly states a company's ethical priorities.

Costco—An Example This chapter includes a foldout exhibit showing a code of ethics created by Costco Wholesale Corporation, a large warehouse-club retailer with over 45 million "members." This code of conduct indicates Costco's commitment to legal compliance, as well as to the welfare of its members (those who purchase its goods), its employees, and its suppliers. The code also details some specific ways in which the interests and welfare of these different groups will be protected. If you look closely at this exhibit, you will also see that Costco acknowledges that by protecting these groups' interests, it will realize its "ultimate goal"—rewarding its shareholders with maximum shareholder value.

Another Necessity—Clear Communication to Employees For an ethical code to be effective, its provisions must be clearly communicated to employees. Most large companies have implemented ethics training programs, in which managers discuss with employees on a face-to-face basis the firm's policies and the importance of ethical conduct. Some firms hold periodic ethics seminars during which employees can openly discuss any ethical problems that they may be experiencing and learn how the firm's ethical policies apply to those specific problems.

Johnson & Johnson—An Example of Web-Based Ethics Training Creating a code of conduct and implementing it are two different activities. In many companies, codes of conduct are simply documents that have very little relevance to day-to-day operations. When Johnson & Johnson wanted to "do better" than other companies with respect to ethical business decision making, it created a Center for Legal and Credo Awareness. (Its code of ethical conduct is called its credo.)

The center created a Web-based set of instructions designed to enhance the corporation's efforts to train employees in the importance of its code of conduct. Given that Johnson & Johnson has over 110,000 employees in fifty-seven countries around the world, reinforcing its code of conduct and its values has not been easy, but Web-based training has helped. The company established a Web-based legal and compliance center, which uses a set of interactive modules to train employees in areas of law and ethics.

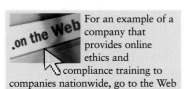

.on the Web For an example of a company that provides online ethics and compliance training to companies nationwide, go to the Web site of Interactive Corporation at **http://www.integrity-interactive.com/welcome.htm**.

CORPORATE COMPLIANCE PROGRAMS

In large corporations, ethical codes of conduct are usually just one part of a comprehensive corporate compliance program. Other components of such a program, some of which were already mentioned, include a corporation's ethics committee, ethical training programs, and internal audits to monitor compliance with applicable laws and the company's standards of ethical conduct.

The Sarbanes-Oxley Act and Web-Based Reporting Systems The Sarbanes-Oxley Act of 2002[1] requires companies to set up confidential systems so that employees and others may "raise red flags" about suspected illegal or unethical auditing and accounting practices. The act required publicly traded companies to have such systems in place by April 2003.

Some companies have implemented online reporting systems. In one Web-based reporting system, employees can click on an icon on their computers that anonymously links them with Ethicspoint, an organization based in Vancouver, Washington. Through Ethicspoint, employees may report suspicious accounting practices, sexual harassment, and other possibly unethical behavior. Ethicspoint, in turn, alerts management personnel or the audit committee at the designated company to the possible problem. Those who have used the system say that it is less inhibiting than calling a company's 800 number.

Compliance Programs Must Be Integrated To be effective, a compliance program must be integrated throughout the firm. For large corporations, such integration is essential. Ethical policies and programs need to be coordinated and monitored by a committee that is separate from various corporate departments. Otherwise, unethical behavior in one department can easily escape the attention of those in control of

1. 15 U.S.C. Sections 7201 *et seq.*

the corporation or the corporate officials responsible for implementing and monitoring the company's compliance program.

ETHICAL ISSUE 2.1 ***Should companies hire chief governance officers?*** According to a survey released by the Ethics Resource Center and the Society for Human Resource Management in April 2003, ethical conduct is not rewarded in today's business world. Indeed, 24 percent of the human resources (HR) managers surveyed felt pressure to compromise ethical standards either all of the time, fairly often, or periodically. In 1997, only 13 percent of the same class of respondents felt the same way. This finding is significant because HR personnel are often caught in the middle between employees who come to them with ethical complaints and company officers who may or may not agree with the HR manager's recommendations as to how the company should respond to specific complaints.

What can companies do to ensure ethical compliance? Should they hire specially trained legal executives, known as chief governance officers (CGOs), to oversee corporate compliance? According to some business ethicists, having a CGO can help a company prevent future governance problems that could be costly. In 1992, pharmaceutical manufacturer Pfizer, Inc., became the first company to hire a CGO. Since then, about sixty other companies have done so. In the wake of the business scandals of the early 2000s and the requirements imposed under the subsequent Sarbanes-Oxley Act of 2002, the number of companies that have CGOs is expected to grow rapidly.[2] ■

Conflicts and Trade-Offs

Management constantly faces ethical trade-offs, some of which may lead to legal problems. As mentioned earlier, firms have implied ethical (and legal) duties to a number of groups, including shareholders and employees.

When a company decides to reduce costs by downsizing and restructuring, the decision may benefit shareholders, but it will harm those employees who are laid off or fired. When downsizing occurs, which employees should be laid off first? Cost-cutting considerations might dictate firing the most senior employees, who generally have higher salaries, and retaining less senior employees, whose salaries are much lower. A company does not necessarily act illegally when it does so. Yet the decision to be made by management clearly involves an important ethical question: Which group's interests—those of the shareholders or those of employees who have been loyal to the firm for a long period of time—should take priority in this situation?

.on the Web You can find articles on issues relating to corporate governance and accountability at the Corporate Governance Web site. Go to **http://www.corpgov.net**.

■ EXAMPLE 2.4 In one case, an employer facing a dwindling market and decreasing sales decided to reduce its costs by eliminating some of its obligations to its employees. It did this by establishing a subsidiary corporation and then transferring some of its employees, and the administration of their retirement benefits, to that entity. The company expected the subsidiary to fail, and when it did, some employees and retirees who were left with no retirement benefits sued the company. The plaintiffs claimed that the company had breached a fiduciary duty under a federal law governing employer-provided pensions. Ultimately, the United States Supreme Court agreed with the plaintiffs, stating, among other things, that "[l]ying is inconsistent with the duty of loyalty owed by all fiduciaries."[3] ■

2. Tamara Loomis, "Companies Are Hiring Chief Governance Officers," *The National Law Journal,* May 5, 2003, p. A15.
3. *Varity Corp. v. Howe,* 516 U.S. 489, 116 S.Ct. 1065, 134 L.Ed.2d 130 (1996).

Business Ethics and the Law

MORAL MINIMUM
The minimum degree of ethical behavior expected of a business firm, which is usually defined as compliance with the law.

Today, legal compliance is regarded as a **moral minimum**—the minimum acceptable standard for ethical business behavior. Had Enron Corporation strictly complied with existing laws and generally accepted accounting practices, very likely the "Enron scandal," which came to light in the early 2000s, would never have happened. Simply obeying the law does not fulfill all business ethics obligations, however. In the interests of preserving personal freedom, as well as for practical reasons, the law does not—and cannot—codify all ethical requirements. No law says, for example, that it is illegal to lie to one's family, but it may be unethical to do so.

It might seem that determining the legality of a given action should be simple. Either something is legal or it is not. In fact, one of the major challenges businesspersons face is that the legality of a particular action is not always clear. In part, this is because business is regulated by so many laws that it is possible to violate one of them without realizing it. The law also contains numerous "gray areas," making it difficult to predict how a court will apply a given law to a particular action. This is especially true when technological developments have raised new types of questions. For example, if a business's trademark is used in a domain name followed by "fraud" or "sucks," is this an infringement of the owner's trademark? For a discussion of this question, see this chapter's *Adapting the Law to the Online Environment* feature on the next page.

Laws Regulating Business

Today's business firms are subject to extensive government regulation. As mentioned in Chapter 1, virtually every action a firm undertakes—from the initial act of going into business, to hiring and firing personnel, to selling products in the marketplace—is subject to statutory law and to numerous rules and regulations issued by administrative agencies. Furthermore, these rules and regulations are changed or supplemented frequently.

Determining whether a planned action is legal thus requires that decision makers keep abreast of the law. Normally, large business firms have attorneys on their staffs to assist them in making key decisions. Small firms must also seek legal advice before making important business decisions because the consequences of just one violation of a regulatory rule may be costly.

Ignorance of the law will not excuse a business owner or manager from liability for violating a statute or regulation. ■ Example 2.5 In one case, the court imposed criminal fines, as well as imprisonment, on a company's supervisory employee for violating a federal environmental act. This punishment was imposed even though the employee was completely unaware of what was required under the provisions of that act.[4] ■

"Gray Areas" in the Law

In many situations, business firms can predict with a fair amount of certainty whether a given action would be legal. For instance, firing an employee solely because of that person's race or gender would clearly violate federal laws prohibiting employment discrimination. In some situations, though, the legality of a particular action may be less clear.

■ Example 2.6 Suppose that a firm decides to launch a new advertising campaign. How far can the firm go in making claims for its products or services? Federal and

4. *United States v. Hanousek,* 176 F.3d 1116 (9th Cir. 1999)—see Case 6.1 in Chapter 6.

ADAPTING THE LAW TO THE ONLINE ENVIRONMENT

"Sucks" Sites—Can They Be Shut Down?

In today's online environment, a recurring challenge for businesses is how to deal with cybergripers—those who complain in cyberspace about corporate products, services, or activities. For trademark owners, the issue becomes particularly thorny when cybergriping sites add "sucks," "fraud," "scam," "ripoff," or some other disparaging term as a suffix to the domain name of a particular company. These sites, sometimes collectively referred to as "sucks" sites, are established solely for the purpose of criticizing the products or services sold by the companies that own the marks. In some cases, they have been used maliciously to harm the reputation of a competitor. Can businesses do anything to ward off these cyber attacks on their reputations and goodwill?

THE TRADEMARK ISSUE

A number of companies have sued the owners of "sucks" sites for trademark infringement in the hope that a court or an arbitrating panel will order the owner of that site to cease using the domain name. To date, however, companies have had little success pursuing this alternative. In one case, Bear Stearns Companies, Inc., sued a cybergriper, Nye Lavalle, alleging that Lavalle infringed its trademark by creating Web sites including "Bear Stearns" in the domain names. Some of these sites were called "BearStearnsFrauds.com," "BearStearnsCriminals.com," and "BearStearnsComplaints.com."

As will be discussed in Chapter 5, one of the tests for trademark infringement is whether consumers would be confused by the use of a similar or identical trademark. Would consumers mistakenly believe that Lavalle's sites were operated by Bear Stearns? In the court's eyes, no. The court concluded that Lavalle's "Frauds.com" and "Criminals.com" sites were "unmistakenly critical" of the target company and that no Internet user would conclude that Bear Stearns sponsored the sites. As to the "Complaints.com" site, however, the court concluded that consumers might be confused—because Bear Stearns could have a "complaints" page on its Web site. Therefore, the "Complaints.com" site violated trademark law, but the other two sites did not.[a]

FOR CYBERGRIPERS, THE MORE OUTRAGEOUS THE SUFFIX, THE BETTER

For cybergripers, the message seems to be clear: the more outrageous or obnoxious the suffix added to a target company's trademark, the less likely it is that the use will constitute trademark infringement. This point is underscored in decisions reached by other courts as well. In *Taubman Co. v. Webfeats,*[b] for example, a cybergriping case decided by the U.S. Court of Appeals for the Sixth Circuit, the court stressed that Internet users were unlikely be confused by "sucks" sites using the Taubman Company name. Because the allegedly infringing domain names all ended with "sucks.com," the court concluded that they were unlikely to mislead Web site visitors into believing that the trademark owner was the source or sponsor of the complaint. The court also noted in its opinion that, generally, the more vicious an attack site's domain name, the less likely that a cybergriper will be found liable for trademark infringement.

FOR CRITICAL ANALYSIS

How might cybergriping sites help to improve the ethical performance of the businesses they criticize? What can business owners do to prevent the use of their marks in "sucks" sites?

a. *Bear Stearns Companies, Inc. v. Lavalle,* 2002 WL 31757771 (N.D.Tex. 2002).
b. 319 F.3d 770 (6th Cir. 2003).

state laws prohibit firms from engaging in "deceptive advertising." At the federal level, the test for deceptive advertising normally used by the Federal Trade Commission is whether an advertising claim would deceive a "reasonable consumer."[5] At what point, though, would a reasonable consumer be deceived by a particular ad? ■

5. See Chapter 13 for a discussion of the Federal Trade Commission's role in regulating deceptive trade practices, including misleading advertising.

In short, business decision makers need to proceed with caution and evaluate an action and its consequences from an ethical perspective. Generally, if a company can demonstrate that it acted in good faith and responsibly in the circumstances, it has a better chance of successfully defending its action in court or before an administrative law judge.

ETHICAL ISSUE 2.2 ***How can a business decide whether a warning is "adequate"?*** One of the "gray areas" in the law has to do with product misuse. As you will read in Chapter 13, product liability laws require manufacturers and sellers to warn consumers of the kind of injuries that might result from the foreseeable misuse of their products. An exception to this rule is made when a risk associated with a product is "open and obvious." Sharp knives, for example, can obviously injure their users. Sometimes, however, a business has no way of predicting how a court might rule in deciding whether a particular risk is open and obvious or whether consumers should be warned of the risk. If consumers should be warned, a further question arises: What constitutes an adequate warning? Even the courts often disagree on such matters.

In one case, for example, a company sold small aerosol cans of butane, a fuel for cigarette lighters. On each can was the warning "DO NOT BREATHE SPRAY." Nonetheless, twenty-year-old Stephen Pavlik died from *intentionally* inhaling the contents of one of the cans. In the lawsuit that followed, brought by Pavlik's father, the trial court and the appellate court came to different conclusions. The trial court reasoned that Pavlik must have been aware of the dangers of inhaling butane and that a more specific warning would not have affected his conduct. The appellate court, though, concluded that the warning gave Pavlik "no notice of the serious nature of the danger posed by inhalation, intentional or otherwise."[6] Cases such as this send a clear message to businesspersons: never assume that a risk that may seem open and obvious to you will necessarily be open and obvious to a court. ■

Technological Developments and Legal Uncertainties

Uncertainties concerning how particular laws may apply to specific factual situations have been compounded in the cyber age. As noted in earlier chapters, the widespread use of the Internet has given rise to situations never before faced by the courts.

The case presented next is illustrative. The case involved an airline pilot who claimed that defamatory, gender-based messages made by her co-workers in an online forum created a hostile working environment. As will be discussed in Chapter 18, federal law prohibits harassment in the workplace, including "hostile-environment harassment," which occurs when an employee is subjected to sexual conduct or comments that he or she perceives as offensive. Generally, employers are expected to take immediate and appropriate corrective action in response to employees' complaints of sexual harassment or abuse. Otherwise, they may be held liable for the harassing actions of an employee's co-workers or supervisors. At issue in the case was whether the online forum could be considered part of the "workplace" over which the employer had control.

6. *Pavlik v. Lane Ltd./Tobacco Exporters International,* 135 F.3d 876 (3d Cir. 1998).

CASE 2.3 Blakey v. Continental Airlines, Inc.

New Jersey Supreme Court, 2000.
751 A.2d 538.
http://lawlibrary.rutgers.edu/search.shtml[a]

HISTORICAL AND TECHNOLOGICAL SETTING *CompuServe, Inc., which is now a wholly owned subsidiary of America Online, Inc., is the Internet service provider for Continental Airlines, Inc. CompuServe provides Continental's pilots and other crew members with online access to their flight schedules. As part of the service, CompuServe makes a "Crew Members Forum" available for the exchange of ideas and information. Through customized software, any individual with a Continental pilot or crew member identification number can access the forum. This includes chief pilots and assistant chief pilots, who are considered management at Continental. Technical assistance is provided by system operators, who are volunteer crew members.*

FACTS Tammy Blakey, a pilot for Continental Airlines since 1984, was the airline's first female captain—and one of only five Continental pilots—to fly an Airbus aircraft. Shortly after qualifying to be a captain on the Airbus A300, Blakey complained about pornographic photos and vulgar gender-based comments directed at her in her plane's cockpit and other work areas by her male co-employees. Blakey pursued claims against Continental with the Equal Employment Opportunity Commission, the agency that administers federal laws prohibiting employment discrimination, and in a federal district court.[b] Meanwhile, Continental pilots published a series of harassing, gender-based, defamatory messages about Blakey on the Internet forum. When the court refused to consider these messages, Blakey filed a complaint against Continental and others in a New Jersey state court. She alleged, in part, gender-based harassment arising from a hostile work environment. Continental filed a motion for summary judgment on this claim, which the court granted. A state intermediate appellate court upheld the summary judgment, and Blakey appealed to the New Jersey Supreme Court.

ISSUE Can an employees' online forum be such an integral part of the workplace that harassment on it may be regarded as an extension of a pattern of harassment in the workplace?

DECISION Yes. The New Jersey Supreme Court reversed the judgment of the lower court and remanded the case for further proceedings. The state supreme court indicated that the trial court was to determine, among other things, which messages were harassing, whether Continental had notice of those messages, and the severity or pervasiveness of the harassing conduct.

REASON The state supreme court explained that "[o]ur common experience tells us how important are the extensions of the workplace where the relations among employees are cemented or sometimes sundered. If an 'old boys' network' continued, in an after-hours setting, the belittling conduct that edges over into harassment, what exactly is the outsider (whether black, Latino, or woman) to do? Keep swallowing the abuse or give up the chance to make the team? We believe that severe or pervasive harassment in a work-related setting that continues a pattern of harassment on the job is sufficiently related to the workplace that an informed employer who takes no effective measures to stop it, sends the harassed employee the message that the harassment is acceptable and that the management supports the harasser." The court compared CompuServe's role to "that of a company that builds an old-fashioned bulletin board. If the maker of an old-fashioned bulletin board provided a better bulletin board by setting aside space on it for employees to post messages, we would have little doubt that messages on the company bulletin board would be part of the workplace setting."

FOR CRITICAL ANALYSIS—Technological Consideration *Does the holding in the* Blakey *case mean that employers have a duty to monitor their employees' e-mail and other online communications? Why or why not?*

a. In the "Search the N.J. Courts Decisions" box, type "Blakey" and click on the "Search" link. When the results appear, scroll down the list and click on the *Blakey* case name to access the opinion. This Web site is maintained by Rutgers School of Law in Camden, New Jersey.

b. In 1997, the federal court ruled in favor of Blakey on a claim of gender-based harassment, awarding her a total of $495,000 in forgone pay and $250,000 for emotional distress, pain, and suffering. The court also found that Blakey had failed to mitigate damages (reduce her damages—by finding other work, for example) and subtracted $120,000 from her back pay award.

Approaches to Ethical Reasoning

ETHICAL REASONING
A reasoning process in which an individual links his or her moral convictions or ethical standards to the particular situation at hand.

Each individual, when faced with a particular ethical dilemma, engages in **ethical reasoning**—that is, a reasoning process in which the individual examines the situation at hand in light of her or his moral convictions or ethical standards. Businesspersons do likewise when making decisions with ethical implications.

How do business decision makers decide whether a given action is the "right" one for their firms? What ethical standards should they apply? Broadly speaking, ethical reasoning relating to business traditionally has been characterized by two fundamental approaches. One approach defines ethical behavior in terms of duty, which also implies certain rights. The other approach determines what is ethical in terms of the consequences, or outcome, of any given action. We examine each of these approaches here.

DUTY-BASED ETHICS

Duty-based ethical standards are often derived from revealed truths, such as religious precepts. They can also be derived through philosophical reasoning.

Religious Ethical Standards In the Judeo-Christian tradition, which is the dominant religious tradition in the United States, the Ten Commandments of the Old Testament establish fundamental rules for moral action. Other religions have their own sources of revealed truth. Religious rules generally are absolute with respect to the behavior of their adherents. ■ EXAMPLE 2.7 The commandment "Thou shalt not steal" is an absolute mandate for a person, such as a Jew or a Christian, who believes that the Ten Commandments reflect revealed truth. Even a benevolent motive for stealing (such as Robin Hood's) cannot justify the act because the act itself is inherently immoral and thus wrong. ■

Ethical standards based on religious teachings also involve an element of *compassion*. ■ EXAMPLE 2.8 Even though it might be profitable for a firm to lay off a less productive employee, if that employee would find it difficult to find employment elsewhere and his or her family would suffer as a result, this potential suffering would be given substantial weight by the decision makers. ■ Compassionate treatment of others is also mandated—to a certain extent, at least—by the Golden Rule of the ancients ("Do unto others as you would have them do unto you"), which has been adopted by most religions.

Kantian Ethics Duty-based ethical standards may also be derived solely from philosophical reasoning. The German philosopher Immanuel Kant (1724–1804), for example, identified some general guiding principles for moral behavior based on what he believed to be the fundamental nature of human beings. Kant held that it is rational to assume that human beings are qualitatively different from other physical objects occupying space. Persons are endowed with moral integrity and the capacity to reason and conduct their affairs rationally. Therefore, their thoughts and actions should be respected. When human beings are treated merely as a means to an end, they are being viewed as the equivalent of objects and are being denied their basic humanity.

A central postulate in Kantian ethics is that individuals should evaluate their actions in light of the consequences that would follow if *everyone* in society acted in

CATEGORICAL IMPERATIVE
A concept developed by the philosopher Immanuel Kant as an ethical guideline for behavior. In deciding whether an action is right or wrong, or desirable or undesirable, a person should evaluate the action in terms of what would happen if everybody else in the same situation, or category, acted the same way.

PRINCIPLE OF RIGHTS
The principle that human beings have certain fundamental rights (to life, freedom, and the pursuit of happiness, for example). Those who adhere to this "rights theory" believe that a key factor in determining whether a business decision is ethical is how that decision affects the rights of various groups. These groups include the firm's owners, its employees, the consumers of its products or services, its suppliers, the community in which it does business, and society as a whole.

the same way. This **categorical imperative** can be applied to any action. ■ EXAMPLE 2.9 Suppose that you are deciding whether to cheat on an examination. If you have adopted Kant's categorical imperative, you will decide not to cheat because if everyone cheated, the examination would be meaningless. ■

The Principle of Rights The principle that human beings have certain fundamental rights (to life, freedom, and the pursuit of happiness, for example) is deeply embedded in Western culture. Those who adhere to this **principle of rights,** or "rights theory," believe that a key factor in determining whether a business decision is ethical is how that decision affects the rights of others. These others include the firm's owners, its employees, the consumers of its products or services, its suppliers, the community in which it does business, and society as a whole.

A potential dilemma for those who support rights theory, however, is that they may disagree on which rights are most important. When considering all those affected by a business decision, for example, how much weight should be given to employees relative to shareholders, customers relative to the community, or employees relative to society as a whole?

In general, rights theorists believe that whichever right is stronger in a particular circumstance takes precedence. ■ EXAMPLE 2.10 Suppose that a firm can either shut down a plant to avoid dumping pollutants into a river that would negatively affect the health of thousands of people or save the jobs of the twelve workers in the plant. In this situation, a rights theorist can easily choose which group to favor. (Not all choices are so clear-cut, however.) ■

OUTCOME-BASED ETHICS: UTILITARIANISM

UTILITARIANISM
An approach to ethical reasoning that evaluates behavior not on the basis of any absolute ethical or moral values but on the consequences of that behavior for those who will be affected by it. In utilitarian reasoning, a "good" decision is one that results in the greatest good for the greatest number of people affected by the decision.

COST-BENEFIT ANALYSIS
A decision-making technique that involves weighing the costs of a given action against the benefits of that action.

"Thou shalt act so as to generate the greatest good for the greatest number." This is a paraphrase of the major premise of the utilitarian approach to ethics. **Utilitarianism** is a philosophical theory developed by Jeremy Bentham (1748–1832) and then advanced, with some modifications, by John Stuart Mill (1806–1873)—both British philosophers. In contrast to duty-based ethics, utilitarianism is outcome oriented. It focuses on the consequences of an action, not on the nature of the action itself or on any set of preestablished moral values or religious beliefs.

Under a utilitarian model of ethics, an action is morally correct, or "right," when, among the people it affects, it produces the greatest amount of good for the greatest number. When an action affects the majority adversely, it is morally wrong. Applying the utilitarian theory thus requires (1) a determination of which individuals will be affected by the action in question; (2) a **cost-benefit analysis,** which involves an assessment of the negative and positive effects of alternative actions on these individuals; and (3) a choice among alternative actions that will produce maximum societal utility (the greatest positive net benefits for the greatest number of individuals).

The utilitarian approach to decision making commonly is employed by businesses, as well as by individuals. Weighing the consequences of a decision in terms of its costs and benefits for everyone affected by it is a useful analytical tool in the decision-making process. At the same time, utilitarianism is often criticized because its objective, calculated approach to problems tends to reduce the welfare of human beings to plus and minus signs on a cost-benefit worksheet and to "justify" human costs that many find totally unacceptable.

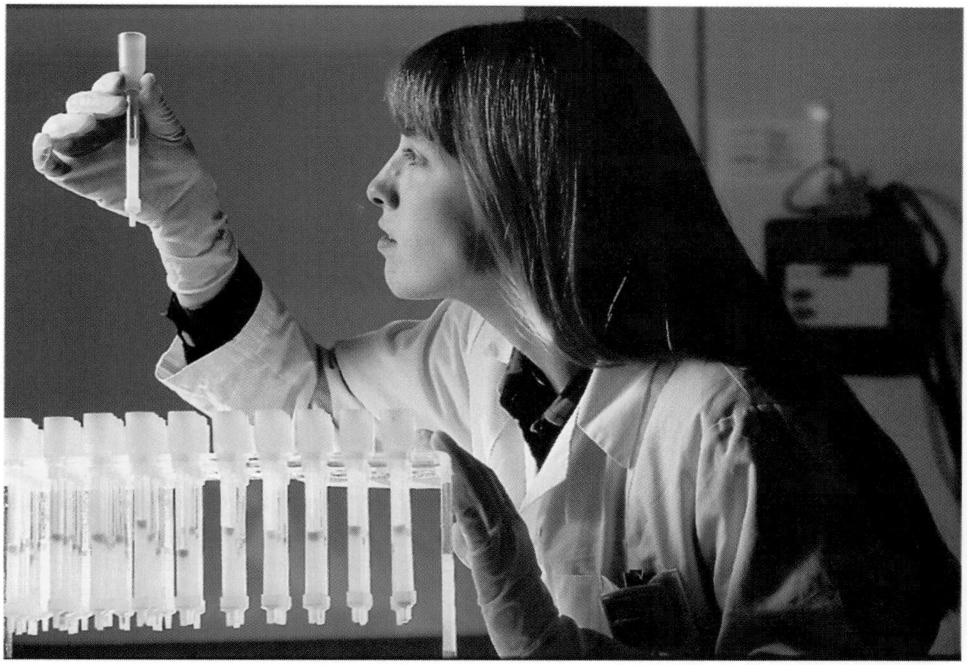

A lab worker conducts research for the development of a drug. If the drug proves beneficial to most people but adverse to a few, would it, under a utilitarian model of ethics, be marketed? Why or why not? (© Ted Horowitz, Getty Images)

Professional Responsibility

Business ethics goes hand in hand with professional responsibility. As you will learn in Chapter 4, all individuals, including businesspersons, owe a duty of care to others. Professionals—those who have knowledge or skills in a specific area such as accounting or law—are expected to perform their work in a manner consistent with that status. Generally, professionals are required to deliver competent services and are obligated to adhere to standards of performance commonly accepted within their professions. A professional who fails to abide by professional standards may be sued for malpractice. If the action also constitutes a statutory violation, the professional may face liability (or even criminal penalties) under the relevant statute.

Here we examine some of the duties owed by two groups of professionals—accountants and attorneys—whose work can significantly affect business decision making. Certainly, the dizzying collapse of Enron Corporation and the failure of other major companies, including WorldCom, Inc., in the early 2000s called attention to the importance of abiding by professional accounting standards. Arthur Andersen, LLP, one of the world's leading public accounting firms, also closed its doors after being convicted on criminal charges for allegedly thwarting the government's investigation into Enron's accounting practices.

After examining the duties owed by accountants and attorneys, we present a case study of Enron's defiance of established accounting rules. Following that, we look at some of the duties subsequently imposed on accountants by the Sarbanes-Oxley Act of 2002.

ACCOUNTANTS' DUTY OF CARE

Accountants play a major role in a business's financial system. Accountants have the necessary expertise and experience in establishing and maintaining accurate financial records to design, control, and audit record-keeping systems; to prepare reliable statements that reflect an individual's or a business's financial status; and to give tax advice and prepare tax returns.

An *audit* is a systematic inspection, by analyses and tests, of a business's financial records. The purpose of an audit is to provide the auditor with evidence to support an opinion on the fairness of the business's financial statements. A normal audit is not intended to uncover fraud or other misconduct. An accountant may be liable for failing to detect misconduct, however, if a normal audit would have revealed it or if the auditor agreed to examine the records for evidence of fraud or other misconduct that should have been obvious.

Standard of Care Generally, an accountant must possess the skills that an ordinarily prudent accountant would have and must exercise the degree of care that an ordinarily prudent accountant would exercise. The level of skill expected of accountants and the degree of care that they should exercise in performing their services are reflected in what are known as **generally accepted accounting principles** (**GAAP**) and **generally accepted auditing standards** (**GAAS**). The Financial Accounting Standards Board (FASB, usually pronounced "faz-bee") determines what accounting conventions, rules, and procedures constitute GAAP at a given point in time. GAAS are standards concerning an auditor's professional qualities and the judgment that he or she exercises in auditing financial records. GAAS are established by the American Institute of Certified Public Accountants. GAAP and GAAS are also reflected in the rules established by the Securities and Exchange Commission (see Chapter 21).

GENERALLY ACCEPTED ACCOUNTING PRINCIPLES (GAAP) The conventions, rules, and procedures necessary to define accepted accounting practices at a particular time. The source of the principles is the Financial Accounting Standards Board (FASB).

GENERALLY ACCEPTED AUDITING STANDARDS (GAAS) Standards concerning an auditor's professional qualities and the judgment exercised by him or her in the performance of an examination and report. The source of the standards is the American Institute of Certified Public Accountants.

Violations of GAAP and GAAS A violation of GAAP and GAAS will be considered *prima facie* (on its face) evidence of negligence on the part of the accountant. Compliance with GAAP and GAAS, however, does not necessarily relieve an accountant from potential legal liability. An accountant may be held to a higher standard of conduct established by state or federal statute and by judicial decisions. If an accountant is found to have been negligent in the performance of accounting services for a client, the client may collect damages for any losses that arose from the accountant's negligence. An accountant may also be liable to third parties, such as investors or corporate managers, who rely on the opinions of accountants when making decisions.

ATTORNEYS' DUTY OF CARE

The conduct of attorneys is governed by rules established by each state and by the American Bar Association's Model Rules of Professional Conduct. All attorneys owe a duty to provide competent and diligent representation. Attorneys are required to be familiar with well-settled principles of law applicable to a case and to discover law that can be found through a reasonable amount of research. The lawyer must also investigate and discover facts that could materially affect the client's legal rights.

Standard of Care In judging an attorney's performance, the standard used will normally be that of a reasonably competent general practitioner of ordinary skill, experience, and capacity. If an attorney holds himself or herself out as having expertise in a special area of law (for example, corporate taxation), then the attorney's standard of care in that area is higher than for attorneys without such expertise.

Liability for Malpractice When an attorney fails to exercise reasonable care and professional judgment, she or he breaches the duty of care and can be held liable for *malpractice* (professional negligence). In malpractice cases—as in all cases involving allegations of negligence—the plaintiff must prove that the attorney's breach of the duty of care actually caused the plaintiff to suffer some injury. ■ EXAMPLE 2.11 Suppose an attorney allows the statute of limitations (a statute that establishes the time period within which a lawsuit may be brought) to lapse on a client's claim. The attorney can be held liable for malpractice because the client can no longer file a cause of action in this case and has lost a potential award of damages. ■

Traditionally, to establish causation, the client normally had to show that "but for" the attorney's negligence, the client would not have suffered the injury. In recent years, however, several courts have held that plaintiffs in malpractice cases need only show that the defendant's negligence was a "substantial factor" in causing the plaintiff's injury.

STATUTORY DUTIES OF ACCOUNTANTS

Both civil and criminal liability may be imposed on accountants under securities laws. Accountants are also subject to criminal liability under the Internal Revenue Code.

The Duty of Accountants under Securities Laws Securities laws are designed to promote disclosure and prevent fraud in the purchase and sale of *securities*—corporate stocks and bonds. As you will read in Chapter 21, the Securities Act of 1933 governs initial sales of stock by businesses. The act requires that all essential information concerning the issuance of securities be made available to the investing public when the securities are registered with the Securities and Exchange Commission (SEC). The SEC is the federal agency that administers and enforces securities laws. The Securities Exchange Act of 1934 regulates the markets in which securities are sold by maintaining a continuous disclosure system for all corporations with securities on the securities exchanges.

.on the Web You can read a variety of articles concerning accounting and business ethics at Questia's online library, at **http://www.questia.com/Index.jsp?CRID=business_ethics&OFFID=se2**.

Accountants frequently prepare and certify the issuer's financial statements that are included in the registration statement that is filed with the SEC. If a financial statement contains a misstatement or omission of a material fact, the accountant may be liable to any purchasers of the security. To avoid liability under the 1933 act, accountants must show that they used *due diligence*—a standard of care that accountants must meet—in the preparation of the financial statements. Among other things, due diligence requires that the accountant follow GAAP and GAAS. Accountants may also face liability for false or deceptive statements, reports, or other documents under the antifraud provisions of the Securities Exchange Act of 1934.

Potential Criminal Liability of Accountants Criminal penalties may also be imposed on accountants for violating securities laws. For *willful* violations of the 1933 act, accountants may be imprisoned for up to five years and/or be subject to a fine of up to $10,000. For willful violations of the 1934 act, an accountant may be imprisoned for up to ten years and fined up to $100,000. The Sarbanes-Oxley Act of 2002, which will be discussed later in this chapter, provides that for a securities filing that is accompanied by an accountant's false or misleading certified audit statement, the accountant may be fined up to $5 million, imprisoned for up to twenty years, or both.

Accountants are also subject to criminal liability under the Internal Revenue Code, as well as under both state and federal criminal codes. The Internal Revenue Code makes aiding or assisting in the preparation of a false tax return a felony punishable by a fine of $100,000 ($500,000 for a corporation) and imprisonment for up to three years. This provision does not apply solely to accountants but to anyone who prepares tax returns for others for compensation. A penalty of $250 per tax return is levied on tax preparers for negligent understatement of the client's tax liability, and a penalty of $1,000 is imposed for willful understatement of tax liability or the reckless or intentional disregard of rules or regulations. In addition, those who prepare tax returns for others may be fined $1,000 per document for aiding and abetting another's understatement of tax liability (the penalty is increased to $10,000 in corporate cases).

Defying the Rules: The Enron Case

Deceptive accounting practices were at the heart of the Enron debacle—one of the largest bankruptcies in the history of U.S. business. For years to come, the Enron scandal will remain a symbol of the cost of unethical behavior to management, employees, suppliers, shareholders, the community, society, and indeed the world. Shareholders lost $62 billion of value in a very short period of time in the early 2000s. This case study of "cooking the books," conflicts of interest, and deviation from accepted ethical standards of business has all of the trappings of an epic novel. Unfortunately, for the thousands of employees who lost millions of dollars and for the millions of shareholders who lost billions of dollars, the Enron story was not fiction.

.on the Web Both CNN and *Time* magazine have published numerous articles on the Enron scandal. See, for example, the articles available at

http://www.time.com/time/business/article/0,8599,193520,00.html

and

http://archives.cnn.com/2002/ALLPOLITICS/07/07/senate.enron.

The Growth of Enron in a Nutshell

In the 1990s, two gas-pipeline companies, Houston Natural Gas Corporation and InterNorth, Inc., merged to create a very large energy trading company, Enron Corporation. It was a "first mover" in a deregulated electricity market and enjoyed impressive growth. By 1998, Enron was the largest energy trader in the world. Then it entered the *online* energy trading market. By December 2000, its shares were selling at $85. Most Enron employees had a large part or even all of their retirement packages tied up in the company's stock.

When competition in energy trading increased, Enron diversified into water, power plants in Brazil and India, and finally fiber optics and high-speed Internet transmission.

Accounting Issues

According to the rules of the Financial Accounting Standards Board, energy traders such as Enron could include in *current* earnings profits that they *anticipated* on energy contracts. Herein lay the beginning of a type of accounting "fudging" that increased over time as the company struggled to improve its reported current earnings. By 2000, 50 percent of Enron's $1.4 billion of reported pretax profits consisted of "anticipated" future earnings on energy contracts.

Because Enron's managers received bonuses based on whether they met earnings goals, they had an incentive to inflate the anticipated earnings on such contracts. Some of the contracts extended as long as twenty years in the future. In retrospect, the temptation to management was too great, and common norms of both ethical and legal business decision making were violated as managers overestimated future earnings in order to inflate current earnings.

OFF-THE-BOOKS TRANSACTIONS

To artificially maintain and even increase its reported earnings, Enron also created a complex network of subsidiaries that enabled it to move losses from the core company to the subsidiaries—companies that did not show up on Enron's books. When it created the subsidiaries, Enron transferred assets to them, assigning a value to the assets that was much greater than their actual market value. The effect was to increase Enron's apparent net worth. Consider one example: Enron sold its unused fiber-optic cable capacity to a subsidiary for $30 million in cash and a $70 million promissory note. This transaction added $53 million to Enron's reported earnings for just one quarter. The value of the unused fiber-optic cable would soon be negligible, however.

For several years, Enron transferred assets from its books, along with the accompanying debt, to partnerships outside the main corporation. Many of these transactions were carried out in the Cayman Islands, a haven for those seeking corporate secrecy as well as a means for avoiding federal income taxes.

SELF-DEALING

Enron's chief executive officer (CEO) frequently did business with companies owned by his son and his daughter. The son created a company that was later bought by Enron. The son was then hired as an executive with a guaranteed pay package of $1 million over three years as well as 20,000 Enron stock options. The CEO's daughter owned a Houston travel agency that received over $10 million—50 percent of the agency's total revenues—from Enron during a three-year period.

Kenneth Lay, a former executive of Enron Corporation, is sworn in during a congressional hearing on Enron's financial affairs in 2002. What legislation did Congress pass in 2002 in an attempt to curb unethical and deceptive accounting practices? (AP Photo/ Ron Edmonds)

THE CORPORATE CULTURE

The many transgressions just described could not have happened without a corporate culture that fostered unethical and, in many instances, illegal business decision making. This case study of unethical behavior is sufficiently important that West Legal Studies in Business has created a project titled "Inside Look" that is accessible on the Web at **http://insidelook.westbuslaw.com**. There you will discover how, on numerous occasions, Enron management was apprised, by both insiders and outsiders, that a "house of cards" had been created. Nonetheless, upper management more often than not refused to investigate and reveal to the public (or to its shareholders and employees) the financial improprieties that had occurred over the previous three years.

The Sarbanes-Oxley Act of 2002

As mentioned earlier, in response to the business scandals of the early 2000s, including the Enron debacle, Congress enacted the Sarbanes-Oxley Act of 2002. The act imposes a number of strict requirements on both domestic and foreign public accounting firms that provide auditing services to companies, or "issuers," whose securities are sold to public investors. (Provisions of the act that are more directly concerned with corporate fraud and the responsibilities of corporate officers and directors will be listed and described in Exhibit 21–4 in Chapter 21.)

THE PUBLIC COMPANY ACCOUNTING OVERSIGHT BOARD

Among other things, the Sarbanes-Oxley Act calls for a greater degree of government oversight over public accounting practices. To this end, the act created the Public Company Accounting Oversight Board, which reports to the Securities and Exchange Commission. The board consists of a chair and four other members.

Generally, the duties of the board are to oversee the audit of companies ("issuers") whose securities are sold to public investors in order to protect the interests of investors and the public interest and to register public accounting firms that prepare audit reports for issuers. The board was also asked to establish or adopt standards relating to the preparation of audit reports for issuers. To enforce compliance with the Sarbanes-Oxley Act, the board is required to inspect registered public accounting firms, investigate firms that violate the act's provisions, and discipline those firms by imposing sanctions. Sanctions range from temporary or permanent suspension to civil penalties that can be as high as $15 million for intentional violations.

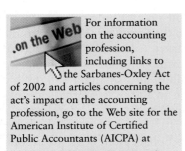

.on the Web For information on the accounting profession, including links to the Sarbanes-Oxley Act of 2002 and articles concerning the act's impact on the accounting profession, go to the Web site for the American Institute of Certified Public Accountants (AICPA) at

http://www.aicpa.org/index.htm.

APPLICABILITY TO PUBLIC ACCOUNTING FIRMS

Titles I and II of the act set forth the key provisions relating to the duties of the new oversight board and the requirements relating to public accounting firms—defined by the act as firms and associated persons that are "engaged in the practice of public accounting or preparing or issuing audit reports."

Auditor Independence To help ensure that auditors remain independent of the firms that they audit, Title II of the Sarbanes-Oxley Act does the following:

1. Makes it unlawful for registered public accounting firms to contemporaneously perform both audit services and nonaudit services (such as management functions).
2. Requires preapproval for most auditing services from the issuer's audit committee.
3. Prohibits registered public accounting firms from providing audit services to an issuer if either the lead audit partner or the audit partner responsible for reviewing the audit has provided such services to the issuer in each of the prior five years.
4. Requires registered public accounting firms to make timely reports to the audit committees of the issuers, indicating all critical accounting policies and practices to be used; all alternative treatments of financial information within generally accepted accounting principles that have been discussed with the issuer's management officials, the ramifications of the use of such alternative treatments, and the treatment preferred by the auditor; and other material written communications between the auditor and the issuer's management.
5. Makes it unlawful for a registered public accounting firm to provide auditing services to an issuer if the issuer's chief executive officer, chief financial officer, chief accounting officer, or controller was previously employed by the auditor and participated in any capacity in the audit of the issuer during the one-year period preceding the date that the audit began.

Document Destruction The Sarbanes-Oxley Act also prohibits the destruction or falsification of records with the intent to obstruct or influence a federal investigation or in relation to bankruptcy proceedings. Violation of this provision can result in a fine, imprisonment for up to twenty years, or both.

Business Ethics on a Global Level

Given the various cultures and religions throughout the world, it is not surprising that conflicts in ethics frequently arise between foreign and U.S. businesspersons. ■ EXAMPLE 2.12 In certain countries, the consumption of alcohol and specific foods is forbidden for religious reasons. Under such circumstances, it would be thoughtless and imprudent for a U.S. businessperson to invite a local business contact out for a drink. ■

The role played by women in other countries may also present some difficult ethical problems for firms doing business internationally. Equal employment opportunity is a fundamental public policy in the United States, and Title VII of the Civil Rights Act of 1964 prohibits discrimination against women in the employment context (see Chapter 18). Some other countries, however, offer little protection for women against gender discrimination in the workplace, including sexual harassment.

We look here at how laws governing workers in other countries, particularly developing countries, have created some especially difficult ethical problems for U.S. sellers of goods manufactured in foreign countries. We also examine some of the ethical ramifications of a U.S. law that prohibits U.S. businesspersons from bribing foreign officials to obtain favorable business contracts.

MONITORING THE EMPLOYMENT PRACTICES OF FOREIGN SUPPLIERS

Many U.S. businesses now contract with companies in developing nations to produce goods, such as shoes and clothing, because the wage rates in those nations are significantly lower than wages in the United States. Yet what if a foreign company exploits its workers—by hiring women and children at below-minimum-wage rates, for example, or by requiring its employees to work long hours in a workplace full of health hazards? What if the company's supervisors routinely engage in workplace conduct that is offensive to women?

> .on the Web Global Exchange offers information on global business activities, including some of the ethical issues stemming from those activities, at **http://www.globalexchange.org**.

Given today's global communications network, few companies can assume that their actions in other nations will go unnoticed by "corporate watch" groups that discover and publicize unethical corporate behavior. As a result, U.S. businesses today usually take steps to avoid such adverse publicity—either by refusing to deal with certain suppliers or by arranging to monitor their suppliers' workplaces to make sure that the employees are not being mistreated.

THE FOREIGN CORRUPT PRACTICES ACT

Another ethical problem in international business dealings has to do with the legitimacy of certain side payments to government officials. In the United States, the majority of contracts are formed within the private sector. In many foreign countries, however, decisions on most major construction and manufacturing contracts

Workers at their sewing machines in a garment plant in Micronesia. How might cultural differences affect what businesspersons consider ethical conduct? If, for example, employees in a particular region typically work twelve-hour days, is it unethical for an American business operating in that region to require the same number of hours? Why or why not? Would it be any more ethical if the American company subcontracted with another company whose employees were required to work twelve-hour days? (AP Photo/Charles Hanley)

are made by government officials because of extensive government regulation and control over trade and industry. Side payments to government officials in exchange for favorable business contracts are not unusual in such countries, nor are they considered to be unethical. In the past, U.S. corporations doing business in these countries largely followed the dictum, "When in Rome, do as the Romans do."

In the 1970s, however, the U.S. press, and government officials as well, uncovered a number of business scandals involving large side payments by U.S. corporations—such as Lockheed Aircraft—to foreign representatives for the purpose of securing advantageous international trade contracts. In response to this unethical behavior, in 1977 Congress passed the Foreign Corrupt Practices Act (FCPA), which prohibits U.S. businesspersons from bribing foreign officials to secure advantageous contracts.

Prohibition against the Bribery of Foreign Officials The first part of the FCPA applies to all U.S. companies and their directors, officers, shareholders, employees, and agents. This part prohibits the bribery of most officials of foreign governments if the purpose of the payment is to get the officials to act in their official capacity to provide business opportunities.

The FCPA does not prohibit payment of substantial sums to minor officials whose duties are ministerial. These payments are often referred to as "grease," or facilitating payments. They are meant to accelerate the performance of administrative services that might otherwise be carried out at a slow pace. Thus, for example, if a firm makes a payment to a minor official to speed up an import licensing process, the firm has not violated the FCPA.

Generally, the act, as amended, permits payments to foreign officials if such payments are lawful within the foreign country. The act also does not prohibit payments to private foreign companies or other third parties unless the U.S. firm knows that the payments will be passed on to a foreign government in violation of the FCPA.

Accounting Requirements In the past, bribes were often concealed in corporate financial records. Thus, the second part of the FCPA is directed toward accountants. All companies must keep detailed records that "accurately and fairly" reflect the company's financial activities. In addition, all companies must have an accounting system that provides "reasonable assurance" that all transactions entered into by the company are accounted for and legal. These requirements assist in detecting illegal bribes. The FCPA further prohibits any person from making false statements to accountants or false entries in any record or account.

Penalties for Violations In 1988, the FCPA was amended to provide that business firms that violate the act may be fined up to $2 million. Individual officers or directors who violate the FCPA may be fined up to $100,000 (the fine cannot be paid by the company) and may be imprisoned for up to five years.

Other Nations Denounce Bribery

For nearly thirty years, the Foreign Corrupt Practices Act (FCPA) of 1977 was the only law of its kind in the world, despite attempts by U.S. political leaders to convince other nations to pass similar legislation. Clearly, U.S. companies, as they often complained, were at a disadvantage relative to companies from other countries that faced no such constraint. That situation is now changing.

In 1997, the Organization for Economic Cooperation and Development created a convention (treaty) that made the bribery of foreign public officials a serious crime. By 2004, at least thirty-five nations had adopted the convention, which obligates them to enact legislation within their own nations in accordance with the convention. In addition, other international institutions, including the European Union, the Organization of American States, and the United Nations, have either passed or are in the process of negotiating rules against bribery in business transactions.

Many are hopeful that these global efforts will go far in preventing corruption and bribery in the awarding of contracts. Others, however, point out that despite antibribery laws, it is often impossible to prosecute bribery cases because of lack of evidence. Evidence of bribery is difficult to discover because, typically, both the party giving the bribe and the party receiving it have a strong incentive to cover it up. That may be one reason why there were less than fifty prosecutions of U.S. companies under the FCPA during the nearly thirty years since its passage. Gathering evidence against foreign parties who take bribes will likely be even more difficult.

APPLICATION How Can You Create an Ethical Workplace?*

If you are a manager, rest assured that unless you are totally committed to the goal of creating and maintaining an ethical workplace, you will not succeed in achieving it. In addition to your attitude toward ethics and your conduct, two other factors help to create an ethical workplace environment: a written code of ethics, or policy statement, and the effective communication of the firm's ethical policies to employees. Finally, you should provide employees with a means by which they can anonymously complain about unethical behavior on the part of their co-workers or supervisors.

THE ROLE OF MANAGEMENT

As mentioned in this chapter, management's behavior is crucial in establishing the ethical tone of a firm. Managers must make it clear, both in their words and by their conduct, that unethical behavior is not acceptable. If an employee persists in unethical behavior, you should consider discharging the employee as a clear example to other employees that you will not tolerate unethical actions. Studies have shown that employees quickly adapt to the "rules" of their workplace environments, but it is up to the company managers to let employees know what those rules are—and to enforce them.

INSTRUCT EMPLOYEES IN ETHICAL STANDARDS

A written ethics code or policy statement helps to make clear to employees how they are expected to relate to their supervisors or managers, to consumers, to suppliers, and to other employees. Above all, it is important to state explicitly what your firm's ethical priorities are and make sure that the firm's employees are aware of those priorities.

A good way to communicate these priorities to employees is by implementing an ethics training program, in which managers discuss with employees—face to face—the firm's policies and the importance of ethical conduct. Ethics seminars should be held at routine intervals so that employees have an opportunity to discuss ethical problems as they arise. Another effective technique is to evaluate periodically the ethical performance of each employee.

Employees should also be instructed in how they can anonymously report unethical behavior. For publicly traded systems, federal law now requires the establishment of confidential reporting systems for this purpose. This can be accomplished through a Web-based reporting system, as described earlier in this chapter, or by using a company "hot line" installed for this purpose.

CHECKLIST FOR THE BUSINESS MANAGER

1. Make sure that management is committed to ethical behavior and sets an ethical example.
2. Create, print, and distribute an ethical code clearly stating your firm's ethical goals and priorities, as well as what behavior is expected of employees in their areas of responsibility.
3. Implement an ethics training program to communicate your firm's ethical policies to employees.
4. Devise a method, such as an ethical checklist, for evaluating the ethical performance of each individual employee.
5. Provide a mechanism through which employees can anonymously complain about unethical behavior in the workplace.

* This *Application* is not meant to substitute for the services of an attorney who is licensed to practice law in your state.

KEY TERMS

CHAPTER SUMMARY Ethics and Professional Responsibility

Business Ethics (See pages 47–48.)	Ethics can be defined as the study of what constitutes right or wrong behavior. Business ethics focuses on how moral and ethical principles are applied in the business context.
Setting the Right Ethical Tone (See pages 48–52.)	1. *Role of management*—Management's commitment and behavior are essential in creating an ethical workplace. Most large firms have ethical codes or policies and corporate compliance programs to help employees determine whether certain actions are ethical. 2. *Ethical trade-offs*—Management constantly faces ethical trade-offs because firms have ethical and legal duties to a number of groups, including shareholders and employees.
Business Ethics and the Law (See pages 53–56.)	1. *The moral minimum*—Lawful behavior is a moral minimum. The law has its limits, though, and some actions may be legal but not ethical. 2. *Legal uncertainties*—It may be difficult to predict with certainty whether particular actions are legal given the numerous and frequent changes in the laws regulating business and the "gray areas" in the law. 3. *Technological developments and legal uncertainties*—Technological developments can also lead to legal uncertainties until it is clear how the law will be applied to the questions raised by these developments.
Approaches to Ethical Reasoning (See pages 57–58.)	1. *Duty-based ethics*—Ethics based on religious beliefs; philosophical reasoning, such as that of Immanuel Kant; and the basic rights of human beings (the principle of rights). 2. *Outcome-based ethics (utilitarianism)*—Ethics based on philosophical reasoning, such as that of John Stuart Mill.
Professional Responsibility (See pages 59–62.)	1. *Duty of care*—Accountants and attorneys are held to standards of care established by their respective professions. Failure to meet the required standard of care may result in liability for negligence. The standard of care expected of accountants is reflected in generally accepted accounting principles (GAAP) and generally accepted auditing standards (GAAS). The standard of care expected of attorneys is reflected in rules established in each state and by the American Bar Association's Model Rules of Professional Conduct. 2. *Statutory duties of accountants*—Accountants are subject to requirements established by securities laws. Violations of these requirements may result in both civil and criminal penalties. Accountants are also subject to criminal liability under the Internal Revenue Code.
Defying the Rules: The Enron Case (See pages 62–63.)	The Enron scandal—involving one of the largest bankruptcies in U.S. history—can serve as a case study of a corporate culture that fostered unethical and, in part, illegal business decision making.
The Sarbanes-Oxley Act of 2002 (See pages 63–65.)	Imposes strict requirements on domestic and foreign public accounting firms that provide auditing services to companies selling securities to the public. Establishes an oversight board and rules to keep auditors independent and prevent the destruction or falsification of records.
Business Ethics on a Global Level (See pages 65–67.)	Businesses must take account of the many cultural, religious, and legal differences among nations. Notable differences relate to the role of women in society, employment laws governing workplace conditions, and the practice of giving side payments to foreign officials to secure favorable contracts.

FOR REVIEW

Answers for the even-numbered questions in this For Review *section can be found in Appendix I at the end of this text.*

1 What is ethics? What is business ethics? Why is business ethics important?

2 How can business leaders encourage their companies to act ethically?

3 How do duty-based ethical standards differ from outcome-based ethical standards?

4 What duties do professionals owe to those who rely on their services?

5 What types of ethical issues might arise in the context of international business transactions?

QUESTIONS AND CASE PROBLEMS

2–1. Business Ethics. Some business ethicists maintain that whereas personal ethics has to do with right or wrong behavior, business ethics is concerned with appropriate behavior. In other words, ethical behavior in business has less to do with moral principles than with what society deems to be appropriate behavior in the business context. Do you agree with this distinction? Do personal and business ethics ever overlap? Should personal ethics play any role in business ethical decision making?

2–2. Business Ethics and Public Opinion. Assume that you are a high-level manager for a shoe manufacturer. You know that your firm could increase its profit margin by producing shoes in Indonesia, where you could hire women for $100 a month to assemble them. You also know, however, that a competing shoe manufacturer recently was accused by human rights advocates of engaging in exploitative labor practices because the manufacturer sold shoes made by Indonesian women for similarly low wages. You personally do not believe that paying $100 a month to Indonesian women is unethical because you know that in their country, $100 a month is a better-than-average wage rate. Assuming that the decision is yours to make, should you have the shoes manufactured in Indonesia and make higher profits for your company? Should you instead avoid the risk of negative publicity and the consequences of that publicity for the firm's reputation and subsequent profits? Are there other alternatives? Discuss fully.

2–3. Business Ethics and Public Opinion. Human rights groups, environmental activists, and other interest groups concerned with unethical business practices have often conducted publicity campaigns against various corporations that those groups feel have engaged in unethical practices. Do you believe that a small group of well-organized activists should dictate how a major corporation conducts its affairs? Discuss fully.

2–4. Ethical Decision Making. Shokun Steel Co. owns many steel plants. One of its plants is much older than the others. Equipment at that plant is outdated and inefficient, and the costs of production at that plant are now twice as high as at any of Shokun's other plants. The company cannot raise the price of steel because of competition, both domestic and international. The plant is located in Twin Firs, Pennsylvania, which has a population of about 45,000, and currently employs over a thousand workers. Shokun is contemplating whether to close the plant. What factors should the firm consider in making its decision? Will the firm violate any ethical duties if it closes the plant? Analyze these questions from the two basic perspectives on ethical reasoning discussed in this chapter.

2–5. Ethical Conduct. Richard and Suzanne Weinstein owned Elm City Cheese Co. Elm City sold its products to three major customers that used the cheese as a "filler" to blend into their cheeses. In 1982, Mark Federico, a certified public accountant, became Elm City's accountant and the Weinsteins' personal accountant. The Weinsteins had known Federico since he was seven years old, and even before he became their accountant, he knew the details of Elm City's business. Federico's duties went beyond typical accounting work, and when the Weinsteins were absent, Federico was put in charge of operations. In 1992, Federico was made a vice president of the company, and a year later he was placed in charge of day-to-day operations. He also continued to serve as Elm City's accountant. The relationship between Federico and the Weinsteins deteriorated, and in 1995, he resigned as Elm City's employee and as its accountant. Less than two years later, Federico opened Lomar Foods, Inc., to make the same products as Elm City by the same process and to sell the products to the same customers. Federico located Lomar closer to Elm City's suppliers. Elm City filed a suit in a Connecticut state court against Federico and Lomar, alleging, among other things, misappropriation of trade secrets. Elm City argued that it was entitled to punitive damages because Federico's conduct was "willful and malicious." Federico responded in part that he did not act willfully and maliciously because he did not know that Elm City's business details were trade secrets. Were Federico's actions "willful and malicious"? Were they ethical? Explain. [*Elm City Cheese Co. v. Federico,* 251 Conn. 59, 752 A.2d 1037 (1999)]

CASE PROBLEM WITH SAMPLE ANSWER

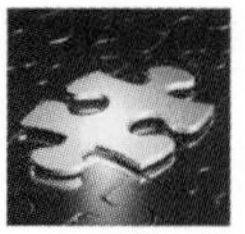

2–6. Richard Fraser was an "exclusive career insurance agent" under a contract with Nationwide Mutual Insurance Co. Fraser leased computer hardware and software from Nationwide for his business. During a dispute between Nationwide and the Nationwide Insurance Independent Contractors Association, an organization representing Fraser and other exclusive career agents, Fraser prepared a letter to Nationwide's competitors asking whether they were interested in acquiring the represented agents' policyholders. Nationwide obtained a copy of the letter and searched its electronic file server for e-mail indicating that the letter had been sent. It found a stored e-mail that Fraser had sent to a co-worker indicating that the letter had been sent to at least one competitor. The e-mail was retrieved from the co-worker's file of already received and discarded messages stored on the receiver. When Nationwide canceled its contract with Fraser, he filed a suit in a federal district court against the firm, alleging, among other things, violations of various federal laws that prohibit the interception of electronic communications during transmission. In whose favor should the court rule, and why? In any case, did Nationwide act ethically in retrieving the e-mail? [*Fraser v. Nationwide Mutual Insurance Co.,* 135 F.Supp.2d 623 (E.D.Pa. 2001)]

After you have answered this problem, compare your answer with the sample answer given on the Web site that accompanies this text. Go to http://blt.westbuslaw.com, select "Chapter 2," and click on "Case Problem with Sample Answer."

2–7. Ethical Conduct. Unable to pay more than $1.2 billion in debt, Big Rivers Electric Corp. filed a petition to declare bankruptcy in a federal bankruptcy court in September 1996. Big Rivers' creditors included Bank of New York (BONY), Chase Manhattan Bank, Mapco Equities, and others. The court appointed J. Baxter Schilling to work as a "disinterested" (neutral) party with Big Rivers and the creditors to resolve their disputes; the court set an hourly fee as Schilling's compensation. Schilling told Chase, BONY, and Mapco that he wanted them to pay him an additional percentage fee based on the "success" he attained in finding "new value" to pay Big Rivers' debts. He said that without such a deal, he would not perform his mediation duties. Chase agreed; the others disputed the deal, but no one told the court. In October 1998, Schilling asked the court for nearly $4.5 million in compensation, including the hourly fees, which totaled about $531,000, and the percentage fees. Big Rivers and others asked the court to deny Schilling any fees on the basis that he had improperly negotiated "secret side agreements." How did Schilling violate his duties as a "disinterested" party? Should he be denied compensation? Why or why not? [*In re Big Rivers Electric Corp.,* 355 F.3d 415 (6th Cir. 2004)]

A QUESTION OF ETHICS

2–8. Hazen Paper Co. manufactured paper and paperboard for use in such products as cosmetic wrap, lottery tickets, and pressure-sensitive items. Walter Biggins, a chemist hired by Hazen in 1977, developed a water-based paper coating that was both environmentally safe and of superior quality. By the mid-1980s, the company's sales had increased dramatically as a result of its extensive use of "Biggins Acrylic." Because of this, Biggins thought he deserved a substantial raise in salary, and from 1984 to 1986, Biggins's persistent requests for a raise became a bone of contention between him and his employers. Biggins ran a business on the side, which involved cleaning up hazardous wastes for various companies. Hazen told Biggins that unless he signed a "confidentiality agreement" promising to restrict his outside activities during the time he was employed by Hazen and for a limited time afterward, he would be fired. Biggins said he would sign the agreement only if Hazen raised his salary to $100,000. Hazen refused to do so, fired Biggins, and hired a younger man to replace him. At the time of his discharge in 1986, Biggins was sixty-two years old, had worked for the company nearly ten years, and was just a few weeks away from being entitled to pension rights worth about $93,000. In view of these circumstances, evaluate and answer the following questions. [*Hazen Paper Co. v. Biggins,* 507 U.S. 604, 113 S.Ct. 1701, 123 L.Ed.2d 338 (1993)]

1. Did the company owe an ethical duty to Biggins to increase his salary, given that its sales increased dramatically as a result of Biggins's efforts and ingenuity in developing the coating? If you were one of the company's executives, would you have raised Biggins's salary? Why or why not?
2. Generally, what public policies come into conflict in cases involving employers who, for reasons of cost and efficiency of operations, fire older, higher-paid workers and replace them with younger, lower-paid workers? If you were an employer facing the need to cut back on personnel to save costs, what would you do, and on what ethical premises would you justify your decision?

FOR CRITICAL ANALYSIS

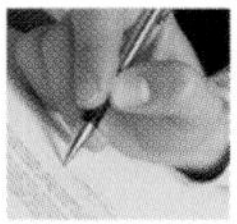

2–9. If a firm engages in "ethically responsible" behavior solely for the purpose of gaining profits from the goodwill it generates, the "ethical" behavior is essentially a means toward a self-serving end (profits and the accumulation of wealth). In this situation, is the firm acting unethically in any way? Should motive or conduct carry greater weight on the ethical scales in this situation?

VIDEO QUESTION

2–10. Go to this text's Web site at http://blt.westbuslaw.com and select "Chapter 2." Click on "Video Questions" and view the video titled *Ethics: Business Ethics an Oxymoron?* Then answer the following questions.

1. According to the instructor in the video, what is the primary reason why businesses act ethically?
2. Which of the two approaches to ethical reasoning that were discussed in the chapter seems to have had more influence on the instructor in the discussion of how business activities are related to societies? Explain your answer.
3. The instructor asserts that "[i]n the end, it is the unethical behavior that becomes costly, and conversely ethical behavior creates its own competitive advantage." Do you agree with this statement? Why or why not?

INTERNET EXERCISES

Go to the *Business Law Today: The Essentials* home page at **http://blt.westbuslaw.com**, select "Chapter 2," and click on "Internet Exercises." There you will find the following Internet research exercises that you can perform to learn more about topics covered in this chapter.

Activity 2–1: LEGAL PERSPECTIVE—Ethics in Business

Activity 2–2: MANAGEMENT PERSPECTIVE—Environmental Self-Audits

BEFORE THE TEST

Go to the *Business Law Today: The Essentials* home page at **http://blt.westbuslaw.com**, select "Chapter 2," and click on "Interactive Quizzes." You will find at least twenty interactive questions relating to this chapter.

CHAPTER 3

Traditional and Online Dispute Resolution

"The Judicial Department comes home in its effects to every man's fireside: it passes on his property, his reputation, his life, his all."

John Marshall, 1755–1835
(Chief justice of the United States Supreme Court, 1801–1835)

CHAPTER OUTLINE

- THE JUDICIARY'S ROLE IN AMERICAN GOVERNMENT
- BASIC JUDICIAL REQUIREMENTS
- THE STATE AND FEDERAL COURT SYSTEMS
- FOLLOWING A STATE COURT CASE
- THE COURTS ADAPT TO THE ONLINE WORLD
- ALTERNATIVE DISPUTE RESOLUTION
- ONLINE DISPUTE RESOLUTION

LEARNING OBJECTIVES

After reading this chapter, you should be able to answer the following questions:

1. What is judicial review? How and when was the power of judicial review established?
2. Before a court can hear a case, it must have jurisdiction. Over what must it have jurisdiction? How are the courts applying traditional jurisdictional concepts to cases involving Internet transactions?
3. What is the difference between a trial court and an appellate court?
4. In a lawsuit, what are the pleadings? What is discovery, and how does electronic discovery differ? What is electronic filing?
5. How are online forums being used to resolve disputes?

As Chief Justice John Marshall remarked in the above quotation, ultimately, we are all affected by what the courts say and do. This is particularly true in the business world—nearly every businessperson will face either a potential or an actual lawsuit at some time or another. For this reason, anyone contemplating a career in business will benefit from an understanding of American court systems, including the mechanics of lawsuits.

In this chapter, after examining the judiciary's overall role in the American governmental scheme, we discuss some basic requirements that must be met before a party may bring a lawsuit before a particular court. We then look at the court systems of the United States in some detail and, to clarify judicial procedures, follow a hypothetical case through a state court system. Even though there are fifty-two court systems—one for each of the fifty states, one for the District of Columbia, plus a federal system—similarities abound. Keep in mind that the federal courts are not superior to the state courts; they are simply an independent system of courts, which derives its authority from Article III, Sections 1 and 2, of the U.S. Constitution. The chapter concludes with an overview of some alternative methods of settling disputes, including methods for settling disputes in online forums.

Note that technological developments are affecting court procedures just as they are affecting all other areas of the law. In this chapter, we will also indicate how court doctrines and procedures, as well as alternative methods of dispute settlement, are being adapted to the needs of a cyber age.

The Judiciary's Role in American Government

As you learned in Chapter 1, the body of American law includes the federal and state constitutions, statutes passed by legislative bodies, administrative law, and the case decisions and legal principles that form the common law. These laws would be meaningless, however, without the courts to interpret and apply them. This is the essential role of the judiciary—the courts—in the American governmental system: to interpret and apply the law.

Judicial Review

JUDICIAL REVIEW
The process by which a court decides on the constitutionality of legislative enactments and actions of the executive branch.

As the branch of government entrusted with interpreting the laws, the judiciary can decide, among other things, whether the laws or actions of the other two branches are constitutional. The process for making such a determination is known as **judicial review.** The power of judicial review enables the judicial branch to act as a check on the other two branches of government, in line with the checks-and-balances system established by the U.S. Constitution.

The Origins of Judicial Review in the United States

The power of judicial review was not mentioned in the Constitution, but the concept was not new at the time the nation was founded. Indeed, prior to 1789 state courts had already overturned state legislative acts that conflicted with state constitutions. Additionally, many of the founders expected the United States Supreme Court to assume a similar role with respect to the federal Constitution. Alexander Hamilton and James Madison both emphasized the importance of judicial review in their essays urging the adoption of the new Constitution. When was the doctrine of judicial review established? See this chapter's *Landmark in the Law* feature for the answer.

Basic Judicial Requirements

Before a court can hear a lawsuit, certain requirements must first be met. These requirements relate to jurisdiction, venue, and standing to sue. We examine each of these important concepts here.

Jurisdiction

JURISDICTION
The authority of a court to hear and decide a specific action.

In Latin, *juris* means "law," and *diction* means "to speak." Thus, "the power to speak the law" is the literal meaning of the term **jurisdiction.** Before any court can hear a case, it must have jurisdiction over the person against whom the suit is brought or over the property involved in the suit. The court must also have jurisdiction over the subject matter.

LANDMARK IN THE LAW

Marbury v. Madison (1803)

In the edifice of American law, the *Marbury v. Madison*[a] decision in 1803 can be viewed as the keystone of the constitutional arch. The facts of the case were as follows. John Adams, who had lost his bid for reelection to the presidency to Thomas Jefferson in 1800, feared the Jeffersonians' antipathy toward business and toward a strong central government. Adams thus worked feverishly to "pack" the judiciary with loyal Federalists (those who believed in a strong national government) by appointing what came to be called "midnight judges" just before Jefferson took office. All of the fifty-nine judicial appointment letters had to be certified and delivered, but Adams's secretary of state (John Marshall) had succeeded in delivering only forty-two of them by the time Jefferson took over as president. Jefferson, of course, refused to order his secretary of state, James Madison, to deliver the remaining commissions.

MARSHALL'S DILEMMA William Marbury and three others to whom the commissions had not been delivered sought a writ of *mandamus* (an order directing a government official to fulfill a duty) from the United States Supreme Court, as authorized by Section 13 of the Judiciary Act of 1789. As fate would have it, John Marshall had stepped down as Adams's secretary of state only to become chief justice of the Supreme Court. Marshall faced a dilemma: If he ordered the commissions delivered, the new secretary of state (Madison) could simply refuse to deliver them—and the Court had no way to compel action, because it had no police force. At the same time, if Marshall simply allowed the new administration to do as it wished, the Court's power would be severely eroded.

MARSHALL'S DECISION Marshall masterfully fashioned his decision. On the one hand, he enlarged the power of the Supreme Court by affirming the Court's power of judicial review. He stated, "It is emphatically the province and duty of the Judicial Department to say what the law is. . . . If two laws conflict with each other, the courts must decide on the operation of each. . . . So if the law be in opposition to the Constitution . . . [t]he Court must determine which of these conflicting rules governs the case. This is the very essence of judicial duty."

On the other hand, his decision did not require anyone to do anything. He stated that the highest court did not have the power to issue a writ of *mandamus* in this particular case. Marshall pointed out that although the Judiciary Act of 1789 specified that the Supreme Court could issue writs of *mandamus* as part of its original jurisdiction, Article III of the Constitution, which spelled out the Court's original jurisdiction, did not mention writs of *mandamus*. Because Congress did not have the right to expand the Supreme Court's jurisdiction, this section of the Judiciary Act of 1789 was unconstitutional—and thus void. The decision still stands today as a judicial and political masterpiece.

APPLICATION TO TODAY'S WORLD

Since the Marbury v. Madison *decision, the power of judicial review has remained unchallenged. Today, this power is exercised by both federal and state courts. For example, as you read in Chapter 1, some of the laws that Congress has passed in*

a. 5 U.S. (1 Cranch) 137, 2 L.Ed. 60 (1803).

(Continued)

LANDMARK IN THE LAW—Continued

an attempt to protect minors from Internet pornography have been held unconstitutional by the courts. If the courts did not have the power of judicial review, the constitutionality of these acts of Congress could not be challenged in court—a congressional statute would remain law until changed by Congress. Because of the importance of Marbury v. Madison *in our legal system, the courts of other countries that have adopted a constitutional democracy often cite this decision as a justification for judicial review.*

RELEVANT WEB SITES

To locate information on the Web concerning the Marbury v. Madison *decision, go to this text's Web site at* **http://blt.westbuslaw.com**, *select "Chapter 3," and click on "URLs for Landmarks."*

James Madison. If Madison had delivered the commissions of the Federalist judges, would the United States Supreme Court today have the power of judicial review? Why did the Court not force Madison to deliver the commissions? (Library of Congress)

Jurisdiction over Persons Generally, a court can exercise personal jurisdiction (*in personam* jurisdiction) over any person or business that resides in a certain geographic area. A state trial court, for example, normally has jurisdictional authority over residents (including businesses) in a particular area of the state, such as a county or district. A state's highest court (often called the state supreme court)[1] has jurisdiction over all residents of that state.

In addition, under the authority of a state **long arm statute,** a court can exercise personal jurisdiction over certain out-of-state defendants based on activities that took place within the state. Before exercising long arm jurisdiction over a nonresident, however, the court must be convinced that the defendant had sufficient contacts, or *minimum contacts,* with the state to justify the jurisdiction.[2] Generally, this means that the defendant must have enough of a connection to the state for the judge to conclude that it is fair for the state to exercise power over the defendant. ■ EXAMPLE 3.1 If an out-of-state defendant caused an automobile accident or sold defective goods within the state, a court will usually find that minimum contacts exist to exercise jurisdiction over that defendant. Similarly, a state may exercise personal jurisdiction over a nonresident defendant who is sued for breaching a contract that was formed within the state. ■

LONG ARM STATUTE
A state statute that permits a state to obtain personal jurisdiction over nonresident defendants. A defendant must have certain "minimum contacts" with that state for the statute to apply.

In regard to corporations,[3] the minimum-contacts requirement is usually met if the corporation does business within the state. ■ EXAMPLE 3.2 Suppose that a Maine corporation has a branch office or a manufacturing plant in Georgia. Does this Maine corporation have sufficient minimum contacts with the state of Georgia to allow a Georgia court to exercise jurisdiction over it? Yes, it does. If the Maine corporation advertises and sells its products in Georgia, those activities will also likely suffice to meet the minimum-contacts requirement, even if the corporate headquarters are located in a different state. ■

In the following case, the issue was whether phone calls and letters constituted sufficient minimum contacts to give a court jurisdiction over a nonresident defendant.

---

1. As will be discussed shortly, a state's highest court is frequently referred to as the state supreme court, but there are exceptions. For example, in New York, the supreme court is a trial court.
2. The minimum-contacts standard was established in *International Shoe Co. v. State of Washington,* 326 U.S. 310, 66 S.Ct. 154, 90 L.Ed. 95 (1945).
3. In the eyes of the law, corporations are "legal persons"—entities that can sue and be sued. See Chapter 20.

CASE 3.1 Cole v. Mileti

United States Court of Appeals,
Sixth Circuit, 1998.
133 F.3d 433.
http://www.law.emory.edu/6circuit/jan98/index.html[a]

FACTS Nick Mileti, a resident of California, co-produced a movie called *Streamers* and organized a corporation, Streamers International Distributors, Inc., to distribute the film. Joseph Cole, a resident of Ohio, bought two hundred shares of Streamers stock. Cole also lent the firm $475,000, which he borrowed from Equitable Bank of Baltimore. The film was unsuccessful. Mileti agreed to repay Cole's loan in a contract arranged through phone calls and correspondence between California and Ohio. When Mileti did not repay the loan, the bank sued Cole, who in turn filed a suit against Mileti in a federal district court in Ohio. The court entered a judgment against Mileti. He appealed to the U.S. Court of Appeals for the Sixth Circuit, arguing in part that the district court's exercise of jurisdiction over him was unfair.

ISSUE Can a federal district court in Ohio[b] exercise personal jurisdiction over a resident of California who does business in Ohio via phone calls and letters?

a. This is a page, at the Web site of the Emory University School of Law, that lists the published opinions of the U.S. Court of Appeals for the Sixth Circuit for January 1998. Scroll down the list of cases to the *Cole* case. To access the opinion, click on the case name.
b. As will be discussed shortly, federal district courts can exercise jurisdiction over disputes between parties living in different states. This is called *diversity-of-citizenship* jurisdiction. When a federal district court exercises diversity jurisdiction, the court normally applies the law of the state in which the court sits—in this case, the law of Ohio.

DECISION Yes. The U.S. Court of Appeals for the Sixth Circuit held that the district court could exercise personal jurisdiction over Mileti.

REASON The appellate court set out a three-part test to determine whether a court has jurisdiction over a nonresident defendant. A defendant must conduct activities in the state in which the suit is filed, the cause of action must arise from those activities, and those activities or their consequences must have a substantial connection to the state. The court reasoned that a nonresident who does business by "negotiating and executing a contract via telephone calls and letters to an Ohio resident" has conducted sufficient activities in the state. A cause of action arises from those activities if it is for breach of that contract. Finally, under those circumstances, the activities have a substantial connection to the state, and "the assertion of personal jurisdiction was proper."

FOR CRITICAL ANALYSIS—Economic Consideration *Why might a defendant prefer to be sued in one state rather than in another?*

Jurisdiction over Property A court can also exercise jurisdiction over property that is located within its boundaries. This kind of jurisdiction is known as *in rem* jurisdiction, or "jurisdiction over the thing." ■ EXAMPLE 3.3 Suppose that a dispute arises over the ownership of a boat in dry dock in Fort Lauderdale, Florida. The boat is owned by an Ohio resident, over whom a Florida court normally cannot exercise personal jurisdiction. The other party to the dispute is a resident of Nebraska. In this situation, a lawsuit concerning the boat could be brought in a Florida state court on the basis of the court's *in rem* jurisdiction. ■

Jurisdiction over Subject Matter Jurisdiction over subject matter is a limitation on the types of cases a court can hear. In both the federal and state court systems, there are courts of *general* (unlimited) *jurisdiction* and courts of *limited jurisdiction.* An example of a court of general jurisdiction is a state trial court or a federal district

PROBATE COURT
A state court of limited jurisdiction that conducts proceedings relating to the settlement of a deceased person's estate.

BANKRUPTCY COURT
A federal court of limited jurisdiction that handles only bankruptcy proceedings. Bankruptcy proceedings are governed by federal bankruptcy law.

court. An example of a state court of limited jurisdiction is a probate court. **Probate courts** are state courts that handle only matters relating to the transfer of a person's assets and obligations after that person's death, including matters relating to the custody and guardianship of children. An example of a federal court of limited subject-matter jurisdiction is a bankruptcy court. **Bankruptcy courts** handle only bankruptcy proceedings, which are governed by federal bankruptcy law (discussed in Chapter 16). In contrast, a court of general jurisdiction can decide a broad array of cases.

A court's jurisdiction over subject matter is usually defined in the statute or constitution creating the court. In both the federal and state court systems, a court's subject-matter jurisdiction can be limited not only by the subject of the lawsuit but also by the amount in controversy, by whether a case is a felony (a more serious type of crime) or a misdemeanor (a less serious type of crime), or by whether the proceeding is a trial or an appeal.

Original and Appellate Jurisdiction The distinction between courts of original jurisdiction and courts of appellate jurisdiction normally lies in whether the case is being heard for the first time. Courts having original jurisdiction are courts of the first instance, or trial courts—that is, courts in which lawsuits begin, trials take place, and evidence is presented. In the federal court system, the *district courts* are trial courts. In the various state court systems, the trial courts are known by various names, as will be discussed shortly.

The key point here is that, normally, any court having original jurisdiction is known as a trial court. Courts having appellate jurisdiction act as reviewing courts, or appellate courts. In general, cases can be brought before appellate courts only on appeal from an order or a judgment of a trial court or other lower court.

Jurisdiction of the Federal Courts Because the federal government is a government of limited powers, the jurisdiction of the federal courts is limited. Article III of the U.S. Constitution establishes the boundaries of federal judicial power. Section 2 of Article III states that "[t]he judicial Power shall extend to all Cases, in Law and Equity, arising under this Constitution, the Laws of the United States, and Treaties made, or which shall be made, under their Authority."

FEDERAL QUESTION
A question that pertains to the U.S. Constitution, acts of Congress, or treaties. A federal question provides a basis for federal jurisdiction.

Whenever a plaintiff's cause of action is based, at least in part, on the U.S. Constitution, a treaty, or a federal law, then a **federal question** arises, and the case comes under the judicial power of the federal courts. Any lawsuit involving a federal question can originate in a federal court. People who claim that their rights under the U.S. Constitution have been violated can begin their suits in a federal court.

DIVERSITY OF CITIZENSHIP
Under Article III, Section 2, of the Constitution, a basis for federal district court jurisdiction over a lawsuit between (1) citizens of different states, (2) a foreign country and citizens of a state or of different states, or (3) citizens of a state and citizens or subjects of a foreign country. The amount in controversy must be more than $75,000 before a federal district court can take jurisdiction in such cases.

Federal district courts can also exercise original jurisdiction over cases involving **diversity of citizenship.** Such cases may arise between (1) citizens of different states, (2) a foreign country and citizens of a state or of different states, or (3) citizens of a state and citizens or subjects of a foreign country. The amount in controversy must be more than $75,000 before a federal court can take jurisdiction in such cases. For purposes of diversity jurisdiction, a corporation is a citizen of both the state in which it is incorporated and the state in which its principal place of business is located. A case involving diversity of citizenship can be filed in the appropriate federal district court, or, if the case starts in a state court, it can sometimes be transferred to a federal court. A large percentage of the cases filed in federal courts each year are based on diversity of citizenship.

Note that in a case based on a federal question, a federal court will apply federal law. In a case based on diversity of citizenship, however, a federal court will apply the relevant state law (which is often the law of the state in which the court sits).

CONCURRENT JURISDICTION
Jurisdiction that exists when two different courts have the power to hear a case. For example, some cases can be heard in a federal or a state court.

EXCLUSIVE JURISDICTION
Jurisdiction that exists when a case can be heard only in a particular court or type of court.

Exclusive versus Concurrent Jurisdiction When both federal and state courts have the power to hear a case, as is true in suits involving diversity of citizenship, **concurrent jurisdiction** exists. When cases can be tried only in federal courts or only in state courts, exclusive jurisdiction exists. Federal courts have **exclusive jurisdiction** in cases involving federal crimes, bankruptcy, patents, and copyrights; in suits against the United States; and in some areas of admiralty law (law governing transportation on the seas and ocean waters). States also have exclusive jurisdiction over certain subject matters—for example, divorce and adoption. The concepts of exclusive and concurrent jurisdiction are illustrated in Exhibit 3–1.

When concurrent jurisdiction exists, a party has a choice of whether to bring a suit in, for example, a federal or a state court. The party's lawyer will consider several factors in counseling the party as to which choice is preferable. The lawyer may prefer to litigate the case in a state court because he or she is more familiar with the state court's procedures, or perhaps the attorney believes that the state's judge or jury would be more sympathetic to the client and the case. Alternatively, the lawyer may advise the client to sue in federal court. Perhaps the state court's **docket** (the court's schedule listing the cases to be heard) is crowded, and the case could be brought to trial sooner in a federal court. Perhaps some feature of federal practice or procedure could offer an advantage in the client's case. Other important considerations include the law in the particular jurisdiction, how that law has been applied in the jurisdiction's courts, and what the results in similar cases have been in that jurisdiction.

DOCKET
The list of cases entered on a court's calendar and thus scheduled to be heard by the court.

JURISDICTION IN CYBERSPACE

The Internet's capacity to bypass political and geographic boundaries undercuts the traditional basic limitations on a court's authority to exercise jurisdiction. These

EXHIBIT 3–1 EXCLUSIVE AND CONCURRENT JURISDICTION

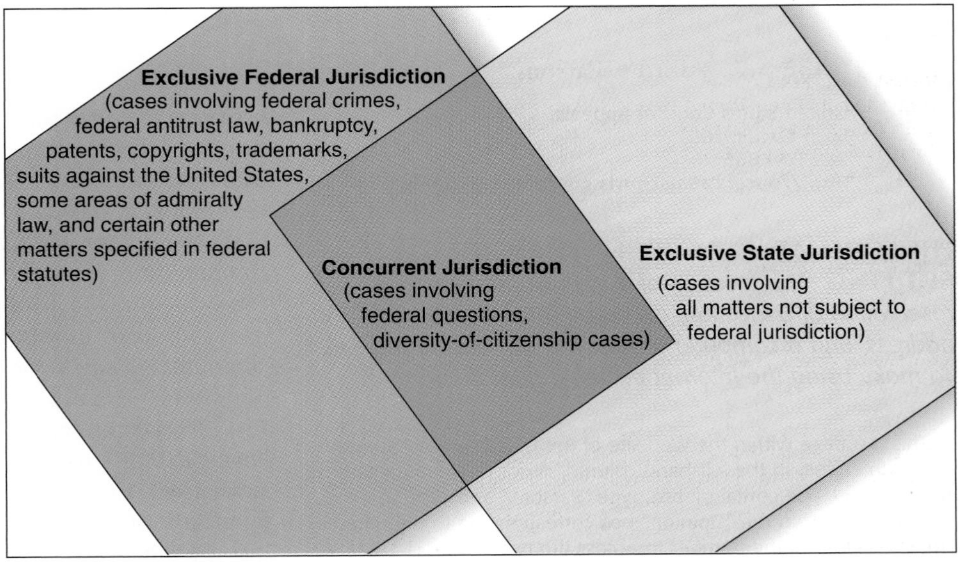
Exclusive Federal Jurisdiction
(cases involving federal crimes, federal antitrust law, bankruptcy, patents, copyrights, trademarks, suits against the United States, some areas of admiralty law, and certain other matters specified in federal statutes)
Concurrent Jurisdiction
(cases involving federal questions, diversity-of-citizenship cases)
Exclusive State Jurisdiction
(cases involving all matters not subject to federal jurisdiction)

limits include a party's contacts with a court's geographic jurisdiction. As already discussed, for a court to compel a defendant to come before it, there must be at least minimum contacts—the presence of a salesperson within the state, for example. Are there sufficient minimum contacts if the only connection to a jurisdiction is an ad on the Web originating from a remote location?

The "Sliding-Scale" Standard Gradually, the courts are developing a standard—called a "sliding-scale" standard—for determining when the exercise of jurisdiction over an out-of-state defendant is proper. In developing this standard, the courts have identified three types of Internet business contacts: (1) substantial business conducted over the Internet (with contracts and sales, for example); (2) some interactivity through a Web site; and (3) passive advertising. Jurisdiction is proper for the first category, improper for the third, and may or may not be appropriate for the second.[4] An Internet communication is typically considered passive if people have to voluntarily access it to read the message and active if it is sent to specific individuals.

In certain situations, even a single contact can satisfy the minimum-contacts requirement. ■ EXAMPLE 3.4 A Texas resident, Davis, sent an unsolicited e-mail message to numerous Mississippi residents advertising a pornographic Web site. Davis falsified the "from" header in the e-mail so that it appeared that Internet Doorway had sent the mail. Internet Doorway filed a lawsuit against Davis in Mississippi claiming that its reputation and goodwill in the community had been harmed. The U.S. district court in Mississippi held that Davis's single e-mail to Mississippi residents satisfied the minimum-contacts requirement for jurisdiction. The court concluded that Davis, by sending the e-mail solicitation, should reasonably have expected that she could be "haled into court in a distant jurisdiction to answer for the ramifications."[5] ■ In the following case, the court considered whether jurisdiction could be exercised over defendants whose only contacts with the jurisdiction were through their Web site.

4. For a leading case on this issue, see *Zippo Manufacturing Co. v. Zippo Dot Com, Inc.,* 952 F.Supp. 1119 (W.D.Pa. 1997).

5. *Internet Doorway, Inc. v. Parks,* 138 F.Supp.2d 773 (S.D.Miss. 2001).

CASE 3.2 Bird v. Parsons

United States Court of Appeals,
Sixth Circuit, 2002.
289 F.3d 865.
http://pacer.ca6.uscourts.gov/opinions/main.php[a]

HISTORICAL AND TECHNOLOGICAL SETTING *The creation of a Web site requires the reservation of a location, called an Internet Protocol (IP) address, and a computer to host the contents of the site. To make using the Internet easier, a domain name is assigned to correspond to an IP address. A person who wants a specific domain name must apply for the name with a domain name registrar. To access a Web site, a user enters in a browser a domain name corresponding to an IP address and then is routed electronically to the computer that hosts the site at that address. Because not every person who establishes a site hosts it on his or her own computer, surrogate hosts license space on their computers to site owners.*

a. This is a page within the Web site of the U.S. Court of Appeals for the Sixth Circuit. In the left-hand column, click on "Opinions Search." In the "Short Title contains" box, type "Parsons" and click on "Submit Query." In the "Opinion" box corresponding to the name of the case, click on the number to access the opinion.

FACTS Darrell Bird, a citizen of Ohio, has operated Financia, Inc., a national computer software business, since 1983. Financia, Inc., owns the domain name financia.com. Dotster, Inc., a domain name registrar incorporated in Washington, operates its registry at

CASE 3.2—Continued

http://www.dotster.com.[b] Dotster allows registrants who lack an Internet server to which a name can be assigned to park their names on Dotster's "Futurehome" page. Marshall Parsons registered the name efinancia.com on Dotster's site in 2000 and "parked" the name on the Futurehome page with the address **http://www.efinancia.com**. George DeCarlo and Steven Vincent, on behalf of Dotster, activated Parsons's site. The name efinancia.com was soon offered for sale at **http://www.afternic.com**, an auction site for the sale of domain names. Bird filed a suit against Dotster and others in a federal district court, alleging, in part, trademark infringement, copyright infringement, and cybersquatting.[c] Dotster, DeCarlo, and Vincent (the "Dotster defendants") asked the court to dismiss the complaint against them for, among other reasons, lack of personal jurisdiction. The court dismissed the suit. Alleging that Dotster sold 4,666 registrations to Ohio residents, Bird appealed to the U.S. Court of Appeals for the Sixth Circuit.

ISSUE Could the state of Ohio assert personal jurisdiction over out-of-state defendants whose only contact with Ohio was through a Web site?

b. Dotster's registration process is in conjunction with the Domain Registration of Internet Assigned Names and Numbers, which is maintained by Network Solutions, Inc. (owned by VeriSign), and regulated by the Internet Corporation for Assigned Names and Numbers (ICANN). Dotster is an ICANN–accredited registrar.

c. *Cybersquatting* is registering another person's trademark as a domain name and offering it for sale. This is a violation of the Anticybersquatting Consumer Protection Act of 1999. Cybersquatting and trademark and copyright infringement are discussed in more detail in Chapter 5.

DECISION Yes. The U.S. Court of Appeals for the Sixth Circuit concluded that the lower court erred in granting the Dotster defendants' motion to dismiss for lack of personal jurisdiction. Bird had established that the court's exercise of jurisdiction over the Dotster defendants was proper.

REASON To be subject to jurisdiction "[f]irst, the defendant must purposefully avail himself of the privilege of acting in the forum state (the state in which a lawsuit is initiated) or causing a consequence in the forum state. Second, the cause of action must arise from the defendant's activities there. Finally, the acts of the defendant or consequences caused by the defendant must have a substantial enough connection with the forum state to make the exercise of jurisdiction over the defendant reasonable." All of these factors were present. Dotster "maintain[s] a website on which Ohio residents can register domain names" and "allegedly accept[ed] the business of 4,666 Ohio residents." Dotster's contacts with Ohio and Bird's claims "stem from [the] defendants' operation of the Dotster website." Also, among other things, "Ohio has a legitimate interest in protecting the business interests of its citizens, even though all of Bird's claims involve federal law." The court ruled against Bird on the substance of his claims, however, and ultimately affirmed the lower court's dismissal of the suit on this ground.

WHY IS THIS CASE IMPORTANT? *This case illustrates how defendants can be sued in states in which they may never have been physically present, provided they have had sufficient contact with that state's residents over the Internet.*

International Jurisdictional Issues Because the Internet is international in scope, international jurisdictional issues understandably have come to the fore. What seems to be emerging in the world's courts is a standard that echoes the "minimum-contacts" requirement applied by the U.S. courts. Most courts are indicating that minimum contacts—doing business within the jurisdiction, for example—are enough to compel a defendant to appear and that a physical presence is not necessary. The effect of this standard is that a business firm has to comply with the laws in any jurisdiction in which it targets customers for its products.

VENUE

VENUE
The geographic district in which an action is tried and from which the jury is selected.

Jurisdiction has to do with whether a court has authority to hear a case involving specific persons, property, or subject matter. **Venue**[6] is concerned with the most appropriate location for a trial. Two state courts (or two federal courts) may have

6. Pronounced *ven*-yoo.

the authority to exercise jurisdiction over a case, but it may be more appropriate or convenient to hear the case in one court than in the other.

Basically, the concept of venue reflects the policy that a court trying a suit should be in the geographic neighborhood (usually the county) where the incident leading to the lawsuit occurred or where the parties involved in the lawsuit reside. Venue in a civil case typically is where the defendant resides, whereas venue in a criminal case is normally where the crime occurred. Pretrial publicity or other factors, though, may require a change of venue to another community, especially in criminal cases when the defendant's right to a fair and impartial jury has been impaired. ■ EXAMPLE 3.5 A change of venue from Oklahoma City to Denver, Colorado, was ordered for the trials of Timothy McVeigh and Terry Nichols, who had been indicted in connection with the 1995 bombing of the Alfred P. Murrah Federal Building in Oklahoma City. (At trial, both McVeigh and Nichols were convicted. McVeigh received the death penalty and was put to death by lethal injection in early 2001. Nichols was sentenced to life imprisonment.) ■

STANDING TO SUE

STANDING TO SUE
The requirement that an individual must have a sufficient stake in a controversy before he or she can bring a lawsuit. The plaintiff must demonstrate that he or she has been either injured or threatened with injury.

Before a person can bring a lawsuit before a court, the party must have **standing to sue,** or a sufficient "stake" in a matter to justify seeking relief through the court system. In other words, to have standing, a party must have a legally protected and tangible interest at stake in the litigation. The party bringing the lawsuit must have suffered a harm, or have been threatened by a harm, as a result of the action about which she or he has complained. At times, a person will have standing to sue on behalf of another person. ■ EXAMPLE 3.6 Suppose that a child suffered serious injuries as a result of a defectively manufactured toy. Because the child is a minor, a lawsuit could be brought on his or her behalf by another person, such as the child's parent or legal guardian. ■

JUSTICIABLE CONTROVERSY
A controversy that is not hypothetical or academic but real and substantial; a requirement that must be satisfied before a court will hear a case.

Standing to sue also requires that the controversy at issue be a **justiciable**[7] **controversy**—a controversy that is real and substantial, as opposed to hypothetical or academic. ■ EXAMPLE 3.7 In the above example, the child's parent could not sue the toy manufacturer merely on the ground that the toy was defective. The issue would become justiciable only if the child had actually been injured due to the defect in the toy as marketed. In other words, the parent normally could not ask the court to determine, for example, what damages might be obtained if the child had been injured, because this would be merely a hypothetical question. ■

The State and Federal Court Systems

As mentioned earlier in this chapter, each state has its own court system. Additionally, there is a system of federal courts. Although state court systems differ, Exhibit 3–2 illustrates the basic organizational structure characteristic of the court systems in many states. The exhibit also shows how the federal court system is structured. We turn now to an examination of these court systems, beginning with the state courts.

7. Pronounced jus-*tish*-uh-bul.

EXHIBIT 3–2 FEDERAL COURTS AND STATE COURT SYSTEMS

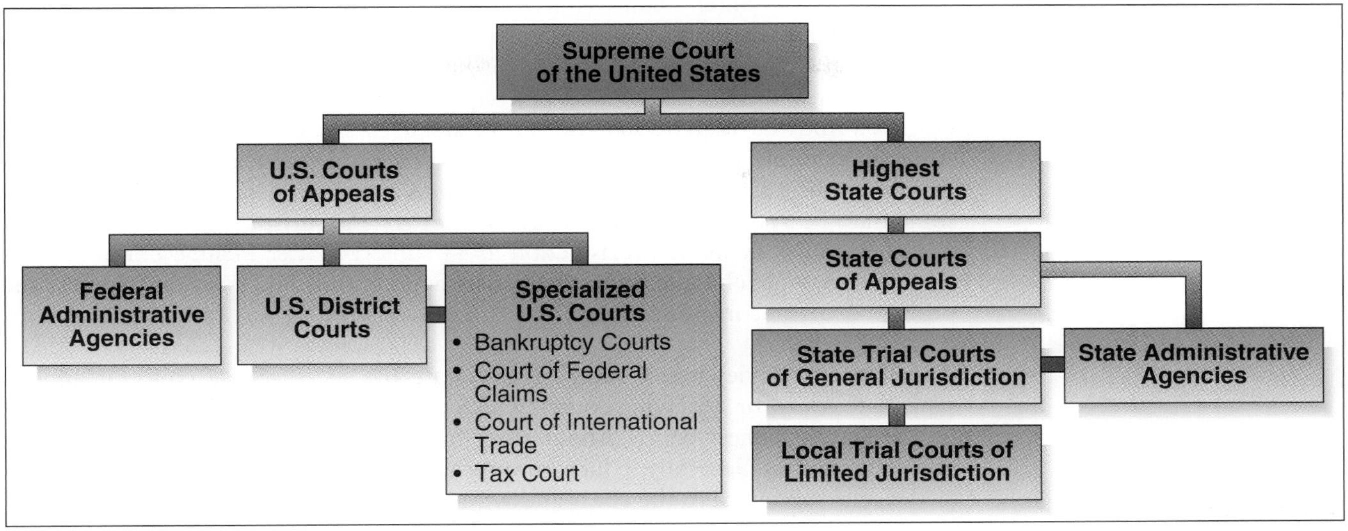

State Court Systems

Typically, a state court system will include several levels, or tiers, of courts. As indicated in Exhibit 3–2, state courts may include (1) trial courts of limited jurisdiction, (2) trial courts of general jurisdiction, (3) appellate courts, and (4) the state's highest court (often called the state supreme court). Generally, any person who is a party to a lawsuit has the opportunity to plead the case before a trial court and then, if he or she loses, before at least one level of appellate court. Finally, if a federal statute or federal constitutional issue is involved in the decision of the state supreme court, that decision may be further appealed to the United States Supreme Court.

Judges in the state court system are usually elected by the voters for a specified term. State judicial elections or appointments vary significantly, however, from state to state. For example, in Iowa the governor appoints judges, and then the general population decides whether to confirm their appointment in the next general election. The states usually specify the number of years that the judge will serve. In contrast, as you will read shortly, judges in the federal court system are appointed by the president of the United States and, if they are confirmed by the Senate, hold office for life—unless they engage in blatantly illegal conduct.

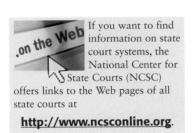

.on the Web If you want to find information on state court systems, the National Center for State Courts (NCSC) offers links to the Web pages of all state courts at **http://www.ncsconline.org**.

Trial Courts Trial courts are exactly what their name implies—courts in which trials are held and testimony taken. State trial courts have either general or limited jurisdiction. Trial courts that have general jurisdiction as to subject matter may be called county, district, superior, or circuit courts.[8] The jurisdiction of these courts is often determined by the size of the county in which the court sits. State trial courts of general jurisdiction have jurisdiction over a wide variety of subjects, including both civil disputes and criminal prosecutions. (In some states, trial courts of general jurisdiction may hear appeals from courts of limited jurisdiction.)

A mother talks with a social worker after a court awarded the mother custody of her child. Are child-custody matters decided by federal or state courts? (Albuquerque Journal, Mark Holm/AP Photo)

8. The name in Ohio is court of common pleas; the name in New York is supreme court.

SMALL CLAIMS COURT
A special court in which parties may litigate small claims (such as $5,000 or less). Attorneys are not required in small claims courts and, in some states, are not allowed to represent the parties.

Some courts of limited jurisdiction are called special inferior trial courts or minor judiciary courts. **Small claims courts** are inferior trial courts that hear only civil cases involving claims of less than a certain amount, such as $5,000 (the amount varies from state to state). Suits brought in small claims courts are generally conducted informally, and lawyers are not required. In a minority of states, lawyers are not even allowed to represent people in small claims courts for most purposes. Another example of an inferior trial court is a local municipal court that hears mainly traffic cases. Decisions of small claims courts and municipal courts may sometimes be appealed to a state trial court of general jurisdiction.

Other courts of limited jurisdiction as to subject matter include domestic relations courts, which handle primarily divorce actions and child-custody disputes, and probate courts, as mentioned earlier.

Appellate, or Reviewing, Courts Every state has at least one court of appeals (appellate court, or reviewing court), which may be an intermediate appellate court or the state's highest court. About three-fourths of the states have intermediate appellate courts. Generally, courts of appeals do not conduct new trials, in which evidence is submitted to the court and witnesses are examined. Rather, an appellate court panel of three or more judges reviews the record of the case on appeal, which includes a transcript of the trial proceedings, and determines whether the trial court committed an error.

Usually, appellate courts do not look at questions of *fact* (such as whether a party did, in fact, commit a certain action, such as burning a flag) but at questions of *law* (such as whether the act of flag-burning is a form of speech protected by the First Amendment to the Constitution). Only a judge, not a jury, can rule on questions of law. Appellate courts normally defer to a trial court's findings on questions of fact because the trial court judge and jury were in a better position to evaluate testimony—by directly observing witnesses' gestures, demeanor, and nonverbal behavior during the trial. At the appellate level, the judges review the written transcript of the trial, which does not include these nonverbal elements.

An appellate court will challenge a trial court's finding of fact only when the finding is clearly erroneous (that is, when it is contrary to the evidence presented at trial) or when there is no evidence to support the finding. ■ **EXAMPLE 3.8** Suppose that a jury concluded that a manufacturer's product harmed the plaintiff but no evidence was submitted to the court to support that conclusion. In that situation, the appellate court would hold that the trial court's decision was erroneous. The options exercised by appellate courts will be further discussed later in this chapter. ■

BE CAREFUL The decisions of a state's highest court are final on questions of state law.

Highest State Courts The highest appellate court in a state is usually called the supreme court but may be called by some other name. For example, in both New York and Maryland, the highest state court is called the court of appeals. The decisions of each state's highest court are final on all questions of state law. Only when issues of federal law are involved can a decision made by a state's highest court be overruled by the United States Supreme Court.

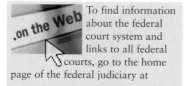

on the Web To find information about the federal court system and links to all federal courts, go to the home page of the federal judiciary at **http://www.uscourts.gov**.

THE FEDERAL COURT SYSTEM

The federal court system is basically a three-tiered model consisting of (1) U.S. district courts (trial courts of general jurisdiction) and various courts of limited jurisdiction, (2) U.S. courts of appeals (intermediate courts of appeals), and (3) the United States Supreme Court.

Unlike state court judges, who are usually elected, federal court judges—including the justices of the Supreme Court—are appointed by the president of the United States and confirmed by the U.S. Senate. All federal judges receive lifetime appointments (because under Article III they "hold their offices during Good Behavior").

U.S. District Courts At the federal level, the equivalent of a state trial court of general jurisdiction is the district court. There is at least one federal district court in every state. The number of judicial districts can vary over time, primarily owing to population changes and corresponding caseloads. Currently, there are ninety-four federal judicial districts.

U.S. district courts have original jurisdiction in federal matters. Federal cases typically originate in district courts. There are other courts with original, but special (or limited), jurisdiction, such as the federal bankruptcy courts and others shown in Exhibit 3–2 on page 83.

U.S. Courts of Appeals In the federal court system, there are thirteen U.S. courts of appeals—also referred to as U.S. circuit courts of appeals. The federal courts of appeals for twelve of the circuits, including the U.S. Court of Appeals for the District of Columbia Circuit, hear appeals from the federal district courts located within their respective judicial circuits. The Court of Appeals for the Thirteenth Circuit, called the Federal Circuit, has national appellate jurisdiction over certain types of cases, such as cases involving patent law and cases in which the U.S. government is a defendant.

.on the Web The decisions of all of the U.S. courts of appeals, as well as those of the United States Supreme Court, are now published online shortly after the decisions are rendered. You can find these decisions and obtain information about the federal court system by accessing the Federal Court Locator at **http://www.law.vill.edu/library/researchguides/fedcourtlocator.asp**.

The decisions of the circuit courts of appeals are final in most cases, but appeal to the United States Supreme Court is possible. Exhibit 3–3 on the following page shows the geographic boundaries of the U.S. circuit courts of appeals and the boundaries of the U.S. district courts within each circuit.

The United States Supreme Court The highest level of the three-tiered model of the federal court system is the United States Supreme Court. According to the language of Article III of the U.S. Constitution, there is only one national Supreme Court. All other courts in the federal system are considered "inferior." Congress is empowered to create other inferior courts as it deems necessary. The inferior courts that Congress has created include the second tier in our model—the U.S. courts of appeals—as well as the district courts and any other courts of limited, or specialized, jurisdiction.

The United States Supreme Court consists of nine justices. Although the Supreme Court has original, or trial, jurisdiction in rare instances (set forth in Article III, Section 2), most of its work is as an appeals court. The Supreme Court can review any case decided by any of the federal courts of appeals, and it also has appellate authority over some cases decided in the state courts.

WRIT OF *CERTIORARI*
A writ from a higher court asking the lower court for the record of a case.

RULE OF FOUR
A rule of the United States Supreme Court under which the Court will not issue a writ of *certiorari* unless at least four justices approve of the decision to issue the writ.

Appeals to the Supreme Court. To bring a case before the Supreme Court, a party requests the Court to issue a writ of *certiorari*. A **writ of *certiorari***[9] is an order issued by the Supreme Court to a lower court requiring the latter to send it the record of the case for review. The Court will not issue a writ unless at least four of the nine justices approve of it. This is called the **rule of four.** Whether the Court will issue a writ of *certiorari* is entirely within its discretion. The Court is not required

9. Pronounced sur-shee-uh-*rah*-ree.

EXHIBIT 3–3 BOUNDARIES OF THE U.S. COURTS OF APPEALS AND U.S. DISTRICT COURTS

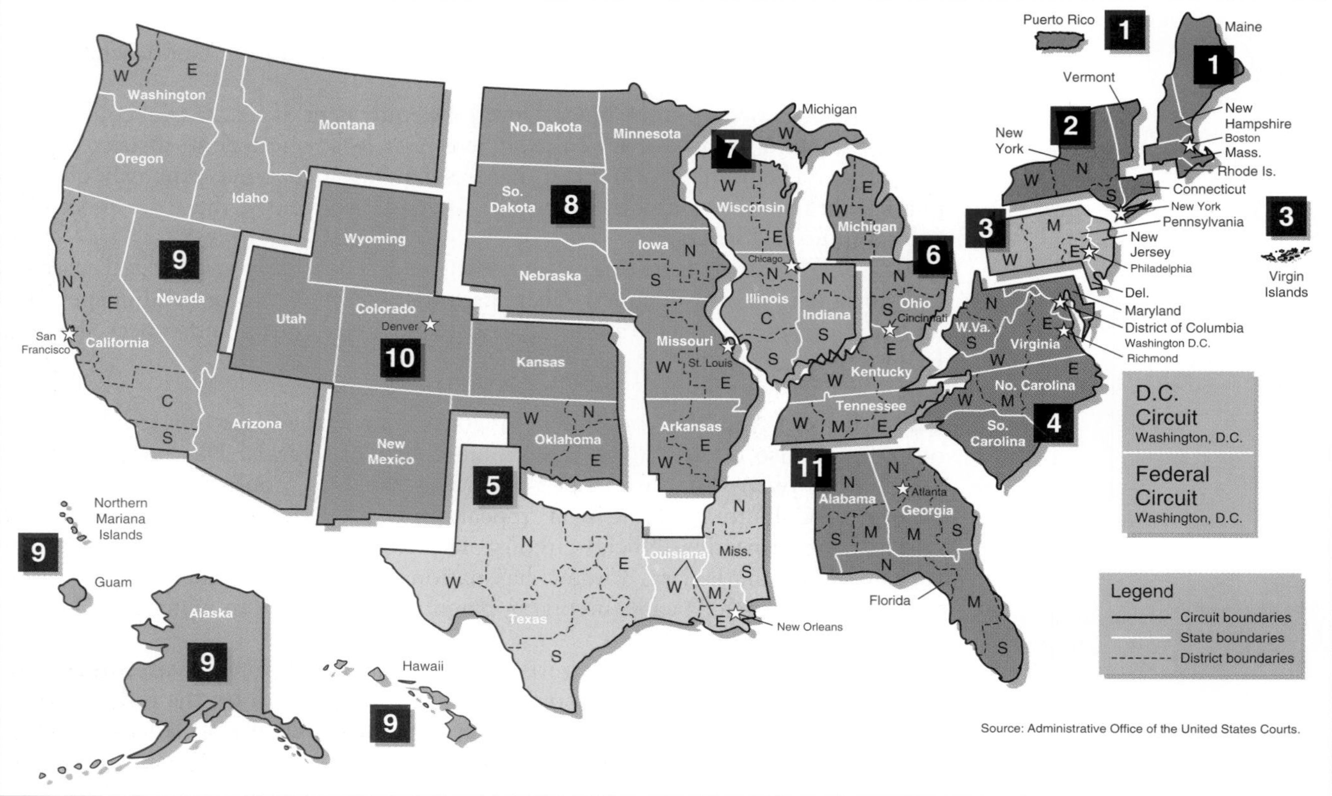

Source: Administrative Office of the United States Courts.

to issue one, and most petitions for writs are denied. (Thousands of cases are filed with the Supreme Court each year; yet it hears, on average, fewer than one hundred of these cases.)[10] A denial is not a decision on the merits of a case, nor does it indicate agreement with the lower court's opinion. Furthermore, a denial of the writ has no value as a precedent.

> **.on the Web** To access Supreme Court opinions, as well as information about the history and function of the Court, go to the Court's official Web site at
> **http://supremecourtus.gov**.

Petitions Granted by the Court. Typically, the Court grants petitions when cases raise important constitutional questions or conflict with other state or federal court decisions. Similarly, if federal appellate courts are rendering inconsistent opinions on an important issue, the Supreme Court may review the case and issue a decision to define the law on the matter. The justices, however, never explain their reasons for hearing certain cases and not others, so it is difficult to predict which type of case the Court might select.

10. From the mid-1950s through the early 1990s, the Supreme Court reviewed more cases per year than it has in the last few years. In the Court's 1982–1983 term, for example, the Court issued opinions in 151 cases. In contrast, in its 2002–2003 term, the Court issued opinions in only 80 cases.

The justices of the United States Supreme Court (as of 2004) are, seated left to right, Antonin Scalia, John Paul Stevens, Chief Justice William H. Rehnquist, Sandra Day O'Connor, and Anthony M. Kennedy; and standing left to right, Ruth Bader Ginsburg, David H. Souter, Clarence Thomas, and Stephen Breyer. Does the fact that these justices are appointed for life have any effect on the decisions they reach in the cases they hear? Explain. (Photo by Richard Strauss, Smithsonian Institution, Collection of the Supreme Court of the United States)

Following a State Court Case

To illustrate the procedures that would be followed in a civil lawsuit brought in a state court, we present a hypothetical case and follow it through the state court system. The case involves an automobile accident in which Kevin Anderson, driving a Mercedes, struck Lisa Marconi, driving a Ford Taurus. The accident occurred at the intersection of Wilshire Boulevard and Rodeo Drive in Beverly Hills, California. Marconi suffered personal injuries, incurring medical and hospital expenses as well as lost wages for four months. Anderson and Marconi are unable to agree on a settlement, and Marconi sues Anderson. Marconi is the plaintiff, and Anderson is the defendant. Both are represented by lawyers.

LITIGATION
The process of resolving a dispute through the court system.

During each phase of the **litigation** (the process of working a lawsuit through the court system), Marconi and Anderson will be required to observe strict procedural requirements. A large body of law—procedural law—establishes the rules and standards for determining disputes in courts. Procedural rules are very complex, and they vary from court to court and from state to state. There is a set of federal rules of procedure as well as various sets of rules for state courts. Additionally, the applicable procedures will depend on whether the case is a civil or criminal proceeding. Generally, the Marconi-Anderson civil lawsuit will involve the procedures discussed in the following subsections. Keep in mind that attempts to settle the case may be ongoing throughout the trial.

The Pleadings

PLEADINGS
Statements made by the plaintiff and the defendant in a lawsuit that detail the facts, charges, and defenses involved in the litigation. The complaint and answer are part of the pleadings.

The complaint and answer (and the counterclaim and reply)—all of which are discussed below—taken together are called the **pleadings.** The pleadings inform each party of the other's claims and specify the issues (disputed questions) involved in the case. Because the rules of procedure vary depending on the jurisdiction of the court, the style and form of the pleadings may look quite different in different states.

COMPLAINT
The pleading made by a plaintiff alleging wrongdoing on the part of the defendant; the document that, when filed with a court, initiates a lawsuit.

The Plaintiff's Complaint Marconi's suit against Anderson commences when her lawyer files a **complaint** with the appropriate court. The complaint contains a statement alleging (asserting to the court, in a pleading) the facts necessary for the court to take jurisdiction, a brief summary of the facts necessary to show that the plaintiff is entitled to a remedy, and a statement of the remedy the plaintiff is seeking. Exhibit 3–4 illustrates how the complaint might read in the Marconi-Anderson case.

EXHIBIT 3–4 EXAMPLE OF A TYPICAL COMPLAINT

IN THE LOS ANGELES SUPERIOR COURT
COUNTY OF LOS ANGELES, STATE OF CALIFORNIA

Lisa Marconi Plaintiff, v. Kevin Anderson Defendant.	CIVIL NO. 8–1026 COMPLAINT

Comes now the plaintiff and for her cause of action against the defendant alleges and states as follows:

1. The jurisdiction of this court is based on Section 86 of the California Civil Code.
2. This action is between plaintiff, a California resident living at 1434 Palm Drive, Anaheim, California, and defendant, a California resident living at 6950 Garrison Avenue, Los Angeles, California.
3. On September 10, 2005, plaintiff, Lisa Marconi, was exercising good driving habits and reasonable care in driving her car through the intersection of Rodeo Drive and Wilshire Boulevard when defendant, Kevin Anderson, negligently drove his vehicle through a red light at the intersection and collided with plaintiff's vehicle. Defendant was negligent in the operation of the vehicle as to:
   a. Speed,
   b. Lookout,
   c. Management and control.
4. As a result of the collision plaintiff suffered severe physical injury that prevented her from working and property damage to her car. The costs she incurred included $10,000 in medical bills, $9,000 in lost wages, and $5,000 for automobile repairs.

WHEREFORE, plaintiff demands judgment against the defendant for the sum of $24,000 plus interest at the maximum legal rate and the costs of this action.

By *Roger Harrington*
Roger Harrington
Attorney for the Plaintiff
800 Orange Avenue
Anaheim, CA 91426

Complaints may be lengthy or brief, depending on the complexity of the case and the rules of the jurisdiction.

After the complaint has been filed, the sheriff, a deputy of the county, or another *process server* (one who delivers a complaint and summons) serves a **summons** and a copy of the complaint on defendant Anderson. The summons notifies Anderson that he must file an answer to the complaint with both the court and the plaintiff's attorney within a specified time period (usually twenty to thirty days). The summons also informs Anderson that failure to answer may result in a **default judgment** for the plaintiff, meaning the plaintiff will be awarded the damages alleged in her complaint.

SUMMONS
A document informing a defendant that a legal action has been commenced against him or her and that the defendant must appear in court on a certain date to answer the plaintiff's complaint. The document is delivered by a sheriff or any other person so authorized.

DEFAULT JUDGMENT
A judgment entered by a court against a defendant who has failed to appear in court to answer or defend against the plaintiff's claim.

The Defendant's Answer The defendant's **answer** either admits the statements or allegations set forth in the complaint or denies them and outlines any defenses that the defendant may have. If Anderson admits to all of Marconi's allegations in his answer, the court will enter a judgment for Marconi. If Anderson denies any of Marconi's allegations, the litigation will go forward.

Anderson can deny Marconi's allegations and set forth his own claim that Marconi was in fact negligent and therefore owes him money for damages to his Mercedes. This is appropriately called a **counterclaim.** If Anderson files a counterclaim, Marconi will have to answer it with a pleading, normally called a **reply,** which has the same characteristics as an answer.

Anderson can also admit the truth of Marconi's complaint but raise new facts that may result in dismissal of the action. This is called raising an affirmative defense. For example, Anderson could assert the expiration of the time period under the relevant statute of limitations (a state or federal statute that sets the maximum time period during which a certain action can be brought or rights enforced) as an affirmative defense.

ANSWER
Procedurally, a defendant's response to the plaintiff's complaint.

COUNTERCLAIM
A claim made by a defendant in a civil lawsuit against the plaintiff. In effect, the defendant is suing the plaintiff.

REPLY
Procedurally, a plaintiff's response to a defendant's answer.

Motion to Dismiss A **motion to dismiss** requests the court to dismiss the case for stated reasons. A defendant often makes a motion to dismiss before filing an answer to the plaintiff's complaint. Grounds for dismissal of a case include improper delivery of the complaint and summons, improper venue, and the plaintiff's failure to state a claim for which a court could grant relief (a remedy). For example, if Marconi had suffered no injuries or losses as a result of Anderson's negligence, Anderson could move to have the case dismissed because Marconi had not stated a claim for which relief could be granted.

If the judge grants the motion to dismiss, the plaintiff generally is given time to file an amended complaint. If the judge denies the motion, the suit will go forward, and the defendant must then file an answer. Note that if Marconi wishes to discontinue the suit because, for example, an out-of-court settlement has been reached, she can likewise move for dismissal. The court can also dismiss the case on its own motion.

MOTION TO DISMISS
A pleading in which a defendant asserts that the plaintiff's claim fails to state a cause of action (that is, has no basis in law) or that there are other grounds on which a suit should be dismissed.

Pretrial Motions

Either party may attempt to get the case dismissed before trial through the use of various pretrial motions. We have already mentioned the motion to dismiss. Two other important pretrial motions are the motion for judgment on the pleadings and the motion for summary judgment.

At the close of the pleadings, either party may make a **motion for judgment on the pleadings,** or on the merits of the case. The judge will grant the motion only when there is no dispute over the facts of the case and the sole issue to be resolved

MOTION FOR JUDGMENT ON THE PLEADINGS
A motion by either party to a lawsuit at the close of the pleadings requesting the court to decide the issue solely on the pleadings without proceeding to trial. The motion will be granted only if no facts are in dispute.

is a question of law. In deciding on the motion, the judge may consider only the evidence contained in the pleadings.

MOTION FOR SUMMARY JUDGMENT A motion requesting the court to enter a judgment without proceeding to trial. The motion can be based on evidence outside the pleadings and will be granted only if no facts are in dispute.

In contrast, in a **motion for summary judgment** the court may consider evidence outside the pleadings, such as sworn statements (affidavits) by parties or witnesses or other documents relating to the case. A motion for summary judgment can be made by either party. As with the motion for judgment on the pleadings, a motion for summary judgment will be granted only if there are no genuine questions of fact and the sole question is a question of law.

DISCOVERY

DISCOVERY A phase in the litigation process during which the opposing parties may obtain information from each other and from third parties prior to trial.

Before a trial begins, each party can use a number of procedural devices to obtain information and gather evidence about the case from the other party or from third parties. The process of obtaining such information is known as **discovery.** Discovery includes gaining access to witnesses, documents, records, and other types of evidence.

The Federal Rules of Civil Procedure and similar rules in the states set forth the guidelines for discovery activity. The rules governing discovery are designed to make sure that a witness or a party is not unduly harassed, that privileged material (communications that need not be presented in court) is safeguarded, and that only matters relevant to the case at hand are discoverable.

Discovery prevents surprises at trial by giving parties access to evidence that might otherwise be hidden. This allows both parties to learn as much as they can about what to expect at a trial before they reach the courtroom. It also serves to narrow the issues so that trial time is spent on the main questions in the case.

DEPOSITION The testimony of a party to a lawsuit or a witness taken under oath before a trial.

Depositions and Interrogatories Discovery can involve the use of depositions or interrogatories, or both. **Depositions** are sworn testimony by a party to the lawsuit or any witness. The person being deposed (the deponent) answers questions asked by the attorneys, and the questions and answers are recorded by an authorized court official and sworn to and signed by the deponent. (Occasionally, written depositions are taken when witnesses are unable to appear in person.) The answers given to depositions will, of course, help the attorneys prepare their cases. They can also be used in court to impeach (challenge the credibility of) a party or a witness who changes testimony at the trial. In addition, the answers given in a deposition can be used as testimony if the witness is not available at trial.

INTERROGATORIES A series of written questions for which written answers are prepared, usually with the assistance of the party's attorney, and then signed under oath by a party to a lawsuit.

Interrogatories are written questions for which written answers are prepared and then signed under oath. The main difference between interrogatories and written depositions is that interrogatories are directed to a party to the lawsuit (the plaintiff or the defendant), not to a witness, and the party can prepare answers with the aid of an attorney. The scope of interrogatories is broader because parties are obligated to answer questions, even if that means disclosing information from their records and files.

Other Information A party can serve a written request on the other party for an admission of the truth of matters relating to the trial. Any matter admitted under such a request is conclusively established for the trial. For example, Marconi can ask Anderson to admit that he was driving at a speed of forty-five miles an hour. A request for admission saves time at trial because the parties will not have to spend time proving facts on which they already agree.

A party can also gain access to documents and other items not in her or his possession in order to inspect and examine them. Likewise, a party can gain "entry on land" to inspect the premises. Anderson's attorney, for example, normally can gain permission to inspect and duplicate Marconi's car repair bills.

When the physical or mental condition of one party is in question, the opposing party can ask the court to order a physical or mental examination. If the court is willing to make the order, which it will do only if the need for the information outweighs the right to privacy of the person to be examined, the opposing party can obtain the results of the examination.

E-EVIDENCE
A type of evidence that consists of computer-generated or electronically recorded information, including e-mail, voice mail, spreadsheets, word processing documents, and other data.

Electronic Discovery Any relevant material, including information stored electronically, can be the object of a discovery request. Electronic evidence, or **e-evidence,** consists of all types of computer-generated or electronically recorded information, including e-mail, voice mail, spreadsheets, word processing documents, and other data. E-evidence is important because it can reveal significant facts that are not discoverable by other means. For example, whenever a person is working on a computer, information is being recorded on the hard drive disk without ever being saved by the user. This information includes the file's location, path, creator, date created, date last accessed, concealed notes, earlier versions, passwords, and formatting. It reveals information about how, when, and by whom a document was created, accessed, modified, and transmitted. This information can be obtained from the file only in its electronic format—not from printed-out versions.

The federal rules and most state rules (as well as court decisions) now specifically allow parties to obtain discovery of electronic "data compilations" (or e-evidence). Although traditional means, such as interrogatories and depositions, may still be used to find out about the e-evidence, the parties must usually hire an expert to retrieve the evidence in its electronic format. Using special software, the expert can reconstruct e-mail exchanges to establish who knew what and when they knew it. The expert can even recover files from a computer that the user thought had been deleted. Reviewing back-up copies of documents and e-mail can provide useful—and often quite damaging—information about how a particular matter progressed over several weeks or months.

Although electronic discovery has significant advantages over paper discovery, it is also time consuming and expensive. Who should pay the costs associated with electronic discovery? This chapter's *Adapting the Law to the Online Environment* feature on the next page discusses how the law is evolving to address this issue.

PRETRIAL CONFERENCE

Either party or the court can request a pretrial conference, or hearing. Usually, the hearing consists of an informal discussion between the judge and the opposing attorneys after discovery has taken place. The purpose of the hearing is to explore the possibility of a settlement without trial and, if this is not possible, to identify the matters that are in dispute and to plan the course of the trial.

JURY SELECTION

.on the Web Picking the "right" jury is often an important aspect of litigation strategy, and a number of firms now specialize in jury consulting services. You can learn more about these services by going to the Web site of the Jury Research Institute at **http://www.jri-inc.com**.

A trial can be held with or without a jury. The Seventh Amendment to the U.S. Constitution guarantees the right to a jury trial for cases in federal courts when the amount in controversy exceeds $20. Most states have similar guarantees in their own constitutions (although the threshold dollar amount is higher than $20). The right to a trial by jury does not have to be exercised, and many cases are tried without a jury. In most states and in federal courts, one of the parties must request a jury, or the right is presumed to be waived.

ADAPTING THE LAW TO THE ONLINE ENVIRONMENT

Who Bears the Costs of Electronic Discovery?

Traditionally, the party responding to a discovery request must pay the expenses involved in obtaining the requested materials. If compliance would be too burdensome or too costly, however, the judge can either limit the scope of the request or shift some or all of the costs to the requesting party. How do these traditional rules governing discovery apply to requests for electronic evidence?

WHY COURTS MIGHT SHIFT THE COSTS OF ELECTRONIC DISCOVERY

Electronic discovery has dramatically increased the costs associated with complying with discovery requests. It is no longer simply a matter of photocopying paper documents. Now the responding party may need to hire computer forensics experts to make "image" copies of desktop, laptop, and server hard drives, as well as removable storage media (including CD-ROMs, DVDs, and Zip drives), back-up tapes, voice mail, cell phones, and any other device that digitally stores data.

In cases involving multiple parties or large corporations with many offices and employees, the electronic discovery process can easily run into hundreds of thousands—if not millions—of dollars. For example, in one case concert promoters alleged that thirty separate defendant companies had engaged in discriminatory practices. The federal district court hearing the case found that the complete restoration of the back-up tapes of just one of those defendants would cost $9.75 million. Acquiring 200,000 e-mail messages from another defendant would cost between $43,000 and $84,000, with an additional $247,000 to have an attorney review the retrieved documents. Restoring the 523 back-up tapes of a third defendant would cost $395,000 and another $120,000 for the attorney to review them. The judge hearing the case decided that both plaintiffs and defendants would share in these discovery costs.[a]

WHAT FACTORS DO COURTS CONSIDER IN DECIDING WHETHER TO SHIFT COSTS?

Increasingly, the courts are shifting part of the costs of obtaining electronic discovery to the party requesting it (which is usually the plaintiff). At what point, however, should this cost-shifting occur? In *Zubulake v. UBS Warburg LLC*,[b] the court identified a three-step analysis for deciding disputes over discovery costs. First, if the data are kept in an accessible format, the usual rules of discovery apply: the responding party should pay the costs of producing responsive data. A court should consider cost-shifting *only* when electronic data are in a relatively inaccessible form, such as in back-up tapes or deleted files. Second, the court should determine what data may be found on the inaccessible media. Requiring the responding party to restore and produce responsive documents from a small sample of the requested medium is a sensible approach in most cases. Third, the court should consider a series of other factors, including, for example, the availability of the information from other sources, the total cost of production compared to the amount in controversy, and each party's ability to pay these costs.

FOR CRITICAL ANALYSIS

The court in the Zubulake *case noted that "as large companies increasingly move to entirely paper-free environments, the frequent use of cost-shifting will have the effect of crippling discovery," especially in cases in which private parties are suing large corporations. Why might cost-shifting thwart discovery? Who would benefit if courts considered cost-shifting in every case involving electronic discovery?*

a. *Rowe Entertainment Inc. v. William Morris Agency*, 2002 WL 975713 (S.D.N.Y.).
b. 2003 WL 21087884 (S.D.N.Y.).

VOIR DIRE
An old French phrase meaning "to speak the truth." In legal language, the phrase refers to the process in which the attorneys question prospective jurors to learn about their backgrounds, attitudes, biases, and other characteristics that may affect their ability to serve as impartial jurors.

Before a jury trial commences, a jury must be selected. The jury selection process is known as ***voir dire***.[11] During *voir dire* in most jurisdictions, attorneys for the plaintiff and the defendant ask prospective jurors oral questions to determine whether a potential jury member is biased or has any connection with a party to the action or with a prospective witness. In some jurisdictions, the judge may do all or part of the questioning based on written inquiries submitted by counsel for the parties.

11. Pronounced vwahr *deehr.*

During *voir dire,* a party may challenge a certain number of prospective jurors *peremptorily*—that is, ask that an individual not be sworn in as a juror without providing any reason. Alternatively, a party may challenge a prospective juror *for cause*—that is, provide a reason why an individual should not be sworn in as a juror. If the judge grants the challenge, the individual is asked to step down. A prospective juror may not be excluded from the jury by the use of discriminatory challenges, however, such as those based on racial criteria[12] or gender.[13]

TAKE NOTE A prospective juror cannot be excluded solely on the basis of his or her race or gender.

AT THE TRIAL

At the beginning of the trial, the attorneys present their opening arguments, setting forth the facts that they expect to provide during the trial. Then the plaintiff's case is presented. In our hypothetical case, Marconi's lawyer would introduce evidence (relevant documents, exhibits, and the testimony of witnesses) to support Marconi's position. The defendant has the opportunity to challenge any evidence introduced and to cross-examine any of the plaintiff's witnesses.

At the end of the plaintiff's case, the defendant's attorney has the opportunity to ask the judge to direct a verdict for the defendant on the ground that the plaintiff has presented no evidence that would justify the granting of the plaintiff's remedy. This is called a **motion for a directed verdict** (known in federal courts as a *motion for judgment as a matter of law*). If the motion is not granted (it seldom is), the defendant's attorney then presents the evidence and witnesses for the defendant's case. At the conclusion of the defendant's case, the defendant's attorney has another opportunity to make a motion for a directed verdict. The plaintiff's attorney can challenge any evidence introduced and cross-examine the defendant's witnesses.

After the defense concludes its presentation, the attorneys present their closing arguments, each urging a verdict in favor of her or his client. The judge instructs the jury in the law that applies to the case (these instructions are often called *charges*), and the jury retires to the jury room to deliberate a verdict. In the Marconi-Anderson case, the jury will not only decide for the plaintiff or for the defendant but, if it finds for the plaintiff, will also decide on the amount of the **award** (the money to be paid to her).

MOTION FOR A DIRECTED VERDICT
In a jury trial, a motion for the judge to take the decision out of the hands of the jury and to direct a verdict for the party who filed the motion on the ground that the other party has not produced sufficient evidence to support her or his claim.

AWARD
In litigation, the amount of money awarded to a plaintiff in a civil lawsuit as damages. In the context of alternative dispute resolution, the decision rendered by an arbitrator.

MOTION FOR JUDGMENT *N.O.V.*
A motion requesting the court to grant judgment in favor of the party making the motion on the ground that the jury's verdict against him or her was unreasonable and erroneous.

MOTION FOR A NEW TRIAL
A motion asserting that the trial was so fundamentally flawed (because of error, newly discovered evidence, prejudice, or other reason) that a new trial is necessary to prevent a miscarriage of justice.

POSTTRIAL MOTIONS

After the jury has rendered its verdict, either party may make a posttrial motion. If Marconi wins, and Anderson's attorney has previously moved for a directed verdict, Anderson's attorney may make a **motion for judgment *n.o.v.*** (from the Latin *non obstante veredicto,* which means "notwithstanding the verdict"—called a *motion for judgment as a matter of law* in the federal courts) in Anderson's favor on the ground that the jury's verdict in favor of Marconi was unreasonable and erroneous. If the judge decides that the jury's verdict was reasonable in light of the evidence presented at trial, the motion will be denied. If the judge agrees with Anderson's attorney, then he or she will set the jury's verdict aside and enter a judgment in favor of Anderson.

Alternatively, Anderson could make a **motion for a new trial,** requesting the judge to set aside the adverse verdict and to hold a new trial. The motion will be granted if the judge is convinced, after looking at all the evidence, that the jury was in error

12. *Batson v. Kentucky,* 476 U.S. 79, 106 S.Ct. 1712, 90 L.Ed.2d 69 (1986).
13. *J.E.B. v. Alabama ex rel. T.B.,* 511 U.S. 127, 114 S.Ct. 1419, 128 L.Ed.2d 89 (1994). (*Ex rel.* is Latin for *ex relatione.* The phrase refers to an action brought on behalf of the state, by the attorney general, at the instigation of an individual who has a private interest in the matter.)

but does not feel it is appropriate to grant judgment for the other side. A new trial may also be granted on the ground of newly discovered evidence, misconduct by the participants or the jury during the trial, or error by the judge.

THE APPEAL

Assume here that any posttrial motion is denied and that Anderson appeals the case. (If Marconi wins but receives a smaller money award than she sought, she can appeal also.) A notice of appeal must be filed with the clerk of the trial court within a prescribed time. Anderson now becomes the appellant, or petitioner, and Marconi becomes the appellee, or respondent.

BRIEF
A formal legal document submitted by the attorney for the appellant or the appellee (in answer to the appellant's brief) to an appellate court when a case is appealed. The appellant's brief outlines the facts and issues of the case, the judge's rulings or jury's findings that should be reversed or modified, the applicable law, and the arguments on the client's behalf.

Filing the Appeal Anderson's attorney files with the appellate court the record on appeal, which includes the pleadings, the trial transcript, the judge's rulings on motions made by the parties, and other trial-related documents. Anderson's attorney will also provide a condensation of the record, known as an *abstract,* which is filed with the reviewing court along with the brief. The **brief** is a formal legal document outlining the facts and issues of the case, the judge's rulings or jury's findings that should be reversed or modified, the applicable law, and arguments on Anderson's behalf (citing applicable statutes and relevant cases as precedents).

Marconi's attorney will file an answering brief. Anderson's attorney can file a reply to Marconi's brief, although it is not required. The reviewing court then considers the case.

Appellate Review As mentioned earlier, a court of appeals does not hear evidence. Rather, it reviews the record for errors of law. Its decision concerning a case is based on the record on appeal, the abstracts, and the attorneys' briefs. The attorneys can present oral arguments, after which the case is taken under advisement. In general, appellate courts do not reverse findings of fact unless the findings are unsupported or contradicted by the evidence.

If the reviewing court believes that an error was committed during the trial or that the jury was improperly instructed, the judgment will be *reversed.* Sometimes the case will be *remanded* (sent back to the court that originally heard the case) for a new trial. Even when a case is remanded to a trial court for further proceedings, however, the appellate court normally spells out how the relevant law should be interpreted and applied to the case.

■ EXAMPLE 3.9 A case may be remanded for several reasons. For instance, if the appellate court decides that a judge improperly granted summary judgment, the case will be remanded for a trial. If the appellate court decides that the trial judge erroneously applied the law, the case will be remanded for a new trial, with instructions to the trial court to apply the law as clarified by the appellate court. If the appellate court decides that the trial jury's award of damages was too high, the case will be remanded with instructions to reduce the damages award. ■ In most cases, the judgment of the lower court is *affirmed,* resulting in the enforcement of the court's judgment or decree.

Appeal to a Higher Appellate Court If the reviewing court is an intermediate appellate court, the losing party normally may appeal to the state supreme court (the highest state court). Such a petition corresponds to a petition for a writ of *certiorari* from the United States Supreme Court. If the petition is granted (in some states, a petition is automatically granted), new briefs must be filed before the state supreme court, and the attorneys may be allowed or requested to present oral arguments. Like the intermediate appellate court, the supreme court may reverse or affirm the appellate court's decision or remand the case. At this point, unless a federal question is at issue, the case has reached its end.

ENFORCING THE JUDGMENT

The uncertainties of the litigation process are compounded by the lack of guarantees that any judgment will be enforceable. Even if a plaintiff wins an award of damages in court, the defendant may not have sufficient assets or insurance to cover that amount. Usually, one of the factors considered before a lawsuit is initiated is whether the defendant has sufficient assets to cover the amount of damages sought, should the plaintiff win the case. What other factors should be considered when deciding whether to initiate a lawsuit? See the *Application* at the end of this chapter for answers to this question.

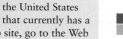

.on the Web For links to every trial-level court in the United States that currently has a Web site, go to the Web site of the Nation's Courts Directory at

http://www.courts.net.

The Courts Adapt to the Online World

We have already mentioned that the courts have attempted to adapt traditional jurisdictional concepts to the online world. Not surprisingly, the Internet has also brought about changes in court procedures and practices, including new methods for filing pleadings and other documents and issuing decisions and opinions. Several courts are experimenting with electronic delivery, such as via the Internet or CD-ROM. Some jurisdictions are exploring the possibility of cyber courts, in which legal proceedings could be conducted totally online.

ELECTRONIC FILING

The federal court system first experimented with an electronic filing system in January 1996, in an asbestos case heard by the U.S. District Court for the Northern District of Ohio. Currently, a number of federal courts permit attorneys to file documents electronically in certain types of cases. At last count, more than 130,000 documents in approximately 10,000 cases had been filed electronically in federal courts. The Administrative Office of the U.S. Courts is considering permitting electronic filing in all U.S. district courts nationwide.

State and local courts are also setting up electronic filing systems. Since the late 1990s, the court system in Pima County, Arizona, has been accepting pleadings via e-mail. The supreme court of the state of Washington also now accepts online filings of litigation documents. In addition, electronic filing projects are being developed in other states, including California, Idaho, Kansas, Maryland, Michigan, Texas, Utah, and Virginia. The state of Colorado implemented the first statewide court e-filing system and currently allows e-filing in over sixty courts. Generally, when electronic filing is made available, it is optional. In early 2001, however, a trial court judge in the District of Columbia launched a pilot project that *required* attorneys to use electronic filing for all documents relating to certain types of civil cases.

The expenses associated with an appeal can be considerable, and e-filing can add substantially to the cost. In some cases, appellants who successfully appeal a judgment are entitled to be awarded their costs, including an amount for printing the copies of the record on appeal and the briefs. In the following case, the appellants spent $16,112 for the paper copies and an additional $16,065 to prepare and submit briefs and other documents in an electronic format. Should the appellants be reimbursed for these expenses?

CASE 3.3 Phansalkar v. Andersen, Weinroth & Co.

United States Court of Appeals,
Second Circuit, 2004.
356 F.3d 188.

FACTS Andersen, Weinroth & Company (AW) is a small firm that finds and creates investment opportunities for itself, its partners, and other investors. AW's income includes returns on its investments, fees paid by its investors, and the compensation and other benefits earned by its employees for their service on boards of directors of the companies with which AW does business. Some AW employees receive stock and "investment opportunities" rather than salaries. Rohit Phansalkar worked for AW from February 1998 until June 2000, when he became the chairman and chief executive officer of Osicom Technologies, Inc. After Phansalkar left, AW refused to pay him the returns on certain "investment opportunities" that he had been given while at AW. Phansalkar filed a suit in a federal district court against AW, alleging in part breach of contract. The court awarded Phansalkar more than $4.4 million. AW appealed to the U.S. Court of Appeals for the Second Circuit, which reversed this judgment on the ground that Phansalkar had acted with disloyalty during his employment with AW by failing to disclose compensation and benefits that he received for serving on various boards. AW then asked for an award of the amount that it spent to create copies of the briefs and other documents involved in the appeal in hyperlinked CD-ROM format.

ISSUE Could AW recover the costs associated with preparing and submitting electronic copies of the appeal documents?

DECISION No. The U.S. Court of Appeals for the Second Circuit ruled that AW could not recover these costs.

REASON The court recognized that it had been one of the first courts to encourage the submission of electronic briefs. "The submission of an electronic version of a paper brief very likely entails small incremental costs. CD-ROM submissions that hyperlink briefs to relevant sections of the appellate record are more versatile, more useful, and considerably more expensive," however. The court could find "no local rule or holding * * * that allocates CD-ROM costs," and "[n]o guidance" in the *Federal Rules of Civil Procedure,* which authorize an award of costs incurred to produce "necessary" copies of briefs and other costs of an appeal. Factors that are important in determining if a cost is authorized by the rules include "whether the party seeking disallowance has clearly consented to the expense; whether a court has previously approved the expense; and whether the alternative arrangement costs less than the expense specifically authorized." None of these factors was present in this case. In fact, because AW "incurred costs both to produce hard copies of their appellate materials *and* to produce hyperlinked CD-ROM copies, * * * the CD-ROM costs in this case were duplicative." The court also noted that "there is no written stipulation or understanding between the parties concerning the allocation of the incremental costs of this useful technology."

FOR CRITICAL ANALYSIS—Social Consideration *How might the result in this case have been different if the court had required, rather than merely encouraged, the submission of electronic copies of the appeal documents?*

COURTS ONLINE

Most courts today have sites on the Web. Of course, each court decides what to make available at its site. Some courts display only the names of court personnel and office phone numbers. Others add court rules and forms. Many include judicial decisions, although generally the sites do not feature archives of old decisions. Instead, decisions usually are available online for a limited time. For example, California keeps opinions online for only sixty days. In addition, in some states, such as California and Florida, court clerks offer docket information and other searchable databases online.

Appellate court decisions are often posted online immediately after they are rendered. Recent decisions of the U.S. courts of appeals, for example, are available online at their Web sites. The United States Supreme Court also has an official Web site and publishes its opinions there immediately after they are announced to the public. (These Web sites are listed elsewhere in this chapter in the *On the Web* features.) In fact, even decisions that are designated as unpublished opinions by the appellate courts are often published online. What is the value of an unpublished decision in today's courts? See this chapter's *Letter of the Law* feature for a discussion of this issue.

LETTER OF THE LAW Should "Unpublished" Opinions Be Law?

Appellate courts churn out thousands of decisions that are labeled "unpublished" and are not included in appellate reporters. Typically, these decisions do not contain the same detailed recital of facts or comprehensive legal analysis as published opinions. The idea is that by designating the opinion as unpublished, the judges will be able to spend less time writing and editing the decision. Traditionally, the rules of many courts banned the citation of unpublished decisions.

The rules regarding unpublished decisions may be changing, however. As a 2000 opinion by the U.S. Court of Appeals for the Eighth Circuit pointed out, it goes against the doctrine of precedent *not* to allow these unpublished decisions to affect later court decisions, and it may even be unconstitutional.[a] After all, the role of the judge is not to invent new law but to interpret the law in a particular context by looking at previous court decisions. This opinion—as well as the online posting of unpublished decisions—has influenced judges' views around the nation. Some courts now permit unpublished decisions to be cited, though usually as persuasive rather than binding authority. In 2002, for example, the U.S. Court of Appeals for the D.C. Circuit adopted new rules that allow unpublished decisions to be cited as precedent. Some state courts, such as those in Texas, are also beginning to allow unpublished opinions to be cited.

THE BOTTOM LINE

Increasingly, judges are allowing unpublished opinions to be cited as authority in their courtrooms and permitting the reasoning used in those cases to persuade their way of thinking.

a. *Anastasoff v. United States,* 223 F.3d 898 (8th Cir. 2000); opinion withdrawn on rehearing *en banc,* 235 F.3d 1054 (8th Cir. 2000). This opinion involved a woman who sought a tax refund for overpaid taxes. When the Internal Revenue Service refunded the taxes, the decision was withdrawn because the tax issue was resolved.

CYBER COURTS AND PROCEEDINGS

Someday, litigants may be able to use cyber courts, in which judicial proceedings take place only on the Internet. The parties to a case could meet online to make their arguments and present their evidence. This might be done with e-mail submissions, through video cameras, in designated "chat" rooms, at closed sites, or through the use of other Internet facilities. These courtrooms could be efficient and economical. We might also see the use of virtual lawyers, judges, and juries—and possibly the replacement of court personnel with computer software. Already the state of Michigan has passed legislation creating cyber courts that will hear cases involving technology issues and high-tech businesses. Many lawyers predict that other states will follow suit.

.on the Web Smith & Johnson, P.C., a Michigan law firm, offers a summary of Michigan's cyber court legislation on its Web page at **http://www.smith-johnson.com/businesslaw/cybercourt.htm**.

The courts may also use the Internet in other ways. In a groundbreaking decision in early 2001, for example, a Florida county court granted "virtual" visitation rights in a couple's divorce proceeding. Although the court granted custody of the couple's ten-year-old daughter to the father, the court also ordered each parent to buy a computer and a videoconferencing system so that the mother could "visit" with her child via the Internet at any time.[14]

ETHICAL ISSUE 3.1

How will online access to courts affect privacy? From a practical perspective, trial court records, although normally available to the public, remain obscure. Because the decisions of most state trial courts (and some federal courts) are not published, someone must be strongly motivated to go to the trouble of traveling to the relevant courthouse in person to access the documents. As online access to court records increases and electronic filing becomes the norm, this "practical obscurity," as lawyers call it, may soon disappear. Electronic filing on a nationwide basis would open up all court documents to anyone with an Internet connection and a Web browser. Utilizing special "data-mining" software, anyone could go online and within just a few minutes access information—ranging from personal health records to financial reports to criminal violations—from dozens of courts. This means that serious privacy issues are at stake. Should the courts restrict public access to certain types of documents, such as bankruptcy records or documents containing personal information that is not directly related to the legal issue being decided? Many courts are struggling with these questions and have taken a myriad of different approaches. Some courts make civil case information available but restrict Internet access to criminal case information. Other courts, such as those in Florida, have deemed certain types of documents and court proceedings confidential and no longer post this information online. ■ [15]

Alternative Dispute Resolution

ALTERNATIVE DISPUTE RESOLUTION (ADR) The resolution of disputes in ways other than those involved in the traditional judicial process. Negotiation, mediation, and arbitration are forms of ADR.

Litigation is expensive. It is also time consuming. Because of the backlog of cases pending in many courts, several years may pass before a case is actually tried. For these and other reasons, more and more businesspersons are turning to **alternative dispute resolution** (ADR) as a means of settling their disputes.

14. For a discussion of this case, see Shelley Emling, "After the Divorce, Internet Visits?" *Austin American-Statesman,* January 30, 2001, pp. A1 and A10.

15. *In re Report of Supreme Court Workgroup on Public Records,* 825 So.2d 889 (Fla. 2002).

Methods of ADR range from neighbors sitting down over a cup of coffee in an attempt to work out their differences to huge multinational corporations agreeing to resolve a dispute through a formal hearing before a panel of experts. The great advantage of ADR is its flexibility. Normally, the parties themselves can control how the dispute will be settled, what procedures will be used, and whether the decision reached (either by themselves or by a neutral third party) will be legally binding or nonbinding.

Today, approximately 95 percent of cases are settled before trial through some form of ADR. Indeed, most states either require or encourage parties to undertake ADR prior to trial. Several federal courts have instituted ADR programs as well. In the following pages, we examine various forms of ADR. Keep in mind, though, that new methods of ADR—and new combinations of existing methods—are constantly being devised and employed. In addition, ADR services are now being offered via the Internet. After looking at traditional forms of ADR, we examine some of the ways in which disputes are being resolved in various online forums.

ETHICAL ISSUE 3.2

Should "secret" settlements be allowed? Perhaps one of the greatest incentives for settling a case is to avoid the publicity of a trial. Often an individual or business defendant is willing to pay a significant amount of money in return for the plaintiff's silence about the terms of the settlement. This practice, however, is increasingly coming under fire, particularly when the lawsuit involves a potential public safety or health hazard. For example, suppose that you are seriously injured by a defective product and sue the manufacturer of that product (product liability will be discussed in Chapter 13). Rather than proceed to trial, the manufacturer offers to pay you several million dollars provided that you agree to keep the terms of the settlement confidential. Many plaintiffs would find it difficult to refuse such an offer.

In most states, confidential or sealed settlement agreements are perfectly legal, even when they may not be perceived as ethical. A few states, such as South Carolina and New York, have passed laws attempting to prohibit—or at least limit—the use of secrecy provisions in settlement agreements. Several federal jurisdictions have also attempted to address the problem. So far, however, there is no uniform approach to resolving this issue, and many critics argue that limiting secrecy will only reduce the number of cases that settle. ■

NEGOTIATION

NEGOTIATION
A process in which parties attempt to settle their dispute informally, with or without attorneys to represent them.

One of the simplest forms of ADR is **negotiation,** a process in which the parties attempt to settle their dispute informally, with or without attorneys to represent them. Attorneys frequently advise their clients to negotiate a settlement voluntarily before they proceed to trial.

Negotiation traditionally involves just the parties themselves and (typically) their attorneys. The attorneys, though, are advocates—they are obligated to put their clients' interests first. Often parties find it helpful to have the opinion and guidance of a neutral (unbiased) third party when deciding whether or how to negotiate a settlement of their dispute. The methods of ADR discussed next all involve neutral third parties.

MEDIATION
A method of settling disputes outside of court by using the services of a neutral third party, who acts as a communicating agent between the parties and assists them in negotiating a settlement.

MEDIATION

In the **mediation** process, the parties themselves attempt to negotiate an agreement, but with the assistance of a neutral third party, a mediator. In mediation, the mediator talks with the parties separately as well as jointly. The mediator emphasizes points of agreement, helps the parties evaluate their positions, and proposes solutions. The mediator, however, does not make a decision on the matter being disputed. The mediator, who need not be a lawyer, usually charges a fee for his or her services (which can be split between the parties). States that require parties to undergo ADR before trial often offer mediation as one of the ADR options or (as in Florida) the only option.

Mediation is not adversarial in nature, as lawsuits are. In litigation, the parties "do battle" with each other in the courtroom, while the judge is the neutral party. Because of its nonadversarial nature, the mediation process tends to reduce the antagonism between the disputants and to allow them to resume their former relationship. For this reason, mediation is often the preferred form of ADR for disputes involving business partners, employers and employees, or other parties involved in long-term relationships. ■ EXAMPLE 3.10 Suppose that two business partners have a dispute over how the profits of their firm should be distributed. If the dispute is litigated, the parties will be adversaries, and their respective attorneys will emphasize how the parties' positions differ, not what they have in common. In contrast, when a dispute is mediated, the mediator emphasizes the common ground shared by the parties and helps them work toward agreement. ■

.on the Web For a guide to alternative dispute resolution, mediation, and arbitration, go to the Web site of Hieros Gamos at **http://www.hg.org/adr.html**.

Today, characteristics of mediation are being combined with those of arbitration (to be discussed next). In *binding mediation,* for example, the parties agree that if they cannot resolve the dispute, the mediator can make a legally binding decision on the issue. In *mediation-arbitration,* or "med-arb," the parties agree to first attempt to settle their dispute through mediation. If no settlement is reached, the dispute will be arbitrated.

ARBITRATION

ARBITRATION
The settling of a dispute by submitting it to a disinterested third party (other than a court), who renders a decision that is (most often) legally binding.

A more formal method of ADR is **arbitration,** in which an arbitrator (a neutral third party or a panel of experts) hears a dispute and renders a decision. The key difference between arbitration and the forms of ADR just discussed is that in arbitration, the third party hearing the dispute makes the decision for the parties. Usually, the parties in arbitration agree that the third party's decision will be *legally binding,* although the parties can also agree to *nonbinding* arbitration. Additionally, arbitration that is mandated by the courts often is not binding on the parties. If the parties do not agree with the arbitrator's decision, they can go forward with the lawsuit.

In some respects, formal arbitration resembles a trial, although usually the procedural rules are much less restrictive than those governing litigation. In the typical hearing format, the parties present opening arguments to the arbitrator and state what remedies should or should not be granted. Evidence is then presented, and witnesses may be called and examined by both sides. The arbitrator then renders a decision, which is called an *award.*

KEEP IN MIND Litigation—even of a dispute over whether a particular matter should be submitted to arbitration—can be time consuming and expensive.

An arbitrator's award is usually the final word on the matter. Although the parties may appeal an arbitrator's decision, a court's review of the decision will be much more restricted in scope than an appellate court's review of a trial court's decision. The general view is that because the parties were free to frame the issues and set the powers of the arbitrator at the outset, they cannot complain about the results. The award will be set aside only if the arbitrator's conduct or "bad faith" substantially prejudiced the rights of one of the parties, if the award violates an established public policy, or if the arbitrator exceeded her or his powers (arbitrated issues that the parties did not agree to submit to arbitration).

ARBITRATION CLAUSE
A clause in a contract that provides that, in the event of a dispute, the parties will submit the dispute to arbitration rather than litigate the dispute in court.

Arbitration Clauses and Statutes Virtually any commercial matter can be submitted to arbitration. Frequently, parties include an **arbitration clause** in a contract (a written agreement—see Chapter 7); the clause provides that any dispute that arises under the contract will be resolved through arbitration rather than through the court system. Parties can also agree to arbitrate a dispute after a dispute arises.

Most states have statutes (often based in part on the Uniform Arbitration Act of 1955) under which arbitration clauses will be enforced, and some state statutes compel arbitration of certain types of disputes, such as those involving public employees. At the federal level, the Federal Arbitration Act (FAA), enacted in 1925, enforces arbitration clauses in contracts involving maritime activity and interstate commerce (though its applicability to employment contracts has been controversial, as discussed in a later subsection). Because of the breadth of the commerce clause (see Chapter 1), arbitration agreements involving transactions only slightly connected to the flow of interstate commerce may fall under the FAA.

The Issue of Arbitrability When a dispute arises as to whether the parties have agreed in an arbitration clause to submit a particular matter to arbitration, one party may file suit to compel arbitration. The court before which the suit is brought will decide *not* the basic controversy but rather the issue of arbitrability—that is, whether the matter is one that must be resolved through arbitration. If the court finds that the subject matter in controversy is covered by the agreement to arbitrate, then a party may be compelled to arbitrate the dispute. Even when a claim involves a violation of a statute passed to protect a certain class of people, such as employees, a court may determine that the parties must nonetheless abide by their agreement to arbitrate the dispute. Usually, a court will allow the claim to be arbitrated if the court, in interpreting the statute, can find no legislative intent to the contrary.

No party, however, will be ordered to submit a particular dispute to arbitration unless the court is convinced that the party consented to do so.[16] Additionally, the courts will not compel arbitration if it is clear that the prescribed arbitration rules and procedures are inherently unfair to one of the parties. ■ **EXAMPLE 3.11** In one case, an employer asked a court to issue an order compelling a former employee to submit to arbitration in accordance with an arbitration agreement that the parties had signed. Under that agreement, the employer was to establish the procedure and the rules for the arbitration. The court held that the employee did not have to submit her claim to arbitration because "the rules were so one-sided that their only possible purpose is to undermine the neutrality of the proceeding." According to the court, the biased rules created "a sham system unworthy even of the name of arbitration" in violation of the parties' contract to arbitrate.[17] ■

Mandatory Arbitration in the Employment Context A significant question in the last several years has concerned mandatory arbitration clauses in employment contracts. Many claim that employees' rights are not sufficiently protected when they are forced, as a condition of hiring, to agree to arbitrate all disputes and thus waive their rights under statutes specifically designed to protect employees. The United States Supreme Court, however, has generally held that mandatory arbitration clauses in employment contracts are enforceable.

---

16. See, for example, *Wright v. Universal Maritime Service Corp.,* 525 U.S. 70, 119 S.Ct. 391, 142 L.Ed.2d 361 (1998).
17. *Hooters of America, Inc. v. Phillips,* 173 F.3d 933 (4th Cir. 1999).

■ EXAMPLE 3.12 In a landmark 1991 decision, *Gilmer v. Interstate/Johnson Lane Corp.*,[18] the Supreme Court held that a claim brought under a federal statute prohibiting age discrimination (see Chapter 18) could be subject to arbitration. The Court concluded that the employee had waived his right to sue when he agreed, as part of a required registration application to be a securities representative with the New York Stock Exchange, to arbitrate "any dispute, claim, or controversy" relating to his employment. ■ The *Gilmer* decision was controversial and generated much discussion during the 1990s. By the early 2000s, some lower courts had begun to question whether Congress intended the Federal Arbitration Act (FAA)—which expressly excludes the employment contracts of seamen, railroad employees, or any other class of workers engaged in foreign or interstate commerce—to apply to any employment contracts.

In 2001, the United States Supreme Court addressed this issue in *Circuit City Stores, Inc. v. Adams.*[19] In that case, as part of the application process, a sales employee was required to sign an arbitration clause. Two years later, the employee, Adams, filed suit against Circuit City for violating state employment-discrimination laws, and the employer asked the court to compel arbitration. Adams argued that the FAA did not apply to employment contracts, and the U.S. Court of Appeals for the Ninth Circuit agreed. The Supreme Court reversed, however, holding that the act applied to most employment contracts, except those that involve interstate transportation workers.

ETHICAL ISSUE 3.3

Should the courts enforce mandatory arbitration clauses that inherently favor the employer? The Supreme Court's holding in *Circuit City* permits employers to require employees (and prospective employees) to sign arbitration agreements as a condition of their employment. Is this fair? Should the courts enforce arbitration clauses even when they appear to be disproportionately weighted in favor of the employer? Some courts are finding reasons not to enforce such clauses.

For example, the federal appellate court that reviewed the *Circuit City* case on remand declined to enforce the arbitration agreement on the ground that it was unconscionable. (An unconscionable contract or clause is one that is so one sided and unfair as to "shock the conscience" of the court—see Chapter 8.) The court noted that Circuit City drafted the agreement and required the plaintiff to sign it without modification as a prerequisite to employment. Under the terms of the agreement, only the employees were required to arbitrate their disputes, while Circuit City remained free to litigate in court any claims it had against its employees. Moreover, Circuit City's contract severely limited the relief that was available to employees, required employees to split the arbitrator's fee, and imposed a strict one-year statute of limitations on claims. For all of these reasons, the court held the entire arbitration agreement unenforceable.[20] Other courts have cited similar reasons for deciding not to enforce one-sided arbitration clauses.[21] ■

OTHER TYPES OF ADR

The three forms of ADR just discussed are the oldest and traditionally the most commonly used. In recent years, a variety of new types of ADR have emerged, some of which were mentioned earlier in the discussion of mediation. Other ADR forms

---

18. 500 U.S. 20, 111 S.Ct. 1647, 114 L.Ed.2d 26 (1991).
19. 532 U.S. 105, 121 S.Ct. 1302, 149 L.Ed.2d 234 (2001).
20. *Circuit City Stores, Inc. v. Adams,* 279 F.3d 889 (9th Cir. 2002).
21. See, for example, *Hardwick v. Sherwin Williams Co.,* 2002 WL 31992364 (Ohio App. 8 Dist. 2003).

that are used today are sometimes referred to as "assisted negotiation" because they involve a third party in what is essentially a negotiation process. For example, in **early neutral case evaluation,** the parties select a neutral third party (generally an expert in the subject matter of the dispute) to evaluate their respective positions. The parties explain their positions to the case evaluator in any manner they choose. The case evaluator then assesses the strengths and weaknesses of the parties' positions, and this evaluation forms the basis for negotiating a settlement.

EARLY NEUTRAL CASE EVALUATION
A form of alternative dispute resolution in which a neutral third party evaluates the strengths and weaknesses of the disputing parties' positions. The evaluator's opinion then forms the basis for negotiating a settlement.

Another form of assisted negotiation that is often used by business parties is the **mini-trial,** in which each party's attorney briefly argues the party's case before representatives of each firm who have the authority to settle the dispute. Typically, a neutral third party (usually an expert in the area being disputed) acts as an adviser. If the parties fail to reach an agreement, the adviser renders an opinion as to how a court would likely decide the issue. The proceeding assists the parties in determining whether they should negotiate a settlement or take the dispute to court.

MINI-TRIAL
A private proceeding in which each party to a dispute argues its position before the other side and vice versa. A neutral third party may be present as an adviser and may render an opinion if the parties fail to reach an agreement.

Today's courts are also experimenting with a variety of ADR alternatives to speed up (and reduce the cost of) justice. Numerous federal courts now hold **summary jury trials (SJTs),** in which the parties present their arguments and evidence and the jury renders a verdict. The jury's verdict is not binding, but it does act as a guide to both sides in reaching an agreement during the mandatory negotiations that immediately follow the trial. Other alternatives being employed by the courts include summary procedures for commercial litigation and the appointment of special masters to assist judges in deciding complex issues.

SUMMARY JURY TRIAL (SJT)
A method of settling disputes, used in many federal courts, in which a trial is held, but the jury's verdict is not binding. The verdict acts only as a guide to both sides in reaching an agreement during the mandatory negotiations that immediately follow the summary jury trial.

Providers of ADR Services

ADR services are provided by both government agencies and private organizations. A major provider of ADR services is the American Arbitration Association (AAA), which was founded in 1926 and now handles over 200,000 claims a year in its numerous offices around the country. Most of the largest U.S. law firms are members of this nonprofit association.

Cases brought before the AAA are heard by an expert or a panel of experts in the area relating to the dispute and are usually settled quickly. Generally, about half of the panel members are lawyers. To cover its costs, the AAA charges a fee, paid by the party filing the claim. In addition, each party to the dispute pays a specified amount for each hearing day, as well as a special additional fee for cases involving personal injuries or property loss.

Hundreds of for-profit firms around the country also provide various forms of dispute-resolution services. Typically, these firms hire retired judges to conduct arbitration hearings or otherwise assist parties in settling their disputes. The judges follow procedures similar to those of the federal courts and use similar rules. Usually, each party to the dispute pays a filing fee and a designated fee for a hearing session or conference.

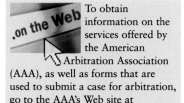

on the Web To obtain information on the services offered by the American Arbitration Association (AAA), as well as forms that are used to submit a case for arbitration, go to the AAA's Web site at **http://www.adr.org**.

Online Dispute Resolution

An increasing number of companies and organizations offer dispute-resolution services using the Internet. The settlement of disputes in these online forums is known as **online dispute resolution (ODR).** To date, the disputes resolved in these forums have most commonly involved disagreements over the rights to domain names (Web site addresses—see Chapter 5) and disagreements over the quality of goods sold via the Internet, including goods sold through Internet auction sites.

ONLINE DISPUTE RESOLUTION (ODR)
The resolution of disputes with the assistance of organizations that offer dispute-resolution services via the Internet.

Currently, ODR may be best for resolving small- to medium-sized business liability claims, which may not be worth the expense of litigation or traditional ADR methods. Rules being developed in online forums, however, may ultimately become a code of conduct for all of those who do business in cyberspace. Most online forums do not automatically apply the law of any specific jurisdiction. Instead, results are often based on general, universal legal principles. As with most offline methods of dispute resolution, any party may appeal to a court at any time.

NEGOTIATION AND MEDIATION SERVICES

The online negotiation of a dispute is generally simpler and more practical than litigation. Typically, one party files a complaint, and the other party is notified by e-mail. Password-protected access is possible twenty-four hours a day, seven days a week. Fees are generally low (often 2 to 4 percent, or less, of the disputed amount).

CyberSettle.com, clickNsettle.com, U.S. Settlement Corporation (ussettle.com), and other Web-based firms offer online forums for negotiating monetary settlements. The parties to a dispute may agree to submit offers; if the offers fall within a previously agreed-on range, they will end the dispute, and the parties will split the difference. Special software keeps secret any offers that are not within the range. If there is no agreed-on range, typically an offer includes a deadline within which the other party must respond before the offer expires. The parties can drop the negotiations at any time.

Mediation providers have also tried resolving disputes online. SquareTrade, for example, has provided mediation services for the online auction site eBay and also resolves disputes among other parties. SquareTrade uses Web-based software that walks participants through a five-step e-resolution process. Negotiation between the parties occurs on a secure page within SquareTrade's Web site. The parties may consult a mediator. The entire process takes as little as ten to fourteen days, and at present no fee is charged unless the parties use a mediator.

ARBITRATION PROGRAMS

A number of organizations, including the American Arbitration Association, offer online arbitration programs. The Internet Corporation for Assigned Names and Numbers (ICANN), a nonprofit corporation that the federal government set up to oversee the distribution of domain names, has issued special rules for the resolution of domain name disputes.[22] ICANN has also authorized several organizations to arbitrate domain name disputes in accordance with ICANN's rules.

Resolution Forum, Inc. (RFI), a nonprofit organization associated with the Center for Legal Responsibility at South Texas College of Law, offers arbitration services through its CAN-WIN conferencing system. Using standard browser software and an RFI password, the parties to a dispute access an online conference room. When multiple parties are involved, private communications and breakout sessions are possible via private messaging facilities. RFI also offers mediation services.

.on the Web To read about the policies and goals of the Virtual Magistrate Project, go to **http://www.vmag.org/docs/concept.html**.

The Virtual Magistrate Project (VMAG) is affiliated with the American Arbitration Association, Chicago-Kent College of Law, Cyberspace Law Institute, National Center for Automated Information Research, and other organizations. VMAG offers arbitration for disputes involving users of online systems; victims of wrongful messages, postings, and files; and system operators subject to complaints or similar

22. ICANN's Rules for Uniform Domain Name Dispute Resolution Policy are online at **http://www.icann.org/udrp/udrp-rules-24oct99.htm**. Domain names will be discussed in more detail in Chapter 5, in the context of trademark law.

demands. VMAG also arbitrates intellectual property, personal property, real property, and tort disputes related to online contracts. VMAG attempts to resolve a dispute within seventy-two hours. The proceedings occur in a password-protected online newsgroup setting, and private e-mail among the participants is possible. A VMAG arbitrator's decision is issued in a written opinion. A party may appeal the outcome to a court.

APPLICATION To Sue or Not to Sue?

Wrongs are committed every minute of every day in the United States. These wrongs may be committed inadvertently or intentionally. Sometimes businesspersons believe that wrongs have been committed against them by other businesspersons, by consumers, or by the local, state, or federal government. If you are deciding whether or not to sue for a wrong that has been committed against you or your business, you must consider many issues.

THE QUESTION OF COST

Competent legal advice is not inexpensive. Good commercial business law attorneys charge $100 to $500 an hour, plus expenses. It is almost always worthwhile to make an initial visit to an attorney who has skills in the area in which you are going to sue to get an estimate of the expected costs of pursuing a redress for your grievance. You may be charged for the initial visit as well.

Note that less than 10 percent of all corporate lawsuits end up in trial—the rest are settled beforehand. You may end up settling for far less than you think you are "owed" simply because of the length of time it takes your attorney to bring your case to trial and to finish the trial. And then you might not win, anyway!

Basically, therefore, you must do a cost-benefit analysis to determine whether you should sue. Your attorney can give you an estimate of the dollar costs involved in litigating the dispute. Realize, though, that litigation also involves nondollar costs. These costs include time away from your business, stress, inconvenience, and publicity—to name but a few. You need to weigh all of these costs against the benefits. You can "guesstimate" the benefits by multiplying the probable size of the award by the probability of obtaining that award.

* This *Application* is not meant to substitute for the services of an attorney who is licensed to practice law in your state.

THE ALTERNATIVES BEFORE YOU

Another method of settling your grievance is by alternative dispute resolution (ADR). Negotiation, mediation, arbitration, and other ADR forms are becoming increasingly attractive alternatives to court litigation because they usually yield quick results at a comparatively low cost. Most disputes relating to business can be mediated or arbitrated through the American Arbitration Association (AAA), which can be accessed online at **http://www.adr.org**.

There are numerous other ADR centers as well. You can obtain information on ADR from the AAA, courthouses, chambers of commerce, law firms, state bar associations, or the American Bar Association. The latter's Web site can be accessed at **http://www.abanet.org**. The Yellow Pages in large metropolitan areas usually list agencies and firms that can help you settle your dispute out of court; look under "Mediation" or "Social Service Agencies."

Depending on the nature of the dispute and the amount of damages you seek, you might wish to contact an organization that offers online dispute-resolution services, such as one of those discussed in this chapter.

CHECKLIST FOR DECIDING WHETHER TO SUE

1. Are you prepared to pay for going to court? Make this decision only after you have consulted an attorney to get an estimate of the costs of litigating the dispute.
2. Do you have the patience to follow a court case through the judicial system, even if it takes several years?
3. Is there a way for you to settle your grievance without going to court? Even if the settlement is less than you think you are owed—in net terms corrected for future expenses, lost time, and frustration—you may be better off settling now for the smaller figure.
4. Can you use some form of alternative dispute resolution? Before you say no, investigate these alternatives—they are usually cheaper and quicker to use than the standard judicial process.

KEY TERMS

CHAPTER SUMMARY Traditional and Online Dispute Resolution

The Judiciary's Role in American Government (See page 74.)	The role of the judiciary—the courts—in the American governmental system is to interpret and apply the law. Through the process of judicial review—determining the constitutionality of laws—the judicial branch acts as a check on the executive and legislative branches of government.
Basic Judicial Requirements (See pages 74–82.)	1. *Jurisdiction*—Before a court can hear a case, it must have jurisdiction over the person against whom the suit is brought or the property involved in the suit, as well as jurisdiction over the subject matter. a. Limited versus general jurisdiction—Limited jurisdiction exists when a court is limited to a specific subject matter, such as probate or divorce. General jurisdiction exists when a court can hear any kind of case. b. Original versus appellate jurisdiction—Original jurisdiction exists with courts that have authority to hear a case for the first time (trial courts). Appellate jurisdiction exists with courts of appeals, or reviewing courts; generally, appellate courts do not have original jurisdiction. c. Federal jurisdiction—Arises (1) when a federal question is involved (when the plaintiff's cause of action is based, at least in part, on the U.S. Constitution, a treaty, or a federal law) or (2) when a case involves diversity of citizenship (citizens of different states, for example) and the amount in controversy exceeds $75,000. d. Concurrent versus exclusive jurisdiction—Concurrent jurisdiction exists when two different courts have authority to hear the same case. Exclusive jurisdiction exists when only state courts or only federal courts have authority to hear a case. 2. *Jurisdiction in cyberspace*—Because the Internet does not have physical boundaries, traditional jurisdictional concepts have been difficult to apply in cases involving activities

CHAPTER SUMMARY Traditional and Online Dispute Resolution—Continued

Basic Judicial Requirements—Continued	conducted via the Web. Gradually, the courts are developing standards to use in determining when jurisdiction over a Web owner or operator in another state is proper. 3. *Venue*—Venue has to do with the most appropriate location for a trial, which is usually the geographic area where the event leading to the dispute took place or where the parties reside. 4. *Standing to sue*—A requirement that a party must have a legally protected and tangible interest at stake sufficient to justify seeking relief through the court system. The controversy at issue must also be a justiciable controversy—one that is real and substantial, as opposed to hypothetical or academic.
The State and Federal Court Systems (See pages 82–86.)	1. *Trial courts*—Courts of original jurisdiction, in which legal actions are initiated. a. State—Courts of general jurisdiction can hear any case; courts of limited jurisdiction include divorce courts, probate courts, traffic courts, small claims courts, and so on. b. Federal—The federal district court is the equivalent of the state trial court. Federal courts of limited jurisdiction include the U.S. Tax Court, the U.S. Bankruptcy Court, and the U.S. Court of Federal Claims. 2. *Intermediate appellate courts*—Courts of appeals, or reviewing courts; generally without original jurisdiction. Many states have an intermediate appellate court; in the federal court system, the U.S. circuit courts of appeals are the intermediate appellate courts. 3. *Supreme (highest) courts*—Each state has a supreme court, although it may be called by some other name; appeal from the state supreme court to the United States Supreme Court is possible only if a federal question is involved. The United States Supreme Court is the highest court in the federal court system and the final arbiter of the Constitution and federal law.
Following a State Court Case (See pages 87–95.)	Rules of procedure prescribe the way in which disputes are handled in the courts. Rules differ from court to court, and separate sets of rules exist for federal and state courts, as well as for criminal and civil cases. A sample civil court case in a state court would involve the following procedures: 1. *The pleadings*— a. Complaint—Filed by the plaintiff with the court to initiate the lawsuit; served with a summons on the defendant. b. Answer—Admits or denies allegations made by the plaintiff; may assert a counterclaim or an affirmative defense. c. Motion to dismiss—A request to the court to dismiss the case for stated reasons, such as the plaintiff's failure to state a claim for which relief can be granted. 2. *Pretrial motions (in addition to the motion to dismiss)*— a. Motion for judgment on the pleadings—May be made by either party; will be granted if the parties agree on the facts and the only question is how the law applies to the facts. The judge bases the decision solely on the pleadings. b. Motion for summary judgment—May be made by either party; will be granted if the parties agree on the facts. The judge applies the law in rendering a judgment. The judge can consider evidence outside the pleadings when evaluating the motion. 3. *Discovery*—The process of gathering evidence concerning the case. Discovery involves depositions (sworn testimony by a party to the lawsuit or any witness), interrogatories (written questions and answers to these questions made by parties to the action with the aid of their attorneys), and various requests (for admissions, documents, and medical examinations, for example). Discovery may also involve electronically recorded information, such as e-mail, voice mail, word processing documents, and other data compilations.

(Continued)

CHAPTER SUMMARY Traditional and Online Dispute Resolution—Continued

Following a State Court Case—Continued	Although electronic discovery has significant advantages over paper discovery, it is also more time consuming and expensive and often requires the parties to hire experts. 4. *Pretrial conference*—Either party or the court can request a pretrial conference to identify the matters in dispute after discovery has taken place and to plan the course of the trial. 5. *Trial*—Following jury selection *(voir dire),* the trial begins with opening statements from both parties' attorneys. The following events then occur: a. The plaintiff's introduction of evidence (including the testimony of witnesses) supporting the plaintiff's position. The defendant's attorney can challenge evidence and cross-examine witnesses. b. The defendant's introduction of evidence (including the testimony of witnesses) supporting the defendant's position. The plaintiff's attorney can challenge evidence and cross-examine witnesses. c. Closing arguments by the attorneys in favor of their respective clients, the judge's instructions to the jury, and the jury's verdict. 6. *Posttrial motions*— a. Motion for judgment *n.o.v.* ("notwithstanding the verdict")—Will be granted if the judge is convinced that the jury was in error. b. Motion for a new trial—Will be granted if the judge is convinced that the jury was in error; can also be granted on the grounds of newly discovered evidence, misconduct by the participants during the trial, or error by the judge. 7. *Appeal*—Either party can appeal the trial court's judgment to an appropriate court of appeals. After reviewing the record on appeal, the abstracts, and the attorneys' briefs, the appellate court holds a hearing and renders its opinion.
The Courts Adapt to the Online World (See pages 95–98.)	A number of state and federal courts now allow parties to file litigation-related documents with the courts via the Internet or other electronic means. The federal courts are considering the implementation of electronic filing systems in all federal district courts. Virtually every court now has a Web page offering information about the court and its procedures, and increasingly courts are publishing their opinions online. In the future, we may see "cyber courts," in which all trial proceedings are conducted online.
Alternative Dispute Resolution (See pages 98–103.)	1. *Negotiation*—The parties come together, with or without attorneys to represent them, and try to reach a settlement without the involvement of a third party. 2. *Mediation*—The parties themselves reach an agreement with the help of a neutral third party, called a mediator, who proposes solutions. At the parties' request, a mediator may make a legally binding decision. 3. *Arbitration*—A more formal method of ADR in which the parties submit their dispute to a neutral third party, the arbitrator, who renders a decision. The decision may or may not be legally binding, depending on the circumstances. 4. *Other types of ADR*—These include early neutral case evaluation, mini-trials, and summary jury trials (SJTs); generally, these are forms of "assisted negotiation." 5. *Providers of ADR services*—The leading nonprofit provider of ADR services is the American Arbitration Association. Hundreds of for-profit firms also provide ADR services.
Online Dispute Resolution (See pages 103–105.)	A number of organizations and firms are now offering negotiation, mediation, and arbitration services through online forums. To date, these forums have been a practical alternative for the resolution of domain name disputes and e-commerce disputes in which the amount in controversy is relatively small.

FOR REVIEW

Answers for the even-numbered questions in this For Review *section can be found in Appendix I at the end of this text.*

1. What is judicial review? How and when was the power of judicial review established?
2. Before a court can hear a case, it must have jurisdiction. Over what must it have jurisdiction? How are the courts applying traditional jurisdictional concepts to cases involving Internet transactions?
3. What is the difference between a trial court and an appellate court?
4. In a lawsuit, what are the pleadings? What is discovery, and how does electronic discovery differ? What is electronic filing?
5. How are online forums being used to resolve disputes?

QUESTIONS AND CASE PROBLEMS

3–1. **Arbitration.** In an arbitration proceeding, the arbitrator need not be a judge or even a lawyer. How, then, can the arbitrator's decision have the force of law and be binding on the parties involved?

3–2. **Jurisdiction.** Marya Callais, a citizen of Florida, was walking near a busy street in Tallahassee one day when a large crate flew off a passing truck and hit her, resulting in numerous injuries to Callais. She incurred a great deal of pain and suffering plus numerous medical expenses, and she could not work for six months. She wishes to sue the trucking firm for $300,000 in damages. The firm's headquarters are in Georgia, although the company does business in Florida. In what court may Callais bring suit—a Florida state court, a Georgia state court, or a federal court? What factors might influence her decision?

3–3. **Standing.** Blue Cross and Blue Shield insurance companies (the Blues) provide 68 million Americans with health-care financing. The Blues have paid billions of dollars for care attributable to illnesses related to tobacco use. In an attempt to recover some of this amount, the Blues filed a suit in a federal district court against tobacco companies and others, alleging fraud, among other things. The Blues claimed that beginning in 1953, the defendants conspired to addict millions of Americans, including members of Blue Cross plans, to cigarettes and other tobacco products. The conspiracy involved misrepresentation about the safety of nicotine and its addictive properties, marketing efforts targeting children, and agreements not to produce or market safer cigarettes. As a result of the defendants' efforts, many tobacco users developed lung, throat, and other cancers, as well as heart disease, stroke, emphysema, and other illnesses. The defendants asked the court to dismiss the case on the ground that the plaintiffs did not have standing to sue. Do the Blues have standing in this case? Why or why not? [*Blue Cross and Blue Shield of New Jersey, Inc. v. Philip Morris, Inc.*, 36 F.Supp.2d 560 (E.D.N.Y. 1999)]

3–4. **Jurisdiction.** George Noonan, a Boston police detective and a devoted nonsmoker, has spent most of his career educating Bostonians about the health risks of tobacco use. In 1992, an ad for Winston cigarettes featuring Noonan's image appeared in several French magazines. Some of the magazines were on sale at newsstands in Boston. Noonan filed a suit in a federal district court against The Winston Co., Lintas:Paris (the French ad agency that created the ads), and others. Lintas:Paris and the other French defendants claimed that they did not know the magazines would be sold in Boston and filed a motion to dismiss the suit for lack of personal jurisdiction. Does the court have jurisdiction? Why or why not? [*Noonan v. The Winston Co.*, 135 F.3d 85 (1st Cir. 1998)]

CASE PROBLEM WITH SAMPLE ANSWER

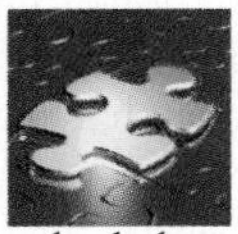

3–5. Ms. Thompson filed a suit in a federal district court against her employer, Altheimer & Gray, seeking damages for alleged racial discrimination in violation of federal law. During *voir dire,* the judge asked the prospective jurors whether "there is something about this kind of lawsuit for money damages that would start any of you leaning for or against a particular party." Ms. Leiter, one of the prospective jurors, raised her hand and explained that she had "been an owner of a couple of businesses and am currently an owner of a business, and I feel that as an employer and owner of a business that will definitely sway my judgment in this case." She explained, "I am constantly faced with people that want various benefits or different positions in the company or better contacts or, you know, a myriad of issues that employers face on a regular basis, and I have to decide whether or not that person should get them." Asked by Thompson's lawyer whether "you believe that people file lawsuits just because they don't get something they want," Leiter answered, "I believe there are some people that do." In answer to another question, she said, "I think I bring a lot of background to this case, and I can't say that it's not going to cloud my judgment. I can try to be as fair as I can, as I do every day." Thompson filed a motion to strike Leiter for cause. Should the judge grant the motion? Explain. [*Thompson v. Altheimer & Gray,* 248 F.3d 621 (7th Cir. 2001)]

After you have answered this problem, compare your answer with the sample answer given on the Web site that accompanies this text. Go to http://blt.westbuslaw.com, select "Chapter 3," and click on "Case Problem with Sample Answer."

3–6. Arbitration. Alexander Little worked for Auto Stiegler, Inc., an automobile dealership in Los Angeles County, California, eventually becoming the service manager. While employed, Little signed an arbitration agreement that required all employment-related disputes to be submitted to arbitration. The agreement also provided that any award over $50,000 could be appealed to a second arbitrator. Little was later demoted and terminated. Alleging that these actions were in retaliation for investigating and reporting warranty fraud and thus were in violation of public policy, Little filed a suit in a California state court against Auto Stiegler. The defendant filed a motion with the court to compel arbitration. Little responded that the arbitration agreement should not be enforced in part because the appeal provision was unfairly one sided. Is this provision enforceable? Should the court grant Auto Stiegler's motion? Why or why not? [*Little v. Auto Stiegler, Inc.,* 29 Cal.4th 1064, 63 P.3d 979, 130 Cal.Rptr.2d 892 (2003)]

3–7. Standing to Sue. Lamar Advertising of Penn, LLC, an outdoor advertising business, wanted to erect billboards of varying sizes in a multiphase operation throughout the town of Orchard Park, New York. An Orchard Park ordinance restricted the signs to certain sizes in certain areas, to advertising products and services available for sale only on the premises, and to other limits. Lamar asked Orchard Park for permission to build signs in some areas larger than the ordinance allowed in those locations (but not as large as allowed in other areas). When the town refused, Lamar filed a suit in a federal district court, claiming that the ordinance violated the First Amendment. Did Lamar have standing to challenge the ordinance? If the court could sever the provisions of the ordinance restricting a sign's content from the provisions limiting a sign's size, would your answer be the same? Explain. [*Lamar Advertising of Penn, LLC v. Town of Orchard Park, New York,* 356 F.3d 365 (2d Cir. 2004)]

A QUESTION OF ETHICS

3–8. Linda Bender brought an action in a federal court against her supervisor at A. G. Edwards & Sons, Inc., a stockbrokerage firm (the defendants). Bender alleged sexual harassment in violation of Title VII of the Civil Rights Act of 1964, which prohibits, among other things, employment discrimination based on gender. In her application for registration as a stockbroker, Bender had agreed to arbitrate any disputes with her employer. The defendants moved to compel arbitration. The district court judge denied the motion, holding that Bender could not be forced to waive her right to adjudicate Title VII claims in federal court. The appellate court reversed, ruling that Title VII claims are arbitrable. The court held that compelling Bender to submit her claim for arbitration did not deprive her of the right to a judicial forum, because if the arbitration proceedings were somehow legally deficient, she could still take her case to a federal court for review. [*Bender v. A. G. Edwards & Sons, Inc.,* 971 F.2d 698 (11th Cir. 1992)]

1. Does the right to a postarbitration judicial forum equate to the right to initial access to a judicial forum in employment disputes?
2. Should the fact that reviewing courts rarely set aside arbitrators' awards have any bearing on the arbitrability of certain types of claims, such as those brought under Title VII?

FOR CRITICAL ANALYSIS

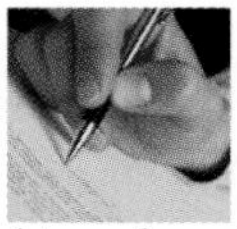

3–9. American courts are forums for adversarial justice, in which attorneys defend the interests of their respective clients before the court. This means that an attorney may end up claiming in court that his or her client is innocent, even though the attorney knows that the client acted wrongfully. Is it ethical for attorneys to try to "deceive" the court in these situations? Can the adversarial system of justice really lead to "truth"?

VIDEO QUESTION

DIGITAL VIDEO LIBRARY
WEST LEGAL STUDIES IN BUSINESS

3–10. Go to this text's Web site at http://blt.westbuslaw.com and select "Chapter 3." Click on "Video Questions" and view the video titled *Jurisdiction in Cyberspace.* Then answer the following questions.

1. What standard would a court apply to determine whether it has jurisdiction over the out-of-state computer firm in the video?
2. What factors is a court likely to consider in assessing whether sufficient contacts existed when the only connection to the jurisdiction is through a Web site?
3. How do you think the court would resolve the issue in this case?

INTERNET EXERCISES

Go to the *Business Law Today: The Essentials* home page at **http://blt.westbuslaw.com**, select "Chapter 3," and click on "Internet Exercises." There you will find the following Internet research exercises that you can perform to learn more about topics covered in this chapter.

Activity 3–1: LEGAL PERSPECTIVE—The Judiciary's Role in American Government

Activity 3–2: MANAGEMENT PERSPECTIVE—Alternative Dispute Resolution

Activity 3–3: SOCIAL PERSPECTIVE—Resolve a Dispute Online

BEFORE THE TEST

Go to the *Business Law Today: The Essentials* home page at **http://blt.westbuslaw.com**, select "Chapter 3," and click on "Interactive Quizzes." You will find at least twenty interactive questions relating to this chapter.

CHAPTER 4
Torts and Cyber Torts

"'Tort' more or less means 'wrong' . . . . One of my friends [in law school] said that Torts is the course which proves that your mother was right."

Scott Turow, 1949–
(American lawyer and author)

CHAPTER OUTLINE

- THE BASIS OF TORT LAW
- INTENTIONAL TORTS AGAINST PERSONS
- INTENTIONAL TORTS AGAINST PROPERTY
- UNINTENTIONAL TORTS (NEGLIGENCE)
- STRICT LIABILITY
- CYBER TORTS

LEARNING OBJECTIVES

After reading this chapter, you should be able to answer the following questions:

1. What is a tort?
2. What is the purpose of tort law? What are two basic categories of torts?
3. What are the four elements of negligence?
4. What is meant by strict liability? In what circumstances is strict liability applied?
5. What is a cyber tort, and how are tort theories being applied in cyberspace?

TORT
A civil wrong not arising from a breach of contract. A breach of a legal duty that proximately causes harm or injury to another.

As Scott Turow's statement in the above quotation indicates, **torts** are wrongful actions.[1] Through tort law, society compensates those who have suffered injuries as a result of the wrongful conduct of others. Although some torts, such as assault and trespass, originated in the English common law, the field of tort law continues to expand. As new ways to commit wrongs are discovered, such as the use of the Internet to commit wrongful acts, the courts are extending tort law to cover these wrongs.

As you will see in later chapters of this book, many of the lawsuits brought by or against business firms are based on the tort theories discussed in this chapter. Some of the torts examined here can occur in any context, including the business environment.

1. The word *tort* is French for "wrong."

BUSINESS TORT
Wrongful interference with another's business rights.

Others traditionally have been referred to as **business torts,** which are defined as wrongful interferences with the business rights of others. Included in business torts are such vague concepts as *unfair competition* and *wrongfully interfering with the business relations of others.*

The Basis of Tort Law

Two notions serve as the basis of all torts: wrongs and compensation. Tort law is designed to compensate those who have suffered a loss or injury due to another person's wrongful act. In a tort action, one person or group brings a personal suit against another person or group to obtain compensation (money **damages**) or other relief for the harm suffered.

DAMAGES
Money sought as a remedy for a breach of contract or a tortious action.

THE PURPOSE OF TORT LAW

Generally, the purpose of tort law is to provide remedies for the invasion of various *protected interests.* Society recognizes an interest in personal physical safety, and tort law provides remedies for acts that cause physical injury or that interfere with physical security and freedom of movement. Society recognizes an interest in protecting real and personal property, and tort law provides remedies for acts that cause destruction or damage to property. Society also recognizes an interest in protecting certain intangible interests, such as personal privacy, family relations, reputation, and dignity, and tort law provides remedies for invasion of these protected interests.

.on the Web You can find cases and articles on torts in the tort law library at the Internet Law Library's Web site. Go to **http://www.lawguru.com/ilawlib**.

CLASSIFICATIONS OF TORTS

There are two broad classifications of torts: *intentional torts* and *unintentional torts* (torts involving negligence). The classification of a particular tort depends largely on how the tort occurs (intentionally or negligently) and the surrounding circumstances. In the following pages, you will read about these two classifications of torts.

Torts committed via the Internet are sometimes referred to as **cyber torts.** We look at how the courts have applied traditional tort law to wrongful actions in the online environment in the concluding pages of this chapter.

CYBER TORT
A tort committed in cyberspace.

Intentional Torts against Persons

INTENTIONAL TORT
A wrongful act knowingly committed.

TORTFEASOR
One who commits a tort.

An **intentional tort,** as the term implies, requires *intent.* The **tortfeasor** (the one committing the tort) must intend to commit an act, the consequences of which interfere with the personal or business interests of another in a way not permitted by law. An evil or harmful motive is not required—in fact, the actor may even have a beneficial motive for committing what turns out to be a tortious act. In tort law, intent means only that the actor intended the consequences of his or her act or knew with substantial certainty that certain consequences would result from the act. The law generally assumes that individuals intend the *normal* consequences of their actions. Thus, forcefully pushing another—even if done in jest and without any evil motive—is an intentional tort (if injury results), because the object of a strong push can ordinarily be expected to fall down.

This section discusses intentional torts against persons, which include assault and battery, false imprisonment, infliction of emotional distress, defamation, invasion of the right to privacy, appropriation, misrepresentation, and wrongful interference.

ASSAULT AND BATTERY

ASSAULT
Any word or action intended to make another person fearful of immediate physical harm; a reasonably believable threat.

Any intentional, unexcused act that creates in another person a reasonable apprehension or fear of immediate harmful or offensive contact is an **assault.** Apprehension is not the same as fear. If a contact is such that a reasonable person would want to avoid it, and if there is a reasonable basis for believing that the contact will occur, then the plaintiff suffers apprehension whether or not he or she is afraid. The interest protected by tort law concerning assault is the freedom from having to expect harmful or offensive contact. The occurrence of apprehension is enough to justify compensation.

BATTERY
The unprivileged, intentional touching of another.

The *completion* of the act that caused the apprehension, if it results in harm to the plaintiff, is a **battery,** which is defined as an unexcused and harmful or offensive physical contact *intentionally* performed. For example, suppose that Ivan threatens Jean with a gun, then shoots her. The pointing of the gun at Jean is an assault; the firing of the gun (if the bullet hits Jean) is a battery. The interest protected by tort law concerning battery is the right to personal security and safety. The contact can be harmful, or it can be merely offensive (such as an unwelcome kiss). Physical injury need not occur. The contact can involve any part of the body or anything attached to it—for example, a hat or other item of clothing, a purse, or a chair or an automobile in which one is sitting. Whether the contact is offensive or not is determined by the *reasonable person standard.*[2] The contact can be made by the defendant or by some force the defendant sets in motion—for example, a rock thrown, food poisoned, or a stick swung.

MALICE
A desire to cause pain, injury, or distress to another.

Compensation If the plaintiff shows that there was contact, and the jury agrees that the contact was offensive, the plaintiff has a right to compensation. There is no need to show that the defendant acted out of **malice;** the person could have just been joking or playing around. The underlying motive does not matter, only the intent to bring about the harmful or offensive contact to the plaintiff. In fact, proving a motive is never necessary (but is sometimes relevant). A plaintiff may be compensated for the emotional harm or loss of reputation resulting from a battery, as well as for physical harm.

DEFENSE
A reason offered and alleged by a defendant in an action or suit as to why the plaintiff should not recover or establish what she or he seeks.

BE AWARE Some of these same four defenses can be raised by a defendant who is sued for other torts.

Defenses to Assault and Battery A number of legally recognized **defenses** (reasons why plaintiffs should not obtain what they are seeking) can be raised by a defendant who is sued for assault or battery, or both:

1. *Consent.* When a person consents to the act that damages her or him, there is generally no liability (legal responsibility) for the damage done.
2. *Self-defense.* An individual who is defending his or her life or physical well-being can claim self-defense. In situations of both *real* and *apparent* danger, a person may use whatever force is *reasonably* necessary to prevent harmful contact.
3. *Defense of others.* An individual can act in a reasonable manner to protect others who are in real or apparent danger.
4. *Defense of property.* Reasonable force may be used in attempting to remove intruders from one's home, although force that is likely to cause death or great bodily injury can never be used just to protect property.

2. The *reasonable person standard* is an objective test of how a reasonable person would have acted under the same circumstances. See "The Duty of Care and Its Breach" later in this chapter.

FALSE IMPRISONMENT

False imprisonment is the intentional confinement or restraint of another person's activities without justification. False imprisonment interferes with the freedom to move without restraint. The confinement can be accomplished through the use of physical barriers, physical restraint, or threats of physical force. Moral pressure or threats of future harm do not constitute false imprisonment. It is essential that the person being restrained not comply with the restraint willingly.

Businesspersons are often confronted with suits for false imprisonment after they have attempted to confine a suspected shoplifter for questioning. Under the "privilege to detain" granted to merchants in some states, a merchant can use the defense of *probable cause* to justify delaying a suspected shoplifter. Probable cause exists when there is sufficient evidence to support the belief that a person is guilty. Although laws governing false imprisonment vary from state to state, generally they require that any detention be conducted in a *reasonable* manner and for only a *reasonable* length of time.

INTENTIONAL INFLICTION OF EMOTIONAL DISTRESS

The tort of *intentional infliction of emotional distress* can be defined as an intentional act that amounts to extreme and outrageous conduct resulting in severe emotional distress to another. ■ **EXAMPLE 4.1** A prankster telephones an individual and says that the individual's spouse has just been in a horrible accident. As a result, the individual suffers intense mental pain or anxiety. The caller's behavior is deemed to be extreme and outrageous conduct that exceeds the bounds of decency accepted by society and is therefore **actionable** (capable of serving as the ground for a lawsuit). ■

ACTIONABLE
Capable of serving as the basis of a lawsuit. An actionable claim can be pursued in a lawsuit or other court action.

The tort of intentional infliction of emotional distress poses several problems for the courts. One problem is the difficulty of proving the existence of emotional suffering. For this reason, courts in some jurisdictions require that the emotional distress be evidenced by some physical symptom or illness or some emotional disturbance that can be documented by a psychiatric consultant or other medical professional.

Another problem is that emotional distress claims must be subject to some limitation, or they could flood the courts with lawsuits. A society in which individuals are rewarded if they are unable to endure the normal emotional stresses of day-to-day living is obviously undesirable. Therefore, the law usually holds that indignity or annoyance alone is not enough to support a lawsuit based on the intentional infliction of emotional distress. Repeated annoyances (such as those experienced by a person who is being stalked), however, coupled with threats, are enough. In the business context, the repeated use of extreme methods to collect a delinquent account may be actionable.

DEFAMATION

DEFAMATION
Anything published or publicly spoken that causes injury to another's good name, reputation, or character.

SLANDER
Defamation in oral form.

LIBEL
Defamation in writing or other permanent form (such as a digital recording) having the quality of permanence.

Defamation of character involves wrongfully hurting a person's good reputation. The law has imposed a general duty on all persons to refrain from making false, defamatory statements about others. Breaching this duty orally involves the tort of **slander;** breaching it in writing involves the tort of **libel.** The tort of defamation also arises when a false statement is made about a person's product, business, or title to property. We deal with these torts later in the chapter.

The Publication Requirement The basis of the tort of defamation is the publication of a statement or statements that hold an individual up to contempt, ridicule, or hatred. *Publication* here means that the defamatory statements are communicated to persons other than the defamed party. ■ EXAMPLE 4.2 If Thompson writes Andrews a private letter accusing him of embezzling funds, the action does not constitute libel. If Peters calls Gordon dishonest, unattractive, and incompetent when no one else is around, the action does not constitute slander. In neither case was the message communicated to a third party. ■

The courts have generally held that even dictating a letter to a secretary constitutes publication, although the publication may be *privileged* (privileged communications will be discussed shortly). Moreover, if a third party overhears defamatory statements by chance, the courts usually hold that this also constitutes publication. Defamatory statements made via the Internet are also actionable, as you will read later in this chapter. Note further that any individual who republishes or repeats defamatory statements is liable even if that person reveals the source of such statements.

Damages for Defamation Generally, in a case alleging slander, the plaintiff must prove "special damages" to establish the defendant's liability. The plaintiff must show that the slanderous statement caused her or him to suffer actual economic or monetary losses. This requirement is imposed in cases involving slander because slanderous statements have a temporary quality. In contrast, a libelous (written) statement has the quality of permanence, can be circulated widely, and usually results from some degree of deliberation on the part of the author. For that reason, a plaintiff can recover "general damages" for libel and need not prove any special damages.

Exceptions to the burden of proving special damages in cases alleging slander are made for certain types of slanderous statements. If a false statement constitutes "slander *per se,*" no proof of special damages is required for it to be actionable. The following four types of utterances are considered to be slander *per se:*

1. A statement that another has a loathsome communicable disease.
2. A statement that another has committed improprieties while engaging in a profession or trade.
3. A statement that another has committed or has been imprisoned for a serious crime.
4. A statement that a woman is unchaste or has engaged in serious sexual misconduct.

Defenses against Defamation Truth is normally an absolute defense against a defamation charge. In other words, if the defendant in a defamation suit can prove that his or her allegedly defamatory statements were true, the defendant will not be liable.

PRIVILEGE
A legal right, exemption, or immunity granted to a person or a class of persons. In the context of defamation, an absolute privilege immunizes the actor from suit, regardless of whether the actor's statements were malicious. A qualified privilege immunizes an actor from suit only when the privilege is properly exercised in the performance of a legal or moral duty.

Privileged Communications. Another defense that is sometimes raised is that the statements were **privileged** communications, and thus the defendant is immune from liability. Privileged communications are of two types: absolute and qualified. Only in judicial proceedings and certain government proceedings is *absolute* privilege granted. For example, statements made in the courtroom by attorneys and judges during a trial are absolutely privileged. So are statements made by government officials during legislative debate, even if the officials make such statements maliciously—that is, knowing them to be untrue. An absolute privilege is granted in these situations because government personnel deal with matters that are so much in the public interest that the parties involved should be able to speak out fully and freely without restriction.

A *qualified,* or *conditional,* privilege applies when a statement is related to a matter of public interest or when the statement is necessary to protect a person's private interest and is made to another person with an interest in the same subject matter. ■ EXAMPLE 4.3 Jorge applies for membership at the local country club. After the country club's board rejects his application, Jorge sues the club's office manager for making allegedly defamatory statements to the board concerning a conversation she had with Jorge. Assuming that the office manager had simply relayed what she thought was her duty to convey to the club's board, her statements would likely be protected by a qualified privilege.[3] ■

Public Figures. In general, false and defamatory statements that are made about *public figures* (public officials who exercise substantial governmental power and any persons in the public limelight) and that are published in the press are privileged if they are made without **actual malice.**[4] To be made with actual malice, a statement must be made *with either knowledge of falsity or a reckless disregard of the truth.* Statements made about public figures, especially when they are made via a public medium, are usually related to matters of general interest; they are made about people who substantially affect all of us. Furthermore, public figures generally have some access to a public medium for answering disparaging (belittling, discrediting) falsehoods about themselves; private individuals do not. For these reasons, public figures have a greater burden of proof in defamation cases (they must prove actual malice) than do private individuals.

ACTUAL MALICE
In a defamation suit, a statement made about a public figure normally must be made with actual malice (with either knowledge of its falsity or a reckless disregard of the truth) for liability to be incurred.

INVASION OF THE RIGHT TO PRIVACY

A person has a right to solitude and freedom from prying public eyes—in other words, to privacy. As discussed in Chapter 1, the Supreme Court has held that a fundamental right to privacy is also implied by various amendments to the U.S. Constitution. Some state constitutions explicitly provide for privacy rights. In addition, a number of federal and state statutes have been enacted to protect individual rights in specific areas. Tort law also safeguards these rights through the tort of *invasion of privacy.* Four acts qualify as an invasion of privacy:

1. *The use of a person's name, picture, or other likeness for commercial purposes without permission.* This tort, which is usually referred to as the tort of appropriation, will be examined shortly.
2. *Intrusion into an individual's affairs or seclusion.* For example, invading someone's home or illegally searching someone's briefcase is an invasion of privacy. The tort has been held to extend to eavesdropping by wiretap, the unauthorized scanning of a bank account, compulsory blood testing, and window peeping.
3. *Publication of information that places a person in a false light.* This could be a story attributing to the person ideas not held or actions not taken by the person. (Publishing such a story could involve the tort of defamation as well.)
4. *Public disclosure of private facts about an individual that an ordinary person would find objectionable.* A newspaper account of a private citizen's sex life or financial affairs could be an actionable invasion of privacy.

on the Web You can find information and cases relating to employee privacy rights with respect to electronic monitoring at the Web site of the American Civil Liberties Union (ACLU). Go to **http://www.aclu.org/library/pbr2.html**.

3. For a case involving a qualified privilege, see *Hickson Corp. v. Northern Crossarm Co.,* 235 F.Supp.2d 1352 (N.D.Ga. 2002).
4. *New York Times Co. v. Sullivan,* 376 U.S. 254, 84 S.Ct. 710, 11 L.Ed.2d 686 (1964).

APPROPRIATION

APPROPRIATION
In tort law, the use by one person of another person's name, likeness, or other identifying characteristic without permission and for the benefit of the user.

The use by one person of another person's name, likeness, or other identifying characteristic, without permission and for the benefit of the user, constitutes the tort of **appropriation.** Under the law, an individual's right to privacy normally includes the right to the exclusive use of her or his identity.

■ EXAMPLE 4.4 Vanna White, the hostess of the popular television game show *Wheel of Fortune*, brought a case against Samsung Electronics America, Inc. Without White's permission, Samsung included in an advertisement for its videocassette recorders (VCRs) a depiction of a robot dressed in a wig, gown, and jewelry, posed in a scene that resembled the *Wheel of Fortune* set, in a stance for which White is famous. The court held in White's favor, holding that the tort of appropriation does not require the use of a celebrity's name or likeness. The court stated that Samsung's robot ad left "little doubt" as to the identity of the celebrity whom the ad was meant to depict.[5] ■

Cases of wrongful appropriation, or misappropriation, may also involve the rights of those who invest time and funds in the creation of a special system, such as a method of broadcasting sports events. Commercial misappropriation may also occur when a person takes and uses the property of another for the sole purpose of capitalizing unfairly on the goodwill or reputation of the property owner.

MISREPRESENTATION (FRAUD)

FRAUDULENT MISREPRESENTATION
Any misrepresentation, either by misstatement or omission of a material fact, knowingly made with the intention of deceiving another and on which a reasonable person would and does rely to his or her detriment.

PUFFERY
A salesperson's often exaggerated claims concerning the quality of property offered for sale. Such claims involve opinions rather than facts and are not considered to be legally binding promises or warranties.

A misrepresentation leads another to believe in a condition that is different from the condition that actually exists. This is often accomplished through a false or incorrect statement. Misrepresentations may be innocently made by someone who is unaware of the existing facts, but the tort of **fraudulent misrepresentation,** or fraud, involves intentional deceit for personal gain. The tort includes several elements:

1. The misrepresentation of facts or conditions with knowledge that they are false or with reckless disregard for the truth.
2. An intent to induce another to rely on the misrepresentation.
3. Justifiable reliance by the deceived party.
4. Damages suffered as a result of the reliance.
5. A causal connection between the misrepresentation and the injury suffered.

For fraud to occur, more than mere **puffery,** or *seller's talk,* must be involved. Fraud exists only when a person represents as a fact something he or she knows is untrue. For example, it is fraud to claim that a building does not leak when one knows it does. Facts are objectively ascertainable, whereas seller's talk is not. "I am the best accountant in town" is seller's talk. The speaker is not trying to represent something as fact because the term *best* is a subjective, not an objective, term.[6]

Normally, the tort of misrepresentation or fraud occurs only when there is reliance on a *statement of fact.* Sometimes, however, reliance on a *statement of opinion* may involve the tort of misrepresentation if the individual making the statement of opinion has a superior knowledge of the subject matter. For example, when a lawyer makes a statement of opinion about the law in a state in which the lawyer

5. *White v. Samsung Electronics America, Inc.,* 971 F.2d 1395 (9th Cir. 1992).

6. In contracts for the sale of goods, Article 2 of the Uniform Commercial Code distinguishes, for warranty purposes, between statements of opinion ("puffery") and statements of fact. See Chapter 13 for a further discussion of this issue.

is licensed to practice, a court would construe reliance on such a statement to be equivalent to reliance on a statement of fact. We examine fraudulent misrepresentation in further detail in Chapter 8, in the context of contract law.

on the Web The 'Lectric Law Library's Legal Lexicon includes an informative discussion of the elements of fraud, as well as different types of fraud. To access this page, go to **http://www.lectlaw.com/def/1079.htm**.

WRONGFUL INTERFERENCE

Business torts involving wrongful interference are generally divided into two categories: wrongful interference with a contractual relationship and wrongful interference with a business relationship.

Wrongful Interference with a Contractual Relationship The body of tort law relating to *intentional interference with a contractual relationship* has expanded greatly in recent years. A landmark case involved an opera singer, Joanna Wagner, who was under contract to sing for a man named Lumley for a specified period of years. A man named Gye, who knew of this contract, nonetheless "enticed" Wagner to refuse to carry out the agreement, and Wagner began to sing for Gye. Gye's action constituted a tort because it wrongfully interfered with the contractual relationship between Wagner and Lumley.[7] (Of course, Wagner's refusal to carry out the agreement also entitled Lumley to sue Wagner for breach of contract.)

Three elements are necessary for wrongful interference with a contractual relationship to occur:

1. A valid, enforceable contract must exist between two parties.
2. A third party must know that this contract exists.
3. The third party must *intentionally* cause either of the two parties to breach the contract.

REMEMBER It is the intent to do an act that is important in tort law, not the motive behind the intent.

The contract may be between a firm and its employees or a firm and its customers. Sometimes a competitor of a firm draws away one of the firm's key employees. If the original employer can show that the competitor induced the breach—that is, that the former employee would not otherwise have broken the contract—damages can be recovered from the competitor.

Wrongful Interference with a Business Relationship Businesspersons devise countless schemes to attract customers, but they are forbidden by the courts to interfere unreasonably with another's business in their attempts to gain a share of the market. There is a difference between competitive methods and **predatory behavior**—actions undertaken with the intention of unlawfully driving competitors completely out of the market.

PREDATORY BEHAVIOR
Business behavior that is undertaken with the intention of unlawfully driving competitors out of the market.

The distinction usually depends on whether a business is attempting to attract customers in general or to solicit only those customers who have shown an interest in a similar product or service of a specific competitor. If a shopping center contains two shoe stores, an employee of Store A cannot be positioned at the entrance of Store B for the purpose of diverting customers to Store A. This type of activity constitutes the tort of wrongful interference with a business relationship, which is commonly considered to be an unfair trade practice. If this type of activity were permitted, Store A would reap the benefits of Store B's advertising.

Defenses to Wrongful Interference A person will not be liable for the tort of wrongful interference with a contractual or business relationship if it can be shown that the

7. *Lumley v. Gye,* 118 Eng.Rep. 749 (1853).

REMEMBER What society and the law consider permissible often depends on the circumstances.

interference was justified, or permissible. Bona fide competitive behavior is a permissible interference even if it results in the breaking of a contract. ■ EXAMPLE 4.5 If Antonio's Meats advertises so effectively that it induces Beverly's Restaurant Chain to break its contract with Otis Meat Company, Otis Meat Company will be unable to recover against Antonio's Meats on a wrongful interference theory. After all, the public policy that favors free competition in advertising outweighs any possible instability that such competitive activity might cause in contractual relations. ■

Intentional Torts against Property

Intentional torts against property include trespass to land, trespass to personal property, conversion, and disparagement of property. These torts are wrongful actions that interfere with individuals' legally recognized rights with regard to their land or personal property. The law distinguishes real property from personal property (see Chapters 23 and 24). *Real property* is land and things "permanently" attached to the land. *Personal property* consists of all other items, which are basically movable. Thus, a house and lot are real property, whereas the furniture inside a house is personal property. Money and stocks and bonds are also personal property.

TRESPASS TO LAND

TRESPASS TO LAND
The entry onto, above, or below the surface of land owned by another without the owner's permission or legal authorization.

A **trespass to land** occurs whenever a person, without permission, enters onto, above, or below the surface of land that is owned by another; causes anything to enter onto the land; remains on the land; or permits anything to remain on it. Actual harm to the land is not an essential element of this tort because the tort is designed to protect the right of an owner to exclusive possession of his or her property. Common types of trespass to land include walking or driving on someone else's land, shooting a gun over the land, throwing rocks at a building that belongs to someone else, building a dam across a river and thereby causing water to back up on someone else's land, and constructing a building so that part of it is on an adjoining landowner's property.

A sign warns trespassers. Should the law allow a trespasser to recover from a landowner for injuries sustained on the premises? Why or why not? (Frederick D. Bodling/Stock Boston)

Trespass Criteria, Rights, and Duties Before a person can be a trespasser, the owner of the real property (or other person in actual and exclusive possession of the property) must establish that person as a trespasser. For example, "posted" trespass signs expressly establish as a trespasser a person who ignores these signs and enters onto the property. A guest in your home is not a trespasser—unless she or he has been asked to leave but refuses. Any person who enters onto your property to commit an illegal act (such as a thief entering a lumberyard at night to steal lumber) is established impliedly as a trespasser, without posted signs.

At common law, a trespasser is liable for damages caused to the property and generally cannot hold the owner liable for injuries sustained on the premises. This common law rule is being abandoned in many jurisdictions in favor of a "reasonable duty of care" rule that varies depending on the status of the parties; for example, a landowner may have a duty to post a notice that the property is patrolled by guard dogs. Furthermore, under the "attractive nuisance" doctrine, children do not assume the risks of the premises if they are attracted to the property by some object, such as a swimming pool, an abandoned building, or a sand pile. Trespassers normally can be removed from the premises through the use of reasonable force without the owner's being liable for assault and battery.

Defenses against Trespass to Land Trespass to land involves wrongful interference with another person's real property rights. One defense against a trespass claim is to show that the trespass was warranted, as when a trespasser enters to assist someone in danger. Another defense exists when the trespasser can show that he or she had a license to come onto the land. A *licensee* is one who is invited (or allowed to enter) onto the property of another for the licensee's benefit. A person who enters another's property to read an electric meter, for example, is a licensee. When you purchase a ticket to attend a movie or sporting event, you are licensed to go onto the property of another to view that movie or event. Note that licenses to enter on another's property are *revocable* by the property owner. If a property owner asks a meter reader to leave and the meter reader refuses to do so, the meter reader at that point becomes a trespasser.

Trespass to Personal Property

TRESPASS TO PERSONAL PROPERTY The unlawful taking or harming of another's personal property; interference with another's right to the exclusive possession of his or her personal property.

Whenever an individual unlawfully harms the personal property of another or otherwise interferes with the personal property owner's right to exclusive possession and enjoyment of that property, **trespass to personal property**—also called *trespass to personalty*[8]—occurs. If a student takes a classmate's business law book as a practical joke and hides it so that the owner is unable to find it for several days prior to the final examination, the student has engaged in a trespass to personal property.

If it can be shown that the trespass to personal property was warranted, then a complete defense exists. Most states, for example, allow automobile repair shops to hold a customer's car (under what is called an *artisan's lien,* discussed in Chapter 16) when the customer refuses to pay for repairs already completed. Trespass to personal property was one of the allegations in the following case. (For a discussion of whether spamming constitutes trespass to personal property, see the examination of cyber torts later in this chapter.)

8. Pronounced *per*-sun-ul-tee.

CASE 4.1 Register.com, Inc. v. Verio, Inc.

United States Court of Appeals,
Second Circuit, 2004.
356 F.3d 393.

FACTS The Internet Corporation for Assigned Names and Numbers (ICANN) administers the Internet domain name system. (Domain names will be discussed in detail in Chapter 5.) ICANN appoints registrars to issue the names to persons preparing to establish Web sites on the Internet. An applicant for a name must provide certain information, including an e-mail address. An agreement between ICANN and its registrars refers to this information as "WHOIS information" and requires the registrars to provide public access to it through the Internet "for any lawful purposes" except "the transmission of mass unsolicited, commercial advertising or solicitations via email (spam)." A party who wishes to obtain this information must also agree not to use it for this purpose.
Register.com, Inc., is an ICANN registrar. Verio, Inc., sells Web site design and other services. Verio devised an automated software program (robot, or bot) to submit daily queries for Register's WHOIS data. Verio would then send ads by e-mail and other methods to the identified parties. Despite Register's request, Verio refused to stop. Register filed a suit in a federal district court against Verio, alleging in part trespass to personal property. The court ordered Verio to, among other things, stop accessing Register's computers by bot. Verio appealed to the U.S. Court of Appeals for the Second Circuit.

ISSUE Did Verio's use of its search bot constitute trespass to personal property?

DECISION Yes. The U.S. Court of Appeals for the Second Circuit affirmed the lower court's order. Trespass

(Continued)

CASE 4.1—Continued

to personal property occurs when one party impairs the condition, quality, or value of another's computer.

REASON The court explained that trespass to personal property is committed when one intentionally uses or interferes with a chattel [an item of personal property] in the possession of another in such a way as to impair its condition, quality, or value. In this case, Verio used search robots, which are software programs that perform multiple automated successive queries. Verio's use of these robots consumed a significant portion of the capacity of Register's computer systems. While Verio's robots alone might not incapacitate Register's systems, the court found that "if Verio were permitted to continue to access Register's computers through such robots, it was highly probable that other Internet service providers would devise similar programs to access Register's data, and that the system would be overtaxed and would crash." The court dismissed Verio's argument that it could not be liable for trespass because Register had never instructed it not to use its robot programs. Register had requested Verio to stop and this, in the court's view, was sufficient to advise Verio that its use of robots was not authorized and could cause harm to Register's systems.

FOR CRITICAL ANALYSIS—Technological Consideration *Why should the use of a bot to initiate "multiple automated successive queries" have a different legal effect than typing and submitting queries manually?*

Conversion

CONVERSION
Wrongfully taking or retaining possession of an individual's personal property and placing it in the service of another.

Whenever personal property is wrongfully taken from its rightful owner or possessor and placed in the service of another, the act of **conversion** occurs. Conversion is defined as any act depriving an owner of personal property without that owner's permission and without just cause. When conversion occurs, the tort of trespass to personal property usually occurs as well. If the initial taking of the property was unlawful, there is trespass; retention of that property is conversion. If the initial taking of the property was permitted by the owner or for some other reason is not a trespass, failure to return it may still be conversion. Conversion is the civil side of crimes related to theft. A store clerk who steals merchandise from the store commits a crime and engages in the tort of conversion at the same time.

Even if a person mistakenly believed that she or he was entitled to the goods, the tort of conversion may occur. In other words, good intentions are not a defense against conversion; in fact, conversion can be an entirely innocent act. Someone who buys stolen goods, for example, is guilty of conversion even if he or she did not know that the goods were stolen. If the true owner brings a tort action against the buyer, the buyer must either return the property to the owner or pay the owner the full value of the property, despite having already paid the thief.

A successful defense against the charge of conversion is that the purported owner does not in fact own the property or does not have a right to possess it that is superior to the right of the holder. Necessity is another possible defense against conversion. ■ EXAMPLE 4.6 If Abrams takes Mendoza's cat, Abrams is guilty of conversion. If Mendoza sues Abrams, Abrams must return the cat or pay damages. If, however, the cat has rabies and Abrams took the cat to protect the public, Abrams has a valid defense—necessity (and perhaps even self-defense, if he can prove that he was in danger because of the cat). ■

Disparagement of Property

DISPARAGEMENT OF PROPERTY
An economically injurious falsehood made about another's product or property. A general term for torts that are more specifically referred to as slander of quality or slander of title.

Disparagement of property occurs when economically injurious falsehoods are made about another's product or property, not about another's reputation. Disparagement of property is a general term for torts that can be more specifically referred to as *slander of quality* or *slander of title.*

SLANDER OF QUALITY (TRADE LIBEL) The publication of false information about another's product, alleging that it is not what its seller claims.

Slander of Quality Publication of false information about another's product, alleging that it is not what its seller claims, constitutes the tort of **slander of quality,** or **trade libel.** The plaintiff must prove that actual damages proximately resulted from the slander of quality. In other words, the plaintiff must show not only that a third person refrained from dealing with the plaintiff because of the improper publication but also that there were associated damages. The economic calculation of such damages—they are, after all, conjectural—is often extremely difficult.

An improper publication may be both a slander of quality and a defamation. For example, a statement that disparages the quality of a product may also, by implication, disparage the character of the person who would sell such a product.

SLANDER OF TITLE The publication of a statement that denies or casts doubt on another's legal ownership of any property, causing financial loss to that property's owner.

Slander of Title When a publication denies or casts doubt on another's legal ownership of any property, and this results in financial loss to that property's owner, the tort of **slander of title** may exist. Usually, this is an intentional tort in which someone knowingly publishes an untrue statement about property with the intent of discouraging a third person from dealing with the person slandered. For example, it would be difficult for a car dealer to attract customers after competitors published a notice that the dealer's stock consisted of stolen autos.

Unintentional Torts (Negligence)

NEGLIGENCE The failure to exercise the standard of care that a reasonable person would exercise in similar circumstances.

The tort of **negligence** occurs when someone suffers injury because of another's failure to live up to a required *duty of care.* In contrast to intentional torts, in torts involving negligence, the tortfeasor neither wishes to bring about the consequences of the act nor believes that they will occur. The actor's conduct merely creates a *risk* of such consequences. If no risk is created, there is no negligence.

Many of the actions discussed in the section on intentional torts constitute negligence if the element of intent is missing. ■ EXAMPLE 4.7 Suppose that Juarez walks up to Natsuyo and intentionally shoves her. Natsuyo falls and breaks an arm as a result. In this situation, Juarez will have committed the intentional tort of assault and battery. If Juarez carelessly bumps into Natsuyo, however, and she falls and breaks an arm as a result, Juarez's action will constitute negligence. In either situation, Juarez has committed a tort. ■

In examining a question of negligence, one should ask the following four questions (each of these elements of negligence will be discussed below):

1. Did the defendant owe a duty of care to the plaintiff?
2. Did the defendant breach that duty?
3. Did the plaintiff suffer a legally recognizable injury as a result of the defendant's breach of the duty of care?
4. Did the defendant's breach cause the plaintiff's injury?

THE DUTY OF CARE AND ITS BREACH

DUTY OF CARE The duty of all persons, as established by tort law, to exercise a reasonable amount of care in their dealings with others. Failure to exercise due care, which is normally determined by the "reasonable person standard," constitutes the tort of negligence.

The concept of a **duty of care** arises from the notion that if we are to live in society with other people, some actions can be tolerated and some cannot; some actions are right and some are wrong; and some actions are reasonable and some are not. The basic principle underlying the duty of care is that people are free to act as they please so long as their actions do not infringe on the interests of others.

When someone fails to comply with the duty to exercise reasonable care, a potentially tortious act may have been committed. Failure to live up to a standard of care may be an act (setting fire to a building) or an omission (neglecting to put out a

"To answer your question. Yes, if you shoot an arrow into the air and it falls to earth you should know not where, you could be liable for any damage it may cause."

campfire). It may be a careless act or a carefully performed but nevertheless dangerous act that results in injury. Courts consider the nature of the act (whether it is outrageous or commonplace), the manner in which the act is performed (cautiously versus heedlessly), and the nature of the injury (whether it is serious or slight) in determining whether the duty of care has been breached.

REASONABLE PERSON STANDARD
The standard of behavior expected of a hypothetical "reasonable person"; the standard against which negligence is measured and that must be observed to avoid liability for negligence.

The Reasonable Person Standard Tort law measures duty by the **reasonable person standard.** In determining whether a duty of care has been breached, the courts ask how a reasonable person would have acted in the same circumstances. The reasonable person standard is said to be (though in an absolute sense it cannot be) objective. It is not necessarily how a particular person would act. It is society's judgment on how people *should* act. If the so-called reasonable person existed, he or she would be careful, conscientious, even tempered, and honest. The courts frequently use this hypothetical reasonable person in decisions relating to other areas of law as well.

That individuals are required to exercise a reasonable standard of care in their activities is a pervasive concept in business law, and many of the issues discussed in subsequent chapters of this text have to do with this duty. What constitutes reasonable care varies, of course, with the circumstances.

ETHICAL ISSUE 4.1

Does a person's duty of care include a duty to come to the aid of a stranger in peril? Suppose that you are walking down a city street and notice that a pedestrian is about to step directly in front of an oncoming bus. Do you have a legal duty to warn that individual? No. Although most people would probably concede that the observer has an *ethical* or moral duty to warn the other in this situation, tort law does not impose a general duty to rescue others in peril. People involved in special relationships, however, have been held to have a duty to rescue other parties within the relationship. A person has a duty to rescue his or her child or spouse if either is in danger, for example. Other special relationships, such as those between teachers and students or hiking and hunting partners, may also give rise to a duty to rescue. In addition, if a person who has no duty to rescue undertakes to rescue another, then the rescuer is charged with a duty to follow through with due care in the rescue attempt. ■

The Duty of Landowners Landowners are expected to exercise reasonable care to protect persons coming onto their property from harm. As mentioned earlier, in some jurisdictions, landowners are held to owe a duty to protect even trespassers against certain risks. Landowners who rent or lease premises to tenants (see Chapter 24) are expected to exercise reasonable care to ensure that the tenants and their guests are not harmed in common areas, such as stairways, entryways, laundry rooms, and the like.

Retailers and other firms that explicitly or implicitly invite persons to come onto their premises are usually charged with a duty to exercise reasonable care to protect those persons, who are considered **business invitees.** For example, if you entered a supermarket, slipped on a wet floor, and sustained injuries as a result, the owner of the supermarket would be liable for damages if when you slipped there was no sign warning that the floor was wet. A court would hold that the business owner was negligent because the owner failed to exercise a reasonable degree of care in protecting the store's customers against foreseeable risks about which the owner knew or *should have known.* That a patron might slip on the wet floor and be injured as a result was a foreseeable risk, and the owner should have taken care to avoid this risk or to warn the customer of it. The landowner also has a duty to discover and remove any hidden dangers that might injure a customer or other invitee.

BUSINESS INVITEE
A person, such as a customer or a client, who is invited onto business premises by the owner of those premises for business purposes.

Some risks, of course, are so obvious that the owner need not warn of them. For instance, a business owner does not need to warn customers to open a door before attempting to walk through it. Other risks, however, even though they may seem obvious to a business owner, may not be so in the eyes of another, such as a child. For example, a hardware store owner may not think it is necessary to warn customers not to climb a stepladder leaning against the back wall of the store. It is possible, though, that a child could climb up and tip the ladder over and be hurt as a result and that the store could be held liable.

In the following case, the court had to decide whether a store owner should be held liable for a customer's injury on the premises. The question was whether the owner had notice of the condition that led to the customer's injury.

CASE 4.2 Martin v. Wal-Mart Stores, Inc.

United States Court of Appeals,
Eighth Circuit, 1999.
183 F.3d 770.
http://guide.lp.findlaw.com/casecode/courts/8th.html[a]

a. This URL will take you to a Web site maintained by FindLaw, which is now a part of West Group. When you access the site, enter "Wal-Mart" in the "Party Name Search" box and then click on "Search." Scroll down the list on the page that opens and select the link to "Harold Martin v. Wal-Mart Stores."

FACTS Harold Martin was shopping in the sporting goods department of a Wal-Mart store. There was one employee in the department at that time. In front of the sporting goods section, in the store's main aisle (which the employees referred to as "action alley"), there was a large display of stacked cases of shotgun shells. On top of the cases were individual boxes of shells. Shortly after the sporting

(Continued)

CASE 4.2—Continued

goods employee walked past the display, Martin did so, but Martin slipped on some loose shotgun shell pellets and fell to the floor. He immediately lost feeling in, and control of, his legs. Sensation and control returned, but during the next week, he lost the use of his legs several times for periods of ten to fifteen minutes. Eventually, sensation and control did not return to the front half of his left foot. Doctors diagnosed the condition as permanent. Martin filed a suit against Wal-Mart in a federal district court, seeking damages for his injury. The jury found in his favor, and the court denied Wal-Mart's motion for a directed verdict. Wal-Mart appealed to the U.S. Court of Appeals for the Eighth Circuit.

ISSUE Should Wal-Mart be held liable for Martin's injury?

DECISION Yes. The U.S. Court of Appeals for the Eighth Circuit affirmed the judgment of the lower court.

REASON The appellate court stated, "The traditional rule * * * required a plaintiff in a slip and fall case to establish that the defendant store had either actual or constructive notice[b] of the dangerous condition." The court, however, explained that this case involved the self-service store exception to the traditional slip-and-fall rule. A self-service store has notice that certain dangers arising through customer involvement are likely to occur and has a duty to anticipate them. Part of this duty is to "warn customers or protect them from the danger." Here, Wal-Mart had constructive notice of the pellets on the floor in the main aisle. Martin slipped on pellets next to a large display of shotgun shells immediately abutting the sporting goods department. The chance that merchandise will wind up on the floor (or merchandise will be spilled on the floor) in the department in which that merchandise is sold or displayed is "exactly the type of foreseeable risk" that is part of the self-service store exception.

FOR CRITICAL ANALYSIS—Ethical Consideration *Why do the courts impose constructive notice requirements on owners of self-service stores but not on owners of other stores?*

b. *Constructive notice* is notice that is implied by law, in view of the circumstances.

.on the Web You can locate the professional standards for various organizations at **http://www.lib.uwaterloo.ca/society/standards.html**.

MALPRACTICE
Professional misconduct or the lack of the requisite degree of skill as a professional. Negligence—the failure to exercise due care—on the part of a professional, such as a physician, is commonly referred to as malpractice.

The Duty of Professionals If an individual has knowledge, skill, or intelligence superior to that of an ordinary person, the individual's conduct must be consistent with that status. Professionals—including physicians, dentists, architects, engineers, accountants, lawyers, and others—are required to have a standard minimum level of special knowledge and ability. Therefore, in determining what constitutes reasonable care in the case of professionals, their training and expertise are taken into account. In other words, an accountant cannot defend against a lawsuit for negligence by stating, "But I was not familiar with that principle of accounting."

If a professional violates her or his duty of care toward a client, the professional may be sued for **malpractice.** For example, a patient might sue a physician for *medical malpractice.* A client might sue an attorney for *legal malpractice.*

THE INJURY REQUIREMENT AND DAMAGES

For a tort to have been committed, the plaintiff must have suffered a *legally recognizable* injury. To recover damages (receive compensation), the plaintiff must have suffered some loss, harm, wrong, or invasion of a protected interest. Essentially, the purpose of tort law is to compensate for legally recognized injuries resulting from wrongful acts. If no harm or injury results from a given negligent action, there is nothing to compensate—and no tort exists. ■ EXAMPLE 4.8 If you carelessly bump into a passerby, who stumbles and falls as a result, you may be liable in tort if the passerby is injured in the fall. If the person is unharmed, however, there normally could be no suit for damages, because no injury was suffered. ■

As already mentioned, the purpose of tort law is not to punish people for tortious acts but to compensate the injured parties for harm suffered by awarding damages.

COMPENSATORY DAMAGES
A money award equivalent to the actual value of injuries or damages sustained by the aggrieved party.

PUNITIVE DAMAGES
Money damages that may be awarded to a plaintiff to punish the defendant and deter future similar conduct.

Compensatory damages are intended to reimburse a plaintiff for actual losses—to make the plaintiff whole. Occasionally, **punitive damages** are also awarded to punish the wrongdoer and deter others from similar wrongdoing. Punitive damages are rarely awarded in lawsuits for ordinary negligence and usually are given only in cases involving intentional torts. They may be awarded, however, in suits involving *gross negligence,* which can be defined as an intentional failure to perform a manifest duty in reckless disregard of the consequences of such a failure for the life or property of another.

In *State Farm Mutual Automobile Insurance Co. v. Campbell,*[9] the United States Supreme Court held that to the extent an award of punitive damages is grossly excessive, it furthers no legitimate purpose and violates due process requirements (discussed in Chapter 1). While this case dealt with intentional torts (fraud and intentional infliction of emotional distress), the Court's holding applies equally to punitive damages awards in gross negligence cases.

CAUSATION

Another element necessary to a tort is *causation.* If a person fails in a duty of care and someone suffers injury, the wrongful activity must have caused the harm for a tort to have been committed. In deciding whether there is causation, the court must address two questions:

CAUSATION IN FACT
An act or omission without which an event would not have occurred.

1. *Is there causation in fact?* Did the injury occur because of the defendant's act, or would it have occurred anyway? If an injury would not have occurred without the defendant's act, then there is causation in fact. **Causation in fact** can usually be determined by the use of the *but for* test: "but for" the wrongful act, the injury would not have occurred. Theoretically, causation in fact is limitless. One could claim, for example, that "but for" the creation of the world, a particular injury would not have occurred. Thus, as a practical matter, the law has to establish limits, and it does so through the concept of proximate cause.

PROXIMATE CAUSE
Legal cause; exists when the connection between an act and an injury is strong enough to justify imposing liability.

2. *Was the act the proximate cause of the injury?* **Proximate cause,** or legal cause, exists when the connection between an act and an injury is strong enough to justify imposing liability. ■ EXAMPLE 4.9 Ackerman carelessly leaves a campfire burning. The fire not only burns down the forest but also sets off an explosion in a nearby chemical plant that spills chemicals into a river, killing all the fish for a hundred miles downstream and ruining the economy of a tourist resort. Should Ackerman be liable to the resort owners? To the tourists whose vacations were ruined? These are questions of proximate cause that a court must decide. ■

Probably the most cited case on proximate cause is the *Palsgraf* case, discussed in this chapter's *Landmark in the Law* feature on the next page. In determining the issue of proximate cause, the court addressed the following question: Does a defendant's duty of care extend only to those who may be injured as a result of a foreseeable risk, or does it extend also to a person whose injury could not reasonably be foreseen?

NOTE Proximate cause can be thought of as a question of social policy. Should the defendant be made to bear the loss instead of the plaintiff?

DEFENSES TO NEGLIGENCE

Defendants often defend against negligence claims by asserting that the plaintiffs failed to prove the existence of one or more of the required elements for negligence. Additionally, there are three basic *affirmative* defenses in negligence cases (defenses that defendants can use to avoid liability even if the facts are as the plaintiffs state):

9. 538 U.S. 408, 123 S.Ct. 1513, 155 L.Ed.2d 585 (2003).

LANDMARK IN THE LAW

Palsgraf v. Long Island Railroad Co. (1928)

In 1928, the New York Court of Appeals (that state's highest court) issued its decision in *Palsgraf v. Long Island Railroad Co.,*[a] a case that has become a landmark in negligence law with respect to proximate cause.

THE FACTS OF THE CASE The plaintiff, Palsgraf, was waiting for a train on a station platform. A man carrying a small package wrapped in newspaper was rushing to catch a train that had begun to move away from the platform. As the man attempted to jump aboard the moving train, he seemed unsteady and about to fall. A railroad guard on the train car reached forward to grab him, and another guard on the platform pushed him from behind to help him board the train. In the process, the man's package fell on the railroad tracks and exploded, because it contained fireworks. The repercussions of the explosion caused scales at the other end of the train platform to fall on Palsgraf, who was injured as a result. She sued the railroad company for damages in a New York state court.

THE QUESTION OF PROXIMATE CAUSE At the trial, the jury found that the railroad guards were negligent in their conduct. On appeal, the question before the New York Court of Appeals was whether the conduct of the railroad guards was the proximate cause of Palsgraf's injuries. In other words, did the guards' duty of care extend to Palsgraf, who was outside the zone of danger and whose injury could not reasonably have been foreseen?

The court stated that the question of whether the guards were negligent *with respect to Palsgraf* depended on whether her injury was *reasonably foreseeable* to the railroad guards. Although the guards may have acted negligently with respect to the man boarding the train, this had no bearing on the question of their negligence with respect to Palsgraf. This was not a situation in which a person committed an act so potentially harmful (for example, firing a gun at a building) that he or she would be held responsible for any harm that resulted. The court stated that here "there was nothing in the situation to suggest to the most cautious mind that the parcel wrapped in newspaper would spread wreckage through the station." The court thus concluded that the railroad guards were not negligent with respect to Palsgraf because her injury was not reasonably foreseeable.

APPLICATION TO TODAY'S WORLD

The Palsgraf *case established* foreseeability *as the test for proximate cause. Today, the courts continue to apply this test in determining proximate cause—and thus tort liability for injuries. Generally, if the victim of a harm or the consequences of a harm done are unforeseeable, there is no proximate cause. Note, though, that in the online environment, distinctions based on physical proximity, such as the "zone of danger" cited by the court in this case, are largely inapplicable.*

RELEVANT WEB SITES

To locate information on the Web concerning the Palsgraf *decision, go to this text's Web site at* **http://blt.westbuslaw.com**, *select "Chapter 4," and click on "URLs for Landmarks."*

a. 248 N.Y. 339, 162 N.E. 99 (1928).

(1) assumption of risk, (2) superseding cause, and (3) contributory and comparative negligence.

ASSUMPTION OF RISK A doctrine under which a plaintiff may not recover for injuries or damages suffered from risks he or she knows of and has voluntarily assumed.

CONTRIBUTORY NEGLIGENCE A rule in tort law that completely bars the plaintiff from recovering any damages if the damage suffered is partly the plaintiff's own fault; used in a minority of states.

COMPARATIVE NEGLIGENCE A rule in tort law that reduces the plaintiff's recovery in proportion to the plaintiff's degree of fault, rather than barring recovery completely; used in the majority of states.

Assumption of Risk A plaintiff who voluntarily enters into a risky situation, knowing the risk involved, will not be allowed to recover. This is the defense of **assumption of risk.** The requirements of this defense are (1) knowledge of the risk and (2) voluntary assumption of the risk.

The risk can be assumed by express agreement, or the assumption of risk can be implied by the plaintiff's knowledge of the risk and subsequent conduct. For example, a driver entering a race knows that there is a risk of being killed or injured in a crash. Of course, the plaintiff does not assume a risk different from or greater than the risk normally carried by the activity. In our example, the race driver would not assume the risk that the banking in the curves of the racetrack will give way during the race because of a construction defect.

Risks are not deemed to be assumed in situations involving emergencies. Neither are they assumed when a statute protects a class of people from harm and a member of the class is injured by the harm. For example, employees are protected by statute from harmful working conditions and therefore do not assume the risks associated with the workplace. An employee who is injured will generally be compensated regardless of fault under state workers' compensation statutes (discussed in Chapter 18).

Superseding Cause An unforeseeable intervening event may break the connection between a wrongful act and an injury to another. If so, the event acts as a *superseding cause*—that is, it relieves a defendant of liability for injuries caused by the intervening event. ■ **EXAMPLE 4.10** Suppose that Derrick keeps a can of gasoline in the trunk of his car. The presence of the gasoline creates a foreseeable risk and is thus a negligent act. If Derrick's car skids and crashes into a tree, causing the gasoline can to explode, Derrick would be liable for injuries sustained by passing pedestrians because of his negligence. If the explosion had been caused by lightning striking the car, however, the lightning would supersede Derrick's original negligence as a cause of the damage, because the lightning was not foreseeable. ■

A bungee jumper leaps from a platform. If the jumper is injured and sues the operator of the jump for negligence, what defenses might the operator use to avoid liability? (Paul Thompson/Image State)

Contributory and Comparative Negligence All individuals are expected to exercise a reasonable degree of care in looking out for themselves. In the past, under the common law doctrine of **contributory negligence,** a plaintiff who was also negligent (failed to exercise a reasonable degree of care) could not recover anything from the defendant. Under this rule, no matter how insignificant the plaintiff's negligence was relative to the defendant's negligence, the plaintiff would be precluded from recovering any damages. Today, only a few jurisdictions still hold to this doctrine. In the majority of states, the doctrine of contributory negligence has been replaced by a **comparative negligence** standard.

Under the comparative negligence standard, both the plaintiff's and the defendant's negligence are computed, and the liability for damages is distributed accordingly. Some jurisdictions have adopted a "pure" form of comparative negligence that allows the plaintiff to recover, even if the extent of his or her fault is greater than that of the defendant. For example, if the plaintiff was 80 percent at fault and the defendant 20 percent at fault, the plaintiff may recover 20 percent of his or her damages. Many states' comparative negligence statutes, however, contain a "50 percent" rule that precludes the plaintiff from any recovery if she or he was more than 50 percent at fault.

SPECIAL NEGLIGENCE DOCTRINES AND STATUTES

There are a number of special doctrines and statutes relating to negligence. We examine a few of them here.

Res Ipsa Loquitur Generally, in lawsuits involving negligence, the plaintiff has the burden of proving that the defendant was negligent. In certain situations, however, when negligence is very difficult or impossible to prove, the courts may infer that negligence has occurred; then the burden of proof rests on the defendant—to prove he or she was *not* negligent. The inference of the defendant's negligence is known as the doctrine of ***res ipsa loquitur,***[10] which translates as "the facts speak for themselves."

RES IPSA LOQUITUR
A doctrine under which negligence may be inferred simply because an event occurred, if it is the type of event that would never occur in the absence of negligence. Literally, the term means "the facts speak for themselves."

This doctrine is applied only when the event creating the damage or injury is one that ordinarily would occur only as a result of negligence. ■ EXAMPLE 4.11 If a person undergoes knee surgery and following the surgery has a severed nerve in the knee area, that person can sue the surgeon under a theory of *res ipsa loquitur.* In this instance, the injury would never occur in the absence of the surgeon's negligence.[11] ■ For the doctrine of *res ipsa loquitur* to apply, the event must have been within the defendant's power to control, and it must not have been due to any voluntary action or contribution on the part of the plaintiff.

Negligence *Per Se* Certain conduct, whether it consists of an action or a failure to act, may be treated as **negligence *per se*** (*per se* means "in or of itself"). Negligence *per se* may occur if an individual violates a statute or an ordinance providing for a criminal penalty and that violation causes another to be injured. The injured person must prove (1) that the statute clearly sets out what standard of conduct is expected, when and where it is expected, and of whom it is expected; (2) that he or she is in the class intended to be protected by the statute; and (3) that the statute was designed to prevent the type of injury that he or she suffered. The standard of conduct required by the statute is the duty that the defendant owes to the plaintiff, and a violation of the statute is the breach of that duty.

NEGLIGENCE *PER SE*
An action or failure to act in violation of a statutory requirement.

■ EXAMPLE 4.12 A statute may require a landowner to maintain a building in safe condition and may also subject the owner to a criminal penalty, such as a fine, if the building is not kept safe. The statute is meant to protect those who are rightfully in the building. Thus, if the owner, without a sufficient excuse, violates the statute and a tenant is thereby injured, then a majority of courts will hold that the owner's unexcused violation of the statute conclusively establishes a breach of a duty of care—that is, that the owner's violation is negligence *per se.* ■

"Danger Invites Rescue" Doctrine Typically, if an individual takes a defensive action, such as swerving to avoid an oncoming car, the original wrongdoer will not be relieved of liability even if the injury actually resulted from the attempt to escape harm. The same is true under the "danger invites rescue" doctrine. ■ EXAMPLE 4.13 If Lemming commits an act that endangers Salter, and Yokem sustains an injury trying to protect Salter, then Lemming will be liable for Yokem's injury. Lemming will also be liable for any injuries Salter may sustain. ■ Rescuers can injure themselves, or the person rescued, or even a stranger, but the original wrongdoer will still be liable.

10. Pronounced *rehz ihp*-suh *low*-kwuh-tuhr.
11. *Edwards v. Boland,* 41 Mass.App.Ct. 375, 670 N.E.2d 404 (1996).

GOOD SAMARITAN STATUTE
A state statute stipulating that persons who provide emergency services to, or rescue, someone in peril cannot be sued for negligence, unless they act recklessly, thereby causing further harm.

DRAM SHOP ACT
A state statute that imposes liability on the owners of bars and taverns, as well as those who serve alcoholic drinks to the public, for injuries resulting from accidents caused by intoxicated persons when the sellers or servers of alcoholic drinks contributed to the intoxication.

Special Negligence Statutes A number of states have enacted statutes prescribing duties and responsibilities in certain circumstances. For example, most states now have what are called **Good Samaritan statutes.** Under these statutes, someone who is aided voluntarily by others cannot turn around and sue the "Good Samaritans" for negligence. These laws were passed largely to protect physicians and medical personnel who voluntarily render services in emergency situations to those in need, such as individuals hurt in car accidents.

Many states have also passed **dram shop acts,** under which a tavern owner or bartender may be held liable for injuries caused by a person who became intoxicated while drinking at the bar or who was already intoxicated when served by the bartender. In some states, statutes impose liability on *social hosts* (persons hosting parties) for injuries caused by guests who became intoxicated at the hosts' homes. Under these statutes, it is unnecessary to prove that the tavern owner, bartender, or social host was negligent.

Strict Liability

STRICT LIABILITY
Liability regardless of fault. In tort law, strict liability is imposed on a manufacturer or seller that introduces into commerce a good that is unreasonably dangerous when in a defective condition.

Another category of torts is called **strict liability,** or *liability without fault.* Intentional torts and torts of negligence involve acts that depart from a reasonable standard of care and cause injuries. Under the doctrine of strict liability, liability for injury is imposed for reasons other than fault. Strict liability for damages proximately caused by an abnormally dangerous or exceptional activity is one application of this doctrine. Courts apply the doctrine of strict liability in such cases because of the extreme risk of the activity. Even if blasting with dynamite is performed with all reasonable care, there is still a risk of injury. Balancing that risk against the potential for harm, it seems reasonable to ask the person engaged in the activity to pay for injuries caused by that activity. Although there is no fault, there is still responsibility because of the dangerous nature of the undertaking.

There are other applications of the strict liability principle. Persons who keep dangerous animals, for example, are strictly liable for any harm inflicted by the animals. A significant application of strict liability is in the area of *product liability*—liability of manufacturers and sellers for harmful or defective products. Liability here is a matter of social policy and is based on two factors: (1) the manufacturer or seller can better bear the cost of injury because it can spread the cost throughout society by increasing prices of goods and services, and (2) the manufacturer or seller is making a profit from its activities and therefore should bear the cost of injury as an operating expense. We will discuss product liability in greater detail in Chapter 13.

Cyber Torts

It should come as no surprise that torts can also be committed in the online environment. Torts committed via the Internet are often called *cyber torts.* Over the last ten years, the courts have had to decide how to apply traditional tort law to torts committed in cyberspace. Consider, for example, issues of proof. How can it be proved that an online defamatory remark was "published" (which requires that a third party see or hear it)? How can the identity of the person who made the remark be discovered? Can an Internet service provider (ISP), such as AOL, be forced to reveal the source of an anonymous comment made by one of its subscribers? We explore some of these questions in this section, as well as some of the legal questions that have arisen with respect to bulk e-mail advertising.

DEFAMATION ONLINE

Recall from the discussion of defamation earlier in this chapter that one who repeats or otherwise republishes a defamatory statement can be subject to liability as if he or she had originally published it. Thus, publishers generally can be held liable for defamatory contents in the books and periodicals that they publish. Now consider online forums. These forums allow anyone—customers, employees, or crackpots—to complain about a firm's personnel, policies, practices, or products. Whatever the truth of the complaint is, it might have an impact on the business of the firm. One of the early questions in the online legal arena was whether the providers of such forums could be held liable, as publishers, for defamatory statements made in those forums.

.on the Web For an interesting article discussing the increasing number of online defamation cases and the associated costs, go to the Web site of Computer Times at

http://computertimes.asia1.com/issues/story/0,5104,1577,00.html.

Liability of Internet Service Providers Prior to the passage of the Communications Decency Act (CDA) of 1996, the courts grappled on several occasions with the question of whether ISPs should be regarded as publishers and thus be held liable for defamatory messages made by users of their services. The CDA resolved the issue by stating that "[n]o provider or user of an interactive computer service shall be treated as the publisher or speaker of any information provided by another information content provider."[12] In a number of key cases, the ISP provisions of the CDA have been invoked to shield ISPs from liability for defamatory postings on their bulletin boards.

■ EXAMPLE 4.14 In a leading case on this issue, decided the year after the CDA was enacted, America Online, Inc. (AOL, now part of Time Warner, Inc.), was not held liable even though it did not promptly remove defamatory messages of which it had been made aware. In upholding a U.S. district court's ruling in AOL's favor, a federal appellate court stated that the CDA "plainly immunizes computer service providers like AOL from liability for information that originates with third parties." The court explained that the purpose of the statute is "to maintain the robust nature of Internet communication and, accordingly, to keep government interference in the medium to a minimum."[13] ■

In subsequent cases, the courts have reached similar conclusions.[14] The courts have also extended the immunity to liability provided by the CDA to auction houses, such as eBay.[15] At issue in the following case was whether the CDA also shields secondary publishers, or distributors, from liability.

12. 47 U.S.C. Section 230.

13. *Zeran v. America Online, Inc.,* 129 F.3d 327 (4th Cir. 1997); *cert.* denied, 524 U.S. 934, 118 S.Ct. 2341, 141 L.Ed.2d 712 (1998).

14. See, for example, *Noah v. AOL Time Warner, Inc.,* 261 F.Supp.2d 532 (E.D.Va. 2003).

15. *Stoner v. eBay, Inc.,* 2000 WL 1705637 (Cal.Super.Ct. 2000).

CASE 4.3 Barrett v. Rosenthal

California Court of Appeal,
First District,
Division 2, 2004.
9 Cal.Rptr.3d 142.

FACTS Stephen Barrett and Terry Polevoy are physicians engaged in combating illegal or unsubstantiated alternative health-care practices and products. Each maintains Web sites that expose "health frauds and quackery" and provide guides to help consumers make intelligent health-care decisions. Ilena Rosenthal directs the Humantics Foundation for Women and participates in Usenet newsgroups that focus on alternative medicine. Among her postings, Rosenthal distributed an e-mail message that she received from another individual, Timothy Bolen, accusing Polevoy of stalking women. Polevoy informed Rosenthal that the message was not true and asked her to withdraw it, but she refused and reposted the message many times, referring to Barrett and Polevoy as "quacks." She also posted statements that the two physicians were "a power-hungry, misguided bunch of pseudoscientific socialist bigots" and were "being sued by many doctors and health organizations." Barrett and Polevoy filed a suit in a California state court against Rosenthal and others, alleging libel and other torts. The court ruled in part that under the CDA, Rosenthal was immune from liability for the reposting of Bolen's statements. The plaintiffs appealed to a state intermediate appellate court.

ISSUE Is a secondary publisher, or distributor, of another's libelous statements immune from liability under the CDA?

DECISION No. The state intermediate appellate court vacated the lower court's ruling on this issue and remanded the case for further proceedings.[a]

a. The lower court's decision on remand was not available at the time this book went to press, but it may be by the time you read this. If you have purchased access to Westlaw Campus, you might be able to locate the remanded decision using that database. Alternatively, you may be able to find the case online at some other site. (See this text's inside front cover for information on Westlaw Campus and URLs for online court decisions.)

REASON The court reasoned: "It is true that defamation requires a publication, and that every repetition is a publication, whether it is effectuated by a primary publisher or by a distributor; this is why distributors are sometimes referred to as 'secondary publishers.' However, the common law subjects the two types of publishers to distinctly different standards of liability for the transmission of the defamation of a third person. Because primary publishers ordinarily exercise control over content, they have a duty to monitor content; distributors, who have no such control, therefore have no such duty. It is entirely reasonable to assume Congress was aware of this significant and very well-established distinction, and that if it intended [the CDA] to immunize providers and users not merely from primary publisher liability but also from distributor liability it would have made this clear, as, for example, by adding the word 'distributor,' and not merely barring liability 'as the publisher or speaker' of information provided by another. * * * Legislative use of the legally uncertain word 'publisher' is simply too flimsy a basis upon which to grant providers and users of interactive computer services what amounts to an absolute protection requiring the total sacrifice of the competing value served by the law of defamation and the subordination of a concept at the root of any decent system of ordered liberty."

WHY IS THIS CASE IMPORTANT? *In this case, the court refused to extend to secondary publishers (distributors) the immunity that the CDA gives to primary publishers. The court concluded that if Congress had intended to protect providers and users from distributor liability, Congress would have made that intent clear. This ruling establishes that, on some level, secondary publishers can be held responsible for the libelous materials that they distribute.*

Piercing the Veil of Anonymity A threshold barrier to anyone who seeks to bring an action for online defamation is discovering the identity of the person who posted the defamatory message online. ISPs can disclose personal information about their customers only when ordered to do so by a court. Consequently, businesses and individuals are increasingly resorting to lawsuits against "John Does." Then, using the authority of the courts, they can obtain from the ISPs the identities of the persons responsible for the messages.

■ EXAMPLE 4.15 In one case, Eric Hvide, a former chief executive of a company called Hvide Marine, sued a number of "John Does" who had posted allegedly defamatory statements about his company on various online message boards. Hvide, who eventually lost his job, sued the John Does for libel in a Florida court. The court ruled that Yahoo and AOL had to reveal the identities of the defendant Does.[16] ■

In other cases, however, the courts have refused to order an ISP to disclose the identity of subscribers.[17] Generally, in these cases the courts must decide which right should take priority: the right to free (anonymous) speech under the First Amendment or the right not to be defamed.

SPAM

SPAM
Bulk, unsolicited ("junk") e-mail.

Bulk, unsolicited e-mail ("junk" e-mail) sent to all of the users on a particular e-mailing list is often called **spam.**[18] Typically, spam consists of a product ad sent to all of the users on an e-mailing list or all of the members of a newsgroup.

Spam wastes user time and network bandwidth (the amount of data that can be transmitted within a certain time). It also imposes a burden on an ISP's equipment as well as on e-mail recipients' computer systems. Does this mean that spamming may constitute a form of trespass to personal property? For a discussion of this question, see this chapter's *Adapting the Law to the Online Environment.*

In the last few years, the number of e-mail ads traveling through cyberspace has escalated significantly, and today spam accounts for an estimated 60 percent of all e-mail. Indeed, many contend that unwanted e-mail is threatening the viability of e-mail as a communications tool and an instrument of commerce. Because of the problems associated with spam, a majority of the states now have laws regulating spam. In 2003, the U.S. Congress also enacted a law to regulate the use of spam.

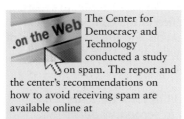

.on the Web The Center for Democracy and Technology conducted a study on spam. The report and the center's recommendations on how to avoid receiving spam are available online at

http://www.cdt.org/speech/spam/030319spamreport.shtml.

State Regulation of Spam Because of the problems associated with spam, thirty-six states have enacted laws that prohibit or regulate its use. A few states, such as Washington, prohibit unsolicited e-mail that is promoting goods, services, or real estate for sale or lease. In some other states, including Minnesota, an unsolicited e-mail ad must state in its subject line that it is an ad ("ADV:"). Many state laws regulating spam require the senders of e-mail ads to instruct the recipients on how they can "opt out" of further e-mail ads from the same sources. For instance, in some states an unsolicited e-mail ad must include a toll-free phone number or return e-mail address through which the recipient can contact the sender to request that no more ads be e-mailed.

The most stringent state law is California's antispam law, which went into effect on January 1, 2004. That law follows the "opt-in" model favored by consumer groups and antispam advocates. In other words, the law prohibits any person or business from sending e-mail ads to or from any e-mail address in California unless

16. *Does v. Hvide,* 770 So.2d 1237 (Fla.App.3d 2000).
17. See, for example, *Graham v. Oppenheimer,* 2000 WL 33381418 (E.D.Va. 2000).
18. The term *spam* is said to come from a Monty Python song with the lyrics, "Spam spam spam spam, spam spam spam spam, lovely spam, wonderful spam." Like these lyrics, spam online is often considered to be a repetition of worthless text.

ADAPTING THE LAW TO THE ONLINE ENVIRONMENT

Can Spamming Constitute a Tort?

Spam-related issues are, of course, unique to the cyber age. Can traditional tort law apply to such issues? For example, when spam overloads a business's computer system or impairs its computer equipment, can the recipient of the spam bring an action under tort law? Since the latter half of the 1990s, a number of plaintiffs have done so, with some success, by claiming that spamming constitutes a trespass to personal property, or *chattels*—a term used under the common law to denote all forms of personal property. The term *trespass to chattels* is usually defined as any unauthorized interference with the use of the personal property of another.

SPAMMING AS A FORM OF TRESPASS

In a leading case on this issue, decided in 1997, Cyber Promotions, Inc., sent bulk e-mail to subscribers of CompuServe, Inc., an ISP. CompuServe subscribers complained to the service about the ads, and many canceled their subscriptions. Handling the ads also placed a tremendous burden on CompuServe's equipment.

CompuServe told Cyber Promotions to stop using CompuServe's equipment to process and store the ads—in effect, to stop sending the ads to CompuServe subscribers. Ignoring the demand, Cyber Promotions stepped up the volume of its ads. After CompuServe attempted unsuccessfully to block the flow with screening software, it filed a suit against Cyber Promotions in a federal district court, seeking an injunction on the ground that the ads constituted trespass to personal property. The court agreed and ordered Cyber Promotions to stop sending its ads to e-mail addresses maintained by CompuServe.[a]

NEW DIRECTIONS IN CALIFORNIA

A 2003 decision by the California Supreme Court may make it more difficult for plaintiffs in that state's courts to combat spammers using tort law. The case was brought by Intel Corporation against one of its former employees, Ken Hamidi. After he was fired, Hamidi sent a series of six e-mail messages to 35,000 Intel employees over a twenty-one-month period. In the messages, Hamidi criticized the company's labor practices and urged employees to leave the company.

Intel sought a court order to stop the e-mail campaign, arguing that Hamidi's actions constituted a trespass to chattels because the e-mail significantly interfered with productivity, thus causing economic damage. When the case reached the California Supreme Court, the court held that under California law, the tort of trespass to chattels requires some evidence of injury to the plaintiff's personal property. Because Hamidi's e-mail had neither damaged Intel's computer system nor impaired its functioning, Hamidi's actions did not amount to a trespass to chattels.

The court distinguished Intel's case from cases in which spamming actually interfered with a computer system or threatened to do so. The court did not reject the idea that trespass theory could apply to cyberspace. Rather, the court simply held that to succeed in a lawsuit for trespass to chattels, a plaintiff must demonstrate that some concrete harm resulted from the unwanted e-mail. Although Hamidi's e-mail messages may have diverted employees' time and attention, thereby interfering with their productivity, the e-mails did not overburden Intel's computer systems—and thus did not amount to a concrete harm in the eyes of the court.[b]

FOR CRITICAL ANALYSIS

Three dissenting justices in the California case maintained that intruding on private property, regardless of injury, should be sufficient to demonstrate trespass to chattels. Do you agree? Why or why not?

a. *CompuServe, Inc. v. Cyber Promotions, Inc.,* 962 F.Supp. 1015 (S.D. Ohio 1997).

b. *Intel Corp. v. Hamidi,* 30 Cal.4th 1342, 71 P.3d 296, 1 Cal.Rptr.3d 32 (2003).

the recipient has expressly agreed to receive e-mails from the sender. An exemption is made for e-mail sent to consumers with whom the advertiser has a "preexisting or current business relationship."

The Federal CAN-SPAM Act In 2003, Congress enacted the Controlling the Assault of Non-Solicited Pornography and Marketing (CAN-SPAM) Act, which took effect on January 1, 2004. The legislation applies to any "commercial electronic mail messages" that are sent to promote a commercial product or service. Significantly, the statute preempts state antispam laws except for those provisions in state laws that prohibit false and deceptive e-mailing practices.

Generally, the act permits the use of unsolicited commercial e-mail but prohibits certain types of spamming activities, including the use of a false return address and the use of false, misleading, or deceptive information when sending e-mail. The statute also prohibits the use of "dictionary attacks"—sending messages to randomly generated e-mail addresses—and the "harvesting" of e-mail addresses from Web sites through the use of specialized software. Additionally, the law requires senders of commercial e-mail to do the following:

1. Include a return address on the e-mail.
2. Include a clear notification that the message is an ad and provide a valid physical postal address.
3. Provide a mechanism that allows recipients to "opt out" of further e-mail ads from the same source.
4. Take action on a recipient's "opt-out" request within ten days.
5. Label any sexually oriented materials as such.

ETHICAL ISSUE 4.2

Who benefits from the CAN-SPAM Act? Some of the stricter state laws regulating spam, such as California's law, favor the members of the public who are not engaged in e-mail advertising. Through its "opt-in" provisions requiring e-mail advertisers to obtain the recipient's consent before sending ads, California's law would have significantly curbed Internet advertising campaigns. The federal CAN-SPAM Act, however, preempts state laws, except for certain provisions relating to deceptive e-mailing practices. This means that these stricter provisions in state laws will no longer be effective.

Clearly, the federal act reflects Congress's intent to protect the e-mail marketing industry against state laws, such as California's, that would make e-mail advertising extremely difficult. The federal government also sought to eliminate advertising by peddlers of financial scams and pornography. Yet critics point out that the new law will do little to reduce the amount of unsolicited e-mail flowing through cyberspace. For one thing, many of the Internet ads being sent today already meet the requirements of the CAN-SPAM Act. For another, because the federal act uses an "opt-out" approach, it places the burden on e-mail recipients to prevent the delivery of further ads from the same source. Additionally, the act cannot regulate spam sent from foreign servers. Indeed, a survey showed that during the first two months after the act became effective, 56 percent of the respondents saw no noticeable reduction in the amount of spam received through e-mail, and 16 percent reported that they had received more spam since the law went into effect.[19] ■

19. Pew Internet and American Life Project survey conducted from February 3 to March 1, 2004.

KEY TERMS

CHAPTER SUMMARY Torts and Cyber Torts

Intentional Torts against Persons (See pages 113–120.)	1. *Assault and battery*—An assault is an unexcused and intentional act that causes another person to be apprehensive of immediate harm. A battery is an assault that results in physical contact. 2. *False imprisonment*—The intentional confinement or restraint of another person's movement without justification. 3. *Intentional infliction of emotional distress*—An intentional act that amounts to extreme and outrageous conduct resulting in severe emotional distress to another. 4. *Defamation (libel or slander)*—A false statement of fact, not made under privilege, that is communicated to a third person and that causes damage to a person's reputation. For public figures, the plaintiff must also prove actual malice. 5. *Invasion of the right to privacy*—The use of a person's name or likeness for commercial purposes without permission, wrongful intrusion into a person's private activities, publication of information that places a person in a false light, or disclosure of private facts that an ordinary person would find objectionable. 6. *Appropriation*—The use of another person's name, likeness, or other identifying characteristic, without permission and for the benefit of the user. 7. *Misrepresentation (fraud)*—A false representation made by one party, through misstatement of facts or through conduct, with the intention of deceiving another and on which the other reasonably relies to his or her detriment. 8. *Wrongful interference*—The knowing, intentional interference by a third party with an enforceable contractual relationship or an established business relationship between other parties for the purpose of advancing the economic interests of the third party.

(Continued)

CHAPTER SUMMARY Torts and Cyber Torts—Continued

Intentional Torts against Property (See pages 120–123.)	1. *Trespass to land*—The invasion of another's real property without consent or privilege. Specific rights and duties apply once a person is expressly or impliedly established as a trespasser. 2. *Trespass to personal property*—Unlawfully damaging or interfering with the owner's right to use, possess, or enjoy her or his personal property. 3. *Conversion*—Wrongfully taking personal property from its rightful owner or possessor and placing it in the service of another. 4. *Disparagement of property*—Any economically injurious falsehood that is made about another's product or property; an inclusive term for the torts of *slander of quality* and *slander of title.*
Unintentional Torts (Negligence) (See pages 123–131.)	1. *Negligence*—The careless performance of a legally required duty or the failure to perform a legally required act. Elements that must be proved are that a legal duty of care exists, that the defendant breached that duty, and that the breach caused damage or injury to another. 2. *Defenses to negligence*—The basic affirmative defenses in negligence cases are (a) assumption of risk, (b) superseding cause, and (c) contributory or comparative negligence. 3. *Special negligence doctrines and statutes*— a. *Res ipsa loquitur*—A doctrine under which a plaintiff need not prove negligence on the part of the defendant because "the facts speak for themselves." b. Negligence *per se*—A type of negligence that may occur if a person violates a statute or an ordinance providing for a criminal penalty and the violation causes another to be injured. c. Special negligence statutes—State statutes that prescribe duties and responsibilities in certain circumstances, the violation of which will impose civil liability. Dram shop acts and Good Samaritan statutes are examples of special negligence statutes.
Strict Liability (See page 131.)	Under the doctrine of strict liability, a person may be held liable, regardless of the degree of care exercised, for damages or injuries caused by her or his product or activity. Strict liability includes liability for harms caused by abnormally dangerous activities, by dangerous animals, and by defective products (product liability).
Cyber Torts (See pages 131–136.)	General tort principles are being extended to cover cyber torts, or torts that occur in cyberspace, such as online defamation and spamming (which may constitute trespass to personal property). Federal and state statutes may also apply to certain forms of cyber torts. For example, under the federal Communications Decency Act of 1996, Internet service providers (ISPs) are not liable for defamatory messages posted by their subscribers. A majority of the states and the federal government now regulate unwanted e-mail ads (spam).

FOR REVIEW

Answers for the even-numbered questions in this For Review *section can be found in Appendix I at the end of this text.*

1. What is a tort?
2. What is the purpose of tort law? What are two basic categories of torts?
3. What are the four elements of negligence?
4. What is meant by strict liability? In what circumstances is strict liability applied?
5. What is a cyber tort, and how are tort theories being applied in cyberspace?

QUESTIONS AND CASE PROBLEMS

4–1. Defenses to Negligence. Corinna was riding her bike on a city street. While she was riding, she frequently looked back to verify that the books that she had fastened to the rear part of her bike were still attached. On one occasion while she was looking behind her, she failed to notice a car that was entering an intersection just as she was crossing it. The car hit her, causing her to sustain numerous injuries. Three eyewitnesses stated that the driver of the car had failed to stop at the stop sign before entering the intersection. Corinna sued the driver of the car for negligence. What defenses might the defendant driver raise in this lawsuit? Discuss fully.

4–2. Liability to Business Invitees. Kim went to Ling's Market to pick up a few items for dinner. It was a rainy, windy day, and the wind had blown water through the door of Ling's Market each time the door opened. As Kim entered through the door, she slipped and fell in the approximately one-half inch of rainwater that had accumulated on the floor. The manager knew of the weather conditions but had not posted any sign to warn customers of the water hazard. Kim injured her back as a result of the fall and sued Ling's for damages. Can Ling's be held liable for negligence in this situation? Discuss.

4–3. Negligence. In which of the following situations will the acting party be liable for the tort of negligence? Explain fully.

(a) Mary goes to the golf course on Sunday morning, eager to try out a new set of golf clubs she has just purchased. As she tees off on the first hole, the head of her club flies off and injures a nearby golfer.

(b) Mary's doctor gives her some pain medication and tells her not to drive after she takes it, as the medication induces drowsiness. In spite of the doctor's warning, Mary decides to drive to the store while on the medication. Owing to her lack of alertness, she fails to stop at a traffic light and crashes into another vehicle, injuring a passenger.

4–4. Causation. Ruth carelessly parks her car on a steep hill, leaving the car in neutral and failing to engage the parking brake. The car rolls down the hill, knocking down an electric line. The sparks from the broken line ignite a grass fire. The fire spreads until it reaches a barn one mile away. The barn houses dynamite, and the burning barn explodes, causing part of the roof to fall on and injure a passing motorist, Jim. Can Jim recover from Ruth? Why or why not?

4–5. Duty of Care. As pedestrians exited at the close of an arts and crafts show, Jason Davis, an employee of the show's producer, stood near the exit. Suddenly and without warning, Davis turned around and collided with Yvonne Esposito, an eighty-year-old woman. Esposito was knocked to the ground, fracturing her hip. After hip-replacement surgery, she was left with a permanent physical impairment. Esposito filed a suit in a federal district court against Davis and others, alleging negligence. What are the factors that indicate whether Davis owed Esposito a duty of care? What do those factors indicate in these circumstances? [*Esposito v. Davis,* 47 F.3d 164 (5th Cir. 1995)]

CASE PROBLEM WITH SAMPLE ANSWER

4–6. During the spring and summer of 1999, Edward and Geneva Irvine received numerous "hang up" phone calls, including three calls in the middle of the night. With the help of their local phone company, the Irvines learned that many of the calls were from the telemarketing department of the *Akron Beacon Journal* in Akron, Ohio. The *Beacon*'s sales force was equipped with an automatic dialing machine. During business hours, the dialer was used to maximize productivity by calling multiple phone numbers at once and connecting a call to a sales representative only after it was answered. After business hours, the dialer was used to dial a list of disconnected numbers to determine whether they had been reconnected. If the dialer detected a ring, it recorded the information and dropped the call. If the automated dialing system crashed, which it did frequently, it redialed the entire list. The Irvines filed a suit in an Ohio state court against the *Beacon* and others, alleging in part invasion of privacy. In whose favor should the court rule, and why? [*Irvine v. Akron Beacon Journal,* 147 Ohio App.3d 428, 770 N.E.2d 1105 (9 Dist. 2002)]

After you have answered this problem, compare your answer with the sample answer given on the Web site that accompanies this text. Go to http://blt.westbuslaw.com, select "Chapter 4," and click on "Case Problem with Sample Answer."

4–7. Defamation. Lydia Hagberg went to her bank, California Federal Bank, FSB, to cash a check made out to her by Smith Barney (SB), an investment services firm. Nolene Showalter, a bank employee, suspected that the check was counterfeit. Showalter phoned SB and was told that the check was not valid. As she phoned the police, Gary Wood, a bank security officer, contacted SB again and was told that its earlier statement was "erroneous" and that the check was valid. Meanwhile, a police officer arrived, drew Hagberg away from the teller's window, spread her legs, patted her down, and handcuffed her. The officer searched her purse, asked her whether she had any weapons or stolen property and whether she was driving a stolen vehicle, and arrested her. Hagberg filed a suit in a California state court against the bank and others, alleging, among other things, slander. Should the absolute privilege for communications made in judicial or other official proceedings apply to statements made when a citizen contacts the police to report suspected criminal activity? Why or why not? [*Hagberg v. California Federal Bank, FSB,* 32 Cal.4th 39, 81 P.3d 244, 7 Cal.Rptr.3d 803 (2004)]

A QUESTION OF ETHICS

4–8. Patsy Slone, while a guest at the Dollar Inn, a hotel, was stabbed in the thumb by a hypodermic needle concealed in the tube of a roll of toilet paper. Slone, fearing that she might have been exposed to the virus that causes acquired immune deficiency syndrome (AIDS), sued the hotel for damages to compensate her for the emotional distress she suffered after the needle stab. An Indiana trial court held for Slone and awarded her $250,000 in damages. The hotel appealed, and one of the issues before the court was whether Slone had to prove that she was actually exposed to AIDS to recover for emotional distress. The appellate court held that she did not and that her fear of getting AIDS was reasonable in these circumstances. [*Slone v. Dollar Inn, Inc.*, 695 N.E.2d 185 (Ind.App. 1998)]

1. Should the plaintiff in this case have been required to show that she was actually exposed to the AIDS virus in order to recover for emotional distress? Should she have been required to show that she actually acquired the AIDS virus as a result of the needle stab?
2. In some states, plaintiffs are barred from recovery in emotional distress cases unless the distress is evidenced by some kind of physical symptoms. Is this fair?

FOR CRITICAL ANALYSIS

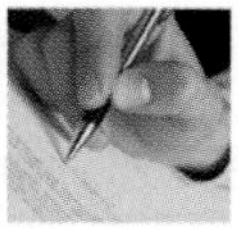

4–9. What general principle underlies the common law doctrine that business owners have a duty of care toward their customers? Does the duty of care unfairly burden business owners? Why or why not?

VIDEO QUESTION

4–10. Go to this text's Web site at **http://blt.westbuslaw.com** and select "Chapter 4." Click on "Video Questions" and view the video titled *Jaws*. Then answer the following questions.

1. In the video, the mayor (Murray Hamilton) and a few other men try to persuade Chief Brody (Roy Scheider) not to close the town's beaches. If Brody keeps the beaches open and a swimmer is injured or killed because he failed to warn swimmers about the potential shark danger, has Brody committed a tort? If so, what kind of tort (intentional tort against persons, intentional tort against property, negligence)? Explain your answer.
2. Can Chief Brody be held liable for any injuries or deaths to swimmers under the doctrine of strict liability? Why or why not?
3. If Chief Brody goes against the mayor's instructions and warns swimmers to stay off the beach, and the town suffers economic damages as a result, has he committed the tort of disparagement of property? Why or why not?

INTERNET EXERCISES

Go to the *Business Law Today: The Essentials* home page at **http://blt.westbuslaw.com**, select "Chapter 4," and click on "Internet Exercises." There you will find the following Internet research exercises that you can perform to learn more about topics covered in this chapter.

Activity 4–1: LEGAL PERSPECTIVE—Negligence and the *Titanic*

Activity 4–2: MANAGEMENT PERSPECTIVE—Legal and Illegal Uses of Spam

BEFORE THE TEST

Go to the *Business Law Today: The Essentials* home page at **http://blt.westbuslaw.com**, select "Chapter 4," and click on "Interactive Quizzes." You will find at least twenty interactive questions relating to this chapter.

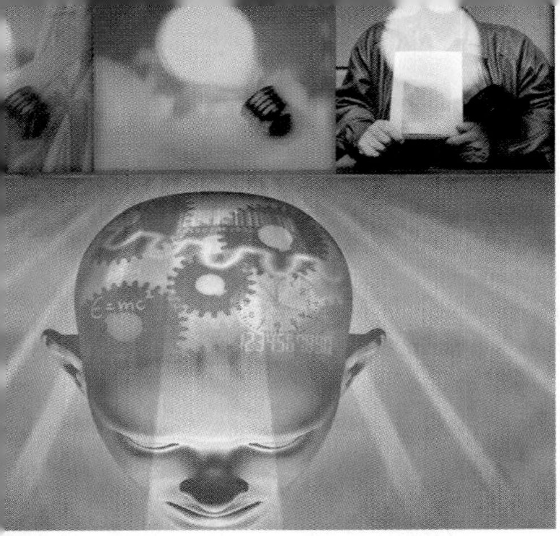

CHAPTER 5

Intellectual Property

The Internet, by virtue of its ability to
:sh what will be hundreds of millions of
eople together, . . . is . . . a profoundly
:erent capability that by and large human
beings have not had before."

Tony Rutkowski, 1943–
Executive director of the Internet Society, 1994–1996)

CHAPTER OUTLINE

- TRADEMARKS AND RELATED PROPERTY
- CYBER MARKS
- PATENTS
- COPYRIGHTS
- TRADE SECRETS
- INTERNATIONAL PROTECTION FOR INTELLECTUAL PROPERTY

LEARNING OBJECTIVES

After reading this chapter, you should be able to answer the following questions:

1. What is intellectual property?
2. Why are trademarks and patents protected by the law?
3. What laws protect authors' rights in the works they generate?
4. What are trade secrets, and what laws offer protection for this form of intellectual property?
5. What steps have been taken to protect intellectual property rights in today's digital age?

INTELLECTUAL PROPERTY
Property resulting from intellectual, creative processes.

Of significant concern to businesspersons today is the need to protect their rights in intellectual property. **Intellectual property** is any property resulting from intellectual, creative processes—the products of an individual's mind. Although it is an abstract term for an abstract concept, intellectual property is nonetheless wholly familiar to virtually everyone. The information contained in books and computer files is intellectual property. The software you use, the movies you see, and the music you listen to are all forms of intellectual property. In fact, in today's information age, it should come as no surprise that the value of the world's intellectual property now exceeds the value of physical property, such as machines and houses.

The need to protect creative works was voiced by the framers of the U.S. Constitution over two hundred years ago: Article I, Section 8, of the Constitution authorized Congress "[t]o promote the Progress of Science and useful Arts, by securing for limited Times to Authors and Inventors the exclusive Right to their respective Writings and Discoveries." Laws protecting patents, trademarks, and copyrights are explicitly designed to protect and reward inventive and artistic creativity. Exhibit 5–1 offers a comprehensive summary of these forms of intellectual property, as well as intellectual property that consists of *trade secrets*.

EXHIBIT 5–1 FORMS OF INTELLECTUAL PROPERTY

	DEFINITION	HOW ACQUIRED	DURATION	REMEDY FOR INFRINGEMENT
Patent	A grant from the government that gives an inventor exclusive rights to an invention.	By filing a patent application with the U.S. Patent and Trademark Office and receiving its approval.	Twenty years from the date of the application; for design patents, fourteen years.	Money damages, including royalties and lost profits, *plus* attorneys' fees. Damages may be tripled for intentional infringements.
Copyright	The right of an author or originator of a literary or artistic work, or other production that falls within a specified category, to have the exclusive use of that work for a given period of time.	Automatic (once the work or creation is put in tangible form). Only the *expression* of an idea (and not the idea itself) can be protected by copyright.	For authors: the life of the author plus 70 years. For publishers: 95 years after the date of publication or 120 years after creation.	Actual damages plus profits received by the party who infringed *or* statutory damages under the Copyright Act, *plus* costs and attorneys' fees in either situation.
Trademark (Service Mark and Trade Dress)	Any distinctive word, name, symbol, or device (image or appearance), or combination thereof, that an entity uses to distinguish its goods or services from those of others. The owner has the exclusive right to use that mark or trade dress.	1. At common law, ownership created by use of the mark. 2. Registration with the appropriate federal or state office gives notice and is permitted if the mark is currently in use or will be within the next six months.	Unlimited, as long as it is in use. To continue notice by registration, owner must renew by filing between the fifth and sixth years, and thereafter, every ten years.	1. Injunction prohibiting the future use of the mark. 2. Actual damages plus profits received by the party who infringed (can be increased under the Lanham Act). 3. Destruction of articles that infringed. 4. *Plus* costs and attorneys' fees.
Trade Secret	Any information that a business possesses and that gives the business an advantage over competitors (including formulas, lists, patterns, plans, processes, and programs).	Through the originality and development of the information and processes that constitute the business secret and are unknown to others.	Unlimited, so long as not revealed to others. Once revealed to others, they are no longer trade secrets.	Money damages for misappropriation (the Uniform Trade Secrets Act also permits punitive damages if willful), *plus* costs and attorneys' fees.

An understanding of intellectual property law is important because intellectual property has taken on increasing significance, not only in the United States but globally as well. Today, ownership rights in intangible intellectual property are more important to the prosperity of many U.S. companies than are their tangible assets. As you will read in this chapter, protecting these assets in today's online world has proved particularly challenging. This is because, as indicated in the chapter-opening quotation, the Internet's capability is "profoundly different" from anything we have had in the past.

Trademarks and Related Property

TRADEMARK
A distinctive mark, motto, device, or emblem that a manufacturer stamps, prints, or otherwise affixes to the goods it produces so that they may be identified on the market and their origins made known. Once a trademark is established (under the common law or through registration), the owner is entitled to its exclusive use.

A **trademark** is a distinctive mark, motto, device, or emblem that a manufacturer stamps, prints, or otherwise affixes to the goods it produces so that they can be identified on the market and their origin vouched for. At common law, the person who used a symbol or mark to identify a business or product was protected in the use of that trademark. Clearly, by using another's trademark, a business could lead consumers to believe that its goods were made by the other business. The law seeks to avoid this kind of confusion. In the following classic case concerning Coca-Cola, the defendants argued that the Coca-Cola trademark was entitled to no protection under the law because the term did not accurately represent the product.

LANDMARK AND CLASSIC CASES

CASE 5.1 The Coca-Cola Co. v. Koke Co. of America

Supreme Court of the United States, 1920.
254 U.S. 143,
41 S.Ct. 113,
65 L.Ed. 189.
http://www.findlaw.com/casecode/supreme.html[a]

COMPANY PROFILE *John Pemberton, an Atlanta pharmacist, invented a caramel-colored, carbonated soft drink in 1886. His bookkeeper, Frank Robinson, named the beverage Coca-Cola after two of the ingredients, coca leaves and kola nuts. Asa Candler bought the Coca-Cola Company in 1891, and within seven years, he made the soft drink available in all of the United States, as well as in parts of Canada and Mexico. Candler continued to sell Coke aggressively and to open up new markets, reaching Europe before 1910. In doing so, however, he attracted numerous competitors, some of whom tried to capitalize directly on the Coke name.*

FACTS The Coca-Cola Company brought an action in a federal district court to enjoin other beverage companies from using the words "Koke" and "Dope" for the defendants' products. The defendants contended that the Coca-Cola trademark was a fraudulent representation and that Coca-Cola was therefore not entitled to any help from the courts. By use of the Coca-Cola name, the defendants alleged, the Coca-Cola Company represented that the beverage contained cocaine (from coca leaves). The district court granted the injunction, but the federal appellate court reversed. The Coca-Cola Company appealed to the United States Supreme Court.

ISSUE Did the marketing of products called Koke and Dope by the Koke Company of America and other firms constitute an infringement on Coca-Cola's trademark?

DECISION Yes for Koke, but no for Dope. The Supreme Court enjoined the competing beverage companies from calling their products Koke but did not prevent them from calling their products Dope.

(Continued)

a. This is the "U.S. Supreme Court Opinions" page within the Web site of the "FindLaw Internet Legal Resources" database. This page provides several options for accessing an opinion. Because you know the citation for this case, you can go to the "Citation Search" box, type in the appropriate volume and page numbers for the *United States Reports* ("254" and "143," respectively, for the *Coca-Cola* case), and click on "Get It."

CASE 5.1—Continued

REASON The Court noted that, to be sure, prior to 1900 the Coca-Cola beverage had contained a small amount of cocaine, but this ingredient had been deleted from the formula by 1906 at the latest, and the Coca-Cola Company had advertised to the public that no cocaine was present in its drink. Coca-Cola was a widely popular drink "to be had at almost any soda fountain." Because of the public's widespread familiarity with Coca-Cola, the retention of the name of the beverage (referring to coca leaves and kola nuts) was not misleading: "Coca-Cola probably means to most persons the plaintiff's familiar product to be had everywhere rather than a compound of particular substances." The name "Coke" was found to be so common a term for the trademarked product Coca-Cola that the defendants' use of the similar-sounding "Koke" as a name for their beverages was disallowed. The Court could find no reason to restrain the defendants from using the name "Dope," however.

COMMENTS *In this classic case, the United States Supreme Court made it clear that trademarks and trade names (and nicknames for those marks and names, such as the nickname "Coke" for "Coca-Cola") that are in common use receive protection under the common law. This holding is significant historically because the federal statute later passed to protect trademark rights (the Lanham Act of 1946, to be discussed shortly) in many ways represented a codification of common law principles governing trademarks.*

RELEVANT WEB SITES *To locate information on the Web concerning the* Coca-Cola Co. *decision, go to this text's Web site at* **http://blt.westbuslaw.com**, *select "Chapter 5," and click on "URLs for Landmarks."*

STATUTORY PROTECTION OF TRADEMARKS

Statutory protection of trademarks and related property is provided at the federal level by the Lanham Act of 1946.[1] The Lanham Act was enacted in part to protect manufacturers from losing business to rival companies that used confusingly similar trademarks. The Lanham Act incorporates the common law of trademarks and provides remedies for owners of trademarks who wish to enforce their claims in federal court. Many states also have trademark statutes.

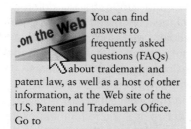

.on the Web You can find answers to frequently asked questions (FAQs) about trademark and patent law, as well as a host of other information, at the Web site of the U.S. Patent and Trademark Office. Go to **http://www.uspto.gov**.

Trademark Dilution In 1995, Congress amended the Lanham Act by passing the Federal Trademark Dilution Act,[2] which extended the protection available to trademark owners by creating a federal cause of action for trademark *dilution*. Until the passage of this amendment, federal trademark law only prohibited the unauthorized use of the same mark on competing—or on noncompeting but "related"—goods or services when such use would likely confuse consumers as to the origin of those goods and services. Trademark dilution laws protect "distinctive" or "famous" trademarks (such as Jergens, McDonald's, RCA, and Macintosh) from certain unauthorized uses of the marks *regardless* of a showing of competition or a likelihood of confusion. More than half of the states have also enacted trademark dilution laws.

Although Congress passed the Federal Trademark Dilution Act in an effort to create uniformity and consistency in dilution cases, until recently, the federal courts were split on the level of proof required to show dilution. Some courts required proof that the defendant's use would cause an "actual lessening" of selling power, whereas other courts required only a showing of a "likelihood of dilution."

1. 15 U.S.C. Sections 1051–1128.
2. 15 U.S.C. Section 1125.

In 2003, the United States Supreme Court resolved this issue in favor of the higher standard in the case of *Moseley v. V Secret Catalogue, Inc.*[3] In that case, famous lingerie maker Victoria's Secret brought a trademark dilution action against "Victor's Little Secret," a small retail store that sold adult videos, lingerie, and other items. The lower courts had granted Victoria's Secret an injunction prohibiting the adult store from diluting the trademark. The Supreme Court, however, concluded that likelihood of dilution is not enough and reversed the lower court's decision. The Court held that to establish dilution under the federal act, some evidence must establish that the allegedly infringing user's mark actually reduces the value of the famous mark or lessens its capacity to identify goods and services.

Use of a Similar Mark May Constitute Trademark Dilution A famous mark may be diluted not only by the use of an *identical* mark but also by the use of a *similar* mark. ■ EXAMPLE 5.1 Ringling Bros.–Barnum & Bailey, Combined Shows, Inc., brought a suit against the state of Utah, claiming that Utah's use of the slogan "The Greatest Snow on Earth"—to attract visitors to the state's recreational and scenic resorts—diluted the distinctiveness of the circus's famous trademark, "The Greatest Show on Earth." Utah moved to dismiss the suit, arguing that the 1995 provisions protect owners of famous trademarks only against the unauthorized use of identical marks. A federal court disagreed and refused to grant Utah's motion to dismiss the case.[4] ■

TRADEMARK REGISTRATION

Trademarks may be registered with the state or with the federal government. To register for protection under federal trademark law, a person must file an application with the U.S. Patent and Trademark Office in Washington, D.C. Under current law, a mark can be registered (1) if it is currently in commerce or (2) if the applicant intends to put the mark into commerce within six months.

.on the Web To access the federal database of registered trademarks, go to **http://www.uspto.gov/main/trademarks.htm**.

In special circumstances, the six-month period can be extended by thirty months, giving the applicant a total of three years from the date of notice of trademark approval to make use of the mark and file the required use statement. Registration is postponed until the mark is actually used. Nonetheless, during this waiting period, any applicant can legally protect his or her trademark against a third party who previously has neither used the mark nor filed an application for it. Registration is renewable between the fifth and sixth years after the initial registration and every ten years thereafter (every twenty years for trademarks registered before 1990).

ETHICAL ISSUE 5.1

Should the courts cancel existing trademarks that are disparaging? The Lanham Act prohibits the U.S. Patent and Trademark Office from registering trademarks that are immoral, scandalous, or disparaging. Trademark examiners review applications and reject any proposed trademarks that are disparaging (demeaning) by today's standards. But what if a trademark that was registered some time ago is perceived as disparaging to a group of people today? Can that registration be canceled? According to a federal district court in 2003, the answer is no. The case involved the Washington Redskins, a professional football team, and six Native Americans

3. 537 U.S. 418, 123 S.Ct. 1115, 155 L.Ed.2d 1 (2003).

4. *Ringling Bros.–Barnum & Bailey, Combined Shows, Inc. v. Utah Division of Travel Development,* 935 F.Supp. 763 (E.D.Va. 1996).

Various billboards in New York City's Times Square. Why are trademarks protected by the law? (Photo by Bill Stryker)

(the plaintiffs) who argued that the trademark should be canceled because the term *Redskins* is the most derogatory one used for native people.

The federal district court held that the plaintiffs had not presented enough evidence to prove the mark was disparaging. According to the court, the test is not whether the trademark is disparaging to Native Americans today but whether it was disparaging at the time it was originally registered. Here, the plaintiffs presented evidence that a number of Native Americans found the term insulting today. The plaintiffs also presented some evidence, including survey results and the testimony of historians and linguists, suggesting that the mark was disparaging when it was first registered in 1967. The court found that evidence insufficient, however, and held that the plaintiffs had waited too long to complain about the trademark.[5] Some contend that this ruling is unfair because what is considered disparaging may change over time. ■

TRADEMARK INFRINGEMENT

Registration of a trademark with the U.S. Patent and Trademark Office gives notice on a nationwide basis that the trademark belongs exclusively to the registrant. The registrant is also allowed to use the symbol ® to indicate that the mark has been registered. Whenever that trademark is copied to a substantial degree or used in its entirety by another, intentionally or unintentionally, the trademark has been *infringed* (used without authorization). When a trademark has been infringed, the owner of the mark has a cause of action against the infringer. A person need not have registered a trademark in order to sue for trademark infringement, but registration does furnish proof of the date of inception of the trademark's use.

Only those trademarks that are deemed sufficiently distinctive from all competing trademarks will be protected, however. The trademarks must be sufficiently distinct to enable consumers to identify the manufacturer of the goods easily and to differentiate among competing products.

Strong Marks Fanciful, arbitrary, or suggestive trademarks are generally considered to be the most distinctive (strongest) trademarks because they are normally taken from outside the context of the particular product and thus provide the best means of distinguishing one product from another.

■ **EXAMPLE 5.2** Fanciful trademarks include invented words, such as "Xerox" for one manufacturer's copiers and "Kodak" for another company's photographic products. Arbitrary trademarks include actual words that have no literal connection to the product, such as "English Leather" used as a name for an aftershave lotion (and not for leather processed in England). Suggestive trademarks are those that suggest something about a product without describing the product directly. For instance, "Dairy Queen" suggests an association between its products and milk, but it does not directly describe ice cream. ■

Secondary Meaning Descriptive terms, geographic terms, and personal names are not inherently distinctive and do not receive protection under the law *until* they acquire a secondary meaning. A secondary meaning may arise when customers begin to associate a specific term or phrase, such as "London Fog," with specific trademarked items (coats with "London Fog" labels). Whether a secondary meaning becomes attached to a term or name usually depends on how extensively the

5. *Pro-Football, Inc. v. Harjo,* 284 F.Supp.2d 96 (D.D.C. 2003).

product is advertised, the market for the product, the number of sales, and other factors. The United States Supreme Court has held that even a color can qualify for trademark protection.[6] Once a secondary meaning is attached to a term or name, a trademark is considered distinctive and is protected.

Generic Terms Generic terms (general, commonly used terms that refer to an entire class of products, such as *bicycle* or *computer*) receive no protection, even if they acquire secondary meanings. A particularly thorny problem arises when a trademark acquires generic use. For instance, *aspirin* and *thermos* were originally trademarked products, but today the words are used generically. Other examples are *escalator, trampoline, raisin bran, dry ice, lanolin, linoleum, nylon,* and *corn flakes.*

Note that a generic term will not be protected under trademark law even if the term has acquired a secondary meaning. ■ EXAMPLE 5.3 In one case, America Online, Inc. (AOL), sued AT&T Corporation, claiming that AT&T's use of "You Have Mail" on its WorldNet Service infringed AOL's trademark rights in the same phrase. The court ruled, however, that because each of the three words in the phrase was a generic term, the phrase as a whole was generic. Although the phrase had become widely associated with AOL's e-mail notification service, and thus may have acquired a secondary meaning, this issue was of no significance in this case. The court stated that it would not consider whether the mark had acquired any secondary meaning because "generic marks with secondary meaning are still not entitled to protection."[7] ■

6. *Qualitex Co. v. Jacobson Products Co.,* 514 U.S. 159, 115 S.Ct. 1300, 131 L.Ed.2d 248 (1995).
7. *America Online, Inc. v. AT&T Corp.,* 243 F.3d 812 (4th Cir. 2001).

The purple and orange colors displayed on FedEx envelopes, packets, and delivery vehicles, including this airplane, are a distinctive feature of that company. If a start-up company specializing in courier delivery services used those same colors, would the new company be infringing on FedEx's trademark? (Photo Courtesy of Federal Express)

A "UL" certification mark. How does a certification mark differ from a trademark?

SERVICE, CERTIFICATION, AND COLLECTIVE MARKS

SERVICE MARK
A mark used in the sale or the advertising of services to distinguish the services of one person from those of others. Titles, character names, and other distinctive features of radio and television programs may be registered as service marks.

A **service mark** is similar to a trademark but is used to distinguish the services of one person or company from those of another. For instance, each airline has a particular mark or symbol associated with its name. Titles and character names used in radio and television are frequently registered as service marks.

Other marks protected by law include certification marks and collective marks. A *certification mark* is used by one or more persons other than the owner to certify the region, materials, mode of manufacture, quality, or accuracy of the owner's goods or services. When used by members of a cooperative, association, or other organization, it is referred to as a *collective mark*. ■ EXAMPLE 5.4 Certification marks include such marks as "Good Housekeeping Seal of Approval" and "UL Tested." Collective marks appear at the ends of the credits of movies to indicate the various associations and organizations that participated in making the movie. The union marks found on the tags of certain products are also collective marks. ■

TRADE NAMES

TRADE NAME
A term that is used to indicate part or all of a business's name and that is directly related to the business's reputation and goodwill. Trade names are protected under the common law (and under trademark law, if the name is the same as the firm's trademarked property).

Trademarks apply to *products*. The term **trade name** is used to indicate part or all of a business's name, whether the business is a sole proprietorship, a partnership, or a corporation. Generally, a trade name is directly related to a business and its goodwill. Trade names may be protected as trademarks if the trade name is the same as the company's trademarked product—for example, Coca-Cola. Unless also used as a trademark or service mark, a trade name cannot be registered with the federal government. Trade names are protected under the common law, however. As with trademarks, words must be unusual or fancifully used if they are to be protected as trade names. The word *Safeway,* for instance, was held by the courts to be sufficiently fanciful to obtain protection as a trade name for a grocery chain.[8]

TRADE DRESS

TRADE DRESS
The image and overall appearance of a product–for example, the distinctive decor, menu, layout, and style of service of a particular restaurant. Basically, trade dress is subject to the same protection as trademarks.

The term **trade dress** refers to the image and overall appearance of a product. Basically, trade dress is subject to the same protection as trademarks. ■ EXAMPLE 5.5 The distinctive decor, menu, layout, and style of service of a particular restaurant may be regarded as the restaurant's trade dress. Similarly, if a golf course is distinguished from other golf courses by prominent features, such as a golf hole designed to look like a lighthouse, those features may be considered the golf course's trade dress. ■ In cases involving trade dress infringement, as in trademark infringement cases, a major consideration is whether consumers are likely to be confused by the allegedly infringing use. Also, features that enhance a product's function will not be protected as trade dress.

Cyber Marks

CYBER MARK
A trademark in cyberspace.

In cyberspace, trademarks are sometimes referred to as **cyber marks.** We turn now to a discussion of trademark-related issues in cyberspace and how new laws and the courts are addressing these issues. One concern relates to the rights of a trademark's owner to use the mark as part of a domain name (Internet address). Other issues have to do with cybersquatting, meta tags, and trademark dilution on the Web. The use of licensing as a way to avoid liability for infringing on another's intellectual property rights in cyberspace will also be discussed.

8. *Safeway Stores v. Suburban Foods,* 130 F.Supp. 249 (E.D.Va. 1955).

DOMAIN NAMES

In the real world, one business can often use the same name as another without causing any conflict, particularly if the businesses are small, their goods or services are different, and the areas where they do business are separate. In the online world, however, there is only one area of business—cyberspace. Thus, disputes between parties over which one has the right to use a particular domain name have become common. A **domain name** is part of an Internet address, such as "westlaw.com." The top level domain (TLD) is the part of the name to the right of the period and indicates the type of entity that operates the site (for example, "com" is an abbreviation for "commercial"). The second level (the part of the name to the left of the period) is chosen by the business entity or individual registering the domain name.

DOMAIN NAME
The last part of an Internet address, such as "westlaw.com." The top level (the part of the name to the right of the period) indicates the type of entity that operates the site ("com" is an abbreviation for "commercial"). The second level (the part of the name to the left of the period) is chosen by the entity.

Conflicts over rights to domain names emerged during the 1990s as e-commerce expanded on a worldwide scale. As e-commerce grew, the *.com* TLD came to be widely used by businesses on the Web. Competition among firms with similar names and products preceding the *.com* TLD led, understandably, to numerous disputes over domain name rights. By using the same, or a similar, domain name, parties have attempted to profit from the goodwill of a competitor, to sell pornography, to offer for sale another party's domain name, and to otherwise infringe on others' trademarks.

As noted in Chapter 3, the federal government set up the Internet Corporation for Assigned Names and Numbers (ICANN), a nonprofit corporation, to oversee the distribution of domain names. ICANN has also played a leading role in facilitating the settlement of domain name disputes worldwide. Since January 2000, ICANN has been operating an online arbitration system to resolve domain name disputes and approve dispute-resolution providers. By 2003, ICANN–approved online arbitration providers were handling over one thousand disputes annually.

ANTICYBERSQUATTING LEGISLATION

In the late 1990s, Congress passed legislation prohibiting another practice that had given rise to numerous disputes over domain names: cybersquatting. **Cybersquatting** occurs when a person registers a domain name that is the same as, or confusingly similar to, the trademark of another and then offers to sell the domain name back to the trademark owner. During the 1990s, cybersquatting became a contentious issue and led to much litigation. Although it was not always easy for the courts to separate cybersquatting from legitimate business activity, many cases held that cybersquatting violated trademark law.[9]

CYBERSQUATTING
The act of registering a domain name that is the same as, or confusingly similar to, the trademark of another and then offering to sell that domain name back to the trademark owner.

In 1999, Congress addressed this issue by passing the Anticybersquatting Consumer Protection Act (ACPA), which amended the Lanham Act—the federal law protecting trademarks, discussed earlier in this chapter. The ACPA makes it illegal for a person to "register, traffic in, or use" a domain name (1) if the name is identical or confusingly similar to the trademark of another and (2) if the one registering, trafficking in, or using the domain name has a "bad faith intent" to profit from that trademark. The act does not define what constitutes bad faith. Instead, it lists several factors that courts can consider in deciding whether bad faith exists. Some of these factors are the trademark rights of the other person, whether there is an intent to divert consumers in a way that could harm the goodwill represented by the trademark, whether there is an offer to transfer or sell the domain name to the

9. See, for example, *Panavision International, L.P. v. Toeppen,* 141 F.3d 1316 (9th Cir. 1998).

trademark owner, and whether there is an intent to use the domain name to offer goods and services.

The ACPA applies to all domain name registrations of trademarks, even domain names registered before the passage of the act. Successful plaintiffs in suits brought under the act can collect actual damages and profits, or elect to receive statutory damages of from $1,000 to $100,000.

META TAGS

META TAGS
Words inserted into a Web site's key-word field to increase the site's inclusion in search engine results.

Search engines compile their results by looking through a Web site's key-word field. **Meta tags,** or key words, may be inserted into this field to increase the site's inclusion in search engine results, even though the site may have nothing to do with the inserted words. Using this same technique, one site may appropriate the key words of other sites with more frequent hits, so that the appropriating site appears in the same search engine results as the more popular sites. Using another's trademark in a meta tag without the owner's permission, however, constitutes trademark infringement. One use of meta tags was at issue in the following case.

CASE 5.2 Playboy Enterprises, Inc. v. Welles

United States Court of Appeals,
Ninth Circuit, 2002.
279 F.3d 796.

FACTS Playboy Enterprises, Inc. (PEI), maintains Web sites to promote *Playboy* magazine and PEI models. PEI's trademarks include the terms "Playboy," "Playmate," and "Playmate of the Year." Terri Welles is a self-employed model and spokesperson, who was featured as the "Playmate of the Year" in June 1981. Welles maintains a Web site titled "Terri Welles—Playmate of the Year 1981." As meta tags, Welles's site uses the terms "Playboy" and "Playmate," among others. PEI asked Welles to stop using these terms, but she refused. PEI filed a suit in a federal district court against Welles, asking the court to order her to, among other things, stop using those terms as meta tags. On this issue, the court granted a summary judgment in Welles's favor. PEI appealed to the U.S. Court of Appeals for the Ninth Circuit.

ISSUE Did Welles's use of PEI's meta tags to direct users to her Web site constitute trademark infringement?

DECISION No. The U.S. Court of Appeals for the Ninth Circuit concluded that Welles's use of PEI's trademarks as meta tags was a permissible, nominative use.[a]

a. A *nominative use* of a trademark is one that does not imply sponsorship or endorsement of a product because the product's mark is used only to describe the thing, rather than to identify its source. See *New Kids on the Block v. News America Publishing, Inc.*, 971 F.2d 302 (9th Cir. 1992).

REASON The U.S. Court of Appeals for the Ninth Circuit explained that the test for nominative use is "[f]irst, the product or service in question must be one not readily identifiable without use of the trademark; second, only so much of the mark or marks may be used as is reasonably necessary to identify the product or service; and third, the user must do nothing that would, in conjunction with the mark, suggest sponsorship or endorsement by the trademark holder." The court reasoned that "[t]here is simply no descriptive substitute for the trademarks used in Welles' meta tags. Precluding their use would have the unwanted effect of hindering the free flow of information on the Internet, something which is certainly not a goal of trademark law." Also, "[t]he meta tags use only so much of the marks as reasonably necessary and nothing is done in conjunction with them to suggest sponsorship or endorsement by the trademark holder."

WHY IS THIS CASE IMPORTANT? *This case illustrates how some uses of another's trademark are permissible and not infringing, provided that the user does not suggest that the trademark owner authorized or sponsored the use.*

DILUTION IN THE ONLINE WORLD

As discussed earlier, trademark *dilution* occurs when a trademark is used, without authorization, in a way that diminishes the distinctive quality of the mark. Unlike trademark infringement, a dilution cause of action does not require proof that consumers are likely to be confused by a connection between the unauthorized use and the mark. For this reason, the products involved do not have to be similar. In the first case alleging dilution on the Web, a court precluded the use of "candyland.com" as the URL for an adult site. The suit was brought by the maker of the "Candyland" children's game and owner of the "Candyland" mark.[10]

In another case, a court issued an injunction on the ground that spamming under another's logo is trademark dilution. In that case, Hotmail, Inc., provided e-mail services and worked to dissociate itself from spam. Van$ Money Pie, Inc., and others spammed thousands of e-mail customers, using the free e-mail Hotmail as a return address. The court ordered the defendants to stop.[11]

LICENSING

One of the ways to make use of another's trademark or other form of intellectual property, while avoiding litigation, is to obtain a license to do so. A license in this context is essentially an agreement permitting the use of a trademark, copyright, patent, or trade secret for certain purposes. For instance, a licensee (the party obtaining the license) might be allowed to use the trademark of the licensor (the party issuing the license) as part of the name of its company, or as part of its domain name, without otherwise using the mark on any products or services. (Like all contracts, contracts granting licenses must be carefully drafted—see, for example, the problems faced by the parties in the case discussed in this chapter's *Letter of the Law* feature on the following page.)

Patents

PATENT
A government grant that gives an inventor the exclusive right or privilege to make, use, or sell his or her invention for a limited time period.

A **patent** is a grant from the government that gives an inventor the exclusive right to make, use, and sell an invention for a period of twenty years from the date of filing the application for a patent. Patents for designs, as opposed to inventions, are given for a fourteen-year period. For either a regular patent or a design patent, the applicant must demonstrate to the satisfaction of the U.S. Patent and Trademark Office that the invention, discovery, process, or design is genuine, novel, useful, and not obvious in light of current technology. A patent holder gives notice to all that an article or design is patented by placing on it the word *Patent* or *Pat.* plus the patent number. In contrast to patent law in other countries, in the United States patent protection is given to the first person to invent a product or process, even though someone else may have been the first to file for a patent on that product or process.

At one time, it was difficult for developers and manufacturers of software to obtain patent protection because many software products simply automate procedures that can be performed manually. In other words, the computer programs do not meet the "novel" and "not obvious" requirements previously mentioned. Also,

10. *Hasbro, Inc. v. Internet Entertainment Group, Ltd.,* 1996 WL 84853 (W.D.Wash. 1996).
11. *Hotmail Corp. v. Van$ Money Pie, Inc.,* 47 U.S.P.Q.2d 1020 (N.D.Cal. 1998).

LETTER OF THE LAW A Book Is a Book Is a Book—But Is It an "E-Book"?

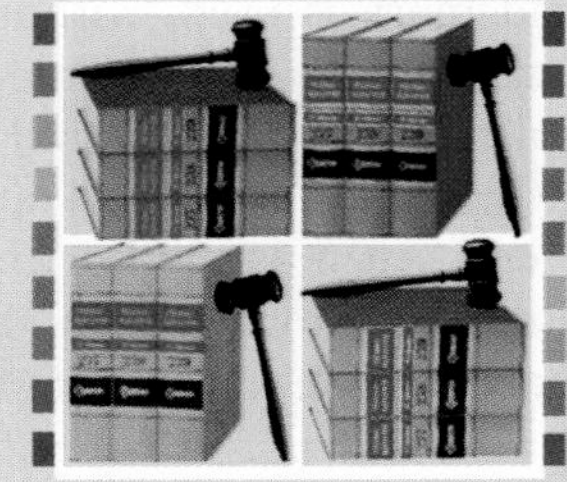

One of the significant issues raised by the cyber age has to do with whether copyrights in printed materials extend to the same materials presented in digital form over the Internet. A related issue involving licensing agreements came before a federal district court in 2001. The case was brought by the well-known publishing firm Random House, Inc., against Rosetta Books, LLC,[a] with which several authors had arranged to publish works electronically. At issue in the case was the following question: Did contracts in which the authors had licensed Random House to "print, publish and sell" their works in "book form" include the right to publish their works in electronic formats (as "e-books") as well?

In evaluating the issue, the court looked to the letter of the law, as decided by other court cases, but found little guidance. Hence, it looked to the words of the contract and to the definition of the term *book* given by the *Random House Webster's Unabridged Dictionary.* That dictionary defines a "book" as "a written or printed work of fiction or nonfiction, usually on sheets of paper fastened or bound together within covers." The court ultimately concluded that a book is not an e-book and therefore refused to grant Random House's motion to enjoin (prohibit) Rosetta Books from publishing the authors' works as e-books.[b]

THE BOTTOM LINE

To avoid litigation, anyone signing a licensing contract should make sure that the specific wording in the contract makes very clear what rights are or are not being conveyed.

a. *LLC* stands for "Limited Liability Company," a form of business organization that will be discussed in Chapter 19.

b. *Random House, Inc. v. Rosetta Books, LLC,* 150 F.Supp.2d 613 (S.D.N.Y. 2001).

the basis for software is often a mathematical equation or formula, which is not patentable. In 1981, however, the United States Supreme Court held that it is possible to obtain a patent for a process that incorporates a computer program—providing, of course, that the process itself is patentable.[12] Subsequently, many patents have been issued for software-related inventions.

A significant development relating to patents is the availability online of the world's patent databases. The Web site of the U.S. Patent and Trademark Office provides searchable databases covering U.S. patents granted since 1976. The Web site of the European Patent Office maintains databases covering all patent documents in sixty-five nations and the legal status of patents in twenty-two of those countries.

PATENT INFRINGEMENT

If a firm makes, uses, or sells another's patented design, product, or process without the patent owner's permission, it commits the tort of patent infringement. Patent infringement may exist even though the patent owner has not put the patented product in commerce. Patent infringement may also occur even though not all features or parts of an invention are copied. (With respect to a patented process, however, all steps or their equivalent must be copied for infringement to exist.)

.on the Web A good online source for information on patents can be found at **http://www.patents.com**.

Often, litigation for patent infringement is so costly that the patent holder will instead offer to sell to the infringer a license to use the patented design, product, or process. Indeed, in many cases the costs of detection, prosecution, and monitoring

12. *Diamond v. Diehr,* 450 U.S. 175, 101 S.Ct. 1048, 67 L.Ed.2d 155 (1981).

are so high that patents are valueless to their owners; the owners cannot afford to protect them.

Should a software program that allows consumers to make offers for vacation packages via the Internet be considered a "new and useful" process that can be the subject of a business process patent? Why or why not?

Business Process Patents

Traditionally, patents have been granted for inventions that are "new and useful processes, machines, manufactures, or compositions of matter, or any new and useful improvements thereof." The U.S. Patent and Trademark Office routinely rejected computer systems and software applications because they were deemed not to be useful processes, machines, articles of manufacture, or compositions of matter. They were simply considered to be mathematical algorithms, abstract ideas, or "methods of doing business." In a landmark 1998 case, however, *State Street Bank & Trust Co. v. Signature Financial Group, Inc.*,[13] the U.S. Court of Appeals for the Federal Circuit ruled that only three categories of subject matter will always remain unpatentable: (1) the laws of nature, (2) natural phenomena, and (3) abstract ideas. This decision meant, among other things, that business processes were patentable.

After this decision, numerous technology firms applied for business process patents. Walker Digital applied for a business process patent for its "Dutch auction" system, which allowed consumers to make offers for airline tickets on the Internet and led to the creation of Priceline.com. Amazon.com obtained a business process patent for its "one-click" ordering system, a method of processing credit-card orders securely. Indeed, since the *State Street* decision, the number of Internet-related patents issued by the U.S. Patent and Trademark Office has increased more than 800 percent.

Ease of interactivity is a key ingredient in the success of the Internet. From the user's perspective, easily communicating via e-mail and accessing information on the Web are among the benefits of current computer technology. The Web browsers of the early 1990s, however, had limited capability for interactivity. Now, interactivity seems nearly effortless because of the patented device at the center of the following case.

13. 149 F.3d 1368 (Fed. Cir. 1998).

CASE 5.3 Eolas Technologies, Inc. v. Microsoft Corp.

United States District Court,
Northern District of Illinois,
Eastern Division, 2004.
__ F.Supp.2d __.

FACTS In 1994, at the University of California, Michael Doyle, David Martin, and Cheong Ang invented a method for building a Web browser that could display interactive objects embedded in a single Web page and could use other applications to enable interactivity, allowing users to manipulate images and other data in a single window. They obtained a patent for this method and licensed its use exclusively to Eolas Technologies, Inc. Without Eolas's permission, Microsoft Corporation included the method's features in its Internet Explorer browser, which was bundled with the Windows operating system. Eolas filed a suit in a federal district court against Microsoft, alleging patent infringement. A jury found Microsoft liable to Eolas and assessed $512 million in damages. Eolas filed a motion to enjoin (prevent) Microsoft from continuing to use the patented method. Microsoft responded that the Explorer and Windows bundled product "is in such widespread use that a broad injunction would impose unacceptably high costs on the product's users. These costs will include not only dollars but also other irreparable injuries such as loss of time and interruption of work. * * * Moreover, Web-based business will be affected because Web pages may

(Continued)

CASE 5.3—Continued

have to be redesigned. The redesign may, in some cases, require upgrades to millions of older Windows systems."

ISSUE Should Microsoft be barred from distributing versions of Explorer that include the features of Eolas's patented method?

DECISION Yes. The court upheld the jury's verdict and granted the injunction. The court stayed (postponed) the injunction, however, while Microsoft appealed the judgment.

REASON The court explained that inventors have a right to keep their invention to themselves, to share it with whom they choose, or to completely prevent others from using it. According to the court, "It is the loss of these rights that cause the irreparable injury that can be vindicated only by an injunction, not by damages." Thus, the court found that Eolas was entitled to an injunction but further held that the injunction should be limited in scope so as to minimize the harm to Microsoft and to the public. The court stated, "The injunction should be carefully crafted to preclude [prevent] infringement only with respect to future conduct by Microsoft; infringements in the past are to be remedied by damages." The court noted that it is important to distinguish between past and future infringements here because the infringement occurs many times each day when Windows users display interactive objects embedded in Web pages. These infringements, in the court's view, belong in the category of past infringements because the operating system (the device used to infringe) was made and sold long before the judgment in this case was rendered. "The future infringement is limited to new versions of Microsoft's Windows operating system or any major service pack [updates] of any existing versions of the Windows operating system containing Internet Explorer that Microsoft releases to manufacturing."

FOR CRITICAL ANALYSIS—Technological Consideration *If Microsoft loses on appeal, should the firm be given time to devise and release noninfringing technology before being held in violation of the injunction? Why or why not?*

Copyrights

COPYRIGHT
The exclusive right of "authors" to publish, print, or sell an intellectual production for a statutory period of time. A copyright has the same monopolistic nature as a patent or trademark, but it differs in that it applies exclusively to works of art, literature, and other works of authorship (including computer programs).

A **copyright** is an intangible property right granted by federal statute to the author or originator of certain literary or artistic productions. Currently, copyrights are governed by the Copyright Act of 1976,[14] as amended. Works created after January 1, 1978, are automatically given statutory copyright protection for the life of the author plus 70 years. For copyrights owned by publishing houses, the copyright expires 95 years from the date of publication or 120 years from the date of creation, whichever is first. For works by more than one author, the copyright expires 70 years after the death of the last surviving author.

These time periods reflect the extensions of the length of copyright protection enacted by Congress in the Copyright Term Extension Act of 1998.[15] Critics challenged this act as overstepping the bounds of Congress's power and violating the constitutional requirement that copyrights endure for only a limited time. In 2003, however, the United States Supreme Court upheld the act in *Eldred v. Ashcroft*.[16] This ruling obviously favored copyright holders by preventing copyrighted works from the 1920s and 1930s from losing protection and falling into the public domain for an additional two decades.

Copyrights can be registered with the U.S. Copyright Office in Washington, D.C. A copyright owner no longer needs to place a © or *Copr.* or *Copyright* on the work, however, to have the work protected against infringement. Chances are that if somebody created it, somebody owns it.

on the Web For information on copyrights, go to the U.S. Copyright Office at **http://lcweb.loc.gov/copyright**.

14. 17 U.S.C. Sections 101 *et seq.*
15. 17 U.S.C.A. Section 302.
16. 537 U.S. 186, 123 S.Ct. 769, 154 L.Ed.2d 683 (2003).

What Is Protected Expression?

BE CAREFUL If a creative work does not fall into a certain category, it may not be copyrighted, but it may be protected by other intellectual property law.

Works that are copyrightable include books, records, films, artworks, architectural plans, menus, music videos, product packaging, and computer software. To obtain protection under the Copyright Act, a work must be original and fall into one of the following categories: (1) literary works; (2) musical works; (3) dramatic works; (4) pantomimes and choreographic works; (5) pictorial, graphic, and sculptural works; (6) films and other audiovisual works; and (7) sound recordings. To be protected, a work must be "fixed in a durable medium" from which it can be perceived, reproduced, or communicated. Protection is automatic. Registration is not required.

Section 102 Exclusions Section 102 of the Copyright Act specifically excludes copyright protection for any "idea, procedure, process, system, method of operation, concept, principle, or discovery, regardless of the form in which it is described, explained, illustrated, or embodied." Note that it is not possible to copyright an *idea*. The underlying ideas embodied in a work may be freely used by others. What is copyrightable is the particular way in which an idea is *expressed*. Whenever an idea and an expression are inseparable, the expression cannot be copyrighted. Generally, anything that is not an original expression will not qualify for copyright protection. Facts widely known to the public are not copyrightable. Page numbers are not copyrightable because they follow a sequence known to everyone. Mathematical calculations are not copyrightable.

Compilations of Facts *Compilations* of facts, however, are copyrightable. Section 103 of the Copyright Act defines a compilation as "a work formed by the collection and assembling of preexisting materials of data that are selected, coordinated, or arranged in such a way that the resulting work as a whole constitutes an original work of authorship." The key requirement for the copyrightability of a compilation is originality. ■ **EXAMPLE 5.6** The white pages of a telephone directory do not qualify for copyright protection when the information that makes up the directory (names, addresses, and telephone numbers) is not selected, coordinated, or arranged in an original way.[17] In one case, even the Yellow Pages of a telephone directory did not qualify for copyright protection.[18] ■

on the Web You can find a host of information on copyright law, including the Copyright Act and significant United States Supreme Court cases in the area of copyright law, at **http://supct.law.cornell.edu/supct/cases/copyrt.htm**.

Copyright Infringement

Whenever the form or expression of an idea is copied, an infringement of copyright occurs. The reproduction does not have to be exactly the same as the original, nor does it have to reproduce the original in its entirety. If a substantial part of the original is reproduced, there is copyright infringement.

Damages for Copyright Infringement Those who infringe copyrights may be liable for damages or criminal penalties. These range from actual damages or statutory damages, imposed at the court's discretion, to criminal proceedings for willful violations. Actual damages are based on the harm caused to the copyright holder by

---

17. *Feist Publications, Inc. v. Rural Telephone Service Co.,* 499 U.S. 340, 111 S.Ct. 1282, 113 L.Ed.2d 358 (1991).
18. *Bellsouth Advertising & Publishing Corp. v. Donnelley Information Publishing, Inc.,* 999 F.2d 1436 (11th Cir. 1993).

the infringement, while statutory damages, not to exceed $150,000, are provided for under the Copyright Act. In addition, criminal proceedings may result in fines and/or imprisonment.

The "Fair Use" Exception An exception to liability for copyright infringement is made under the "fair use" doctrine. In certain circumstances, a person or organization can reproduce copyrighted material without paying royalties (fees paid to the copyright holder for the privilege of reproducing the copyrighted material). Section 107 of the Copyright Act provides as follows:

> [T]he fair use of a copyrighted work, including such use by reproduction in copies or phonorecords or by any other means specified by [Section 106 of the Copyright Act,] for purposes such as criticism, comment, news reporting, teaching (including multiple copies for classroom use), scholarship, or research, is not an infringement of copyright. In determining whether the use made of a work in any particular case is a fair use the factors to be considered shall include—
>
> (1) the purpose and character of the use, including whether such use is of a commercial nature or is for nonprofit educational purposes;
>
> (2) the nature of the copyrighted work;
>
> (3) the amount and substantiality of the portion used in relation to the copyrighted work as a whole; and
>
> (4) the effect of the use upon the potential market for or value of the copyrighted work.

Because these guidelines are very broad, the courts determine whether a particular use is fair on a case-by-case basis. Thus, anyone reproducing copyrighted material may be committing a violation. In determining whether a use is fair, courts have often considered the fourth factor to be the most important.

Copyright Protection for Software

In 1980, Congress passed the Computer Software Copyright Act, which amended the Copyright Act of 1976 to include computer programs in the list of creative works protected by federal copyright law. The 1980 statute, which classifies computer programs as "literary works," defines a computer program as a "set of statements or instructions to be used directly or indirectly in a computer in order to bring about a certain result."

Because of the unique nature of computer programs, the courts have had many problems applying and interpreting the 1980 act. Generally, though, the courts have held that copyright protection extends not only to those parts of a computer program that can be read by humans, such as the high-level language of a source code, but also to the binary-language object code of a computer program, which is readable only by the computer.[19] Additionally, such elements as the overall structure, sequence, and organization of a program were deemed copyrightable.[20] The courts have disagreed as to whether the "look and feel"—the general appearance, command structure, video images, menus, windows, and other screen displays—of computer programs should also be protected by copyright. The courts have tended, however, not to extend copyright protection to look-and-feel aspects of computer programs.

---

19. See *Stern Electronics, Inc. v. Kaufman*, 669 F.2d 852 (2d Cir. 1982); and *Apple Computer, Inc. v. Franklin Computer Corp.*, 714 F.2d 1240 (3d Cir. 1983).

20. *Whelan Associates, Inc. v. Jaslow Dental Laboratory, Inc.*, 797 F.2d 1222 (3d Cir. 1986).

Copyrights in Digital Information

Copyright law is probably the most important form of intellectual property protection on the Internet. This is because much of the material on the Internet consists of works of authorship (including multimedia presentations, software, and database information), which are the traditional focus of copyright law. Copyright law is also important because the nature of the Internet requires that data be "copied" to be transferred online. Copies are a significant part of the traditional controversies arising in this area of the law.

.on the Web The University of Michigan provides information on copyrights generally and copyrights in digital information at **http://www.copyright.umich.edu/law.html**.

The Copyright Act of 1976 When Congress drafted the principal U.S. law governing copyrights, the Copyright Act of 1976, cyberspace did not exist for most of us. The threat to copyright owners was posed not by computer technology but by unauthorized *tangible* copies of works and the sale of rights to movies, television, and other media.

Some issues that were unimagined when the Copyright Act was drafted have posed thorny questions for the courts. For instance, to sell a copy of a work, permission of the copyright holder is necessary. Because of the nature of cyberspace, however, one of the early controversies involved determining at what point an intangible, electronic "copy" of a work has been made. The courts have held that loading a file or program into a computer's random access memory, or RAM, constitutes the making of a "copy" for purposes of copyright law.[21] RAM is a portion of a computer's memory into which a file, for instance, is loaded so that it can be accessed (read or written over). Thus, a copyright is infringed when a party downloads

21. *MAI Systems Corp. v. Peak Computer, Inc.,* 991 F.2d 511 (9th Cir. 1993).

software into RAM without owning the software or otherwise having a right to download it.[22]

Other rights, including those relating to the revision of "collective works" such as magazines, were acknowledged thirty years ago but were considered to have only limited economic value. Today, technology has made some of those rights vastly more significant. How does the old law apply to these rights? That was one of the questions in the following case.

22. *DSC Communications Corp. v. Pulse Communications, Inc.*, 170 F.3d 1354 (Fed. Cir. 1999).

CASE 5.4 New York Times Co. v. Tasini

Supreme Court of the United States, 2001.
533 U.S. 483,
121 S.Ct. 2381,
150 L.Ed.2d 500.
http://supct.law.cornell.edu/supct[a]

FACTS Magazines and newspapers, including the *New York Times,* buy and publish articles written by freelance writers. Besides circulating hard copies of their periodicals, these publishers sell the contents to e-publishers for inclusion in online and other electronic databases. Jonathan Tasini and other freelance writers filed a suit in a federal district court against the New York Times Company and other publishers, including the e-publishers, contending that the e-publication of the articles violated the Copyright Act. The publishers responded that, among other things, the Copyright Act gave them a right to produce "revisions" of their publications. The writers argued that the Copyright Act did not cover electronic "revisions." The court granted a summary judgment in the publishers' favor, which was reversed on the writers' appeal to the U.S. Court of Appeals for the Second Circuit. The publishers appealed to the United States Supreme Court.

ISSUE To put the contents of periodicals into e-databases and onto CD-ROMs, do publishers need to obtain the permission of the writers whose contributions are included in the periodicals?

DECISION Yes. The United States Supreme Court affirmed the lower court's judgment. The Supreme Court remanded the case for a determination as to how the writers should be compensated.

REASON The Court pointed out that databases are "vast domain[s] of diverse texts," consisting of "thousands or millions of files containing individual articles from thousands of collective works." The Court found that these databases have little relationship to the articles' original publication. The databases are not "revisions," as the publishers argued, because the databases reproduce and distribute articles "clear of the context provided by the original periodical editions"—not "as part of that particular collective work" to which the author contributed, not "as part of * * * any revision," and not "as part of * * * any later collective work in the same series," as the Copyright Act provides. The Court reasoned that a database composed of such articles was no more a revision of an original work than "a 400-page novel quoting a sonnet in passing would represent a 'revision' of that poem."

FOR CRITICAL ANALYSIS—Economic Consideration *When rights such as those in this case become more valuable as a result of new technology, should the law be changed to redistribute the economic benefit of those rights? Explain.*

a. In the "Search" box at the top of the page, enter "Tasini." Click on "submit." In the result, scroll to the case name and select the appropriate link to access the opinion.

Further Developments in Copyright Law In the last several years, Congress has enacted legislation designed specifically to protect copyright holders in a digital age. Prior to 1997, criminal penalties under copyright law could be imposed only if unauthorized copies were exchanged for financial gain. Yet much piracy of copyrighted materials was "altruistic" in nature; that is, unauthorized copies were made and distributed not for financial gain but simply for reasons of generosity—to share the copies with others.

Cary Sherman, president of the Recording Industry Association of America (RIAA). Sherman is talking with reporters after announcing that the RIAA was filing hundreds of lawsuits against individuals who shared copyrighted music files via the Internet. Under what theories can a company that distributes file-sharing software also be held liable if individuals use the software to exchange copyrighted music? (AP Photo/George Nikitin)

To combat altruistic piracy and for other reasons, Congress passed the No Electronic Theft (NET) Act of 1997. This act extends criminal liability for the piracy of copyrighted materials to persons who exchange unauthorized copies of copyrighted works, such as software, even though they realize no profit from the exchange. The act also imposes penalties on those who make unauthorized electronic copies of books, magazines, movies, or music for *personal* use, thus altering the traditional "fair use" doctrine. The criminal penalties for violating the act are steep; they include fines as high as $250,000 and incarceration for up to five years.

In 1998, Congress passed further legislation to protect copyright holders—the Digital Millennium Copyright Act. Because of its significance in protecting against the piracy of copyrighted materials in the online environment, this act is presented as this chapter's *Landmark in the Law* feature on pages 160 and 161.

MP3 AND FILE-SHARING TECHNOLOGY

At one time, music fans swapped compact discs (CDs) and recorded the songs that they liked from others' CDs onto their own cassettes. This type of "file-sharing" was awkward at best. Soon after the Internet became popular, a few enterprising programmers created software to compress large data files, particularly those associated with music. The reduced file sizes make transmitting music over the Internet feasible. The most widely known compression and decompression system is MP3, which enables music fans to download songs or entire CDs onto their computers or onto a portable listening device, such as Rio or iPod. The MP3 system also made it possible for music fans to access other music fans' files by engaging in file-sharing via the Internet.

PEER-TO-PEER (P2P) NETWORKING
The sharing of resources (such as files, hard drives, and processing styles) among multiple computers without necessarily requiring a central network server.

DISTRIBUTED NETWORK
A network that can be used by persons located (distributed) around the country or the globe to share computer files.

Peer-to-Peer (P2P) Networking File-sharing via the Internet is accomplished through what is called **peer-to-peer (P2P) networking.** The concept is simple. Rather than going through a central Web server, P2P involves numerous personal computers (PCs) that are connected to the Internet. Files stored on one PC can be accessed by others who are members of the same network. Sometimes this is called a **distributed network.** In other words, parts of the network are distributed all over the country or the world. File-sharing offers an unlimited number of uses for distributed networks. Currently, for instance, many researchers allow their home computers' computing power to be accessed through file-sharing software so that very large mathematical problems can be solved quickly. Additionally, persons scattered throughout the country or the world can work together on the same project by using file-sharing programs.

Sharing Stored Music Files When file-sharing is used to download others' stored music files, copyright issues arise. Recording artists and their labels stand to lose large amounts of royalties and revenues if relatively few CDs are purchased and then made available on distributed networks, from which everyone can get them for free. The issue of file-sharing infringement has been the subject of an ongoing debate over the last few years.

■ EXAMPLE 5.7 In the highly publicized case of *A&M Records, Inc. v. Napster, Inc.,*[23] several firms in the recording industry sued Napster, Inc., the owner of the

23. 239 F.3d 1004 (9th Cir. 2001).

LANDMARK IN THE LAW

The Digital Millennium Copyright Act of 1998

The United States leads the world in the production of creative products, including books, films, videos, recordings, and software. In fact, as indicated earlier in this chapter, the creative industries are more important to the U.S. economy than the traditional product industries are. Exports of U.S. creative products, for example, surpass those of every other U.S. industry in value. Creative industries are growing at nearly three times the rate of the economy as a whole.

Steps have been taken, both nationally and internationally, to protect ownership rights in intellectual property, including copyrights. As you will read later in this chapter, to curb unauthorized copying of copyrighted materials, the World Intellectual Property Organization (WIPO) enacted a treaty in 1996 to upgrade global standards of copyright protection, particularly for the Internet.

IMPLEMENTING THE WIPO TREATY In 1998, Congress implemented the provisions of the WIPO treaty by updating U.S. copyright law. The new law—the Digital Millennium Copyright Act of 1998—is a landmark step in the protection of copyright owners and, because of the leading position of the United States in the creative industries, serves as a model for other nations. Among other things, the act established civil and criminal penalties for anyone who circumvents (bypasses, or gets around—through clever maneuvering, for example) encryption software or other technological antipiracy protection. Also prohibited are the manufacture, import, sale, and distribution of devices or services for circumvention.

The act provides for exceptions to fit the needs of libraries, scientists, universities, and others. In general, the law does not restrict the "fair use" of circumvention methods for educational and other noncommercial purposes. For example, circumvention is allowed to test computer security, conduct encryption research, protect personal privacy, and enable parents to monitor their children's use of the Internet. The exceptions are to be reconsidered every three years.

then-popular Napster Web site. The Napster site provided registered users with free software that enabled them to transfer exact copies of the contents of MP3 files from one computer to another via the Internet. Napster also maintained centralized search indices so that users could locate specific titles or artists' recordings on the computers of other members. The firms argued that Napster should be liable for contributory and vicarious[24] copyright infringement because it assisted others in obtaining copies of copyrighted music without the copyright owners' permission. Both the federal district court and the U.S. Court of Appeals for the Ninth Circuit agreed and held Napster liable for violating copyright laws. ■

Since the 2001 *Napster* decision, the recording industry has filed and won numerous lawsuits against companies that distribute online file-sharing software. The courts have held these Napsterlike companies liable based on two theories: contributory infringement, which applies if the company had reason to know about a user's infringement and failed to stop it; and vicarious liability, which exists if the company was able to control the users' activities and stood to benefit financially from

24. Vicarious (indirect) liability exists when one person is subject to liability for another's actions. A common example occurs in the employment context, when an employer is held vicariously liable by third parties for torts committed by employees in the course of their employment.

LANDMARK IN THE LAW

The Digital Millennium Copyright Act of 1998—Continued

LIMITING THE LIABILITY OF INTERNET SERVICE PROVIDERS The 1998 act also limited the liability of Internet service providers (ISPs). Under the act, an ISP is not liable for any copyright infringement by its customer *unless* the ISP is aware of the subscriber's violation. An ISP may be held liable only if it fails to take action to shut the subscriber down after learning of the violation. A copyright holder has to act promptly, however, by pursuing a claim in court, or the subscriber has the right to be restored to online access.

APPLICATION TO TODAY'S WORLD

The application of the Digital Millennium Copyright Act of 1998 to today's world is fairly self-evident. If Congress had not enacted this legislation, copyright owners would have a far more difficult time obtaining legal redress against those who, without authorization, decrypt and/or copy copyrighted materials. Of course, problems remain, particularly because of the global nature of the Internet. From a practical standpoint, the degree of protection afforded to copyright holders depends on the extent to which other nations that have signed the WIPO treaty actually implement its provisions and agree on the interpretation of terms, such as what constitutes an electronic copy.

RELEVANT WEB SITES

To locate information on the Web concerning the Digital Millennium Copyright Act of 1998, go to this text's Web site at **http://blt.westbuslaw.com**, *select "Chapter 5," and click on "URLs for Landmarks."*

their infringement. In the *Napster* case, the court held the company liable under both doctrines, largely because the technology that Napster had used was centralized and gave it "the ability to locate infringing material listed on its search indices, and the right to terminate users' access to the system."

New File-Sharing Technologies In the wake of the *Napster* decision, other companies developed new technologies that allow P2P network users to share stored music files, without paying a fee, more quickly and efficiently than ever. Today's file-sharing software is decentralized and does not use search indices. Thus, the companies have no ability to supervise or control which music (or other media files) their users are exchanging. Unlike the Napster system, in which the company played a role in connecting people who were downloading and uploading songs, the new systems are designed to work without the company's input.

Software such as Morpheus and KaZaA, for example, provides users with an interface that is similar to a Web browser. This technology is different from that used by Napster. Instead of the company locating songs for users on other members' computers, the software automatically annotates files with descriptive information so that the music can easily be categorized and cross-referenced (by artist and title, for instance). When a user performs a search, the software is able to locate a list of peers that have the file available for downloading. Also, to expedite the P2P transfer and ensure that the complete file is received, the software distributes the download task over the entire list of peers simultaneously. By downloading even one file, the user becomes a point of distribution for that file, which is then automatically shared with others on the network.

How will the courts decide the legality of these new digital technologies? See this chapter's *Adapting the Law to the Online Environment* feature for a discussion of this issue.

ADAPTING THE LAW TO THE ONLINE ENVIRONMENT

New File-Sharing Technology and Copyright Law

Over 18 million Americans downloaded music from the Internet in 2004. It is not known what percentage of those downloaded copies were unauthorized, or "pirated." Clearly, any person who downloads copyrighted music without permission from the copyright holder is liable for copyright infringement. But what about the companies that provide the software that enables users to swap copyrighted music? In what circumstances will the companies be held liable? It has been difficult for the courts to apply traditional doctrines of contributory and vicarious copyright liability to new file-sharing technologies.

THE *GROKSTER* CASE

Consider the situation faced by the court in *Metro-Goldwyn-Mayer Studios, Inc. v. Grokster, Ltd.*[a] In that case, organizations in the music and film industry (the plaintiffs) sued several companies that distribute file-sharing software used in P2P networks, including Grokster, Ltd., and StreamCast Networks, Inc. (the defendants). The plaintiffs claimed that the companies were contributorily and vicariously liable for the infringement of their end users.

The federal district court examined the technology involved and concluded that the defendants were not liable for contributory infringement because they lacked the requisite level of knowledge. It was not enough that the defendants *generally* knew that the software they provided might be used to infringe on copyrights; they also had to have *specific knowledge* of the infringement "at a time when they can use that knowledge to stop the particular infringement." Here, the companies had merely distributed free software. They had no knowledge of whether users were swapping copyrighted files and no ability to stop users from infringing activities. Further, the two defendants could not be held vicariously liable for the infringement because it was not possible for the companies to supervise or control their users' conduct.

A SIGNIFICANT DEFEAT FOR THE ENTERTAINMENT INDUSTRY

The *Grokster* case represents a significant defeat for the entertainment and recording industries. The district court's decision was appealed to the U.S. Court of Appeals for the Ninth Circuit—the same court that decided the *Napster* case—and was affirmed. The appellate court noted that "we live in a quicksilver technological environment with courts ill suited to fix the flow of Internet innovation." The court went on to find that "it is prudent for courts to exercise caution before restructuring liability theories for the purpose of addressing specific market abuses, despite their apparent present magnitude." The court also acknowledged that according to the United States Supreme Court, such matters should be left to Congress. After all, Congress has the power to promote the progress of science and the arts, and the sign of how far Congress has chosen to go with respect to this protection can come only from Congress.[b]

FOR CRITICAL ANALYSIS

On appeal, the defense compared distributing file-sharing software to selling copy machines, arguing that the courts would not hold Xerox Corporation liable simply because people frequently use its machines to make infringing copies of copyrighted material. Should different rules apply to providers of file-sharing software than to makers of copy machines or videocassette recorders, both of which can be used to infringe on copyrights? Why or why not?

a. 243 F.Supp.2d 1073 (C.D.Cal. 2003).

b. *Metro-Goldwyn-Mayer Studios, Inc. v. Grokster, Ltd.*, 380 F.3d 1154 (9th Cir. 2004).

Trade Secrets

TRADE SECRET
Information or processes that give a business an advantage over competitors that do not know the information or processes.

Some business processes and information that are not or cannot be patented, copyrighted, or trademarked are nevertheless protected against appropriation by a competitor as trade secrets. **Trade secrets** consist of customer lists, plans, research and development, pricing information, marketing techniques, production methods, and generally anything that makes an individual company unique and that would have value to a competitor.

Unlike copyright and trademark protection, protection of trade secrets extends both to ideas and to their expression. (For this reason, and because a trade secret involves no registration or filing requirements, trade secret protection may be well suited for software.) Of course, the secret formula, method, or other information must be disclosed to some persons, particularly to key employees. Businesses generally attempt to protect their trade secrets by having all employees who use the process or information agree in their contracts, or in confidentiality agreements, never to divulge it. For further information on how trade secrets can be protected, see the *Application* feature at the end of this chapter.

State and Federal Law on Trade Secrets

Under Section 757 of the *Restatement of Torts,* those who disclose or use another's trade secret, without authorization, are liable to that other party if (1) they discovered the secret by improper means, or (2) their disclosure or use constitutes a breach of a duty owed to the other party. The theft of confidential business data by industrial espionage, as when a business taps into a competitor's computer, is a theft of trade secrets without any contractual violation and is actionable in itself.

Until twenty years ago, virtually all law with respect to trade secrets was common law. In an effort to reduce the unpredictability of the common law in this area, a model act, the Uniform Trade Secrets Act, was presented to the states for adoption in 1979. Parts of this act have been adopted in more than thirty states. Typically, a state that has adopted parts of the act has adopted only those parts that encompass its own existing common law. Additionally, in 1996 Congress passed the Economic Espionage Act, which made the theft of trade secrets a federal crime. We will examine the provisions and significance of this act in Chapter 6, in the context of crimes related to business.

.on the Web The Cyberspace Law Institute offers articles and information on such topics as trade secrets at **http://www.cli.org**.

Trade Secrets in Cyberspace

The nature of new computer technology undercuts a business firm's ability to protect its confidential information, including trade secrets.[25] For instance, a dishonest employee could e-mail trade secrets in a company's computer to a competitor or a future employer. If e-mail is not an option, the employee might walk out with the information on a computer disk.

ETHICAL ISSUE 5.2

Does preventing a Web site from posting computer codes that reveal trade secrets violate free speech rights? An ongoing issue with ethical dimensions is the point at which free speech rights come into conflict with the right of copyright holders to protect their property by using encryption technology. This issue came before the California Supreme Court in 2003 in the case of *DVD Copy Control Association v. Bunner.*[26] Trade associations in the movie industry (the plaintiffs) sued an Internet Web site operator (the defendant) who had posted the code of a computer program

25. Note that the courts have even found that customers' e-mail addresses may constitute trade secrets. See *T-N-T Motorsports, Inc. v. Hennessey Motorsports, Inc.,* 965 S.W.2d 18 (Tex.App.—Hous. [1 Dist.] 1998); rehearing overruled (1998); petition dismissed (1998).
26. 31 Cal.4th 864, 75 P.3d 1, 4 Cal.Rptr.3d 69 (2003).

that cracked technology used to encrypt DVDs. This posed a significant threat to the plaintiffs because, by using the code-cracking software, users would be able to duplicate the copyrighted movies stored on the DVDs. In their suit, the plaintiffs claimed that the defendant had misappropriated trade secrets. The defendant argued that software programs designed to break encryption programs were a form of constitutionally protected speech. When the case reached the California Supreme Court, the court held that although the First Amendment applies to computer code, computer code is not a form of "pure speech" and the courts can therefore protect it to a lesser extent. The court reinstated the trial court's order that enjoined (prevented) the defendant from continuing to post the code. ■

International Protection for Intellectual Property

For many years, the United States has been a party to various international agreements relating to intellectual property rights. For example, the Paris Convention of 1883, to which about ninety countries are signatory, allows parties in one country to file for patent and trademark protection in any of the other member countries. Other international agreements include the Berne Convention and the TRIPS agreement.

THE BERNE CONVENTION

Under the Berne Convention of 1886, an international copyright agreement, if an American writes a book, every country that has signed the convention must recognize the American author's copyright in the book. Also, if a citizen of a country that has not signed the convention first publishes a book in a country that has signed, all other countries that have signed the convention must recognize that author's copyright. Copyright notice is not needed to gain protection under the Berne Convention for works published after March 1, 1989.

.on the Web The Web site of Cornell University's Legal Information Institute includes the texts of the Berne Convention and other international treaties on copyright issues at **http://www.law.cornell.edu/topics/copyright.html**.

This convention and other international agreements have given some protection to intellectual property on a worldwide level. None of them, however, has been as significant and far reaching in scope as the agreement on Trade-Related Aspects of Intellectual Property Rights, or, more simply, TRIPS.

THE TRIPS AGREEMENT

Representatives from over one hundred nations signed the TRIPS agreement in 1994. The agreement established, for the first time, standards for the international protection of intellectual property rights, including patents, trademarks, and copyrights for movies, computer programs, books, and music. Prior to the agreement, U.S. sellers of intellectual property in the international market faced difficulties because many other countries had no laws protecting intellectual property rights or failed to enforce existing laws. To address this problem, the TRIPS agreement provides that each member country must include in its domestic laws broad intellectual property rights and effective remedies (including civil and criminal penalties) for violations of those rights.

Generally, the TRIPS agreement provides that each member nation must not discriminate (in the administration, regulation, or adjudication of intellectual property rights) against foreign owners of such rights. In other words, a member nation cannot give its own nationals (citizens) favorable treatment without offering the same treatment to nationals of all member countries. For instance, if a U.S. software manufacturer brings a suit for the infringement of intellectual property rights under a member nation's national laws, the U.S. manufacturer is entitled to receive the same treatment as a domestic manufacturer. Each member nation must also ensure that legal procedures are available for parties who wish to bring actions for infringement of intellectual property rights. Additionally, a related document established a mechanism for settling disputes among member nations.

Particular provisions of the TRIPS agreement relate to patent, trademark, and copyright protection for intellectual property. The agreement specifically provides copyright protection for computer programs by stating that compilations of data, databases, and other materials are "intellectual creations" and that they are to be protected as copyrightable works. Other provisions relate to trade secrets and the rental of computer programs and cinematographic works.

APPLICATION How Can You Protect Your Trade Secrets?*

Most successful businesses have trade secrets. The law protects trade secrets indefinitely, provided that the information is not generally known, is kept a secret, and has commercial value. Sometimes, of course, a business needs to disclose secret information to a party in the course of conducting business. For example, a company may need to hire a consultant to revamp a computer system, an engineer to design a manufacturing system, or a marketing firm to implement a sales program. All of these individuals may need access to some of the company's trade secrets. One way to protect against the unauthorized disclosure of such information is through confidentiality agreements.

Confidentiality Agreements

In a confidentiality agreement, one party promises not to divulge information about the other party to anyone else or to use the other party's confidential information for his or her own benefit. Confidentiality agreements are often included in licensing and employment contracts, but they can also be separate contracts. The key is to make sure that the agreement adequately protects the trade secrets and applies to any related transactions between the parties. For instance, if you execute a separate confidentiality agreement with a marketing firm, you need to make sure that it refers to any other contracts you have made with that firm prior to the confidentiality agreement. Also, subsequent contracts with the firm should either refer back to the confidentiality agreement or include a new confidentiality provision.

Defining the Scope of the Agreement

Confidentiality agreements must be reasonable. Businesspersons should consider what information needs to be protected and for how long. Make certain to define what you mean by *confidential information* in the agreement. Do you want to protect just your customer list or all financial, technical, and other business information? Think ahead, cover the bases, and be specific.

The duration of the agreement usually depends on the nature of the information. Very important secret information should remain confidential for a longer time than less important secrets. Sometimes, as with an advertising campaign, the time period for confidentiality may be self-evident (if the campaign ends in six months, for example). Tailor the agreement to your needs as much as possible. If the party to whom you are disclosing information will no longer need the information after a certain date—such as when the project is completed—include a provision requiring the return of confidential information after that date. This will alleviate concerns that your confidential trade secrets might later fall into the hands of a stranger.

* This *Application* is not meant to substitute for the services of an attorney who is licensed to practice law in your state.

Checklist for the Owner of Trade Secrets

1. Determine what your trade secrets are and who may need access to them.
2. Make sure that confidentiality agreements define, in an all-inclusive manner, what information should be considered confidential.
3. Specify a time period that is reasonable under the circumstances.
4. Identify the agreements to which the confidentiality provisions apply.
5. Require that the confidential materials be returned to you.

KEY TERMS

copyright 154
cyber mark 148
cybersquatting 149
distributed network 159
domain name 149
intellectual property 141
meta tags 150
patent 151
peer-to-peer (P2P) networking 159
service mark 148
trade dress 148
trade name 148
trade secret 163
trademark 143

CHAPTER SUMMARY Intellectual Property

Trademarks and Related Property (See pages 143–148.)	1. A *trademark* is a distinctive mark, motto, device, or emblem that a manufacturer stamps, prints, or otherwise affixes to the goods it produces so that they can be identified on the market and their origin vouched for. 2. The major federal statutes protecting trademarks and related property are the Lanham Act of 1946 and the Federal Trademark Dilution Act of 1995. Generally, to be protected, a trademark must be sufficiently distinctive from all competing trademarks. 3. *Trademark infringement* occurs when one uses a mark that is the same as, or confusingly similar to, the protected trademark, service mark, trade name, or trade dress of another without permission when marketing goods or services.
Cyber Marks (See pages 148–151.)	A *cyber mark* is a trademark in cyberspace. Trademark infringement in cyberspace occurs when one person uses, in a domain name or in meta tags, a name that is the same as, or confusingly similar to, the protected mark of another.
Patents (See pages 151–154.)	1. A *patent* is a grant from the government that gives an inventor the exclusive right to make, use, and sell an invention for a period of twenty years from the date of filing the application for a patent. To be patentable, an invention (or a discovery, process, or design) must be genuine, novel, useful, and not obvious in light of current technology. Computer software may be patented. 2. *Patent infringement* occurs when one uses or sells another's patented design, product, or process without the patent owner's permission.
Copyrights (See pages 154–162.)	1. A *copyright* is an intangible property right granted by federal statute to the author or originator of certain literary or artistic productions. Computer software may be copyrighted. 2. *Copyright infringement* occurs whenever the form or expression of an idea is copied without the permission of the copyright holder. An exception applies if the copying is deemed a "fair use." 3. Copyrights are governed by the Copyright Act of 1976, as amended. To protect copyrights in digital information, Congress passed the No Electronic Theft Act of 1997 and the Digital Millennium Copyright Act of 1998. 4. Technology that allows users to share files via the Internet on distributed networks often raises copyright infringement issues. Companies that provide file-sharing software to users have been held liable in the past for contributory and vicarious copyright liability. The courts, however, are having difficulty applying these doctrines of liability to new file-sharing technologies.
Trade Secrets (See pages 163–164.)	*Trade secrets* include customer lists, plans, research and development, and pricing information, for example. Trade secrets are protected under the common law and, in some states, under statutory law against misappropriation by competitors. The Economic Espionage Act of 1996 made the theft of trade secrets a federal crime (see Chapter 6).

CHAPTER SUMMARY Intellectual Property—Continued

International Protection for Intellectual Property (See pages 164–165.)	Various international agreements provide international protection for intellectual property. A landmark agreement is the 1994 agreement on Trade-Related Aspects of Intellectual Property Rights (TRIPS), which provides for enforcement procedures in all countries signatory to the agreement.

FOR REVIEW

Answers for the even-numbered questions in this For Review *section can be found in Appendix I at the end of this text.*

1. What is intellectual property?
2. Why are trademarks and patents protected by the law?
3. What laws protect authors' rights in the works they generate?
4. What are trade secrets, and what laws offer protection for this form of intellectual property?
5. What steps have been taken to protect intellectual property rights in today's digital age?

QUESTIONS AND CASE PROBLEMS

5–1. **Copyright Infringement.** In which of the following situations would a court likely hold Maruta liable for copyright infringement?

(a) At the library, Maruta photocopies ten pages from a scholarly journal relating to a topic on which she is writing a term paper.

(b) Maruta makes leather handbags and sells them in her small leather shop. She advertises her handbags as "Vutton handbags," hoping that customers might mistakenly assume that they were made by Vuitton, the well-known maker of high-quality luggage and handbags.

(c) Maruta owns a video store. She purchases one copy of all the latest videos from various video manufacturers. Then, using blank videotapes, she makes copies to rent or sell to her customers.

(d) Maruta teaches Latin American history at a small university. She has a videocassette recorder and frequently tapes television programs relating to Latin America. She then takes the videos to her classroom so that her students can watch them.

5–2. **Patent Infringement.** John and Andrew Doney invented a hard-bearing device for balancing rotors. Although they registered their invention with the U.S. Patent and Trademark Office, it was never used as an automobile wheel balancer. Some time later, Exetron Corp. produced an automobile wheel balancer that used a hard-bearing device with a support plate similar to that of the Doneys. Given that the Doneys had not used their device for automobile wheel balancing, does Exetron's use of a similar hard-bearing device infringe on the Doneys' patent?

5–3. **Trademark Infringement.** Elvis Presley Enterprises, Inc. (EPE), owns all of the trademarks of the Elvis Presley estate. None of these marks is registered for use in the restaurant business. Barry Capece registered "The Velvet Elvis" as a service mark for a restaurant and tavern with the U.S. Patent and Trademark Office. Capece opened a nightclub called "The Velvet Elvis" with a menu, decor, advertising, and promotional events that evoked Elvis Presley and his music. EPE filed a suit in a federal district court against Capece and others, claiming, among other things, that "The Velvet Elvis" service mark infringed on EPE's trademarks. During the trial, witnesses testified that they thought the bar was associated with Elvis Presley. Should Capece be ordered to stop using "The Velvet Elvis" mark? Why or why not? [*Elvis Presley Enterprises, Inc. v. Capece,* 141 F.3d 188 (5th Cir. 1998)]

5–4. **Trademark Infringement.** A&H Sportswear, Inc., a swimsuit maker, obtained a trademark for its MIRACLESUIT in 1992. The MIRACLESUIT design makes the wearer appear slimmer. The MIRACLESUIT was widely advertised and discussed in the media. The MIRACLESUIT was also sold for a brief time in the Victoria's Secret (VS) catalogue, which is published by Victoria's Secret Catalogue, Inc. In 1993, Victoria's Secret Stores, Inc., began selling a cleavage-enhancing bra, which was named THE MIRACLE BRA and for which a trademark was obtained. The next year, THE MIRACLE BRA swimwear debuted in the VS catalogue and stores. A&H filed a suit in a federal district court against VS Stores and VS Catalogue, alleging in part that THE MIRACLE BRA mark, when applied to swimwear, infringed on the MIRACLESUIT mark. A&H argued that there was a "possibility of confusion" between the marks. The VS entities contended that the appropriate standard was "likelihood of confusion" and that, in this case, there was no likelihood of confusion. In whose favor will the court rule, and why? [*A&H Sportswear, Inc. v. Victoria's Secret Stores, Inc.,* 166 F.3d 197 (3d Cir. 1999)]

CASE PROBLEM WITH SAMPLE ANSWER

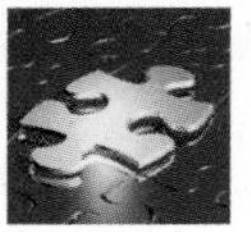

5–5. In 1999, Steve and Pierce Thumann and their father, Fred, created Spider Webs, Ltd., a partnership, to, according to Steve, "develop Internet address names." Spider Webs registered nearly two thousand Internet domain names for an average of $70 each, including the names of cities, the names of buildings, names related to a business or trade (such as air conditioning or plumbing), and the names of famous companies. It offered many of the names for sale on its Web site and through eBay.com. Spider Webs registered the domain name "ERNESTANDJULIOGALLO.COM" in Spider Webs' name. E. and J. Gallo Winery filed a suit against Spider Webs, alleging, in part, violations of the Anticybersquatting Consumer Protection Act. Gallo asked the court for, among other things, statutory damages. Gallo also sought to have the domain name at issue transferred to Gallo. During the suit, Spider Webs published anticorporate articles and opinions, and discussions of the suit, at the URL "ERNESTANDJULIOGALLO.COM." Should the court rule in Gallo's favor? Why or why not? [*E. & J. Gallo Winery v. Spider Webs, Ltd.,* 129 F.Supp.2d 1033 (S.D.Tex. 2001)]

After you have answered this problem, compare your answer with the sample answer given on the Web site that accompanies this text. Go to http://blt.westbuslaw.com, select "Chapter 5," and click on "Case Problem with Sample Answer."

5–6. **Trade Secrets.** Four Pillars Enterprise Co. is a Taiwanese company owned by Pin Yen Yang. Avery Dennison, Inc., a U.S. corporation, is one of Four Pillars' chief competitors in the manufacture of adhesives. In 1989, Victor Lee, an Avery employee, met Yang and Yang's daughter Hwei Chen. They agreed to pay Lee $25,000 a year to serve as a consultant to Four Pillars. Over the next eight years, Lee supplied the Yangs with confidential Avery reports, including information that Four Pillars used to make a new adhesive that had been developed by Avery. The Federal Bureau of Investigation (FBI) confronted Lee, and he agreed to cooperate in an operation to catch the Yangs. When Lee next met the Yangs, he showed them documents provided by the FBI. The documents bore "confidential" stamps, and Lee said that they were Avery's confidential property. The FBI arrested the Yangs with the documents in their possession. The Yangs and Four Pillars were charged with, among other crimes, the attempted theft of trade secrets. The defendants argued in part that it was impossible for them to have committed this crime because the documents were not actually trade secrets. Should the court acquit them? Why or why not? [*United States v. Yang,* 281 F.3d 534 (6th Cir. 2002)]

5–7. **Patent Infringement.** As a cattle rancher in Nebraska, Gerald Gohl used handheld searchlights to find and help calving animals (animals giving birth) in harsh blizzard conditions. Gohl thought that it would be more helpful to have a portable searchlight mounted on the outside of a vehicle and remotely controlled. He and Al Gebhardt developed and patented practical applications of this idea—the Golight and the wireless, remote-controlled Radio Ray, which could rotate 360 degrees—and formed Golight, Inc., to make and market these products. In 1997, Wal-Mart Stores, Inc., began selling a portable, wireless, remote-controlled searchlight that was identical to the Radio Ray except for a stop piece that prevented the light from rotating more than 351 degrees. Golight sent Wal-Mart a letter, claiming that its device infringed Golight's patent. Wal-Mart sold its remaining inventory of the devices and stopped carrying the product. Golight filed a suit in a federal district court against Wal-Mart, alleging patent infringement. How should the court rule? Explain. [*Golight, Inc. v. Wal-Mart Stores, Inc.,* 355 F.3d 1327 (Fed. Cir. 2004)]

A QUESTION OF ETHICS

5–8. Texaco, Inc., conducts research to develop new products and technology in the petroleum industry. As part of the research, Texaco employees routinely photocopy articles from scientific and medical journals without the permission of the copyright holders. The publishers of the journals brought a copyright infringement action against Texaco in a federal district court. The court ruled that the copying was not a fair use. The U.S. Court of Appeals for the Second Circuit affirmed this ruling "primarily because the dominant purpose of the use is 'archival'—to assemble a set of papers for future reference, thereby serving the same purpose for which additional subscriptions are normally sold, or . . . for which photocopying licenses may be obtained." [*American Geophysical Union v. Texaco, Inc.,* 37 F.3d 881 (2d Cir. 1994)]

1. Do you agree with the court's decision that the copying was not a fair use? Why or why not?
2. Do you think that the law should impose a duty on every person to obtain permission to photocopy or reproduce any article under any circumstance? What would be some of the implications of such a duty for society? Discuss fully.

FOR CRITICAL ANALYSIS

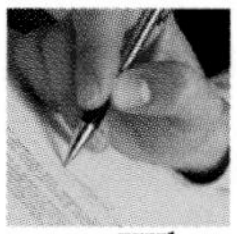

5–9. Patent protection in the United States is granted to the first person to invent a given product or process, even though another person may be the first to file for a patent on the same product or process. What are the advantages of this patenting procedure? Can you think of any disadvantages? Explain.

VIDEO QUESTION

DIGITAL VIDEO LIBRARY
WEST LEGAL STUDIES IN BUSINESS

5–10. Go to this text's Web site at **http://blt.westbuslaw.com** and select "Chapter 5." Click on "Video Questions" and view the video titled *Jerk.* Then answer the following questions.

1. In the video, Navin (Steve Martin) creates a special handle for Mr. Fox's (Bill Macy's) glasses. Can Navin obtain

a patent or a copyright protecting his invention? Explain your answer.

2. Suppose that after Navin legally protects his idea, Fox steals it and decides to develop it for himself, without Navin's permission. Has Fox committed infringement? If so, what kind: trademark, patent, or copyright?
3. Suppose that after Navin legally protects his idea, he realizes he doesn't have the funds to mass-produce the special glasses handle. Navin therefore agrees to allow Fox to manufacture the product. Has Navin granted Fox a license? Explain.
4. Assume that Navin is able to manufacture his invention. What might Navin do to ensure that his product is identifiable and can be distinguished from other products on the market?

INTERNET EXERCISES

Go to the *Business Law Today: The Essentials* home page at **http://blt.westbuslaw.com**, select "Chapter 5," and click on "Internet Exercises." There you will find the following Internet research exercises that you can perform to learn more about topics covered in this chapter.

Activity 5–1: LEGAL PERSPECTIVE—Unwarranted Legal Threats

Activity 5–2: TECHNOLOGICAL PERSPECTIVE—File-Sharing

Activity 5–3: MANAGEMENT PERSPECTIVE—Protecting Intellectual Property across Borders

BEFORE THE TEST

Go to the *Business Law Today: The Essentials* home page at **http://blt.westbuslaw.com**, select "Chapter 5," and click on "Interactive Quizzes." You will find at least twenty interactive questions relating to this chapter.

CHAPTER 6

Criminal Law and Cyber Crimes

"No State shall . . . deprive any person of life, liberty, or property without due process of law, nor deny to any person within its jurisdiction the equal protection of the laws."

Fourteenth Amendment to the U.S. Constitution, July 28, 1868

CHAPTER OUTLINE

- CIVIL LAW AND CRIMINAL LAW
- CLASSIFICATION OF CRIMES
- CRIMINAL LIABILITY
- CORPORATE CRIMINAL LIABILITY
- TYPES OF CRIMES
- DEFENSES TO CRIMINAL LIABILITY
- CONSTITUTIONAL SAFEGUARDS AND CRIMINAL PROCEDURES
- CYBER CRIME

LEARNING OBJECTIVES

After reading this chapter, you should be able to answer the following questions:

1. What two elements must exist before a person can be held liable for a crime? Can a corporation commit crimes?
2. What are five broad categories of crimes? What is white-collar crime?
3. What defenses might be raised by criminal defendants to avoid liability for criminal acts?
4. What constitutional safeguards exist to protect persons accused of crimes? What are the basic steps in the criminal process?
5. What is cyber crime? What laws apply to crimes committed in cyberspace?

Various sanctions are used to bring about a society in which individuals engaging in business can compete and flourish. These sanctions include damages for various types of tortious conduct (as discussed in Chapter 4), damages for breach of contract (to be discussed in Chapter 9), and the equitable remedies discussed in Chapter 1. Additional sanctions are imposed under criminal law. Many statutes regulating business provide for criminal as well as civil sanctions. Therefore, criminal law joins civil law as an important element in the legal environment of business.

In this chapter, following a brief summary of the major differences between criminal and civil law, we look at how crimes are classified and what elements must be present for criminal liability to exist. We then examine various categories of crime, the defenses that can be raised to avoid liability for criminal actions, and criminal procedural law. Criminal procedural law attempts to ensure that a criminal defendant's right to "due process of law" is enforced. This right is guaranteed by the Fourteenth Amendment to the U.S. Constitution, as stated in the chapter-opening quotation.

Since the advent of computer networks and, more recently, the Internet, new types of crimes or new variations of traditional crimes have been committed in cyberspace. For that reason, they are often referred to as **cyber crime.** Generally, cyber crime refers more to the way particular crimes are committed than to a new category of crimes. We devote the concluding pages of this chapter to a discussion of this increasingly significant area of criminal activity.

CYBER CRIME
A crime that occurs online, in the virtual community of the Internet, as opposed to the physical world.

Civil Law and Criminal Law

Remember from Chapter 1 that *civil law* spells out the duties that exist between persons or between persons and their governments, excluding the duty not to commit crimes. Contract law, for example, is part of civil law. The whole body of tort law, which deals with the infringement by one person on the legally recognized rights of another, is also an area of civil law.

Criminal law, in contrast, has to do with crime. A **crime** can be defined as a wrong against society proclaimed in a statute and, if committed, punishable by society through fines and/or imprisonment—and, in some cases, death. As mentioned in Chapter 1, because crimes are *offenses against society as a whole,* they are prosecuted by a public official, such as a district attorney (D.A.), not by victims.

CRIME
A wrong against society proclaimed in a statute and, if committed, punishable by society through fines and/or imprisonment—and, in some cases, death.

Key Differences between Civil Law and Criminal Law

Because the state has extensive resources at its disposal when prosecuting criminal cases, there are numerous procedural safeguards to protect the rights of defendants. One of these safeguards is the higher burden of proof that applies in a criminal case. As you can see in Exhibit 6–1 on the next page, which summarizes some of the key differences between civil law and criminal law, in a civil case the plaintiff usually must prove his or her case by a *preponderance of the evidence.* Under this standard, the plaintiff must convince the court that, based on the evidence presented by both parties, it is more likely than not that the plaintiff's allegation is true.

In a criminal case, however, the state must prove its case **beyond a reasonable doubt.** For the defendant to be convicted, *every* juror in a criminal case must be convinced, beyond a reasonable doubt, that the defendant has committed each essential element of the offense with which she or he is charged. In contrast, in civil cases typically only three-fourths of the jurors need to agree that it is more likely than not that the defendant caused the plaintiff's harm. In a criminal case, the verdict normally must be unanimous. The higher burden of proof in criminal cases reflects a fundamental social value—the belief that it is worse to convict an innocent individual than to let a guilty person go free. We will look at other safeguards later in the chapter, in the context of criminal procedure.

BEYOND A REASONABLE DOUBT
The burden of proof used in criminal cases. If there is any reasonable doubt that a criminal defendant did not commit the crime with which she or he has been charged, then the verdict must be "not guilty."

EXHIBIT 6–1 KEY DIFFERENCES BETWEEN CIVIL AND CRIMINAL LAW

ISSUE	CIVIL LAW	CRIMINAL LAW
Party who brings suit	Person who suffered harm	The state
Burden of proof	Preponderance of the evidence	Beyond a reasonable doubt
Verdict	Three-fourths majority (typically)	Unanimous
Remedy	Damages to compensate for the harm or a decree to achieve an equitable result	Punishment (fine, imprisonment, or death)

CIVIL LIABILITY FOR CRIMINAL ACTS

Those who commit crimes may be subject to both civil and criminal liability. ■ EXAMPLE 6.1 Joe is walking down the street, minding his own business, when suddenly a person attacks him. In the ensuing struggle, the attacker stabs Joe several times, seriously injuring him. A police officer restrains and arrests the wrongdoer. In this situation, the attacker may be subject both to criminal prosecution by the state and to a tort lawsuit brought by Joe. ■ Exhibit 6–2 illustrates how the same act can result in both a tort action and a criminal action against the wrongdoer.

Classification of Crimes

FELONY
A crime—such as arson, murder, rape, or robbery—that carries the most severe sanctions, which range from more than one year in a state or federal prison to the death penalty.

MISDEMEANOR
A lesser crime than a felony, punishable by a fine or incarceration in jail for up to one year.

Depending on their degree of seriousness, crimes are classified as felonies or misdemeanors. **Felonies** are serious crimes punishable by death or by imprisonment in a federal or state penitentiary for more than a year. The Model Penal Code[1] provides for four degrees of felony: (1) capital offenses, for which the maximum penalty is death; (2) first degree felonies, punishable by a maximum penalty of life imprisonment; (3) second degree felonies, punishable by a maximum of ten years' imprisonment; and (4) third degree felonies, punishable by a maximum of five years' imprisonment.

Under federal law and in most states, any crime that is not a felony is considered a **misdemeanor.** Misdemeanors are crimes punishable by a fine or by confinement for up to a year. If incarcerated (imprisoned), the guilty party goes to a local jail instead of a prison. Disorderly conduct and trespass are common misdemeanors. Some states have different classes of misdemeanors. For example, in Illinois misdemeanors are either Class A (confinement for up to a year), Class B (not more than six months), or Class C (not more than thirty days). Whether a crime is a felony or a misdemeanor can also determine whether the case is tried in a magistrate's court (for example, by a justice of the peace) or in a general trial court.

1. The American Law Institute issued the Official Draft of the Model Penal Code in 1962. The Model Penal Code is not a uniform code. Uniformity of criminal law among the states is not as important as uniformity in other areas of the law. Types of crimes vary with local circumstances, and it is appropriate that punishments vary accordingly. The Model Penal Code contains four parts: (1) general provisions, (2) definitions of special crimes, (3) provisions concerning treatment and corrections (such as incarceration in a prison or a jail), and (4) provisions on the organization of corrections.

EXHIBIT 6–2 TORT LAWSUIT AND CRIMINAL PROSECUTION FOR THE SAME ACT

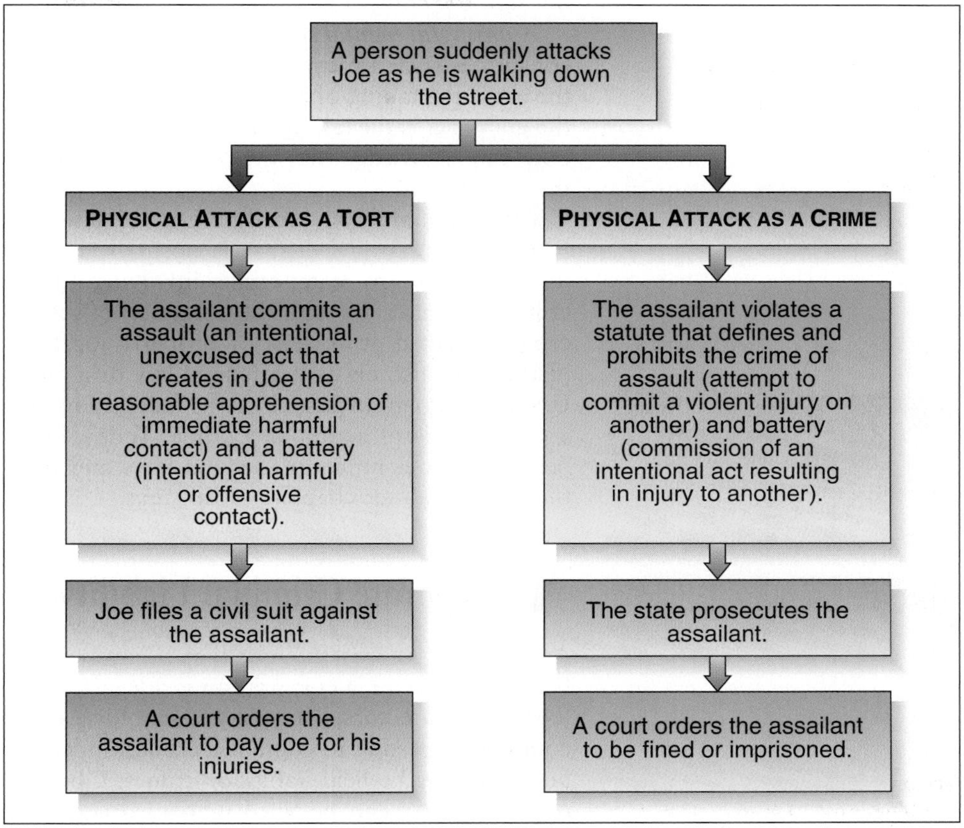

PETTY OFFENSE
In criminal law, the least serious kind of criminal offense, such as a traffic or building-code violation.

In most jurisdictions, **petty offenses** are considered to be a subset of misdemeanors. Petty offenses are minor violations, such as jaywalking or violations of building codes. Even for petty offenses, however, a guilty party can be put in jail for a few days, fined, or both, depending on state or local law.

Criminal Liability

Two elements must exist simultaneously for a person to be convicted of a crime: (1) the performance of a prohibited act and (2) a specified state of mind or intent on the part of the actor. Every criminal statute prohibits certain behavior. Most crimes require an act of *commission;* that is, a person must *do* something in order to be accused of a crime.[2] In some instances, an act of *omission* can be a crime, but only when a person has a legal duty to perform the omitted act. Failure to file a tax return is an example of an omission that is a crime.

The *guilty act* requirement is based on one of the premises of criminal law—that a person is punished for harm done to society. Thinking about killing someone or about

2. Called the *actus reus* (pronounced *ak*-tuhs *ray*-uhs), or "guilty act."

stealing a car may be wrong, but the thoughts do no harm until they are translated into action. Of course, a person can be punished for attempting murder or robbery, but normally only if he or she took substantial steps toward the criminal objective.

A *wrongful mental state*[3] is generally required to establish criminal liability. What constitutes such a mental state varies according to the wrongful action. For murder, the act is the taking of a life, and the mental state is the intent to take life. For theft, the guilty act is the taking of another person's property, and the mental state involves both the knowledge that the property belongs to another and the intent to deprive the owner of it.

Criminal liability typically arises for actions that violate state criminal statutes. Federal criminal jurisdiction is normally limited to crimes that occur outside the jurisdiction of any state, crimes involving interstate commerce or communications, crimes that interfere with the operation of the federal government or its agents, and crimes directed at citizens or property located outside the United States. Federal jurisdiction also exists if a federal law or a federal government agency (such as the U.S. Department of Justice or the federal Environmental Protection Agency) defines a certain type of action as a crime. Today, businesspersons are subject to criminal penalties under numerous federal laws and regulations. We will examine many of these laws in later chapters of this text.

.on the Web Many state criminal codes are now online. To find your state's code, go to

http://www.findlaw.com

and select "State" under the link to "US Laws: Cases and Codes."

Corporate Criminal Liability

At one time, it was thought that a corporation could not incur criminal liability because, although a corporation is a legal person, it can act only through its agents (corporate directors, officers, and employees). Therefore, the corporate entity itself could not "intend" to commit a crime. Under modern criminal law, however, a corporation may be held liable for crimes. Obviously, corporations cannot be imprisoned, but they can be fined or denied certain legal privileges (such as a license). Today, corporations are normally liable for the crimes committed by their agents and employees within the course and scope of their employment.

Corporate directors and officers are personally liable for the crimes they commit, regardless of whether the crimes were committed for their personal benefit or on the corporation's behalf. Additionally, corporate directors and officers may be held liable for the actions of employees under their supervision. Under what has become known as the "responsible corporate officer" doctrine, a court may impose criminal liability on a corporate officer regardless of whether she or he participated in, directed, or even knew about a given criminal violation.

■ **EXAMPLE 6.2** In *United States v. Park,*[4] the chief executive officer of a national supermarket chain was held personally liable for sanitation violations in corporate warehouses, in which the food was exposed to contamination by rodents. The United States Supreme Court imposed personal liability on the corporate officer not because he intended the crime or even knew about it but because he was in a "responsible relationship" to the corporation and had the power to prevent the violation. ■ Since the *Park* decision, courts have applied this "responsible corporate officer" doctrine on a number of occasions to hold corporate officers liable for their employees' statutory violations. The following case illustrates that corporate offi-

3. Called the *mens rea* (pronounced mehns *ray*-uh), or "evil intent."

4. 421 U.S. 658, 95 S.Ct. 1903, 44 L.Ed.2d 489 (1975).

cers and supervisors who oversee operations causing environmental harm may be held liable under the criminal provisions of environmental statutes.

CASE 6.1 United States v. Hanousek

United States Court of Appeals,
Ninth Circuit, 1999.
176 F.3d 1116.
http://www.ca9.uscourts.gov/ca9/newopinions.nsf[a]

FACTS Edward Hanousek worked for Pacific & Arctic Railway and Navigation Company (P&A) as a roadmaster of the White Pass & Yukon Railroad in Alaska. Hanousek was responsible "for every detail of the safe and efficient maintenance and construction of track, structures and marine facilities of the entire railroad," including special projects. One project was a rock quarry, known as "6-mile," above the Skagway River. Next to the quarry, and just beneath the surface, ran a high-pressure oil pipeline owned by Pacific & Arctic Pipeline, Inc., P&A's sister company. When the quarry's backhoe operator punctured the pipeline, an estimated 1,000 to 5,000 gallons of oil were discharged into the river. Hanousek was charged with, among other things, negligently discharging a harmful quantity of oil into a navigable water of the United States in violation of the criminal provisions of the Clean Water Act (CWA). After a trial in a federal district court, a jury convicted Hanousek, and the court imposed a sentence of six months' imprisonment, six months in a halfway house, six months' supervised release, and a fine of $5,000. Hanousek appealed to the U.S. Court of Appeals for the Ninth Circuit, arguing in part that the statute under which he was convicted violated his right to due process because he was not aware of what the CWA required.

a. The U.S. Court of Appeals for the Ninth Circuit maintains this Web site. Click on the "OPINIONS BY DATE" link. From that page, click on the "1999" icon, and when the menu opens, click on "March." Scroll down and click on "USA V HANOUSEK" to access the case.

ISSUE Were Hanousek's due process rights violated?

DECISION No. The U.S. Court of Appeals for the Ninth Circuit affirmed Hanousek's conviction.

REASON A corporate manager who has responsibility for operations with the potential to cause harm can be held criminally liable for harm that results even if he or she does not actually know of the specific statute under which liability may be imposed. The CWA is public-welfare legislation, which "is designed to protect the public from potentially harmful or injurious items and may render criminal a type of conduct that a reasonable person should know is subject to stringent public regulation." The court stated,"[I]t is well established that a public welfare statute may subject a person to criminal liability for his or her ordinary negligence without violating due process." When "dangerous or deleterious [harmful] devices or products or obnoxious waste materials are involved, the probability of regulation is so great that anyone who is aware that he is in possession of them or dealing with them must be presumed to be aware of the regulation." Hanousek knew about the pipeline and the danger that a puncture would pose. "Therefore, Hanousek should have been alerted to the probability of strict regulation."

WHY IS THIS CASE IMPORTANT? *This case illustrates the liability that corporate managers and others who take responsibility for corporate operations might face if those operations cause harm to others or, as in this case, to the environment. It underscores the need for corporate managers to become aware of the laws that might come into play during any operations for which the managers assume responsibility.*

Types of Crimes

The number of acts that are defined as criminal is nearly endless. Federal, state, and local laws provide for the classification and punishment of hundreds of thousands of different criminal acts. Traditionally, though, crimes have been grouped into five broad categories, or types: violent crime (crimes against persons), property crime, public order crime, white-collar crime, and organized crime. Cyber crime—which consists of crimes committed in cyberspace with the use of computers—is, as mentioned earlier in this chapter, less a category of crime than a new way to commit crime. We will examine cyber crime later in this chapter.

VIOLENT CRIME

ROBBERY
The act of forcefully and unlawfully taking personal property of any value from another. Force or intimidation is usually necessary for an act of theft to be considered a robbery.

Crimes against persons, because they cause others to suffer harm or death, are referred to as *violent crimes*. Murder is a violent crime. So is sexual assault, or rape. Assault and battery, which were discussed in Chapter 4 in the context of tort law, are also classified as violent crimes. **Robbery**—defined as the taking of money, personal property, or any other article of value from a person by means of force or fear—is also a violent crime. Typically, states have more severe penalties for *aggravated robbery*—robbery with the use of a deadly weapon.

Each of these violent crimes is further classified by degree, depending on the circumstances surrounding the criminal act. These circumstances include the intent of the person committing the crime, whether a weapon was used, and (in cases other than murder) the level of pain and suffering experienced by the victim.

PROPERTY CRIME

The most common type of criminal activity is property crime—crimes in which the goal of the offender is some form of economic gain or the damaging of property. Robbery is a form of property crime, as well as a violent crime, because the offender seeks to gain the property of another. We look here at a number of other crimes that fall within the general category of property crime.

BURGLARY
The unlawful entry or breaking into a building with the intent to commit a felony. (Some state statutes expand this to include the intent to commit any crime.)

Burglary Traditionally, **burglary** was defined under the common law as breaking and entering the dwelling of another at night with the intent to commit a felony. Originally, the definition was aimed at protecting an individual's home and its occupants. Most state statutes have eliminated some of the requirements found in the common law definition. The time at which the breaking and entering occurs, for example, is usually immaterial. State statutes frequently omit the element of breaking, and some states do not require that the building be a dwelling. Aggravated burglary, which is defined as burglary with the use of a deadly weapon, burglary of a dwelling, or both, incurs a greater penalty.

LARCENY
The wrongful taking and carrying away of another person's personal property with the intent to permanently deprive the owner of the property. Some states classify larceny as either grand or petit, depending on the property's value.

Larceny Any person who wrongfully or fraudulently takes and carries away another person's personal property is guilty of **larceny.** Larceny includes the fraudulent intent to deprive an owner permanently of property. Many business-related larcenies entail fraudulent conduct. Whereas robbery involves force or fear, larceny does not. Therefore, picking pockets is larceny. Similarly, taking company products and supplies home for personal use, if one is not authorized to do so, is larceny.

In most states, the definition of property that is subject to larceny statutes has expanded. Stealing computer programs may constitute larceny even though the "property" consists of magnetic impulses. Stealing computer time can also constitute larceny. So, too, can the theft of natural gas. Trade secrets can be subject to larceny statutes. Obtaining another's phone-card number and then using that number, without authorization, to place long-distance calls is a form of property theft. These types of larceny are covered by "theft of services" statutes in many jurisdictions.

The common law distinguishes between grand and petit larceny depending on the value of the property taken. Many states have abolished this distinction, but in those that have not, grand larceny is a felony and petit larceny, a misdemeanor.

Obtaining Goods by False Pretenses It is a criminal act to obtain goods by means of false pretenses—for example, buying groceries with a check, knowing that one has insufficient funds to cover it. Statutes dealing with such illegal activities vary widely from state to state.

Receiving Stolen Goods It is a crime to receive stolen goods. The recipient of such goods need not know the true identity of the owner or the thief. All that is necessary is that the recipient knows or should have known that the goods are stolen, which implies an intent to deprive the owner of those goods.

ARSON
The intentional burning of another's dwelling. Some statutes have expanded this to include any real property regardless of ownership and the destruction of property by other means—for example, by explosion.

Arson The willful and malicious burning of a building (and in some states, personal property) owned by another is the crime of **arson.** At common law, arson traditionally applied only to burning down another person's house. The law was designed to protect human life. Today, arson statutes have been extended to cover the destruction of any building, regardless of ownership, by fire or explosion.

Every state has a special statute that covers a person's burning a building for the purpose of collecting insurance. ■ EXAMPLE 6.3 If Smith owns an insured apartment building that is falling apart and sets fire to it himself or pays someone else to do so, he is guilty not only of arson but also of defrauding insurers, which is an attempted larceny. ■ Of course, the insurer need not pay the claim when insurance fraud is proved.

FORGERY
The fraudulent making or altering of any writing in a way that changes the legal rights and liabilities of another.

Forgery The fraudulent making or altering of any writing in a way that changes the legal rights and liabilities of another is **forgery.** If, without authorization, Severson signs Bennett's name to the back of a check made out to Bennett, Severson is committing forgery. Forgery also includes changing trademarks, falsifying public records, counterfeiting, and altering a legal document.

PUBLIC ORDER CRIME

Historically, societies have always outlawed activities that are considered to be contrary to public values and morals. Today, the most common public order crimes include public drunkenness, prostitution, gambling, and illegal drug use. These crimes are sometimes referred to as victimless crimes because they normally harm only the offender. From a broader perspective, however, they are deemed detrimental to society as a whole because they might create an environment that gives rise to property and violent crimes. (Is swearing in public a crime? See this chapter's *Letter of the Law* feature on the next page for a discussion of this question.)

WHITE-COLLAR CRIME

WHITE-COLLAR CRIME
Nonviolent crime committed by individuals or corporations to obtain a personal or business advantage.

Crimes that typically occur only in the business context are commonly referred to as **white-collar crimes.** Although there is no official definition of white-collar crime, the term is popularly used to mean an illegal act or series of acts committed by an individual or business entity using some nonviolent means. Usually, this kind of crime is committed in the course of a legitimate occupation. Corporate crimes fall into this category.

EMBEZZLEMENT
The fraudulent appropriation of funds or other property by a person to whom the funds or property has been entrusted.

Embezzlement When a person entrusted with another person's property or money fraudulently appropriates it, **embezzlement** occurs. Typically, embezzlement involves an employee who steals funds. Banks face this problem, and so do a number of businesses in which corporate officers or accountants "jimmy" the books to cover up

LETTER OF THE LAW The Case of the "Cussing Canoeist"

Timothy Boomer, then a twenty-eight-year-old engineer, went on a swearing rampage when his canoe tipped over on the Rifle River in Michigan. Others heard the swearing, including a couple and their two children, and a sheriff, who wrote him a ticket for violating an 1897 Michigan law that banned cursing in front of women and children. Specifically, the law made it illegal for anyone to use indecent, immoral, obscene, vulgar, or insulting language near children and women. Boomer was convicted and ordered to pay a fine of $75 and volunteer four days in a child-care program. Boomer, with the assistance of the American Civil Liberties Union, appealed the decision, arguing that the law was unconstitutionally vague. After all, what might be considered "vulgar" or "obscene" by one person might not be by another. A Michigan appellate court agreed and struck down the law.[a]

THE BOTTOM LINE

Eight other states—Louisiana, New Mexico, Oklahoma, South Carolina, South Dakota, Texas, Virginia, and Wisconsin—also have "swearing laws." Whether these laws will survive challenges remains to be seen.

a. *Michigan v. Boomer,* 250 Mich.App. 534, 655 N.W.2d 255 (2002). This case is also discussed in Tresa Baldas, "A 'Cussing Canoeist' Cans a Controversial Michigan Law," *The National Law Journal,* May 6, 2002, p. A6.

the fraudulent conversion of funds for their own benefit. Embezzlement is not larceny, because the wrongdoer does not physically take the property from the possession of another, and it is not robbery, because force or fear is not used.

It does not matter whether the accused takes the funds from the victim or from a third person. If, as the financial officer of a large corporation, Saunders pockets a certain number of checks from third parties that were given to her to deposit into the corporate account, she is embezzling.

Ordinarily, an embezzler who returns what has been taken will not be prosecuted because the owner usually will not take the time to make a complaint, give depositions, and appear in court. That the accused intended eventually to return the embezzled property, however, does not constitute a sufficient defense to the crime of embezzlement.

Mail and Wire Fraud One of the most potent weapons against white-collar criminals is the Mail Fraud Act of 1990.[5] Under this act, it is a federal crime (mail fraud) to use the mails to defraud the public. Illegal use of the mails must involve (1) mailing or causing someone else to mail a writing—something written, printed, or photocopied—for the purpose of executing a scheme to defraud and (2) a contemplated or an organized scheme to defraud by false pretenses. If, for example, Johnson advertises by mail the sale of a cure for cancer that he knows to be fraudulent because it has no medical validity, he can be prosecuted for fraudulent use of the mails.

Federal law also makes it a crime to use wire (for example, the telephone), radio, or television transmissions to defraud.[6] Violators may be fined up to $1,000, imprisoned for up to five years, or both. If the violation affects a financial institution, the violator may be fined up to $1 million, imprisoned for up to thirty years, or both.

5. 18 U.S.C. Sections 1341–1342.

6. 18 U.S.C. Section 1343.

Bribery Basically, three types of bribery are considered crimes: bribery of public officials, commercial bribery, and bribery of foreign officials. The attempt to influence a public official to act in a way that serves a private interest is a crime. As an element of this crime, intent must be present and proved. The bribe can be anything the recipient considers to be valuable. Realize that *the crime of bribery occurs when the bribe is offered.* It does not matter whether the person to whom the bribe is offered accepts the bribe or agrees to perform whatever action is desired by the person offering the bribe. *Accepting a bribe* is a separate crime.

Typically, people make commercial bribes to obtain proprietary information, cover up an inferior product, or secure new business. Industrial espionage sometimes involves commercial bribes. For example, a person in one firm may offer an employee in a competing firm some type of payoff in exchange for trade secrets or pricing schedules. So-called kickbacks, or payoffs for special favors or services, are a form of commercial bribery in some situations.

Bribing foreign officials to obtain favorable business contracts is a crime. The Foreign Corrupt Practices Act of 1977, which was discussed in Chapter 2, was passed to curb the use of bribery by American businesspersons in securing foreign contracts.

Bankruptcy Fraud Today, federal bankruptcy law (see Chapter 16) allows individuals and businesses to be relieved of oppressive debt through bankruptcy proceedings. Numerous white-collar crimes may be committed during the many phases of a bankruptcy proceeding. A creditor, for example, may file a false claim against the debtor, which is a crime. Also, a debtor may fraudulently transfer assets to favored parties before or after the petition for bankruptcy is filed. For example, a company-owned automobile may be "sold" at a bargain price to a trusted friend or relative. Closely related to the crime of fraudulent transfer of property is the crime of fraudulent concealment of property, such as hiding gold coins.

The Theft of Trade Secrets As discussed in Chapter 5, trade secrets constitute a form of intellectual property that for many businesses can be extremely valuable. The Economic Espionage Act of 1996[7] made the theft of trade secrets a federal crime. The act also made it a federal crime to buy or possess trade secrets of another person, knowing that the trade secrets were stolen or otherwise acquired without the owner's authorization.

Violations of the act can result in steep penalties. An individual who violates the act can be imprisoned for up to ten years and fined up to $500,000. If a corporation or other organization violates the act, it can be fined up to $5 million. Additionally, the law provides that any property acquired as a result of the violation and any property used in the commission of the violation are subject to criminal *forfeiture*—meaning that the government can take the property. A theft of trade secrets conducted via the Internet, for example, could result in the forfeiture of every computer, printer, or other device used to commit or facilitate the violation.

Insider Trading An individual who obtains "inside information" about the plans of a publicly listed corporation can often make stock-trading profits by using the information to guide decisions relating to the purchase or sale of corporate securities.

7. 18 U.S.C. Sections 1831–1839.

INSIDER TRADING
The purchase or sale of securities on the basis of "inside information" (information that has not been made available to the public).

Insider trading is a violation of securities law and will be considered more fully in Chapter 21. Generally, the rule is that a person who possesses inside information and has a duty not to disclose it to outsiders may not profit from the purchase or sale of securities based on that information until the information is available to the public.

ORGANIZED CRIME

As mentioned, white-collar crime takes place within the confines of the legitimate business world. *Organized crime,* in contrast, operates *illegitimately* by, among other things, providing illegal goods and services. For organized crime, the traditional preferred markets are gambling, prostitution, illegal narcotics, and loan sharking (lending funds at higher than legal maximum interest rates), along with more recent ventures into counterfeiting and credit-card scams.

.on the Web You can find a wealth of information on famous criminal trials at a Web site maintained by the University of Missouri–Kansas City law school. Go to **http://www.law.umkc.edu/faculty/projects/ftrials/ftrials.html**.

Money Laundering The profits from illegal activities amount to billions of dollars a year, particularly the profits from illegal drug transactions and, to a lesser extent, from racketeering, prostitution, and gambling. Under federal law, banks, savings and loan associations, and other financial institutions are required to report currency transactions involving more than $10,000. Consequently, those who engage in illegal activities face difficulties in depositing their cash profits from illegal transactions.

As an alternative to simply storing cash from illegal transactions in a safe-deposit box, wrongdoers and racketeers have invented ways to launder "dirty" money to make it "clean." This **money laundering** is done through legitimate businesses.

MONEY LAUNDERING
Falsely reporting income that has been obtained through criminal activity as income obtained through a legitimate business enterprise—in effect, "laundering" the "dirty money."

■ EXAMPLE 6.4 Matt, a successful drug dealer, becomes a partner with a restaurateur. Little by little, the restaurant shows an increasing profit. As a partner in the restaurant, Matt is able to report the "profits" of the restaurant as legitimate income on which he pays federal and state income taxes. He can then spend those after-tax funds without worrying that his lifestyle may exceed the level possible with his reported income. ■

Jeffrey Skilling, former chief executive officer (CEO) of Enron Corporation, testifies before a congressional committee concerning allegations that Enron insiders profited at the company's expense while improperly concealing losses and inflating earnings. About a month after Skilling resigned as CEO, he sold nearly $60 million of his stock in Enron. This led prosecutors to believe that he sold those shares knowing of the bankruptcy that Enron was facing. Skilling was subsequently indicted on numerous counts of fraud and insider trading. If Skilling knew that the company was on the brink of bankruptcy at the time that he sold his stock, is he guilty of a crime? Explain your answer. (AP Photo/Kenneth Lambert)

The Federal Bureau of Investigation estimates that organized crime has invested tens of billions of dollars in as many as a hundred thousand business establishments in the United States for the purpose of money laundering. Globally, it is estimated that more than $500 billion in illegal money moves through the world banking system every year.

The Racketeer Influenced and Corrupt Organizations Act In 1970, in an effort to curb the apparently increasing entry of organized crime into the legitimate business world, Congress passed the Racketeer Influenced and Corrupt Organizations Act (RICO).[8] The act, which was enacted as part of the Organized Crime Control Act, makes it a federal crime to (1) use income obtained from racketeering activity to purchase any interest in an enterprise, (2) acquire or maintain an interest in an enterprise through racketeering activity, (3) conduct or participate in the affairs of an enterprise through racketeering activity, or (4) conspire to do any of the preceding activities.

Racketeering activity is not a new type of substantive crime created by RICO; rather, RICO incorporates by reference twenty-six separate types of federal crimes and nine types of state felonies[9] and declares that if a person commits two of these offenses, he or she is guilty of "racketeering activity." Additionally, RICO is more often used today to attack white-collar crimes than organized crime.

In the event of a violation, the statute permits the government to seek civil penalties, including the divestiture of a defendant's interest in a business (called forfeiture) or the dissolution of the business. Perhaps the most controversial aspect of RICO is that, in some cases, private individuals are allowed to recover three times their actual losses (treble damages), plus attorneys' fees, for business injuries caused by a violation of the statute. Under criminal provisions of RICO, any individual found guilty of a violation is subject to a fine of up to $25,000 per violation, imprisonment for up to twenty years, or both. Additionally, the statute provides that those who violate RICO may be required to forfeit (give up) any assets, in the form of property or cash, that were acquired as a result of the illegal activity or that were "involved in" or an "instrumentality of" the activity.

.on the Web You can gain insights into criminal law and procedures, including a number of the defenses that can be raised to avoid criminal liability, by looking at some of the famous criminal law cases included on Court TV's Web site. Go to **http://www.courttv.com/index.html**.

Defenses to Criminal Liability

Among the most important defenses to criminal liability are infancy, intoxication, insanity, mistake, consent, duress, justifiable use of force, entrapment, and the statute of limitations. Many of these defenses involve assertions that the intent requirement for criminal liability is lacking. Also, in some cases, defendants are given immunity and thus relieved, at least in part, of criminal liability for crimes they committed. We look at each of these defenses here.

Note that procedural violations, such as obtaining evidence without a valid search warrant, may also operate as defenses. As you will read later in this chapter, evidence obtained in violation of a defendant's constitutional rights normally may not be admitted in court. If the evidence is suppressed, then there may be no basis for prosecuting the defendant.

8. 18 U.S.C. Sections 1961–1968.
9. See 18 U.S.C. Section 1961(1)(A).

INFANCY

The term *infant,* as used in the law, refers to any person who has not yet reached the age of majority (see Chapter 8). In all states, certain courts handle cases involving children who are alleged to have violated the law. In some states, juvenile courts handle children's cases exclusively. In other states, however, courts that handle children's cases may also have jurisdiction over additional matters.

Originally, juvenile court hearings were informal, and lawyers were rarely present. Since 1967, however, when the United States Supreme Court ruled that a child charged with delinquency must be allowed to consult with an attorney before being committed to a state institution,[10] juvenile court hearings have become more formal. In some states, a child may be treated as an adult and tried in a regular court if she or he is above a certain age (usually fourteen) and is charged with a felony, such as rape or murder.

INTOXICATION

The law recognizes two types of intoxication, whether from drugs or from alcohol: *involuntary* and *voluntary.* Involuntary intoxication occurs when a person either is physically forced to ingest or inject an intoxicating substance or is unaware that a substance contains drugs or alcohol. Involuntary intoxication is a defense to a crime if its effect was to make a person incapable of obeying the law or incapable of understanding that the act committed was wrong. Voluntary intoxication is rarely a defense, but it may be effective in cases in which the defendant was *extremely* intoxicated when committing the wrong.

INSANITY

Someone suffering from a mental illness may be judged incapable of having the state of mind required to commit a crime. Thus, insanity may be a defense to a criminal charge. The courts have had difficulty deciding what the test for legal insanity should be, however, and psychiatrists as well as lawyers are critical of the tests used. Almost all federal courts and some states use the relatively liberal standard set forth in the Model Penal Code:

> A person is not responsible for criminal conduct if at the time of such conduct as a result of mental disease or defect he [or she] lacks substantial capacity either to appreciate the wrongfulness of his [or her] conduct or to conform his [or her] conduct to the requirements of the law.

Some states use the *M'Naghten* test,[11] under which a criminal defendant is not responsible if, at the time of the offense, he or she did not know the nature and quality of the act or did not know that the act was wrong. Other states use the irresistible-impulse test. A person operating under an irresistible impulse may know an act is wrong but cannot refrain from doing it.

MISTAKE

Everyone has heard the saying, "Ignorance of the law is no excuse." Ordinarily, ignorance of the law or a mistaken idea about what the law requires is not a valid defense. In some states, however, that rule has been modified. Criminal defendants who claim that they honestly did not know that they were breaking a law may have a valid

10. *In re Gault,* 387 U.S. 1, 87 S.Ct. 1428, 18 L.Ed.2d 527 (1967).

11. A rule derived from *M'Naghten's* case, 8 Eng.Rep. 718 (1843).

Three suspects were charged with assaulting Matthew Shepard, a gay University of Wyoming student. Shepard was beaten, burned, and tied to a fence like a scarecrow. Should the court allow the defendants to claim that they were temporarily insane because of "homosexual rage"? Why or why not? (AP Photo/Ed Andrieski)

defense if (1) the law was not published or reasonably made known to the public or (2) the defendant relied on an official statement of the law that was erroneous.

COMPARE "Ignorance" is a lack of information. "Mistake" is a confusion of information.

A *mistake of fact,* as opposed to a *mistake of law,* operates as a defense if it negates the mental state necessary to commit a crime. ■ EXAMPLE 6.5 If Oliver Wheaton mistakenly walks off with Julie Cabrera's briefcase because he thinks it is his, there is no theft. Theft requires knowledge that the property belongs to another. (If Wheaton's act causes Cabrera to incur damages, however, Wheaton may be subject to liability for trespass to personal property or conversion, torts that were discussed in Chapter 4.) ■

CONSENT

CONSENT
The voluntary agreement to a proposition or an act of another; a concurrence of wills.

What if a victim consents to a crime or even encourages the person intending a criminal act to commit it? Ordinarily, **consent** does not operate as a bar to criminal liability. In some rare circumstances, however, the law may allow consent to be used as a defense. In each case, the question is whether the law forbids an act that was committed against the victim's will or forbids the act without regard to the victim's wish. The law forbids murder, prostitution, and drug use regardless of whether the victim consents to it. Also, if the act causes harm to a third person who has not consented, there is no escape from criminal liability. Consent or forgiveness given after a crime has been committed is not really a defense, though it can affect the likelihood of prosecution or the severity of the sentence. Consent operates most successfully as a defense in crimes against property.

■ EXAMPLE 6.6 Barry gives Phong permission to hunt for deer on Barry's land while staying in Barry's lakeside cabin. After observing Phong carrying a gun into the cabin at night, a neighbor calls the police, and an officer subsequently arrests Phong. If charged with burglary (or aggravated burglary, because he had a weapon), Phong can assert the defense of consent. He had obtained Barry's consent to enter the premises. ■

DURESS

DURESS
Unlawful pressure brought to bear on a person, causing the person to perform an act that she or he would not otherwise perform.

Duress exists when the *wrongful threat* of one person induces another person to perform an act that she or he would not otherwise perform. In such a situation, duress is said to negate the mental state necessary to commit a crime. For duress to qualify as a defense, the following requirements must be met:

1. The threat must be of serious bodily harm or death.
2. The harm threatened must be greater than the harm caused by the crime.
3. The threat must be immediate and inescapable.
4. The defendant must have been involved in the situation through no fault of his or her own.

JUSTIFIABLE USE OF FORCE

SELF-DEFENSE
The legally recognized privilege to protect oneself or one's property against injury by another. The privilege of self-defense protects only acts that are reasonably necessary to protect oneself, one's property, or another person.

Probably the best-known defense to criminal liability is **self-defense.** Other situations, however, also justify the use of force: the defense of one's dwelling, the defense of other property, and the prevention of a crime. In all of these situations, it is important to distinguish between deadly and nondeadly force. *Deadly force* is likely to result in death or serious bodily harm. *Nondeadly force* is force that reasonably appears necessary to prevent the imminent use of criminal force.

Generally speaking, people can use the amount of nondeadly force that seems necessary to protect themselves, their dwellings, or other property or to prevent the commission of a crime. Deadly force can be used in self-defense if there is a *reasonable belief* that imminent death or grievous bodily harm will otherwise result, if the attacker is using unlawful force (an example of lawful force is that exerted by a police officer), and if the defender has not initiated or provoked the attack. Deadly force normally can be used to defend a dwelling only if the unlawful entry is violent and the person believes deadly force is necessary to prevent imminent death or great bodily harm or—in some jurisdictions—if the person believes deadly force is necessary to prevent the commission of a felony (such as arson) in the dwelling.

ENTRAPMENT

ENTRAPMENT
In criminal law, a defense in which the defendant claims that he or she was induced by a public official—usually an undercover agent or police officer—to commit a crime that he or she would otherwise not have committed.

Entrapment is a defense designed to prevent police officers or other government agents from encouraging crimes in order to apprehend persons wanted for criminal acts. In the typical entrapment case, an undercover agent *suggests* that a crime be committed and somehow pressures or induces an individual to commit it. The agent then arrests the individual for the crime.

For entrapment to be considered a defense, both the suggestion and the inducement must take place. The defense is intended not to prevent law enforcement agents from setting a trap for an unwary criminal but rather to prevent them from pushing the individual into it. The crucial issue is whether the person who committed a crime was predisposed to do so or acted because the agent induced it.

STATUTE OF LIMITATIONS

With some exceptions, such as for the crime of murder, statutes of limitations apply to crimes just as they do to civil wrongs. In other words, criminal cases must be prosecuted within a certain number of years. If a criminal action is brought after the statutory time period has expired, the accused person can raise the statute of limitations as a defense.

IMMUNITY

At times, the state may wish to obtain information from a person accused of a crime. Accused persons are understandably reluctant to give information if it will be used to prosecute them, and they cannot be forced to do so. The privilege against self-incrimination is granted by the Fifth Amendment to the Constitution, which reads, in part, "nor shall [any person] be compelled in any criminal case to be a witness against himself." In cases in which the state wishes to obtain information from a person accused of a crime, the state can grant *immunity* from prosecution or agree to prosecute for a less serious offense in exchange for the information. Once immunity is given, the person can no longer refuse to testify on Fifth Amendment grounds, because he or she now has an absolute privilege against self-incrimination.

PLEA BARGAINING
The process by which a defendant and the prosecutor in a criminal case work out a mutually satisfactory disposition of the case, subject to court approval; usually involves the defendant's pleading guilty to a lesser offense in return for a lighter sentence.

Often, a grant of immunity from prosecution for a serious crime is part of the **plea bargaining** between the defendant and the prosecuting attorney. The defendant may be convicted of a lesser offense, while the state uses the defendant's testimony to prosecute accomplices for serious crimes carrying heavy penalties.

Constitutional Safeguards and Criminal Procedures

Criminal law brings the power of the state, with all its resources, to bear against the individual. Criminal procedures are designed to protect the constitutional rights of individuals and to prevent the arbitrary use of power on the part of the government.

The U.S. Constitution provides specific safeguards for those accused of crimes. Most of these safeguards protect individuals against state government actions, as well as federal government actions, by virtue of the due process clause of the Fourteenth Amendment. These safeguards are set forth in the Fourth, Fifth, Sixth, and Eighth Amendments.

FOURTH AMENDMENT PROTECTIONS

SEARCH WARRANT
An order granted by a public authority, such as a judge, that authorizes law enforcement personnel to search particular premises or property.

PROBABLE CAUSE
Reasonable grounds for believing that a person should be arrested or searched.

The Fourth Amendment protects the "right of the people to be secure in their persons, houses, papers, and effects." Before searching or seizing private property, law enforcement officers must obtain a **search warrant**—an order from a judge or other public official authorizing the search or seizure. To obtain a search warrant, the officers must convince a judge that they have reasonable grounds, or **probable cause,** to believe a search will reveal a specific illegality. Probable cause requires law enforcement officials to have trustworthy evidence that would convince a reasonable person that the proposed search or seizure is more likely justified than not. Furthermore, the Fourth Amendment prohibits general warrants. It requires a particular description of what is to be searched or seized. General searches through a person's belongings are impermissible. The search cannot extend beyond what is described in the warrant.

There are exceptions to the requirement of a search warrant, as when it is likely that the items sought will be removed before a warrant can be obtained. For example, if a police officer has probable cause to believe an automobile contains evidence of a crime and the vehicle is likely to be unavailable by the time a warrant is obtained, the officer can search the vehicle without a warrant.

on the Web You can learn about some of the constitutional questions raised by various criminal laws and procedures by going to the Web site of the American Civil Liberties Union at **http://www.aclu.org**.

Constitutional protection against unreasonable searches and seizures is important to businesses and professionals. As federal and state regulation of commercial activities increased, frequent and unannounced government inspections were conducted to ensure compliance with the regulations. Such inspections were extremely disruptive at times. In *Marshall v. Barlow's, Inc.,*[12] the United States Supreme Court held that government inspectors do not have the right to enter business premises without a warrant, although the standard of probable cause is not the same as that required in nonbusiness contexts. The existence of a general and neutral enforcement plan will justify issuance of the warrant.

BE AWARE The Fifth Amendment protection against self-incrimination does not cover partnerships or corporations.

FIFTH AMENDMENT PROTECTIONS

The Fifth Amendment offers significant protections for accused persons. One is the guarantee that no one can be deprived of "life, liberty, or property without due process of law" (see Chapter 1 for a discussion of the due process clause). The Fifth Amendment also protects persons from **double jeopardy** (being tried twice for the same criminal offense). The prohibition against double jeopardy means that once a criminal defendant is acquitted (found "not guilty") of a particular crime, the government may not reindict the person and retry him or her for the same crime.

DOUBLE JEOPARDY
A situation occurring when a person is tried twice for the same criminal offense; prohibited by the Fifth Amendment to the Constitution.

Additionally, the Fifth Amendment guarantees that no person "shall be compelled in any criminal case to be a witness against himself." Thus, in any criminal proceeding, an accused person cannot be compelled to give testimony that might subject her or him to any criminal prosecution. The Fifth Amendment's guarantee against **self-incrimination** extends only to natural persons. Protection against self-incrimination does not apply to corporations or partnerships.[13]

SELF-INCRIMINATION
The giving of testimony that may subject the testifier to criminal prosecution. The Fifth Amendment to the Constitution protects against self-incrimination by providing that no person "shall be compelled in any criminal case to be a witness against himself."

PROTECTIONS UNDER THE SIXTH AND EIGHTH AMENDMENTS

The Sixth Amendment guarantees several important rights for criminal defendants: the right to a speedy trial, the right to a jury trial, the right to a public trial, the right to confront witnesses, and the right to counsel. The Eighth Amendment prohibits excessive bail and fines, and cruel and unusual punishment.

The Sixth Amendment right to counsel is one of the rights of which a suspect must be advised when he or she is arrested under the *Miranda* rule (discussed later in this chapter). In many cases, a statement that a criminal suspect makes in the absence of counsel is not admissible at trial unless the suspect has knowingly and voluntarily waived this right. Is this right to counsel triggered when judicial proceedings are initiated through any preliminary step? Or is this right triggered only when a suspect is "interrogated" by the police? In the following case, the Supreme Court considered these questions.

12. 436 U.S. 307, 98 S.Ct. 1816, 56 L.Ed.2d 305 (1978).

13. The privilege has been applied to some small family partnerships. See *United States v. Slutsky,* 352 F.Supp. 1105 (S.D.N.Y. 1972).

CASE 6.2 Fellers v. United States

Supreme Court of the United States, 2004.
540 U.S. 519,
124 S.Ct. 1019,
157 L.Ed.2d 1016.
http://supct.law.cornell.edu/supct[a]

a. In the "Search" box, type "Fellers," select "Current decisions only," and click on "submit." In the result, scroll to the name of the case, and click on it to access the opinion. The Legal Information Institute of Cornell Law School in Ithaca, New York, maintains this Web site.

FACTS In February 2000, an indictment was issued charging John Fellers, a resident of Lincoln, Nebraska, with conspiracy to distribute methamphetamine. Police officers Michael Garnett and Jeff Bliemeister went to Fellers's home to arrest him. They told Fellers that the purpose of their visit was to discuss his use and distribution of methamphetamine. They said that they had a warrant for his arrest and that the charges referred to his involvement with four indi-

CASE 6.2—Continued

viduals. Fellers responded that he knew the persons and had used methamphetamine with them. The officers took Fellers to jail and advised him for the first time of his right to counsel. He waived this right and repeated his earlier statements. Before Fellers's trial, the court ruled that his "jailhouse statements" could be admitted at his trial because he had waived his right to counsel before making them. After Fellers's conviction, he appealed to the U.S. Court of Appeals for the Eighth Circuit, arguing that the officers had elicited his incriminating "home statements" without advising him of his right to counsel and that his "jailhouse statements" should thus have been excluded from his trial as "fruits" of his earlier statements. The appellate court affirmed the lower court's judgment, holding that Fellers had not had a right to counsel at his home because he had not been subject to police "interrogation." Fellers appealed to the United States Supreme Court.

ISSUE Did Garnett and Bliemeister violate Fellers's right to counsel by deliberately eliciting information from him during their visit to his home without advising him of his right to counsel?

DECISION Yes. The United States Supreme Court reversed the lower court's decision and remanded the case for the determination of a different issue.[b] The Supreme Court held that the Sixth Amendment bars the use at trial of a suspect's incriminating words, deliberately elicited by police after an indictment, in the absence of either counsel or a waiver of the right to counsel, regardless of whether police conduct constitutes an "interrogation."

b. The lower court's decision on remand was not available at the time this book went to press, but it may be by the time you read this book. If you have purchased access to Westlaw Campus, you may be able to locate the remanded decision using that database. Alternatively, you might be able to find the case online at some other site. (See this text's inside front cover for information on Westlaw Campus and URLs for online court decisions.)

REASON The Court explained, "The Sixth Amendment right to counsel is triggered at or after the time that judicial proceedings have been initiated * * * . [A]n accused is denied the basic protections of the Sixth Amendment when there is used against him at his trial evidence of his own incriminating words, which federal agents * * * deliberately elicited from him after he had been indicted and in the absence of his counsel." In this case, "there is no question that the officers * * * deliberately elicited information from petitioner [Fellers]. Indeed, the officers, upon arriving at petitioner's house, informed him that their purpose in coming was to discuss his involvement in the distribution of methamphetamine and his association with certain charged co-conspirators. * * * [T]he ensuing discussion took place after petitioner had been indicted, outside the presence of counsel, and in the absence of any waiver of petitioner's Sixth Amendment rights."

FOR CRITICAL ANALYSIS—Social Consideration *Should Fellers's "jailhouse statements" also have been excluded from his trial? Why or why not?*

THE EXCLUSIONARY RULE AND THE *MIRANDA* RULE

Two other procedural protections for criminal defendants are the exclusionary rule and the *Miranda* rule.

EXCLUSIONARY RULE
In criminal procedure, a rule under which any evidence that is obtained in violation of the accused's constitutional rights guaranteed by the Fourth, Fifth, and Sixth Amendments, as well as any evidence derived from illegally obtained evidence, will not be admissible in court.

The Exclusionary Rule Under what is known as the **exclusionary rule,** all evidence obtained in violation of the constitutional rights spelled out in the Fourth, Fifth, and Sixth Amendments, as well as all evidence derived from the illegally obtained evidence, normally must be excluded from the trial. Evidence derived from illegally obtained evidence is known as the "fruit of the poisonous tree." For example, if a confession is obtained after an illegal arrest, the arrest is "the poisonous tree," and the confession, if "tainted" by the arrest, is the "fruit."

The purpose of the exclusionary rule is to deter police from conducting warrantless searches and from engaging in other misconduct. The rule is sometimes criticized because it can lead to injustice. Many a defendant has "gotten off on a technicality" because law enforcement personnel failed to observe procedural requirements. Even though a defendant may be obviously guilty, if the evidence of that guilt was obtained improperly (without a valid search warrant, for example), it normally cannot be used against the defendant in court. In the following case, the court had to decide whether a lost computer printout should cause evidence to be excluded.

CASE 6.3 People v. McFarlan

New York Supreme Court, 2002.[a]
191 Misc.2d 531,
744 N.Y.S.2d 287.

FACTS In May 2001, Lisa Kordes saw two men picking pockets on a Lexington Avenue bus in Manhattan, in New York City. Based on Kordes's description of the men, a police department computer produced a six-photo array of possible suspects. Kordes selected a photo of Kevin McFarlan as one of the men she had seen. Five days later, on a bus, Neal Ariano, a police officer, arrested McFarlan after seeing him bump an elderly woman while placing his hand near her pocketbook. At the police station, Kordes viewed a lineup including McFarlan and identified him as the man she had seen on the Lexington Avenue bus. McFarlan was charged in a New York state court with various crimes. The printout of the computer-generated photo array that Kordes had been shown was lost, but the "People" (the state of New York) introduced into evidence a second printout to show what Kordes had seen. McFarlan argued, among other things, that the first printout was the original photo array and that because that printout had been lost, the court should presume the photo-array procedure had been illegal. Thus, McFarlan's arrest and Kordes's identification of him in the lineup should be excluded as "fruit of the poisonous tree."

ISSUE Should the second printout of the photo array be considered "fruit of the poisonous tree" and thus inadmissible?

a. In New York, a supreme court is a trial court.

DECISION No. The New York state court held that the second printout of the photo array was not "fruit of the poisonous tree" and could be properly accepted into evidence.

REASON The court concluded that because both printouts were generated in the same format, there could be no prejudice from the fact that the defendant was selected from the first printout and that a second identical printout was later introduced into evidence. Because the printouts were identical and conveyed the full recoverable information, the court held that to decide otherwise would be absurd. "Where, for example, a witness is shown only the screen display, what must the People [public prosecutor] keep? For on such an analysis the printout of the screen could not be the 'original.' " The court pointed out that the purpose of requiring the preservation of a record was clear. According to the court, concern for the integrity of information has always led the courts to prefer the original and has led to many rules to bar or limit the use of nonoriginal material. "Here," said the court, "the original array was in electronic form in the computer memory, the testimony was unequivocal that [both] printout[s] * * * were generated in the same manner. * * * [A]s a result, defendant's argument crumbles."

FOR CRITICAL ANALYSIS—Technological Consideration *When a record is stored on a computer, which should be considered the "original" record—the version on the computer or a printout of the computer version? Why?*

REMEMBER Once a suspect has been informed of his or her rights, anything that person says can be used as evidence in a trial.

The *Miranda* Rule In *Miranda v. Arizona,*[14] a case decided in 1966, the United States Supreme Court established the rule that individuals who are arrested must be informed of certain constitutional rights, including their Fifth Amendment right to remain silent and their Sixth Amendment right to counsel. If the arresting officers fail to inform a criminal suspect of these constitutional rights, any statements the suspect makes normally will not be admissible in court.

14. 384 U.S. 436, 86 S.Ct. 1602, 16 L.Ed.2d 694 (1966).

If you are interested in reading the Supreme Court's opinion in *Miranda v. Arizona*, go to

http://supct.law.cornell.edu:8080/supct/cases/name.htm.

Select "M" from the menu at the top of the page, and scroll down the page that opens to the *Miranda v. Arizona* case.

The Supreme Court's *Miranda* decision was controversial, and Congress subsequently attempted to overrule it by enacting Section 3501 of the Omnibus Crime Control Act[15] of 1968. Essentially, Section 3501 reinstated the rule that had been in effect for 180 years before *Miranda*—namely, that statements by defendants can be used against them as long as the statements are made voluntarily. Section 3501, however, was never enforced. The Supreme Court has held that the *Miranda* rights enunciated by the Court in the 1966 case were constitutionally based and thus could not be overruled by a legislative act.[16]

Exceptions to the *Miranda* Rule Over time, as part of a continuing attempt to balance the rights of accused persons against the rights of society, the United States Supreme Court has carved out numerous exceptions to the *Miranda* rule. In 1984, for example, the Court recognized a "public safety" exception to the *Miranda* rule. The need to protect the public warranted the admissibility of statements made by the defendant (in this case, indicating where he placed the gun) as evidence at trial, even though the defendant had not been informed of his *Miranda* rights.[17]

In 1986, the Supreme Court further held that a confession need not be excluded even though the police failed to inform a suspect in custody that his attorney had tried to reach him by telephone.[18] In an important 1991 decision, the Court stated that a suspect's conviction will not be automatically overturned if the suspect was coerced into making a confession. If other, legally obtained evidence admitted at trial is strong enough to justify the conviction without the confession, then the fact that the confession was obtained illegally can, in effect, be ignored.[19]

15. 42 U.S.C. Section 3789d.
16. *Dickerson v. United States,* 530 U.S. 428, 120 S.Ct. 2326, 147 L.Ed.2d 405 (2000).
17. *New York v. Quarles,* 467 U.S. 649, 104 S.Ct. 2626, 81 L.Ed.2d 550 (1984).
18. *Moran v. Burbine,* 475 U.S. 412, 106 S.Ct. 1135, 89 L.Ed.2d 410 (1985).
19. *Arizona v. Fulminante,* 499 U.S. 279, 111 S.Ct. 1246, 113 L.Ed.2d 302 (1991).

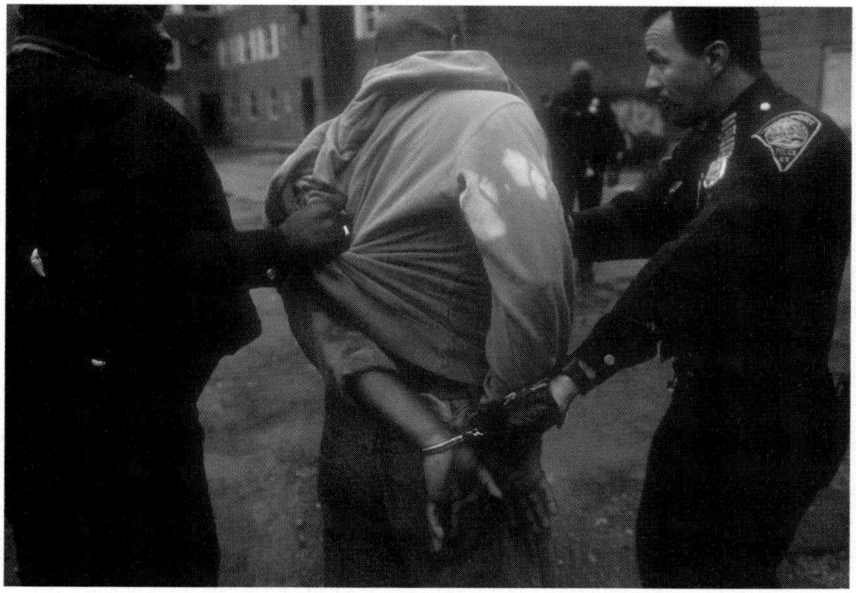

Police officers take a suspect into custody. Why must a criminal suspect be informed of his or her legal rights? (© Corbis. All rights reserved.)

In yet another case, in 1994, the Supreme Court ruled that a suspect must unequivocally and assertively request to exercise his or her right to counsel in order to stop police questioning. Saying, "Maybe I should talk to a lawyer" during an interrogation after being taken into custody is not enough. The Court held that police officers are not required to decipher the suspect's intentions in such situations.[20]

.on the Web To learn more about criminal procedures, access the following site and select "Anatomy of a Murder: A Trip through Our Nation's Legal Justice System": **http://library.thinkquest.org/2760/home.htm**.

CRIMINAL PROCEDURES AND SENTENCING

As mentioned, a criminal prosecution differs significantly from a civil case in several respects. These differences reflect the desire to safeguard the rights of the individual against the state. Exhibit 6–3 summarizes the major procedural steps in processing a criminal case.

Traditionally, persons who committed the same crime might receive very different sentences, depending on the judge hearing the case, the jurisdiction in which it was heard, and many other factors. Today, however, court judges typically must follow state or federal guidelines when sentencing convicted persons.

At the federal level, the Sentencing Reform Act created the U.S. Sentencing Commission, which was charged with the task of standardizing sentences for federal crimes. The commission fulfilled its task, and since 1987 its sentencing guidelines for all federal crimes have been applied by federal court judges. The guidelines establish a range of possible penalties for each federal crime. Depending on the defendant's criminal record, the seriousness of the offense, and other factors specified in the guidelines, federal judges must select a sentence from within this range.

.on the Web The U.S. Sentencing Guidelines can be found online at **http://www.ussc.gov**.

The commission also created specific guidelines for the punishment of crimes committed by corporate employees (white-collar crimes). These guidelines established stiffer penalties for criminal violations of securities laws (see Chapter 21), antitrust laws (see Chapter 22), employment laws (see Chapter 18), mail and wire fraud, commercial bribery, and kickbacks and money laundering.[21] The guidelines allow federal judges to take into consideration a number of factors when selecting from the range of possible penalties for a specified crime. These factors include the defendant company's history of past violations, the extent of management's cooperation with federal investigators, and the extent to which the firm has undertaken specific programs and procedures to prevent criminal activities by its employees.

Cyber Crime

COMPUTER CRIME
Any act that is directed against computers and computer parts, that uses computers as instruments of crime, or that involves computers and constitutes abuse.

Some years ago, the American Bar Association defined **computer crime** as any act that is directed against computers and computer parts, that uses computers as instruments of crime, or that involves computers and constitutes abuse. Today, because much of the crime committed with the use of computers occurs in cyberspace, many computer crimes fall under the broad label of cyber crime. Here we look at several types of activity that constitute cyber crimes against persons or property. Other cyber crimes will be discussed in later chapters of this text as they relate to particular topics, such as banking or consumer law.

20. *Davis v. United States,* 512 U.S. 452, 114 S.Ct. 2350, 129 L.Ed.2d 362 (1994).

21. The sentencing guidelines were amended in 2003, as required under the Sarbanes-Oxley Act of 2002, to impose stiffer penalties for corporate securities fraud—see Chapter 21.

EXHIBIT 6–3 MAJOR PROCEDURAL STEPS IN A CRIMINAL CASE

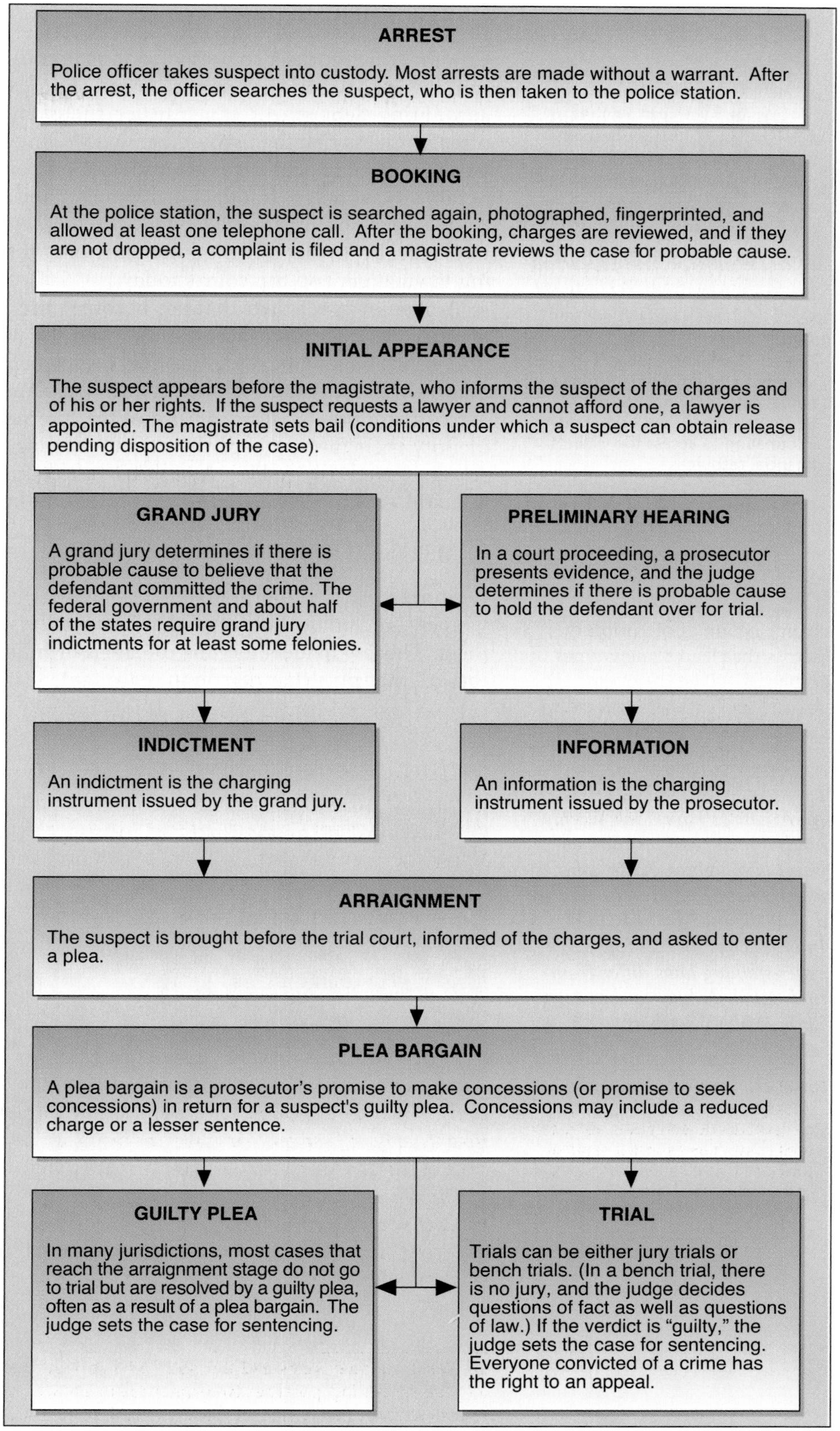
ARREST
Police officer takes suspect into custody. Most arrests are made without a warrant. After the arrest, the officer searches the suspect, who is then taken to the police station.
BOOKING
At the police station, the suspect is searched again, photographed, fingerprinted, and allowed at least one telephone call. After the booking, charges are reviewed, and if they are not dropped, a complaint is filed and a magistrate reviews the case for probable cause.
INITIAL APPEARANCE
The suspect appears before the magistrate, who informs the suspect of the charges and of his or her rights. If the suspect requests a lawyer and cannot afford one, a lawyer is appointed. The magistrate sets bail (conditions under which a suspect can obtain release pending disposition of the case).
GRAND JURY
A grand jury determines if there is probable cause to believe that the defendant committed the crime. The federal government and about half of the states require grand jury indictments for at least some felonies.
PRELIMINARY HEARING
In a court proceeding, a prosecutor presents evidence, and the judge determines if there is probable cause to hold the defendant over for trial.
INDICTMENT
An indictment is the charging instrument issued by the grand jury.
INFORMATION
An information is the charging instrument issued by the prosecutor.
ARRAIGNMENT
The suspect is brought before the trial court, informed of the charges, and asked to enter a plea.
PLEA BARGAIN
A plea bargain is a prosecutor's promise to make concessions (or promise to seek concessions) in return for a suspect's guilty plea. Concessions may include a reduced charge or a lesser sentence.
GUILTY PLEA
In many jurisdictions, most cases that reach the arraignment stage do not go to trial but are resolved by a guilty plea, often as a result of a plea bargain. The judge sets the case for sentencing.
TRIAL
Trials can be either jury trials or bench trials. (In a bench trial, there is no jury, and the judge decides questions of fact as well as questions of law.) If the verdict is "guilty," the judge sets the case for sentencing. Everyone convicted of a crime has the right to an appeal.

CYBER THEFT

The U.S. Department of Justice offers an impressive collection of statistics on crime, including cyber crime, at the following Web site:

http://www.ojp.usdoj.gov/bjs.

Computer networks also provide opportunities for employees to commit crimes that can involve serious economic losses. For example, employees of a company's accounting department can transfer funds among accounts with little effort and often with less risk than would be involved in transactions evidenced by paperwork. Generally, the dependence of businesses on computer operations has left firms vulnerable to sabotage, fraud, embezzlement, and the theft of proprietary data, such as trade secrets or other intellectual property. As noted in Chapter 5, the piracy of intellectual property via the Internet is one of the most serious legal challenges facing lawmakers and the courts today.

IDENTITY THEFT
The act of stealing another's identifying information—such as a name, date of birth, or Social Security number—and using that information to access the victim's financial resources.

A form of cyber theft that has become particularly troublesome in recent years is **identity theft.** Identity theft occurs when the wrongdoer steals a form of identification—such as a name, date of birth, or Social Security number—and uses the information to access the victim's financial resources. This crime existed to a certain extent before the widespread use of the Internet. The Internet, however, has turned identity theft into perhaps the fastest-growing financial crime in the United States. An estimated 10 million Americans are victims of identity theft each year, and annual losses are estimated to exceed $50 billion.

CYBER-STALKING

BE AWARE Technological change is one of the primary factors that lead to new types of crime.

California enacted the first stalking law in 1990, in response to the murders of six women—including Rebecca Schaeffer, a television star—by men who had harassed them. The law made it a crime to harass or follow a person while making a "credible threat" that puts that person in reasonable fear for his or her safety or the safety of

An Arkansas man, Rick Woody, holds a picture of his thirteen-year-old daughter, Kacie, who was kidnapped and murdered by a man she met through an Internet chat room. How do cyber-stalking laws differ from traditional stalking laws? (AP Photo/Mike Wintroath)

the person's immediate family.[22] Since then, all other states have enacted some form of stalking laws. In about half of the states, these laws require a physical act such as following the victim.

CYBER STALKER
A person who commits the crime of stalking in cyberspace. Generally, stalking consists of harassing a person and putting that person in reasonable fear for his or her safety or the safety of the person's immediate family.

Cyber stalkers (stalkers who commit their crimes in cyberspace), however, find their victims through Internet chat rooms, Usenet newsgroups or other bulletin boards, or e-mail. To close this "loophole" in existing stalking laws, more than three-fourths of the states now have laws specifically designed to combat cyber-stalking and other forms of online harassment.

Note that cyber-stalking can be even more threatening than physical stalking in some respects. While it takes a great deal of effort to physically stalk someone, it is relatively easy to harass a victim with electronic messages. Furthermore, the possibility of personal confrontation may discourage a stalker from actually following a victim. This disincentive is removed in cyberspace. Also, there is always the possibility that a cyber stalker will eventually pose a physical threat to her or his target. Finally, the Internet makes it easier to obtain information about the victim, such as where he or she lives or works. (Can Internet sellers of personal information be held responsible for crimes by stalkers who use that information to locate their victims? For a discussion of this issue, see this chapter's *Adapting the Law to the Online Environment* feature on the following page.)

Hacking and Cyber Terrorism

HACKER
A person who uses one computer to break into another. Professional computer programmers refer to such persons as "crackers."

CYBER TERRORIST
A hacker whose purpose is to exploit a target computer for a serious impact, such as corrupting a program to sabotage a business.

Persons who use one computer to break into another are sometimes referred to as **hackers.** Hackers who break into computers without authorization often commit cyber theft. Sometimes, however, their principal aim is to prove how smart they are by gaining access to others' password-protected computers and causing random data errors or making unpaid-for telephone calls.[23] **Cyber terrorists** are hackers who, rather than trying to attract attention, strive to remain undetected so that they can exploit computers for a serious impact. Just as "real" terrorists destroyed the World Trade Center towers and a portion of the Pentagon in September 2001, cyber terrorists might explode "logic bombs" to shut down central computers. Such activities can pose a danger to national security.

Businesses may be targeted by cyber terrorists as well as hackers. The goals of a hacking operation might include a wholesale theft of data, such as a merchant's customer files, or the monitoring of a computer to discover a business firm's plans and transactions. A cyber terrorist might also want to insert false codes or data. For example, the processing control system of a food manufacturer could be changed to alter the levels of ingredients so that consumers of the food would become ill.

on the Web The Computer Crime Research Center is a nonprofit organization that provides up-to-date information and articles on cyber crime and cyber terrorism at **http://www.crime-research.org**.

A cyber terrorist attack on a major financial institution such as the New York Stock Exchange or a large bank could leave securities or money markets in flux and seriously affect the daily lives of millions of citizens. Similarly, any prolonged disruption of computer, cable, satellite, or telecommunications systems due to the actions of expert hackers would have serious repercussions on business operations—and national security—on a global level. Computer viruses are another tool that can be used by cyber terrorists to cripple communications networks.

22. See, for example, Cal. Penal Code Section 646.9.

23. The total cost of crime on the Internet is estimated to be several billion dollars annually, but two-thirds of that total is said to consist of unpaid-for toll calls.

ADAPTING THE LAW TO THE ONLINE ENVIRONMENT

Stalking and Internet Data Brokers

A cutting-edge issue coming before today's courts has to do with stalking and Internet data brokers—those in the business of selling personal information via the Internet. Suppose that a stalker purchases personal information (such as a home address) from a Web broker and then uses that information to commit a crime (such as murder). The stalker, of course, can be prosecuted under criminal law for the crime of murder. At issue is the broker's responsibility for the crime. Can the broker be sued under tort law (see Chapter 4) for damages?

ONE COURT WEIGHS IN

At least one court has weighed in on this issue. In *Remsburg v. Docusearch, Inc.,*[a] the Supreme Court of New Hampshire concluded that an Internet data broker had a duty to exercise reasonable care when selling personal information online. The case involved Liam Youens, a New Hampshire resident, and Docusearch, Inc., an Internet-based investigation and information service. Youens contacted Docusearch through its Web site and requested information about Amy Boyer. Youens provided his name, address, and phone number and paid Docusearch's fee by credit card. In return, Docusearch provided Boyer's home address, birth date, and Social Security number. Youens also asked for Boyer's workplace address, which Docusearch obtained for him. After Youens had obtained the address of Boyer's place of employment, he drove to the workplace, fatally shot her, and then shot and killed himself.

a. 149 N.H. 148, 816 A.2d 1001 (2003).

Helen Remsburg, Boyer's mother, sued Docusearch, claiming that the defendant had acted wrongfully. The federal district court referred the case to the New Hampshire Supreme Court for a determination of the parties' duties under the state's common law. The state supreme court held that an information broker who sells information about a third person to a client has a duty to exercise reasonable care in disclosing the information.

A FORESEEABLE RISK?

One of the key issues for the court was whether the crime committed by Youens was a foreseeable risk to Docusearch. Remember from Chapter 4 that under tort law, the test for proximate cause—and the extent of a defendant's duty of care—is the foreseeability of a risk of harm. If certain consequences of an action are not foreseeable, there is no proximate cause.

In determining whether a risk of criminal misconduct was foreseeable to Docusearch, the Supreme Court of New Hampshire found that Docusearch's information disclosure presented two foreseeable risks: stalking and identity theft. Therefore, the company had a duty to exercise reasonable care in disclosing personal information about Boyer to Youens. Because Docusearch had not exercised reasonable care (taken steps to find out if Youens's requests were for a legitimate purpose), Docusearch could be sued for damages for breaching this duty.

FOR CRITICAL ANALYSIS

What other crimes can you think of, in addition to stalking and identity theft, that might qualify as "foreseeable risks" created by the online sale of personal data by information brokers?

ETHICAL ISSUE 6.1

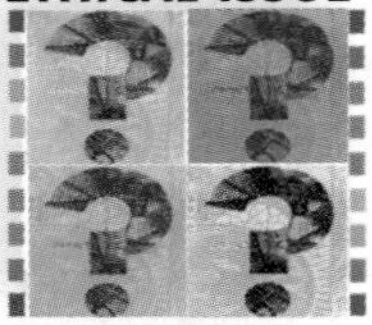

Is it possible to control cyber crime without sacrificing some civil liberties? Governments in some countries, such as China, have succeeded in controlling Internet crime to a certain extent by monitoring the e-mail and other electronic transmissions of users of specific Internet service providers. In the United States, however, Americans have been reluctant to allow the government to monitor Internet use to detect criminal conspiracies or terrorist activities. The traditional attitude has been that civil liberties must be safeguarded to the greatest extent feasible.

As noted in Chapter 1, however, after the terrorist attacks on the World Trade Center and the Pentagon in September 2001, Congress enacted legislation, including the USA Patriot Act, to give law enforcement personnel more authority to conduct electronic surveillance, such as monitoring Web sites and e-mail exchanges. For a time, it seemed that the terrorist attacks might have made Americans more willing to trade off some of their civil liberties for greater national security. Today, however, many complain that this legislation has gone too far in curbing traditional civil liberties guaranteed by the U.S. Constitution. ■

PROSECUTING CYBER CRIMES

The "location" of cyber crime (cyberspace) has raised new issues in the investigation of crimes and the prosecution of offenders. A threshold issue is, of course, jurisdiction. A person who commits an act against a business in California, where the act is a cyber crime, might never have set foot in California but might instead reside in New York, or even in Canada, where the act may not be a crime. If the crime was committed via e-mail, the question arises as to whether the e-mail would constitute sufficient "minimum contacts" (see Chapter 3) for the victim's state to exercise jurisdiction over the perpetrator.

.on the Web Professor Brenner at the University of Dayton Law School posts numerous articles on combating cyber crime, as well as information and links to the relevant laws of other nations, the policies of the European Council, and the United Nations' approach. You can access the site at

http://www.cybercrimes.net/International/IntLinks.html.

The U.S. Department of Justice maintains a site dedicated to cyber crime at

http://www.usdoj.gov/criminal/cybercrime.

Identifying the wrongdoers can also be difficult. Cyber criminals do not leave physical traces, such as fingerprints or DNA samples, as evidence of their crimes. Even electronic "footprints" can be hard to find and follow. For example, e-mail may be sent through a remailer, an online service that guarantees that a message cannot be traced to its source.

For these reasons, laws written to protect physical property are difficult to apply in cyberspace. Nonetheless, governments at both the state and federal levels have taken significant steps toward controlling cyber crime, both by applying existing criminal statutes and by enacting new laws that specifically address wrongs committed in cyberspace. For suggestions on how to protect your business from losses caused by cyber crime, see the *Application* at the end of this chapter.

The Computer Fraud and Abuse Act Perhaps the most significant federal statute specifically addressing cyber crime is the Counterfeit Access Device and Computer Fraud and Abuse Act of 1984 (commonly known as the Computer Fraud and Abuse Act, or CFAA). This act, as amended by the National Information Infrastructure Protection Act of 1996,[24] provides, among other things, that a person who accesses a computer online, without authority, to obtain classified, restricted, or protected data, or attempts to do so, is subject to criminal prosecution. Such data could include financial and credit records, medical records, legal files, military and national security files, and other confidential information in government or private computers. The crime has two elements: accessing a computer without authority and taking the data.

This theft is a felony if it is committed for a commercial purpose or for private financial gain, or if the value of the stolen data (or computer time) exceeds $5,000. Penalties include fines and imprisonment for up to twenty years. A victim of computer theft can also bring a civil suit against the violator to obtain damages, an injunction, and other relief.

Other Federal Statutes The federal wire fraud statute, the Economic Espionage Act of 1996, and RICO, all of which were discussed earlier in this chapter, extend to crimes committed in cyberspace as well. Other federal statutes that may apply include the Electronic Fund Transfer Act of 1978, which makes the unauthorized

24. 18 U.S.C. Section 1030.

access to an electronic fund transfer system a crime; the Anticounterfeiting Consumer Protection Act of 1996, which increased penalties for stealing copyrighted or trademarked property; and the National Stolen Property Act of 1988, which concerns the interstate transport of stolen property. Recall from Chapter 1 that the federal government has also enacted laws (many of which have been challenged on constitutional grounds) to protect minors from online pornographic materials. In later chapters of this text, you will read about other federal statutes and regulations that are designed to address wrongs committed in cyberspace in specific areas of the law.

APPLICATION How Can You Protect against Cyber Crime?*

In addition to protecting their physical property, business owners today also are concerned about protecting their intangible property—such as computer data or files—from unauthorized access. U.S. business firms lose millions of dollars to industrial espionage and sabotage every year. Once a computer system has been corrupted, it can be difficult to recover. To prevent losses through computer systems, some firms hire experts to improve the security of the systems.

Computer System Safeguards

Many sources of software offer security programs that can easily be used to protect computers that are connected to an internal network or to the Internet. For example, most word processing programs include a "password" function. To gain access to information within the program, a user must know the password. A document that can be unlocked only with the password can be e-mailed as an attachment, providing some security.

Cryptography also provides increased protection for computer data and files. Encryption hardware is available in the form of computer chips and is commonly used in automated teller machines. These chips quickly encrypt or decrypt information. The same results can be achieved using encryption software.

Additionally, effective "firewalls" can be installed at the interface between computers and the Internet to protect against unwanted intruders. Firewall software can also be used to keep internal network segments secure.

Employment Policies

Although outside hackers are a threat, employees, former employees, and other "insiders" are responsible for most computer abuse, including breaches of information security. Generally, employees should be given access only to information that they need to know. Additionally, employees and other insiders should be instructed in what constitutes proper and improper use of your company's computer systems. They should also be told that any form of computer abuse is against company policy, is illegal, and will be the basis for termination of employment and even criminal prosecution.

Another safeguard is to have employees agree, in a written confidentiality agreement (see the *Application* feature in Chapter 5), not to disclose confidential information during or after employment without the employer's consent. Monitoring certain computer-related employee activities may be appropriate, but if monitoring is to take place, employees should be informed (see Chapter 18). Still other security measures include the use of digital signatures (see Chapter 10), facility lockups, visitor screenings, and announced briefcase checks.

Checklist for the Business Owner

1. Consider protecting your computer security and documents through the use of passwords, encryption, and firewalls.
2. Instruct your employees in how computers and computer information are to be used and not used.
3. Consider using confidentiality agreements, monitoring, and digital signatures to protect your computer system and data against unauthorized use.

* This *Application* is not meant to substitute for the services of an attorney who is licensed to practice law in your state.

KEY TERMS

CHAPTER SUMMARY Criminal Law and Cyber Crimes

Civil Law and Criminal Law (See pages 171–172.)	1. *Civil law*—Spells out the duties that exist between persons or between citizens and their governments, excluding the duty not to commit crimes. 2. *Criminal law*—Has to do with crimes, which are defined as wrongs against society proclaimed in statutes and, if committed, punishable by society through fines, and/or imprisonment—and, in some cases, death. Because crimes are *offenses against society as a whole,* they are prosecuted by a public official, not by victims. 3. *Key differences*—An important difference between civil and criminal law is that the burden of proof is higher in criminal cases (see Exhibit 6–1 on page 172 for other differences between criminal and civil law). 4. *Civil liability for criminal acts*—A criminal act may give rise to both criminal liability and tort liability (see Exhibit 6–2 on page 173 for an example of criminal and tort liability for the same act).
Classification of Crimes (See pages 172–173.)	1. *Felonies*—Serious crimes punishable by death or by imprisonment in a penitentiary for more than one year. 2. *Misdemeanors*—Under federal law and in most states, any crimes that are not felonies.
Criminal Liability (See pages 173–174.)	1. *Guilty act*—In general, some form of harmful act must be committed for a crime to exist. 2. *Intent*—An intent to commit a crime, or a wrongful mental state, is generally required for a crime to exist.
Corporate Criminal Liability (See pages 174–175.)	1. *Liability of corporations*—Corporations normally are liable for the crimes committed by their agents and employees within the course and scope of their employment. Corporations cannot be imprisoned, but they can be fined or denied certain legal privileges. 2. *Liability of corporate officers and directors*—Corporate directors and officers are personally liable for the crimes they commit and may be held liable for the actions of employees under their supervision.
Types of Crimes (See pages 175–181.)	Crimes fall into five general categories: violent crime, property crime, public order crime, white-collar crime, and organized crime.

(Continued)

CHAPTER SUMMARY Criminal Law and Cyber Crimes—Continued

Defenses to Criminal Liability (See pages 181–185.)	Defenses to criminal liability include infancy, intoxication, insanity, mistake, consent, duress, justifiable use of force, entrapment, and the statute of limitations. Also, in some cases defendants may be relieved of criminal liability, at least in part, if they are given immunity.
Constitutional Safeguards and Criminal Procedures (See pages 185–190.)	1. *Fourth Amendment*—Provides protection against unreasonable searches and seizures and requires that probable cause exist before a warrant for a search or an arrest can be issued. 2. *Fifth Amendment*—Requires due process of law, prohibits double jeopardy, and protects against self-incrimination. 3. *Sixth Amendment*—Provides guarantees of a speedy trial, a trial by jury, a public trial, the right to confront witnesses, and the right to counsel. 4. *Eighth Amendment*—Prohibits excessive bail and fines, and cruel and unusual punishment. 5. *Exclusionary rule*—A criminal procedural rule that prohibits the introduction at trial of all evidence obtained in violation of constitutional rights, as well as any evidence derived from the illegally obtained evidence. 6. *Miranda rule*—A rule set forth by the Supreme Court in *Miranda v. Arizona* that individuals who are arrested must be informed of certain constitutional rights, including their right to counsel. 7. *Arrest, indictment, and trial*—Procedures governing arrest, indictment, and trial for a crime are designed to safeguard the rights of the individual against the state. See Exhibit 6–3 for a summary of the procedural steps involved in prosecuting a criminal case. 8. *Sentencing guidelines*—Both the federal government and the states have established sentencing laws or guidelines. The federal sentencing guidelines indicate a range of penalties for each federal crime; federal judges must abide by these guidelines when imposing sentences on those convicted of federal crimes.
Cyber Crime (See pages 190–196.)	Cyber crime is any crime that occurs in cyberspace. Examples include cyber theft (financial crimes committed with the aid of computers, as well as identity theft), cyber-stalking, hacking, and cyber terrorism. Significant federal statutes addressing cyber crimes include the Electronic Fund Transfer Act of 1978 and the Counterfeit Access Device and Computer Fraud and Abuse Act of 1984, as amended by the National Information Infrastructure Protection Act of 1996.

FOR REVIEW

Answers for the even-numbered questions in this For Review *section can be found in Appendix I at the end of this text.*

1. What two elements must exist before a person can be held liable for a crime? Can a corporation commit crimes?
2. What are five broad categories of crimes? What is white-collar crime?
3. What defenses might be raised by criminal defendants to avoid liability for criminal acts?
4. What constitutional safeguards exist to protect persons accused of crimes? What are the basic steps in the criminal process?
5. What is cyber crime? What laws apply to crimes committed in cyberspace?

QUESTIONS AND CASE PROBLEMS

6–1. Criminal versus Civil Trials. In criminal trials, the defendant must be proved guilty beyond a reasonable doubt, whereas in civil trials, the defendant need only be proved guilty by a preponderance of the evidence. Discuss why a higher burden of proof is required in criminal trials.

6–2. Types of Crimes. The following situations are similar (all involve the theft of Makoto's television set), yet they represent three different crimes. Identify the three crimes, noting the differences among them.

(a) While passing Makoto's house one night, Sarah sees a portable television set left unattended on Makoto's lawn. Sarah takes the television set, carries it home, and tells everyone she owns it.
(b) While passing Makoto's house one night, Sarah sees Makoto outside with a portable television set. Holding Makoto at gunpoint, Sarah forces him to give up the set. Then Sarah runs away with it.
(c) While passing Makoto's house one night, Sarah sees a portable television set in a window. Sarah breaks the front-door lock, enters, and leaves with the set.

6–3. Types of Crimes. Which, if any, of the following crimes necessarily involve illegal activity on the part of more than one person?

(a) Bribery.
(b) Forgery.
(c) Embezzlement.
(d) Larceny.
(e) Receiving stolen property.

6–4. Double Jeopardy. Armington, while robbing a drugstore, shot and seriously injured Jennings, a drugstore clerk. Armington was subsequently convicted in a criminal trial of armed robbery and assault and battery. Jennings later brought a civil tort suit against Armington for damages. Armington contended that he could not be tried again for the same crime, as that would constitute double jeopardy, which is prohibited by the Fifth Amendment to the Constitution. Is Armington correct? Explain.

6–5. Fifth Amendment. The federal government was investigating a corporation and its employees. The alleged criminal wrongdoing, which included the falsification of corporate books and records, occurred between 1993 and 1996 in one division of the corporation. In 1999, the corporation pleaded guilty and agreed to cooperate in an investigation of the individuals who might have been involved in the improper corporate activities. "Doe I," "Doe II," and "Doe III" were officers of the corporation during the period when the illegal activities occurred and worked in the division where the wrongdoing took place. They were no longer working for the corporation, however, when, as part of the subsequent investigation, the government asked them to provide specific corporate documents in their possession. All three asserted the Fifth Amendment privilege against self-incrimination. The government asked a federal district court to order the three to produce the records. Corporate employees can be compelled to produce corporate records in a criminal proceeding because they hold the records as representatives of the corporation, to which the Fifth Amendment privilege against self-incrimination does not apply. Should *former* employees also be compelled to produce corporate records in their possession? Why or why not? [*In re Three Grand Jury Subpoenas* Duces Tecum *Dated January 29, 1999,* 191 F.3d 173 (2d Cir. 1999)]

CASE PROBLEM WITH SAMPLE ANSWER

6–6. The District of Columbia Lottery Board licensed Soo Young Bae, a Washington, D.C., merchant, to operate a terminal that prints and dispenses lottery tickets for sale. Bae used the terminal to generate tickets with a face value of $525,586, for which he did not pay. The winning tickets among these had a total redemption value of $296,153, of which Bae successfully obtained all but $72,000. Bae pleaded guilty to computer fraud, and the court sentenced him to eighteen months in prison. In sentencing a defendant for fraud, a federal court must make a reasonable estimate of the victim's loss. The court determined that the value of the loss due to the fraud was $503,650—the market value of the tickets less the commission Bae would have received from the lottery board had he sold those tickets. Bae appealed, arguing that "[a]t the instant any lottery ticket is printed," it is worth whatever value the lottery drawing later assigns to it; that is, losing tickets have no value. Bae thus calculated the loss at $296,153, the value of his winning tickets. Should the U.S. Court of Appeals for the District of Columbia Circuit affirm or reverse Bae's sentence? Why? [*United States v. Bae,* 250 F.3d 774 (C.A.D.C. 2001)]

After you have answered this problem, compare your answer with the sample answer given on the Web site that accompanies this text. Go to http://blt.westbuslaw.com, select "Chapter 6," and click on "Case Problem with Sample Answer."

6–7. Larceny. In February 2001, a homeowner hired Jimmy Smith, a contractor claiming to employ a crew of thirty workers, to build a garage. The homeowner paid Smith $7,950 and agreed to make additional payments as needed to complete the project, up to $15,900. Smith promised to start the next day and finish within eight weeks. Nearly a month passed with no work, while Smith lied to the homeowner that materials were on "back order." During a second month, footings were created for the foundation, and a subcontractor poured the concrete slab, but Smith did not return the homeowner's phone calls. After eight weeks, the homeowner confronted Smith, who promised to complete the job, worked on the site that day until lunch, and never returned. Three months later, the homeowner again confronted Smith, who promised to "pay [him] off" later that day but did not do so. In March 2002, the state of Georgia filed criminal charges against Smith. While his trial was pending, he promised to pay the homeowner "next week," but again failed to refund any money. The value of the labor performed before Smith abandoned the project was between $800 and $1,000, the value of the materials was $367, and the subcontractor was paid $2,270. Did Smith commit larceny? Explain. [*Smith v. State of Georgia,* __ S.E.2d __ (Ga.App. 2004)]

A QUESTION OF ETHICS

6–8. A troublesome issue concerning the constitutional privilege against self-incrimination has to do with "jail plants"—that is, undercover police officers placed in cells with criminal suspects to gain information from the suspects. For example, in one case the police placed an undercover agent, Parisi, in a jail cell block with Lloyd Perkins, who had been imprisoned on charges unrelated to the murder that Parisi was investigating. When Parisi asked Perkins if he had ever killed anyone, Perkins made statements implicating himself in the murder. Perkins was then charged with the murder. [*Illinois v. Perkins,* 496 U.S. 292, 110 S.Ct. 2394, 110 L.Ed.2d 243 (1990)]

1. Review the discussion of *Miranda v. Arizona* in this chapter. Should Perkins's statements be suppressed—that is, not be admissible as evidence at trial—because he was not "read his rights," as required by the *Miranda* decision, prior to making his self-incriminating statements? Does *Miranda* apply to Perkins's situation?
2. Do you think that it is fair for the police to resort to trickery and deception to bring those who have committed crimes to justice? Why or why not? What rights or public policies must be balanced in deciding this issue?

FOR CRITICAL ANALYSIS

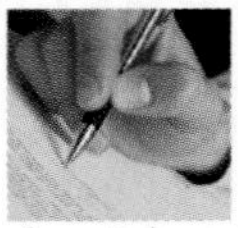

6–9. Do you think that criminal procedure in this country is weighted too heavily in favor of accused persons? Can you think of a fairer way to balance the constitutional rights of accused persons against the right of society to be protected against criminal behavior? Should different criminal procedures be used when terrorism is involved? Explain.

VIDEO QUESTION

6–10. Go to this text's Web site at **http://blt.westbuslaw.com** and select "Chapter 6." Click on "Video Questions" and view the video titled *Casino.* Then answer the following questions.

1. In the video, a casino manager, Ace (Robert DeNiro), discusses how politicians "won their 'comp life' when they got elected." "Comps" are the free gifts that casinos give to high-stakes gamblers to keep their business. If an elected official accepts comps, is he or she committing a crime? If so, what type of crime? Explain your answers.
2. Assume that Ace committed a crime by giving politicians comps. Can the casino, Tangiers Corporation, be held liable for that crime? Why or why not? How could a court punish the corporation?
3. Suppose that the Federal Bureau of Investigation (FBI) wants to search the premises of Tangiers for evidence of criminal activity. If casino management refuses to consent to the search, what constitutional safeguards and criminal procedures, if any, protect Tangiers?

INTERNET EXERCISES

Go to the *Business Law Today: The Essentials* home page at **http://blt.westbuslaw.com,** select "Chapter 6," and click on "Internet Exercises." There you will find the following Internet research exercises that you can perform to learn more about topics covered in this chapter.

Activity 6–1: LEGAL PERSPECTIVE—Revisiting *Miranda*

Activity 6–2: MANAGEMENT PERSPECTIVE—Hackers

Activity 6–3: INTERNATIONAL PERSPECTIVE—Fighting Cyber Crime Worldwide

BEFORE THE TEST

Go to the *Business Law Today: The Essentials* home page at **http://blt.westbuslaw.com,** select "Chapter 6," and click on "Interactive Quizzes." You will find at least twenty interactive questions relating to this chapter.

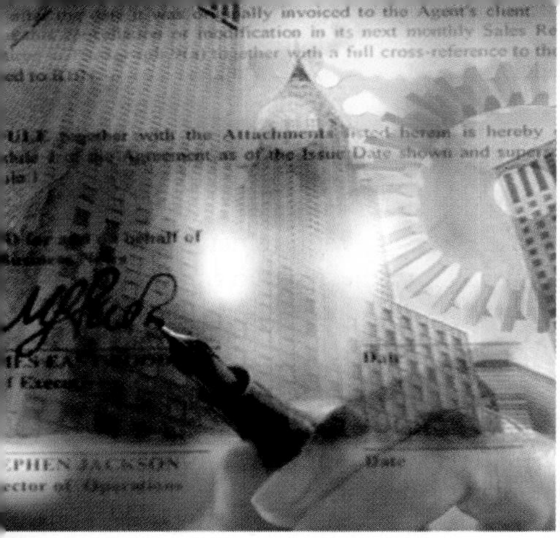

CHAPTER 7

Contracts: Nature, Classification, Agreement, and Consideration

"The social order rests upon the stability and predictability of conduct, of which keeping promises is a large item."

Roscoe Pound, 1870–1964
(American jurist)

CHAPTER OUTLINE

- THE NATURE AND FUNCTION OF CONTRACTS
- TYPES OF CONTRACTS
- AGREEMENT
- CONSIDERATION

LEARNING OBJECTIVES

After reading this chapter, you should be able to answer the following questions:

1. What is a contract? What are the four elements necessary to the formation of a valid contract?
2. What are the various types of contracts?
3. What are the requirements of an offer?
4. How can an offer be accepted?
5. What are the elements of consideration?

As Roscoe Pound—an eminent jurist—observed in the above quotation, "keeping promises" is important to a stable social order. Contract law deals with, among other things, the formation and keeping of promises. A **promise** is an assertion that something either will or will not happen in the future.

PROMISE
An assertion that something either will or will not happen in the future.

Like other types of law, contract law reflects our social values, interests, and expectations at a given point in time. It shows, for example, what kinds of promises our society thinks should be legally binding. It shows what excuses our society accepts for breaking such promises. Additionally, it shows what promises are considered to be contrary to public policy, or against the interests of society, and therefore legally void. If a promise goes against the interests of society as a whole, it will be invalid. Also, if it was made by a child or a mentally incompetent person, or on the basis of false information, a question will arise as to whether the promise should be enforced. Resolving such questions is the essence of contract law.

In this chapter, we first discuss the nature and function of contracts and the various types of contracts that exist. We also consider the basic requirements for a valid and enforceable contract. We then look closely at two of these requirements—*agreement* and *consideration*.

The Nature and Function of Contracts

No aspect of modern life is entirely free of contractual relationships. You acquire rights and obligations, for example, when you borrow funds, when you buy or lease a house, when you procure insurance, when you form a business, and when you purchase goods or services. Contract law is designed to provide stability and predictability for both buyers and sellers in the marketplace.

Contract law assures the parties to private agreements that the promises they make will be enforceable. Clearly, many promises are kept because the parties involved feel a moral obligation to do so or because keeping a promise is in their mutual self-interest, not because the **promisor** (the person making the promise) or the **promisee** (the person to whom the promise is made) is conscious of the rules of contract law. Nevertheless, the rules of contract law are often followed in business agreements to avoid potential problems.

PROMISOR
A person who makes a promise.

PROMISEE
A person to whom a promise is made.

By supplying procedures for enforcing private agreements, contract law provides an essential condition for the existence of a market economy. Without a legal framework of reasonably assured expectations within which to plan and venture, businesspersons would be able to rely only on the good faith of others. Duty and good faith are usually sufficient, but when dramatic price changes or adverse economic conditions make it costly to comply with a promise, these elements may not be enough. Contract law is necessary to ensure compliance with a promise or to entitle the innocent party to some form of relief.

THE LAW GOVERNING CONTRACTS

Although aspects of contract law vary from state to state, much of it is based on the common law. In 1932, the American Law Institute compiled the *Restatement of the Law of Contracts*. This work is a nonstatutory, authoritative exposition of the present law on the subject of contracts and is currently in its second edition (a third edition is in the process of being drafted). Throughout the following chapters on contracts, we will refer to the second edition of the *Restatement of the Law of Contracts* as simply the *Restatement (Second) of Contracts*.

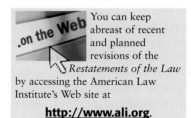

.on the Web You can keep abreast of recent and planned revisions of the *Restatements of the Law* by accessing the American Law Institute's Web site at

http://www.ali.org.

The Uniform Commercial Code (UCC), which governs contracts and other transactions relating to the sale and lease of goods, occasionally departs from common law contract rules. Generally, the different treatment of contracts falling under the UCC stems from the general policy of encouraging commerce. The ways in which the UCC changes common law contract rules will be discussed in later chapters. When discussing the common law of contracts, we indicate only briefly or in footnotes those common law rules that have been altered significantly by the UCC for sales and lease contracts.[1]

1. Note that throughout the chapters on the common law of contracts, we cite in the footnotes the section numbers of the UCC that are used in the UCC version that is currently in effect in most states. As you will read in later chapters covering sales contracts, the UCC was amended in 2003, and thus some of the section numbers may have been changed by those amendments.

Definition of a Contract

CONTRACT
An agreement that can be enforced in court; formed by two or more competent parties who agree, for consideration, to perform or to refrain from performing some legal act now or in the future.

A **contract** is an agreement that can be enforced in court. It is formed by two or more parties who agree to perform or to refrain from performing some act now or in the future. Generally, contract disputes arise when there is a promise of future performance. If the contractual promise is not fulfilled, the party who made it is subject to the sanctions of a court (see Chapter 9). That party may be required to pay money damages for failing to perform the contractual promise; in limited instances, the party may be required to perform the promised act.

Requirements of a Contract

The following list describes the four requirements that must be met for a valid contract to exist. Each item will be explained more fully in the chapter indicated.

.on the Web An extensive definition of the term *contract* is offered by the 'Lectric Law Library at **http://www.lectlaw.com/def/c123.htm**.

1. *Agreement.* An agreement includes an offer and an acceptance. One party must offer to enter into a legal agreement, and another party must accept the terms of the offer (this chapter).
2. *Consideration.* Any promises made by parties must be supported by legally sufficient and bargained-for consideration (something of value received or promised, to convince a person to make a deal) (this chapter).
3. *Contractual capacity.* Both parties entering into the contract must have the contractual capacity to do so; the law must recognize them as possessing characteristics that qualify them as competent parties (Chapter 8).
4. *Legality.* The contract's purpose must be to accomplish some goal that is legal and not against public policy (Chapter 8).

If any of these four elements is lacking, no contract will have been formed. Even if all of these elements exist, however, a contract may be unenforceable if the following requirements are not met. These requirements typically are raised as *defenses* to the enforceability of an otherwise valid contract.

1. *Genuineness of assent.* The apparent consent of both parties must be genuine (Chapter 8).
2. *Form.* The contract must be in whatever form the law requires; for example, some contracts must be in writing to be enforceable (Chapter 8).

Freedom of Contract and Freedom from Contract

As a general rule, the law recognizes everyone's ability to enter freely into contractual arrangements. This recognition is called *freedom of contract,* a freedom protected by the U.S. Constitution in Article I, Section 10. Because freedom of contract is a fundamental public policy of the United States, courts rarely interfere with contracts that have been voluntarily made.

Of course, as in other areas of the law, there are many exceptions to the general rule that contracts voluntarily negotiated will be enforced. For example, illegal bargains, agreements that unreasonably restrain trade, and certain unfair contracts made between one party with a great amount of bargaining power and another with little power are generally not enforced. In addition, as you will read in Chapter 8, certain contracts and clauses may not be enforceable if they are contrary to public policy, fairness, and justice. These exceptions provide freedom from contract for persons who may have been forced into making contracts unfavorable to themselves.

Types of Contracts

There are numerous types of contracts. They are categorized based on legal distinctions as to their formation, performance, and enforceability. Exhibit 7–1 illustrates three classifications, or categories, of contracts based on their mode of formation.

.on the Web For an excellent overview of the basic principles of contract law, go to **http://profs.lp.findlaw.com/contracts/index.html**.

Contract Formation

As you can see in Exhibit 7–1, three classifications, or categories, of contracts are based on how and when a contract is formed. The best way to explain each type of contract is to compare one type with another, as we do in the following pages.

OFFEROR
A person who makes an offer.

OFFEREE
A person to whom an offer is made.

Bilateral versus Unilateral Contracts Every contract involves at least two parties. The **offeror** is the party making the offer. The **offeree** is the party to whom the offer is made. The offeror always promises to do or not to do something and thus is also a promisor. Whether the contract is classified as *bilateral* or *unilateral* depends on what the offeree must do to accept the offer and bind the offeror to a contract.

BILATERAL CONTRACT
A type of contract that arises when a promise is given in exchange for a return promise.

Bilateral Contracts. If to accept the offer the offeree must only promise to perform, the contract is a **bilateral contract.** Hence, a bilateral contract is a "promise for a promise." An example of a bilateral contract is a contract in which one person agrees to buy another person's automobile for a specified price. No performance, such as the payment of money or delivery of goods, need take place for a bilateral contract to be formed. The contract comes into existence at the moment the promises are exchanged.

UNILATERAL CONTRACT
A contract that results when an offer can be accepted only by the offeree's performance.

Unilateral Contracts. If the offer is phrased so that the offeree can accept only by completing the contract performance, the contract is a **unilateral contract.** Hence, a unilateral contract is a "promise for an act." In other words, the contract is formed not at the moment when promises are exchanged but rather when the contract is *performed.* ■ EXAMPLE 7.1 Joe says to Celia, "If you drive my car from New York to Los Angeles, I'll give you $1,000." Only on Celia's completion of the act—bringing the car to Los Angeles—does she fully accept Joe's offer to pay $1,000. If she chooses not to accept the offer to drive the car to Los Angeles, there are no legal consequences. ■

EXHIBIT 7–1 CLASSIFICATIONS BASED ON CONTRACT FORMATION

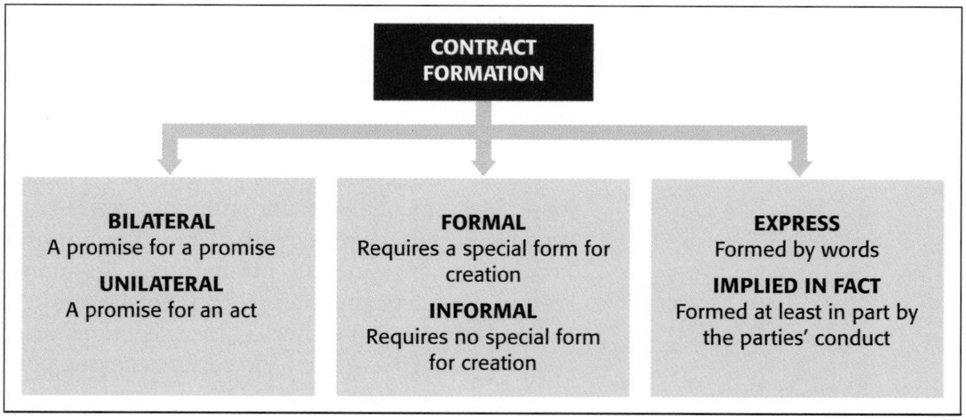

Contests, lotteries, and other competitions offering prizes are also examples of offers for unilateral contracts. If a person complies with the rules of the contest—such as by submitting the right lottery number at the right place and time—a unilateral contract is formed, binding the organization offering the prize to a contract to perform as promised in the offer.

Can a school's, or an employer's, letter of tentative acceptance to a prospective student, or a possible employee, qualify as a unilateral contract? That was the issue in the following case.

CASE 7.1 Ardito v. City of Providence

United States District Court, District of Rhode Island, 2003.
263 F.Supp.2d 358.

FACTS In 2001, the city of Providence, Rhode Island, decided to begin hiring police officers to fill vacancies in its police department. Because only individuals who had graduated from the Providence Police Academy were eligible, the city also decided to conduct two training sessions, the "60th and 61st Police Academies." To be admitted, an applicant had to pass a series of tests and be deemed qualified by members of the department after an interview. The applicants judged most qualified were sent a letter informing them that they had been selected to attend the academy if they successfully completed a medical checkup and a psychological examination. The letter for the applicants to the 61st Academy, dated October 15, stated that it was "a conditional offer of employment." Meanwhile, a new chief of police, Dean Esserman, decided to revise the selection process, which caused some of those who had received the letter to be rejected. Derek Ardito and thirteen other newly rejected applicants filed a suit in a federal district court against the city, seeking a halt to the 61st Academy unless they were allowed to attend. They alleged in part that the city was in breach of contract.

ISSUE Was the October 15 letter a unilateral offer that the plaintiffs had accepted by passing the required medical and psychological examinations?

DECISION Yes. The court issued an injunction to prohibit the city from conducting the 61st Police Academy unless the plaintiffs were included.

REASON The court found the October 15 letter to be "a classic example of an offer to enter into a unilateral contract. The October 15 letter expressly stated that it was a 'conditional offer of employment' and the message that it conveyed was that the recipient would be admitted into the 61st Academy if he or she successfully completed the medical and psychological examinations." The court contrasted the letter with "notices sent to applicants by the City at earlier stages of the selection process. Those notices merely informed applicants that they had completed a step in the process and remained eligible to be considered for admission into the Academy. Unlike the October 15 letter, the prior notices did not purport to extend a 'conditional offer' of admission." The court concluded that "[t]he plaintiffs accepted the City's offer of admission into the Academy by satisfying the specified conditions. Each of the plaintiffs submitted to and passed lengthy and intrusive medical and psychological examinations."

FOR CRITICAL ANALYSIS—Social Consideration *How might the city have phrased the October 15 letter to avoid its being considered a unilateral contract?*

Revocation of Offers for Unilateral Contracts. A problem arises in unilateral contracts when the promisor attempts to *revoke* (cancel) the offer after the promisee has begun performance but before the act has been completed. ■ EXAMPLE 7.2 Suppose that Roberta offers to buy Ed's sailboat, moored in San Francisco, on delivery of the boat to Roberta's dock in Newport Beach, three hundred miles south of San Francisco. Ed rigs the boat and sets sail. Shortly before his arrival at Newport Beach, Ed receives a radio message from Roberta withdrawing her offer. Roberta's offer is an offer for a unilateral contract, and only Ed's delivery of the sailboat at her dock is an acceptance. ■

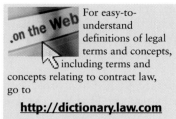

on the Web For easy-to-understand definitions of legal terms and concepts, including terms and concepts relating to contract law, go to

http://dictionary.law.com

and key in a term, such as "contract" or "consideration."

In contract law, offers are normally *revocable* (capable of being taken back, or canceled) until accepted. Under the traditional view of unilateral contracts, Roberta's revocation would terminate the offer. Because of the harsh effect on the offeree of the revocation of an offer to form a unilateral contract, the modern-day view is that once performance has been *substantially* undertaken, the offeror cannot revoke the offer. Thus, in our example, even though Ed has not yet accepted the offer by complete performance, Roberta is prohibited from revoking it. Ed can deliver the boat and bind Roberta to the contract.

FORMAL CONTRACT
A contract that by law requires a specific form, such as being executed under seal, for its validity.

Formal versus Informal Contracts Contracts that require a special form or method of creation (formation) to be enforceable are known as **formal contracts.** Formal contracts include (1) contracts under seal, (2) recognizances, (3) negotiable instruments, and (4) letters of credit.[2]

KEEP IN MIND Not every contract is a document with "Contract" printed in block letters at the top. A contract can be expressed in a letter, a memo, or another document.

Contracts under seal are formalized writings with a special seal attached.[3] The significance of the seal has lessened, although about ten states require no consideration for formation of a valid contract when a contract is under seal. A *recognizance* is an acknowledgment in court by a person that he or she will perform some specified obligation or pay a certain sum if he or she fails to perform. One form of recognizance is the surety bond.[4] Another is the personal recognizance bond used as bail in a criminal matter. As will be discussed at length in subsequent chapters, *negotiable instruments* include checks, notes, drafts, and certificates of deposit; letters of credit are agreements to pay contingent on the purchaser's receipt of invoices and bills of lading (documents evidencing receipt of, and title to, goods shipped).

INFORMAL CONTRACT
A contract that does not require a specified form or formality to be valid.

Informal contracts (also called *simple contracts*) include all other contracts. No special form is required (except for certain types of contracts that must be in writing), as the contracts are usually based on their substance rather than their form. Typically, businesspersons put their contracts in writing to ensure that there is some proof of a contract's existence should problems arise.

Express versus Implied Contracts Contracts may also be formed and categorized as express or implied by the conduct of the parties. We look here at the differences between these two types of contracts.

EXPRESS CONTRACT
A contract in which the terms of the agreement are stated in words, oral or written.

Express Contracts. An **express contract** is one in which the terms of the agreement are fully and explicitly stated in words, oral or written. A signed lease for an apartment or a house is an express written contract. If a classmate accepts your offer to sell your textbooks from last semester for $75, an express oral contract has been made.

IMPLIED-IN-FACT CONTRACT
A contract formed in whole or in part from the conduct of the parties (as opposed to an express contract).

Implied Contracts. A contract that is implied from the conduct of the parties is called an **implied-in-fact contract,** or an implied contract. This type of contract differs from an express contract in that the *conduct* of the parties, rather than their words, creates and defines at least some of the terms of the contract.

■ **EXAMPLE 7.3** Suppose that you need an accountant to fill out your tax return this year. You look through the Yellow Pages and find an accounting firm located in

2. *Restatement (Second) of Contracts,* Section 6.

3. A seal may be actual (made of wax or some other durable substance), impressed on the paper, or indicated simply by the word *seal* or the letters *L.S.* at the end of the document. *L.S.* stands for *locus sigilli,* which means "the place for the seal."

4. An obligation of a party who guarantees that he or she will pay a second party if a third party does not perform.

What determines whether a contract for accounting, tax preparation, or any other service is an express contract or an implied-in-fact contract? (© Getty Images)

your neighborhood. You drop by the firm's office, explain your problem to an accountant, and learn what fees will be charged. The next day you return and give the receptionist all of the necessary information and documents, such as canceled checks, W-2 forms, and so on. Then you walk out the door without saying anything expressly to the receptionist. In this situation, you have entered into an implied-in-fact contract to pay the accountant the usual and reasonable fees for the accounting services. The contract is implied by your conduct. The accountant expects to be paid for completing your tax return. By bringing in the records the accountant will need to do the work, you have implied an intent to pay for the services. ■ (For another example of how an implied-in-fact contract can arise, see this chapter's *Application* feature at the end of this chapter.)

Requirements for an Implied-in-Fact Contract. For an implied-in-fact contract to arise, certain requirements must be met. Normally, if the following conditions exist, a court will hold that an implied contract was formed:

1. The plaintiff furnished some service or property.
2. The plaintiff expected to be paid for that service or property, and the defendant knew or should have known that payment was expected.
3. The defendant had a chance to reject the services or property and did not.

CONTRACT PERFORMANCE

EXECUTED CONTRACT
A contract that has been completely performed by both parties.

EXECUTORY CONTRACT
A contract that has not as yet been fully performed.

Contracts are also classified according to their state of performance. A contract that has been fully performed on both sides is called an **executed contract.** A contract that has not been fully performed on either side is called an **executory contract.** If one party has fully performed but the other has not, the contract is said to be executed on the one side and executory on the other, but the contract is still classified as executory.

■ EXAMPLE 7.4 Assume that you agree to buy ten tons of coal from Western Coal Company. Further assume that Western has delivered the coal to your steel mill, where it is now being burned. At this point, the contract is an executory contract—it is executed on the part of Western and executory on your part. After you pay Western for the coal, the contract will be executed on both sides. ■

CONTRACT ENFORCEABILITY

VALID CONTRACT
A contract that results when the elements necessary for contract formation (agreement, consideration, legal purpose, and contractual capacity) are present.

A **valid contract** has the four elements necessary for contract formation: (1) an agreement (offer and acceptance) (2) supported by legally sufficient consideration (3) for a legal purpose and (4) made by parties who have the legal capacity to enter into the contract. As mentioned, we will discuss each of these elements in this chapter and the one that follows.

As you can see in Exhibit 7–2, valid contracts may be enforceable, voidable, or unenforceable. Additionally, a contract may be referred to as a *void contract.* We look next at the meaning of the terms *voidable, unenforceable,* and *void* in relation to contract enforceability.

VOIDABLE CONTRACT
A contract that may be legally avoided (canceled, or annulled) at the option of one or both of the parties.

Voidable Contracts A **voidable contract** is a *valid* contract but one that can be avoided at the option of one or both of the parties. The party having the option can elect either to avoid any duty to perform or to *ratify* (make valid) the contract. If the contract is avoided, both parties are released from it. If it is ratified, both parties must fully perform their respective legal obligations.

EXHIBIT 7–2 ENFORCEABLE, VOID, VOIDABLE, AND UNENFORCEABLE CONTRACTS

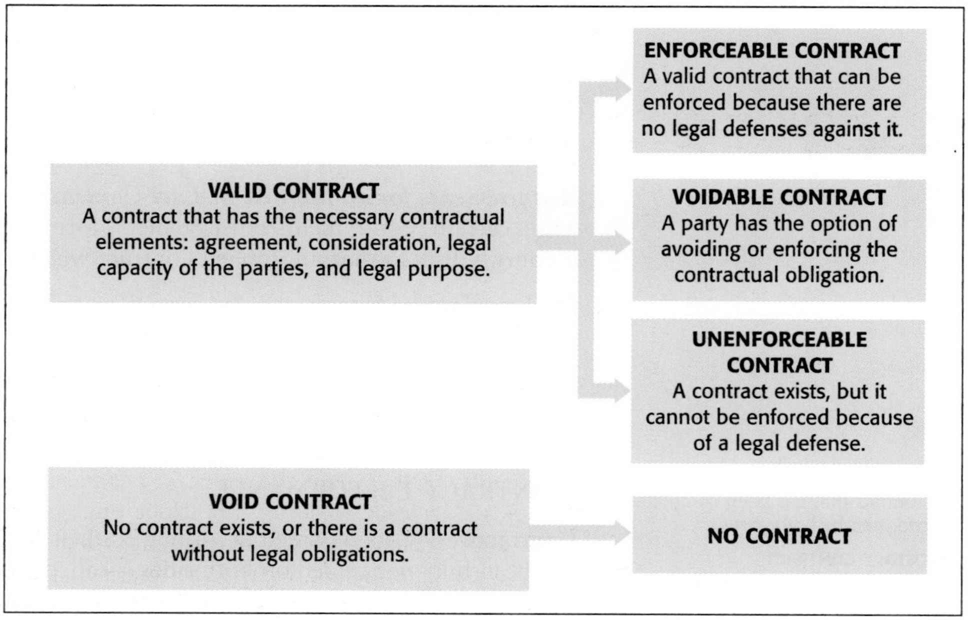

ENFORCEABLE CONTRACT
A valid contract that can be enforced because there are no legal defenses against it.
VALID CONTRACT
A contract that has the necessary contractual elements: agreement, consideration, legal capacity of the parties, and legal purpose.
VOIDABLE CONTRACT
A party has the option of avoiding or enforcing the contractual obligation.
UNENFORCEABLE CONTRACT
A contract exists, but it cannot be enforced because of a legal defense.
VOID CONTRACT
No contract exists, or there is a contract without legal obligations.
NO CONTRACT

As you will read in Chapter 8, contracts made by minors, insane persons, and intoxicated persons may be voidable. As a general rule, for example, contracts made by minors are voidable at the option of the minor. Additionally, contracts entered into under fraudulent conditions are voidable at the option of the defrauded party. Contracts entered into under legally defined duress or undue influence are voidable (see Chapter 8).

UNENFORCEABLE CONTRACT
A valid contract rendered unenforceable by some statute or law.

Unenforceable Contracts An **unenforceable contract** is one that cannot be enforced because of certain legal defenses against it. It is not unenforceable because a party failed to satisfy a legal requirement of the contract; rather, it is a valid contract rendered unenforceable by some statute or law. For example, some contracts must be in writing (see Chapter 8), and if they are not, they will not be enforceable except in certain exceptional circumstances.

VOID CONTRACT
A contract having no legal force or binding effect.

Void Contracts A **void contract** is no contract at all. The terms *void* and *contract* are contradictory. None of the parties has any legal obligations if a contract is void. A contract can be void because, for example, one of the parties was previously determined by a court to be legally insane (and thus lacked the legal capacity to enter into a contract) or because the purpose of the contract was illegal.

Quasi Contracts

QUASI CONTRACT
A fictional contract imposed on parties by a court in the interests of fairness and justice; usually imposed to avoid the unjust enrichment of one party at the expense of another.

Quasi contracts, or contracts *implied in law,* are wholly different from actual contracts. Express contracts and implied-in-fact contracts are actual, or true, contracts. The word *quasi* is Latin for "as if" or "analogous to." Quasi contracts are thus not true contracts. They do not arise from any agreement, express or implied, between the parties themselves. Rather, quasi contracts are fictional contracts imposed on parties by courts "as if" the parties had entered into an actual contract. Usually, quasi contracts are imposed to avoid the *unjust enrichment* of one party at the expense of another. The doctrine of unjust enrichment is based on the theory that individuals should not be allowed to profit or enrich themselves inequitably at the expense of others.

■ EXAMPLE 7.5 Suppose that a vacationing physician is driving down the highway and encounters Emerson, who is lying unconscious on the side of the road. The physician renders medical aid that saves Emerson's life. Although the injured, unconscious Emerson did not solicit the medical aid and was not aware that the aid had been rendered, Emerson received a valuable benefit, and the requirements for a quasi contract were fulfilled. In such a situation, the law normally will impose a quasi contract, and Emerson will have to pay the physician for the reasonable value of the medical services provided. ■

ETHICAL ISSUE 7.1

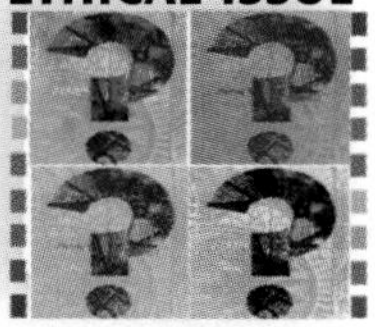

When does enrichment qualify as "unjust enrichment"? Sometimes a party is enriched by (benefits from) the actions of another, yet the benefits do not necessarily constitute unjust enrichment. For example, in one case the owner of a building (the lessor) leased the building to a commercial tenant (the lessee) for five years. The lessee, which assumed all responsibility for repairs, maintenance, and alterations, hired DCB Construction Company to make alterations to the premises that cost about $300,000. The lessor told DCB that it would not be responsible for any of the costs. Nonetheless, when the lessee quit paying rent, was evicted, and failed to pay DCB for the completed work, DCB sued the lessor for the amount still owing ($280,000). In this case, clearly the lessor had benefited from DCB's work. Yet did this benefit amount to unjust enrichment under the law? No, stated the court. The

A worker takes apart machinery. If the worker, without a contract, makes a design modification that the manufacturer incorporates into later models of the machine, should the worker be compensated? Why or why not? (Billy E. Barnes, PhotoEdit)

court pointed out that DCB did the work for the lessee and was notified by the lessor that it would not be held liable for the costs of the work. Further, no fraud or mistake was involved. The court noted that the courts almost always reject unjust enrichment claims such as this one.[5] ■

Limitations on Quasi-Contractual Recovery Although quasi contracts exist to prevent unjust enrichment, in some situations the party who obtains a benefit will not be deemed to have been unjustly enriched. Basically, the quasi-contractual principle cannot be invoked by a party who has conferred a benefit on someone else unnecessarily or as a result of misconduct or negligence.

■ EXAMPLE 7.6 You take your car to the local car wash and ask to have it run through the washer and to have the gas tank filled. While your car is being washed, you go to a nearby shopping center for two hours. In the meantime, one of the workers at the car wash mistakenly assumes that your car is the one that he is supposed to hand wax. When you come back, you are presented with a bill for a full tank of gas, a wash job, and a hand wax. Clearly, you have received a benefit, but this benefit was conferred because of a mistake by the car wash employee. You have not been *unjustly* enriched under these circumstances. People normally cannot be forced to pay for benefits "thrust" on them. ■

When a Contract Already Exists The doctrine of quasi contract generally cannot be used when an actual contract covers the area in controversy. This is because a remedy already exists if a party is unjustly enriched as a result of a breach of contract: the nonbreaching party can sue the breaching party for breach of contract. In this instance, a court does not need to impose a quasi contract to achieve justice.

Agreement

AGREEMENT
A meeting of two or more minds in regard to the terms of a contract; usually broken down into two events—an offer by one party to form a contract, and an acceptance of the offer by the person to whom the offer is made.

OFFER
A promise or commitment to perform or refrain from performing some specified act in the future.

An essential element for contract formation is **agreement**—the parties must agree on the terms of the contract. Ordinarily, agreement is evidenced by two events: an *offer* and an *acceptance.* One party offers a certain bargain to another party, who then accepts that bargain.

Because words often fail to convey the precise meaning intended, the law of contracts generally adheres to the *objective theory of contracts.* Under this theory, a party's words and conduct are held to mean whatever a reasonable person in the offeree's position would think they meant. The court will give words their usual meanings even if "it were proved by twenty bishops that [the] party . . . intended something else."[6]

REQUIREMENTS OF THE OFFER

An **offer** is a promise or commitment to perform or refrain from performing some specified act in the future. As discussed earlier, the party making an offer is called the *offeror,* and the party to whom the offer is made is called the *offeree.*

5. *DCB Construction Co. v. Central City Development Co.,* 940 P.2d 958 (Colo.App. 1997).

6. Judge Learned Hand in *Hotchkiss v. National City Bank of New York,* 200 F. 287 (2d Cir. 1911); aff'd 231 U.S. 50, 34 S.Ct. 20, 58 L.Ed. 115 (1913). (The term *aff'd* is an abbreviation for *affirmed;* an appellate court can affirm a lower court's judgment, decree, or order, thereby declaring that it is valid and must stand as rendered.)

Three elements are necessary for an offer to be effective:

1. There must be a serious, objective intention by the offeror.
2. The terms of the offer must be reasonably certain, or definite, so that the parties and the court can ascertain the terms of the contract.
3. The offer must be communicated to the offeree.

Once an effective offer has been made, the offeree's acceptance of that offer creates a legally binding contract (providing the other essential elements for a valid and enforceable contract are present).

In today's e-commerce world, offers are frequently made online. Essentially, the requirements for traditional offers apply to online offers as well, as you will read in Chapter 10.

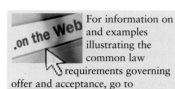

> **.on the Web** For information on and examples illustrating the common law requirements governing offer and acceptance, go to FindLaw's Web site at
>
> **http://profs.lp.findlaw.com/contracts/index.html.**

Intention The first requirement for an effective offer to exist is a serious, objective intention on the part of the offeror. Intent is not determined by the *subjective* intentions, beliefs, or assumptions of the offeror. Rather, it is determined by what a reasonable person in the offeree's position would conclude the offeror's words and actions meant. Offers made in obvious anger, jest, or undue excitement do not meet the serious-and-objective-intent test. Because these offers are not effective, an offeree's acceptance does not create an agreement.

■ **EXAMPLE 7.7** You and three classmates ride to school each day in Julio's new automobile, which has a market value of $18,000. One cold morning the four of you get into the car, but Julio cannot get it started. He yells in anger, "I'll sell this car to anyone for $500!" You drop $500 in his lap. A reasonable person, taking into consideration Julio's frustration and the obvious difference in value between the car's market price and the purchase price, would declare that Julio's offer was not made with serious and objective intent and that you do not have an agreement. ■ In the subsections that follow, we further examine the concept of intention as we look at the distinctions between offers and nonoffers.

Lucy v. Zehmer, presented next, is a classic case in the area of contractual agreement. The case involved a business transaction in which boasts, brags, and dares "after a few drinks" resulted in a contract to sell certain property. The sellers claimed that the offer had been made in jest and that, in any event, the contract was voidable at their option because they were intoxicated when the offer was made and thus lacked contractual capacity (see Chapter 8). The court, however, looked to the words and actions of the parties—not their secret intentions—to determine whether a contract had been formed.

LANDMARK AND CLASSIC CASES

CASE 7.2 Lucy v. Zehmer

Supreme Court of Appeals of Virginia, 1954.
196 Va. 493,
84 S.E.2d 516.

FACTS Lucy and Zehmer had known each other for fifteen to twenty years. For some time, Lucy had been wanting to buy Zehmer's farm. Zehmer had always told Lucy that he was not interested in selling. One night, Lucy stopped in to visit with the Zehmers at a restaurant they operated. Lucy said to Zehmer, "I bet you wouldn't take $50,000 for that place." Zehmer replied, "Yes, I would, too; you wouldn't give fifty." Throughout the evening, the conversation returned to the sale of the farm. At the same time, the parties were drinking whiskey. Eventually, Zehmer wrote up an agreement, on the back of a restaurant check, for the sale of the farm, and he asked his wife

(Continued)

CASE 7.2—Continued

to sign it—which she did. When Lucy brought an action in a Virginia state court to enforce the agreement, Zehmer argued that he had been "high as a Georgia pine" at the time and that the offer had been made in jest: "two dog-goned drunks bluffing to see who could talk the biggest and say the most." Lucy claimed that he had not been intoxicated and did not think Zehmer had been, either, given the way Zehmer handled the transaction. The trial court ruled in favor of the Zehmers, and Lucy appealed.

ISSUE Can the agreement be avoided on the basis of intoxication?

DECISION No. The agreement to sell the farm was binding.

REASON The opinion of the court was that the evidence given about the nature of the conversation, the appearance and completeness of the agreement, and the signing all tended to show that a serious business transaction, not a casual jest, was intended. The court had to look into the objective meaning of the words and acts of the Zehmers: "An agreement or mutual assent is of course essential to a valid contract, but the law imputes to a person an intention corresponding to the reasonable meaning of his words and acts. If his words and acts, judged by a reasonable standard, manifest an intention to agree, it is immaterial what may be the real but unexpressed state of mind."

COMMENTS *This is a classic case in contract law because it illustrates so clearly the objective theory of contracts with respect to determining whether an offer was intended. Today, the objective theory of contracts continues to be applied by the courts, and* Lucy v. Zehmer *is routinely cited as a significant precedent in this area. Note that in cases involving contracts formed online, the issue of contractual intent rarely arises. Perhaps this is because an online offer is, by definition, "objective" in the sense that it consists of words only—the offeror's physical actions and behavior are not evidenced.*

RELEVANT WEB SITES *To locate information on the Web concerning* Lucy v. Zehmer, *go to this text's Web site at* **http://blt.westbuslaw.com**, *select "Chapter 7," and click on "URLs for Landmarks."*

Expressions of Opinion. An expression of opinion is not an offer. It does not evidence an intention to enter into a binding agreement. ■ EXAMPLE 7.8 In *Hawkins v. McGee*,[7] Hawkins took his son to McGee, a doctor, and asked McGee to operate on the son's hand. McGee said that the boy would be in the hospital three or four days and that the hand would *probably* heal a few days later. The son's hand did not heal for a month, but nonetheless the father did not win a suit for breach of contract. The court held that McGee did not make an offer to heal the son's hand in three or four days. He merely expressed an opinion as to when the hand would heal. ■

Statements of Intention. A statement of an *intention* to do something in the future is not an offer. ■ EXAMPLE 7.9 If Ari says, "I *plan* to sell my stock in Novation, Inc., for $150 per share," a contract is not created if John "accepts" and tenders $150 per share for the stock. Ari has merely expressed his intention to enter into a future contract for the sale of the stock. If John accepts and tenders the $150 per share, no contract is formed because a reasonable person would conclude that Ari was only *thinking about* selling his stock, not promising to sell it. ■

BE CAREFUL An opinion is not an offer and not a contract term. Goods or services can be "perfect" in one party's opinion and "poor" in another's.

Preliminary Negotiations. A request or invitation to negotiate is not an offer; it only expresses a willingness to discuss the possibility of entering into a contract. Examples are statements such as "Will you sell Forest Acres?" and "I wouldn't sell my car for less than $1,000." A reasonable person in the offeree's position would

7. 84 N.H. 114, 146 A. 641 (1929).

not conclude that such a statement evidenced an intention to enter into a binding obligation. Likewise, when the government and private firms need to have construction work done, contractors are invited to submit bids. The *invitation* to submit bids is not an offer, and a contractor does not bind the government or private firm by submitting a bid. (The bids that the contractors submit are offers, however, and the government or private firm can bind the contractor by accepting the bid.)

Advertisements, Catalogues, and Circulars. In general, advertisements, mail-order catalogues, price lists, and circular letters (meant for the general public) are treated as invitations to negotiate, not as offers to form a contract.[8] ■ EXAMPLE 7.10 Suppose that you put an ad in the classified section of your local newspaper offering to sell your guitar for $75. Seven people call and "accept" your "offer" before you can remove the ad from the newspaper. If the ad were truly an offer, you would be bound by seven contracts to sell your guitar. Because advertisements are treated as *invitations* to make offers rather than offers, however, you will have seven offers to choose from, and you can accept the best one without incurring any liability for the six you reject. ■ On some occasions, though, courts have construed advertisements to be offers because the ads contained definite terms that invited acceptance (such as an ad offering a reward for the return of a lost dog).[9]

KEEP IN MIND Advertisements are not binding, but they cannot be deceptive.

Price lists are another form of invitation to negotiate or trade. A seller's price list is not an offer to sell at that price; it merely invites the buyer to offer to buy at that price. In fact, the seller usually puts "prices subject to change" on the price list. Only in rare circumstances will a price quotation be construed as an offer.[10]

ETHICAL ISSUE 7.2

Should promises of prizes made in ads and circulars always be enforced? Businesses and other organizations commonly promote their products or services by offering prizes, rewards, and the like for certain performance. Ordinarily, these ads for prizes present few problems. At times, though, people perform whatever is necessary to win advertised prizes only to learn that the offers were made in jest—that is, the ads' sponsors had no real intention of giving anyone the prizes. Consider an example. PepsiCo launched an ad campaign in which consumers could use "Pepsi Points"—which could be found on specially marked packages of Pepsi or purchased for ten cents each—to obtain T-shirts and other merchandise with the Pepsi logo. One of the ads featured a Harrier fighter jet, which was listed at 7,000,000 Pepsi Points. When a consumer, John Leonard, raised $700,000, purchased 7,000,000 Pepsi Points, and laid claim to the prize, however, PepsiCo contended that the Harrier jet in the commercial was "fanciful" and that the offer was made in jest.

In the lawsuit that followed, the court agreed, stating that "no objective person could reasonably have concluded that the commercial actually offered consumers a Harrier jet."[11] Yet Leonard obviously did draw that conclusion, and in a number of other cases, individuals have undertaken serious efforts to win nonexistent prizes. Some claim that not enforcing such promises is unfair to individuals who rely on the promises, as John Leonard did in the *PepsiCo* case. ■

8. *Restatement (Second) of Contracts,* Section 26, Comment b.
9. The classic example is *Lefkowitz v. Great Minneapolis Surplus Store, Inc.,* 251 Minn. 188, 86 N.W.2d 689 (1957).
10. See, for example, *Fairmount Glass Works v. Grunden-Martin Woodenware Co.,* 106 Ky. 659, 51 S.W. 196 (1899).
11. *Leonard v. PepsiCo,* 88 F.Supp.2d 116 (S.D.N.Y. 1999); aff'd 210 F.3d 88 (2d Cir. 2000).

Auctions. In an auction, a seller "offers" goods for sale through an auctioneer. This is not, however, an offer to form a contract. Rather, it is an invitation asking bidders to submit offers. In the context of an auction, a bidder is the offeror, and the auctioneer is the offeree. The offer is accepted when the auctioneer strikes the hammer. Before the fall of the hammer, a bidder may revoke (take back) her or his bid, or the auctioneer may reject that bid or all bids. Typically, an auctioneer will reject a bid that is below the price the seller is willing to accept.

When the auctioneer accepts a higher bid, he or she rejects all previous bids. Because rejection terminates an offer (as will be discussed later), those bids represent offers that have been terminated. Thus, if the highest bidder withdraws his or her bid before the hammer falls, none of the previous bids is reinstated. If the bid is not withdrawn or rejected, the contract is formed when the auctioneer announces, "Going once, going twice, sold!" (or something similar) and lets the hammer fall.

Traditionally, auctions have been either "with reserve" or "without reserve." In an auction with reserve, the seller (through the auctioneer) may withdraw the goods at any time before the auctioneer closes the sale by announcement or by the fall of the hammer. All auctions are assumed to be auctions with reserve unless the terms of the auction are explicitly stated to be *without reserve.* In an auction without reserve, the goods cannot be withdrawn by the seller and must be sold to the highest bidder. In auctions with reserve, the seller may reserve the right to confirm or reject the sale even after "the hammer has fallen." In this situation, the seller is obligated to notify those attending the auction that sales of goods made during the auction are not final until confirmed by the seller.[12]

How do these rules apply to an online auction of rights to a domain name? For a discussion of a case involving this issue, see this chapter's *Adapting the Law to the Online Environment* feature.

Agreements to Agree. Traditionally, agreements to agree—that is, agreements to agree to the material terms of a contract at some future date—were not considered

12. These rules apply under both the common law of contracts and the Uniform Commercial Code, or UCC. See UCC 2–328.

In an auction, such as this one in Boonesville, Missouri, is the party selling the goods the "offeror" for purposes of contract law? Why or why not? (AP Photo/L.G. Patterson)

ADAPTING THE LAW TO THE ONLINE ENVIRONMENT

Can an Online Bid Constitute an Acceptance?

Under the Uniform Commercial Code, or UCC (see Chapter 11), a bid at an auction constitutes an offer. The offer (the highest bid) is accepted when the auctioneer's hammer falls. The UCC also states that auctions are "with reserve" unless the seller specifies otherwise. As just noted, in an auction with reserve, the seller reserves the right not to sell the goods to the highest bidder. Hence, even after the hammer falls, the contract for sale remains conditioned on the seller's approval. The question of how these rules should be applied to an online auction of a domain name, in which no hammer falls, came before a California court.

THE BID (OR OFFER?)

The case involved an online auction conducted by The.TV Corporation International (DotTV) on its Web site. DotTV posted an announcement on its Web site asking for bids for rights to the "Golf.tv" domain name and stating that the name would go to the highest bidder. Je Ho Lim submitted a bid for $1,010 and authorized DotTV to charge that amount to his credit card if his bid was the highest. Later, DotTV sent Lim an e-mail message stating that he had "won the auction" and charged the bid price of $1,010 to Lim's credit card. When DotTV subsequently refused to transfer the name, Lim sued DotTV for, among other things, breach of contract. Lim argued that his bid constituted an acceptance of DotTV's offer to sell the name. DotTV contended that Lim's bid was an offer, which it had not accepted. Furthermore, even if it had accepted Lim's offer, because the auction was "with reserve," DotTV could withdraw the domain name from the auction even after acceptance. The trial court held for DotTV, and Lim appealed.

THE COURT'S ANALYSIS

The appellate court first looked at the UCC's provisions concerning auctions but noted that the UCC did not apply in this case because the UCC applies only to "goods" and domain names are not goods. The court then looked at common law principles as codified in the *Restatement (Second) of Contracts*. The rules under the *Restatement* are similar to those of the UCC: a bid in an auction is an offer that is accepted when the "hammer falls," and an auction is with reserve unless otherwise specified by the seller.

The court also pointed out, however, that DotTV's charging of the bid price to Lim's credit card was inconsistent with DotTV's claim that it could withdraw the domain name from the bidding because the auction was with reserve. Furthermore, stated the court, even if it concluded that Lim's bid was an offer and not an acceptance, DotTV had accepted the offer by its e-mail to Lim stating that he had won the auction. In all, held the court, there was no evidence that a contract between DotTV and Lim had *not* been formed, and Lim had stated a valid claim against DotTV for breach of contract. The court thus reversed the lower court's decision and remanded the case for further deliberation consistent with the appellate court's opinion.[a]

FOR CRITICAL ANALYSIS

Should the UCC rules governing auctions apply to items sold on online auction sites, such as eBay? Why or why not? How can you know whether eBay's auctions are "with reserve" or "without reserve"?

a. *Lim v. The.TV Corp. International,* 99 Cal.App.4th 684, 121 Cal.Rptr.2d 333 (2d Dist. 2002).

to be binding contracts. The modern view, however, is that agreements to agree may be enforceable agreements (contracts) if it is clear that the parties intend to be bound by the agreements. In other words, under the modern view the emphasis is on the parties' intent rather than on form.

■ **EXAMPLE 7.11** When the Pennzoil Company discussed with the Getty Oil Company the possible purchase of Getty's stock, a memorandum of agreement was drafted to reflect the terms of the conversations. After more negotiations over the price, both companies issued press releases announcing an agreement in principle on the terms of the memorandum. The next day, Texaco, Inc., offered to buy all of

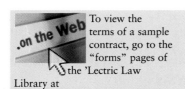

.on the Web To view the terms of a sample contract, go to the "forms" pages of the 'Lectric Law Library at

http://www.lectlaw.com/formb.htm

and select one of the types of contracts listed there to review.

Getty's stock at a higher price. The day after that, Getty's board of directors voted to accept Texaco's offer, and Texaco and Getty signed a merger agreement. When Pennzoil sued Texaco for tortious interference with its "contractual" relationship with Getty, a jury concluded that Getty and Pennzoil had intended to form a binding contract, with only the details left to be worked out, before Texaco made its offer. Texaco was held liable for wrongfully interfering with this contract.[13] ■

Definiteness The second requirement for an effective offer involves the definiteness of its terms. An offer must have reasonably definite terms so that a court can determine if a breach has occurred and give an appropriate remedy.[14]

An offer may invite an acceptance to be worded in such specific terms that the contract is made definite. ■ **EXAMPLE 7.12** Suppose that Marcus Business Machines contacts your corporation and offers to sell "from one to ten MacCool copying machines for $1,600 each; state number desired in acceptance." Your corporation agrees to buy two copiers. Because the quantity is specified in the acceptance, the terms are definite, and the contract is enforceable. ■

Communication A third requirement for an effective offer is communication—the offer must be communicated to the offeree. ■ **EXAMPLE 7.13** Suppose that Tolson advertises a reward for the return of her lost cat. Dirlik, not knowing of the reward, finds the cat and returns it to Tolson. Ordinarily, Dirlik cannot recover the reward because an essential element of a reward contract is that the one who claims the reward must have known it was offered. A few states would allow recovery of the reward, but not on contract principles—Dirlik would be allowed to recover on the basis that it would be unfair to deny him the reward just because he did not know about it. ■

TERMINATION OF THE OFFER

The communication of an effective offer to an offeree gives the offeree the power to transform the offer into a binding, legal obligation (a contract) by an acceptance. This power of acceptance, however, does not continue forever. It can be terminated by action of the parties or by operation of law.

Termination by Action of the Parties An offer can be terminated by the action of the parties in any of three ways: by revocation, by rejection, or by counteroffer.

REVOCATION
In contract law, the withdrawal of an offer by an offeror. Unless the offer is irrevocable, it can be revoked at any time prior to acceptance without liability.

Revocation of the Offer. The offeror's act of withdrawing an offer is referred to as **revocation.** Unless an offer is irrevocable, the offeror usually can revoke the offer (even if he or she has promised to keep the offer open), as long as the revocation is communicated to the offeree before the offeree accepts. Revocation may be accomplished by an express repudiation of the offer (for example, with a statement such as "I withdraw my previous offer of October 17") or by the performance of acts that are inconsistent with the existence of the offer and that are made known to the offeree.

13. *Texaco, Inc. v. Pennzoil Co.,* 729 S.W.2d 768 (Tex.App.—Houston [1st Dist.] 1987, writ ref'd n.r.e.). (Generally, a complete Texas Court of Appeals citation includes the writ-of-error history showing the Texas Supreme Court's disposition of the case. In this case, *writ ref'd n.r.e.* is an abbreviation for "writ refused, no reversible error," which means that Texas's highest court refused to grant the appellant's request to review the case, because the court did not think there was any reversible error.)

14. *Restatement (Second) of Contracts,* Section 33. The UCC has relaxed the requirements regarding the definiteness of terms in contracts for the sale of goods. See UCC 2–204(3).

■ EXAMPLE 7.14 Geraldine offers to sell some land to Gary. A week passes, and Gary, who has not yet accepted the offer, learns from his friend Konstantine that Geraldine has in the meantime sold the property to Nunan. Gary's knowledge of Geraldine's sale of the land to Nunan, even though he learned of it through a third party, effectively revokes Geraldine's offer to sell the land to Gary. Geraldine's sale of the land to Nunan is inconsistent with the continued existence of the offer to Gary, and thus the offer to Gary is revoked. ■

The general rule followed by most states is that a revocation becomes effective when the offeree or the offeree's agent (a person who acts on behalf of another) actually receives it. Therefore, a letter of revocation mailed on April 1 and delivered at the offeree's residence or place of business on April 3 becomes effective on April 3.

An offer made to the general public can be revoked in the same manner in which the offer was originally communicated. ■ EXAMPLE 7.15 Suppose that a department store offers a $10,000 reward to anyone giving information leading to the apprehension of the persons who burglarized its downtown store. The offer is published in three local papers and in four papers in neighboring communities. To revoke the offer, the store must publish the revocation in all seven papers for the same number of days it published the offer. The revocation is then accessible to the general public, and the offer is revoked even if some particular offeree does not know about the revocation. ■

Irrevocable Offers. Although most offers are revocable, some can be made irrevocable. Increasingly, courts refuse to allow an offeror to revoke an offer when the offeree has changed position because of justifiable reliance on the offer (under the doctrine of detrimental reliance, or promissory estoppel, discussed later in this chapter). In some circumstances, "firm offers" made by merchants may also be considered irrevocable. We discuss these offers in Chapter 11.

A poster offers a reward for a missing seven-year-old girl. How can this offer be revoked? (AP Photo/Denis Poroy)

OPTION CONTRACT
A contract under which the offeror cannot revoke his or her offer for a stipulated time period, and the offeree can accept or reject the offer during this period without fear that the offer will be made to another person. The offeree must give consideration for the option (the irrevocable offer) to be enforceable.

Another form of irrevocable offer is an option contract. An **option contract** is created when an offeror promises to hold an offer open for a specified period of time in return for a payment (consideration) given by the offeree. An option contract takes away the offeror's power to revoke an offer for the period of time specified in the option. If no time is specified, then a reasonable period of time is implied. ■ EXAMPLE 7.16 Suppose that you are in the business of writing movie scripts. Your agent contacts the head of development at New Line Cinema and offers to sell New Line your most recent movie script. New Line likes your script and agrees to pay you $5,000 for a six-month option. In this situation, you (through your agent) are the offeror, and New Line is the offeree. You cannot revoke your offer to sell New Line your script for the next six months. If after six months no contract has been formed, however, New Line loses the $5,000, and you are free to sell your movie script to another firm. ■

Option contracts are also frequently used in conjunction with the sale of real estate. ■ EXAMPLE 7.17 You might agree with a landowner to lease a home and include in the lease contract a clause stating that you will pay $2,000 for an option to purchase the home within a specified period of time. If you decide not to purchase the home after the specified period has lapsed, you lose the $2,000, and the landlord is free to sell the property to another buyer. ■

Rejection of the Offer by the Offeree. If the offeree rejects the offer, the offer is terminated. Any subsequent attempt by the offeree to accept will be construed as a new offer, giving the original offeror (now the offeree) the power of acceptance. A rejection is ordinarily accomplished by words or by conduct evidencing an intent not to accept the offer.

BE CAREFUL The way in which a response to an offer is phrased can determine whether the offer has legally been accepted or rejected.

As with revocation, rejection of an offer is effective only when it is actually received by the offeror or the offeror's agent. ■ EXAMPLE 7.18 Suppose that Growgood Farms mails a letter to Campbell Soup Company offering to sell carrots at ten cents a pound. (Of course, today, such offers tend to be sent electronically rather than by mail, as will be discussed in Chapter 10.) Campbell Soup Company could reject the offer by mailing, faxing, or e-mailing a letter to Growgood Farms expressly rejecting the offer, or by returning the offer back to Growgood, evidencing an intent to reject it. Alternatively, Campbell could offer to buy the carrots at eight cents per pound (a counteroffer), necessarily rejecting the original offer. ■

Merely inquiring about an offer does not constitute rejection. ■ EXAMPLE 7.19 A friend offers to buy your CD-ROM library for $300. You respond, "Is this your best offer?" or "Will you pay me $375 for it?" A reasonable person would conclude that you did not reject the offer but merely made an inquiry for further consideration of the offer. You can still accept and bind your friend to the $300 purchase price. When the offeree merely inquires as to the firmness of the offer, there is no reason to presume that she or he intends to reject it. ■

COUNTEROFFER
An offeree's response to an offer in which the offeree rejects the original offer and at the same time makes a new offer.

MIRROR IMAGE RULE
A common law rule that requires that the terms of the offeree's acceptance adhere exactly to the terms of the offeror's offer for a valid contract to be formed.

Counteroffer by the Offeree. A **counteroffer** is a rejection of the original offer and the simultaneous making of a new offer. ■ EXAMPLE 7.20 Suppose that Burke offers to sell his home to Lang for $170,000. Lang responds, "Your price is too high. I'll offer to purchase your house for $165,000." Lang's response is called a counteroffer because it rejects Burke's offer to sell at $170,000 and creates a new offer by Lang to purchase the home at a price of $165,000. ■

At common law, the **mirror image rule** requires that the offeree's acceptance match the offeror's offer exactly. In other words, the terms of the acceptance must "mirror" those of the offer. If the acceptance materially changes or adds to the terms of the original offer, it will be considered not an acceptance but a counteroffer—which, of course, need not be accepted. The original offeror can, however, accept the terms of the counteroffer and create a valid contract.[15]

Termination by Operation of Law The offeree's power to transform an offer into a binding, legal obligation can be terminated by operation of law if any of four conditions occur: lapse of time, destruction of the specific subject matter, death or incompetence of the offeror or offeree, or supervening illegality of the proposed contract.

Lapse of Time. An offer terminates automatically by law when the period of time *specified in the offer* has passed. If the offer states that it will be left open until a particular date, then the offer will terminate at midnight on that day. If the offer states that it will be left open for a number of days, such as ten days, this time period normally begins to run when the offer is actually received by the offeree, not when it is formed or sent. When the offer is delayed (through the misdelivery of mail, for example), the period begins to run from the date the offeree would have received the offer, but only if the offeree knows or should know that the offer is delayed.[16]

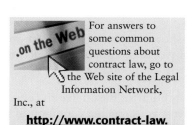

.on the Web For answers to some common questions about contract law, go to the Web site of the Legal Information Network, Inc., at **http://www.contract-law.com/TheLaw.htm**.

■ EXAMPLE 7.21 Suppose that Beth offers to sell her boat to Jonah, stating that the offer will remain open until May 20. Unless Jonah accepts the offer by midnight on May 20, the offer will lapse (terminate). Now suppose that Beth writes a letter to Jonah, offering to sell him her boat if Jonah accepts the offer within twenty days of the letter's date, which is May 1. Jonah must accept within twenty days after May 1, or the offer will terminate. The same rule would apply even if Beth had used improper postage when mailing the offer, and Jonah received the letter ten days after May 1, not knowing of the improper mailing. If, however, Jonah knew about the improper mailing, the offer would lapse twenty days after the day Jonah ordinarily would have received the offer had Beth used proper postage. ■

If the offer does not specify a time for acceptance, the offer terminates at the end of a *reasonable* period of time. A reasonable period of time is determined by the subject matter of the contract, business and market conditions, and other relevant circumstances. An offer to sell farm produce, for example, will terminate sooner than an offer to sell farm equipment because farm produce is perishable and subject to greater fluctuations in market value.

Destruction of the Subject Matter. An offer is automatically terminated if the specific subject matter of the offer is destroyed before the offer is accepted. For example, if Bekins offers to sell his prize cow to Yatsen, but the cow is struck by lightning and dies before Yatsen can accept, the offer is automatically terminated. (Note that if Yatsen accepted the offer just before lightning struck the cow, a contract would have been formed, but, because of the cow's death, a court would likely excuse Bekins's obligation to perform the contract on the basis of impossibility of performance—see Chapter 9.)

Death or Incompetence of the Offeror or Offeree. An offeree's power of acceptance is terminated when the offeror or offeree dies or is deprived of legal capacity to enter

15. The mirror image rule has been greatly modified in regard to sales contracts. Section 2–207 [Section 2–206(3) in the 2003 amendments] of the UCC provides that a contract is formed if the offeree makes a definite expression of acceptance (such as signing the form in the appropriate location), even though the terms of the acceptance modify or add to the terms of the original offer (see Chapter 11).

16. *Restatement (Second) of Contracts,* Section 49.

into the proposed contract, *unless the offer is irrevocable.*[17] An offer is personal to both parties and normally cannot pass to the decedent's heirs, guardian, or estate. This rule applies whether or not one party had notice of the death or incompetence of the other party. ■ EXAMPLE 7.22 Kapola, who is quite ill, writes to her friend Amanda, offering to sell Amanda her grand piano for only $400. That night, Kapola dies. The next day, Amanda, not knowing of Kapola's death, writes a letter to Kapola accepting the offer and enclosing a check for $400. Is there a contract? No. There is no contract because the offer automatically terminated on Kapola's death. ■

Supervening Illegality of the Proposed Contract. A statute or court decision that makes an offer illegal automatically terminates the offer. ■ EXAMPLE 7.23 If Acme Finance Corporation offers to lend Jack $20,000 at 15 percent annually, and the state legislature enacts a statute prohibiting loans at interest rates greater than 12 percent before Jack can accept, the offer is automatically terminated. (If the statute is enacted after Jack accepts the offer, a valid contract is formed, but the contract may still be unenforceable—see Chapter 8.) ■

ACCEPTANCE

ACCEPTANCE
A voluntary act by the offeree that shows assent, or agreement, to the terms of an offer; may consist of words or conduct.

An **acceptance** is a voluntary act by the offeree that shows assent, or agreement, to the terms of an offer. The offeree's act may consist of words or conduct. The acceptance must be unequivocal and must be communicated to the offeror.

Who Can Accept? Generally, a third person cannot substitute for the offeree and effectively accept the offer. After all, the identity of the offeree is as much a condition of a bargaining offer as any other term contained therein. Thus, except in special circumstances, only the person to whom the offer is made or that person's agent can accept the offer and create a binding contract. For example, Lottie makes an offer to Paul. Paul is not interested, but Paul's friend José accepts the offer. No contract is formed.

Unequivocal Acceptance To exercise the power of acceptance effectively, the offeree must accept unequivocally. This is the *mirror image rule* previously discussed. If the acceptance is subject to new conditions or if the terms of the acceptance materially change the original offer, the acceptance may be deemed a counteroffer that implicitly rejects the original offer.

DON'T FORGET When an offer is rejected, it is terminated.

Certain terms, when added to an acceptance, will not qualify the acceptance sufficiently to constitute rejection of the offer. ■ EXAMPLE 7.24 Suppose that in response to a person offering to sell a painting by a well-known artist, the offeree replies, "I accept; please send a written contract." The offeree is requesting a written contract but is not making it a condition for acceptance. Therefore, the acceptance is effective without the written contract. If the offeree replies, "I accept *if* you send a written contract," however, the acceptance is expressly conditioned on the request for a writing, and the statement is not an acceptance but a counteroffer. (Notice how important each word is!)[18] ■

17. *Restatement (Second) of Contracts,* Section 48. If the offer is irrevocable, it is not terminated when the offeror dies. Also, if the offer is such that it can be accepted by the performance of a series of acts, and those acts began before the offeror died, the offeree's power of acceptance is not terminated.

18. As noted in footnote 15, in regard to sales contracts, the UCC provides that an acceptance may still be effective even if some terms are added. The new terms are simply treated as proposals for additions to the contract, unless both parties are merchants—in which case the additional terms (with some exceptions) become part of the contract [UCC 2–207(2)].

Silence as Acceptance Ordinarily, silence cannot constitute acceptance, even if the offeror states, "By your silence and inaction, you will be deemed to have accepted this offer." This general rule applies because an offeree should not be put under a burden of liability to act affirmatively in order to reject an offer. No consideration—that is, nothing of value—has passed to the offeree to impose such a liability.

In some instances, however, the offeree does have a duty to speak; if so, his or her silence or inaction will operate as an acceptance. Silence may be an acceptance when an offeree takes the benefit of offered services even though he or she had an opportunity to reject them and knew that they were offered with the expectation of compensation. ■ EXAMPLE 7.25 Suppose that John, a college student who earns extra income by washing store windows, taps on the window of a store and catches the attention of the store's manager. John points to the window and raises his cleaner, signaling that he will be washing the window. The manager does nothing to stop him. Here, the store manager's silence constitutes an acceptance, and an implied-in-fact contract is created. The store is bound to pay a reasonable value for John's work. ■

Silence can also operate as an acceptance when the offeree has had prior dealings with the offeror. If a merchant, for example, routinely receives shipments from a supplier and in the past has always notified the supplier when defective goods are rejected, then silence constitutes acceptance. Also, if a buyer solicits an offer specifying that certain terms and conditions are acceptable, and the seller makes the offer in response to the solicitation, the buyer has a duty to reject—that is, a duty to tell the seller that the offer is not acceptable. Failure to reject (silence) would operate as an acceptance.

REMEMBER A bilateral contract is a promise for a promise, and a unilateral contract is performance for a promise.

Communication of Acceptance Whether the offeror must be notified of the acceptance depends on the nature of the contract. In a bilateral contract, communication of acceptance is necessary because acceptance is in the form of a promise (not performance), and the contract is formed when the promise is made (rather than when the act is performed). Communication of acceptance is not necessary, however, if the offer dispenses with the requirement. Also, if the offer can be accepted by silence, no communication is necessary.[19]

19. Under the UCC, an order or other offer to buy goods that are to be promptly shipped may be treated as either a bilateral or a unilateral offer and can be accepted by a promise to ship or by actual shipment. See UCC 2–206(1)(b).

This photo shows a letter from a DVD club that was sent to a club member. If the recipient (offeree) does nothing, has he or she accepted the offer? Why or why not?

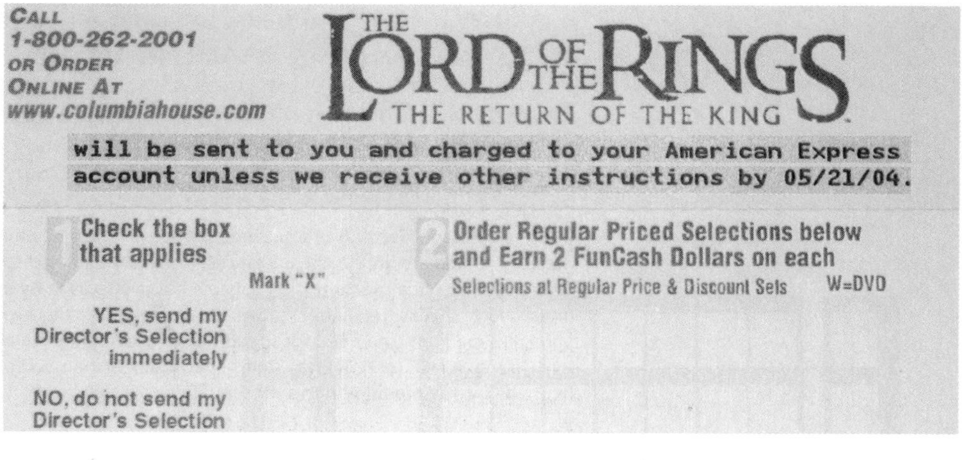

In a unilateral contract, the full performance of some act is called for; therefore, acceptance is usually evident, and notification is unnecessary. Exceptions do exist, however. When the offeror requests notice of acceptance or has no adequate means of determining whether the requested act has been performed, or when the law (such as Article 2 of the UCC) requires notice of acceptance, then notice is necessary.[20]

Mode and Timeliness of Acceptance The general rule is that acceptance in a bilateral contract is timely if it is effected within the duration of the offer. Problems arise, however, when the parties involved are not dealing face to face. In such situations, the offeree may use an authorized mode of communication.

MAILBOX RULE
A rule providing that an acceptance of an offer becomes effective on dispatch (on being placed in an official mailbox), if mail is, expressly or impliedly, an authorized means of communication of acceptance to the offeror.

The Mailbox Rule. Acceptance takes effect, thus completing formation of the contract, at the time the offeree sends or delivers the communication via the mode expressly or impliedly authorized by the offeror. This is the so-called **mailbox rule,** also called the "deposited acceptance rule," which the majority of courts uphold. Under this rule, if the authorized mode of communication is the mail, then an acceptance becomes valid when it is dispatched (placed in the control of the U.S. Postal Service)—*not* when it is received by the offeror.

The mailbox rule was formed to prevent the confusion that arises when an offeror sends a letter of revocation but, before it arrives, the offeree sends a letter of acceptance. Thus, whereas a revocation becomes effective only when it is *received* by the offeree, an acceptance becomes effective on *dispatch* (even if it is never received), provided that an *authorized* means of communication is used.

Authorized Means of Communication. Authorized means of communicating an acceptance can be either expressly authorized—that is, expressly stipulated in the offer—or impliedly authorized by facts or law.[21] An acceptance sent by means not expressly or impliedly authorized is normally not effective until it is received by the offeror.

When an offeror specifies how acceptance should be made (for example, by first class mail or express delivery), *express authorization* is said to exist. Moreover, both the offeror and the offeree are bound in contract the moment that such means of acceptance are employed. Most offerors do not expressly specify the means by which the offeree is to accept. Thus, the common law recognizes the following implied authorized means of acceptance:[22]

1. The offeror's choice of a particular means in making the offer implies that the offeree is authorized to use the same *or a faster* means for acceptance.
2. When two parties are at a distance, mailing is impliedly authorized.

Exceptions. There are three basic exceptions to the rule that a contract is formed when acceptance is sent by authorized means:

20. UCC 2–206(2).

21. *Restatement (Second) of Contracts,* Section 30, provides that an offer invites acceptance "by any medium reasonable in the circumstances," unless the offer is specific about the means of acceptance. Under Section 65, a medium is reasonable if it is one used by the offeror or one customary in similar transactions, unless the offeree knows of circumstances that would argue against the reasonableness of a particular medium (the need for speed because of rapid price changes, for example).

22. Note that UCC 2–206(1)(a) states specifically that an acceptance of an offer for the sale of goods can be made by any medium that is *reasonable* under the circumstances.

If an offer expressly authorizes acceptance of the offer by first-class mail or express delivery, can the offeree accept by a faster means, such as by fax or e-mail? Why or why not? (© Michael Newman, PhotoEdit)

1. If the acceptance is not properly dispatched (if a letter is incorrectly addressed, for example, or lacks the proper postage), in most states it will not be effective until it is received by the offeror.
2. The offeror can stipulate in the offer that an acceptance will not be effective until it is received (usually by a specified time) by the offeror.
3. Sometimes an offeree sends a rejection first, then later changes his or her mind and sends an acceptance. Obviously, this chain of events could cause confusion and even detriment to the offeror, depending on whether the rejection or the acceptance arrived first. In such situations, the law cancels the rule of acceptance on dispatch, and the first communication received by the offeror determines whether a contract is formed. If the rejection arrives first, there is no contract.[23]

Technology and Acceptances Technology, and particularly the Internet, has all but eliminated the need for the mailbox rule because online acceptances typically are communicated instantaneously to the offeror. As you will learn in Chapter 10, while online offers are not significantly different from traditional offers contained in paper documents, online acceptances have posed some unusual problems.

Consideration

In every legal system, some promises will be enforced, and other promises will not be enforced. The simple fact that a party has made a promise, then, does not mean the promise is enforceable. Under the common law, a primary basis for the enforcement of promises is consideration. **Consideration** is usually defined as the value given in return for a promise. We look here at the basic elements of consideration and then at some other contract doctrines relating to consideration.

CONSIDERATION
Generally, the value given in return for a promise. The consideration must result in a detriment to the promisee (something of legally sufficient value and bargained for) or a benefit to the promisor.

ELEMENTS OF CONSIDERATION

Often, consideration is broken down into two parts: (1) something of *legally sufficient value* must be given in exchange for the promise, and (2) there must be a *bargained-for exchange.*

Legal Value The "something of legally sufficient value" may consist of (1) a promise to do something that one has no prior legal duty to do (to pay money on receipt of certain goods, for example), (2) the performance of an action that one is otherwise not obligated to undertake (such as providing accounting services), or (3) the refraining from an action that one has a legal right to undertake (called a **forbearance**).

FORBEARANCE
The act of refraining from an action that one has a legal right to undertake.

23. *Restatement (Second) of Contracts,* Section 40.

Consideration in bilateral contracts normally consists of a promise in return for a promise, as explained earlier in this chapter. ■ EXAMPLE 7.26 Suppose that in a contract for the sale of goods, the seller promises to ship specific goods to the buyer, and the buyer promises to pay for those goods when they are received. Each of these promises constitutes consideration for the contract. ■ In contrast, unilateral contracts involve a promise in return for a performance. ■ EXAMPLE 7.27 Suppose that Anita says to her neighbor, "If you paint my garage, I will pay you $100." Anita's neighbor paints the garage. The act of painting the garage is the consideration that creates Anita's contractual obligation to pay her neighbor $100. ■

What if, in return for a promise to pay, a person forbears to pursue harmful habits, such as the use of tobacco and alcohol? Does such forbearance create consideration for the contract? This was the issue before the court in *Hamer v. Sidway,* a classic case concerning consideration that we present as this chapter's *Landmark in the Law* feature.

Bargained-for Exchange The second element of consideration is that it must provide the basis for the bargain struck between the contracting parties. The promise given by the promisor must induce the promisee to incur a legal detriment either now or in the future, and the detriment incurred must induce the promisor to make the promise. This element of bargained-for exchange distinguishes contracts from gifts.

■ EXAMPLE 7.28 Suppose that Roberto says to his son, "In consideration of the fact that you are not as wealthy as your brothers, I will pay you $500." This promise is not enforceable because Roberto's son has not given any return consideration for the $500 promised.[24] The son (the promisee) incurs no legal detriment; he does not have to promise anything or undertake (or refrain from undertaking) any action to receive the $500. Here, Roberto has simply stated his motive for giving his son a gift. The fact that the word *consideration* is used does not, by itself, mean that consideration has been given. ■

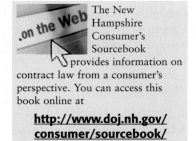

on the Web The New Hampshire Consumer's Sourcebook provides information on contract law from a consumer's perspective. You can access this book online at

http://www.doj.nh.gov/consumer/sourcebook/index.html.

BE AWARE A consumer's signature on a contract does not always guarantee that the contract will be enforced. Ultimately, the terms must be fair.

LEGAL SUFFICIENCY AND ADEQUACY OF CONSIDERATION

Legal sufficiency of consideration involves the requirement that consideration be something of value in the eyes of the law. Adequacy of consideration involves "how much" consideration is given. Essentially, adequacy of consideration concerns the fairness of the bargain. On the surface, fairness would appear to be an issue when the items exchanged are of unequal value. In general, however, courts do not question the adequacy of consideration if the consideration is legally sufficient. Under the doctrine of freedom of contract, parties are usually free to bargain as they wish. If people could sue merely because they had entered into an unwise contract, the courts would be overloaded with frivolous suits.

In extreme cases, however, a court of law may look to the amount or value (the adequacy) of the consideration because apparently inadequate consideration can indicate that fraud, duress, or undue influence was involved or that a gift was made (if a father "sells" a $100,000 house to his daughter for only $1, for example). Additionally, when the consideration is grossly inadequate, the courts may declare the contract unenforceable on the ground that it is *unconscionable,*[25] meaning that, generally speaking, it is so one sided under the circumstances as to be clearly unfair. (Unconscionability will be discussed further in Chapter 8.)

24. See *Fink v. Cox,* 18 Johns. 145, 9 Am.Dec. 191 (N.Y. 1820).

25. Pronounced un-*kon*-shun-uh-bul.

LANDMARK IN THE LAW

Hamer v. Sidway (1891)

In *Hamer v. Sidway,*[a] the issue before the court arose from a contract created in 1869 between William Story, Sr., and his nephew, William Story II. The uncle promised his nephew that if the nephew refrained from drinking alcohol, using tobacco, and playing billiards and cards for money until he reached the age of twenty-one, the uncle would pay him $5,000 (about $75,000 in today's dollars). The nephew, who indulged occasionally in all of these "vices," agreed to refrain from them and did so for the next six years. Following his twenty-first birthday in 1875, the nephew wrote to his uncle that he had performed his part of the bargain and was thus entitled to the promised $5,000. A few days later, the uncle wrote the nephew a letter stating, "[Y]ou shall have the five thousand dollars, as I promised you." The uncle said that the money was in the bank and that the nephew could "consider this money on interest."

THE ISSUE OF CONSIDERATION The nephew left the funds in the care of his uncle, who held it for the next twelve years. When the uncle died in 1887, however, the executor of the uncle's estate refused to pay the $5,000 claim brought by Hamer, a third party to whom the promise had been *assigned.* (The law allows parties to assign, or transfer, rights in contracts to third parties; see Chapter 9.) The executor, Sidway, contended that the contract was invalid because there was insufficient consideration to support it. The uncle had received nothing, and the nephew had actually benefited by fulfilling the uncle's wishes. Therefore, no contract existed.

THE COURT'S CONCLUSION Although a lower court upheld Sidway's position, the New York Court of Appeals reversed and ruled in favor of the plaintiff, Hamer. "The promisee used tobacco, occasionally drank liquor, and he had a legal right to do so," the court stated. "That right he abandoned for a period of years upon the strength of the promise of the testator [one who makes a will] that for such forbearance he would give him $5,000. We need not speculate on the effort which may have been required to give up the use of those stimulants. It is sufficient that he restricted his lawful freedom of action within certain prescribed limits upon the faith of his uncle's agreement."

APPLICATION TO TODAY'S WORLD

Although this case was decided over a century ago, the principles enunciated by the court remain applicable to contracts formed today, including online contracts. For a contract to be valid and binding, consideration must be given, and that consideration must be something of legally sufficient value.

RELEVANT WEB SITES

To locate information on the Web concerning the Hamer v. Sidway *decision, go to this text's Web site at* **http://blt.westbuslaw.com**, *select "Chapter 7," and click on "URLs for Landmarks."*

a. 124 N.Y. 538, 27 N.E. 256 (1891).

In the following case, the issue was whether consideration existed in a contract to accept lower payments for medical services than the maximum fees allowed under state regulations.

CASE 7.3 Seaview Orthopaedics v. National Healthcare Resources, Inc.

Superior Court of New Jersey,
Appellate Division, 2004.
366 N.J.Super. 501, 841 A.2d 917.
http://lawlibrary.rutgers.edu/search.shtml[a]

FACTS Consumer Health Network (CHN) is a large medical-insurance preferred provider organization (PPO) in New Jersey. CHN provides medical services providers (its clients) with a PPO network in three distinct areas: workers' compensation, group health benefits, and auto insurance. The network includes over 11,000 physicians and nearly 14,000 medical services providers (which include physicians, laboratories, and hospitals). By entering into a contract with CHN, a medical services provider gains potential access to 950,000 enrollees in exchange for accepting reimbursement at rates lower than the maximum rates permitted by New Jersey state regulations. Seaview Orthopaedics is a CHN client that renders services to auto accident victims insured by Allstate Indemnity Company. Allstate pays the CHN rates for Seaview's services through Allstate's claims administrator, National Healthcare Resources (NHR). Seaview and others filed a suit in a New Jersey state court against NHR and others to recover the difference between the CHN rates and the state's maximum rates. The court issued a summary judgment in favor of the defendants. The plaintiffs appealed to a state intermediate appellate court, claiming that the CHN contract was not enforceable, in part because it lacked consideration.

ISSUE Did the CHN contract lack consideration?

a. Click on "Search by Party Name." On that page, select "Appellate Division" as the court, and type "Seaview Orthopaedics" in the "First Name" box. Click on "Submit Form" to view a synopsis of the case, and then "click here to get this case" to read the opinion. Rutgers University School of Law in Camden, New Jersey, maintains this Web site.

DECISION No. The state intermediate appellate court affirmed the lower court's summary judgment.

REASON The court acknowledged that contracts are not enforceable in the absence of consideration—that is, both sides must get something out of the exchange. The court explained, however, that the determination of whether consideration exists does not depend on the comparative value of the things exchanged. Instead, stated the court, the consideration must merely be valuable in the sense that it is something that is bargained for in fact. The court noted, "Here, the contract provided benefits to plaintiffs in a variety of ways which either collectively or separately constituted valuable consideration for plaintiffs' promise to accept the CHN rates for reimbursement from auto accident victims (and other types of patients) and not the maximum rate permitted by the [state's] schedule. Plaintiffs, for example, obtained the benefit of marketing their businesses in a directory of providers utilized by numerous payors in the workers' compensation and health benefits markets and many thousands of potential patients. Payors make the list available to the largest PPO membership network in New Jersey and, in the health and workers' compensation settings, are generally offered substantial financial incentives when those patients use the providers on the list." The court concluded that it is the totality of the exchange of promises and benefits that must be considered, and in this case, the exchange was sufficient to create an enforceable contract.

WHY IS THIS CASE IMPORTANT? *As this case illustrates, something need not be of direct economic or financial value to be considered legally sufficient consideration. In many situations, as here, the exchange of promises and potential benefits is deemed sufficient as consideration.*

CONTRACTS THAT LACK CONSIDERATION

Sometimes, one or both of the parties to a contract may think that they have exchanged consideration when in fact they have not. Here we look at some situations in which the parties' promises or actions do not qualify as contractual consideration.

Preexisting Duty Under most circumstances, a promise to do what one already has a legal duty to do does not constitute legally sufficient consideration because no legal detriment is incurred.[26] The preexisting legal duty may be imposed by law or may arise out of a previous contract. A sheriff, for example, cannot collect a reward for information leading to the capture of a criminal if the sheriff already has a legal duty to capture the criminal. Likewise, if a party is already bound by contract to perform a certain duty, that duty cannot serve as consideration for a second contract.

.on the Web To learn more about how the courts decide such issues as whether consideration was lacking for a particular contract, look at relevant case law, which can be accessed through the Web site of Cornell University's School of Law at **http://www.law.cornell.edu/topics/contracts.html**.

■ EXAMPLE 7.29 Suppose that Bauman-Bache, Inc., begins construction on a seven-story office building and after three months demands an extra $75,000 on its contract. If the extra $75,000 is not paid, it will stop working. The owner of the land, having no one else to complete construction, agrees to pay the extra $75,000. The agreement is not enforceable because it is not supported by legally sufficient consideration; Bauman-Bache had a preexisting contractual duty to complete the building. ■

Unforeseen Difficulties. The rule regarding preexisting duty is meant to prevent extortion and the so-called holdup game. What happens, though, when an honest contractor, who has contracted with a landowner to build a house, runs into extraordinary difficulties that were totally unforeseen at the time the contract was formed? In the interests of fairness and equity, the courts sometimes allow exceptions to the preexisting duty rule. In the example just mentioned, if the landowner agrees to pay extra compensation to the contractor for overcoming the unforeseen difficulties (such as having to use dynamite and special equipment to remove an unexpected rock formation to excavate for a basement), the court may refrain from applying the preexisting duty rule and enforce the agreement. When the "unforeseen difficulties" that give rise to a contract modification are the types of risks ordinarily assumed in business, however, the courts will usually assert the preexisting duty rule.[27]

Rescission and New Contract. The law recognizes that two parties can mutually agree to rescind their contract, at least to the extent that it is executory (still to be carried out). **Rescission**[28] is defined as the unmaking of a contract so as to return the parties to the positions they occupied before the contract was made. When rescission and the making of a new contract take place at the same time, the courts frequently are given a choice of applying the preexisting duty rule or allowing rescission and letting the new contract stand.

RESCISSION
A remedy whereby a contract is canceled and the parties are returned to the positions they occupied before the contract was made; may be effected through the mutual consent of the parties, by the parties' conduct, or by court decree.

Past Consideration Promises made in return for actions or events that have already taken place are unenforceable. These promises lack consideration in that the element of bargained-for exchange is missing. In short, you can bargain for something to take place now or in the future but not for something that has already taken place. Therefore, **past consideration** is no consideration.

PAST CONSIDERATION
An act that takes place before the contract is made and that ordinarily, by itself, cannot be consideration for a later promise to pay for the act.

■ EXAMPLE 7.30 Suppose that Elsie, a real estate agent, does her friend Judy a favor by selling Judy's house and not charging any commission. Later, Judy says to Elsie, "In return for your generous act, I will pay you $3,000." This promise is made in return for past consideration and is thus unenforceable; in effect, Judy is stating her intention to give Elsie a gift. ■

26. See *Foakes v. Beer,* 9 App.Cas. 605 (1884).

27. Note that under the UCC, any agreement modifying a contract within Article 2 on Sales needs no consideration to be binding. See UCC 2–209(1).

28. Pronounced reh-*sih*-zhen.

Illusory Promises If the terms of the contract express such uncertainty of performance that the promisor has not definitely promised to do anything, the promise is said to be *illusory*—without consideration and unenforceable. ■ EXAMPLE 7.31 The president of Tuscan Corporation says to his employees, "All of you have worked hard, and if profits remain high, a 10 percent bonus at the end of the year will be given—if management thinks it is warranted." This is an *illusory promise,* or no promise at all, because performance depends solely on the discretion of the president (the management). There is no bargained-for consideration. The statement declares merely that management may or may not do something in the future. ■

Option-to-cancel clauses in contracts for specified time periods sometimes present problems in regard to consideration. ■ EXAMPLE 7.32 Abe contracts to hire Chris for one year at $5,000 per month, reserving the right to cancel the contract at any time. On close examination of these words, you can see that Abe has not actually agreed to hire Chris, as Abe could cancel without liability before Chris started performance. Abe has not given up the opportunity of hiring someone else. This contract is therefore illusory. Now suppose that Abe contracts to hire Chris for a one-year period at $5,000 per month, reserving the right to cancel the contract at any time after Chris has begun performance by giving Chris thirty days' notice. Abe, by saying that he will give Chris thirty days' notice, is relinquishing the opportunity (legal right) to hire someone else instead of Chris for a thirty-day period. If Chris works for one month, at the end of which Abe gives him thirty days' notice, Chris has a valid and enforceable contractual claim for $10,000 in salary. ■

SETTLEMENT OF CLAIMS

Businesspersons or others can settle legal claims in several ways. It is important to understand the nature of the consideration given in these settlement agreements, or contracts. Claims are commonly settled through an *accord and satisfaction,* in which a debtor offers to pay a lesser amount than the creditor purports to be owed. Two other methods that are also often used to settle claims are the *release* and the *covenant not to sue.*

ACCORD AND SATISFACTION
A common means of settling a disputed claim, in which a debtor offers to pay a lesser amount than the creditor purports to be owed. The creditor's acceptance of the offer creates an accord (agreement), and when the accord is executed, satisfaction occurs.

Accord and Satisfaction In an **accord and satisfaction,** a debtor offers to pay, and a creditor accepts, a lesser amount than the creditor originally claimed was owed. Thus, in an accord and satisfaction, the debtor attempts to terminate an existing obligation. The *accord* is the settlement agreement. In an accord, the debtor offers to give or perform something less than the parties originally agreed on, and the creditor accepts that offer in satisfaction of the claim. *Satisfaction* is the performance (usually payment), which takes place after the accord is executed. A basic rule is that there can be no satisfaction unless there is first an accord.

REMEMBER Businesspersons should consider settling potential legal disputes to save both their own time and resources and those of the courts.

For accord and satisfaction to occur, the amount of the debt *must be in dispute.* If a debt is *liquidated,* accord and satisfaction cannot take place. A debt is liquidated if its amount has been ascertained, fixed, agreed on, settled, or exactly determined. An example of a liquidated debt is a loan contract in which the borrower agrees to pay a stipulated amount every month until the amount of the loan is paid. In the majority of states, acceptance of (an accord for) a lesser sum than the entire amount of a liquidated debt is not satisfaction, and the balance of the debt is still legally owed. The rationale for this rule is that the debtor has given no consideration to satisfy the obligation of paying the balance to the creditor—because the debtor has a preexisting legal obligation to pay the entire debt.

An *unliquidated debt* is the opposite of a liquidated debt. Here, reasonable persons may differ over the amount owed. It is not settled, fixed, agreed on, ascertained, or determined. In these circumstances, acceptance of payment of the lesser sum operates as a satisfaction, or discharge, of the debt. One argument to support this rule is that the parties give up a legal right to contest the amount in dispute, and thus consideration is given.

RELEASE
A contract in which one party forfeits the right to pursue a legal claim against the other party.

Release A **release** is a contract in which one party forfeits the right to pursue a legal claim against the other party. Releases will generally be binding if they are (1) given in good faith, (2) stated in a signed writing (required by many states), and (3) accompanied by consideration.[29] Clearly, parties are better off if they know the extent of their injuries or damages before signing releases.

■ EXAMPLE 7.33 Suppose that you are involved in an automobile accident caused by Raoul's negligence. Raoul offers to give you $1,000 if you will release him from further liability resulting from the accident. You believe that this amount will cover your damages, so you agree to and sign the release. Later you discover that the repairs to your car will cost $1,200. Can you collect the balance from Raoul? The answer is normally no; you are limited to the $1,000 in the release. Why? The reason is that a valid contract existed. You and Raoul both assented to the bargain (hence, agreement existed), and sufficient consideration was present. Your consideration for the contract was the legal detriment you suffered (by releasing Raoul from liability, you forfeited your right to sue to recover damages, should they be more than $1,000). This legal detriment was induced by Raoul's promise to give you the $1,000. Raoul's promise was, in turn, induced by your promise not to pursue your legal right to sue him for damages. ■

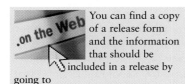

.on the Web You can find a copy of a release form and the information that should be included in a release by going to

http://www.nolo.com/category/cm_home.html

and clicking on "Release from Legal Claims" in the right-hand column of the page.

COVENANT NOT TO SUE
An agreement to substitute a contractual obligation for some other type of legal action based on a valid claim.

Covenant Not to Sue Unlike a release, a **covenant not to sue** does not always bar further recovery. The parties simply substitute a contractual obligation for some other type of legal action based on a valid claim. Suppose (following the earlier example) that you agree with Raoul not to sue for damages in a tort action if he will pay for the damage to your car. If Raoul fails to pay, you can bring an action for breach of contract.

PROMISSORY ESTOPPEL

PROMISSORY ESTOPPEL
A doctrine that applies when a promisor makes a clear and definite promise on which the promisee justifiably relies; such a promise is binding if justice will be better served by the enforcement of the promise.

ESTOPPED
Barred, impeded, or precluded.

Sometimes individuals rely on promises, and such reliance may form a basis for contract rights and duties. Under the doctrine of **promissory estoppel** (also called *detrimental reliance*), a person who has reasonably relied on the promise of another can often obtain some measure of recovery. When the doctrine of promissory estoppel is applied, the promisor (the offeror) is **estopped** (barred, or impeded) from revoking the promise. For the doctrine of promissory estoppel to be applied, the following elements are required:

1. There must be a clear and definite promise.
2. The promisee must justifiably rely on the promise.
3. The reliance normally must be of a substantial and definite character.
4. Justice will be better served by the enforcement of the promise.

29. Under the UCC, a written, signed waiver or renunciation by an aggrieved party discharges any further liability for a breach, even without consideration [UCC 1–107].

■ EXAMPLE 7.34 Your uncle tells you, "I'll pay you $150 a week so you won't have to work anymore." In reliance on your uncle's promise, you quit your job, but your uncle refuses to pay you. Under the doctrine of promissory estoppel, you may be able to enforce his promise.[30] Now your uncle makes a promise to give you $10,000 to buy a car. If you buy the car with your own funds and he does not pay you, you may once again be able to enforce the promise under this doctrine. ■

30. A classic example is *Ricketts v. Scothorn,* 57 Neb. 51, 77 N.W. 365 (1898).

APPLICATION How Can You Avoid Unintended Employment Contracts?*

Employers have learned many lessons from court decisions. In recent years, for example, the message has been clear that employers should be cautious about what they say in their employment manuals.

EMPLOYMENT MANUALS AND IMPLIED-IN-FACT CONTRACTS

Promises made in an employment manual may create an implied-in-fact employment contract. If an employment handbook states that employees will be fired only for specific causes, the employer may be held to that "promise." Even if, by state law, employment is "at will"—that is, the employer is allowed to hire and fire employees at will, with or without cause (see Chapter 18)—the at-will doctrine will not apply if the terms of employment are subject to a contract between the employer and the employee. If a court holds that an implied employment contract exists—on the basis of promises made in an employment manual—the employment is no longer at will. The employer will be bound by the contract and liable for damages for breaching the contract.

TAKING PRECAUTIONS

Employers who wish to avoid potential liability for breaching unintended employment contracts should therefore make it clear to employees that the policies expressed in an employment manual are not to be interpreted as contractual promises. An effective way to do this is to inform employees, when initially giving them the handbook or discussing its contents with them, that the handbook is not intended as a contract and to include a disclaimer to that effect in the employment manual. The disclaimer might read as follows: "This policy manual describes the basic personnel policies and practices of our Company. You should understand that the manual does not modify our Company's 'at will' employment doctrine or provide employees with any kind of contractual rights."

The employer should make the disclaimer clear and prominent so that the applicant cannot later claim that it was the employer's fault that the employee did not see the disclaimer. A disclaimer will be clear and prominent if it is set off from the surrounding text by the use of larger type, a different color, all capital letters, or some other device that calls the reader's attention to it.

In the handbook, the employer should also avoid making definite promises that employees will be fired only for cause, that after they have worked for a certain length of time they will not be fired except for specific reasons, or the like. The handbook itself should include a clear and prominent disclaimer of contractual liability for its contents.

* This *Application* is not meant to substitute for the services of an attorney who is licensed to practice law in your state.

CHECKLIST FOR THE EMPLOYER

1. Inform new employees that statements in an employment handbook are not intended as contractual terms.
2. Include a clear and prominent disclaimer to this effect in employment applications.
3. Avoid including in the handbook any definite promises relating to job security, and include a clear and prominent disclaimer of contractual liability for any statements made within the handbook.

KEY TERMS

acceptance 220
accord and satisfaction 228
agreement 210
bilateral contract 204
consideration 223
contract 203
counteroffer 218
covenant not to sue 229
estopped 229
executed contract 207
executory contract 207
express contract 206
forbearance 223
formal contract 206
implied-in-fact contract 206
informal contract 206
mailbox rule 222
mirror image rule 218
offer 210
offeree 204
offeror 204
option contract 218
past consideration 227
promise 201
promisee 202
promisor 202
promissory estoppel 229
release 229
rescission 227
revocation 216
quasi contract 209
unenforceable contract 209
unilateral contract 204
valid contract 208
void contract 209
voidable contract 208

CHAPTER SUMMARY Contracts: Nature, Classification, Agreement, and Consideration

The Nature and Function of Contracts (See pages 202–203.)	Contract law establishes what kinds of promises will be legally binding and supplies procedures for enforcing legally binding promises, or agreements. A contract is defined as an agreement that can be enforced in court. It is formed by two or more competent parties who agree to perform or to refrain from performing some act now or in the future. For a contract to exist, the following requirements must be met: 1. *Elements of a valid contract*—Agreement, consideration, contractual capacity, and legality. 2. *Possible defenses to the enforcement of a contract*—Genuineness of assent and form.
Types of Contracts (See pages 204–210.)	1. *Bilateral*—A promise for a promise. 2. *Unilateral*—A promise for an act (acceptance is the completed—or substantial—performance of the contract by the offeree). 3. *Formal*—Requires a special form for contract formation. 4. *Informal*—Requires no special form for contract formation. 5. *Express*—Formed by words (oral, written, or a combination). 6. *Implied in fact*—Formed at least in part by the conduct of the parties. 7. *Executed*—A fully performed contract. 8. *Executory*—A contract not yet fully performed. 9. *Valid*—A contract that has the necessary contractual elements of offer and acceptance, consideration, parties with legal capacity, and having been made for a legal purpose. 10. *Voidable*—A contract in which a party has the option of avoiding or enforcing the contractual obligation. 11. *Unenforceable*—A valid contract that cannot be enforced because of a legal defense. 12. *Void*—No contract exists, or there is a contract without legal obligations. 13. *Quasi contract*—A quasi contract, or a contract implied in law, is a contract that is imposed by law to prevent unjust enrichment.

(Continued)

CHAPTER SUMMARY Contracts: Nature, Classification, Agreement, and Consideration—Continued

Requirements of the Offer (See pages 210–216.)	1. *Intent*—There must be a serious, objective intention by the offeror to become bound by the offer. Nonoffer situations include (a) expressions of opinion; (b) statements of intention; (c) preliminary negotiations; (d) generally, advertisements, catalogues, price lists, and circulars; (e) solicitations for bids made by an auctioneer; and (f) traditionally, agreements to agree in the future. 2. *Definiteness*—The terms of the offer must be sufficiently definite to be ascertainable by the parties or by a court. 3. *Communication*—The offer must be communicated to the offeree.
Termination of the Offer (See pages 216–220.)	1. *By action of the parties*— a. Revocation—Unless the offer is irrevocable, it can be revoked at any time before acceptance without liability. Revocation is not effective until received by the offeree or the offeree's agent. Some offers, such as a merchant's firm offer and option contracts, are irrevocable. b. Rejection—Accomplished by words or actions that demonstrate a clear intent not to accept the offer; not effective until received by the offeror or the offeror's agent. c. Counteroffer—A rejection of the original offer and the making of a new offer. 2. *By operation of law*— a. Lapse of time—The offer terminates (1) at the end of the time period specified in the offer or (2) if no time period is stated in the offer, at the end of a reasonable time period. b. Destruction of the specific subject matter of the offer—Automatically terminates the offer. c. Death or incompetence—Terminates the offer unless the offer is irrevocable. d. Illegality—Supervening illegality terminates the offer.
Acceptance (See pages 220–223.)	1. Can be made only by the offeree or the offeree's agent. 2. Must be unequivocal. Under the common law (mirror image rule), if new terms or conditions are added to the acceptance, it will be considered a counteroffer. 3. Acceptance of a unilateral offer is effective on full performance of the requested act. Generally, no communication is necessary. 4. Acceptance of a bilateral offer can be communicated by the offeree by any authorized mode of communication and is effective on dispatch. Unless the mode of communication is expressly specified by the offeror, the following methods are impliedly authorized: a. The same mode used by the offeror or a faster mode. b. Mail, when the two parties are at a distance. c. In sales contracts, by any reasonable medium.
Elements of Consideration (See pages 223–224.)	Consideration is broken down into two parts: (1) something of *legally sufficient value* must be given in exchange for the promise, and (2) there must be a *bargained-for exchange.*
Adequacy of Consideration (See pages 224–226.)	Legal sufficiency of consideration relates to the first element of consideration—something of legal value must be given in exchange for a promise. Adequacy of consideration relates to "how much" consideration is given and whether a fair bargain was reached. Courts will inquire into the adequacy of consideration (whether the consideration is legally sufficient) only when fraud, undue influence, duress, or unconscionability may be involved.

CHAPTER SUMMARY Contracts: Nature, Classification, Agreement, and Consideration—Continued

Contracts That Lack Consideration (See pages 226–228.)	Consideration is lacking in the following situations: 1. *Preexisting duty*—Consideration is not legally sufficient if one is either by law or by contract under a *preexisting duty* to perform the action being offered as consideration for a new contract. 2. *Past consideration*—Actions or events that have already taken place do not constitute legally sufficient consideration. 3. *Illusory promises*—When the nature or extent of performance is too uncertain, the promise is rendered illusory (without consideration and unenforceable).
Settlement of Claims (See pages 228–229.)	1. *Accord and satisfaction*—An *accord* is an agreement in which a debtor offers to pay a lesser amount than the creditor purports to be owed. *Satisfaction* may take place when the accord is executed. 2. *Release*—An agreement in which, for consideration, a party forfeits the right to seek further recovery beyond the terms specified in the release. 3. *Covenant not to sue*—An agreement not to sue on a present, valid claim.
Promissory Estoppel (See pages 229–230.)	The equitable doctrine of promissory estoppel applies when a promisor reasonably expects a promise to induce definite and substantial action or forbearance by the promisee, and the promisee does act in reliance on the promise. Such a promise is binding if injustice can be avoided only by enforcement of the promise. Also known as the doctrine of detrimental reliance.

FOR REVIEW

Answers for the even-numbered questions in this For Review *section can be found in Appendix I at the end of this text.*

1. What is a contract? What are the four elements necessary to the formation of a valid contract?
2. What are the various types of contracts?
3. What are the requirements of an offer?
4. How can an offer be accepted?
5. What are the elements of consideration?

QUESTIONS AND CASE PROBLEMS

7–1. Express versus Implied Contracts. Suppose that a local businessperson, McDougal, is a good friend of Krunch, the owner of a local candy store. Every day on his lunch hour McDougal goes into Krunch's candy store and spends about five minutes looking at the candy. After examining Krunch's candy and talking with Krunch, McDougal usually buys one or two candy bars. One afternoon, McDougal goes into Krunch's candy shop, looks at the candy, and picks up a $1 candy bar. Seeing that Krunch is very busy, he catches Krunch's eye, waves the candy bar at Krunch without saying a word, and walks out. Is there a contract? If so, classify it within the categories presented in this chapter.

7–2. Contract Classification. High-Flying Advertising, Inc., contracted with Big Burger Restaurants to fly an advertisement above the Connecticut beaches. The advertisement offered $5,000 to any person who could swim from the Connecticut beaches to Long Island across Long Island Sound in less than a day. McElfresh saw the streamer and accepted the challenge. He started his marathon swim that same day at 10 A.M. After he had been swimming for four hours and was about halfway across the sound, McElfresh saw another plane pulling a streamer that read, "Big Burger revokes." Is there a contract between McElfresh and Big Burger? If there is a contract, what type(s) of contract is (are) formed?

7–3. **Offers versus Nonoffers.** On June 1, Jason placed an ad in a local newspaper, to be run on the following Sunday, June 5, offering a reward of $100 to anyone who found his wallet. When his wallet had not been returned by June 12, he purchased another wallet and took steps to obtain duplicates of his driver's license, credit cards, and other items that he had lost. He also placed another ad in the same newspaper revoking his offer. The second ad was the same size as the original. On June 15, Sharith, who had seen Jason's first ad in the paper, found Jason's wallet, returned it to Jason, and asked for the $100. Is Jason obligated to pay Sharith the $100? Why or why not?

7–4. **Consideration.** Ben hired Lewis to drive his racing car in a race. Tuan, a friend of Lewis, promised to pay Lewis $3,000 if he won the race. Lewis won the race, but Tuan refused to pay the $3,000. Tuan contended that no legally binding contract had been formed because he had received no consideration from Lewis for his promise to pay the $3,000. Lewis sued Tuan for breach of contract, arguing that winning the race was the consideration given in exchange for Tuan's promise to pay the $3,000. What rule of law discussed in this chapter supports Tuan's claim? Explain.

CASE PROBLEM WITH SAMPLE ANSWER

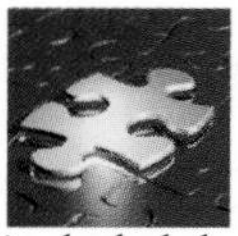

7–5. Professor Dixon was an adjunct professor at Tulsa Community College (TCC) in Tulsa, Oklahoma. Each semester, near the beginning of the term, the parties executed a written contract that always included the following provision: "It is agreed that this agreement may be cancelled by the Administration or the instructor at anytime before the first class session." In the spring semester of Dixon's seventh year, he filed a complaint with TCC alleging that one of his students, Meredith Bhuiyan, had engaged in disruptive classroom conduct. He gave her an incomplete grade and asked TCC to require her to apologize as a condition of receiving a final grade. TCC later claimed, and Dixon denied, that he was told to assign Bhuiyan a grade if he wanted to teach in the fall. Toward the end of the semester, Dixon was told which classes he would teach in the fall, but the parties did not sign a written contract. The Friday before classes began, TCC terminated him. Dixon filed a suit in an Oklahoma state court against TCC and others, alleging breach of contract. Did the parties have a contract? If so, did TCC breach it? Explain. [*Dixon v. Bhuiyan,* 10 P.3d 888 (Okla. 2000)]

After you have answered this problem, compare your answer with the sample answer given on the Web site that accompanies this text. Go to <u>http://blt.westbuslaw.com</u>, select "Chapter 7," and click on "Case Problem with Sample Answer."

7–6. **Bilateral versus Unilateral Contracts.** D.L. Peoples Group (D.L.) placed an ad in a Missouri newspaper to recruit admissions representatives, who were hired to recruit Missouri residents to attend D.L.'s college in Florida. Donald Hawley responded to the ad, his interviewer recommended him for the job, and he signed, in Missouri, an "Admissions Representative Agreement," which was mailed to D.L.'s president, who signed it in his office in Florida. The agreement provided in part that Hawley would devote exclusive time and effort to the business in his assigned territory in Missouri and that D.L. would pay Hawley a commission if he successfully recruited students for the school. While attempting to make one of his first calls on his new job, Hawley was accidentally shot and killed. On the basis of his death, a claim was filed in Florida for workers' compensation. (Under Florida law, when an accident occurs outside Florida, workers' compensation benefits are payable only if the employment contract was made in Florida.) Is this admissions representative agreement a bilateral or a unilateral contract? What are the consequences of the distinction in this case? Explain. [*D.L. Peoples Group, Inc. v. Hawley,* 804 So.2d 561 (Fla.App. 1 Dist. 2002)]

7–7. **Intention.** Music that is distributed on compact discs and similar media generates income in the form of "mechanical" royalties. Music that is publicly performed, such as when a song is played on the radio, included in a movie or commercial, or sampled in another song, produces "performance" royalties. Both types of royalties are divided between the songwriter and the song's publisher. Vincent Cusano is a musician and songwriter who performed under the name "Vinnie Vincent" as a guitarist with the group KISS in the early 1980s. Cusano co-wrote three songs entitled "Killer," "I Love It Loud," and "I Still Love You," which KISS recorded and released in 1982 on an album titled *Creatures of the Night.* Cusano left KISS in 1984. Eight years later, Cusano sold to Horipro Entertainment Group "one hundred (100%) percent undivided interest" of his rights in the songs "other than Songwriter's share of performance income." Later, Cusano filed a suit in a federal district court against Horipro, claiming in part that he never intended to sell the writer's share of the mechanical royalties. Horipro filed a motion for summary judgment. Should the court grant the motion? Explain. [*Cusano v. Horipro Entertainment Group,* 301 F.Supp.2d 272 (S.D.N.Y. 2004)]

A QUESTION OF ETHICS

7–8. When LeRoy McIlravy began working for Kerr-McGee Corp., he was given an employee handbook that listed examples of misconduct that could result in discipline or discharge and spelled out specific procedures that would be used in those instances. When McIlravy was later laid off, he and other former employees filed a suit against Kerr-McGee, contending, among other things, that the handbook constituted an implied contract that Kerr-McGee had breached, because the handbook implied that employees would not be dismissed without "cause." In view of these facts, consider the following questions. [*McIlravy v. Kerr-McGee Corp.*, 119 F.3d 876 (10th Cir. 1997)]

1. Would it be fair to the employer for the court to hold that an implied contract had been created in this case, given that the employer did not *intend* to create a contract? Would it be fair to the employees to hold that no contract was created? If the decision were up to you, how would you decide this issue?
2. Suppose that the handbook contained a disclaimer stating that the handbook was not to be construed as a contract. How would this affect your answers to the above questions? From an ethical perspective, would it ever be fair to hold that an implied contract exists *notwithstanding* such a disclaimer?

FOR CRITICAL ANALYSIS

7–9. Review the list of basic requirements for contract formation given at the beginning of this chapter. In view of those requirements, analyze the relationship entered into when a student enrolls in a college or university. Has a contract been formed? If so, is it a bilateral contract or a unilateral contract? Discuss.

VIDEO QUESTION

7–10. Go to this text's Web site at **http://blt.westbuslaw.com** and select "Chapter 7." Click on "Video Questions" and view the video titled *Bowfinger.* Then answer the following questions.

1. In the video, Renfro (Robert Downey, Jr.) says to Bowfinger (Steve Martin), "You bring me this script and Kit Ramsey and you've got yourself a 'go' picture." Assume for the purposes of this question that their agreement is a contract. Is the contract bilateral or unilateral? Is it express or implied? Is it formal or informal? Is it executed or executory? Explain your answers.
2. What criteria would a court rely on to interpret the terms of the contract?
3. Recall from the video that the contract between Bowfinger and the producer was oral. Suppose that a statute requires contracts of this type to be in writing. In that situation, would the contract be void, voidable, or unenforceable? Explain.

INTERNET EXERCISES

Go to the *Business Law Today: The Essentials* home page at **http://blt.westbuslaw.com**, select "Chapter 7," and click on "Internet Exercises." There you will find the following Internet research exercises that you can perform to learn more about topics covered in this chapter.

Activity 7–1: LEGAL PERSPECTIVE—Contract Terms

Activity 7–2: MANAGEMENT PERSPECTIVE—Implied Employment Contracts

Activity 7–3: HISTORICAL PERSPECTIVE—Contracts in Ancient Mesopotamia

BEFORE THE TEST

Go to the *Business Law Today: The Essentials* home page at **http://blt.westbuslaw.com**, select "Chapter 7," and click on "Interactive Quizzes." You will find at least twenty interactive questions relating to this chapter.

CHAPTER 8

Contracts: Capacity, Legality, Assent, and Form

"Liberty of contract is not an absolute concept. It is relative to many conditions of time and place and circumstance."

Benjamin Cardozo, 1870–1938
(Associate justice of the United States Supreme Court, 1932–1938)

CHAPTER OUTLINE

- CONTRACTUAL CAPACITY
- LEGALITY
- GENUINENESS OF ASSENT
- THE STATUTE OF FRAUDS—REQUIREMENT OF A WRITING
- THE STATUTE OF FRAUDS—SUFFICIENCY OF THE WRITING

LEARNING OBJECTIVES

After reading this chapter, you should be able to answer the following questions:

1. What are some exceptions to the rule that a minor can disaffirm (avoid) any contract?
2. Does an intoxicated person have the capacity to enter into an enforceable contract?
3. In what types of situations might genuineness of assent to a contract's terms be lacking?
4. What elements must exist for fraudulent misrepresentation to occur?
5. What contracts must be in writing to be enforceable?

Courts generally want contracts to be enforceable, and much of the law is devoted to aiding the enforceability of contracts. Nonetheless, as indicated in the opening quotation, "liberty of contract" is not absolute. In other words, not all people can make legally binding contracts at all times. Contracts entered into by persons lacking the capacity to do so may be voidable. Similarly, contracts calling for the performance of an illegal act are illegal and thus void—they are not contracts at all.

In this chapter, we first examine contractual capacity and some aspects of illegal bargains. We then look at genuineness of assent. An otherwise valid contract may still be unenforceable if the parties have not genuinely assented to its terms. As mentioned in Chapter 7, lack of genuine assent is a *defense* to the enforcement of a contract. A contract that is otherwise valid may also be unenforceable if it is not in the proper form. For example, if a contract is required by law to be in writing and there is no written evidence of the contract, it may not be enforceable. In the concluding section of this chapter, we examine the kinds of contracts that require a writing under what is called the *Statute of Frauds.*

Contractual Capacity

CONTRACTUAL CAPACITY
The threshold mental capacity required by law for a party who enters into a contract to be bound by that contract.

Contractual capacity is the legal ability to enter into a contractual relationship. Courts generally presume the existence of contractual capacity, but in some situations, capacity is lacking or may be questionable. A person *adjudged by a court* to be mentally incompetent, for example, cannot form a legally binding contract with another party. In other situations, a party may have the capacity to enter into a valid contract but also have the right to avoid liability under it. For example, minors—or *infants,* as they are commonly referred to legally—usually are not legally bound by contracts. In this section, we look at the effect of youth, intoxication, and mental incompetence on contractual capacity.

MINORS

Today, in virtually all states, the *age of majority* (when a person is no longer a minor) for contractual purposes is eighteen years—the so-called coming of age. (The age of majority may still be twenty-one for other purposes, however, such as the purchase and consumption of alcohol.) In addition, some states provide for the termination of minority on marriage. Subject to certain exceptions, the contracts entered into by a minor are voidable at the option of that minor.

The general rule is that a minor can enter into any contract an adult can, provided that the contract is not one prohibited by law for minors (for example, the sale of alcoholic beverages or tobacco). Although minors have the right to avoid their contracts, there are exceptions (to be discussed shortly).

DISAFFIRMANCE
The legal avoidance, or setting aside, of a contractual obligation.

Disaffirmance The legal avoidance, or setting aside, of a contractual obligation is referred to as **disaffirmance.** To disaffirm, a minor must express his or her intent, through words or conduct, not to be bound to the contract. The minor must disaffirm the entire contract, not merely a portion of it. For instance, a minor cannot decide to keep part of the goods purchased under a contract and return the remaining goods. When a minor disaffirms a contract, the minor can recover any property that he or she transferred to the adult as consideration for the contract, even if it is then in the possession of a third party.[1]

A contract can ordinarily be disaffirmed at any time during minority[2] or for a reasonable time after the minor comes of age. While two months would probably be considered reasonable, a court may not consider it reasonable to wait a year or more after coming of age to disaffirm, depending on the circumstances. If an individual fails to disaffirm an executed contract within a reasonable time after reaching the age of majority, a court will likely hold that the contract has been ratified (ratification will be discussed shortly).

Note that an adult who enters into a contract with a minor cannot avoid his or her contractual duties on the ground that the minor can do so. Unless the minor exercises the option to disaffirm the contract, the adult party normally is bound by it.

1. The Uniform Commercial Code, in Section 2–403(1), allows an exception if the third party is a "good faith purchaser for value."
2. In some states, however, a minor who enters into a contract for the sale of land cannot disaffirm the contract until she or he reaches the age of majority.

A Minor's Obligations on Disaffirmance. Although all states' laws permit minors to disaffirm contracts (with certain exceptions), including executed contracts, state laws differ on the extent of a minor's obligations on disaffirmance. Courts in a majority of states hold that the minor need only return the goods (or other consideration) subject to the contract, provided the goods are in the minor's possession or control. ■ EXAMPLE 8.1 Jim Garrison, a seventeen-year-old, purchases a computer from Radio Shack. While transporting the computer to his home, Garrison, through no fault of his own, is involved in a car accident. As a result of the accident, the plastic casing of the computer is broken. The next day, he returns the computer to Radio Shack and disaffirms the contract. Under the majority view, this return fulfills Garrison's duty even though the computer is now damaged. Garrison is entitled to receive a refund of the purchase price (if paid in cash) or to be relieved of any further obligations under an agreement to purchase the computer on credit. ■

A growing number of states, either by statute or by court decision, place an additional duty on the minor—the duty to restore the adult party to the position she or he held before the contract was made. ■ EXAMPLE 8.2 Sixteen-year-old Joseph Dodson bought a pickup truck for $4,900 from a used-car dealer. Although the truck developed mechanical problems nine months later, Dodson continued to drive it until the engine blew up and it stopped running. Then Dodson disaffirmed the contract and attempted to return the truck to the dealer for a refund of the full purchase price. The dealer refused to accept the pickup or refund the money. Dodson filed suit. Ultimately, the Tennessee Supreme Court allowed Dodson to disaffirm the contract but required the seller to be compensated for the depreciated value—not the purchase price—of the pickup.[3] ■ This example illustrates the trend among

3. *Dodson v. Shrader,* 824 S.W.2d 545 (Tenn. 1992).

Two young men discuss the sale of a car. When a minor disaffirms a contract, such as a contract to buy a car, most states require the minor to return whatever he or she purchased, if it is within his or her control. Why do some states require more? (© Michael Newman, PhotoEdit)

today's courts to hold a minor responsible for damage, ordinary wear and tear, and depreciation of goods that the minor used prior to disaffirmance.

Misrepresentation of Age. Suppose that a minor tells a seller she is twenty-one years old when she is really seventeen. Ordinarily, the minor can disaffirm the contract even though she has misrepresented her age. Moreover, in some jurisdictions the minor is not liable for the tort of fraudulent misrepresentation, the rationale being that such a tort judgment might indirectly force the minor to perform the contract.

In many jurisdictions, however, a minor who has misrepresented his or her age can be bound by a contract under certain circumstances. First, several states have enacted statutes for precisely this purpose. In these states, misrepresentation of age is enough to prohibit disaffirmance. Other statutes prohibit disaffirmance by a minor who has engaged in business as an adult. Second, some courts refuse to allow minors to disaffirm executed (fully performed) contracts unless they can return the consideration received. The combination of the minors' misrepresentations and their unjust enrichment has persuaded these courts to *estop* (prevent) the minors from asserting contractual incapacity.

Finally, some courts allow a misrepresenting minor to disaffirm the contract, but they hold the minor liable for damages in tort. Here, the defrauded party may sue the minor for misrepresentation or fraud. Authority is split on this point because some courts, as previously noted, have recognized that allowing a suit in tort is equivalent to indirectly enforcing the minor's contract.

Contracts for Necessaries, Insurance, and Loans. A minor who enters into a contract for necessaries may disaffirm the contract but remains liable for the reasonable value of the goods used. **Necessaries** are basic needs, such as food, clothing, shelter, and medical services, at a level of value required to maintain the minor's standard of living or financial and social status. Thus, what will be considered a necessary for one person may be a luxury for another. Additionally, what is considered a necessary depends on whether the minor is under the care or control of his or her parents, who are required by law to provide necessaries for the minor. If a minor's parents provide the minor with shelter, for example, then a contract to lease shelter (such as an apartment) normally will not be considered as a contract for necessaries.

NECESSARIES
Necessities required for life, such as food, shelter, clothing, and medical attention; may include whatever is believed to be necessary to maintain a person's standard of living or financial and social status.

Generally, then, to qualify as a contract for necessaries, (1) the item contracted for must be necessary to the minor's existence, (2) the value of the necessary item may be up to a level required to maintain the minor's standard of living or financial and social status, and (3) the minor must not be under the care of a parent or guardian who is required to supply this item. Unless these three criteria are met, the minor can normally disaffirm the contract *without* being liable for the reasonable value of the goods used.

BE AWARE A minor's station in life (including financial and social status and lifestyle) is important in determining whether an item is a necessary or a luxury. For example, clothing is a necessary, but if a minor from a low-income family contracts for the purchase of a $2,000 leather coat, a court may deem the coat a luxury. In this situation, the contract would not be for "necessaries."

Traditionally, insurance has not been viewed as a necessary, so minors can ordinarily disaffirm their insurance contracts and recover all premiums paid. Some jurisdictions, however, prohibit the disaffirmance of insurance contracts—for example, when minors contract for life insurance on their own lives. Financial loans are seldom considered to be necessaries, even if the minor spends the funds borrowed on necessaries. If, however, a lender makes a loan to a minor for the express purpose of enabling the minor to purchase necessaries, and the lender personally makes sure the funds are so spent, the minor normally is obligated to repay the loan. The issue in the following case was whether a medical service provider could collect from a minor the cost of emergency services rendered to the minor when his mother did not pay.

CASE 8.1 Yale Diagnostic Radiology v. Estate of Harun Fountain

Supreme Court of Connecticut, 2004.
267 Conn. 351,
838 A.2d 179.

FACTS In March 1996, Harun Fountain was shot in the back of the head at point-blank range by a playmate. Fountain required extensive lifesaving medical services from a variety of providers, including Yale Diagnostic Radiology. Yale billed Fountain's mother, Vernetta Turner-Tucker, for the cost of its services, $17,694, but she did not pay. Instead, in January 2001, Turner-Tucker filed for bankruptcy (see Chapter 16), and all of her debts, including the amount owed to Yale, were discharged. Meanwhile, she filed a suit in a Connecticut state court against the boy who shot Fountain and obtained money for Fountain's medical care. These funds were deposited in an account—sometimes referred to as an "estate"—established on Fountain's behalf. Yale filed a suit against Fountain's estate, asking the court to order the estate to pay Yale's bill, but the court refused to grant the order. Yale appealed to a state intermediate appellate court, which reversed this ruling and ordered the payment. The estate appealed to the state supreme court.

ISSUE Can a party who provides emergency medical services to a minor collect for those services from the minor if his or her parents do not pay?

DECISION Yes. The Connecticut Supreme Court affirmed the judgment of the lower court. Yale could collect from Fountain's estate for the cost of its services under the doctrine of necessaries.

REASON The state supreme court explained that while Connecticut has long recognized the rule that a minor's contracts are voidable, a minor cannot avoid a contract for goods or services necessary for the minor's health. The court reasoned that this principle is based on the theory of quasi contract (also known as implied-in-law contracts—see Chapter 7). According to the court, two contracts arise when a necessary medical service is provided to a minor. The primary contract is between the provider and the minor's parents and is based on the parents' duty to pay for the child's necessary health expenses. A secondary contract is implied in law between the provider and the minor to prevent unjust enrichment. "Therefore," stated the court, "where necessary medical services are rendered to a minor whose parents do not pay for them, equity and justice demand that a secondary implied-in-law contract arise between the medical services provider and the minor who has received the benefits of those services."

FOR CRITICAL ANALYSIS—Social Consideration
What might have happened in future cases if the court had held that there was no implied-in-law contract between Fountain and Yale?

RATIFICATION
The act of accepting and giving legal force to an obligation that previously was not enforceable.

Ratification In contract law, **ratification** is the act of accepting and giving legal force to an obligation that previously was not enforceable. A minor who has reached the age of majority can ratify a contract expressly or impliedly. Express ratification occurs when the minor expressly states, orally or in writing, that she or he intends to be bound by the contract. Implied ratification exists when the conduct of the minor indicates an intention to be bound by the contract. Ratification will be implied if the minor's conduct is inconsistent with disaffirmance (as when the minor enjoys the benefits of the contract) or if the minor fails to disaffirm an executed (fully performed) contract within a reasonable time after reaching the age of majority. If the contract is still executory (not yet performed or only partially performed), however, failure to disaffirm the contract will not necessarily imply ratification.

■ EXAMPLE 8.3 Lin enters a contract to sell her laptop to Arturo, a minor. If Arturo does not disaffirm the contract and, on reaching the age of majority, writes a letter to Lin stating that he still agrees to buy the laptop, he has expressly ratified the contract. If, instead, Arturo takes possession of the laptop as a minor and continues to use it well after reaching the age of majority, he has impliedly ratified the contract. ■

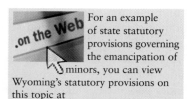

.on the Web For an example of state statutory provisions governing the emancipation of minors, you can view Wyoming's statutory provisions on this topic at **http://legisweb.state.wy.us/statutes/sub14.htm.**

In determining whether implied ratification has occurred, the courts generally look at whether the minor, after reaching the age of majority, has had ample opportunity to consider the nature of the contractual obligations he or she entered into as a minor and at the extent to which the adult party to the contract has performed.

INTOXICATED PERSONS

Contractual capacity also becomes an issue when a party to a contract was intoxicated at the time the contract was made. Intoxication is a condition in which a person's normal capacity to act or think is inhibited by alcohol or some other drug. If the person was sufficiently intoxicated to lack mental capacity, the contract may be voidable even if the intoxication was purely voluntary. For the contract to be voidable, however, the person must prove that the intoxication impaired her or his reason and judgment so severely that she or he did not comprehend the legal consequences of entering into the contract. In addition, to avoid the contract in the majority of states, the person claiming intoxication must be able to return all consideration received.

If, despite intoxication, the person understood the legal consequences of the agreement, the contract is enforceable. The fact that the terms of the contract are foolish or obviously favor the other party does not make the contract voidable (unless the other party fraudulently induced the person to become intoxicated). As a practical matter, courts rarely permit contracts to be avoided on the ground of intoxication because it is difficult to determine whether a party was sufficiently intoxicated to avoid legal duties. Rather than inquire into the intoxicated person's mental state, many courts instead focus on objective indications of capacity to determine whether the contract is voidable.[4]

MENTALLY INCOMPETENT PERSONS

.on the Web For a brief covering contractual capacity and mentally incompetent persons, go to **http://www.zlawyer2b.com/Contract-4-brief.html**.

Contracts made by mentally incompetent persons can be void, voidable, or valid. If a court has previously determined that a person is mentally incompetent and has appointed a guardian to represent the person, any contract made by that mentally incompetent person is *void*—no contract exists. Only the guardian can enter into a binding contract on behalf of the mentally incompetent person.

If a court has not previously judged a person to be mentally incompetent but in fact the person was incompetent at the time, the contract may be *voidable*. A contract is voidable if the person did not know he or she was entering into the contract or lacked the mental capacity to comprehend its nature, purpose, and consequences. In such situations, the contract is voidable at the option of the mentally incompetent person but not the other party. The contract may then be disaffirmed or ratified (if the person regains mental competence). Like intoxicated persons, mentally incompetent persons must return any consideration and pay for the reasonable value of any necessaries they receive.

A contract entered into by a mentally incompetent person (whom a court has not previously declared incompetent) may also be deemed *valid* if the person had capacity *at the time the contract was formed*. For instance, a person may be able to understand the nature and effect of entering into a certain contract yet simultaneously lack capacity to engage in other activities. In such cases, the contract ordinarily will be valid because the person is not legally mentally incompetent for contractual

4. See, for example, the court's decision in *Lucy v. Zehmer*, presented as Case 7.2 in Chapter 7.

purposes.[5] Similarly, an otherwise mentally incompetent person may have a *lucid interval*—a temporary restoration of sufficient intelligence, judgment, and will to enter into contracts—during which he or she will be considered to have full legal capacity.

Legality

To this point, we have discussed three of the requirements for a valid contract to exist—agreement, consideration, and contractual capacity. Now we examine a fourth—legality. For a contract to be valid and enforceable, it must be formed for a legal purpose. A contract to do something that is prohibited by federal or state statutory law is illegal and, as such, void from the outset and thus unenforceable. Additionally, a contract to commit a tortious act or to commit an action that is contrary to public policy is illegal and unenforceable.

Contracts Contrary to Statute

Statutes often set forth rules specifying which terms and clauses may be included in contracts and which are prohibited. We examine here several ways in which contracts may be contrary to a statute and thus illegal.

USURY
Charging an illegal rate of interest.

Usury Virtually every state has a statute that sets the maximum rate of interest that can be charged for different types of transactions, including ordinary loans. A lender who makes a loan at an interest rate above the lawful maximum commits **usury.** The maximum rate of interest varies from state to state.

Although usury statutes place a ceiling on allowable rates of interest, exceptions are made to facilitate business transactions. For example, many states exempt corporate loans from the usury laws. In addition, almost all states have special statutes allowing much higher interest rates on small loans to help those borrowers who need funds and could not otherwise obtain loans.

The consequences for lenders who make usurious loans vary from state to state. A number of states allow the lender to recover only the principal of a loan along with interest up to the legal maximum. In effect, the lender is denied recovery of the excess interest. In other states, the lender can recover the principal amount of the loan but no interest. In a few states, a usurious loan is a void transaction, and the lender cannot recover either the principal or the interest.

Gambling All states have statutes that regulate gambling—defined as any scheme that involves the distribution of property by chance among persons who have paid valuable consideration for the opportunity (chance) to receive the property.[6] Gambling is the creation of risk for the purpose of assuming it. Traditionally, the states have deemed gambling contracts illegal and thus void.

In several states, however, including Louisiana, Nevada, and New Jersey, casino gambling is legal. In other states, certain other forms of gambling are legal. California, for example, has not defined draw poker as a crime, although criminal statutes prohibit numerous other types of gambling games. A number of states allow gambling on horse races, and the majority of states have legalized state-operated lot-

5. Modern courts no longer require a person to be completely incompetent to disaffirm contracts on the basis of mental incompetence. A contract may be voidable if, by reason of a mental illness or defect, an individual was unable to act reasonably with respect to the transaction and the other party had reason to know of the condition.

6. See *Wishing Well Club v. Akron,* 66 Ohio Law Abs. 406, 112 N.E.2d 41 (1951).

teries, as well as lotteries (such as bingo) conducted for charitable purposes. Many states also allow gambling on Indian reservations.

Sometimes it is difficult to distinguish a gambling contract from the risk sharing inherent in almost all contracts. ■ EXAMPLE 8.4 In one case, five co-workers each received a free lottery ticket from a customer and agreed to split the winnings if one of the tickets turned out to be the winning one. At first glance, this may seem entirely legal. The court, however, noted that the oral contract in this case "was an exchange of promises to share winnings from the parties' individually owned lottery tickets upon the happening of the uncertain event" that one of the tickets would win. Consequently, concluded the court, the agreement at issue was "founded on a gambling consideration" and therefore was void.[7] ■

ETHICAL ISSUE 8.1

How can states enforce gambling laws in the age of the Internet? One of the threshold issues in regulating online gambling is jurisdictional in nature. For example, in those states that do not allow casino gambling or offtrack betting, what can a state government do if residents of the state place bets online? After all, as you read in Chapter 1, states have no constitutional authority to regulate activities that occur in other states. Another threshold issue in regulating online gambling involves determining where the physical act of placing a bet on the Internet occurs. Is it where the gambler is located or where the gambling site is based? For example, suppose that a resident of New York places bets via the Internet at a gambling site located in Antigua. Is the actual act of "gambling" taking place in New York or in Antigua?

When this exact question came before a New York court, the court, in a precedent-setting decision, concluded that the act of gambling occurred in New York, because under New York law a bet has to be legal in both the jurisdiction where the bet is placed and the jurisdiction where it is received. According to the court, "if the person engaged in gambling is located in New York, then New York is the location where the gambling occurred." Significantly, the U.S. Court of Appeals for the Second Circuit upheld the New York court's decision.[8] ■

Sabbath (Sunday) Laws Statutes referred to as Sabbath (Sunday) laws prohibit the formation or performance of certain contracts on a Sunday. Under the common law, such contracts are legal in the absence of this statutory prohibition. According to some state and local laws, all contracts entered into on a Sunday are illegal. Laws in other states or municipalities prohibit only the sale of certain types of merchandise, such as alcoholic beverages, on a Sunday.

As noted in Chapter 1, these laws, which date back to colonial times, are often called **blue laws.** Blue laws get their name from the blue paper on which New Haven, Connecticut, printed its new town ordinance in 1781. The ordinance prohibited all work on Sunday and required all shops to close on the "Lord's Day." A number of states and municipalities enacted laws forbidding the carrying on of "all secular labor and business on the Lord's Day." Exceptions to Sunday laws permit contracts for necessities (such as food) and works of charity. Additionally, a fully performed (executed) contract that was entered into on a Sunday normally cannot be rescinded (canceled).

Sunday laws are often not enforced, and some of these laws have been held to be unconstitutional on the ground that they are contrary to the freedom of religion. Nonetheless, as a precaution, business owners contemplating doing business in a particular locality should check to see if any Sunday statutes or ordinances will affect their business activities.

BLUE LAWS
State or local laws that prohibit the performance of certain types of commercial activities on Sunday.

on the Web If you are interested in reading the earliest legislation regulating activities on the Sabbath in colonial America (and about some of the punishments meted out for failing to obey these regulations), go to **http://www.natreformassn.org/statesman/99/charactr.html**.

7. *Dickerson v. Deno,* 770 So.2d 63 (Ala. 2000).
8. *United States v. Cohen,* 260 F.3d. 68 (2d Cir. 2001).

Adults gamble at a casino. Would this same activity be illegal if it were conducted online? If so, could it be prevented? How? (© M. Borchi/Photo Researchers)

Licensing Statutes All states require that members of certain professions obtain licenses allowing them to practice. Physicians, lawyers, real estate brokers, architects, electricians, and stockbrokers are but a few of the people who must be licensed. Some licenses are obtained only after extensive schooling and examinations, which indicate to the public that a special skill has been acquired. Others require only that the particular person be of good moral character and pay a fee.

The Purpose of Licensing Statutes. Generally, business licenses provide a means of regulating and taxing certain businesses and protecting the public against actions that could threaten the general welfare. For example, in nearly all states, a stockbroker must be licensed and must file a bond with the state to protect the public from fraudulent transactions in stock. Similarly, a plumber must be licensed and bonded to protect the public against incompetent plumbers and to protect the public health. Only persons or businesses possessing the qualifications and complying with the conditions required by statute are entitled to licenses. For instance, the owner of a tavern can be required to sell food as a condition of obtaining a license to serve liquor.

Contracts with Unlicensed Practitioners. A contract with an unlicensed practitioner may still be enforceable, depending on the nature of the licensing statute. Some states expressly provide that the lack of a license in certain occupations bars the enforcement of work-related contracts. If the statute does not expressly state this, one must look to the underlying purpose of the licensing requirements for a particular occupation. If the purpose is to protect the public from unauthorized practitioners, a contract involving an unlicensed individual is illegal and unenforceable. If, however, the underlying purpose of the statute is to raise government revenues, a contract with an unlicensed practitioner is enforceable—although the unlicensed person is usually fined.

CONTRACTS CONTRARY TO PUBLIC POLICY

Although contracts involve private parties, some are not enforceable because of the negative impact they would have on society. These contracts are said to be *contrary to public policy.* Examples include a contract to commit an immoral act, such as selling a child (see, for example, the case discussed in this chapter's *Letter of the Law* feature), and a contract that prohibits marriage. ■ **EXAMPLE 8.5** Everett offers a young man $10,000 if he refrains from marrying Everett's daughter. If the young man accepts, no contract is formed (the contract is void) because it is contrary to public policy. Thus, if the man marries Everett's daughter, Everett cannot sue him for breach of contract. ■ Business contracts that may be contrary to public policy include contracts in restraint of trade and unconscionable contracts or clauses.

EMPLOYMENT CONTRACT
A contract between an employer and an employee in which the terms and conditions of employment are stated.

COVENANT NOT TO COMPETE
A contractual promise of one party to refrain from conducting business similar to that of another party for a certain period of time and within a specified geographic area. Courts commonly enforce such covenants if they are reasonable in terms of time and geographic area and part of, or supplemental to, an employment contract or a contract for the sale of a business.

Contracts in Restraint of Trade Contracts in restraint of trade (anticompetitive agreements) usually adversely affect the public policy that favors competition in the economy. Typically, such contracts also violate one or more federal or state statutes.[9] An exception is recognized when the restraint is reasonable and is part of, or supplemental to, a contract for the sale of a business or an **employment contract** (a contract stating the terms and conditions of employment). Many such exceptions involve a type of restraint called a **covenant not to compete,** or a restrictive covenant.

9. Federal statutes prohibiting anticompetitive agreements include the Sherman Antitrust Act, the Clayton Act, and the Federal Trade Commission Act (see Chapter 22).

LETTER OF THE LAW For Sale: "The Most Beautiful Baby in the World"

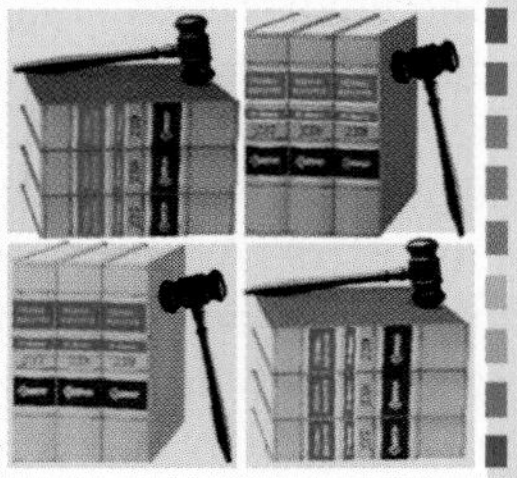

Lawrence Schaub, a former windshield repairman in Detroit, Michigan, was facing financial problems. He was out of work. He was behind in his mobile home payments. He had three children to feed. Desperate to obtain funds, he decided to sell the youngest of his three children. To that end, he created a videotape titled "The Most Beautiful Baby in the World" to show to prospective buyers. Unfortunately for Schaub, his children's babysitter informed the police of his plan, and he was caught in a "sting" operation when undercover police officers posed as a would-be adoptive family. Schaub accepted $10,000 from the officers as a down payment on the $60,000 contract price.

If a case involving a similar contract came before a civil court, the court would likely deem the contract void as against public policy. Schaub's was a criminal case, however, and a significant question immediately arose: What statute had Schaub violated? Until September 1, 2000, Michigan was one of about twenty-five states that did not explicitly outlaw the sale of children. Shortly after Schaub's arrest drew attention to this "oversight" in state law, the Michigan legislature passed a bill making trafficking in humans punishable by up to twenty years in prison and a $100,000 fine. At the time Schaub tried to sell his daughter, however, the law did not exist. At worst, the only state crime that Schaub committed was attempting to profit from an adoption, which is subject to a penalty of ninety days in jail.[a]

THE BOTTOM LINE

Occasionally, bizarre cases such as this one alert state legislatures to loopholes in their laws. Note, though, that the prosecutors in Schaub's case found other ways to keep Schaub in jail for a while—at least until his former wife claimed custody of the children. The prosecutors charged Schaub with child abandonment, driving with a suspended license, and violating his probation stemming from an earlier drug case.

a. For a summary of Schaub's actions and the prosecution's case against him, see M. L. Elrick, "Baby for Sale," *The National Law Journal,* September 11, 2000, pp. A1–A2.

Covenants Not to Compete and the Sale of an Ongoing Business. Covenants not to compete are often contained in contracts concerning the sale of an ongoing business. A covenant not to compete is created when a seller agrees not to open a new store in a certain geographic area surrounding the old store. Such an agreement, when it is ancillary to a sales contract and reasonable in terms of time and geographic area, enables the seller to sell, and the purchaser to buy, the "goodwill" and "reputation" of an ongoing business. If, for example, a well-known merchant sells his or her store and opens a competing business a block away, many of the merchant's customers will likely do business at the new store. This renders valueless the good name and reputation sold to the other merchant for a price. If a covenant not to compete is not ancillary to a sales agreement, however, it will be void because it unreasonably restrains trade and is contrary to public policy.

Covenants Not to Compete in Employment Contracts. Agreements not to compete can also be included in employment contracts. People in middle-level and upper-level management positions commonly agree not to work for competitors or not to start a competing business for a specified period of time after terminating employment. Such agreements are generally legal so long as the specified period of time is not excessive in duration and the geographic restriction is reasonable. Basically, the restriction on competition must be reasonable—that is, not any greater than necessary to protect a legitimate business interest. While a time restriction of one year may be upheld by a court as reasonable, a time restriction of two, three, or five years may not be.

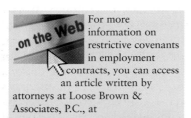

.on the Web For more information on restrictive covenants in employment contracts, you can access an article written by attorneys at Loose Brown & Associates, P.C., at **http://www.loosebrown.com/articles/art009.pdf**.

Determining what constitute "reasonable" time and geographic restrictions in the online environment is a more difficult issue being addressed by the courts. The Internet environment has no physical borders, so geographic restrictions are no longer relevant. Also, a reasonable time period in the online environment may be less than what is reasonable in conventional employment contracts because the restrictions would apply worldwide.

■ EXAMPLE 8.6 Mark Schlack worked as a Web site manager and vice president for EarthWeb, Inc., a company in the information technology industry. At the time he was hired, Schlack signed a covenant not to compete. It stated that, on termination of his employment, he would not work for any competing company for one year. When Schlack later accepted an offer from another company to design a Web site, EarthWeb sued to enforce the covenant not to compete. The federal district court hearing the case decided that the covenant was unreasonable because it prohibited Schlack from working for a competing company located anywhere in the world for one year. According to that court, "in the Internet environment, a one-year hiatus [break] from the work force is several generations, if not an eternity."[10] ■

Enforcement Problems. The laws governing the enforceability of covenants not to compete vary significantly from state to state. In some states, such as Texas, such a covenant will not be enforced unless the employee has received some benefit in return for signing the noncompete agreement. This is true even if the covenant is reasonable as to time and area. If the employee receives no benefit, the covenant will be deemed void. California prohibits the enforcement of covenants not to compete altogether.

Occasionally, depending on the jurisdiction, courts will *reform* covenants not to compete. If a covenant is found to be unreasonable in time or geographic area, the

10. *EarthWeb, Inc. v. Schlack,* 71 F.Supp.2d 299 (S.D.N.Y. 1999).

court may convert the terms into reasonable ones and then enforce the reformed covenant. This presents a problem, however, in that the judge, implicitly, has become a party to the contract. Consequently, courts usually resort to contract **reformation** only when necessary to prevent undue burdens or hardships.

REFORMATION
A court-ordered correction of a written contract so that it reflects the true intentions of the parties.

Unconscionable Contracts or Clauses Ordinarily, a court does not look at the fairness or equity of a contract; for example, a court normally will not inquire into the adequacy of consideration. Persons are assumed to be reasonably intelligent, and the court does not come to their aid just because they have made unwise or foolish bargains. In certain circumstances, however, bargains are so oppressive that the courts relieve innocent parties of part or all of their duties. Such a bargain is called an **unconscionable contract** (or **unconscionable clause**). Both the Uniform Commercial Code (UCC) and the Uniform Consumer Credit Code (UCCC) embody the unconscionability concept—the former with regard to the sale of goods and the latter with regard to consumer loans and the waiver of rights.[11] A contract can be unconscionable on either procedural or substantive grounds, as discussed in the following subsections.

UNCONSCIONABLE CONTRACT (OR UNCONSCIONABLE CLAUSE)
A contract or clause that is void on the basis of public policy because one party, as a result of disproportionate bargaining power, is forced to accept terms that are unfairly burdensome and that unfairly benefit the dominating party.

Procedural Unconscionability. Procedural unconscionability has to do with how a term becomes part of a contract and relates to factors bearing on a party's lack of knowledge or understanding of the contract terms because of inconspicuous print, unintelligible language ("legalese"), lack of opportunity to read the contract, lack of opportunity to ask questions about the contract's meaning, and other factors. Procedural unconscionability sometimes relates to purported lack of voluntariness because of a disparity in bargaining power between the two parties. Contracts entered into because of one party's vastly superior bargaining power may be deemed unconscionable. These situations usually involve an **adhesion contract,** which is a contract drafted by the dominant party and then presented to the other—the adhering party—on a "take-it-or-leave-it" basis.[12]

ADHESION CONTRACT
A "standard-form" contract, such as that between a large retailer and a consumer, in which the stronger party dictates the terms.

Substantive Unconscionability. Substantive unconscionability characterizes those contracts, or portions of contracts, that are oppressive or overly harsh. Courts generally focus on provisions that deprive one party of the benefits of the agreement or leave that party without remedy for nonperformance by the other. For example, suppose that a person with little income and only a fourth-grade education agrees to purchase a refrigerator for $3,000 and signs a two-year installment contract. The same type of refrigerator usually sells for $600 on the market. Despite the general rule that the courts will not inquire into the adequacy of the consideration, some courts hold that this type of contract is unconscionable because the contract terms are so oppressive as to "shock the conscience" of the court.[13] Is a contract to prescribe medications via the Internet unconscionable? For a discussion of this issue, see this chapter's *Adapting the Law to the Online Environment* feature on the next page.

EXCULPATORY CLAUSE
A clause that releases a contractual party from liability in the event of monetary or physical injury, no matter who is at fault.

Exculpatory Clauses Often closely related to the concept of unconscionability are **exculpatory clauses,** which release a party from liability in the event of monetary or physical injury, *no matter who is at fault.* Indeed, some courts refer to such clauses

11. See, for example, UCC Sections 2–302 and 2–719.
12. See, for example, *Henningsen v. Bloomfield Motors, Inc.,* 32 N.J. 358, 161 A.2d 69 (1960).
13. See, for example, *Jones v. Star Credit Corp.,* 59 Misc.2d 189, 298 N.Y.S.2d 264 (1969). This case is presented in Chapter 11 as Case 11.2.

ADAPTING THE LAW TO THE ONLINE ENVIRONMENT

Is It Unconscionable for Physicians to Prescribe Medication Online?

Anyone with an e-mail address has undoubtedly received scores of messages offering to sell prescription medications, such as Viagra, online. In the past, someone who wanted a prescription for a certain medication—whether it was for allergies, weight loss, or sexual enhancement—had to see a physician and, normally, undergo a physical examination to see if that medication was appropriate. Today, however, it is possible to enter into a contract to obtain a prescription for, and order, many medications via the Internet without ever setting foot in a physician's office. Contracting with a physician online to receive prescription drugs may be ill advised, but are such contracts unconscionable?

A VIRTUAL DIAGNOSIS

The hallmark of an unconscionable contract is that its terms are so oppressive, one sided, or unfair as to "shock the conscience" of the court. Thus, the issue is whether Internet prescription contracts are so unfair that they "shock the conscience" of the court. After all, physicians are trained to examine patients, diagnose medical conditions, and evaluate possible treatments. A physician who is prescribing medication for a person online, however, has no objective way to determine the person's health status or whether the person understands the risks involved. For example, in the online context, a physician cannot tell if a person is truthfully reporting his or her age and weight, which can significantly affect whether a medication is recommended. In addition, physicians who prescribe drugs online cannot monitor the use of these drugs and evaluate their effectiveness.

AN EMERGING ISSUE

To date, only a few courts have addressed this issue, and no court as yet has held that prescribing drugs online is unconscionable. For example, in 2003, in a case before the Kansas Supreme Court, the state attorney general claimed that it was unconscionable for an out-of-state physician to contract with residents to prescribe drugs via the Internet. The case involved three Kansas residents, including a minor, who entered into contracts on the Web to obtain prescription weight loss drugs (Meridia and phentermine).[a]

The court held that the physician's conduct and the resulting contracts were not unconscionable because there was no evidence that the physician had deceived, oppressed, or misused superior bargaining power. The Web site used by the physician had included a great deal of general information about the specific drugs and their side effects, online questionnaires to obtain medical histories, and waivers of the physician's liability for the prescriptions. The Web site had also provided an online calculator for body weight so that a person could determine if she or he was twenty-five pounds overweight, as required to obtain a prescription for Meridia. Because the court found that the individuals had gotten exactly what they bargained for—the prescription medications they sought—the court refused to step in and declare the contracts unconscionable.

FOR CRITICAL ANALYSIS

If the physicians are not deceptive, should the courts allow all types of medications to be prescribed over the Internet? Why or why not? Explain whether the practice of prescribing medications via the Internet might reach the point at which it "shocks the conscience" of the court.

a. *State ex rel. Stovall v. DVM Enterprises, Inc.,* 275 Kan. 243, 62 P.3d 653 (2003); see also *State ex rel. Stovall v. Confimed.com, L.L.C.,* 272 Kan. 1313, 38 P.3d 707 (2002). (The Latin phrase *ex rel.* means "by or on the relation of" and is used in case names when the suit is brought by the government on the application of a private party who is interested in the matter.)

in terms of unconscionability. ■ EXAMPLE 8.7 Suppose, for example, that Madison Manufacturing Company hires a laborer and has him sign a contract containing the following clause:

> Said employee hereby agrees with employer, in consideration of such employment, that he will take upon himself all risks incident to his position and will in no case hold the company liable for any injury or damage he may sustain, in his person or otherwise, by accidents or injuries in the factory, or which may result from defective machinery or carelessness or misconduct of himself or any other employee in service of the employer.

REMEMBER Virtually everyone is liable for her or his own torts, and this responsibility cannot be contracted away.

This contract provision attempts to remove Madison's potential liability for injuries occurring to the employee, and it would usually be held contrary to public policy.[14] ■ Additionally, exculpatory clauses found in agreements to lease commercial property are normally held to be contrary to public policy. Such clauses are almost universally held to be illegal and unenforceable when they are included in residential property leases.

Exculpatory clauses may be enforced, however, when the parties seeking their enforcement are not involved in businesses considered important to the public interest. Businesses such as health clubs, amusement parks, horse-rental concessions, golf-cart concessions, and skydiving organizations frequently use exculpatory clauses to limit their liability for patrons' injuries. Because these services are not essential, the firms offering them are sometimes considered to have no relative advantage in bargaining strength, and anyone contracting for their services is considered to do so voluntarily.

THE EFFECT OF ILLEGALITY

In general, an illegal contract is void; that is, the contract is deemed never to have existed, and the courts will not aid either party. In most illegal contracts, both parties are considered to be equally at fault—*in pari delicto*. If the contract is executory (not yet fulfilled), neither party can enforce it. If it has been executed, there can be neither contractual nor quasi-contractual recovery.

That one wrongdoer in an illegal contract is unjustly enriched at the expense of the other is of no concern to the law—except under certain circumstances (to be discussed shortly). The major justification for this hands-off attitude is that it is improper to place the machinery of justice at the disposal of a plaintiff who has broken the law by entering into an illegal bargain. Another justification is the hoped-for deterrent effect of this general rule. A plaintiff who suffers a loss because of an illegal bargain will presumably be deterred from entering into similar illegal bargains in the future.

There are exceptions to the general rule that neither party to an illegal bargain can sue for breach and neither party can recover for performance rendered. We look at these exceptions here.

Justifiable Ignorance of the Facts When one of the parties to a contract is relatively innocent (has no reason to know that the contract is illegal), that party can often recover any benefits conferred in a partially executed contract. In this situation, the courts will not enforce the contract but will allow the parties to return to their original positions.

A court may sometimes permit an innocent party who has fully performed under a contract to enforce the contract against the guilty party. ■ **EXAMPLE 8.8** A trucking company contracts with Gillespie to carry crated goods to a specific destination for a normal fee of $500. The trucker delivers the crates and later finds out that they contained illegal goods. Although the shipment, use, and sale of the goods are illegal under the law, the trucker, being an innocent party, can normally still legally collect the $500 from Gillespie. ■

14. For a case with similar facts, see *Little Rock & Fort Smith Railway Co. v. Eubanks,* 48 Ark. 460, 3 S.W. 808 (1887). In such a case, the exculpatory clause may also be illegal because it violates a state workers' compensation law.

Members of Protected Classes When a statute protects a certain class of people, a member of that class can enforce an illegal contract even though the other party cannot. ■ EXAMPLE 8.9 Statutes prohibit certain employees (such as flight attendants) from working more than a specified number of hours per month. These employees thus constitute a class protected by statute. An employee who is required to work more than the maximum can recover for those extra hours of service. ■

BLUE SKY LAWS
State laws that regulate the offer and sale of securities.

Other examples of statutes designed to protect a particular class of people are **blue sky laws**—state laws that regulate and supervise investment companies for the protection of the public (see Chapter 21)—and state statutes regulating the sale of insurance. If an insurance company violates a statute when selling insurance, the purchaser can nevertheless enforce the policy and recover from the insurer.

Withdrawal from an Illegal Agreement If the illegal part of a bargain has not yet been performed, the party rendering performance can withdraw from the contract and recover the performance or its value. ■ EXAMPLE 8.10 Suppose that Marta and Amil decide to wager (illegally) on the outcome of a boxing match. Each deposits money with a stakeholder, who agrees to pay the winner of the bet. At this point, each party has performed part of the agreement, but the illegal part of the agreement will not occur until the money is paid to the winner. Before such payment occurs, either party is entitled to withdraw from the agreement by giving notice to the stakeholder of his or her withdrawal. ■

Severable, or Divisible, Contracts A contract that is *severable,* or divisible, consists of distinct parts that can be performed separately, with separate consideration provided for each part. With an *indivisible* contract, in contrast, the parties intended that complete performance by each party would be essential, even if the contract contains a number of seemingly separate provisions.

If a contract is divisible into legal and illegal portions, a court may enforce the legal portion but not the illegal one, so long as the illegal portion does not affect the essence of the bargain. This approach is consistent with the basic policy of enforcing the legal intentions of the contracting parties whenever possible. ■ EXAMPLE 8.11 If an employment contract includes an overly broad and thus illegal covenant not to compete, the court might allow the employment contract to be enforceable but reform the unreasonably broad covenant by converting its terms into reasonable ones. Alternatively, the court could declare the covenant illegal (and thus void) and enforce the remaining employment terms. ■

Contracts Illegal through Fraud, Duress, or Undue Influence Often, one party to an illegal contract is more at fault than the other. When a party has been induced to enter into an illegal bargain through fraud, duress, or undue influence on the part of the other party to the agreement, the first party will be allowed to recover for the performance or its value.

Genuineness of Assent

Genuineness of assent may be lacking because of mistake, fraudulent misrepresentation, undue influence, or duress. Generally, a party who demonstrates that he or she did not genuinely assent to the terms of a contract can choose either to carry out the contract or to rescind (cancel) it and thus avoid the entire transaction.

MISTAKES

We all make mistakes, so it is not surprising that mistakes are made when contracts are created. In certain circumstances, contract law allows a contract to be avoided on the basis of mistake. Realize, though, that the concept of mistake in contract law has to do with mistaken assumptions relating to contract formation. For example, the error you make when you send your monthly bank loan payment to your plumber "by mistake" is totally different from the kind of mistake that we are discussing here. In contract law, a mistake may be a defense to the enforcement of a contract if it can be proved that the parties entered into the contract, each having different assumptions relating to the subject matter of the contract.

Courts have considerable difficulty in specifying the circumstances that justify allowing a mistake to invalidate a contract. Generally, though, courts distinguish between *mistakes as to judgment of market value or conditions* and *mistakes as to fact*. Only the latter normally have legal significance.

■ EXAMPLE 8.12 Jud Wheeler contracts to buy ten acres of land because he believes that he can resell the land at a profit to Bart. Can Jud escape his contractual obligations if it later turns out that he was mistaken? Not likely. Jud's overestimation of the value of the land or of Bart's interest in it is an ordinary risk of business for which a court normally will not provide relief. Now suppose that Jud purchases a painting of a landscape from Roth's Gallery. Both Jud and Roth believe that the painting is by the artist Van Gogh. Jud later discovers that the painting is a very clever fake. Because neither Jud nor Roth was aware of this fact when they made their deal, Jud can normally rescind the contract and recover the purchase price of the painting. ■

Mistakes occur in two forms—*unilateral* and *bilateral* (mutual). A unilateral mistake is made by only one of the contracting parties; a mutual mistake is made by both. We look next at these two types of mistakes and illustrate them graphically in Exhibit 8–1.

Unilateral Mistakes A unilateral mistake occurs when only one party is mistaken as to a *material fact*—that is, a fact important to the subject matter of the contract. Generally, a unilateral mistake does not give the mistaken party any right to relief from the contract. In other words, the contract normally is enforceable against the

EXHIBIT 8–1 MISTAKES OF FACT

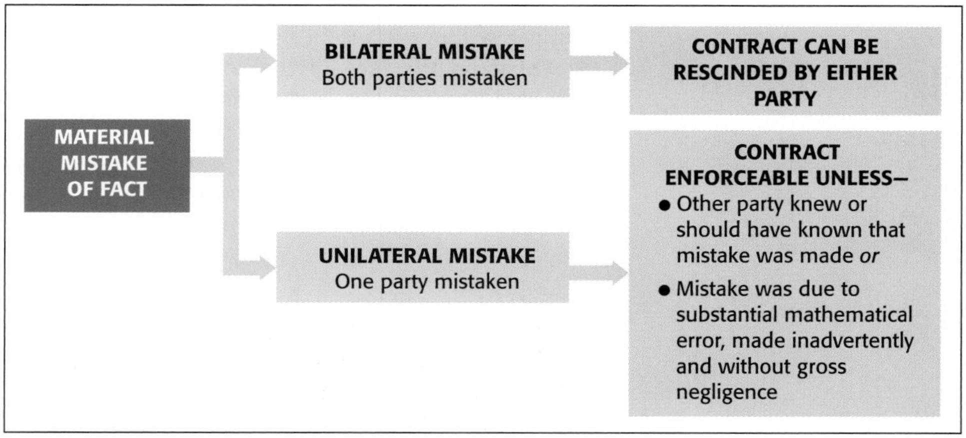

mistaken party. ■ EXAMPLE 8.13 Elena intends to sell her motor home for $17,500. When she learns that Chin is interested in buying a used motor home, she types a letter offering to sell her vehicle to him. When typing the letter, however, she mistakenly keys in the price of $15,700. Chin writes back, accepting Elena's offer. Even though Elena intended to sell her motor home for $17,500, she has made a unilateral mistake and is bound by contract to sell the vehicle to Chin for $15,700. ■

There are at least two exceptions to this rule.[15] First, if the *other* party to the contract knows or should have known that a mistake of fact was made, the contract may not be enforceable. In the above example, if Chin knew that Elena intended to sell her motor home for $17,500, then Elena's unilateral mistake (stating $15,700 in her offer) may render the resulting contract unenforceable. The second exception arises when a unilateral mistake of fact was due to a mathematical error in addition, subtraction, division, or multiplication and was made inadvertently and without gross (extreme) negligence. If a contractor's bid was significantly low because he or she made a mistake in addition when totaling the estimated costs, any contract resulting from the bid normally may be rescinded. Of course, in both situations, the mistake must still involve some *material fact*.

BE CAREFUL What a party to a contract knows or should know can determine whether the contract is enforceable.

Bilateral (Mutual) Mistakes When both parties are mistaken about the same material fact, the contract can be rescinded by either party.[16] Note that, as with unilateral mistakes, the mistake must be about a *material fact* (one that is important and central to the contract—as was the "Van Gogh" painting in Example 8.12). If, instead, a mutual mistake concerns the future market value or quality of the object of the contract, the contract normally can be enforced by either party. This rule is based on the theory that both parties assume certain risks when they enter into a contract. Without this rule, almost any party who did not receive what she or he considered a fair bargain could argue bilateral mistake.

A word or term in a contract may be subject to more than one reasonable interpretation. In that situation, if the parties to the contract attach materially different meanings to the term, their mutual misunderstanding may allow the contract to be rescinded.

■ EXAMPLE 8.14 In *Raffles v. Wichelhaus,*[17] a classic case involving a mutual mistake, Wichelhaus purchased a shipment of cotton from Raffles to arrive on a ship called the *Peerless* from Bombay, India. Wichelhaus meant a ship called the *Peerless* sailing from Bombay in October; Raffles meant another ship called the *Peerless* sailing from Bombay in December. When the goods arrived on the December *Peerless,* Raffles delivered them to Wichelhaus. By that time, however, Wichelhaus was no longer willing to accept them. The British court hearing the case stated, "There is nothing on the face of the contract to show that any particular ship called the 'Peerless' was meant; but the moment it appears that two ships called the 'Peerless' were about to sail from Bombay there is a latent ambiguity. . . . That being so, there was no consensus . . . and therefore no binding contract." ■

In the following case, an injured worker sought to set aside a settlement agreement entered into with his employer, arguing that the agreement was based on a mutual mistake of fact—a physician's mistaken diagnosis of the worker's injury.

15. The *Restatement (Second) of Contracts,* Section 153, liberalizes the general rule to take into account the modern trend of allowing avoidance in some circumstances even though only one party has been mistaken.

16. *Restatement (Second) of Contracts,* Section 152.

17. 159 Eng.Rep. 375 (1864).

CASE 8.2 Roberts v. Century Contractors, Inc.

Court of Appeals of North Carolina, 2004.
592 S.E.2d 215.
http://www.aoc.state.nc.us/www/public/html/opinions.htm[a]

FACTS Bobby Roberts was an employee of Century Contractors, Inc., when a pipe struck him in a work-related accident in July 1993, causing trauma to his neck and back. Dr. James Markworth of Southeastern Orthopaedic Clinic diagnosed Roberts's injuries. After surgery and treatment, Markworth concluded that Roberts was at maximum medical improvement (MMI) and stopped treating him. Roberts agreed with Century to accept $125,000 and payment of related medical expenses, and to waive any right to make further claims in regard to his injury. In June 1998, still experiencing pain, Roberts saw Dr. Allen Friedman, who determined that Roberts was not at MMI. Markworth then admitted that his diagnosis was a mistake. Roberts filed a claim for workers' compensation (see Chapter 18), seeking compensation and medical benefits for his injury. He alleged that his agreement with Century should be set aside due to a mutual mistake of fact. The North Carolina state administrative agency authorized to rule on workers' compensation claims awarded Roberts what he sought. Century appealed to a state intermediate appellate court.

ISSUE Should the agreement between Roberts and Century be set aside on the basis of a mutual mistake of fact?

a. In the "Keywords" box, type "Roberts." In the "What" pull-down menu, select "Title." In the "Additional Search Options" section, choose "Court of Appeals Opinions Only." Click on "Search." In the result, scroll to the name of the case and click on it to access the opinion. The North Carolina Administrative Office of the Courts maintains this Web site.

DECISION Yes. The state intermediate appellate court affirmed the award of compensation and medical benefits to Roberts.

REASON The court explained that compromise settlement agreements, including settlement agreements in workers' compensation cases, are governed by general principles of contract law. The court stated that it is a well-settled principle of contract law that a valid contract exists only where there has been a meeting of the minds as to all essential terms of the agreement. "Therefore," said the court, "where a mistake is common to both parties and concerns a material past or presently existing fact, such that there is no meeting of the minds, a contract may be avoided." The mistake "must be as to a fact which enters into and forms the basis of the contract * * * and must be such that it animates and controls the conduct of the parties." Also, "relief from a contract due to mistake of fact will be had only where *both* parties to an agreement are mistaken." The court pointed out that Markworth's MMI diagnosis was "material to the settlement of this claim" and that both parties relied on this information in entering into settlement negotiations. Later, however, "Dr. Friedman testified, and the [state agency found] as fact, that plaintiff was not at maximum medical improvement." Thus, the court concluded that there was a mutual mistake with regard to the plaintiff's medical condition at the time of the signing of the settlement agreement.

FOR CRITICAL ANALYSIS—Social Consideration
Why did the court consider Markworth's misdiagnosis a bilateral mistake rather than a unilateral mistake?

FRAUDULENT MISREPRESENTATION

Although fraud is a tort, the presence of fraud also affects the genuineness of the innocent party's consent to a contract. When an innocent party consents to a contract with fraudulent terms, the contract usually can be avoided because he or she has not *voluntarily* consented to the terms.[18] Normally, the innocent party can either rescind (cancel) the contract and be restored to his or her original position or enforce the contract and seek damages for injuries resulting from the fraud.

18. *Restatement (Second) of Contracts,* Sections 163 and 164.

Typically, fraud involves three elements:

1. A misrepresentation of a material fact must occur.
2. There must be an intent to deceive.
3. The innocent party must justifiably rely on the misrepresentation.

Additionally, to collect damages, a party must have been injured as a result of the misrepresentation.

REMEMBER To collect damages in almost any lawsuit, there must be some sort of injury.

Fraudulent misrepresentation can also occur in the online environment. Indeed, a major challenge today is how to curb Internet fraud—a topic that will be explored further in Chapter 13, in the context of consumer law.

Misrepresentation Must Occur The first element of proving fraud is to show that misrepresentation of a material fact has occurred. This misrepresentation can take the form of words or actions. For example, an art gallery owner's statement, "This painting is a Picasso" is a misrepresentation of fact if the painting was done by another artist.

A statement of opinion is generally not subject to a claim of fraud. For example, claims such as "This computer will never break down" and "This car will last for years and years" are statements of opinion, not fact, and contracting parties should recognize them as such and not rely on them. A fact is objective and verifiable; an opinion is usually subject to debate. Therefore, a seller is allowed to "huff and puff his [or her] wares" without being liable for fraud. In certain cases, however, particularly when a naïve purchaser relies on an expert's opinion, the innocent party may be entitled to rescission or reformation (an equitable remedy granted by a court in which the terms of a contract are altered to reflect the true intentions of the parties).

Intent to Deceive The second element of fraud is knowledge on the part of the misrepresenting party that facts have been misrepresented. This element, normally

Workers excavate a site and bury a sewer line. Would the party who contracted for this work be liable for fraud if the party knew, or should have known, that subsoil conditions could greatly increase the expense of the work and failed to disclose this to the bidders? Why or why not? (© Mark Mellett, Stock Boston)

SCIENTER
Knowledge by the misrepresenting party that material facts have been falsely represented or omitted with an intent to deceive.

called *scienter*,[19] or "guilty knowledge," generally signifies that there was an intent to deceive. *Scienter* clearly exists if a party knows that a fact is not as stated. *Scienter* also exists if a party makes a statement that he or she believes not to be true or makes a statement recklessly, without regard to whether it is true or false. Finally, this element is met if a party says or implies that a statement is made on some basis, such as personal knowledge or personal investigation, when it is not.

■ EXAMPLE 8.15 Suppose that Alicia Rolando, when selling a house to Cariton, tells Cariton that the plumbing pipe is of a certain quality. Rolando knows nothing about the quality of the pipe but does not believe it to be what she is representing it to be (and in fact it is not what she says it is). Rolando's statement induces Cariton to buy the house. Rolando's statement is a fraudulent misrepresentation because she does not believe that what she says is true and because she knows that she does not have any basis for making the statement. Cariton can avoid the contract. ■

Can an employer avoid liability for the breach of a contract that was induced by an employee's fraud during the hiring process? That was the question in the following case.

19. Pronounced sy-*en*-ter.

CASE 8.3 Sarvis v. Vermont State Colleges

Supreme Court of Vermont, 2001.
772 A.2d 494.

FACTS In 1995, Robert Sarvis was convicted of bank fraud, ordered to pay more than $12 million in restitution, and sentenced to forty-six months in prison. While incarcerated, he worked in the prison's electrical department. Two weeks after his release in 1998, he applied for an adjunct professor position at Community College of Vermont (CCV). On his résumé, he stated that during "1984–1998" he was "President and Chairman of the Board" of "CMI International Inc., Boston, Massachusetts," where he was "[r]esponsible for all operations and financial matters." For a position as CCV's Coordinator of Academic Services, he submitted a second résumé, on which he added, "1998–present. Semi-retired. Adjunct Instructor of Business at Colby-Sawyer College and Franklin Pierce College." He stated that he was "well equipped to teach" business law and business ethics, that he had "a great interest and knowledge of business law," and that he believed he would do "an excellent job" teaching a business ethics class because this subject was "of particular concern" to him. CCV hired him as academic coordinator, teacher, and independent studies instructor. After he began work, his probation officer alerted CCV to Sarvis's criminal history, and CCV terminated his employment. Sarvis filed a suit in a Vermont state court against CCV, alleging, among other things, breach of contract. CCV filed a motion for summary judgment, in part on the ground of fraud, seeking rescission. The court granted CCV's motion, and Sarvis appealed to the Vermont Supreme Court.

ISSUE Can a partial disclosure during the preemployment process, with an intent to deceive, support the termination of an employment contract?

DECISION Yes. The Vermont Supreme Court affirmed the lower court's judgment and rescinded the contract between Sarvis and CCV.

REASON The state supreme court explained that "[t]he misrepresentation in this case occurred through plaintiff's partial disclosure of his past work history and references and his effort to limit defendant's inquiry into his past." The court emphasized that Sarvis "was not silent; he carefully drafted his résumés and supplemental materials to lead defendant to believe he had made a full disclosure about his past and his qualifications. He listed classes in business ethics and law in which he claimed he had the highest level of capability and knowledge but failed to mention his felony bank fraud conviction. Plaintiff assured defendant that making additional inquiries into his background would have revealed 'more of the same' type of information * * * . This was not true. Contact with plaintiff's probation officer or supervisor at the * * * prison would have notified defendant of plaintiff's fraud convictions, period of incarceration, and work history at the prison."

(Continued)

CASE 8.3—Continued

WHY IS THIS CASE IMPORTANT? *This case illustrates the long-applied legal principle that when a contract is formed as a result of fraudulent misrepresentation, the defrauded party can avoid the contract. From the facts in this case, CCV clearly would not have hired Sarvis had he fully disclosed information about his past and his qualifications.*

Reliance on the Misrepresentation The third element of fraud is *justifiable reliance* on the misrepresentation of fact. The deceived party must have a justifiable reason for relying on the misrepresentation, and the misrepresentation must be an important factor (but not necessarily the sole factor) in inducing the party to enter into the contract.

Reliance is not justified if the innocent party knows the true facts or relies on obviously extravagant statements. ■ EXAMPLE 8.16 If a used-car dealer tells you, "This old Cadillac will get over sixty miles to the gallon," you normally would not be justified in relying on this statement. Suppose, however, that Merkel, a bank director, induces O'Connell, a co-director, to sign a statement that the bank's assets will satisfy its liabilities by telling O'Connell, "We have plenty of assets to satisfy our creditors." This statement is false. If O'Connell knows the true facts or, as a bank director, should know the true facts, he is not justified in relying on Merkel's statement. If O'Connell does not know the true facts, however, *and has no way of finding them out,* he may be justified in relying on the statement. ■

REMEMBER An opinion is neither a contract offer, nor a contract term, nor fraud.

ETHICAL ISSUE 8.2

How much information must employers disclose to prospective employees? One of the problems employers face is that it is not always clear what information they should disclose to prospective employees. To lure qualified workers, employers are often tempted to "promise the moon" to prospective employees and paint their companies' prospects as bright. Employers must be careful, though, to avoid any conduct that could be interpreted by a court as intentionally deceptive. In particular, they must avoid making any statements about their companies' future prospects or financial health that they know to be false. If they do make a false statement on which a prospective employee relies to her or his detriment, they may be sued for fraudulent misrepresentation.

In one case, for example, an employee accepted a job with a brokerage firm, relying on assurances that the firm was not about to be sold. In fact, as the employee was able to prove in his later lawsuit against the firm for fraud, negotiations to sell the firm were under way at the time he was hired. The trial court awarded the employee over $6 million in damages, a decision that was affirmed on appeal.[20] Generally, employers must be truthful in their hiring to avoid possible lawsuits for fraudulent misrepresentation. ■

Injury to the Innocent Party Most courts do not require a showing of injury when the action is to *rescind* (cancel) the contract—these courts hold that because rescission returns the parties to the positions they held before the contract was made, a showing of injury to the innocent party is unnecessary.[21]

20. *McConkey v. Aon Corp.,* 804 A.2d 572 (N.J.Super.A.D. 2002).

21. For a leading case on this issue, see *Kaufman v. Jaffe,* 244 App.Div. 344, 279 N.Y.S. 392 (1935).

To recover damages caused by fraud, however, proof of an injury is universally required. The measure of damages is ordinarily equal to the property's value had it been delivered as represented, less the actual price paid for the property. In actions based on fraud, courts often award *punitive,* or *exemplary, damages,* which are granted to a plaintiff over and above the compensation for the actual loss. As pointed out in Chapter 4, punitive damages are based on the public-policy consideration of punishing the defendant or setting an example to deter similar wrongdoing by others.

UNDUE INFLUENCE

.on the Web To read more about contesting contracts on the grounds of fraud and duress, go to **http://www.lawyers.com/lawyers/A~1001073~LDC/CONTESTING+CONTRACT.html**.

Undue influence arises from relationships in which one party can greatly influence another party, thus overcoming that party's free will. Minors and elderly people, for example, are often under the influence of guardians. If a guardian induces a young or elderly ward (a person placed by a court under the care of a guardian) to enter into a contract that benefits the guardian, the guardian may have exerted undue influence.

Undue influence can arise from a number of confidential or fiduciary relationships, including attorney-client, physician-patient, guardian-ward, parent-child, husband-wife, and trustee-beneficiary relationships. The essential feature of undue influence is that the party being taken advantage of does not, in reality, exercise free will in entering into a contract. A contract entered into under excessive or undue influence lacks genuine assent and is therefore voidable.[22]

DURESS

Assent to the terms of a contract is not genuine if one of the parties is forced into the agreement. Forcing a party to enter into a contract because of the fear created by threats is referred to as *duress.*[23] Inducing consent to a contract through blackmail or extortion also constitutes duress. Duress is both a defense to the enforcement of a contract and a ground for rescission, or cancellation, of a contract. Therefore, a party who signs a contract under duress can choose to carry out the contract or to avoid the entire transaction. (The wronged party usually has this choice in cases in which assent is not real or genuine.)

Economic need is generally not sufficient to constitute duress, even when one party exacts a very high price for an item the other party needs. If the party exacting the price also creates the need, however, economic duress may be found. ■ **EXAMPLE 8.17** The Internal Revenue Service (IRS) assessed a large tax and penalty against Weller. Weller retained Eyman to resist the assessment. Two days before the deadline for filing a reply with the IRS, Eyman declined to represent Weller unless he agreed to pay a very high fee for Eyman's services. The agreement was held to be unenforceable.[24] Although Eyman had threatened only to withdraw his services, something that he was legally entitled to do, he was responsible for delaying his withdrawal until the last two days. Because Weller was forced into either signing the contract or losing his right to challenge the IRS assessment, the agreement was secured under duress. ■

22. *Restatement (Second) of Contracts,* Section 177.
23. *Restatement (Second) of Contracts,* Sections 174 and 175.
24. *Thompson Crane & Trucking Co. v. Eyman,* 123 Cal.App.2d 904, 267 P.2d 1043 (1954).

The Statute of Frauds—Requirement of a Writing

STATUTE OF FRAUDS
A state statute under which certain types of contracts must be in writing to be enforceable.

Today, every state has a statute that stipulates what types of contracts must be in writing. In this text, we refer to such statutes as the **Statute of Frauds.** The primary purpose of the statute is to ensure that, for certain types of contracts, there is reliable evidence of the contracts and their terms. These types of contracts are those deemed historically to be important or complex. Although the statutes vary slightly from state to state, the following types of contracts are normally required to be in writing or evidenced by a written memorandum:

1. Contracts involving interests in land.
2. Contracts that cannot by their terms be performed within one year from the date of formation.
3. Collateral contracts, such as promises to answer for the debt or duty of another.
4. Promises made in consideration of marriage.
5. Contracts for the sale of goods priced at $500 or more ($5,000 or more under the 2003 amendments to the Uniform Commercial Code, or UCC—see Chapter 11).

KEEP IN MIND Although only certain types of contracts must be in writing to be enforceable, it is good practice to put other contracts in writing as well to prevent disputes over contract terms.

Agreements or promises that fit into one or more of these categories are said to "fall under" or "fall within" the Statute of Frauds. (Certain exceptions are made to the applicability of the Statute of Frauds in some circumstances, however, as you will read later in this section.)

The actual name of the Statute of Frauds is misleading because it does not apply to fraud. Rather, the statute denies enforceability to certain contracts that do not comply with its requirements. The name derives from an English act passed in 1677, which is presented as this chapter's *Landmark in the Law* feature.

Contracts Involving Interests in Land

Land is a form of *real property,* or real estate, which includes not only land but all physical objects that are permanently attached to the soil, such as buildings, plants, trees, and the soil itself. Under the Statute of Frauds, a contract involving an interest in land must be evidenced by a writing to be enforceable.[25] If Carol, for example, contracts orally to sell Seaside Shelter to Axel but later decides not to sell, Axel cannot enforce the contract. Similarly, if Axel refuses to close the deal, Carol cannot force Axel to pay for the land by bringing a lawsuit. The Statute of Frauds is a *defense* to the enforcement of this type of oral contract.

A contract for the sale of land ordinarily involves the entire interest in the real property, including buildings, growing crops, vegetation, minerals, timber, and anything else affixed to the land. Therefore, a *fixture* (personal property so affixed or so used as to become a part of the realty—see Chapter 24) is treated as real property.

The Statute of Frauds requires written contracts not just for the sale of land but also for the transfer of other interests in land, such as mortgages and leases. We describe these other interests in Chapter 24.

.on the Web Professor Eric Talley of the University of Southern California provides an interesting discussion of the history and current applicability of the Statute of Frauds, both internationally and in the United States, at **http://www-bcf.usc.edu/~etalley/frauds.html**.

The One-Year Rule

Contracts that cannot, *by their own terms,* be performed within one year from the day after the contract is formed must be in writing to be enforceable. Because disputes

25. In some states, the contract will be enforced, however, if each party admits to the existence of the oral contract in court or admits to its existence during discovery before trial (see Chapter 3).

LANDMARK IN THE LAW

The Statute of Frauds

On April 12, 1677, the English Parliament passed "An Act for the Prevention of Frauds and Perjuries." Four days later, the act was signed by King Charles II and became the law of the land. The act contained twenty-five sections and stipulated that if certain types of contracts were to be enforceable by the courts, they would henceforth have to be in writing or evidenced by a written memorandum.[a]

ENFORCEMENT OF ORAL PROMISES The English act was enacted specifically to prevent the many frauds that were being perpetrated through the perjured testimony of witnesses in cases involving breached oral agreements for which no written evidence existed. During the early history of the common law in England, oral contracts were generally not enforced by the courts, but in the fourteenth century, they began to be enforced in certain *assumpsit* actions.[b] These actions, to which the origins of modern contract law are traced, allowed a party to sue and obtain relief when a promise or contract had been breached. During the next two centuries, the king's courts commonly enforced oral promises in actions in *assumpsit*.

PROBLEMS WITH ORAL CONTRACTS Because the courts enforced oral contracts on the strength of oral testimony by witnesses, it was not too difficult to evade justice by alleging that a contract had been breached and then procuring "convincing" witnesses to support the claim. The possibility of fraud in such actions was enhanced by the fact that seventeenth-century English courts did not allow oral testimony to be given by the parties to a lawsuit—or by any parties with an interest in the litigation, such as husbands or wives. Defense against actions for breach of contract was thus limited to written evidence and the testimony of third parties. The Statute of Frauds was enacted to minimize the possibility of fraud in oral contracts relating to certain types of transactions.

APPLICATION TO TODAY'S WORLD

Essentially, the Statute of Frauds offers a defense against contracts that fall under the statute. Indeed, the statute has been criticized by some because, although it was created to protect the innocent, it can also be used as a technical defense by a party who has breached a genuine, mutually agreed-on oral contract—if the contract falls within the Statute of Frauds. For this reason, some legal scholars believe the act has caused more fraud than it has prevented. Nonetheless, U.S. courts continue to apply the Statute of Frauds to disputes involving oral contracts. The definitions of such terms as writing *and* signature, *however, are changing as we move further into an electronic age—as you will read in Chapter 10, which covers e-contracts.*

RELEVANT WEB SITES

To locate information on the Web concerning the Statute of Frauds, go to this text's Web site at **http://blt.westbuslaw.com**, *select "Chapter 8," and click on "URLs for Landmarks."*

a. These contracts are discussed in the text of this chapter.
b. *Assumpsit* is Latin for "he undertook" or "she promised." The emergence of remedies given on the basis of breached promises and duties dates to these actions. One of the earliest occurred in 1370, when the court allowed an individual to sue a person who, in trying to cure the plaintiff's horse, had acted so negligently that the horse died. Another such action was permitted in 1375, when a plaintiff obtained relief for having been maimed by a surgeon hired to cure him.

over such contracts are unlikely to occur until some time after the contracts are made, resolution of these disputes is difficult unless the contract terms have been put in writing. The one-year period begins to run *the day after the contract is made.*

■ EXAMPLE 8.18 Suppose that Superior University forms a contract with Kimi San, stating that San will teach three courses in history during the coming academic year (September 15 through June 15). If the contract is formed in March, it must be in writing to be enforceable—because it cannot be performed within one year. If the contract is not formed until July, however, it will not have to be in writing to be enforceable—because it can be performed within one year. ■ Exhibit 8–2 graphically illustrates the one-year rule.

Normally, the test for determining whether an oral contract is enforceable under the one-year rule of the Statute of Frauds is not whether the agreement is *likely* to be performed within one year from the day after the date of contract formation but whether performance within a year is *possible.* When performance of a contract is objectively impossible during the one-year period, the oral contract will be unenforceable.

COLLATERAL PROMISES

COLLATERAL PROMISE
A secondary promise that is ancillary (subsidiary) to a principal transaction or primary contractual relationship, such as a promise made by one person to pay the debts of another if the latter fails to perform. A collateral promise normally must be in writing to be enforceable.

A **collateral promise,** or secondary promise, is one that is ancillary (subsidiary) to a principal transaction or primary contractual relationship. In other words, a collateral promise is one made by a third party to assume the debts or obligations of a primary party to a contract if that party does not perform. Any collateral promise of this nature falls under the Statute of Frauds and therefore must be in writing to be enforceable. To understand this concept, it is important to distinguish between primary and secondary promises and obligations.

Primary versus Secondary Obligations As a general rule, a contract in which a party assumes a primary obligation does not need to be in writing to be enforceable. ■ EXAMPLE 8.19 Suppose that Kenneth orally contracts with Joanne's Floral

EXHIBIT 8–2 THE ONE-YEAR RULE

Under the Statute of Frauds, contracts that by their terms are impossible to perform within one year from the day after the date of contract formation must be in writing to be enforceable. Put another way, if it is at all possible to perform an oral contract within one year from the day after the contract is made, the contract will fall outside the Statute of Frauds and be enforceable.

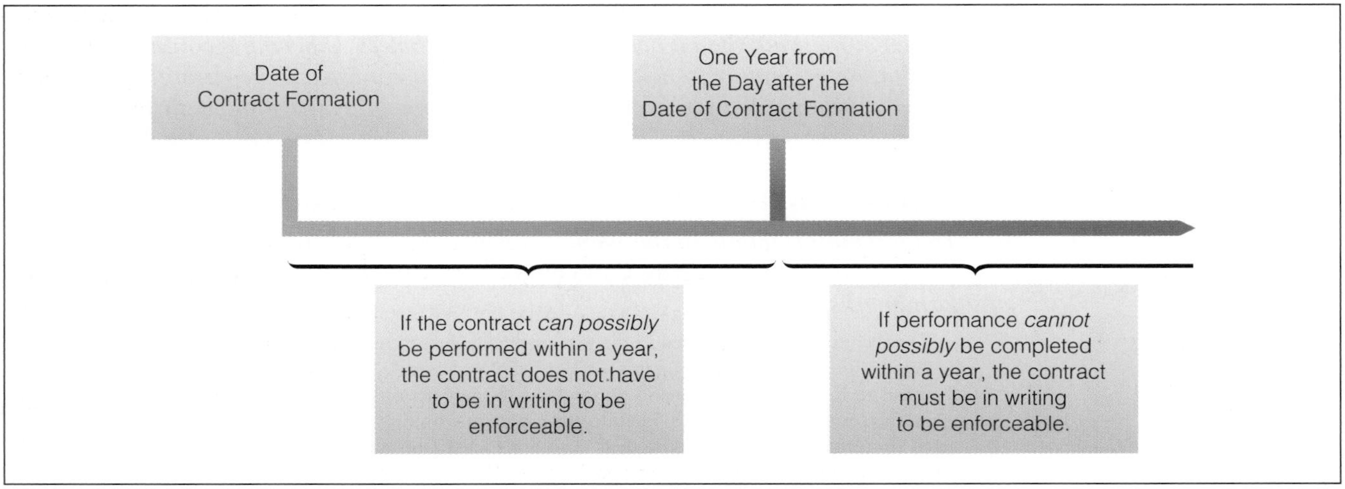

Boutique to send his mother a dozen roses for Mother's Day. Kenneth promises to pay the boutique when he receives the bill for the flowers. Kenneth is a direct party to this contract and has incurred a *primary* obligation under the contract. Because he is a party to the contract and has a primary obligation to Joanne's Floral Boutique, this contract does not fall under the Statute of Frauds and does not have to be in writing to be enforceable. If Kenneth fails to pay the florist and the florist sues him for payment, Kenneth cannot raise the Statute of Frauds as a defense. He cannot claim that the contract is unenforceable because it was not in writing. ■

In contrast, a contract in which a party assumes a secondary obligation does have to be in writing to be enforceable. ■ EXAMPLE 8.20 Suppose that Kenneth's mother borrows $1,000 from the Medford Trust Company on a promissory note payable six months later. Kenneth promises the bank officer handling the loan that he will pay the $1,000 *if his mother does not pay the loan on time*. Kenneth, in this situation, becomes what is known as a *guarantor* on the loan; that is, he is guaranteeing to the bank (the creditor) that he will pay the loan if his mother fails to do so. This kind of collateral promise, in which the guarantor states that he or she will become responsible only if the primary party does not perform, must be in writing to be enforceable. ■ We return to the concept of guaranty and the distinction between primary and secondary obligations in Chapter 16, in the context of creditors' rights.

An Exception—The "Main Purpose" Rule An oral promise to answer for the debt of another is covered by the Statute of Frauds *unless* the guarantor's purpose in accepting secondary liability is to secure a personal benefit. Under the "main purpose" rule, this type of contract need not be in writing.[26] The assumption is that a court can infer from the circumstances of a case whether a "leading objective" of the promisor was to secure a personal benefit.

■ EXAMPLE 8.21 Carrie Oswald contracts with Machine Manufacturing Company to have some machines custom-made for her factory. To ensure that Machine Manufacturing will have the supplies it needs to make the machines, Oswald promises Allrite Materials Supply Company, Machine Manufacturing's supplier, that if Allrite continues to deliver materials to Machine Manufacturing, she will guarantee payment. This promise need not be in writing, even though the effect may be to pay the debt of another, because Oswald's main purpose is to secure a benefit for herself. ■

Another typical application of the so-called main purpose doctrine occurs when one creditor guarantees the debtor's debt to another creditor to forestall litigation. This allows the debtor to remain in business long enough to generate profits sufficient to pay *both* creditors. In this situation, the guaranty does not need to be in writing to be enforceable.

PROMISES MADE IN CONSIDERATION OF MARRIAGE

PRENUPTIAL AGREEMENT
An agreement made before marriage that defines each partner's ownership rights in the other partner's property. Prenuptial agreements must be in writing to be enforceable.

A unilateral promise to pay a sum of money or to give property in consideration of marriage must be in writing. If Mr. Baumann promises to pay Joe Villard $10,000 if Villard marries Baumann's daughter, the promise must be in writing to be enforceable. The same rule applies to **prenuptial agreements**—agreements made before marriage (also called *antenuptial agreements*) that define each partner's ownership rights in the other partner's property. For example, a prospective wife or husband

26. *Restatement (Second) of Contracts,* Section 116.

may wish to limit the amount the prospective spouse can obtain if the marriage ends in divorce. Prenuptial agreements made in consideration of marriage must be in writing to be enforceable.

CONTRACTS FOR THE SALE OF GOODS

The Uniform Commercial Code (UCC) contains Statute of Frauds provisions that require written evidence of a contract. Section 2–201 contains the major provision, which generally requires a writing or memorandum for the sale of goods priced at $500 or more ($5,000 or more under the 2003 amendments to the UCC—see Chapter 11). A writing that will satisfy the UCC requirement need only state the quantity term; other terms agreed on need not be stated "accurately" in the writing, as long as they adequately reflect both parties' intentions. The contract will not be enforceable, however, for any quantity greater than that set forth in the writing. In addition, the writing must be signed by the person against whom enforcement is sought. Beyond these two requirements, the writing need not designate the buyer or the seller, the terms of payment, or the price.

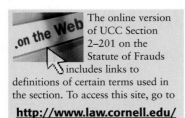

.on the Web The online version of UCC Section 2–201 on the Statute of Frauds includes links to definitions of certain terms used in the section. To access this site, go to **http://www.law.cornell.edu/ucc/2/2-201.html**.

EXCEPTIONS TO THE STATUTE OF FRAUDS

Exceptions to the applicability of the Statute of Frauds are made in certain situations. We describe those situations here.

Partial Performance In cases involving oral contracts for the transfer of interests in land, if the purchaser has paid part of the price, taken possession, and made valuable improvements to the property, and if the parties cannot be returned to their status quo prior to the contract, a court may grant *specific performance* (performance of the contract according to its precise terms). Whether a court will enforce an oral contract for an interest in land when partial performance has taken place is usually determined by the degree of injury that would be suffered if the court chose *not* to enforce the oral contract. In some states, mere reliance on certain types of oral contracts is enough to remove them from the Statute of Frauds.

Under the UCC, an oral contract for goods priced at $500 or more ($5,000 or more under the 2003 amendments) is enforceable to the extent that a seller accepts payment or a buyer accepts delivery of the goods.[27] For example, if Ajax Corporation orders by telephone twenty crates of bleach from Cloney, Inc., and repudiates the contract after ten crates have been delivered and accepted, Cloney can enforce the contract to the extent of the ten crates accepted by Ajax.

Admissions In some states, if a party against whom enforcement of an oral contract is sought admits in pleadings, testimony, or otherwise in court proceedings that a contract for sale was made, the contract will be enforceable.[28] A contract subject to the UCC will be enforceable, but only to the extent of the quantity admitted.[29] Thus, if the president of Ajax Corporation admits under oath that an oral agreement was made with Cloney, Inc., for the twenty crates of bleach, the agreement will be enforceable to that extent.

27. UCC 2–201(3)(c). See Chapter 11.
28. *Restatement (Second) of Contracts,* Section 133.
29. UCC 2–201(3)(b). See Chapter 11.

Promissory Estoppel In some states, an oral contract that would otherwise be unenforceable under the Statute of Frauds may be enforced under the doctrine of promissory estoppel, or detrimental reliance. Recall from Chapter 7 that if a promisor makes a promise on which the promisee justifiably relies to her or his detriment, a court may *estop* (prevent) the promisor from denying that a contract exists. Section 139 of the *Restatement (Second) of Contracts* provides that in these circumstances, an oral promise can be enforceable, notwithstanding the Statute of Frauds, if the reliance was foreseeable to the person making the promise and if injustice can be avoided only by enforcing the promise.

.on the Web For information on the *Restatements of the Law,* including the *Restatement (Second) of Contracts,* go to the American Law Institute's Web site at **http://www.ali.org**.

Special Exceptions under the UCC Special exceptions to the applicability of the Statute of Frauds exist for sales contracts. Oral contracts for customized goods may be enforced in certain circumstances. Another exception has to do with oral contracts between merchants that have been confirmed in writing. We will examine these exceptions in Chapter 11. Exhibit 8–3 graphically summarizes the types of contracts that fall under the Statute of Frauds and the various exceptions that apply.

The Statute of Frauds—Sufficiency of the Writing

A written contract will satisfy the writing requirement of the Statute of Frauds. A *written memorandum* (written evidence of the oral contract) signed by the party against whom enforcement is sought will also satisfy the writing requirement.[30]

30. As mentioned earlier, under the UCC Statute of Frauds, a writing is required only for contracts for the sale of goods priced at $500 or more ($5,000 or more under the 2003 amendments to UCC Article 2). See Chapter 11.

EXHIBIT 8–3 CONTRACTS SUBJECT TO THE STATUTE OF FRAUDS

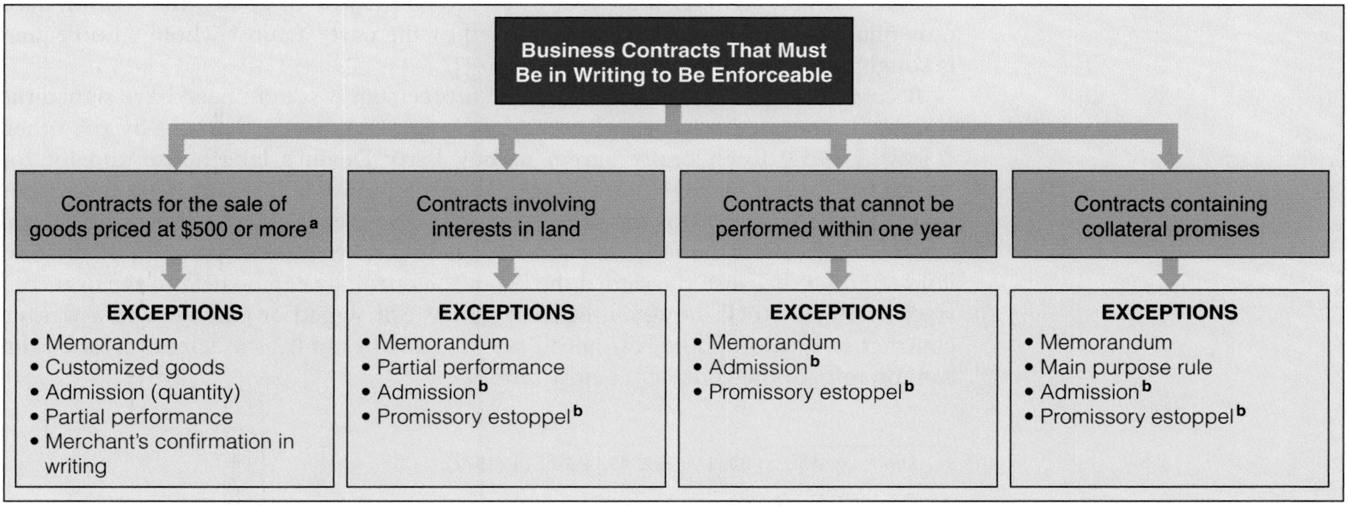

a. Under a 2003 amendment to the UCC, a contract for a sale of goods must involve goods priced at $5,000 or more to be subject to the writing requirement of the Statute of Frauds (see Chapter 11). This amendment also exempts contracts for the sale of goods from the one-year rule.
b. Some states follow Section 133 (on admissions) and Section 139 (on promissory estoppel) of the *Restatement (Second) of Contracts.*

The signature need not be placed at the end of the document but can be anywhere in the writing; it can even be initials rather than the full name. (See the *Application* feature for suggestions on how to prevent problems with oral contracts.)

A significant issue in today's business world has to do with how "signatures" can be created and verified on electronic contracts and other documents. We will examine electronic signatures in Chapter 10.

WHAT CONSTITUTES A WRITING?

A writing can consist of any confirmation, invoice, sales slip, check, or fax—or such items in combination. The written contract need not consist of a single document to constitute an enforceable contract. One document may incorporate another document by expressly referring to it. Several documents may form a single contract if they are physically attached, such as by staple, paper clip, or glue. Several documents may form a single contract even if they are only placed in the same envelope.

■ EXAMPLE 8.22 Sam orally agrees to sell some land next to a shopping mall to Terry. Sam gives Terry an unsigned memo that contains a legal description of the property, and Terry gives Sam an unsigned first draft of their contract. Sam sends Terry a signed letter that refers to the memo and to the first and final drafts of the contract. Terry sends Sam an unsigned copy of the final draft of the contract with a signed check stapled to it. Together, the documents can constitute a writing sufficient to satisfy the Statute of Frauds and bind both parties to the terms of the contract as evidenced by the writings. ■

WHAT MUST BE CONTAINED IN THE WRITING?

A memorandum evidencing the oral contract need only contain the essential terms of the contract. Under most provisions of the Statute of Frauds, the writing must name the parties, subject matter, consideration, and quantity. With respect to contracts for the sale of land, some states require that the memorandum also set forth the essential terms of the contract, such as location and price, with sufficient clarity to allow the terms to be determined from the memo itself, without reference to any outside sources.[31] Under the UCC, in regard to the sale of goods, the writing need only name the quantity term and be signed by the party against whom enforcement is sought.

Because only the party against whom enforcement is sought need have signed the writing, a contract may be enforceable by one of its parties but not by the other. ■ EXAMPLE 8.23 Rock orally agrees to buy Betty Devlin's lake house and lot for $150,000. Devlin writes Rock a letter confirming the sale by identifying the parties and the essential terms of the sales contract—price, method of payment, and legal address—and signs the letter. Devlin has made a written memorandum of the oral land contract. Because she signed the letter, she normally can be held to the oral contract by Rock. Rock, however, because he has not signed or entered into a written contract or memorandum, can plead the Statute of Frauds as a defense, and Devlin cannot enforce the contract against him. ■

31. *Rhodes v. Wilkins,* 83 N.M. 782, 498 P.2d 311 (1972).

APPLICATION How Can You Prevent Problems with Oral Contracts?*

As a general rule, most business contracts should be in writing even when they fall outside the Statute of Frauds. Businesspersons frequently make oral contracts over the telephone, however, particularly when the parties have done business with each other in the past.

CONFIRM THE AGREEMENT IN WRITING

Any time an oral contract is made, it is advisable for one of the parties to send either a written memorandum or a confirmation of the oral agreement by fax or e-mail to the other party. This accomplishes two purposes: (1) it demonstrates the party's clear intention to form a contract, and (2) it provides the terms of the contract as that party understood them. If the party receiving the memorandum or confirmation then disagrees with the terms as described, the issue can be addressed before performance begins.

SPECIAL RULES FOR CONTRACTS BETWEEN MERCHANTS

What about the sale of goods between merchants? Under the UCC, written confirmation received by one merchant removes the Statute of Frauds requirement of a writing unless the merchant receiving the confirmation objects in writing within ten days of its receipt. This law (discussed in Chapter 11) clearly points out the need for the merchant receiving the confirmation to review it carefully to ascertain that the confirmation conforms to the oral contract. If the writing does not so conform, the merchant can object in writing (the Statute of Frauds still applies), and the parties can resolve misunderstandings without legal liability. If the merchant fails to object, the written confirmation can be used as evidence to prove the terms of the oral contract. Note, however, that this ten-day rule does not apply to contracts for interests in realty or for services, to which the UCC does not apply.

* This *Application* is not meant to substitute for the services of an attorney who is licensed to practice law in your state.

CHECKLIST FOR THE BUSINESSPERSON

1. When feasible, use written contracts.
2. If you enter into an oral contract over the telephone, fax or e-mail a written confirmation outlining your understanding of the oral contract.
3. If you receive the other party's written confirmation, read it carefully to make sure that it states the terms already agreed to in the oral contract, as you understand them.
4. If you have any objections, notify the other party of these objections, in writing, within ten days.

KEY TERMS

adhesion contract 247
blue laws 243
blue sky laws 250
collateral promise 260
contractual capacity 237
covenant not to compete 245
disaffirmance 237
employment contract 245
exculpatory clause 247
necessaries 239
prenuptial agreement 261
ratification 240
reformation 247
scienter 255
Statute of Frauds 258
unconscionable contract or unconscionable clause 247
usury 242

CHAPTER SUMMARY Contracts: Capacity, Legality, Assent, and Form

	CONTRACTUAL CAPACITY
Minors (See pages 237–241.)	A minor is a person who has not yet reached the age of majority. In most states, the age of majority is eighteen for contract purposes. Contracts with minors are voidable at the option of the minor. 1. *Disaffirmance*—The legal avoidance of a contractual obligation. a. Disaffirmance can take place (in most states) at any time during minority and within a reasonable time after the minor has reached the age of majority. b. If a minor disaffirms part of a contract, the entire contract must be disaffirmed. c. When disaffirming executed contracts, the minor has a duty to return received goods if they are still in the minor's control or (in some states) to pay their reasonable value. d. A minor who has committed an act of fraud (such as misrepresentation of age) will be denied the right to disaffirm by some courts. e. A minor may disaffirm a contract for necessaries but remains liable for the reasonable value of the goods. 2. *Ratification*—The acceptance, or affirmation, of a legal obligation; may be express or implied. a. Express ratification—Exists when the minor, through a writing or an oral agreement, explicitly assumes the obligations imposed by the contract. b. Implied ratification—Exists when the conduct of the minor is inconsistent with disaffirmance or when the minor fails to disaffirm an executed contract within a reasonable time after reaching the age of majority.
Intoxicated Persons (See page 241.)	1. A contract entered into by an intoxicated person is voidable at the option of the intoxicated person if the person was sufficiently intoxicated to lack mental capacity, even if the intoxication was voluntary. 2. A contract with an intoxicated person is enforceable if, despite being intoxicated, the person understood the legal consequences of entering into the contract.
Mentally Incompetent Persons (See pages 241–242.)	1. A contract made by a person adjudged by a court to be mentally incompetent is void. 2. A contract made by a mentally incompetent person not adjudged by a court to be mentally incompetent is voidable at the option of the mentally incompetent person.
	LEGALITY
Contracts Contrary to Statute (See pages 242–244.)	1. *Usury*—Usury occurs when a lender makes a loan at an interest rate above the lawful maximum. The maximum rate of interest varies from state to state. 2. *Gambling*—Gambling contracts that contravene (go against) state statutes are deemed illegal and thus void. 3. *Sabbath (Sunday) laws*—These laws prohibit the formation or the performance of certain contracts on Sunday. Such laws vary widely from state to state, and many states do not enforce them. 4. *Licensing statutes*—Contracts entered into by persons who do not have a license, when one is required by statute, will not be enforceable *unless* the underlying purpose of the statute is to raise government revenues (and not to protect the public from unauthorized practitioners).
Contracts Contrary to Public Policy (See pages 245–249.)	1. *Contracts in restraint of trade*—Contracts to reduce or restrain free competition are illegal. Most such contracts are now prohibited by statutes. An exception is a *covenant not to compete.* It is usually enforced by the courts if the terms are ancillary to a contract (such as a

CHAPTER SUMMARY Contracts: Capacity, Legality, Assent, and Form—Continued

Contracts Contrary to Public Policy—Continued	contract for the sale of a business or an employment contract) and are reasonable as to time and area of restraint. Courts tend to scrutinize covenants not to compete closely. If a covenant is overbroad, a court may either reform the covenant to make the restraints more reasonable and then enforce the reformed contract or declare the covenant void and thus unenforceable. 2. *Unconscionable contracts and clauses*—When a contract or contract clause is so unfair that it is oppressive to one party, it can be deemed unconscionable; as such, it is illegal and cannot be enforced. 3. *Exculpatory clauses*—An exculpatory clause is a clause that releases a party from liability in the event of monetary or physical injury, no matter who is at fault. In certain situations, exculpatory clauses may be contrary to public policy and thus unenforceable.
Effect of Illegality (See pages 249–250.)	In general, an illegal contract is void, and the courts will not aid either party when both parties are considered to be equally at fault *(in pari delicto)*. If the contract is executory, neither party can enforce it. If the contract is executed, there can be neither contractual nor quasi-contractual recovery. Several exceptions exist to the general rule that neither party to an illegal bargain will be able to recover. In the following situations, the court may grant recovery: 1. *Justifiable ignorance of the facts*—When one party to the contract is relatively innocent. 2. *Members of protected classes*—When one party to the contract is a member of a group of persons protected by statute, such as employees. 3. *Withdrawal from an illegal agreement*—When either party seeks to recover consideration given for an illegal contract before the illegal act is performed. 4. *Severable, or divisible, contracts*—When the court can divide the contract into illegal and legal portions and the illegal portion is not essential to the bargain. 5. *Fraud, duress, or undue influence*—When one party was induced to enter into an illegal bargain through fraud, duress, or undue influence.
	GENUINENESS OF ASSENT
Mistakes (See pages 251–253.)	1. *Unilateral*—Generally, the mistaken party is bound by the contract *unless* (a) the other party knows or should have known of the mistake or (b) the mistake is an inadvertent mathematical error—such as an error in addition or subtraction—committed without gross negligence. 2. *Bilateral* (mutual)—When both parties are mistaken about the same material fact, such as identity, either party can avoid the contract. If the mistake concerns value or quality, either party can enforce the contract.
Fraudulent Misrepresentation (See pages 253–257.)	When fraud occurs, usually the innocent party can enforce or avoid the contract. The elements necessary to establish fraud are as follows: 1. A misrepresentation of a material fact must occur. 2. There must be an intent to deceive. 3. The innocent party must justifiably rely on the misrepresentation.
Undue Influence (See page 257.)	Undue influence arises from special relationships, such as fiduciary or confidential relationships, in which one party's free will has been overcome by the undue influence exerted by the other party. Usually, the contract is voidable.
Duress (See page 257.)	Duress is the tactic of forcing a party to enter a contract under the fear of a threat—for example, the threat of violence or serious economic loss. The party forced to enter the contract can rescind the contract.

(Continued)

CHAPTER SUMMARY Contracts: Capacity, Legality, Assent, and Form—Continued

	FORM
The Statute of Frauds—Requirement of a Writing (See pages 258–263.)	*Applicability*—The following types of contracts fall under the Statute of Frauds and must be in writing to be enforceable: 1. *Contracts involving interests in land*—The statute applies to any contract for an interest in realty, such as a sale, a lease, or a mortgage. 2. *Contracts whose terms cannot be performed within one year*—The statute applies only to contracts objectively impossible to perform fully within one year from the day after the contract's formation. 3. *Collateral promises*—The statute applies only to express contracts made between the guarantor and the creditor whose terms make the guarantor secondarily liable. Exception: the "main purpose" rule. 4. *Promises made in consideration of marriage*—The statute applies to promises to pay money or give property in consideration of a promise to marry and to prenuptial agreements made in consideration of marriage. 5. *Contracts for the sale of goods priced at $500 or more*—Under the UCC Statute of Frauds provision in UCC 2–201. (Under a 2003 amendment to that UCC section, the threshold amount is raised from $500 to $5,000.) *Exceptions*—Partial performance, admissions, and promissory estoppel.
The Statute of Frauds—Sufficiency of the Writing (See pages 263–264.)	To constitute an enforceable contract under the Statute of Frauds, a writing must be signed by the party against whom enforcement is sought, must name the parties, must identify the subject matter, and must state with reasonable certainty the essential terms of the contract. In a sale of land, the price and a description of the property may need to be stated with sufficient clarity to allow them to be determined without reference to outside sources. Under the UCC, a contract for a sale of goods is not enforceable beyond the quantity of goods shown in the contract.

FOR REVIEW

Answers for the even-numbered questions in this For Review *section can be found in Appendix I at the end of this text.*

1. What are some exceptions to the rule that a minor can disaffirm (avoid) any contract?
2. Does an intoxicated person have the capacity to enter into an enforceable contract?
3. In what types of situations might genuineness of assent to a contract's terms be lacking?
4. What elements must exist for fraudulent misrepresentation to occur?
5. What contracts must be in writing to be enforceable?

QUESTIONS AND CASE PROBLEMS

8–1. Contracts by Minors. Kalen is a seventeen-year-old minor who has just graduated from high school. He is attending a university two hundred miles from home and has contracted to rent an apartment near the university for one year at $500 per month. He is working at a convenience store to earn enough income to be self-supporting. After living in the apartment and paying monthly rent for four months, he becomes involved in a dispute with his landlord. Kalen, still a minor, moves out and returns the key to the landlord. The landlord wants to hold Kalen liable for the balance of the payments due under the lease. Discuss fully Kalen's liability in this situation.

8–2. Licensing Statutes. State X requires that persons who prepare and serve liquor in the form of drinks at commercial establishments be licensed by the state to do so. The only requirement for obtaining a yearly license is that the person be at least twenty-one years old. Mickey, aged thirty-five, is hired as a bartender for the Southtown Restaurant. Gerald, a staunch alumnus of a nearby university, brings twenty of his friends to the restaurant to celebrate a football victory one afternoon. Gerald orders four rounds of drinks, and the bill is nearly $200. On learning that Mickey has failed to renew his bartender's license, Gerald refuses to pay, claiming that the contract is unenforceable. Discuss whether Gerald is correct.

8–3. Fraudulent Misrepresentation. Larry offered to sell Stanley his car and told Stanley that the car had been driven only 25,000 miles and had never been in an accident. Stanley hired Cohen, a mechanic, to appraise the condition of the car, and Cohen said that the car probably had at least 50,000 miles on it and probably had been in an accident. In spite of this information, Stanley still thought the car would be a good buy for the price, so he purchased it. Later, when the car developed numerous mechanical problems, Stanley sought to rescind the contract on the basis of Larry's fraudulent misrepresentation of the auto's condition. Will Stanley be able to rescind his contract? Discuss.

8–4. Exculpatory Clause. Norbert Eelbode applied for a job with Travelers Inn in the state of Washington. As part of the application process, Eelbode was sent to Laura Grothe, a physical therapist at Chec Medical Centers, Inc., for a preemployment physical exam. Before the exam, Eelbode signed a document that stated in part, "I hereby release Chec and the Washington Readicare Medical Group and its physicians from all liability arising from any injury to me resulting from my participation in the exam." During the exam, Grothe asked Eelbode to lift an item while bending from the waist using only his back with his knees locked. Eelbode experienced immediate sharp and burning pain in his lower back and down the back of his right leg. Eelbode filed a suit in a Washington state court against Grothe and Chec, claiming that he was injured because of an improperly administered back torso strength test. Citing the document that Eelbode signed, Grothe and Chec filed a motion for summary judgment. Should the court grant the motion? Why or why not? [*Eelbode v. Chec Medical Centers, Inc.,* 984 P.2d 436 (Wash.App. 1999)]

8–5. Oral Contracts. Robert Pinto, doing business as Pinto Associates, hired Richard MacDonald as an independent contractor in March 1992. The parties orally agreed on the terms of employment, including payment to MacDonald of a share of the company's income, but they did not put anything in writing. In March 1995, MacDonald quit. Pinto then told MacDonald that he was entitled to $9,602.17—25 percent of the difference between the accounts receivable and the accounts payable as of MacDonald's last day. MacDonald disagreed and demanded more than $83,500—25 percent of the revenue from all invoices, less the cost of materials and outside processing, for each of the years that he worked for Pinto. Pinto refused. MacDonald filed a suit in a Connecticut state court against Pinto, alleging breach of contract. In Pinto's response and at the trial, he testified that the parties had an oral contract under which MacDonald was entitled to 25 percent of the difference between accounts receivable and payable as of the date of MacDonald's termination. Did the parties have an enforceable contract? How should the court rule, and why? [*MacDonald v. Pinto,* 62 Conn.App. 317, 771 A.2d 156 (2001)]

CASE PROBLEM WITH SAMPLE ANSWER

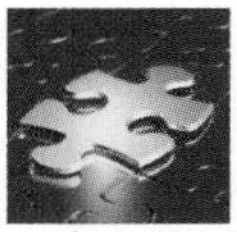

8–6. In 1993, Mutual Service Casualty Insurance Co. and its affiliates (collectively, MSI) hired Thomas Brass as an insurance agent. Three years later, Brass entered into a career agent's contract with MSI. This contract contained provisions regarding Brass's activities after termination. These provisions stated that, for a period of not less than one year, Brass could not solicit any MSI customers to "lapse, cancel, or replace" any insurance contract in force with MSI in an effort to take that business to a competitor. If he did, MSI could at any time refuse to pay the commissions that it otherwise owed him. The contract also restricted Brass from working for American National Insurance Co. for three years after termination. In 1998, Brass quit MSI and immediately went to work for American National, soliciting MSI customers. MSI filed a suit in a Wisconsin state court against Brass, claiming that he had violated the noncompete terms of his MSI contract. Should the court enforce the covenant not to compete? Why or why not? [*Mutual Service Casualty Insurance Co. v. Brass,* 625 N.W.2d 648 (Wis.App. 2001)]

After you have answered this problem, compare your answer with the sample answer given on the Web site that accompanies this text. Go to http://blt.westbuslaw.com, select "Chapter 8," and click on "Case Problem with Sample Answer."

8–7. Covenant Not to Compete. Gary Forsee was an executive officer with responsibility for the U.S. operations of BellSouth Corp., a company providing global telecommunications services. Under a covenant not to compete, Forsee agreed that for a period of eighteen months after termination from employment, he would not "provide services * * * in competition with [BellSouth] * * * to any person or entity which provides products or services identical or similar to products and services provided by [BellSouth] * * * within the territory." *Territory* was defined to include the geographic area in which Forsee provided services to BellSouth. The *services* included "management, strategic planning, business planning, administration, or other participation in or providing advice with respect to the communications services business." Forsee announced his intent to resign and accept a position as chief executive officer of Sprint Corp., a competitor of BellSouth. BellSouth filed a suit in a Georgia state court against Forsee, claiming in part that his acceptance of employment with Sprint would violate the covenant not to compete. Is the covenant legal? Should it be enforced? Why or why not? [*BellSouth Corp. v. Forsee,* 595 S.E.2d 99 (Ga.App. 2004)]

A QUESTION OF ETHICS

8–8. Nancy Levy worked for Health Care Financial Enterprises, Inc., and signed a noncompete agreement in June 1992. When Levy left Health Care and opened her own similar business in 1993, Health Care brought a court action in a Florida state court to enforce the covenant not to compete. The trial court concluded that the noncompete agreement prevented Levy from working in too broad a geographic area and thus refused to enforce the agreement. A Florida appellate court, however, reversed the trial court's ruling and remanded the case with instructions that the trial court modify the geographic area to make it reasonable and then enforce the covenant. [*Health Care Financial Enterprises, Inc. v. Levy,* 715 So.2d 341 (Fla.App.4th 1998)]

1. At one time in Florida, under the common law, noncompete covenants were illegal, although modern Florida statutory law now allows such covenants to be enforced. Generally, what interests are served by refusing to enforce covenants not to compete? What interests are served by allowing them to be enforced?
2. What argument could be made in support of reforming (and then enforcing) illegal covenants not to compete? What argument could be made against this practice?

FOR CRITICAL ANALYSIS

8–9. Do you think that the advent of legalized forms of gambling, such as state-operated lotteries, is consistent with a continued public policy against the enforcement of gambling contracts? Why or why not?

VIDEO QUESTION

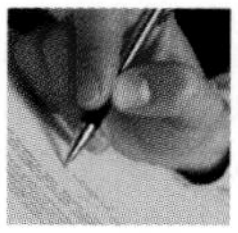

8–10. Go to this text's Web site at **http://blt.westbuslaw.com** and select "Chapter 8." Click on "Video Questions" and view the video titled *Money Pit.* Then answer the following questions.

1. Assume that a valid contract exists between Walter (Tom Hanks) and the plumber. Recall from the video that the plumber had at least two drinks before agreeing to take on the plumbing job. If the plumber was intoxicated, is the contract voidable? Why or why not?
2. Suppose that state law requires plumbers in Walter's state to have a plumber's license and that this plumber does not have a license. Would the contract be enforceable? Why or why not?
3. In the video, the plumber suggests that Walter has been "turned down by every other plumber in the valley." Although the plumber does not even look at the house's plumbing, he agrees to do the repairs if Walter gives him a check for $5,000 right now "before he changes his mind." If Walter later seeks to void the contract because it is contrary to public policy, what should he argue?

INTERNET EXERCISES

Go to the *Business Law Today: The Essentials* home page at **http://blt.westbuslaw.com,** select "Chapter 8," and click on "Internet Exercises." There you will find the following Internet research exercises that you can perform to learn more about topics covered in this chapter.

Activity 8–1: LEGAL PERSPECTIVE—Covenants Not to Compete

Activity 8–2: MANAGEMENT PERSPECTIVE—Minors and the Law

Activity 8–3: HISTORICAL PERSPECTIVE—The English Act for the Prevention of Frauds and Perjuries

BEFORE THE TEST

Go to the *Business Law Today: The Essentials* home page at **http://blt.westbuslaw.com,** select "Chapter 8," and click on "Interactive Quizzes." You will find at least twenty interactive questions relating to this chapter.

CHAPTER 9

Contracts: Third Party Rights, Discharge, Breach, and Remedies

"The laws of a state change with the changing times."
Aeschylus, 525–456 B.C.E.
(Greek dramatist)

CHAPTER OUTLINE

- ASSIGNMENTS AND DELEGATIONS
- THIRD PARTY BENEFICIARIES
- CONTRACT DISCHARGE
- DAMAGES
- EQUITABLE REMEDIES
- RECOVERY BASED ON QUASI CONTRACT
- ELECTION OF REMEDIES

LEARNING OBJECTIVES

After reading this chapter, you should be able to answer the following questions:

1. What is the difference between an assignment and a delegation?
2. What factors indicate that a third party beneficiary is an intended beneficiary?
3. What is the difference between compensatory damages and consequential damages? What are nominal damages, and when do courts award nominal damages?
4. Under what circumstances will equitable remedies be available?
5. What is the rationale underlying the doctrine of election of remedies?

PRIVITY OF CONTRACT
The relationship that exists between the promisor and the promisee of a contract.

Because a contract is a private agreement between the parties who have entered into it, it is fitting that these parties alone should have rights and liabilities under the contract. This concept is referred to as **privity of contract,** and it establishes the basic principle that third parties have no rights in contracts to which they are not parties.

You may be convinced by now that for every rule of contract law, there is an exception. As times change, so must the laws, as indicated in the opening quotation. When justice cannot be served by adherence to a rule of law, exceptions to the rule must be made. In this chapter, we look at some exceptions to the rule of privity of contract. We also examine how contractual obligations can be *discharged.* Normally, contract discharge is accomplished when both parties have performed the acts promised in the contract. In the latter part of this chapter, we look at the degree of performance required to discharge a contractual obligation, as well as at some other ways in which contract discharge can occur.

BREACH OF CONTRACT
The failure, without legal excuse, of a promisor to perform the obligations of a contract.

When it is no longer advantageous for a party to fulfill her or his contractual obligations, that party may breach the contract. A **breach of contract** occurs when a party fails to perform part or all of the required duties under a contract.[1] Once a party fails to perform or performs inadequately, the other party—the nonbreaching party—can choose one or more of several remedies.

Assignments and Delegations

When third parties acquire rights or assume duties arising from contracts, the rights are transferred to them by *assignment,* and the duties are transferred by *delegation.*

ASSIGNMENTS

ASSIGNMENT
The act of transferring to another all or part of one's rights arising under a contract.

ASSIGNOR
A party who transfers (assigns) his or her rights under a contract to another party (called the assignee).

ASSIGNEE
A party to whom the rights under a contract are transferred, or assigned.

OBLIGEE
One to whom an obligation is owed.

OBLIGOR
One who owes an obligation to another.

In a bilateral contract, normally one party has a right to require the other to perform some task, and the other has a duty to perform it. The transfer of contract *rights* to a third person is known as an **assignment.** The party assigning the rights to a third party is known as the **assignor,** and the party receiving the rights is the **assignee.** Other traditional terminology used to describe the parties in assignment relationships are the **obligee** (the person to whom a duty, or obligation, is owed) and the **obligor** (the person who is obligated to perform the duty).

When rights under a contract are assigned unconditionally, the rights of the *assignor* (the party making the assignment) are extinguished.[2] The third party (the *assignee,* or the party receiving the assignment) has a right to demand performance from the other original party to the contract (the *obligor,* the person who is obligated to perform). ■ EXAMPLE 9.1 Brent owes Alex $1,000, and Alex, the assignor, assigns to Carmen the right to receive the $1,000. Here, a valid assignment of a debt exists. Carmen, the assignee, can enforce the contract against Brent, the obligor, if Brent fails to perform. ■ Exhibit 9–1 illustrates assignment relationships.

The assignee takes only those rights that the assignor originally had. Furthermore, the assignee's rights are subject to the defenses that the obligor has against the assignor. ■ EXAMPLE 9.2 Brent owes Alex $1,000 under a contract in which Brent agreed to buy Alex's computer work station. Alex assigns his right to receive the $1,000 to Carmen. Brent, in deciding to purchase the work station, relied on Alex's fraudulent misrepresentation that the computer's hard drive had a storage capacity of 120 gigabytes. When Brent discovers that the computer can store only 20 gigabytes, he tells Alex that he is going to return the work station and cancel the contract. Even though Alex has assigned his "right" to receive the $1,000 to Carmen, Brent need not pay Carmen the $1,000—Brent can raise the defense of Alex's fraudulent misrepresentation to avoid payment. ■

The Importance of Assignments in the Business Context Assignments are important because they are utilized in much business financing. Lending institutions, such as banks, frequently assign the rights to receive payments under their loan contracts to other firms, which pay for those rights. If you obtain a loan from your local bank to purchase a car, you may later receive in the mail a notice stating that your bank has transferred (assigned) its rights to receive payments on the loan to another firm

1. *Restatement (Second) of Contracts,* Section 235(2).
2. *Restatement (Second) of Contracts,* Section 317.

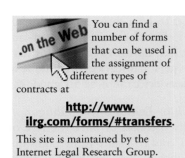

.on the Web You can find a number of forms that can be used in the assignment of different types of contracts at **http://www.ilrg.com/forms/#transfers**. This site is maintained by the Internet Legal Research Group.

and that, when the time comes to repay your loan, you must make the payments to that other firm.

Lenders that make *mortgage loans* (loans to allow prospective home buyers to purchase land or a home) often assign their rights to collect the mortgage payments to a third party, such as GMAC Mortgage Corporation. Following an assignment, the home buyer is notified that future payments must be made not to the lender that loaned the funds but to the third party. Millions of dollars change hands daily in the business world in the form of assignments of rights in contracts. If it were not possible to transfer (assign) contractual rights, many businesses could not continue to operate.

Rights That Cannot Be Assigned As a general rule, all rights can be assigned. Exceptions are made, however, in the following special circumstances.

When a Statute Expressly Prohibits Assignment. If a statute expressly prohibits assignment, the particular right in question cannot be assigned. ■ **EXAMPLE 9.3** Marn is a new employee of CompuFuture, Inc. CompuFuture is an employer under workers' compensation statutes (see Chapter 18) in this state, and thus Marn is a covered employee. Marn has a relatively high-risk job. In need of a loan, she borrows some funds from Stark, assigning to Stark all workers' compensation benefits due her should she be injured on the job. A state statute prohibits the assignment of *future* workers' compensation benefits, and thus such rights cannot be assigned. ■

When a Contract Is Personal in Nature. When a contract is for personal services, the rights under the contract normally cannot be assigned unless all that remains is a

EXHIBIT 9–1 ASSIGNMENT RELATIONSHIPS

In the assignment relationship illustrated here, Alex assigns his *rights* under a contract that he made with Brent to a third party, Carmen. Alex thus becomes the *assignor* and Carmen the *assignee* of the contractual rights. Brent, the *obligor* (the party owing performance under the contract), now owes performance to Carmen instead of Alex. Alex's original contract rights are extinguished after assignment.

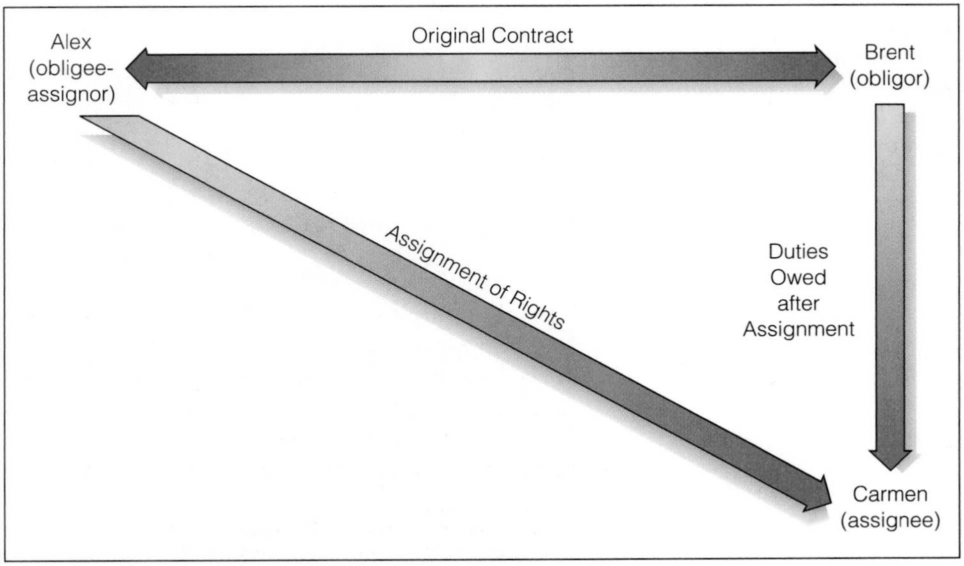

money payment.[3] ■ EXAMPLE 9.4 Brent signs a contract to be a tutor for Alex's children. Alex then attempts to assign to Carmen his right to Brent's services. Carmen cannot enforce the contract against Brent. Brent may not like Carmen's children or may for some other reason not want to tutor them. Because personal services are unique to the person rendering them, rights to receive personal services cannot be assigned. ■

When an Assignment Will Increase or Alter the Risk or Duties of the Obligor. A right cannot be assigned if assignment will materially increase or alter the risk or duties of the obligor.[4] ■ EXAMPLE 9.5 Alex has a hotel, and to insure it, he takes out a policy with Northwest Insurance Company. The policy insures against fire, theft, floods, and vandalism. Alex attempts to assign the insurance policy to Carmen, who also owns a hotel. The assignment is ineffective because it may substantially alter the insurance company's duty of performance and the risk that the company undertakes. An insurance company evaluates the particular risk of a certain party and tailors its policy to fit that risk. If the policy is assigned to a third party, the insurance risk is materially altered. ■

When the Contract Prohibits Assignment. If a contract stipulates that the right cannot be assigned, then *ordinarily* it cannot be assigned. ■ EXAMPLE 9.6 Brent agrees to build a house for Alex. The contract between Brent and Alex states, "This contract cannot be assigned by Alex without Brent's consent. Any assignment without such consent renders this contract void, and all rights hereunder will thereupon terminate." Alex then assigns his rights to Carmen, without first obtaining Brent's consent. Carmen cannot enforce the contract against Brent. ■ This rule has several exceptions:

1. A contract cannot prevent an assignment of the right to receive money. This exception exists to encourage the free flow of funds and credit in modern business settings.

3. *Restatement (Second) of Contracts,* Sections 317 and 318.
4. See Section 2–210(2) of the Uniform Commercial Code (UCC).

A music teacher instructs her pupil. Assuming that the boy's parent contracted with the instructor for her services, can the parent assign the right to receive music lessons to another party? Why or why not? (AP Photo/ Fort Collins Coloradoan, Sherri Barber)

ALIENATION
The process of transferring land out of one's possession (thus "alienating" the land from oneself).

2. The assignment of ownership rights in real estate often cannot be prohibited because such a prohibition is contrary to public policy in most states. Prohibitions of this kind are called restraints against **alienation** (the voluntary transfer of land ownership).
3. The assignment of negotiable instruments (see Chapter 14) cannot be prohibited.
4. In a contract for the sale of goods, the right to receive damages for breach of contract or for payment of an account owed may be assigned even though the sales contract prohibits such assignment.[5]

In the following case, both parties had violated an antiassignment clause. The question before the court was how one party's violation affected that party's recovery for the other party's violation.

5. UCC 2–210(2).

CASE 9.1 Forest Commodity Corp. v. Lone Star Industries, Inc.

Court of Appeals of Georgia, 2002.
564 S.E.2d 755.

FACTS Forest Commodity Corporation (FCC) owns an ocean terminal facility where ships unload and store bulk cargo. FCC, which has no employees or equipment, leases the facility to Woodchips Export Corporation (WEC). Construction Aggregates, Limited, owned by Lone Star Industries, Inc. (jointly referred to as CAL), mines and ships aggregate stone. FCC and CAL entered into a three-year contract under which FCC agreed to provide terminal space for unloading aggregate stone, which FCC would then store, reload onto trucks, and weigh for further shipment. CAL promised to unload a minimum of 150,000 tons per year or pay a higher price. The contract prohibited its assignment without the other party's consent. FCC transferred its obligations under this contract to WEC without CAL's consent. About a year later, after CAL had shipped nearly 200,000 tons, Martin Marietta Materials, Inc., acquired CAL and offered to accept its obligations under the contract with FCC, but FCC refused. At the same time, FCC and Martin Marietta entered into a separate, but substantially similar, contract. The total aggregate shipped under both contracts over a three-year period was 484,868 tons. FCC filed a suit in a Georgia state court against CAL for breach of contract, alleging that CAL had failed to ship the agreed minimum. The court issued a summary judgment in CAL's favor. FCC appealed to a state intermediate appellate court.

ISSUE Was FCC's breach of the antiassignment clause a material breach of the agreement with CAL, which would prevent FCC from holding CAL to the contract?

DECISION Yes. The state intermediate appellate court affirmed the lower court's judgment. FCC breached its contract with CAL by violating the antiassignment clause, and this breach precluded FCC from enforcing the contract.

REASON The court explained that a party's refusal to abide by a contract provision prohibiting assignment amounted to an anticipatory repudiation of the contract.[a] The court stated that "[s]uch a repudiation of the agreement estops [prevents] FCC from seeking to enforce other provisions of the agreement." FCC claimed that any breach of the antiassignment clause was not material, because "the fundamental purpose of the agreement—to provide CAL with a place to discharge and store its aggregate cargo [stone]—was satisfied." The court responded, "FCC's own refusal of CAL's request for consent to an assignment of the agreement to Martin Marietta * * * shows that FCC thought the identity of the parties to the agreement was important or it would have accepted CAL's proposed assignment. In addition, the agreement creates a bailment relationship between FCC and CAL, wherein CAL entrusts aggregate to FCC's safekeeping.[b] Certainly, the uniqueness and identity of the parties is a material term in such a relationship."

FOR CRITICAL ANALYSIS—Social Consideration *Would the result in this case have been different if FCC had not entered into a substantially similar contract with Martin Marietta? Why or why not?*

a. As will be discussed later in this chapter, an anticipatory repudiation of a contract occurs when one party, before the time for performance, indicates by words or actions that the party will not perform the contract.
b. In a bailment relationship, the property of one party is entrusted to another, who is obligated to return the property or otherwise dispose of it as instructed. See Chapter 23.

DELEGATIONS

DELEGATION OF DUTIES
The act of transferring to another all or part of one's duties arising under a contract.

DELEGATOR
A party who transfers (delegates) her or his obligations under a contract to another party (called the delegatee).

DELEGATEE
A party to whom contractual obligations are transferred, or delegated.

Just as a party can transfer rights to a third party through an assignment, a party can also transfer duties. Duties are not assigned, however; they are *delegated.* Normally, a **delegation of duties** does not relieve the party making the delegation (the **delegator**) of the obligation to perform in the event that the party to whom the duty has been delegated (the **delegatee**) fails to perform. No special form is required to create a valid delegation of duties. As long as the delegator expresses an intention to make the delegation, it is effective; the delegator need not even use the word *delegate.* Exhibit 9–2 graphically illustrates delegation relationships.

Duties That Cannot Be Delegated As a general rule, any duty can be delegated. This rule has some exceptions, however. Delegation is prohibited in the following circumstances:

1. When performance depends on the personal skill or talents of the obligor.
2. When special trust has been placed in the obligor.
3. When performance by a third party will vary materially from that expected by the obligee (the one to whom performance is owed) under the contract.
4. When the contract expressly prohibits delegation.

The following examples will help to clarify the kinds of duties that can and cannot be delegated:

1. Brent contracts with Alex to tutor Alex in various aspects of financial underwriting and investment banking. Brent, an experienced businessperson known for his expertise in finance, delegates his duties to a third party, Carmen. This

EXHIBIT 9–2 DELEGATION RELATIONSHIPS

In the delegation relationship illustrated here, Brent delegates his *duties* under a contract that he made with Alex to a third party, Carmen. Brent thus becomes the *delegator* and Carmen the *delegatee* of the contractual duties. Carmen now owes performance of the contractual duties to Alex. Note that a delegation of duties normally does not relieve the delegator (Brent) of liability if the delegatee (Carmen) fails to perform the contractual duties.

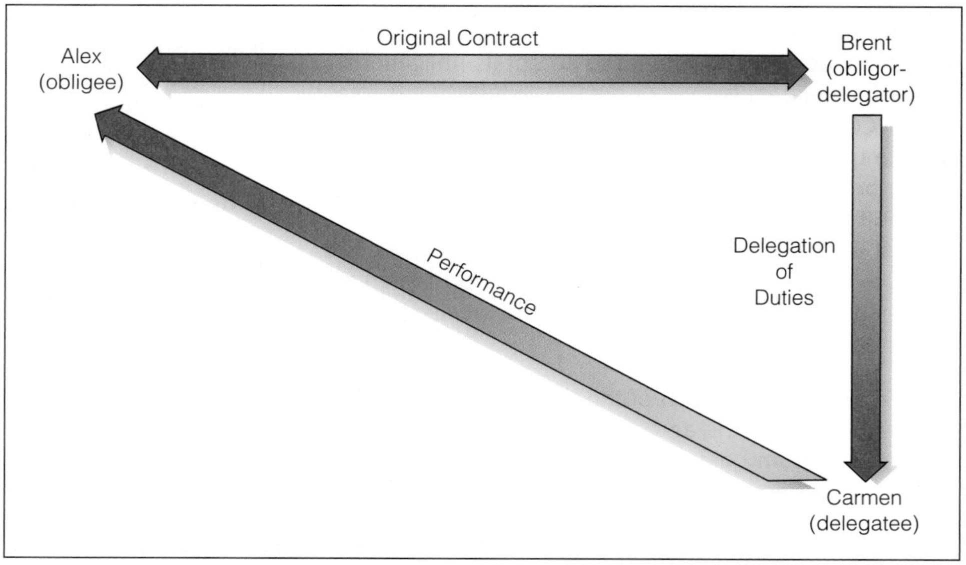

delegation is ineffective because Brent contracted to render a service that is founded on Brent's *expertise,* and the delegation changes Alex's expectancy under the contract.

2 Brent contracts with Alex to *personally* mow Alex's lawn during June, July, and August. Then Brent decides that he would rather spend the summer at the beach. Brent delegates his lawn-mowing duties to Carmen, who is in the business of mowing lawns and doing other landscaping work to earn income to pay for college. No matter how competent Carmen is, the delegation is not effective without Alex's consent. The contract was for *personal* performance.

3 Brent contracts with Alex to pick up and deliver heavy construction machinery to Alex's property. Brent delegates this duty to Carmen, who is in the business of delivering heavy machinery. This delegation is effective. The performance required is of a routine and nonpersonal nature, and the delegation does not change Alex's expectations under the contract.

Effect of a Delegation If a delegation of duties is enforceable, the *obligee* (the one to whom performance is owed) must accept performance from the delegatee (the one to whom the duties are delegated). ■ EXAMPLE 9.7 In the third example in the above list, Brent delegates his duty (to pick up and deliver heavy construction machinery to Alex's property) to Carmen. In that situation, Alex (the obligee) must accept performance from Carmen (the delegatee) because the delegation was effective. The obligee can legally refuse performance from the delegatee only if the duty is one that cannot be delegated. ■

A valid delegation of duties does not relieve the delegator of obligations under the contract.[6] In the above example, if Carmen (the delegatee) fails to perform, Brent (the delegator) is still liable to Alex (the obligee). The obligee can also hold the delegatee liable if the delegatee made a promise of performance that will directly benefit the obligee. In this situation, there is an "assumption of duty" on the part of the delegatee, and breach of this duty makes the delegatee liable to the obligee. For example, if Carmen (the delegatee) promises Brent (the delegator), in a contract, to pick up and deliver the construction equipment to Alex's property but fails to do so, Alex (the obligee) can sue Brent, Carmen, or both. Although there are many exceptions, the general rule today is that the obligee can sue both the delegatee and the delegator.

COMPARE In an assignment, the assignor's original contract rights are extinguished after assignment. In a delegation, the delegator remains liable for performance under the contract if the delegatee fails to perform.

"Assignment of All Rights" Sometimes, a contract provides for an "assignment of all rights." The traditional view was that under this type of assignment, the assignee did not assume any duties. This view was based on the theory that the assignee's agreement to accept the benefits of the contract was not sufficient to imply a promise to assume the duties of the contract.

Modern authorities, however, take the view that the probable intent in using such general words is to create both an assignment of rights and an assumption of duties.[7] Therefore, when general words are used (for example, "I assign the contract" or "all my rights under the contract"), the contract is construed as implying both an assignment of rights and an assumption of duties.

6. For a classic case on this issue, see *Crane Ice Cream Co. v. Terminal Freezing & Heating Co.,* 147 Md. 588, 128 A. 280 (1925).
7. See UCC 2–210(1), (4); *Restatement (Second) of Contracts,* Section 328.

Third Party Beneficiaries

As mentioned earlier in this chapter, to have contractual rights, a person normally must be a party to the contract. In other words, privity of contract must exist. An exception to the doctrine of privity exists when the original parties to the contract intend, at the time of contracting, that the contract performance directly benefit a third person. In this situation, the third person becomes a **third party beneficiary** of the contract. As an **intended beneficiary** of the contract, the third party has legal rights and can sue the promisor directly for breach of the contract.

THIRD PARTY BENEFICIARY
One for whose benefit a promise is made in a contract but who is not a party to the contract.

INTENDED BENEFICIARY
A third party for whose benefit a contract is formed. An intended beneficiary can sue the promisor if such a contract is breached.

TYPES OF INTENDED BENEFICIARIES

The law distinguishes between *intended* beneficiaries and *incidental* beneficiaries. Only intended beneficiaries acquire legal rights in a contract. One type of intended beneficiary is a *creditor beneficiary.* A creditor beneficiary benefits from a contract in which one party (the promisor) promises another party (the promisee) to pay a debt that the promisee owes to a third party (the creditor beneficiary). As an intended beneficiary, the creditor beneficiary can sue the promisor directly to enforce the contract.

Another type of intended beneficiary is a *donee* beneficiary. When a contract is made for the express purpose of giving a *gift* to a third party, the third party (the donee beneficiary) can sue the promisor directly to enforce the promise.[8] The most common donee beneficiary contract is a life insurance contract. ■ EXAMPLE 9.8 Akins (the promisee) pays premiums to Standard Life, a life insurance company, and Standard Life (the promisor) promises to pay a certain amount on Akins's death to anyone Akins designates as a beneficiary. The designated beneficiary is a donee beneficiary under the life insurance policy and can enforce the promise made by the insurance company to pay him or her on Akins's death. ■

As the law concerning third party beneficiaries evolved, numerous cases arose in which the third party beneficiary did not fit readily into either category—creditor beneficiary or donee beneficiary. Thus, the modern view, and the one adopted by the *Restatement (Second) of Contracts,* does not draw such clear lines and distinguishes only between intended beneficiaries (who can sue to enforce contracts made for their benefit) and incidental beneficiaries (who cannot sue, as will be discussed shortly).

ETHICAL ISSUE 9.1

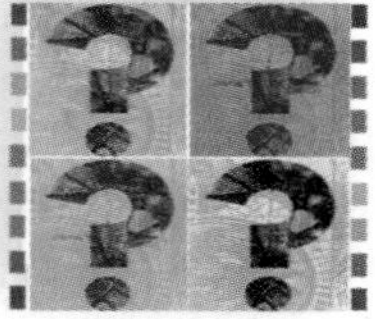

Should third party beneficiaries be able to recover from attorneys on the basis of negligence? Periodically, the courts are asked to decide whether a designated beneficiary under a legal document, such as a will, can sue the attorney who drafted the document to recover for benefits that were lost as a result of the attorney's negligence. This is a significant issue for the beneficiaries of a will because normally the question does not arise until the party who signed the will has died—and thus cannot rectify the problem. Traditionally, the rule was that third party beneficiaries could not sue the attorney in these situations because they were not in privity of contract with the attorney—that is, an attorney's duty of care extends only to her or his client, and thus third parties do not have standing to sue the attorney for negligence.

Clearly, restricting suits against attorneys in these situations can have harsh results for intended beneficiaries. Although some courts continue to adhere to the traditional rule, increasingly courts are allowing third party beneficiaries to sue attorneys in these circumstances.[9] ■

8. This principle was first enunciated in *Seaver v. Ransom,* 224 N.Y. 233, 120 N.E. 639 (1918).

9. See, for example, *Leak-Gilbert v. Fahle,* 55 P.3d 1054 (Okla. 2002).

When the Rights of an Intended Beneficiary Vest

An intended third party beneficiary cannot enforce a contract against the original parties until the rights of the third party have *vested,* meaning that the rights have taken effect and cannot be taken away. Until these rights have vested, the original parties to the contract—the promisor and the promisee—can modify or rescind the contract without the consent of the third party. When do the rights of third parties vest? Generally, the rights vest when one of the following occurs:

1. When the third party demonstrates manifest assent to the contract, such as sending a letter or note acknowledging awareness of and consent to a contract formed for her or his benefit.
2. When the third party materially alters his or her position in detrimental reliance on the contract, such as when a donee beneficiary contracts to have a home built in reliance on the receipt of funds promised to him or her in a donee beneficiary contract.
3. When the conditions for vesting are satisfied. For example, the rights of a beneficiary under a life insurance policy vest when the insured person dies.

If the contract expressly reserves to the contracting parties the right to cancel, rescind, or modify the contract, the rights of the third party beneficiary are subject to any changes that result. In such a situation, the vesting of the third party's rights does not terminate the power of the original contracting parties to alter their legal relationships.[10]

Incidental Beneficiaries

INCIDENTAL BENEFICIARY
A third party who incidentally benefits from a contract but whose benefit was not the reason the contract was formed. An incidental beneficiary has no rights in a contract and cannot sue to have the contract enforced.

The benefit that an **incidental beneficiary** receives from a contract between two parties is unintentional. Therefore, an incidental beneficiary cannot enforce a contract to which he or she is not a party.

■ EXAMPLE 9.9 In one case, spectators at a Mike Tyson boxing match in which Tyson was disqualified for biting his opponent's ear sued Tyson and the fight's promoters for a refund of their money on the basis of breach of contract. The spectators claimed that they had standing to sue the defendants as third party beneficiaries of the contract between Tyson and the fight's promoters. The court, however, held that the spectators did not have standing to sue because they were not in contractual privity with any of the defendants. Furthermore, any benefits they received from the contract were incidental to the contract. The court noted that the spectators got what they paid for: "the right to view whatever event transpired."[11] ■

Is a person who benefits from a contract between another party and a government entity an incidental beneficiary or an intended beneficiary? For a discussion of a case raising this question, see this chapter's *Adapting the Law to the Online Environment* feature on the following page.

Intended versus Incidental Beneficiaries

In determining whether a third party beneficiary is an intended or an incidental beneficiary, the courts generally use the *reasonable person* test—that is, a beneficiary

---

10. Defenses raised against third party beneficiaries are given in the *Restatement (Second) of Contracts,* Section 309.
11. *Castillo v. Tyson,* 268 A.D.2d 336, 701 N.Y.S.2d 423 (Sup.Ct.App.Div. 2000).

ADAPTING THE LAW TO THE ONLINE ENVIRONMENT

Government Contracts and Third Party Beneficiaries

Government entities often contract with private organizations to provide certain services to the public. Are those who benefit under such contracts intended beneficiaries? This question came before the court in a case involving a person who had registered a domain name with an organization that had contracted with the federal government to provide domain name registration services.

THE DOMAIN NAME CONFLICT

In 1994, in the early days of the Internet (as a public surfing/shopping vehicle), domain names were free for the asking. At that time, Network Solutions, Inc. (NSI), was the sole registrar of domain names. NSI had a contract with a federal government agency stating that NSI had the primary responsibility for "ensuring the quality, timeliness, and effective management" of domain name registration services.

Gary Kremen, seeing what he felt was a great opportunity, registered the name "sex.com" with NSI. Unfortunately for Kremen, Stephen Cohen also saw the potential of that domain name. Cohen, who had just gotten out of prison for impersonating a bankruptcy lawyer, knew that Kremen had already registered the name. That fact, however, in the words of the court, "was only a minor impediment for a man of Cohen's boundless resource and bounded integrity." Through forgery and deceit, Cohen succeeded in having NSI transfer the domain name to his company. When Kremen later contacted NSI, he was told that it was too late to undo the transfer. Kremen then turned to the courts for assistance.

THE LEGAL ISSUES

Kremen sued Cohen, seeking as damages the substantial profits that Cohen had made by using the name. The court held in Kremen's favor and awarded him millions of dollars in damages. Kremen could not collect the judgment, however, because Cohen had disappeared—after first transferring large sums to offshore accounts. Kremen then tried to hold NSI responsible for his losses by alleging, among other things, that he was an intended third party beneficiary of NSI's contract with the government. He claimed that because NSI had not "effectively managed" its duties, as it was obligated to do under the contract, his domain name had been wrongfully transferred.

Was Kremen an intended third party beneficiary of the contract? When the case ultimately reached the Court of Appeals for the Ninth Circuit, the court held that Kremen was not an intended third party beneficiary of the contract. The court noted that a third party can enforce a contract if the contract reflects an "express or implied intention of the parties to the contract to benefit the third party." The court emphasized, however, that when a contract is with a government entity, a more stringent test applies: for a third party to be an intended beneficiary, *the contract must express a clear intent to benefit the third party.* If it does not express this clear intent, then anyone who benefits under the contract is regarded as an incidental beneficiary and, as such, cannot sue to enforce the contract.[a]

FOR CRITICAL ANALYSIS

Kremen also alleged that NSI had breached an implied-in-fact contract with him, but the court dismissed this claim. Why would the court hold that no contract existed between Kremen and NSI? Was a required element for a valid contract lacking?

a. *Kremen v. Cohen,* 337 F.3d 1024 (9th Cir. 2003).

will be considered an intended beneficiary if a reasonable person in the position of the beneficiary would believe that the promisee *intended* to confer on the beneficiary the right to bring suit to enforce the contract. In determining whether a party is an intended or an incidental beneficiary, the courts also look at a number of other factors. The presence of one or more of the following factors strongly indicates that the third party is an intended (rather than an incidental) beneficiary to the contract:

1 Performance is rendered directly to the third party.
2 The third party has the right to control the details of performance.
3 The third party is expressly designated as a beneficiary in the contract.

Contract Discharge

DISCHARGE
The termination of an obligation. In contract law, discharge occurs when the parties have fully performed their contractual obligations or when events, conduct of the parties, or operation of law releases the parties from performance.

PERFORMANCE
In contract law, the fulfillment of one's duties arising under a contract with another; the normal way of discharging one's contractual obligations.

The most common way to **discharge,** or terminate, one's contractual duties is by the **performance** of those duties. The duty to perform under a contract may be *conditioned* on the occurrence or nonoccurrence of a certain event, or the duty may be *absolute.* As you can see in Exhibit 9–3, in addition to performance, a contract can be discharged in numerous other ways, including discharge by agreement of the parties and discharge by operation of law.

CONDITIONS OF PERFORMANCE

In most contracts, promises of performance are not expressly conditioned or qualified. Instead, they are *absolute promises.* They must be performed, or the party

EXHIBIT 9–3 CONTRACT DISCHARGE

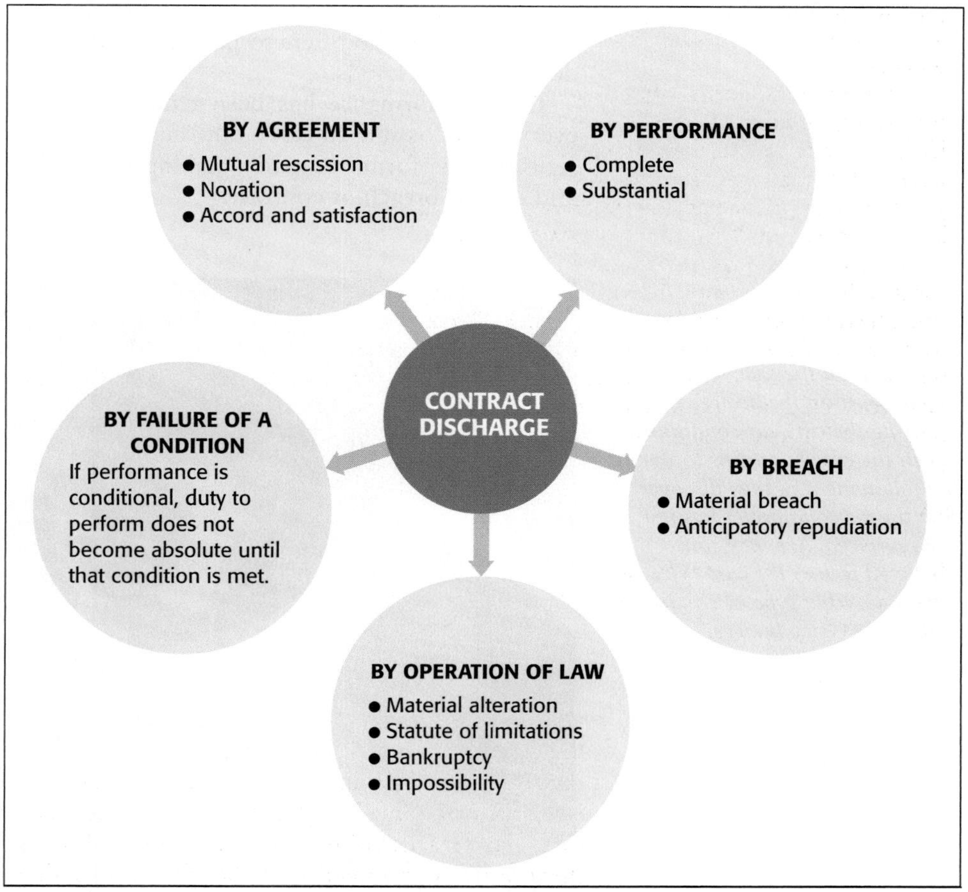

promising the act will be in breach of contract. ■ EXAMPLE 9.10 JoAnne contracts to sell Alfonso a painting for $10,000. The parties' promises are unconditional: JoAnne's transfer of the painting to Alfonso and Alfonso's payment of $10,000 to JoAnne. The payment does not have to be made if the painting is not transferred. ■

CONDITION
A qualification, provision, or clause in a contractual agreement, the occurrence or nonoccurrence of which creates, suspends, or terminates the obligations of the contracting parties.

In some situations, however, contractual promises are conditioned. A **condition** is a possible future event, the occurrence or nonoccurrence of which will trigger the performance of a legal obligation or terminate an existing obligation under a contract. If the condition is not satisfied, the obligations of the parties are discharged. ■ EXAMPLE 9.11 Suppose that Alfonso, in the above example, offers to purchase JoAnne's painting only if an independent appraisal indicates that it is worth at least $10,000. JoAnne accepts Alfonso's offer. Their obligations (promises) are conditioned on the outcome of the appraisal. Should this condition not be satisfied (for example, if the appraiser deems the value of the painting to be only $5,000), their obligations to each other are discharged and cannot be enforced. ■

DISCHARGE BY PERFORMANCE

TENDER
An unconditional offer to perform an obligation by a person who is ready, willing, and able to do so.

The contract comes to an end when both parties fulfill their respective duties by performing the acts they have promised. Performance can also be accomplished by tender. **Tender** is an unconditional offer to perform by a person who is ready, willing, and able to do so. Therefore, a seller who places goods at the disposal of a buyer has tendered delivery and can demand payment according to the terms of the agreement. A buyer who offers to pay for goods has tendered payment and can demand delivery of the goods.

Once performance has been tendered, the party making the tender has done everything possible to carry out the terms of the contract. If the other party then refuses to perform, the party making the tender can consider the duty discharged and sue for breach of contract.

A couple negotiates with a salesperson to purchase a car. Suppose that the parties reach an agreement on the sale, which is conditioned on the dealer's servicing the car's air conditioner. When the couple returns to the lot the following day, they discover that the air conditioner has not been serviced. Are they still obligated to buy the car? Why or why not? What type of condition is this? (© Getty Images)

Different brands of construction supplies displayed at a site. If a contract for the construction of a building or house specifies a particular brand, can a product of a different brand of comparable quality be substituted? Why or why not? (© Tony Freeman, PhotoEdit)

Complete versus Substantial Performance Normally, conditions expressly stated in the contract must fully occur in all aspects for *complete performance* (strict performance) of the contract to occur. Any deviation breaches the contract and discharges the other party's obligations to perform. Although in most contracts the parties fully discharge their obligations by complete performance, sometimes a party fails to fulfill all of the duties or completes the duties in a manner contrary to the terms of the contract. The issue then arises as to whether the performance was nonetheless sufficiently substantial to discharge the contractual obligations.

To qualify as *substantial performance,* the performance must not vary greatly from the performance promised in the contract, and it must create substantially the same benefits as those promised in the contract. If performance is substantial, the other party's duty to perform remains absolute (less damages, if any, for the minor deviations).

■ EXAMPLE 9.12 A couple contracts with a construction company to build a house. The contract specifies that Brand X plasterboard be used for the walls. The builder cannot obtain Brand X plasterboard, and the buyers are on holiday in the mountains of Peru and virtually unreachable. The builder decides to install Brand Y instead, which he knows is identical in quality and durability to Brand X plasterboard. All other aspects of construction conform to the contract. Does this deviation constitute a breach of contract? Can the buyers avoid their contractual obligation to pay the builder because Brand Y plasterboard was used instead of Brand X? Very likely, a court would hold that the builder had substantially performed his end of the bargain, and therefore the couple will be obligated to pay the builder.

What if the plasterboard substituted for Brand X was not of the same quality as Brand X, and the value of the house was reduced by $10,000? Again, a court would likely hold that the contract had been substantially performed and that the contractor should be paid the price agreed on in the contract, less that $10,000. ■

Performance to the Satisfaction of Another Contracts often state that completed work must personally satisfy one of the parties or a third person. The question is whether this satisfaction becomes a contract *condition*, requiring actual personal satisfaction or approval for discharge, or whether the test of satisfaction is performance that would satisfy a *reasonable person* (substantial performance).

When the subject matter of the contract is personal, a contract to be performed to the satisfaction of one of the parties is conditioned, and performance must actually satisfy that party. For example, contracts for portraits, works of art, and tailoring are considered personal. Therefore, only the personal satisfaction of the party fulfills the condition—unless a court finds the party is expressing dissatisfaction only to avoid payment or otherwise is not acting in good faith.

Contracts that involve mechanical fitness, utility, or marketability need be performed only to the satisfaction of a reasonable person unless they *expressly state otherwise.* When such contracts require performance to the satisfaction of a third party (for example, "to the satisfaction of Robert Ames, the supervising engineer"), the courts are divided. A majority of courts require the work to be satisfactory to a

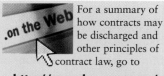

.on the Web For a summary of how contracts may be discharged and other principles of contract law, go to

http://www.lawyers.com/legal_topics/browse_by_topic/index.php?.

Click on "Business Needs." Then, under the heading "General Business," click on "Contracts" and select the appropriate links.

reasonable person, but some courts hold that the personal satisfaction of the third party designated in the contract (Robert Ames, in this example) must be met. Again, the personal judgment must be made honestly, or the condition will be excused.

Material Breach of Contract When a breach of contract is *material*[12]—that is, when performance is not deemed substantial—the nonbreaching party is excused from the performance of contractual duties and has a cause of action to sue for damages caused by the breach. If the breach is *minor* (not material), the nonbreaching party's duty to perform may sometimes be suspended until the breach is remedied, but the duty is not entirely excused. Once the minor breach is cured, the nonbreaching party must resume performance of the contractual obligations that had been undertaken.

A breach entitles the nonbreaching party to sue for damages, but only a material breach discharges the nonbreaching party from the contract. The policy underlying these rules is that contracts should go forward when only minor problems occur, but contracts should be terminated if major problems arise.[13]

Did a seller's failure to repair the plumbing in an apartment building within the eight-month period specified in a contract with the buyers constitute a material breach of the parties' contract? That was the issue in the following case.

12. *Restatement (Second) of Contracts,* Section 241.
13. See UCC 2–612, which deals with installment contracts for the sale of goods.

CASE 9.2 Kim v. Park

Court of Appeals of Oregon, 2004.
192 Or.App. 365,
86 P.3d 63.
http://www.publications.ojd.state.or.us/appeals.htm[a]

FACTS Su Yong Kim sold an apartment building in Portland, Oregon, to Chon Sik Park, Bok Soon Park, Johan Cen, William Itzineag, Johnny Perea, and Patricia Maldonado. At the time, the building's plumbing violated the Portland Housing Code. The contract provided the following: "Seller shall correct the plumbing code violation * * * within eight months * * * . Buyer shall cooperate with seller in * * * providing access to the premises to complete repairs." Kim did not make the repairs within eight months, but twelve months after the date of the contract, Kim cut holes in the walls of the apartments to expose the plumbing. Seven weeks later, early one morning, Kim sent plumbers to the building without notice to the owners, apparently in an attempt to make repairs. The owners ordered the plumbers to leave, refused to allow Kim to send others, and stopped making payments under the contract. Kim filed a suit in an Oregon state court against the buyers, seeking the amount due. The buyers asserted that Kim's failure to repair the plumbing was a material breach that excused the performance of their obligations and counterclaimed for damages for the breach. The court concluded that Kim's breach was not material and ordered relief in his favor. The buyers appealed to a state intermediate appellate court.

ISSUE Was the seller's failure to repair the plumbing according to the parties' contract a material breach excusing the buyers' performance?

DECISION Yes. The state intermediate appellate court reversed the decision of the lower court on this issue and remanded the case for a determination of the amount of damages.[b]

a. Click on "March" under "Cases decided in 2004." In the result, scroll to the name of the case under 3/3/04 and click on it to access the opinion. The state of Oregon's judicial branch maintains this Web site.

b. The lower court's decision on remand was not available at the time this book went to press, but it may be by the time you read this. If you have purchased access to Westlaw Campus, you may be able to locate the remanded decision using that database. Alternatively, you may be able to find the case online at some other site. (See this text's inside front cover for information on Westlaw Campus and URLs for online court decisions.)

CASE 9.2—Continued

REASON The appellate court reasoned that a breach is material if it "goes to the very substance of the contract and defeats the object of the parties entering into the contract." In this case, as a result of the code violations, "the City of Portland continued to assess fines against defendants and defendants lost some tenants." The court pointed out that the requirement that the seller repair the plumbing within eight months was intended to ensure that the building's plumbing would satisfy the city code within a reasonable time after the sale. Also, the buyers had purchased the building from the seller so that they could rent out the apartments in it. According to the court, "[a]lthough the repairs to the plumbing in the building would have caused some temporary inconvenience to the tenants, the failure of plaintiff to make the repairs in accordance with the contract ultimately prevented defendants from using the building as intended by the parties' agreement. In light of that evidence, we hold that as a matter of law the plaintiff's [seller's] failure to perform as promised was a material breach of the contract." The court added that because the seller's breach was material, the buyers were not obligated to continue to perform their obligation to make the payments under the contract.

WHY IS THIS CASE IMPORTANT? *This case emphasizes that when one party's failure to perform a contractual obligation causes another to suffer significant harm, the other party normally is entitled to a remedy. Recall from Chapter 7 that even when no contract exists, if a party justifiably relies to his or her detriment on the promise of another, the party may be able to obtain relief under the doctrine of quasi contract or promissory estoppel.*

ANTICIPATORY REPUDIATION An assertion or action by a party indicating that he or she will not perform an obligation that the party is contractually obligated to perform at a future time.

Anticipatory Repudiation of a Contract Before either party to a contract has a duty to perform, one of the parties may refuse to perform her or his contractual obligations. This is called **anticipatory repudiation.**[14] When anticipatory repudiation occurs, it is treated as a material breach of contract, and the nonbreaching party is permitted to bring an action for damages immediately, even though the scheduled time for performance under the contract may still be in the future.[15] Until the nonbreaching party treats this early repudiation as a breach, however, the breaching party can retract the anticipatory repudiation by proper notice and restore the parties to their original obligations.[16]

An anticipatory repudiation is treated as a present, material breach for two reasons. First, the nonbreaching party should not be required to remain ready and willing to perform when the other party has already repudiated the contract. Second, the nonbreaching party should have the opportunity to seek a similar contract elsewhere and may have the duty to do so to minimize his or her loss.

REMEMBER The risks that prices will fluctuate and values will change are ordinary business risks for which the law does not provide relief.

Quite often, an anticipatory repudiation occurs when a sharp fluctuation in market prices creates a situation in which performance of the contract would be extremely unfavorable to one of the parties. ■ EXAMPLE 9.13 Shasta Manufacturing Company contracts to manufacture and sell 100,000 personal computers to New Age, Inc., a computer retailer with 500 outlet stores. Delivery is to be made two months from the date of the contract. One month later, three suppliers of computer parts raise their prices to Shasta. Because of these higher prices, Shasta stands to lose $500,000 if it sells the computers to New Age at the contract price. Shasta writes to New Age, stating that it cannot deliver the 100,000 computers at the agreed-on contract price. Even though you might sympathize with Shasta, its letter is an anticipatory repudiation of the contract, allowing New Age the option of treating the

14. *Restatement (Second) of Contracts,* Section 253, and UCC 2–610.

15. The doctrine of anticipatory repudiation first arose in the landmark case of *Hochster v. De La Tour,* 2 Ellis and Blackburn Reports 678 (1853), when the English court recognized the delay and expense inherent in a rule requiring a nonbreaching party to wait until the time of performance before suing on an anticipatory repudiation.

16. See UCC 2–611.

repudiation as a material breach and proceeding immediately to pursue remedies, even though the contract delivery date is still a month away. ■

DISCHARGE BY AGREEMENT

Any contract can be discharged by agreement of the parties. The agreement can be contained in the original contract, or the parties can form a new contract for the express purpose of discharging the original contract.

Discharge by Rescission As discussed in Chapter 7, rescission is the process in which the parties cancel the contract and are returned to the positions they occupied prior to the contract's formation. For *mutual rescission* to take place, the parties must make another agreement that also satisfies the legal requirements for a contract—there must be an *offer,* an *acceptance,* and *consideration.* Ordinarily, if the parties agree to rescind the original contract, their promises not to perform those acts promised in the original contract will be legal consideration for the second contract.

Mutual rescission can occur in this manner when the original contract is executory on both sides (that is, neither party has completed performance). The agreement to rescind an executory contract is generally enforceable, even if it is made orally and even if the original agreement was in writing.[17] When one party has fully performed, however, an agreement to rescind the original contract usually is not enforceable unless additional consideration or restitution is made.[18]

NOVATION
The substitution, by agreement, of a new contract for an old one, with the rights under the old one being terminated. Typically, novation involves the substitution of a new person who is responsible for the contract and the removal of the original party's rights and duties under the contract.

Discharge by Novation The process of **novation** substitutes a third party for one of the original parties. Essentially, the parties to the original contract and one or more new parties all get together and agree to the substitution. The requirements of a novation are as follows:

1. The existence of a previous, valid obligation.
2. Agreement by all of the parties to a new contract.
3. The extinguishing of the old obligation (discharge of the prior party).
4. A new, valid contract.

A novation may appear similar to an assignment or delegation. There is an important distinction, however: a novation involves a new contract, and an assignment or delegation involves the old contract.

■ EXAMPLE 9.14 Suppose that you contract with Logan Enterprises to sell it your office equipment business. Logan later learns that it should not expand at this time but knows of another party, MBI Corporation, that is interested in purchasing your business. All three of you get together and agree to a novation. As long as the new contract is supported by consideration, the novation discharges the original contract between you and Logan and replaces it with the new contract between you and MBI Corporation. Logan prefers the novation because it discharges its liabilities under the contract with you. If the original contract had been an installment sales contract requiring twelve monthly payments, and Logan had merely assigned the contract (assigned its rights and delegated its duties under the contract) to MBI Corporation,

---

17. Agreements to rescind contracts involving transfers of realty, however, must be evidenced by a writing. Another exception has to do with the sale of goods under the UCC, when the sales contract requires written rescission.

18. Under UCC 2–209(1), however, no consideration is needed to modify a contract for a sale of goods. See Chapter 11. Also see UCC 1–107.

Logan would have remained liable to you for the payments if MBI Corporation defaulted. ■

Discharge by Accord and Satisfaction As discussed in Chapter 7, in an *accord and satisfaction,* the parties agree to accept performance different from the performance originally promised. An *accord* is an executory contract (one that has not yet been performed) to perform some act in order to satisfy an existing contractual duty that is not yet discharged.[19] A *satisfaction* is the performance of the accord agreement. An *accord* and its *satisfaction* discharge the original contractual obligation.

Once the accord has been made, the original obligation is merely suspended until the accord agreement is fully performed. If it is not performed, the party to whom performance is owed can bring an action on the original obligation or for breach of the accord. ■ **EXAMPLE 9.15** Shea obtains a judgment against Marla for $4,000. Later, both parties agree that the judgment can be satisfied by Marla's transfer of her automobile to Shea. This agreement to accept the auto in lieu of $4,000 in cash is the accord. If Marla transfers her automobile to Shea, the accord agreement is fully performed, and the $4,000 debt is discharged. If Marla refuses to transfer her car, the accord is breached. Because the original obligation is merely suspended, Shea can bring an action to enforce the judgment for $4,000 in cash or bring an action for breach of the accord. ■

DISCHARGE BY OPERATION OF LAW

Under some circumstances, contractual duties may be discharged by operation of law. These circumstances include material alteration of the contract, the running of the relevant statute of limitations, bankruptcy, and impossibility of performance.

Contract Alteration To discourage parties from altering written contracts, the law allows an innocent party to be discharged when one party has materially altered a written contract without the knowledge or consent of the other party. For example, if a party alters a material term of the contract—such as the quantity term or the price term—without the knowledge or consent of the other party, the party who was unaware of the alteration can treat the contract as discharged or terminated.

Statutes of Limitations As mentioned earlier in this text, statutes of limitations limit the period during which a party can sue on a particular cause of action. After the applicable limitations period has passed, a suit can no longer be brought. For example, the limitations period for bringing suits for breach of oral contracts is usually two to three years; for written contracts, four to five years; and for recovery of amounts awarded in judgment, ten to twenty years, depending on state law. Suits for breach of a contract for the sale of goods must be brought within four years after the cause of action has accrued. By original agreement, the parties can reduce this four-year period to a one-year period. They cannot, however, extend it beyond the four-year limitations period.

Bankruptcy A proceeding in bankruptcy attempts to allocate the debtor's assets to the creditors in a fair and equitable fashion. Once the assets have been allocated, the debtor receives a *discharge in bankruptcy* (see Chapter 16). A discharge in bankruptcy ordinarily bars enforcement of most of a debtor's contracts by the creditors.

19. *Restatement (Second) of Contracts,* Section 281.

IMPOSSIBILITY OF PERFORMANCE
A doctrine under which a party to a contract is relieved of his or her duty to perform when performance becomes objectively impossible or totally impracticable (through no fault of either party).

NOTE The doctrine of commercial impracticability does not provide relief from such events as ordinary price increases or easily predictable changes in the weather.

When Performance Is Impossible After a contract has been made, performance may become impossible in an objective sense. This is known as **impossibility of performance** and may discharge the contract.[20]

Objective Impossibility. *Objective impossibility* ("It can't be done") must be distinguished from subjective impossibility ("I'm sorry, I simply can't do it"). An example of subjective impossibility is the inability to pay funds on time because the bank is closed.[21] In effect, the nonperforming party is saying, "It is impossible for *me* to perform," rather than "It is impossible for *anyone* to perform." Accordingly, such excuses do not discharge a contract, and the nonperforming party is normally held in breach of contract. Four basic types of situations will generally qualify as grounds for the discharge of contractual obligations based on impossibility of performance:[22]

1. *When a party whose personal performance is essential to the completion of the contract dies or becomes incapacitated prior to performance.* ■ EXAMPLE 9.16 Fred, a famous dancer, contracts with Ethereal Dancing Guild to play a leading role in its new ballet. Before the ballet can be performed, Fred becomes ill and dies. His personal performance was essential to the completion of the contract. Thus, his death discharges the contract and his estate's liability for his nonperformance. ■
2. *When the specific subject matter of the contract is destroyed.* ■ EXAMPLE 9.17 A-1 Farm Equipment agrees to sell Gudgel the green tractor on its lot and promises to have the tractor ready for Gudgel to pick up on Saturday. On Friday night, however, a truck veers off the nearby highway and smashes into the tractor, destroying it beyond repair. Because the contract was for this specific tractor, A-1's performance is rendered impossible owing to the accident. ■
3. *When a change in the law renders performance illegal.* An example is a contract to build an apartment building, when the zoning laws are changed to prohibit the construction of residential rental property at this location. This change renders the contract impossible to perform.
4. *When performance becomes commercially impracticable.* The inclusion of this type of "impossibility" as a basis for contract discharge results from a growing trend to allow parties to discharge contracts when the originally contemplated performance turns out to be much more difficult or expensive than anticipated. In such situations, courts may excuse parties from their performance obligations under the doctrine of *commercial impracticability.* For example, in one case, a court held that a contract could be discharged because a party would have to pay ten times more than the original estimate to excavate a certain amount of gravel.[23]

Temporary Impossibility. An occurrence or event that makes performance temporarily impossible operates to suspend performance until the impossibility ceases. Then, ordinarily, the parties must perform the contract as originally planned. If, however, the lapse of time and the change in circumstances surrounding the contract make it substantially more burdensome for the parties to perform the promised acts, the contract is discharged.

---

20. *Restatement (Second) of Contracts,* Section 261.
21. *Ingham Lumber Co. v. Ingersoll & Co.,* 93 Ark. 447, 125 S.W. 139 (1910).
22. *Restatement (Second) of Contracts,* Sections 262–266, and UCC 2–615.
23. *Mineral Park Land Co. v. Howard,* 172 Cal. 289, 156 P. 458 (1916).

■ EXAMPLE 9.18 The leading case on the subject, *Autry v. Republic Productions*,[24] involved an actor who was drafted into the army in 1942. Being drafted rendered the actor's contract temporarily impossible to perform, and it was suspended until the end of the war. When the actor got out of the army, the purchasing power of the dollar had so changed that performance of the contract would have been substantially burdensome to him. Therefore, the contract was discharged. ■ Review the *Application* feature at the end of this chapter for more on what to do when a contract cannot be performed.

A production line in a commercial bakery. If a fire incapacitated the bakery's oven, would the bakery be excused from performing its contracts until the oven was fixed? If a contract involved a special holiday order and the oven could not be fixed until after the holiday, would the contract be discharged? Why or why not? (© Dick Luria, Getty Images)

REMEMBER The terms of a contract must be sufficiently definite for a court to determine the amount of damages to award.

Damages

A breach of contract entitles the nonbreaching party to sue for money damages. As you read in Chapter 4, damages are designed to compensate a party for harm suffered as a result of another's wrongful act. In the context of contract law, damages are designed to compensate the nonbreaching party for the loss of the bargain. Often, courts say that innocent parties are to be placed in the position they would have occupied had the contract been fully performed.[25]

TYPES OF DAMAGES

There are basically four broad categories of damages:

1. Compensatory (to cover direct losses and costs).
2. Consequential (to cover indirect and foreseeable losses).
3. Punitive (to punish and deter wrongdoing).
4. Nominal (to recognize wrongdoing when no monetary loss is shown).

Compensatory and punitive damages were discussed in Chapter 4 in the context of tort law. Here, we look at these types of damages, as well as consequential and nominal damages, in the context of contract law.

Compensatory Damages Damages compensating the nonbreaching party for the *loss of the bargain* are known as *compensatory damages*. These damages compensate the injured party only for damages actually sustained and proved to have arisen directly from the loss of the bargain caused by the breach of contract. They simply replace what was lost because of the wrong or damage.

The standard measure of compensatory damages is the difference between the value of the breaching party's promised performance under the contract and the value of her or his actual performance. This amount is reduced by any loss that the injured party has avoided, however.

■ EXAMPLE 9.19 You contract with Marinot Industries to perform certain personal services exclusively for Marinot during August for a payment of $3,500. Marinot cancels the contract and is in breach. You are able to find another job during August but can earn only $1,000. You normally can sue Marinot for breach and recover $2,500 as compensatory damages. You may also recover from Marinot the amount that you spent to find the other job. ■ Expenses that are directly incurred because of a breach of contract—such as those incurred to obtain performance from another source—are called *incidental damages*.

24. 30 Cal.2d 144, 180 P.2d 888 (1947).

25. *Restatement (Second) of Contracts,* Section 347; and Section 1–106(1) of the Uniform Commercial Code (UCC).

The measurement of compensatory damages varies by type of contract. Certain types of contracts deserve special mention—contracts for the sale of goods, contracts for the sale of land, and construction contracts.

Sale of Goods. In a contract for the sale of goods, the usual measure of compensatory damages is the difference between the contract price and the market price.[26] ■ EXAMPLE 9.20 MediQuick Laboratories contracts with Cal Computer Industries to purchase ten model UTS 400 network servers for $8,000 each. If Cal Computer fails to deliver the ten servers, and the current market price of the servers is $8,150, MediQuick's measure of damages is $1,500 (10 × $150) plus any incidental damages (expenses) caused by the breach. ■ If the buyer breaches and the seller has not yet produced the goods, compensatory damages normally equal the seller's lost profits on the sale rather than the difference between the contract price and the market price.

.on the Web For a summary of how contracts may be breached and other information on contract law, go to **http://www.lawyers.com/lawyers/A~1001075~LDC/TERMINATING+A+CONTRACT.html**.

Sale of Land. Ordinarily, because each parcel of land is unique, the remedy for a seller's breach of a contract for a sale of real estate is specific performance—that is, the buyer is awarded the parcel of property for which he or she bargained (specific performance is discussed more fully later in this chapter). When this remedy is unavailable (because the property has been sold, for example) or when the buyer is the party in breach, the measure of damages is typically the difference between the contract price and the market price of the land. The majority of states follow this rule.

Construction Contracts. The measure of damages in a building or construction contract varies depending on which party breaches and when the breach occurs. The owner can breach at three different stages of the construction:

1. Before performance has begun.
2. During performance.
3. After performance has been completed.

If the owner breaches *before performance has begun,* the contractor can recover only the profits that would have been made on the contract (that is, the total contract price less the cost of materials and labor). If the owner breaches *during performance,* the contractor can recover the profits plus the costs incurred in partially constructing the building. If the owner breaches *after the construction has been completed,* the contractor can recover the entire contract price plus interest.

When the contractor breaches the construction contract—either by failing to begin construction or by stopping work partway through the project—the measure of damages is the cost of completion, which includes reasonable compensation for any delay in performance. If the contractor finishes late, the measure of damages is the loss of use. Exhibit 9–4 summarizes the rules concerning the measurement of damages in breached construction contracts.

CONSEQUENTIAL DAMAGES
Special damages that compensate for a loss that does not directly or immediately result from the breach (for example, lost profits). For the plaintiff to collect consequential damages, they must have been reasonably foreseeable at the time the breach or injury occurred.

Consequential Damages Foreseeable damages that result from a party's breach of contract are referred to as **consequential damages,** or *special damages.* Consequential damages differ from compensatory damages in that they are caused by special cir-

26. That is, the difference between the contract price and the market price at the time and place at which the goods were to be delivered or tendered. [See UCC 2–708, 2–713, and 2–715(1), discussed in Chapter 12.]

EXHIBIT 9–4 MEASUREMENT OF DAMAGES—BREACH OF CONSTRUCTION CONTRACTS

PARTY IN BREACH	TIME OF BREACH	MEASUREMENT OF DAMAGES
Owner	Before construction has begun	Profits (contract price less cost of materials and labor)
Owner	During construction	Profits plus costs incurred up to time of breach
Owner	After construction is completed	Contract price plus interest
Contractor	Before construction has begun	Cost above contract price to complete work
Contractor	Before construction is completed	Generally, all costs incurred by owner to complete work

cumstances beyond the contract itself. They flow from the consequences, or results, of a breach. When a seller fails to deliver goods, knowing that the buyer is planning to use or resell those goods immediately, consequential damages are awarded for the loss of profits from the planned resale.

■ EXAMPLE 9.21 Gilmore contracts to have a specific item shipped to her—one that she desperately needs to repair her printing press. In her contract with the shipper, Gilmore states that she must receive the item by Monday or she will not be able to print her paper and will lose $950. If the shipper is late, Gilmore normally can recover the consequential damages caused by the delay (that is, the $950 in losses). ■

NOTE A seller who does not wish to take on the risk of consequential damages can limit the buyer's remedies via contract.

To recover consequential damages, the breaching party must know (or have reason to know) that special circumstances will cause the nonbreaching party to suffer an additional loss.[27] When was this rule first enunciated? See this chapter's *Landmark in the Law* feature on the following pages for a discussion of *Hadley v. Baxendale,* a case decided in England in 1854.

Punitive Damages Recall from Chapter 4 that punitive damages are designed to punish a wrongdoer and set an example to deter similar conduct in the future. Punitive damages, or *exemplary damages,* are generally not awarded in an action for breach of contract. Such damages have no legitimate place in contract law because they are, in essence, penalties, and a breach of contract is not unlawful in a criminal sense. A contract is simply a civil relationship between the parties. The law may compensate one party for the loss of the bargain—no more and no less.

In a few situations, a person's actions can cause both a breach of contract and a tort. ■ EXAMPLE 9.22 Two parties establish by contract a certain reasonable standard or duty of care. Failure to live up to that standard is a breach of the contract. The same act that breached the contract may also constitute negligence, or it may be an intentional tort if, for example, the breaching party committed fraud. In such a situation, it is possible for the nonbreaching party to recover punitive damages for the tort in addition to compensatory and consequential damages for the breach of contract. ■

NOMINAL DAMAGES
A small monetary award (often one dollar) granted to a plaintiff when no actual damage was suffered.

Nominal Damages When no actual damage or financial loss results from a breach of contract and only a technical injury is involved, the court may award **nominal damages** to the innocent party. Nominal damage awards are often small, such as one dollar, but they do establish that the defendant acted wrongfully. Most lawsuits for nominal damages are brought as a matter of principle under the theory that a breach has occurred and some damages must be imposed regardless of actual loss.

27. UCC 2–715(2). See Chapter 12.

LANDMARK IN THE LAW

Hadley v. Baxendale (1854)

The rule that notice of special ("consequential") circumstances must be given if consequential damages are to be recovered was first enunciated in *Hadley v. Baxendale*,[a] a landmark case decided in 1854.

CASE BACKGROUND This case involved a broken crankshaft used in a flour mill run by the Hadley family in Gloucester, England. The crankshaft attached to the steam engine in the mill broke, and the shaft had to be sent to a foundry located in Greenwich so that a new shaft could be made to fit the other parts of the engine.

The Hadleys hired Baxendale, a common carrier, to transport the shaft from Gloucester to Greenwich. Baxendale received payment in advance and promised to deliver the shaft the following day. It was not delivered for several days, however. As a consequence, the mill was closed during those days because the Hadleys had no extra crankshaft on hand to use. The Hadleys sued Baxendale to recover the profits they lost during that time. Baxendale contended that the loss of profits was "too remote."

In the mid-1800s, it was common knowledge that large mills, such as that run by the Hadleys, normally had more than one crankshaft in case the main one broke and had to be repaired, as happened in this case. It is against this background that the parties argued their respective positions on whether the damages resulting from loss of profits while the crankshaft was out for repair were "too remote" to be recoverable.

THE ISSUE BEFORE THE COURT AND THE COURT'S RULING The crucial issue before the court was whether the Hadleys had informed the carrier, Baxendale, of the special circumstances surrounding the crankshaft's repair, particularly that the mill would have to shut down while the crankshaft was being repaired. If Baxendale had been notified of this circumstance at the time the contract was formed, then the

a. 9 Exch. 341, 156 Eng.Rep. 145 (1854).

■ EXAMPLE 9.23 Hernandez contracts to buy potatoes at fifty cents a pound from Lentz. Lentz breaches the contract and does not deliver the potatoes. Meanwhile, the price of potatoes falls. Hernandez is able to buy them in the open market at half the price he agreed to pay Lentz. Hernandez is clearly better off because of Lentz's breach. Thus, in a suit for breach of contract, Hernandez may be awarded only nominal damages for the technical injury he sustained, as no monetary loss was involved. ■

(Note that nominal damages may take on greater significance in tort cases involving defamation or trade libel. If a false statement made by a competing firm calls into question a business's integrity or good reputation, the business may find it desirable to establish the falsity of the statement in public court proceedings. If the business wins in court, the court may award nominal damages because actual damages in such cases are difficult to estimate.)

MITIGATION OF DAMAGES

MITIGATION OF DAMAGES
A rule requiring a plaintiff to do whatever is reasonable to minimize the damages caused by the defendant.

In most situations, when a breach of contract occurs, the injured party is held to a duty to mitigate, or reduce, the damages that he or she suffers. Under this doctrine of **mitigation of damages**, the required action depends on the nature of the situation.

LANDMARK IN THE LAW —Continued

remedy for breaching the contract would have been the amount of damages that would reasonably follow from the breach—including the Hadleys' lost profits.

In the court's opinion, however, the only circumstances communicated by the Hadleys to Baxendale at the time the contract was made were that the item to be transported was a broken crankshaft of a mill and that the Hadleys were the owners and operators of that mill. The court concluded that these circumstances did not reasonably indicate that the mill would have to stop operations if the delivery of the crankshaft was delayed.

APPLICATION TO TODAY'S WORLD

Today, the rule enunciated by the court in this case still applies. When damages are awarded, compensation is given only for those injuries that the defendant could reasonably have foreseen as a probable result of the usual course of events following a breach. If the injury complained of is outside the usual and foreseeable course of events, the plaintiff must show specifically that the defendant had reason to know the facts and foresee the injury. This rule applies to contracts in the online environment as well. For example, suppose that a Web merchant loses business (and profits) due to a computer system's failure. If the failure was caused by malfunctioning software, the merchant normally may recover the lost profits from the software maker if these consequential damages were foreseeable.

RELEVANT WEB SITES

To locate information on the Web concerning Hadley v. Baxendale, *go to this text's Web site at* **http://blt.westbuslaw.com**, *select "Chapter 9," and click on "URLs for Landmarks."*

■ EXAMPLE 9.24 Some states require a landlord to use reasonable means to find a new tenant if a tenant abandons the premises and fails to pay rent. If an acceptable tenant becomes available, the landlord is required to lease the premises to this tenant to mitigate the damages recoverable from the former tenant. The former tenant is still liable for the difference between the amount of the rent under the original lease and the rent received from the new tenant. If the landlord has not used the reasonable means necessary to find a new tenant, a court will likely reduce any award by the amount of rent the landlord could have received had such reasonable means been used. ■

In the majority of states, a person whose employment has been wrongfully terminated has a duty to mitigate damages incurred because of the employer's breach of the employment contract. In other words, wrongfully terminated employees have a duty to take similar jobs if they are available. If the employees fail to do this, the damages they receive will be equivalent to their salaries less the incomes they would have received in similar jobs obtained by reasonable means. The employer has the burden of proving that such jobs existed and that the employee could have been hired. Normally, the employee is under no duty to take a job that is not of the same type and rank.

Liquidated Damages versus Penalties

LIQUIDATED DAMAGES
An amount, stipulated in a contract, that the parties to the contract believe to be a reasonable estimation of the damages that will occur in the event of a breach.

PENALTY
A contractual clause that states that a certain amount of money damages will be paid in the event of a future default or breach of contract. The damages are not a measure of compensation for the contract's breach but rather a punishment for a default. The agreement as to the amount will not be enforced, and recovery will be limited to actual damages.

A **liquidated damages** provision in a contract specifies that a certain dollar amount is to be paid in the event of a future default or breach of contract. (*Liquidated* means determined, settled, or fixed.) Liquidated damages differ from penalties. A **penalty** specifies a certain amount to be paid in the event of a default or breach of contract and is designed to penalize the breaching party. Liquidated damages provisions normally are enforceable. In contrast, if a court finds that a provision calls for a penalty, the agreement as to the amount will not be enforced, and recovery will be limited to actual damages.[28]

To determine whether a particular provision is for liquidated damages or for a penalty, the court must answer two questions:

1. At the time the contract was formed, was it apparent that damages would be difficult to estimate in the event of a breach?
2. Was the amount set as damages a reasonable estimate of those potential damages and not excessive?[29]

If the answers to both questions are yes, the provision normally will be enforced. If either answer is no, the provision will normally not be enforced. In a construction contract, it is difficult to estimate the amount of damages that might be caused by a delay in completing construction, so liquidated damages clauses are often used.

The court in the following case addressed the liquidated damages questions just referred to in evaluating a provision in an agreement for the lease of a hotel.

28. This is also the rule under the UCC. See UCC 2–718(1).
29. *Restatement (Second) of Contracts,* Section 356(1).

CASE 9.3 Green Park Inn, Inc. v. Moore

North Carolina Court of Appeals, 2002.
562 S.E.2d 53.
http://www.nccourts.org[a]

COMPANY PROFILE *Green Park Inn (**http://www.greenparkinn.com**) is one of the oldest hotels in the United States. Established in 1882 and listed on the National Register of Historic Places, it is located in the Blue Ridge Mountains near Blowing Rock, North Carolina. Eminent guests have included Annie Oakley, Herbert Hoover, Eleanor Roosevelt, Margaret Mitchell, Calvin Coolidge, and John D. Rockefeller. Green Park Inn is a full-service, first class hotel and restaurant.*

a. Select the link to "Court Opinions", enter "Green Park" in the box labeled "Key Words", and click on "Search." Select the name of the case from the resulting list to access the opinion. The North Carolina Appellate Division Reporter maintains this Web site.

FACTS Allen and Pat McCain own Green Park Inn, Inc., which operates the Green Park Inn. In 1996, they leased the Inn to GMAFCO, LLC, which is owned by Gary and Gail Moore. The lease agreement provided that, in case of a default by GMAFCO, Green Park Inn, Inc., would be entitled to $500,000 as "liquidated damages." GMAFCO defaulted on the February 2000 rent. Green Park Inn, Inc., gave GMAFCO an opportunity to cure the default, but GMAFCO made no further payments and returned possession of the property to the lessor. When Green Park Inn, Inc., sought the "liquidated damages," the Moores refused to pay. Green Park Inn, Inc., filed a suit in a North Carolina state court against the Moores, GMAFCO, and their bank to obtain the $500,000. The defendants contended in part that the lease clause requiring payment of "liquidated damages" was an unenforceable penalty provision. The court ordered the defendants to pay Green Park Inn, Inc. The defendants appealed to a state intermediate appellate court.

CASE 9.3—Continued

ISSUE Did the liquidated damages provision in the lease agreement constitute an unenforceable penalty clause?

DECISION No. The state intermediate appellate court affirmed the decision of the lower court.

REASON The appellate court quoted from the lease agreement's liquidated damages clause, which listed such items to be included in the lessor's damages as "restoration of the physical plant," "lost lease payments," and "harm to the reputation of the hotel." The clause also stated that the McCains had retired to Florida and would have to relocate back to Blowing Rock if they were "forced out of retirement to take over the operation of the hotel." The parties had agreed in the lease that $500,000 was a fair and reasonable estimate of the damages the McCains would suffer in the event of a default. The court held that these provisions satisfied the two-part test for liquidated damages: the amount of the damages would have been difficult to determine at the time the lease was signed, and the estimate of the damages was reasonable. The court noted that while some of the items listed in the clause could be determined, "others, such as the harm to the hotel's reputation or the cost to the McCains of being forced out of retirement, clearly would have been difficult to ascertain at the time the Lease Agreement was signed." The court also pointed out that after McCain and his wife came out of retirement and were again operating the hotel, he testified that $500,000 was "a fair and reasonable estimate to measure the damages" and that the Moores did not attempt to show that this amount was unreasonable.

FOR CRITICAL ANALYSIS—Economic Consideration *If the lease had specified $3 million in damages, would the result in this case have been different? Why or why not?*

ETHICAL ISSUE 9.2

Should liquidated damages clauses be enforced when no actual damages are incurred? An issue involving liquidated damages clauses that occasionally comes before the courts has to do with deposits on the purchase price of a home or other real estate. For example, in one case a couple signed a contract to buy a home and paid a nonrefundable deposit of $18,000 toward the purchase price. The full agreement was contingent on the buyers' sale of their current home. Because the couple was unable to sell their existing home, they had to back out of the agreement. Shortly thereafter, another buyer agreed to purchase the home for a higher price than the initial buyers had agreed to pay. Thus, the seller incurred no actual damages and, in fact, reaped higher profits as a result of the buyers' inability to perform. In such situations, does a clause requiring the buyers to forgo their deposit constitute a penalty clause rather than a liquidated damages clause?

Not in most cases. The courts routinely hold that such clauses are enforceable liquidated damages clauses. Although this may seem unfair to home buyers who cannot perform due to events beyond their control, consider the alternative: if the courts refused to enforce liquidated damages clauses in these circumstances, it would, in the words of one court, undermine "the peace of mind and certainty of result the parties sought when they contracted for liquidated damages."[30] ■

Equitable Remedies

In some situations, damages are an inadequate remedy for a breach of contract. In these cases, the nonbreaching party may ask the court for an equitable remedy. Equitable remedies include rescission and restitution, specific performance, and reformation.

30. *Kelly v. Marx,* 705 N.E.2d 1114 (Mass. 1999).

Rescission and Restitution

As discussed earlier, *rescission* is essentially an action to undo, or cancel, a contract—to return nonbreaching parties to the positions that they occupied prior to the transaction. When fraud, mistake, duress, or failure of consideration is present, rescission is available. The failure of one party to perform under a contract entitles the other party to rescind the contract.[31] The rescinding party must give prompt notice to the breaching party.

RESTITUTION
An equitable remedy under which a person is restored to his or her original position prior to loss or injury, or placed in the position he or she would have been in had the breach not occurred.

Restitution To rescind a contract, both parties generally must make **restitution** to each other by returning goods, property, or money previously conveyed.[32] If the physical property or goods can be returned, they must be. If the property or goods have been consumed, restitution must be made in an equivalent dollar amount.

Essentially, restitution involves the recapture of a benefit conferred on the defendant that has unjustly enriched her or him. ■ EXAMPLE 9.25 Andrea pays $12,000 to Myles in return for his promise to design a house for her. The next day, Myles calls Andrea and tells her that he has taken a position with a large architectural firm in another state and cannot design the house. Andrea decides to hire another architect that afternoon. Andrea can require restitution of $12,000 because Myles has received an unjust benefit of $12,000. ■

CONTRAST Restitution offers several advantages over traditional damages. First, restitution may be available in situations when damages cannot be proved or are difficult to prove. Second, restitution can be used to recover specific property. Third, restitution sometimes results in a greater overall award.

Restitution Is Not Limited to Rescission Cases Restitution may be required when a contract is rescinded, but the right to restitution is not limited to rescission cases. Restitution may be sought in actions for breach of contract, tort actions, and other actions at law or in equity. Usually, restitution can be obtained when funds or property has been transferred by mistake or because of fraud. An award in a case may include restitution of money or property obtained through embezzlement, conversion, theft, copyright infringement, or misconduct by a party in a confidential or other special relationship.

Specific Performance

SPECIFIC PERFORMANCE
An equitable remedy requiring exactly the performance that was specified in a contract; usually granted only when money damages would be an inadequate remedy and the subject matter of the contract is unique (for example, real property).

The equitable remedy of **specific performance** calls for the performance of the act promised in the contract. This remedy is often attractive to a nonbreaching party because it provides the exact bargain promised in the contract. It also avoids some of the problems inherent in a suit for money damages. First, the nonbreaching party need not worry about collecting the judgment.[33] Second, the nonbreaching party need not look around for another contract. Third, the actual performance may be more valuable than the money damages.

Normally, however, specific performance will not be granted unless the party's legal remedy (money damages) is inadequate.[34] For this reason, contracts for the

31. The rescission discussed here refers to *unilateral* rescission, in which only one party wants to undo the contract. In *mutual* rescission, both parties agree to undo the contract. Mutual rescission discharges the contract; unilateral rescission is generally available as a remedy for breach of contract.
32. *Restatement (Second) of Contracts,* Section 370.
33. Courts dispose of cases, after trials, by entering judgments. A judgment may order the losing party to pay money damages to the winning party. Collecting a judgment, however, can pose problems. For example, the judgment debtor may be insolvent (cannot pay his or her bills when they come due) or have only a small net worth, or exemption laws may prevent a creditor from seizing the debtor's assets to satisfy a debt (see Chapter 16).
34. *Restatement (Second) of Contracts,* Section 359.

sale of goods rarely qualify for specific performance. Money damages ordinarily are adequate in such situations because substantially identical goods can be bought or sold in the market. Only if the goods are unique will a court of equity grant specific performance. For instance, paintings, sculptures, and rare books and coins are often unique, and money damages will not enable a buyer to obtain substantially identical substitutes in the market.

Sale of Land A court will grant specific performance to a buyer in a contract for the sale of land. The legal remedy for breach of a land sales contract is inadequate because every parcel of land is considered to be unique. Money damages will not compensate a buyer adequately because the same land in the same location obviously cannot be obtained elsewhere. Only when specific performance is unavailable (for example, when the seller has sold the property to someone else) will money damages be awarded instead.

Contracts for Personal Services Personal-service contracts require one party to work personally for another party. Courts normally refuse to grant specific performance of contracts for personal services. This is because to order a party to perform personal services against his or her will amounts to a type of involuntary servitude, which is contrary to the public policy expressed in the Thirteenth Amendment to the Constitution. Moreover, the courts do not want to monitor contracts for personal services.

■ EXAMPLE 9.26 If you contract with a brain surgeon to perform brain surgery on you and the surgeon refuses to perform, the court will not compel (and you certainly would not want) the surgeon to perform under these circumstances. There is no way the court can assure meaningful performance in such a situation.[35] ■

35. Similarly, courts often refuse to order specific performance of construction contracts because courts are not set up to operate as construction supervisors or engineers.

Suppose that a seller contracts to sell some valuable coins to a buyer. If the seller breaches the contract, would specific performance be an appropriate remedy for the buyer to seek? Why or why not? (Elizabeth Simpson, Getty Images)

REFORMATION

Reformation is an equitable remedy used when the parties have *imperfectly* expressed their agreement in writing. Reformation allows the contract to be rewritten to reflect the parties' true intentions. It applies most often when fraud or mutual mistake is present. ■ EXAMPLE 9.27 If Keshan contracts to buy a forklift from Shelley but the written contract refers to a crane, a mutual mistake has occurred. Accordingly, a court could reform the contract so that the writing conforms to the parties' original intention as to which piece of equipment is being sold. ■

Courts frequently reform contracts in two other situations. The first occurs when two parties who have made a binding oral contract agree to put the oral contract in writing but, in doing so, make an error in stating the terms. Universally, the courts allow into evidence the correct terms of the oral contract, thereby reforming the written contract. The second situation occurs when the parties have executed a written covenant not to compete (see Chapter 8). If the covenant not to compete is for a valid and legitimate purpose (such as the sale of a business) but the area or time restraints are unreasonable, some courts will reform the restraints by making them reasonable and will enforce the entire contract as reformed. Other courts, however, will throw the entire restrictive covenant out as illegal. Exhibit 9–5 summarizes the remedies, including reformation, that are available to the nonbreaching party.

Recovery Based on Quasi Contract

Recall from Chapter 7 that a quasi contract is not a true contract but rather a fictional contract that a court imposes on the parties to prevent unjust enrichment. Hence, quasi contract provides a basis for relief when no enforceable contract exists. The legal obligation arises because the law considers that a promise to pay for benefits received is implied by the party accepting the benefits. Generally, when one party confers a benefit on another party, justice requires that the party receiving the benefit pay a reasonable value for it.

DON'T FORGET The function of a quasi contract is to impose a legal obligation on a party who made no actual promise.

WHEN QUASI CONTRACTS ARE USED

Quasi contract is a legal theory under which an obligation is imposed in the absence of an agreement. It allows the courts to act as if a contract exists when there is no actual contract or agreement between the parties. The courts can also use this theory when the parties have a contract, but it is unenforceable for some reason.

EXHIBIT 9–5 REMEDIES FOR BREACH OF CONTRACT

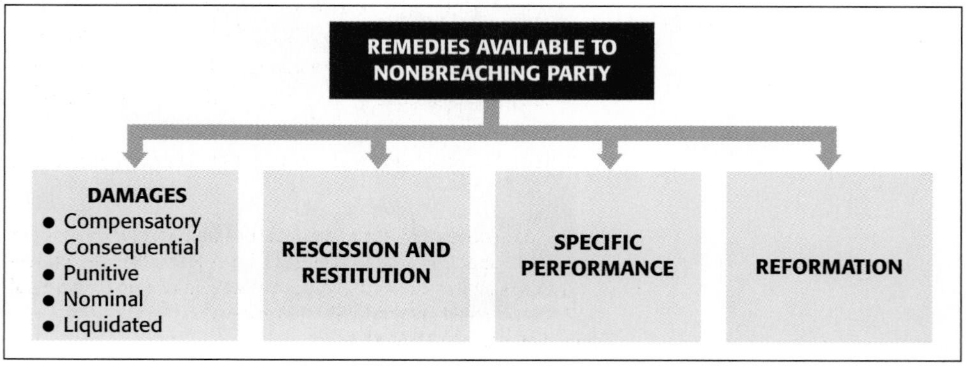

Quasi-contractual recovery is often granted when one party has partially performed under a contract that is unenforceable. It provides an alternative to suing for damages and allows the party to recover the reasonable value of the partial performance. ■ EXAMPLE 9.28 Ericson contracts to build two oil derricks for Petro Industries. The derricks are to be built over a period of three years, but the parties do not create a written contract. Therefore, the Statute of Frauds will bar the enforcement of the contract.[36] After Ericson completes one derrick, Petro Industries informs him that it will not pay for the derrick. Ericson can sue Petro Industries under the theory of quasi contract. ■

THE REQUIREMENTS OF QUASI CONTRACT

To recover on quasi contract, the party seeking recovery must show the following:

1. The party conferred a benefit on the other party.
2. The party conferred the benefit with the reasonable expectation of being paid.
3. The party did not act as a volunteer in conferring the benefit.
4. The party receiving the benefit would be unjustly enriched by retaining the benefit without paying for it.

In the example just given, Ericson can sue in quasi contract because all of the conditions for quasi-contractual recovery have been fulfilled. Ericson built the oil derrick with the expectation of being paid. The derrick conferred an obvious benefit on Petro Industries, and Petro Industries would be unjustly enriched if it was allowed to keep the derrick without paying Ericson for the work. Therefore, Ericson should be able to recover the reasonable value of the oil derrick that was built (under the theory of *quantum meruit*[37]—"as much as he deserves"). The reasonable value is ordinarily equal to the fair market value.

Election of Remedies

BE AWARE Which remedy a plaintiff elects depends on the subject of the contract, the defenses of the breaching party, the advantages that might be gained in terms of tactics against the defendant, and what the plaintiff can prove with respect to the remedy sought.

In many cases, a nonbreaching party has several remedies available. Because the remedies may be inconsistent with one another, the common law of contracts requires the party to choose which remedy to pursue. This is called *election of remedies*. The purpose of the doctrine of election of remedies is to prevent double recovery. ■ EXAMPLE 9.29 Suppose that Jefferson agrees to sell his land to Adams. Then Jefferson changes his mind and repudiates the contract. Adams can sue for compensatory damages or for specific performance. If Adams receives damages as a result of the breach, she should not also be granted specific performance of the sales contract because that would mean she would unfairly end up with both the land and the damages. The doctrine of election of remedies requires Adams to choose the remedy she wants, and it eliminates any possibility of double recovery. ■

In contrast, remedies under the UCC are cumulative. They include all of the remedies available under the UCC for breach of a sales or lease contract.[38] We will examine the UCC provisions on limited remedies in Chapter 12, in the context of the remedies available on the breach of a contract for the sale or lease of goods.

---

36. Contracts that by their terms cannot be performed within one year from the day after the date of contract formation must be in writing to be enforceable. See Chapter 8. (Under the 2003 amendments to the Uniform Commercial Code, the one-year rule will no longer apply to sales contracts. See Chapter 11.)
37. Pronounced *kwahn*-tuhm *mehr*-oo-wuht.
38. See UCC 2–703 and 2–711.

APPLICATION What Do You Do When You Cannot Perform?*

Not every contract can be performed. If you are a contractor, you may take on a job that, for one reason or another, you cannot or do not wish to perform. Simply walking away from the job and hoping for the best normally is not the most effective way to avoid litigation—which can be costly, time consuming, and emotionally draining. Instead, you should consider different options that may reduce the likelihood of litigation.

For example, suppose that you are a building contractor and you sign a contract to build a home for the Andersons. Performance is to begin on June 15. On June 1, Central Enterprises offers you a position that will yield you two and a half times the amount of net income you could earn as an independent builder. To take the job, you have to start on June 15. You cannot be in two places at the same time, so to accept the new position, you must breach the contract with the Andersons.

CONSIDER YOUR OPTIONS

What can you do in this situation? One option is to subcontract the work to another builder and oversee the work yourself to make sure it conforms to the contract. Another option is to negotiate with the Andersons for a release. You can offer to find another qualified builder who will build a house of the same quality at the same price. Alternatively, you can offer to pay any additional costs if another builder takes the job and is more expensive. In any event, this additional cost would be the measure of damages that a court would impose on you if the Andersons prevailed in a suit for breach of contract. Thus, by making the offer, you might be able to avoid the expense of litigation—if the Andersons accept your offer.

SETTLEMENT OFFERS

Often, parties are reluctant to propose compromise settlements because they fear that what they say will be used against them in court if litigation ensues. The general rule, however, is that offers for settlement cannot be used in court to prove that you are liable for a breach of contract.

* This *Application* is not meant to substitute for the services of an attorney who is licensed to practice law in your state.

CHECKLIST FOR THE CONTRACTOR WHO CANNOT PERFORM

1. Consider a compromise.
2. Subcontract out the work and oversee it.
3. Offer to find an alternative contractor to fulfill your obligation.
4. Make a cash offer to "buy" a release from your contract. If anything other than an insignificant amount of money is involved, however, work with an attorney in making the offer.

KEY TERMS

alienation 275
anticipatory repudiation 285
assignee 272
assignment 272
assignor 272
breach of contract 272
condition 282
consequential damages 290
delegatee 276
delegation of duties 276
delegator 276
discharge 281
impossibility of performance 288
incidental beneficiary 279
intended beneficiary 278
liquidated damages 294
mitigation of damages 292
nominal damages 291
novation 286
obligee 272
obligor 272
penalty 294
performance 281
privity of contract 271
restitution 296
specific performance 296
tender 282
third party beneficiary 278

CHAPTER SUMMARY Contracts: Third Party Rights, Discharge, Breach, and Remedies

	THIRD PARTY RIGHTS
Assignments (See pages 272–275.)	1. An assignment is the transfer of rights under a contract to a third party. The person assigning the rights is the *assignor,* and the party to whom the rights are assigned is the *assignee.* The assignee has a right to demand performance from the other original party to the contract. 2. Generally, all rights can be assigned, except in the following circumstances: a. When assignment is expressly prohibited by statute (for example, workers' compensation benefits). b. When a contract calls for the performance of personal services. c. When the assignment will materially increase or alter the risks or duties of the *obligor* (the party that is obligated to perform). d. When the contract itself stipulates that the rights cannot be assigned (with some exceptions).
Delegations (See pages 276–277.)	1. A delegation is the transfer of duties under a contract to a third party (the *delegatee*), who then assumes the obligation of performing the contractual duties previously held by the one making the delegation (the *delegator*). 2. As a general rule, any duty can be delegated, except in the following circumstances: a. When performance depends on the personal skill or talents of the obligor. b. When special trust has been placed in the obligor. c. When performance by a third party will vary materially from that expected by the obligee (the one to whom the duty is owed) under the contract. d. When the contract expressly prohibits delegation. 3. A valid delegation of duties does not relieve the delegator of obligations under the contract. If the delegatee fails to perform, the delegator is still liable to the obligee. 4. An "assignment of all rights" or an "assignment of the contract" is often construed to mean that both the rights and the duties arising under the contract are transferred to a third party.
Third Party Beneficiaries (See pages 278–281.)	A third party beneficiary contract is one made for the purpose of benefiting a third party. 1. *Intended beneficiary*—One for whose benefit a contract is created. When the promisor (the one making the contractual promise that benefits a third party) fails to perform as promised, the third party can sue the promisor directly. Examples of third party beneficiaries are creditor and donee beneficiaries. 2. *Incidental beneficiary*—A third party who indirectly (incidentally) benefits from a contract but for whose benefit the contract was not specifically intended. Incidental beneficiaries have no rights to the benefits received and cannot sue to have the contract enforced.
	CONTRACT DISCHARGE
Discharge by Performance (See pages 282–286.)	A contract may be discharged by complete (strict) performance or by substantial performance. In some cases, performance must be to the satisfaction of another. Totally inadequate performance constitutes a material breach of contract. An anticipatory repudiation of a contract allows the other party to sue immediately for breach of contract.
Discharge by Agreement (See pages 286–287.)	Parties may agree to discharge their contractual obligations in several ways: 1. *By rescission*—The parties mutually agree to rescind (cancel) the contract. 2. *By novation*—A new party is substituted for one of the primary parties to a contract. 3. *By accord and satisfaction*—The parties agree to render and accept performance different from that on which they originally agreed.

(Continued)

CHAPTER SUMMARY Contracts: Third Party Rights, Discharge, Breach, and Remedies—Continued

Discharge by Operation of Law (See pages 287–289.)	Parties' obligations under contracts may be discharged by operation of law owing to one of the following: 1. Contract alteration. 2. Statutes of limitations. 3. Bankruptcy. 4. Impossibility of performance.
	COMMON REMEDIES AVAILABLE TO NONBREACHING PARTY
Damages (See pages 289–295.)	The legal remedy designed to compensate the nonbreaching party for the loss of the bargain. By awarding money damages, the court tries to place the parties in the positions that they would have occupied had the contract been fully performed. The nonbreaching party frequently has a duty to *mitigate* (lessen or reduce) the damages incurred as a result of the contract's breach. There are five broad categories of damages: 1. *Compensatory damages*—Damages that compensate the nonbreaching party for injuries actually sustained and proved to have arisen directly from the loss of the bargain resulting from the breach of contract. a. In breached contracts for the sale of goods, the usual measure of compensatory damages is the difference between the contract price and the market price. b. In breached contracts for the sale of land, the measure of damages is ordinarily the same as in contracts for the sale of goods. c. In breached construction contracts, the measure of damages depends on which party breaches and at what stage of construction the breach occurs. 2. *Consequential damages*—Damages resulting from special circumstances beyond the contract itself; the damages flow only from the consequences of a breach. For a party to recover consequential damages, the damages must be the foreseeable result of a breach of contract, and the breaching party must have known at the time the contract was formed that special circumstances existed that would cause the nonbreaching party to incur additional loss on breach of the contract. Also called *special damages.* 3. *Punitive damages*—Damages awarded to punish the breaching party. Usually not awarded in an action for breach of contract unless a tort is involved. 4. *Nominal damages*—Damages small in amount (such as one dollar) that are awarded when a breach has occurred but no actual damages have been suffered. Awarded only to establish that the defendant acted wrongfully. 5. *Liquidated damages*—Damages that may be specified in a contract as the amount to be paid to the nonbreaching party in the event the contract is breached in the future. Clauses providing for liquidated damages are enforced if the damages were difficult to estimate at the time the contract was formed and if the amount stipulated is reasonable. If the amount is construed to be a penalty, the clause will not be enforced.
Rescission and Restitution (See page 296.)	1. *Rescission*—A remedy whereby a contract is canceled and the parties are restored to the original positions that they occupied prior to the transaction. Available when fraud, a mistake, duress, or failure of consideration is present. The rescinding party must give prompt notice of the rescission to the breaching party. 2. *Restitution*—When a contract is rescinded, both parties must make restitution to each other by returning the goods, property, or funds previously conveyed. Restitution prevents the unjust enrichment of the parties.

CHAPTER SUMMARY Contracts: Third Party Rights, Discharge, Breach, and Remedies—Continued

Specific Performance (See pages 296–297.)	An equitable remedy calling for the performance of the act promised in the contract. This remedy is available only in special situations—such as those involving contracts for the sale of unique goods or land—and when monetary damages would be an inadequate remedy. Specific performance is not available as a remedy in breached contracts for personal services.
Reformation (See page 298.)	An equitable remedy allowing a contract to be "reformed," or rewritten, to reflect the parties' true intentions. Available when an agreement is imperfectly expressed in writing.
Recovery Based on Quasi Contract (See pages 298–299.)	An equitable theory imposed by the courts to obtain justice and prevent unjust enrichment in a situation in which no enforceable contract exists. The party seeking recovery must show the following: 1. A benefit was conferred on the other party. 2. The party conferring the benefit did so with the expectation of being paid. 3. The benefit was not volunteered. 4. Retaining the benefit without paying for it would result in the unjust enrichment of the party receiving the benefit.
	CONTRACT DOCTRINE RELATING TO REMEDIES
Election of Remedies (See page 299.)	A common law doctrine under which a nonbreaching party must choose one remedy from those available. This doctrine prevents double recovery. Under the UCC, remedies are cumulative for the breach of a contract for the sale of goods.

FOR REVIEW

Answers for the even-numbered questions in this For Review *section can be found in Appendix I at the end of this text.*

1. What is the difference between an assignment and a delegation?
2. What factors indicate that a third party beneficiary is an intended beneficiary?
3. What is the difference between compensatory damages and consequential damages? What are nominal damages, and when do courts award nominal damages?
4. Under what circumstances will equitable remedies be available?
5. What is the rationale underlying the doctrine of election of remedies?

QUESTIONS AND CASE PROBLEMS

9–1. Third Party Beneficiaries. Wilken owes Rivera $2,000. Howie promises Wilken that he will pay Rivera the $2,000 in return for Wilken's promise to give Howie's children guitar lessons. Is Rivera an intended beneficiary of the Howie-Wilken contract? Explain.

9–2. Assignments. Aron, a college student, signs a one-year lease agreement that runs from September 1 to August 31. The lease agreement specifies that the lease cannot be assigned without the landlord's consent. In late May, Aron decides not to go to summer school and assigns the balance of the lease (three months) to a close friend, Erica. The landlord objects to the assignment and denies Erica access to the apartment. Aron claims that Erica is financially sound and should be allowed the full rights and privileges of an assignee. Discuss fully whether the landlord or Aron is correct.

9–3. **Impossibility of Performance.** Millie contracted to sell Frank 1,000 bushels of corn to be grown on Millie's farm. Owing to a drought during the growing season, Millie's yield was much less than anticipated, and she could deliver only 250 bushels to Frank. Frank accepted the lesser amount but sued Millie for breach of contract. Can Millie defend successfully on the basis of objective impossibility of performance? Explain.

9–4. **Measure of Damages.** Ben owns and operates a famous candy store. He makes most of the candy sold in the store, and business is particularly heavy during the Christmas season. Ben contracts with Sweet, Inc., to purchase ten thousand pounds of sugar, to be delivered on or before November 15. Ben informs Sweet that this particular order is to be used for the Christmas season business. Because of production problems, the sugar is not tendered to Ben until December 10, at which time Ben refuses the order because it is so late. Ben has been unable to purchase the quantity of sugar needed to meet the Christmas orders and has had to turn down numerous regular customers, some of whom have indicated that they will purchase candy elsewhere in the future. The sugar that Ben has been able to purchase has cost him ten cents per pound above Sweet's price. Ben sues Sweet for breach of contract, claiming as damages the higher price paid for the sugar from other suppliers, lost profits from this year's lost Christmas sales, future lost profits from customers who have indicated that they will discontinue doing business with him, and punitive damages for failure to meet the contracted-for delivery date. Sweet claims Ben is limited to compensatory damages only. Discuss who is correct, and why.

CASE PROBLEM WITH SAMPLE ANSWER

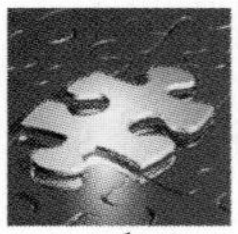

9–5. In May 1996, O'Brien-Shiepe Funeral Home, Inc., in Hempstead, New York, hired Teramo & Co. to build an addition to O'Brien's funeral home. The parties' contract did not specify a date for the completion of the work. The city of Hempstead issued a building permit for the project on June 14, and Teramo began work about two weeks later. There was some delay in construction because O'Brien asked that no work be done during funeral services, but by the end of March 1997, the work was substantially complete. The city of Hempstead issued a "Certificate of Completion" on April 15. During the construction, O'Brien made periodic payments to Teramo, but there was a balance due of $17,950, which O'Brien did not pay. To recover this amount, Teramo filed a suit in a New York state court against O'Brien. O'Brien filed a counterclaim to recover lost profits for business allegedly lost due to the time Teramo took to build the addition, and for $6,180 spent to correct problems caused by poor work. Which, if any, party is entitled to an award in this case? Explain. [*Teramo & Co. v. O'Brien-Shiepe Funeral Home, Inc.*, 725 N.Y.S.2d 87 (A.D. 2 Dept. 2001)]

After you have answered this problem, compare your answer with the sample answer given on the Web site that accompanies this text. Go to http://blt.westbuslaw.com, select "Chapter 9," and click on "Case Problem with Sample Answer."

9–6. **Third Party Beneficiaries.** Action Steel, Inc., entered into a contract with Systems Builders, Inc., a general contractor, to construct an addition to a commercial building in Indianapolis, Indiana. The contract provided that after the addition's completion, Action Steel would obtain insurance, which "shall include the interest of . . . subcontractors." The parties would then "waive all rights against . . . any of their subcontractors." Varco-Pruden Building, a subcontractor, designed the addition, which was completed in the summer of 1995. Action Steel obtained an insurance policy from Midwestern Indemnity Co. In January 1996, a snowstorm hit the Indianapolis area, and the new addition collapsed. Midwestern paid over $1.3 million to Action Steel for the loss. Because Midwestern paid for the loss, it stood in Action Steel's place in a suit filed in an Indiana state court against Varco-Pruden and others to recover this amount. Varco-Pruden filed a motion for summary judgment, arguing in part that it was a third party beneficiary of the waiver clause in the contract between Action Steel and Systems Builders. Should the court grant this motion? Why or why not? [*Midwestern Indemnity Co. v. Systems Builders, Inc.*, 801 N.E.2d 661 (Ind.App. 2004)]

9–7. **Liquidated Damages versus Penalties.** Every homeowner in the Putnam County, Indiana, subdivision of Stardust Hills must be a member of the Stardust Hills Owners Association, Inc., and must pay annual dues of $200 for the maintenance of common areas and other community services. Under the Association's rules, dues paid more than ten days late "shall bear a delinquent fee at a rate of $2.00 per day." Phyllis Gaddis failed to pay the dues on a Stardust Hills lot that she owned. Late fees began to accrue. Nearly two months later, the Association filed a suit in an Indiana state court to collect the unpaid dues and the late fees. Gaddis argued in response that the delinquent fee was an unenforceable penalty. What questions should be considered in determining the status of this fee? Should the Association's rule regarding assessment of the fee be enforced? Explain. [*Gaddis v. Stardust Hills Owners Association, Inc.*, 804 N.E.2d 231 (Ind.App. 2004)]

A QUESTION OF ETHICS

9–8. Bath Iron Works (BIW) offered a job to Thomas Devine, contingent on Devine's passing a drug test. The testing was conducted by NorDx, a subcontractor of Roche Biomedical Laboratories. When NorDx found that Devine's urinalysis showed the presence of opiates, a result confirmed by Roche, BIW refused to offer Devine permanent employment. Devine claimed that the ingestion of poppy seeds can lead to a positive result and that he tested positive for opiates only because of his daily consumption of poppy seed muffins. In Devine's suit against Roche, Devine argued, among other things, that he was a third party beneficiary of the contract between his employer (BIW) and NorDx (Roche). Given this factual background, consider the following questions. [*Devine v. Roche Biomedical Laboratories*, 659 A.2d 868 (Me. 1995)]

1. Is Devine an intended third party beneficiary of the BIW–NorDx contract? In deciding this issue, should the court focus on the nature of the promises made in the contract itself or on the consequences of the contract for Devine, a third party?
2. Should employees whose job security and reputation have suffered as a result of false test results be allowed to sue drug-testing labs for the tort of negligence? In such situations, do drug-testing labs have a duty to the employees to exercise reasonable care in conducting the tests?

FOR CRITICAL ANALYSIS

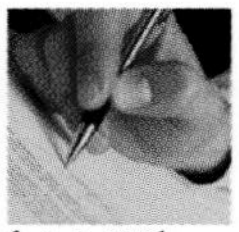

9–9. The concept of substantial performance permits a party to be discharged from a contract even though the party has not fully performed his or her obligations according to the contract's terms. Is this fair? What policy interests are at issue here?

VIDEO QUESTION

9–10. Go to this text's Web site at **http://blt.westbuslaw.com** and select "Chapter 9." Click on "Video Questions" and view the video titled *Midnight Run*. Then answer the following questions.

1. In the video, Eddie (Joe Pantoliano) and Jack (Robert DeNiro) negotiate a contract for Jack to find the Duke, a mob accountant who embezzled funds, and bring him back for trial. Assume that the contract is valid. If Jack breaches the contract by failing to bring in the Duke, what kinds of remedies, if any, can Eddie seek? Explain your answer.
2. Would the equitable remedy of specific performance be available to either Jack or Eddie in the event of a breach? Why or why not?
3. Now assume the contract between Eddie and Jack is unenforceable. Nevertheless, Jack performs his side of the bargain (brings in the Duke). Is any remedy available to him? Why or why not?

INTERNET EXERCISES

Go to the *Business Law Today: The Essentials* home page at **http://blt.westbuslaw.com**, select "Chapter 9," and click on "Internet Exercises." There you will find the following Internet research exercises that you can perform to learn more about topics covered in this chapter.

Activity 9–1: LEGAL PERSPECTIVE—Anticipatory Repudiation

Activity 9–2: MANAGEMENT PERSPECTIVE—Commercial Impracticability

Activity 9–3: MANAGEMENT PERSPECTIVE—The Duty to Mitigate

BEFORE THE TEST

Go to the *Business Law Today: The Essentials* home page at **http://blt.westbuslaw.com**, select "Chapter 9," and click on "Interactive Quizzes." You will find at least twenty interactive questions relating to this chapter.

CHAPTER 10
E-Contracts

"[B]usiness models and methods for doing business have evolved to take advantage of the speed, efficiencies, and cost benefits of electronic technologies."

Prefatory Note, Uniform Electronic Transactions Act

CHAPTER OUTLINE

- FORMING CONTRACTS ONLINE
- E-SIGNATURES
- PARTNERING AGREEMENTS
- THE UNIFORM ELECTRONIC TRANSACTIONS ACT
- THE UNIFORM COMPUTER INFORMATION TRANSACTIONS ACT

LEARNING OBJECTIVES

After reading this chapter, you should be able to answer the following questions:

1. What are some important clauses to include when making offers to form electronic contracts, or e-contracts?
2. How do shrink-wrap and click-on agreements differ from other contracts? How have traditional laws been applied to these agreements?
3. What is an electronic signature? Are electronic signatures valid?
4. What is a partnering agreement? What purpose does it serve?
5. What is the Uniform Electronic Transactions Act (UETA)? What are some of the major provisions of this act?

As the chapter-opening quotation indicates, electronic technology offers businesses several advantages, including speed, efficiency, and lower costs. In the 1990s, many observers argued that the development of cyberspace was revolutionary. Therefore, new legal theories, and new laws, would be needed to govern **e-contracts**, or contracts entered into electronically. To date, however, most courts have adapted traditional contract law principles and, when applicable, provisions of the Uniform Commercial Code to cases involving e-contract disputes.

E-CONTRACT
A contract that is formed electronically.

In the first part of this chapter, we look at how traditional laws are being applied to contracts formed online. We then examine some new laws that have been created to apply in situations in which traditional laws governing contracts have sometimes been thought inadequate. For example, traditional laws governing signature and writing requirements are not easily adapted to contracts formed in the online environment. Thus, new laws have been created to address these issues.

Forming Contracts Online

Today, numerous contracts are being formed online. Although the medium through which these contracts are generated has changed, the age-old problems attending contract formation have not. Disputes concerning contracts formed online continue to center around contract terms and whether the parties voluntarily assented to those terms.

Note that online contracts may be formed not only for the sale of goods and services but also for *licensing*. ■ EXAMPLE 10.1 The "sale" of software generally involves a license, or a right to use the software, rather than the passage of title (ownership rights) from the seller to the buyer. ■ As you read through the following pages, keep in mind that although we typically refer to the offeror and the offeree as a *seller* and a *buyer*, in many transactions these parties would be more accurately described as a *licensor* and a *licensee*.

ONLINE OFFERS

Sellers doing business via the Internet can protect themselves against contract disputes and legal liability by creating offers that clearly spell out the terms that will govern their transactions if the offers are accepted. All important terms should be conspicuous and easily viewed by potential buyers.

An important rule to keep in mind is that the offeror controls the offer and thus the resulting contract. The seller should therefore anticipate the terms he or she wants to include in a contract and provide for them in the offer. In some instances, a standardized contract form may suffice—the *Application* at the end of this chapter offers suggestions on how to find and use online contract forms.

At a minimum, an online offer should include the following provisions:

1. A provision specifying the remedies available to the buyer if the goods are found to be defective or if the contract is otherwise breached. Any limitation of remedies should be clearly spelled out.
2. A clause that clearly indicates what constitutes the buyer's agreement to the terms of the offer.
3. A provision specifying how payment for the goods and of any applicable taxes must be made.
4. A statement of the seller's refund and return policies.
5. Disclaimers of liability for certain uses of the goods. For example, an online seller of business forms may add a disclaimer that the seller does not accept responsibility for the buyer's reliance on the forms rather than on an attorney's advice.
6. A statement indicating how the seller will use the information gathered about the buyer.

Dispute-Settlement Provisions In addition to the above provisions, many online offers include provisions relating to dispute settlement. For example, the offer might include an arbitration clause specifying that any dispute arising under the contract will be arbitrated in a designated forum.

FORUM-SELECTION CLAUSE
A provision in a contract designating the court, jurisdiction, or tribunal that will decide any disputes arising under the contract.

Many online contracts also contain a **forum-selection clause** (indicating the forum, or location, for the resolution of any dispute arising under the contract). As discussed in Chapter 3, significant jurisdictional issues may occur when parties are at a great distance, as they often are when they form contracts via the Internet. A forum-selection clause will help to avert future jurisdictional problems and also help to ensure that the seller will not be required to appear in court in a distant state.

ETHICAL ISSUE 10.1

Are forum-selection clauses fair to online purchasers? One of the issues that has come before the courts over the last several years has to do with forum-selection clauses included in online contracts. Online businesses typically include such clauses so that they will not have to travel to other states to defend against lawsuits brought by dissatisfied customers. This seems fair to businesses, but is it fair to consumers? Should the courts always enforce these clauses? Generally, the courts do enforce forum-selection clauses that are freely and voluntarily entered into by the parties.[1]

If, however, the enforcement of a forum-selection clause would significantly deprive a plaintiff of her or his rights under state law, a court may refuse to enforce the clause. In one case, for example, a group of Florida subscribers of America Online, Inc. (AOL), brought a suit in a Florida state court, claiming that AOL had continued to debit their credit cards for monthly service fees, without authorization, for some time after they had terminated their subscriptions. AOL sought to enforce its forum-selection clause, which was included in its "Terms of Service" agreement with its subscribers. The clause provided that all lawsuits under the agreement had to be brought in Virginia, AOL's home state. In this case, a Florida court refused to enforce the clause because the "purpose and effectiveness" of the Florida consumer statutes would be "seriously undermined" if the plaintiffs were required to bring their suit in Virginia.[2] ■

Displaying the Offer The seller's Web site should include a hypertext link to a page containing the full contract so that potential buyers are made aware of the terms to which they are assenting. The contract generally must be displayed online in a readable format such as a twelve-point typeface. All provisions should be reasonably clear. ■ EXAMPLE 10.2 Suppose that Netquip sells a variety of heavy equipment, such as trucks and trailers, online at its Web site. Because Netquip's pricing schedule is very complex, the schedule must be fully provided and explained on the Web site. ■

Indicating How the Offer Can Be Accepted An online offer should also include some mechanism by which the customer may accept the offer. Typically, online sellers include boxes containing the words "I agree" or "I accept the terms of the offer" that offerees can click on to indicate acceptance. The contract resulting from such an acceptance is often called a **click-on agreement.**

CLICK-ON AGREEMENT
An agreement that arises when a buyer, engaging in a transaction on a computer, indicates his or her assent to be bound by the terms of an offer by clicking on a button that says, for example, "I agree"; sometimes referred to as a *click-on license* or a *click-wrap agreement.*

SHRINK-WRAP AGREEMENT
An agreement whose terms are expressed in a document located inside a box in which goods (usually software) are packaged; sometimes called a *shrink-wrap license.*

ONLINE ACCEPTANCES

In many ways, click-on agreements are the Internet equivalents of **shrink-wrap agreements** (or *shrink-wrap licenses,* as they are sometimes called). A *shrink-wrap agreement* is an agreement whose terms are expressed inside a box in which the goods are packaged. (The term *shrink-wrap* refers to the plastic that covers the box.) Usually, the party who opens the box is told that she or he agrees to the terms by keeping whatever is in the box. Similarly, when the purchaser opens a software package, he or she agrees to abide by the terms of the limited license agreement.

■ EXAMPLE 10.3 John orders a new computer from a national company, which ships the computer to him. Along with the computer, the box contains an agreement setting forth the terms of the sale, including what remedies are available. The

1. See, for example, *Freedman v. America Online, Inc.,* 294 F.Supp.2d 238 (D.Conn. 2003).
2. *America Online, Inc. v. Pasieka,* 870 So.2d 170 (Fla.App.—1st Dist. 2004).

document also states that John's retention of the computer for longer than thirty days will be construed as an acceptance of the terms. ■

In most cases, a shrink-wrap agreement is not between a retailer and a buyer, but between the manufacturer of the hardware or software and the ultimate buyer-user of the product. The terms generally concern warranties, remedies, and other issues associated with the use of the product.

We look next at how the law has been applied to both shrink-wrap and click-on agreements.

Shrink-Wrap Agreements—Enforceable Contract Terms The *Restatement (Second) of Contracts*—a compilation of common law contract principles—states that parties may agree to a contract "by written or spoken words or by other action or by failure to act."[3] The Uniform Commercial Code (UCC)—the law governing sales contracts—has a similar provision. Section 2–204 of the UCC states that any contract for the sale of goods "may be made in any manner sufficient to show agreement, including conduct by both parties which recognizes the existence of such a contract." The courts have used these provisions to conclude that a binding contract can be created by conduct, including conduct accepting the terms in either a shrink-wrap agreement or a click-on agreement. Thus, a buyer's failure to object to terms contained within a shrink-wrapped software package (or an online offer) may constitute an acceptance of the terms by conduct.[4]

.on the Web You can access the Uniform Commercial Code, including Article 2, at the Web site of the University of Pennsylvania Law School. Go to

http://www.law.upenn.edu/bll/ulc/ulc.htm.

In many cases, the courts have enforced the terms of shrink-wrap agreements the same as the terms of other contracts. Some courts have reasoned that by including the terms with the product, the seller proposed a contract that the buyer could accept by using the product after having an opportunity to read the terms. Also, it seems practical from a business's point of view to enclose a full statement of the legal terms of a sale with the product rather than to read the statement over the phone, for example, when a buyer calls in an order for the product.

Shrink-Wrap Terms That May Not Be Enforced Not all of the terms included in shrink-wrap agreements have been enforced, however. One important consideration is whether the parties form their contract before or after the seller communicates the terms of the shrink-wrap agreement to the buyer. If a court finds that the buyer learned of the shrink-wrap terms *after* the parties entered into a contract, the court may conclude that those terms were proposals for additional terms and were not part of the contract unless the buyer expressly agreed to them.[5] Could any other problems arise with shrink-wrap agreements? For a discussion of a case involving an issue that arose for one firm, see this chapter's *Adapting the Law to the Online Environment* feature on the following two pages.

Click-On Agreements As described earlier, a click-on agreement (also sometimes called a *click-on license* or *click-wrap agreement*) arises when a buyer, completing a transaction on a computer, indicates his or her assent to be bound by the terms of an offer by clicking on a button that says, for example, "I agree." The terms may be contained on a Web site through which the buyer is obtaining goods or services, or they may appear on a computer screen when software is loaded. Exhibit 10–1 on the next page contains the language of a click-on agreement that accompanies a package of software made and marketed by Microsoft.

3. *Restatement (Second) of Contracts,* Section 19.
4. For a leading case on this issue, see *ProCD, Inc. v. Zeidenberg,* 86 F.3d 1447 (7th Cir. 1996).
5. See, for example, *Klocek v. Gateway, Inc.,* 104 F.Supp.2d 1332 (D.Kan. 2000).

EXHIBIT 10–1 A CLICK-ON AGREEMENT

This exhibit illustrates an online offer to form a contract. To accept the offer, the user simply scrolls down the page and clicks on the "Accept" box.

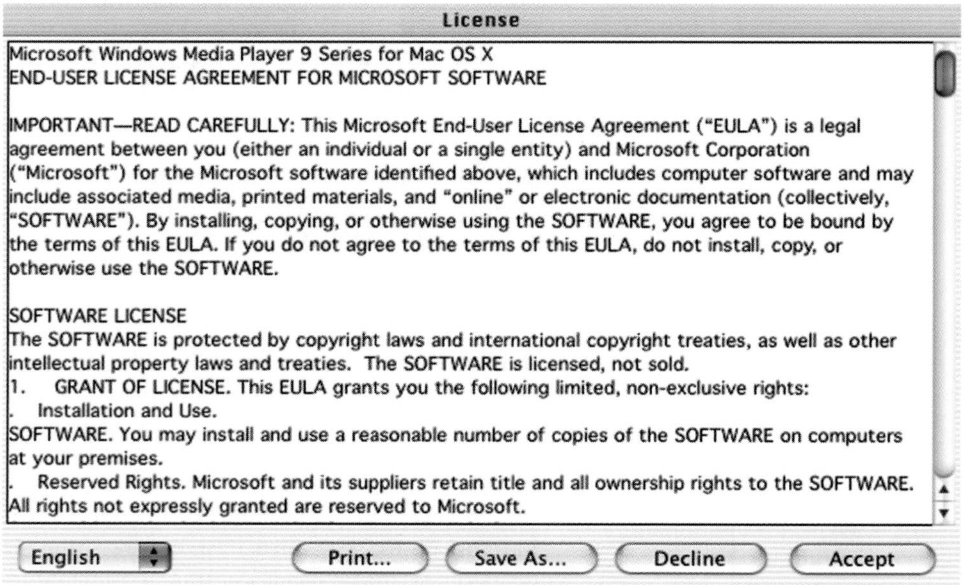
License

Microsoft Windows Media Player 9 Series for Mac OS X
END-USER LICENSE AGREEMENT FOR MICROSOFT SOFTWARE

IMPORTANT—READ CAREFULLY: This Microsoft End-User License Agreement ("EULA") is a legal agreement between you (either an individual or a single entity) and Microsoft Corporation ("Microsoft") for the Microsoft software identified above, which includes computer software and may include associated media, printed materials, and "online" or electronic documentation (collectively, "SOFTWARE"). By installing, copying, or otherwise using the SOFTWARE, you agree to be bound by the terms of this EULA. If you do not agree to the terms of this EULA, do not install, copy, or otherwise use the SOFTWARE.

SOFTWARE LICENSE
The SOFTWARE is protected by copyright laws and international copyright treaties, as well as other intellectual property laws and treaties. The SOFTWARE is licensed, not sold.
1. GRANT OF LICENSE. This EULA grants you the following limited, non-exclusive rights:
. Installation and Use.
SOFTWARE. You may install and use a reasonable number of copies of the SOFTWARE on computers at your premises.
. Reserved Rights. Microsoft and its suppliers retain title and all ownership rights to the SOFTWARE. All rights not expressly granted are reserved to Microsoft.

English | Print... | Save As... | Decline | Accept

ADAPTING THE LAW TO THE ONLINE ENVIRONMENT

Avoiding Deception in Software Sales

Sometimes, businesspersons who include shrink-wrap licenses with their products may have some terms elsewhere, such as on a disk or on a download page of the Internet. Not including all of the terms in the shrink-wrap agreement, however, can lead to problems—as one software producer learned when the state of New York brought an action against its company for fraud.

THE LAWSUIT AGAINST NETWORK ASSOCIATES, INC.

Network Associates, Inc. (NA), develops and sells software, including Gauntlet, a software firewall product, via the Internet. NA included on its disks and on its Internet download page—but not in its license agreement that accompanied its products—a restrictive clause.

The restrictive clause provided that anyone installing the Gauntlet software accepted the terms and conditions of the license agreement in the box and urged users to read the license before installing the software. The clause also stated, among other things, that the customer "will not publish reviews of this product without prior consent from Network Associates." The problem was that the license agreement in the box stated that the agreement contained all of the rights and duties of the parties. How, then, did the restrictive clause apply to the sale?

When *Network World Fusion,* an online magazine, published a comparative review of firewall software products, including NA's Gauntlet, without NA's permission, NA protested. Ultimately, the state attorney general of New York brought an action against NA for fraud.

THE FRAUD ISSUE

According to the New York court hearing the case, NA's restrictive clause misled customers and was thus deceptive. First, the license agreement stated that it contained all of the terms of the agreement. Therefore, the rules and regulations listed in the restrictive clause appeared to be

ADAPTING THE LAW TO THE ONLINE ENVIRONMENT—Continued

Avoiding Deception in Software Sales—Continued

independent of the license contract. This could mislead purchasers of the software because they might believe that the restriction was created by some other entity, such as the federal government.

For these reasons, the court concluded that the restrictive clause was deceptive and constituted fraud. The court ordered NA to stop including the clause in its software. The court also ordered NA to reveal "the number of instances in which software was sold on disks or through the Internet containing the above-mentioned language in order for the court to determine what, if any, penalties and costs should be ordered."[a]

FOR CRITICAL ANALYSIS

What is the difference, if any, between reading a restrictive clause in a shrink-wrap agreement and accessing it through a link as part of a click-on agreement?

a. *People v. Network Associates, Inc.*, 195 Misc.2d 384, 758 N.Y.S.2d 466 (2003).

Generally, under the law governing contracts, including sales and lease contracts under the UCC, there is no requirement that all of the terms in a contract must actually have been read by all of the parties to be effective. For example, clicking on a button or box that states "I accept" to certain terms can be enough.

In the following case, the court considered the enforceability of a click-on (click-wrap) agreement under Article 2 of the UCC.

CASE 10.1 i.LAN Systems, Inc. v. NetScout Service Level Corp.

United States District Court,
District of Massachusetts, 2002.
183 F.Supp.2d 328.

COMPANY PROFILE *i.LAN Systems, Inc.* (**http://www.ilan.com**)*, helps companies monitor their computer networks. Based in Los Angeles, California, with a staff that includes approximately forty technicians, i.LAN can troubleshoot network problems almost anywhere in the world. Over the Internet, many problems can be solved remotely using the software tools already built into a network. These tools include software designed and sold by NetScout Service Level Corporation, formerly known as NextPoint Networks, Inc.*

FACTS A click-wrap provision in the NextPoint software states that the seller's liability is limited to the price paid for the software unless a different term is "specifically accepted by NextPoint in writing." In 1998, i.LAN and NextPoint signed an agreement under which i.LAN agreed to resell the software. In 1999, under a different purchase order, i.LAN bought what it thought was the unlimited right to rent, rather than sell, the software, complete with perpetual upgrades and technical support. When NextPoint disputed this interpretation, i.LAN filed a suit in a federal district court, alleging, among other things, breach of contract. i.LAN sought specific performance (a remedy in which a court orders the breaching party to perform as specified in the contract—see Chapter 9) that included unlimited upgrades and support. The defendant argued that even if the allegations were true, the click-wrap provision limited its liability to the price paid for the software. Both parties filed motions for summary judgment.

ISSUE Was the click-wrap agreement enforceable?

DECISION Yes. The court denied the plaintiff's motion for summary judgment and instead issued a summary judgment in favor of the defendant (NextPoint).

REASON The court reasoned that the plaintiff agreed to the click-wrap terms when it clicked on the "I agree"

(Continued)

CASE 10.1—Continued

box. Those terms effectively limited the defendant's liability. In the words of the court, "pursuant to UCC 2–204, the analysis is simple: i.LAN manifested assent to the click-wrap license agreement when it clicked on the box stating 'I agree,' so the agreement is enforceable."[a] The court reasoned that "money now, terms later" forms a contract when the purchaser receives the box of software, sees the license agreement, and does not return the software. The court noted that "money now, terms later" is a practical way to form contracts, especially with purchasers of software. The court concluded that if it is "correct to enforce a shrink-wrap license agreement, where any assent is implicit, then it must also be correct to enforce a click-wrap license agreement, where the assent is explicit."

a. As pointed out earlier, under UCC 2–204 a contract "may be made in any manner sufficient to show agreement, including conduct by both parties which recognizes the existence of such a contract."

FOR CRITICAL ANALYSIS—Economic Consideration *If click-wrap agreements were not enforceable, what would be the effect on the software industry?*

BROWSE-WRAP TERMS
Terms and conditions of use that are presented to an Internet user at the time certain products, such as software, are being downloaded but that need not be agreed to (by clicking "I agree," for example) before the user is able to install or use the product.

Browse-Wrap Terms Like the terms of a click-on agreement, **browse-wrap terms** can occur in a transaction conducted over the Internet. Unlike a click-on agreement, however, browse-wrap terms do not require an Internet user to assent to the terms before, say, downloading or using certain software. In other words, a person can install the software without clicking "I agree" to the terms of a license. Offerors of browse-wrap terms generally assert that the terms are binding without the user's active consent.

Critics contend that browse-wrap terms are not enforceable because they do not satisfy the basic elements of contract formation. It has been suggested that to form a valid contract online, a user must at least be presented with the terms before indicating assent.[6] With respect to a browse-wrap term, this would require that a user navigate past it and agree to it before being able to obtain whatever is being granted to the user.

The following case involved the enforceability of a clause in an agreement that the court characterized as a browse-wrap license.

6. American Bar Association Committee on the Law of Cyberspace, "Click-Through Agreements: Strategies for Avoiding Disputes on the Validity of Assent" (document presented at the annual American Bar Association meeting in August 2001).

CASE 10.2 Specht v. Netscape Communications Corp.

United States District Court,
Southern District of New York, 2001.
150 F.Supp.2d 585.

FACTS Netscape Communications Corporation's "SmartDownload" software makes it easier for users to download files from the Internet without losing progress if they pause to do some other task or their Internet connection is interrupted. Netscape offers SmartDownload free of charge on its Web site to those who indicate, by clicking the mouse in a designated box, that they wish to obtain it. John Gibson clicked in the box and downloaded the software. On the Web site's download page is a reference to a license agreement that is visible only by scrolling to the next screen. Affirmatively indicating assent to the agreement is not required to download the software. The agreement provides that any disputes arising from use of the software are to be submitted to arbitration in California. Believing that the use of SmartDownload transmits private information about its users, Gibson and others filed a suit in a federal district court in New York against Netscape, alleging violations of federal law. Netscape asked the court to order the parties to arbitration in California, according to the license agreement.

ISSUE Was the arbitration clause in the license agreement enforceable?

DECISION No. The court denied the motion to compel arbitration.

REASON The court applied UCC Article 2 because "[a]lthough in this case the product was provided free of charge, the roles are essentially the same as when an individual uses the Internet to purchase software from a

CASE 10.2—Continued
company: here, the Plaintiff requested Defendant's product by clicking on an icon marked 'Download,' and Defendant then tendered the product." The court emphasized that unless the plaintiffs agreed to the license contract, they could not be bound by the arbitration clause. The court discussed the forms of license agreements that accompany sales of software (shrink-wrap, click-on, and browse-wrap licenses) and their enforceability, and characterized Netscape's license in this case as a browse-wrap license. According to the court, Netscape's SmartDownload "allows a user to download and use the software without taking any action that plainly manifests assent to the terms of the associated license or indicates an understanding that a contract is being formed." The court pointed out that "the individual obtaining SmartDownload is not made aware that he is entering into a contract * * * . [T]he user need not view any license agreement terms or even any reference to a license agreement, and need not do anything to manifest assent." The court reasoned that the plaintiffs did not assent to the license agreement, and thus they were not subject to the arbitration clause.

WHY IS THIS CASE IMPORTANT? *The ruling in this case is significant because it marks an application of traditional contract principles to a type of dispute that can arise only in the online context. In the case, the court clearly applied a long-standing principle of contract law: a person will not be bound to an agreement to which he or she did not assent.*

E-Signatures

In many instances, a contract cannot be enforced unless it is signed by the party against whom enforcement is sought. A significant issue in the context of e-commerce has to do with how electronic signatures, or **e-signatures,** can be created and verified on e-contracts.

E-SIGNATURE
As defined by the Uniform Electronic Transactions Act, "an electronic sound, symbol, or process attached to or logically associated with a record and executed or adopted by a person with the intent to sign the record."

In the days when many people could not write, they signed documents with an "X." Then handwritten signatures became common, followed by typed signatures, printed signatures, and, most recently, digital signatures that are transmitted electronically. Throughout the evolution of signature technology, the question of what constitutes a valid signature has arisen again and again, and with good reason—without some consensus on what constitutes a valid signature, less business or legal work could be accomplished.

E-Signature Technologies

Today, numerous technologies allow electronic documents to be signed. These include digital signatures and alternative technologies.

Digital Signatures The most prevalent e-signature technology is the *asymmetric cryptosystem,* which creates a digital signature using two different (asymmetric) cryptographic "keys." With this system, a person attaches a digital signature to a document using a private key, or code. The key has a publicly available counterpart. Anyone with the appropriate software can use the public key to verify that the digital signature was made using the private key. A **cybernotary,** or legally recognized certification authority, issues the key pair, identifies the owner of the keys, and certifies the validity of the public key. The cybernotary also serves as a repository for public keys.

CYBERNOTARY
A legally recognized authority that can certify the validity of digital signatures.

Signature Dynamics With another type of signature technology, known as *signature dynamics,* a sender's signature is captured using a stylus and an electronic digitizer pad. A computer program takes the signature's measurements, the sender's identity,

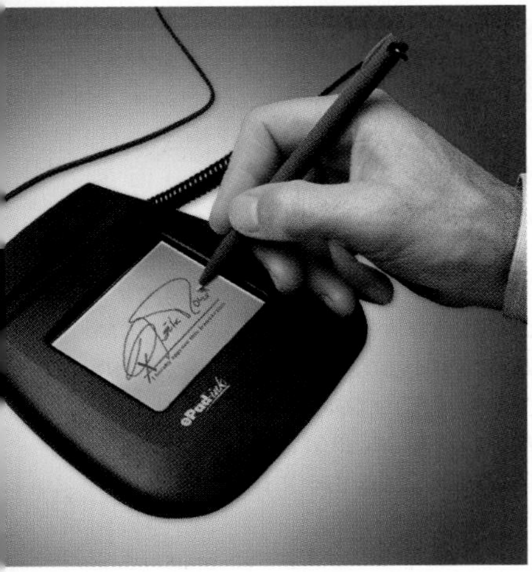

The ePad-Ink is an electronic signature pad that can be used to insert handwritten signatures into electronic documents. What type of e-signature technology does this device utilize? What procedure is used to verify the authenticity of a signature created using this ePad? (Photo courtesy of Interlink Electronics)

the time and date of the signature, and the identity of the hardware. This information is then placed in an encrypted *biometric token* attached to the document being transmitted. To verify the authenticity of the signature, the recipient of the document compares the measurements of the signature with the measurements in the token. When this type of e-signature is used, it is not necessary to have a third party verify the signatory's identity.

Other E-Signature Forms Other forms of e-signatures have been—or are now being—developed as well. ■ EXAMPLE 10.4 Some e-signatures use "smart cards." As you will read in Chapter 15, a smart card is a device the size of a credit card that is embedded with code and other data. Like credit and debit cards, a smart card can be inserted into computers to transfer information. Unlike those other cards, however, a smart card can be used to establish a person's identity as validly as a signature on a piece of paper. ■ In addition, technological innovations now under way will allow an e-signature to be evidenced by an image of a person's retina, fingerprint, or face that is scanned by a computer and then matched to a numeric code. The scanned image and the numeric code are registered with security companies that maintain files on an accessible server that can be used to authenticate a transaction.

STATE LAWS GOVERNING E-SIGNATURES

Most states have laws governing e-signatures. The problem is that the state e-signature laws are not uniform. Some states—California is a notable example—provide that many types of documents cannot be signed with e-signatures, while other states are more permissive. Additionally, some states recognize only digital signatures as valid, while others permit other types of e-signatures.

The National Conference of Commissioners on Uniform State Laws, in an attempt to create more uniformity among the states, promulgated the Uniform Electronic Transactions Act (UETA) in 1999. To date, the UETA has been adopted, at least in part, by more than forty states. The UETA provides, among other things, that a signature may not be denied legal effect or enforceability solely because it is in electronic form. (Other aspects of the UETA will be discussed shortly.)

FEDERAL LAW ON E-SIGNATURES AND E-DOCUMENTS

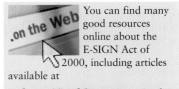

on the Web You can find many good resources online about the E-SIGN Act of 2000, including articles available at **http://archives.cnn.com/2000/ALLPOLITICS/stories/06/30/clinton.e.signatures.04/index.html** and **http://www.bizjournals.com/albany/stories/2000/09/11/editorial5.html**.

In 2000, Congress enacted the Electronic Signatures in Global and National Commerce Act (E-SIGN Act) to provide that no contract, record, or signature may be "denied legal effect" solely because it is in an electronic form. In other words, under this law, an electronic signature is as valid as a signature on paper, and an electronic document can be as enforceable as a paper one.

For an electronic signature to be enforceable, the contracting parties must have agreed to use electronic signatures. For an electronic document to be valid, it must be in a form that can be retained and accurately reproduced.

The E-SIGN Act does not apply to all types of documents, however. Contracts and documents that are exempt include court papers, divorce decrees, evictions, foreclosures, health-insurance terminations, prenuptial agreements, and wills. Also, the only agreements governed by the UCC that fall under this law are those covered by Articles 2 and 2A and UCC 1–107 and 1–206.

Despite these limitations, the E-SIGN Act greatly expands the possibilities for contracting online. ■ EXAMPLE 10.5 From a remote location, anyone can now open an account with a financial institution, obtain a mortgage or other loan, buy insurance, and purchase real estate over the Internet. Payments and transfers of funds can be done entirely online. Thus, using e-contracts can avoid the time and costs associated with producing, delivering, signing, and returning paper documents. ■

At issue in the following case was whether an exchange of e-mail between the representatives of a seller and its buyers constituted a "writing."

CASE 10.3 In re Cafeteria Operators, L.P.[a]

United States Bankruptcy Court,
Northern District of Texas, 2003.
299 Bankr. 411.

FACTS Under the Perishable Agricultural Commodities Act (PACA) of 1930, a seller of fruits and vegetables has a right to the proceeds from their sale but loses this right if he or she agrees in *writing* to extend the time for payment beyond thirty days. Cafeteria Operators, L.P., operates cafeterias primarily in the Southwest. In 2002, Cafeteria Operators and other buyers ordered cherries from Cherrco, Inc., a wholesale food distributor, through Tim Dent of George E. Dent Sales, Inc. Cherrco bought the fruit from Peterson Farms, Inc., and others and delivered it as specified in invoices that required payment within thirty days. When the buyers failed to pay, Dent and Gene Baldwin, the buyers' representative, tried to negotiate a new payment schedule via e-mail. In January 2003, with $25,269.12 still owed, the buyers filed a petition in a federal bankruptcy court, seeking permission to pay less than this amount. Cherrco objected, asserting that it had a right to the full amount under PACA. The buyers claimed that Cherrco had waived this right in the e-mail exchanged between Dent and Baldwin. Cherrco argued in part that this e-mail was not a "writing."

ISSUE Did the e-mail exchanged between Dent and Baldwin constitute a "writing"?

DECISION Yes. The court rejected Cherrco's argument, holding that the e-mail constituted a "writing" under the E-SIGN Act. The court also held, however, that Cherrco had not waived its PACA right and awarded the seller the full amount of its claim.

REASON The court noted that an e-mail message to Dent from Sarah Peterson-Schlukebir, a Peterson Farms representative, stated, "[B]oth Peterson Farms and Cherrco are not willing to sign" a release of the original payment terms. "If we sign the release, we are no longer covered by PACA." Dent e-mailed this message to Baldwin, who, after further negotiations, e-mailed the last note between the parties, "[W]e do not need a formal [contract]. We will just start making the payments starting today. All we really want is the agreement from them that the payment plan is ok." The court quoted from the E-SIGN Act, which provides that "with respect to any transaction in or affecting interstate or foreign commerce * * * a contract * * * may not be denied legal effect, validity, or enforceability solely because an electronic signature or electronic record was used in its formation." In other words, in a transaction involving interstate commerce, e-mail can constitute a "writing." The court concluded, "The transactions between Cherrco and the Debtor[s] occurred in 2002, and clearly qualify for the requirement that the transaction is in or affects interstate commerce." Thus, the court concluded that the e-mails between the parties satisfied the writing requirement under PACA.

FOR CRITICAL ANALYSIS—Social Consideration *Did the e-mail between Dent and Baldwin constitute an agreement between the parties to extend the original payment terms beyond thirty days? Why or why not?*

a. *L.P.* stands for "limited partnership," a special form of business organization discussed in Chapter 19.

Partnering Agreements

PARTNERING AGREEMENT
An agreement between a seller and a buyer who frequently do business with each other concerning the terms and conditions that will apply to all subsequently formed electronic contracts.

One way that online sellers and buyers can prevent disputes over signatures in their e-contracts, as well as disputes over the terms and conditions of those contracts, is to form partnering agreements. In a **partnering agreement,** a seller and a buyer who frequently do business with each other agree in advance on the terms and conditions that will apply to all transactions subsequently conducted electronically. The partnering agreement can also establish special access and identification codes to be used by the parties when transacting business electronically.

A partnering agreement reduces the likelihood that disputes will arise under the contract because the buyer and the seller have agreed in advance to the terms and conditions that will accompany each sale. Furthermore, if a dispute does arise, a court or arbitration forum will be able to refer to the partnering agreement when determining the parties' intent with respect to subsequent contracts. Of course, even with a partnering agreement fraud remains a possibility. If an unauthorized person uses a purchaser's designated access number and identification code, it may be some time before the problem is discovered.

The Uniform Electronic Transactions Act

As noted earlier, the Uniform Electronic Transactions Act (UETA) was promulgated in 1999. The UETA represents one of the first comprehensive efforts to create uniform laws pertaining to e-commerce.

The primary purpose of the UETA is to remove barriers to e-commerce by giving the same legal effect to electronic records and signatures as is currently given to paper documents and signatures. The UETA broadly defines an *e-signature* as "an electronic sound, symbol, or process attached to or logically associated with a record and executed or adopted by a person with the intent to sign the record."[7] An e-signature includes encrypted digital signatures, names (intended as signatures) at the ends of e-mail messages, and "clicks" on a Web page if the click includes the identification of the person. A **record** is "information that is inscribed on a tangible medium or that is stored in an electronic or other medium and is retrievable in perceivable [visual] form."[8]

RECORD
According to the Uniform Electronic Transactions Act, information that is either inscribed on a tangible medium or stored in an electronic or other medium and that is retrievable. The Uniform Computer Information Transactions Act also uses the term *record* instead of *writing.*

THE SCOPE AND APPLICABILITY OF THE UETA

The UETA does not create new rules for electronic contracts but rather establishes that records, signatures, and contracts may not be denied enforceability solely due to their electronic form. The UETA does not apply to all writings and signatures but only to electronic records and electronic signatures *relating to a transaction.* A *transaction* is defined as an interaction between two or more people relating to business, commercial, or governmental activities.[9]

The act specifically does not apply to laws governing wills or testamentary trusts, to the UCC (other than Articles 2 and 2A), or to the Uniform Computer Information Transactions Act (discussed later in this chapter).[10] In addition, the provisions of the UETA allow the states to exclude its application to other areas of law.

As described earlier, Congress passed the E-SIGN Act in 2000, a year after the UETA was presented to the states for adoption. Thus, a significant issue is whether and to what extent the federal E-SIGN Act preempts the UETA as adopted by the states.

.on the Web The Web site of the National Conference of Commissioners on Uniform State Laws includes an update of the list of states that have adopted the UETA or considered it for adoption. The site also contains a summary of the act and "Question and Answer" sections concerning this law. Go to **http://www.nccusl.org**.

THE FEDERAL E-SIGN ACT AND THE UETA

The E-SIGN Act refers explicitly to the UETA and provides that if a state has enacted the uniform version of the UETA, it is not preempted by the E-SIGN Act.[11]

7. UETA 102(8).
8. UETA 102(15).
9. UETA 2(12) and 3.
10. UETA 3(b).
11. 15 U.S.C. Section 7002(2)(A)(i).

In other words, if the state has enacted the UETA *without modification,* state law will govern. The problem is that many states have enacted nonuniform (modified) versions of the UETA, largely for the purpose of excluding other areas of state law from the UETA's terms. The E-SIGN Act specifies that those exclusions will be preempted to the extent that they are inconsistent with the E-SIGN Act's provisions.

The E-SIGN Act, however, explicitly allows the states to enact alternative requirements for the use of electronic records or electronic signatures. Generally, though, the requirements must be consistent with the provisions of the E-SIGN Act, and the state must not give greater legal status or effect to one specific type of technology. Additionally, if a state has enacted alternative requirements *after* the E-SIGN Act was adopted, the state law must specifically refer to the E-SIGN Act. The relationship between the UETA and the E-SIGN Act is illustrated in Exhibit 10–2.

HIGHLIGHTS OF THE UETA

We look next at selected provisions of the UETA. Our discussion is, of course, based on the act's uniform provisions. Keep in mind that the states that have enacted the UETA may have adopted slightly different versions.

The Parties Must Agree to Conduct Transactions Electronically The UETA will not apply to a transaction unless each of the parties has previously agreed to conduct transactions by electronic means. The agreement need not be explicit, however, and it may be implied by the conduct of the parties and the surrounding circumstances.[12] In the comments that accompany the UETA, the drafters stated that it may be reasonable to infer that a person who gives out a business card with an

12. UETA 5(b).

EXHIBIT 10–2 THE E-SIGN ACT AND THE UETA

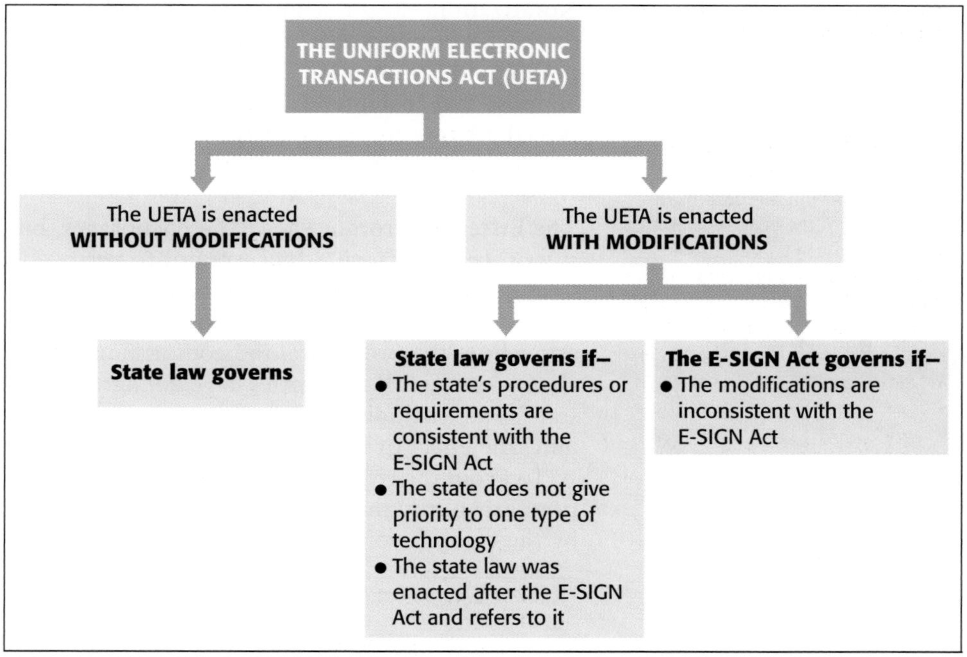

e-mail address on it has consented to transact business electronically.[13] The parties' agreement may also be inferred from a letter or other writing, as well as from some verbal communications.

A person who has previously agreed to an electronic transaction can also withdraw his or her consent and refuse to conduct further business electronically. Additionally, the act expressly gives parties the power to vary the UETA's provisions by contract. In other words, *parties can opt out of all or some of the terms of the UETA*. If the parties do not opt out of the terms of the UETA, however, the UETA will govern their electronic transactions.

Attribution In the context of electronic transactions, the term *attribution* refers to the procedures that may be used to ensure that the person sending an electronic record is the same person whose e-signature accompanies the record. Under the UETA, if an electronic record or signature is the act of a particular person, the record or signature may be attributed to that person. If a person types her or his name at the bottom of an e-mail purchase order, that name would qualify as a "signature" and be attributed to the person whose name appeared. Just as in paper contracts, one may use any relevant evidence to prove that the record or signature is or is not the act of the person.[14]

Note that even if an individual's name does not appear on a record, the UETA states that the effect of the record is to be determined from the context and surrounding circumstances. In other words, a record may have legal effect even if no one has signed it. ■ **EXAMPLE 10.6** Suppose that Darby sends a fax to Corina. The fax contains a letterhead identifying Darby as the sender, but the document is not signed by Darby. Depending on the circumstances, the fax may be attributed to Darby. ■

The UETA does not contain any express provisions about what constitutes fraud or whether an agent (a person who acts on behalf of another—see Chapter 17) is authorized to enter into a contract. Under the UETA, other state laws control if any issues relating to agency, authority, forgery, or contract formation arise.

Notarization If a document is required to be notarized under existing state law, the UETA provides that this requirement is satisfied by the electronic signature of a notary public or other person authorized to verify signatures. ■ **EXAMPLE 10.7** Suppose that Joel intends to accept an offer to purchase real estate via e-mail. Under the UETA, the requirement is satisfied if a notary public is present to verify Joel's identity and to affix an electronic signature to the e-mail acceptance. ■

.on the Web At the Web site of the Consumers Union, you can read an article discussing some concerns that consumer groups have about many of the provisions in the UETA. Go to **http://www.consumersunion.org/finance/899nclcwc.htm**.

The Effect of Errors The UETA encourages, but does not require, the use of security procedures (such as encryption) to verify changes to electronic documents and to correct errors. Section 10 of the UETA provides that if the parties have agreed to a security procedure and one party does not detect an error because he or she did not follow the procedure, the conforming party can legally avoid the effect of the change or error. If the parties have not agreed to use a security procedure, then other state laws (including contract law governing mistakes—see Chapter 9) will determine the effect of the error on the parties' agreement.

To avoid the effect of errors, a party must take certain steps. First, the party must promptly notify the other party of the error and of her or his intent not to be bound by the error. Second, the party must take reasonable steps to return any benefit or

13. UETA 5, Comment 4B.
14. UETA 9.

consideration received. Parties cannot avoid a transaction from which they have benefited. ■ EXAMPLE 10.8 Suppose that Marissa, as the result of an error, received access to valuable information. Because she cannot "give back" or make restitution for the valuable information she now knows, the transaction may be unavoidable. ■ In all other situations in which a change or error occurs in an electronic record (and the parties' agreement does not specifically address errors), the UETA states that the traditional law governing mistakes will apply.

Timing Section 15 of the UETA sets forth provisions relating to the sending and receiving of electronic records. These provisions apply unless the parties agree to different terms. Under Section 15, an electronic record is considered *sent* when it is properly directed to the intended recipient in a form readable by the recipient's computer system. Once the electronic record leaves the control of the sender or comes under the control of the recipient, the UETA deems it to have been sent. An electronic record is considered *received* when it enters the recipient's processing system in a readable form—*even if no individual is aware of its receipt.*

Additionally, the UETA provides that, unless otherwise agreed, an electronic record is to be sent from or received at the party's principal place of business. If a party has no place of business, the provision then authorizes the place of sending or receipt to be the party's residence. If a party has multiple places of business, the record should be sent from or received at the location that has the closest relationship to the underlying transaction.

The Uniform Computer Information Transactions Act

COMPUTER INFORMATION
As defined by the Uniform Computer Information Transactions Act, "information in an electronic form obtained from or through use of a computer, or that is in digital or an equivalent form capable of being processed by a computer."

The National Conference of Commissioners on Uniform State Laws (NCCUSL) promulgated the Uniform Computer Information Transactions Act (UCITA) in 1999. The primary purpose of the UCITA is to validate e-contracts to license or purchase software, or contracts that give access to—or allow the distribution of—**computer information.** The UCITA is controversial, and only two states (Maryland and Virginia) have adopted it, while four states (Iowa, North Carolina, Vermont, and West Virginia) have passed anti–UCITA provisions. In 2003, the NCCUSL withdrew its support of the UCITA. Although the UCITA remains a legal resource, the NCCUSL will no longer seek its adoption by the states, which are thus unlikely to consider it further.

APPLICATION How Can You Find and Use Online Contract Forms?*

Before the printing press, every contract form had to be handwritten. Since the advent of printing, however, most standard contract forms have been readily available at low cost. Now the Internet has made available an even larger variety of contract forms, as well as other legal and business forms.

* This *Application* is not meant to substitute for the services of an attorney who is licensed to practice law in your state.

WHERE TO OBTAIN ONLINE CONTRACT FORMS

The 'Lectric Law Library has a collection of forms at **http://www.lectlaw.com/form.html**. The site includes forms for the assignment of a contract, a contract for the sale of a motor vehicle, and many others. In addition to actual forms, there are comments on how the forms should be used and filled out. Another excellent online resource for

(Continued)

APPLICATION How Can You Find and Use Online Contract Forms?—Continued

various types of forms is FindForms, at http://www.findforms.com.

Other online forms collections can be found at LegalWiz.com (go to http://www.legalwiz.com/forms.htm), a Web site that provides free legal forms, including a form that can be used to sell personal property. At http://www.legaldocs.com, you will find an electronic forms book that offers hundreds of standardized legal forms, some of which are free. Washburn University School of Law has a Web page containing links to an extensive number of forms archives at http://www.washlaw.edu/legalforms.

A special Web site for small-business owners is http://www.lawvantage.com/index.shtml. Some documents are free; others require a fee or an annual subscription. Many law firms post legal forms, including contract forms, on their Web sites. For example, see the Web site of Bornstein & Naylor (at http://lbnlaw.com/Freedownload2.htm).

Finally, a number of forms are available from FindLaw. Go to http://forms.lp.findlaw.com and scroll down the screen to "Other Form Resources." FindLaw is now a part of West Group.

CHECKLIST FOR THE ONLINE SELLER

1. When looking for a contract form appropriate to your business, "shop around" for a form that most closely meets your needs.
2. Consider customizing any standardized contract form that you use to ensure that it will cover all of the contingencies that you deem important.
3. When using a standardized contract form, make sure that you provide for a means of acceptance—for example, by including a box stating "I accept" or "I agree."
4. Consider posting your own customized contract forms on your Web site for prospective customers or others to use.

KEY TERMS

CHAPTER SUMMARY E-Contracts

Online Offers (See pages 307–308.)	Businesspersons who present contract offers via the Internet should keep in mind that the terms of the offer should be just as inclusive as the terms in an offer made in a written (paper) document. All possible contingencies should be anticipated and provided for in the offer. Because jurisdictional issues frequently arise with online transactions, it is particularly important to include dispute-settlement provisions in the offer, as well as a forum-selection clause. The offer should be displayed in an easily readable and clear format. An online offer should also include some mechanism, such as an "I agree" or "I accept" box, by which the customer may accept the offer.

CHAPTER SUMMARY E-Contracts—Continued

Online Acceptances (See pages 308–313.)	1. *Shrink-wrap agreement*— a. Definition—An agreement whose terms are expressed inside a box in which the goods are packaged. The party who opens the box is informed that, by keeping the goods that are in the box, he or she agrees to the terms of the shrink-wrap agreement. b. Enforceability—The courts have often enforced shrink-wrap agreements, even if the purchaser-user of the goods did not read the terms of the agreement. A court may deem a shrink-wrap agreement unenforceable, however, if the buyer learns of the shrink-wrap terms *after* the parties entered into the agreement. 2. *Click-on agreement*— a. Definition—An agreement created when a buyer, completing a transaction on a computer, is required to indicate her or his assent to be bound by the terms of an offer by clicking on a button that says, for example, "I agree." The terms of the agreement may appear on the Web site through which the buyer is obtaining goods or services, or they may appear on a computer screen when software is downloaded. b. Enforceability—The courts have enforced click-on agreements, holding that by clicking "I agree," the offeree has indicated acceptance by conduct. Browse-wrap terms, however (terms in a license that an Internet user does not have to read prior to downloading the product, such as software), may not be enforced on the ground that the user is not made aware that he or she is entering into a contract.
E-Signatures (See pages 313–315.)	1. *Definition*—The Uniform Electronic Transactions Act (UETA) defines the term *e-signature* as "an electronic sound, symbol, or process attached to or logically associated with a record and executed or adopted by a person with the intent to sign the record." 2. *E-signature technologies*—These include the *asymmetric cryptosystem* (which creates a digital signature using two different cryptographic "keys"); *signature dynamics* (which involves capturing a sender's signature using a stylus and an electronic digitizer pad); a *smart card* (a device the size of a credit card that is embedded with code and other data); and, probably in the near future, scanned images of retinas, fingerprints, or other physical characteristics that are linked to numeric codes. 3. *State laws governing e-signatures*—Although most states have laws governing e-signatures, these laws are not uniform. The UETA provides for the validity of e-signatures and may ultimately create more uniformity among the states in this respect. 4. *Federal law on e-signatures and e-documents*—The Electronic Signatures in Global and National Commerce Act (E-SIGN Act) of 2000 gave validity to e-signatures by providing that no contract, record, or signature may be "denied legal effect" solely because it is in an electronic form.
Partnering Agreements (See pages 315–316.)	To reduce the likelihood that disputes will arise under their e-contracts, parties who frequently do business with each other may form a *partnering agreement.* In effect, the parties agree in advance on the terms and conditions that will apply to all transactions subsequently conducted electronically. The agreement can also establish access and identification codes to be used by the parties when transacting business electronically.
The Uniform Electronic Transactions Act (UETA) (See pages 316–319.)	1. *Definition*—A uniform act submitted to the states for adoption by the National Conference of Commissioners on Uniform State Laws (NCCUSL). 2. *Purpose*—To create rules to support the enforcement of e-contracts. Under the UETA, contracts entered into online, as well as other documents, are presumed to be valid. The UETA does not apply to transactions governed by the UCC or to wills or testamentary trusts.

(Continued)

CHAPTER SUMMARY E-Contracts—Continued

The Uniform Computer Information Transactions Act (See page 319.)	1. *Definition*—A uniform act previously submitted to the states for adoption by the NCCUSL. The NCCUSL withdrew its support in 2003. 2. *Purpose*—To validate e-contracts to license or purchase software, or contracts that give access to—or allow the distribution of—computer information.

FOR REVIEW

Answers for the even-numbered questions in this For Review *section can be found in Appendix I at the end of this text.*

1. What are some important clauses to include when making offers to form electronic contracts, or e-contracts?
2. How do shrink-wrap and click-on agreements differ from other contracts? How have traditional laws been applied to these agreements?
3. What is an electronic signature? Are electronic signatures valid?
4. What is a partnering agreement? What purpose does it serve?
5. What is the Uniform Electronic Transactions Act (UETA)? What are some of the major provisions of this act?

QUESTIONS AND CASE PROBLEMS

10–1. Click-On Agreements. Paul is a financial analyst for King Investments, Inc., a brokerage firm. He uses the Internet to investigate the background and activities of companies that might be good investments for King's customers. While visiting the Web site of Business Research, Inc., Paul sees on his screen a message that reads, "Welcome to businessresearch.com. By visiting our site, you have been entered as a subscriber to our e-publication, *Companies Unlimited*. This publication will be sent to you daily at a cost of $7.50 per week. An invoice will be included with *Companies Unlimited* every four weeks. You may cancel your subscription at any time." Has Paul entered into an enforceable contract to pay for *Companies Unlimited?* Why or why not?

10–2. Click-On Agreements. Anne is a reporter for *Daily Business Journal,* a print publication consulted by investors and other businesspersons. She often uses the Internet to perform research for the articles that she writes for the publication. While visiting the Web site of Cyberspace Investments Corp., Anne reads a pop-up window that states, "Our business newsletter, *E-Commerce Weekly,* is available at a one-year subscription rate of $5 per issue. To subscribe, enter your e-mail address below and click 'SUBSCRIBE.' By subscribing, you agree to the terms of the subscriber's agreement. To read this agreement, click 'AGREEMENT.' " Anne enters her e-mail address, but does not click on "AGREEMENT" to read the terms. Has Anne entered into an enforceable contract to pay for *E-Commerce Weekly?* Explain.

10–3. Online Acceptance. Bob, a sales representative for Central Computer Co., occasionally uses the Internet to obtain information about his customers and to look for new sales leads. While visiting the Web site of Marketing World, Inc., Bob is presented with an on-screen message that offers, "To improve your ability to make deals, read our monthly online magazine, *Sales Genius,* available at a subscription rate of $15 a month. To subscribe, fill in your name, company name, and e-mail address below, and click 'YES!' By clicking 'YES!' you agree to the terms of the subscription contract. To read this contract, click 'TERMS.'" Among those terms is a clause that allows Marketing World to charge interest for subscription bills not paid within a certain time. The terms also prohibit subscribers from copying or distributing part or all of *Sales Genius* in any form. Bob subscribes without reading the terms. Marketing World later files a suit against Bob, based on his failure to pay for his subscription. Should the court hold that Bob is obligated to pay interest on the amount? Explain.

10–4. Shrink-Wrap/Click-On Agreements. 1-A Equipment Co. signed a sales order to lease Accware 10 User NT software, which is made and marketed by ICode, Inc. Just above the signature line, the order stated: "Thank you for your order. No returns or refunds will be issued for software license and/or services. All sales are final. Please read the End User License and Service Agreement." The software was delivered in a sealed envelope inside a box. On the outside of the envelope, an "End

User Agreement" provided in part, "BY OPENING THIS PACKAGING, CLICKING YOUR ACCEPTANCE OF THE AGREEMENT DURING DOWNLOAD OR INSTALLATION OF THIS PRODUCT, OR BY USING ANY PART OF THIS PRODUCT, YOU AGREE TO BE LEGALLY BOUND BY THE TERMS OF THE AGREEMENT. . . . This agreement will be governed by the laws in force in the Commonwealth of Virginia . . . and exclusive venue for any litigation shall be in Virginia." Later, dissatisfied with the software, 1-A filed a suit in a Massachusetts state court against ICode, alleging breach of contract and misrepresentation. ICode asked the court to dismiss the case on the basis of the "End User Agreement." Is the agreement enforceable? Should the court dismiss the suit? Why or why not? [*1-A Equipment Co. v. ICode, Inc.*, 43 UCC Rep.Serv.2d 807 (Mass.Dist. 2000)]

CASE PROBLEM WITH SAMPLE ANSWER

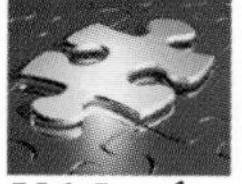

10–5. Peerless Wall & Window Coverings, Inc., is a small business in Pennsylvania. To run the cash registers in its stores, manage inventory, and link the stores electronically, in 1994 Peerless installed Point of Sale V6.5 software produced by Synchronics, Inc., a small corporation in Tennessee that develops and markets business software. Point of Sale V6.5 was written with code that used only a two-digit year field—for example, 1999 was stored as "99." This meant that all dates were interpreted as falling within the twentieth century (2001, stored as "01," would be mistaken for 1901). In other words, Point of Sale V6.5 was not "Year 2000" (Y2K) compliant. The software was licensed under a shrink-wrap agreement printed on the envelopes containing the disks. The agreement included a clause that, among other things, limited remedies to replacement within ninety days if there was a defect in the disks and stated, "The entire risk as to the quality and performance of the Software is with you." In 1995, Synchronics stopped selling and supporting Point of Sale V6.5. Two years later, Synchronics told Peerless that the software was not Y2K compliant and should be replaced. Peerless sued Synchronics in a federal district court, alleging, in part, breach of contract. Synchronics filed a motion for summary judgment. Who is more likely to bear the cost of replacing the software? Why? [*Peerless Wall & Window Coverings, Inc. v. Synchronics, Inc.*, 85 F.Supp.2d 519 (W.D.Pa. 2000), aff'd 234 F.3d 1265 (3d Cir. 2000)]

After you have answered this problem, compare your answer with the sample answer given on the Web site that accompanies this text. Go to <u>http://blt.westbuslaw.com</u>, select "Chapter 10," and click on "Case Problem with Sample Answer."

10–6. Click-On Agreements. America Online, Inc. (AOL), provided e-mail service to Walter Hughes and other members under a click-on agreement titled "Terms of Service." This agreement consisted of three parts: a "Member Agreement," "Community Guidelines," and a "Privacy Policy." The "Member Agreement" included a forum-selection clause that read, "You expressly agree that exclusive jurisdiction for any claim or dispute with AOL or relating in any way to your membership or your use of AOL resides in the courts of Virginia." When Officer Thomas McMenamon of the Methuen, Massachusetts, Police Department received threatening e-mail sent from an AOL account, he requested and obtained from AOL Hughes's name and other personal information. Hughes filed a suit in a federal district court against AOL, which filed a motion to dismiss on the basis of the forum-selection clause. Considering that the clause was a click-on provision, is it enforceable? Explain. [*Hughes v. McMenamon*, 204 F.Supp.2d 178 (D.Mass. 2002)]

10–7. Shrink-Wrap Agreements/Browse-Wrap Terms. Mary DeFontes bought a computer and a service contract from Dell Computers Corp. DeFontes was charged $950.51, of which $13.51 was identified on the invoice as "tax." This amount was paid to the state of Rhode Island. DeFontes and other Dell customers filed a suit in a Rhode Island state court against Dell, claiming that Dell was overcharging its customers by collecting a tax on service contracts and transportation costs. Dell asked the court to order DeFontes to submit the dispute to arbitration. Dell cited its "Terms and Conditions Agreement," which provides in part that by accepting delivery of Dell's products or services, a customer agrees to submit any dispute to arbitration. Customers can view this agreement through an *inconspicuous* link at the bottom of Dell's Web site, and Dell encloses a copy with an order when it is shipped. Dell argued that DeFontes accepted these terms by failing to return her purchase within thirty days, although the agreement did not state this. Is DeFontes bound to the "Terms and Conditions Agreement"? Should the court grant Dell's request? Why or why not? [*DeFontes v. Dell Computers Corp.*, __ A.2d __ (R.I. 2004)]

A QUESTION OF ETHICS

10–8. Over the phone, Rich and Enza Hill ordered a computer from Gateway 2000, Inc. Inside the box were the computer and a list of contract terms, which provided that the terms governed the transaction unless the customers returned the computer within thirty days. Among those terms was a clause that required any claims to be submitted to arbitration. The Hills kept the computer for more than thirty days before complaining to Gateway about the computer's components and its performance. When the matter was not resolved to their satisfaction, the Hills filed a suit in a federal district court against Gateway, arguing, among other things, that the computer was defective. Gateway asked the court to enforce the arbitration clause. The Hills claimed that this term was not part of a contract to buy the computer because the list on which it appeared had been in the box and they did not see the list until after the computer was delivered. In view of these facts, consider the following questions. [*Hill v. Gateway 2000, Inc.*, 105 F.3d 1147 (7th Cir. 1997)]

1. Should the court enforce the arbitration clause in this case? If you were the judge, how would you rule on this issue?
2. In your opinion, do shrink-wrap agreements impose too great a burden on purchasers? Why or why not?

3. An ongoing complaint about shrink-wrap and click-wrap agreements is that all too often the terms of these agreements go unread. Should purchasers be bound in contract by terms that they have not even read? Why or why not?

FOR CRITICAL ANALYSIS

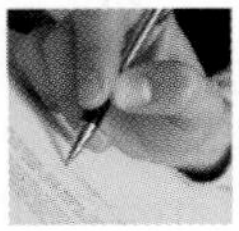

10–9. Would you say that, on balance, most of the legal issues presented by e-commerce and e-contracting are unique to the cyber age or simply old legal issues in a new form?

VIDEO QUESTION

DIGITAL VIDEO LIBRARY WEST LEGAL STUDIES IN BUSINESS

10–10. Go to this text's Web site at **http://blt.westbuslaw.com** and select "Chapter 10." Click on "Video Questions" and view the video titled *E-Contracts: Agreeing Online.* Then answer the following questions.

1. According to the instructor in the video, what is the key factor in determining whether a particular term in an online agreement is enforceable?
2. Suppose that you click on "I accept" in order to download software from the Internet. You do not read the terms of the agreement before accepting it, even though you know that such agreements often contain forum-selection and arbitration clauses. The software later causes irreparable harm to your computer system, and you want to sue. When you go to the Web site and view the agreement, however, you discover that a choice-of-law clause in the contract specified that the law of Nigeria controls. Is this term enforceable? Is it a term that should reasonably be expected in an online contract?
3. Does it matter what the term actually says if it is a type of term that one could reasonably expect to be in the contract? What arguments can be made for and against enforcing a choice-of-law clause in an online contract?

INTERNET EXERCISES

Go to the *Business Law Today: The Essentials* home page at **http://blt.westbuslaw.com**, select "Chapter 10," and click on "Internet Exercises." There you will find the following Internet research exercises that you can perform to learn more about topics covered in this chapter.

Activity 10–1: LEGAL PERSPECTIVE—E-Contract Formation

Activity 10–2: MANAGEMENT PERSPECTIVE—E-Signatures

BEFORE THE TEST

Go to the *Business Law Today: The Essentials* home page at **http://blt.westbuslaw.com**, select "Chapter 10," and click on "Interactive Quizzes." You will find at least twenty interactive questions relating to this chapter.

CHAPTER 23

Personal Property, Bailments, and Insurance

"The great . . . end . . . of men united into commonwealths, and putting themselves under government, is the preservation of their property."

John Locke, 1632–1704
(English political philosopher)

CHAPTER OUTLINE

- PROPERTY OWNERSHIP
- ACQUIRING OWNERSHIP OF PERSONAL PROPERTY
- MISLAID, LOST, AND ABANDONED PROPERTY
- BAILMENTS
- INSURANCE

LEARNING OBJECTIVES

After reading this chapter, you should be able to answer the following questions:

1. What is real property? What is personal property?
2. What are the three elements necessary for an effective gift? How else can property be acquired?
3. What are the three elements of a bailment? What are the basic rights and duties of a bailee? What are the rights and duties of a bailor?
4. What is an insurable interest? When must an insurable interest exist—at the time the insurance policy is obtained, at the time the loss occurs, or both?
5. What clauses are typically included in insurance contracts?

PROPERTY
Legally protected rights and interests in anything with an ascertainable value that is subject to ownership.

REAL PROPERTY
Land and everything attached to it, such as trees and buildings.

PERSONAL PROPERTY
Property that is movable; any property that is not real property.

CHATTEL
All forms of personal property.

Property consists of the legally protected rights and interests a person has in anything with an ascertainable value that is subject to ownership. Property would have little value (and the word would have little meaning) if the law did not define the right to use it, to sell or dispose of it, and to prevent trespass on it. Indeed, John Locke, as indicated in the opening quotation, considered the preservation of property to be the primary reason for the establishment of government.

Property is divided into real property and personal property. **Real property** (sometimes called *realty* or *real estate*) means the land and everything permanently attached to it. Everything else is **personal property,** or *personalty.* Attorneys sometimes refer to personal property as **chattel,** a term used under the common law to denote all forms of personal property. Personal property can be tangible or intangible. *Tangible* personal property, such as a television set or a car, has physical substance. *Intangible* personal property represents some set of rights and interests but has no real physical existence. Stocks and bonds, patents, and copyrights are examples of intangible personal property.

In the first part of this chapter, we look at the ways in which title to property is held; the methods of acquiring ownership of personal property; and issues relating to mislaid, lost, and abandoned personal property. In the second part of the chapter, we examine bailment relationships. A *bailment* is created when personal property is temporarily delivered into the care of another without a transfer of title. This is the distinguishing characteristic of a bailment compared with a sale or a gift—there is no passage of title and no intent to transfer title. In the last part of this chapter, we consider insurance, which is a foremost concern of property owners and others. By insuring our property, and our lives, we protect ourselves against damage and loss.

Property Ownership

Property ownership[1] can be viewed as a bundle of rights, including the right to possess property and to dispose of it—by sale, gift, lease, or other means.

Fee Simple

FEE SIMPLE
An absolute form of property ownership entitling the property owner to use, possess, or dispose of the property as he or she chooses during his or her lifetime. On death, the interest in the property descends to the owner's heirs.

A person who holds the entire bundle of rights to property is said to be the owner in **fee simple.** The owner in fee simple is entitled to use, possess, or dispose of the property as he or she chooses during his or her lifetime, and on this owner's death, the interests in the property descend to his or her heirs. We will return to this form of property ownership in Chapter 24, in the context of ownership rights in real property.

Concurrent Ownership

CONCURRENT OWNERSHIP
Joint ownership.

Persons who share ownership rights simultaneously in a particular piece of property are said to be *concurrent* owners. There are two principal types of **concurrent ownership:** *tenancy in common* and *joint tenancy.* Other types of concurrent ownership include tenancy by the entirety and community property.

TENANCY IN COMMON
Co-ownership of property in which each party owns an undivided interest that passes to her or his heirs at death.

Tenancy in Common The term **tenancy in common** refers to a form of co-ownership in which each of two or more persons owns an *undivided* interest in the property. The interest is undivided because each tenant has rights in the *whole* property. ■ EXAMPLE 23.1 Rosa and Chad own a rare stamp collection together as tenants in common. This does not mean that Rosa owns some particular stamps and Chad others. Rather, it means that Rosa and Chad each have rights in the *entire* collection. (If Rosa owned some of the stamps and Chad owned others, then the interest would be *divided.*) ■

On the death of a tenant in common, that tenant's interest in the property passes to her or his heirs. ■ EXAMPLE 23.2 Should Rosa die before Chad, a one-half interest in the stamp collection will become the property of Rosa's heirs. If Rosa sells her interest to Fred before she dies, Fred and Chad will be co-owners as tenants in common. If Fred dies, his interest in the personal property will pass to his heirs, and they in turn will own the property with Chad as tenants in common. ■

1. The principles discussed in this section apply equally to real property ownership, discussed in Chapter 24.

How should the value of the property owned by two tenants in common be apportioned when neither tenant has died but both agree that their interests should be divided? This was the question in the following case.

CASE 23.1 Clark v. Dady

Missouri Court of Appeals,
Western District, 2004.
131 S.W.3d 382.
http://www.findlaw.com/11stategov/mo/moca.html[a]

FACTS In 1998, John Dady and Mary Clark bought a mobile home in Missouri for $35,848. Clark made a $4,000 down payment. Greentree Financial financed the $31,848 balance through a promissory note signed by both parties, in whose names title was issued. They lived together until August 2001 when Dady moved out. Clark made the subsequent payments on the note and for the lot rental and utilities. Less than six months later, Clark filed a petition in a Missouri state court against Dady, asking in part that she be adjudged "the rightful owner of [the] personal property due to the care and amount of money that she has contributed to the purchase." A balance of $31,964.19, including interest, was due on the note. John Dady asked to be reimbursed for the cost of adding a $10,000 deck, a $1,500 barn, and $2,000 worth of landscaping, plus "hours of painting" and his portion of the rental value of the mobile home after he had moved out. The court awarded the mobile home to Clark and ordered Dady to pay her $3,050 for his half of the lot and loan payments that she made after he had left. Dady appealed to a state intermediate appellate court.

ISSUE Did the trial court properly determine the respective interests of the owners of the property?

DECISION No. The state intermediate appellate court reversed the judgment of the lower court and remanded the case for a decision as to which expenses should be credited to the parties.[b]

REASON The court held that tenants in common own property in equal shares if the transfer that created their interests does not state otherwise, or if there is no other evidence showing the contributions of the owners toward the acquisition of the property to be unequal. Contributions toward acquisition include liability incurred in financing any part of the purchase price. Here, Clark made the down payment, but the parties jointly obligated themselves for the payment of the balance by signing a promissory note. The court explained, "As a result of the appellant's [Dady's] being jointly obligated on the note, he is considered to have contributed $15,924 to the acquisition of the mobile home ($31,848/2)." In other words, he owned "a 44.42% ($15,924/$35,848) share." The court acknowledged its responsibility to make a final determination of the parties' interests, but remanded the case because "the record is insufficient to allow us to determine what, if any, expenditures should be reimbursed to the parties."

WHY IS THIS CASE IMPORTANT? *As this case illustrates, how property is held can have a significant impact on the respective rights of the parties. In the absence of conflicting evidence, courts will presume that tenants in common own equal shares of the property, even if the parties' contributions to the property were unequal.*

a. In the "Court of Appeals" section, in the "2004" row, click on "April." On the next page, in the "04/06/2004" section, click on the docket number beside the name of the case to access the opinion.

b. The lower court's decision on remand was not available at the time this book went to press, but it may be by the time you read this. If you have purchased access to Westlaw Campus, you may be able to locate the remanded decision using that database. Alternatively, you might be able to find the case online at some other site. (See this text's inside front cover for information on Westlaw Campus and URLs for online court decisions.)

JOINT TENANCY
The joint ownership of property by two or more co-owners in which each co-owner owns an undivided portion of the property. On the death of one of the joint tenants, his or her interest automatically passes to the surviving joint tenant(s).

Joint Tenancy In a **joint tenancy,** each of two or more persons owns an undivided interest in the property, and a deceased joint tenant's interest passes to the surviving joint tenant or tenants. The rights of a surviving joint tenant to inherit a deceased joint tenant's ownership interest—which are referred to as *survivorship rights*—distinguish the joint tenancy from the tenancy in common. A joint tenancy can be terminated before a joint tenant's death by gift or by sale; in this situation, the person who receives the property as a gift or who purchases the property becomes a tenant in common, not a joint tenant.

■ EXAMPLE 23.3 If, in the preceding example, Rosa and Chad held their stamp collection in a joint tenancy and if Rosa died before Chad, the entire collection would become the property of Chad; Rosa's heirs would receive absolutely no interest in the collection. If Rosa, while living, sold her interest to Fred, however, the sale would terminate the joint tenancy, and Fred and Chad would become owners as tenants in common. ■

Generally, it is presumed that a co-tenancy is a tenancy in common unless there is a clear intention to establish a joint tenancy. Thus, language such as "to Jerrold and Eva as joint tenants with right of survivorship, and not as tenants in common" would be necessary to create a joint tenancy.

TENANCY BY THE ENTIRETY
The joint ownership of property by a husband and wife. Neither party can transfer her or his interest in the property without the consent of the other.

Tenancy by the Entirety A **tenancy by the entirety** is a less common form of ownership that can be created by a conveyance (transfer) of real property to a husband and wife. It differs from a joint tenancy only by the fact that neither spouse can make a separate lifetime transfer of his or her interest without the consent of the other spouse. In some states where statutes give the wife the right to convey her property, this form of concurrent ownership has been effectively abolished. A divorce, either spouse's death, or mutual agreement will terminate a tenancy by the entirety.

COMMUNITY PROPERTY
A form of concurrent ownership of property in which each spouse technically owns an undivided one-half interest in property acquired during the marriage. This form of joint ownership occurs in only ten states and Puerto Rico.

Community Property A married couple is allowed to own property as **community property** in only a limited number of states.[2] If property is held as community property, each spouse technically owns an undivided one-half interest in property acquired during the marriage. Generally, community property does not include property acquired prior to the marriage or property acquired by gift or inheritance as separate property during the marriage. After a divorce, community property is divided equally in some states and according to the discretion of the court in other states.

Acquiring Ownership of Personal Property

The most common way of acquiring personal property is by purchasing it. We have already discussed the purchase and sale of personal property (goods) in Chapters 11 and 12. Often, property is acquired by will or inheritance. Here we look at additional ways in which ownership of personal property can be acquired, including acquisition by possession, production, gift, accession, and confusion.

POSSESSION

One example of acquiring ownership by possession is the capture of wild animals. Wild animals belong to no one in their natural state, and the first person to take possession of a wild animal normally owns it. The killing of a wild animal amounts to assuming ownership of it. Merely being in hot pursuit does not give title, however. This basic rule has two exceptions. First, any wild animals captured by a trespasser are the property of the landowner, not the trespasser. Second, if wild animals are captured or killed in violation of wild-game statutes, the state, and not the capturer,

2. These states include Alaska, Arizona, California, Idaho, Louisiana, Nevada, New Mexico, Texas, Washington, and Wisconsin. Puerto Rico allows property to be owned as community property as well.

obtains title to the animals. (Sometimes, a question arises as to what is a wild animal—see this chapter's *Letter of the Law* feature.)

Those who find lost or abandoned property can also acquire ownership rights through mere possession of the property, as will be discussed later in the chapter. (Ownership rights in real property can also be acquired through possession, such as adverse possession—see Chapter 24.)

PRODUCTION

Production—the fruits of labor—is another means of acquiring ownership of personal property. For instance, writers, inventors, and manufacturers all produce personal property and thereby acquire title to it. (In some situations, though, as when a researcher is hired to invent a new product or technique, the researcher-producer may not own what is produced—see Chapter 17.)

GIFTS

GIFT
Any voluntary transfer of property made without consideration, past or present.

A **gift** is another fairly common means of acquiring and transferring ownership of real and personal property. A gift is essentially a voluntary transfer of property ownership for which no consideration is given. As discussed in Chapter 7, the presence of consideration is what distinguishes a contract from a gift.

To be an effective gift, three requirements must be met—donative intent on the part of the *donor* (the one giving the gift), delivery, and acceptance by the *donee* (the one receiving the gift). We examine each of these requirements here, as well as the requirements of a gift made in contemplation of imminent death. Until these three requirements are met, no effective gift has been made. ■ EXAMPLE 23.4 Suppose that your aunt tells you that she *intends* to give you a new Mercedes-Benz for your next birthday. This is simply a promise to make a gift. It is not considered a gift until the Mercedes-Benz is delivered and accepted. ■

LETTER OF THE LAW Are Clams "Wild Animals"?

Timothy Longshore was arrested and convicted for stealing clams from a private beach near Puget Sound, Washington. On appeal to the Supreme Court of Washington, Longshore argued that he had not committed theft because the landowner did not own the clams. He asserted that because clams are wild animals, or *ferae naturae,* they are not owned by anyone until someone takes possession of them. The court, however, viewed the matter differently. The court emphasized that clams "ordinarily live in the soil under the waters" and belong with the land. "When taken, they must be wrenched from their beds, made well down in the soil itself." Therefore, said the court, it must follow that a private landowner "has the right to exercise dominion [control] and ownership over what is upon the land, and especially over things so closely related to the soil as clams." The court also had the letter of Washington law on its side: the Washington legislature had enacted a statute that, among other things, stated that the term *wildlife* "does not include . . . fish, shellfish, and marine invertebrates classified as food fish or shellfish."[a]

THE BOTTOM LINE

In the state of Washington, an individual who privately owns tidelands also owns any naturally occurring clams embedded in the soil.

a. *State v. Longshore,* 141 Wash.2d 414, 5 P.3d 1256 (2000).

ETHICAL ISSUE 23.1

Who owns the engagement ring? Often, when a couple decides to marry, one party gives the other an engagement ring. What if the engagement is called off? Etiquette authorities routinely counsel that if the woman breaks the engagement, she should return the ring, but if the man calls the wedding off, the woman is entitled to keep the ring. Interestingly, the courts are coming up with a different approach. Courts in Kansas, Michigan, New York, Ohio, and a number of other states have held that an engagement ring is not a real gift. Rather, it is a "conditional gift" that becomes final only if the marriage occurs. If the marriage does not take place, the ring is returned to the donor regardless of who broke the engagement.[3] This so-called modern trend among the courts is actually similar to the law of ancient Rome, which mandated that when an engagement was broken, the woman had to return the ring, as a penalty, regardless of who was at fault. Some judges, however, disagree with the conditional-gift theory and contend that an engagement ring is a gift, and, as such, it belongs to the donee, even if the engagement is broken. As one judge stated, "Those jurisdictions that rely on the analysis that an engagement ring is a conditional gift ignore general gift law, which holds that a gift is complete if there is intent, delivery, and acceptance."[4] ■

Donative Intent When a gift is challenged in court, the court will determine whether donative intent exists by looking at the language of the donor and the surrounding circumstances. ■ EXAMPLE 23.5 A court may look at the relationship between the parties and the size of the gift in relation to the donor's other assets. A gift to a mortal enemy is viewed with suspicion. Similarly, when a gift represents a large portion of a person's assets, the court will scrutinize the transaction closely to determine the mental capacity of the donor and ascertain whether any element of fraud or duress is present. ■

> **.on the Web** Who owns a gift received by a married person—the spouse who received the gift or the husband and wife jointly? To learn the answer to this question, go to Scott Law Firm's Web page at **http://www.scottlawfirm.com/property.htm**.

Delivery The gift must be delivered to the donee. Delivery is obvious in most cases, but some objects cannot be relinquished physically. Then the question of delivery depends on the surrounding circumstances.

Constructive Delivery. When the object itself cannot be physically delivered, a symbolic, or constructive, delivery will be sufficient. **Constructive delivery** does not confer actual possession of the object in question, only the right to take actual possession. Thus, constructive delivery is a general term used to describe an action that the law holds to be the equivalent of real delivery. ■ EXAMPLE 23.6 Suppose that you want to make a gift of various old rare coins that you have stored in a safe-deposit box at your bank. You certainly cannot deliver the box itself to the donee, and you do not want to take the coins out of the bank. In this situation, you can simply deliver the key to the box to the donee and authorize the donee's access to the box and its contents. This action constitutes a constructive delivery of the contents of the box. ■

CONSTRUCTIVE DELIVERY
An act equivalent to the actual, physical delivery of property that cannot be physically delivered because of difficulty or impossibility. For example, the transfer of a key to a safe constructively delivers the contents of the safe.

The delivery of intangible property—such as stocks, bonds, insurance policies, and contracts, for example—must always be accomplished by symbolic, or constructive, delivery. This is because the documents represent rights and are not, in themselves, the true property.

Delivery by Agents. Delivery may be accomplished by means of a third person who is the agent of either the donor or the donee. If the third person is the agent of the donor, the delivery is effective when the agent delivers the gift to the donee. If the third person is the agent of the donee, the gift is effectively delivered when the donor deliv-

3. See, for example, *Meyer v. Mitnick,* 244 Mich.App. 697, 625 N.W.2d 136 (2001).
4. See the dissenting opinion in *Heiman v. Parrish,* 262 Kan. 926, 942 P.2d 631 (1997).

ers the property to the donee's agent.[5] Naturally, no delivery is necessary if the gift is already in the hands of the donee. All that is necessary to complete the gift in such a situation is that the donor had the required intent and the donee accepted the gift.

DOMINION
Ownership rights in property, including the right to possess and control the property.

Relinquishing Dominion and Control. An effective delivery also requires giving up complete control and **dominion** (ownership rights) over the subject matter of the gift. The outcome of disputes often turns on whether control has actually been relinquished. The Internal Revenue Service scrutinizes transactions between relatives when one claims to have given income-producing property to the other. A relative who does not relinquish complete control over a piece of property will have to pay taxes on the income from that property, as opposed to the family member who received the "gift."

In the following case, the court focused on the requirement that a donor must relinquish complete control and dominion over property given to the donee before a gift can be effectively delivered.

5. *Bickford v. Mattocks,* 95 Me. 547, 50 A. 894 (1901).

LANDMARK AND CLASSIC CASES

CASE 23.2 In re Estate of Piper

Missouri Court of Appeals, 1984.
676 S.W.2d 897.

FACTS Gladys Piper died intestate (without a will) in 1982. At her death, she owned miscellaneous personal property worth $5,000 and had in her purse $200 in cash and two diamond rings, known as the Andy Piper rings. The contents of her purse were taken by her niece Wanda Brown, allegedly to preserve them for the estate. Clara Kaufmann, a friend of Piper's, filed a claim against the estate for $4,800. From October 1974 until Piper's death, Kaufmann had taken Piper to the doctor, beauty shop, and grocery store; had written her checks to pay her bills; and had helped her care for her home. Kaufmann maintained that Piper had promised to pay her for these services and had given her the diamond rings as a gift. A Missouri state trial court denied her request for payment; the court found that her services had been voluntary. Kaufmann then filed a petition for delivery of personal property—the rings—which was granted by the trial court. Brown, other heirs, and the administrator of Piper's estate appealed.

ISSUE Had Gladys Piper made an effective gift of the rings to Clara Kaufmann?

DECISION No. The state appellate court reversed the judgment of the trial court on the ground that Piper had never delivered the rings to Kaufmann.

REASON Kaufmann claimed that the rings belonged to her by reason of a "consummated gift long prior to the death of Gladys Piper." Two witnesses testified for Kaufmann at the trial that Piper had told them the rings belonged to Kaufmann but that she was going to wear them until she died. The appellate court found "no evidence of any actual delivery." The court held that the essentials of a gift are (1) a present intention to make a gift on the part of the donor, (2) a delivery of the property by the donor to the donee, and (3) an acceptance by the donee. The evidence in the case showed only an intent to make a gift. Because there was no delivery—either actual or constructive—a valid gift was not made. For Piper to have made a gift, her intention would have to have been executed by the complete and unconditional delivery of the property or the delivery of a proper written instrument evidencing the gift. As this did not occur, the court found that there had been no gift.

COMMENTS *Although this case is relatively recent in the long span of the law governing gifts, we present it here as a classic case because it so clearly illustrates the delivery requirement when making a gift. Assuming that Piper did, indeed, intend for Kaufmann to have the rings, it was unfortunate that Kaufmann had no right to receive them after Piper's death. Yet the alternative could lead to perhaps even more unfairness. The policy behind the delivery requirement is to protect alleged donors and their heirs from fraudulent claims based solely on parol evidence. If not for this policy, an alleged donee could easily claim that a gift was made when, in fact, it was not.*

RELEVANT WEB SITES *To locate information on the Web concerning* In re Estate of Piper, *go to this text's Web site at* **http://blt.westbuslaw.com**, *select "Chapter 23," and click on "URLs for Landmarks."*

Acceptance The final requirement of a valid gift is acceptance by the donee. This rarely presents any problem, as most donees readily accept their gifts. The courts generally assume acceptance unless the circumstances indicate otherwise.

GIFT *INTER VIVOS*
A gift made during one's lifetime and not in contemplation of imminent death, in contrast to a gift *causa mortis.*

GIFT *CAUSA MORTIS*
A gift made in contemplation of death. If the donor does not die of that ailment, the gift is revoked.

Gifts *Inter Vivos* and Gifts *Causa Mortis* A gift made during one's lifetime is termed a **gift *inter vivos.*** **Gifts *causa mortis*** (so-called *deathbed gifts*), in contrast, are made in contemplation of imminent death. A gift *causa mortis* does not become absolute until the donor dies from the contemplated illness, and it is automatically revoked if the donor recovers from the illness. Moreover, the donee must survive to take the gift. To be effective, a gift *causa mortis* must also meet the three requirements discussed earlier—donative intent, delivery, and acceptance by the donee.

■ EXAMPLE 23.7 Suppose that Yang is to be operated on for a cancerous tumor. Before the operation, he delivers an envelope to a close business associate. The envelope contains a letter saying, "I realize my days are numbered, and I want to give you this check for $1 million in the event of my death from this operation." The business associate cashes the check. The surgeon performs the operation and removes the tumor. Yang recovers fully. Several months later, Yang dies from a heart attack that is totally unrelated to the operation. If Yang's personal representative (the party charged with administering Yang's estate) tries to recover the $1 million, normally she will succeed. The gift *causa mortis* is automatically revoked if the donor recovers. The *specific event* that was contemplated in making the gift was death from a particular operation. Because Yang's death was not the result of this event, the gift is revoked, and the $1 million passes to Yang's estate. ■

ACCESSION

ACCESSION
Occurs when an individual adds value to personal property by either labor or materials. In some situations, a person may acquire ownership rights in another's property through accession.

Accession means "something added." Accession occurs when someone adds value to an item of personal property by use of either labor or materials. Generally, there is no dispute about who owns the property after the accession occurs, especially when the accession is accomplished with the owner's consent. ■ EXAMPLE 23.8 A Corvette-customizing specialist comes to Hoshi's house. Hoshi has all the materials necessary to customize the car. The customizing specialist uses them to add a unique bumper to Hoshi's Corvette. Hoshi simply pays the customizer for the value of the labor, obviously retaining title to the property. ■

When a Party Wrongfully Causes the Accession When accession occurs without the permission of the owner, the courts will tend to favor the owner over the improver—the one who improves the property—provided that the accession was wrongful and undertaken in bad faith. This is true even if the accession increased the value of the property substantially. In addition, many courts will deny the improver (wrongdoer) any compensation for the value added. ■ EXAMPLE 23.9 Patti steals a car and puts new tires on it. Obviously, a car thief will not be compensated for the value of the new tires if the rightful owner recovers the car. ■

Increased Property Value Due to a Good Faith Accession If the accession is performed in good faith, however, even without the owner's consent, ownership of the improved item most often depends on whether the accession has increased the value of the property or changed its identity. The greater the increase in value, the more likely that ownership will pass to the improver. If ownership does pass, the improver must compensate the original owner for the value of the property prior to the accession. If the increase in value is not sufficient for ownership to pass to the improver, most courts will require the owner to compensate the improver for the value added.

CONFUSION

CONFUSION
The mixing together of goods belonging to two or more owners so that the separately owned goods cannot be identified.

Confusion is the commingling (mixing together) of goods so that one person's personal property cannot be distinguished from another's. Confusion frequently occurs when the goods are *fungible*. *Fungible goods* are goods consisting of identical particles, such as grain or oil. For instance, if two farmers put their number 2–grade winter wheat into the same storage bin, confusion will occur and the farmers become tenants in common.

When goods are confused due to a wrongful and willful act and the wrongdoer is unable to prove what percentage of the confused goods belongs to him or her, then the innocent party ordinarily acquires title to the whole. If confusion occurs as a result of agreement, an honest mistake, or the act of some third party, the owners share ownership as tenants in common and will share any loss in proportion to their ownership interests in the property.

■ EXAMPLE 23.10 Five farmers in a small Iowa community enter a cooperative arrangement. Each fall, the farmers harvest the same amount of number 2–grade yellow corn and store it in silos that are held by the cooperative. Each farmer thus owns one-fifth of the total corn in the silos. If, however, one farmer harvests and stores more corn than the others in the cooperative silos and wants to claim a greater ownership interest, that farmer must keep careful records. Otherwise, the courts will presume that each farmer has an equal interest in the corn. ■

Mislaid, Lost, and Abandoned Property

As already mentioned, one of the methods of acquiring ownership of property is to possess it. Simply finding something and holding on to it, however, does not necessarily give the finder any legal rights in the property. Different rules apply, depending on whether the property was mislaid, lost, or abandoned.

MISLAID PROPERTY

MISLAID PROPERTY
Property with which the owner has voluntarily parted and then cannot find or recover.

Property that has voluntarily been placed somewhere by the owner and then inadvertently forgotten is **mislaid property.** ■ EXAMPLE 23.11 Suppose that you go to the theater. You leave your gloves on the concession stand and then forget about them. The gloves are mislaid property, and the theater owner is entrusted with the duty of reasonable care for them. ■ When mislaid property is found, the finder does not obtain title to the goods. Instead, the owner of the place where the property was mislaid becomes the caretaker of the property because it is highly likely that the true owner will return.[6]

LOST PROPERTY

LOST PROPERTY
Property with which the owner has involuntarily parted and then cannot find or recover.

Property that is involuntarily left and forgotten is **lost property.** A finder of the property can claim title to the property against the whole world *except the true owner.*[7] If the true owner demands that the lost property be returned, the finder must return

6. The finder of mislaid property is an involuntary bailee (to be discussed later in this chapter).
7. See *Armory v. Delamirie,* discussed in this chapter's *Landmark in the Law* feature on the following pages.

it. If a third party attempts to take possession of lost property from a finder, the third party cannot assert a better title than the finder.

■ EXAMPLE 23.12 Suppose that Kamul works in a large library at night. In the courtyard on her way home, she finds a piece of gold jewelry set with stones that look like precious stones to her. She takes it to a jeweler to have it appraised. While pretending to weigh the jewelry, an employee of the jeweler removes several of the stones. If Kamul brings an action to recover the stones from the jeweler, she normally will win because she found lost property and holds valid title against everyone *except the true owner.* Because the property was lost, rather than mislaid, the finder is the caretaker of the jewelry, and the finder acquires title good against the whole world (except the true owner). ■

.on the Web Some states and government agencies now post online a list of unclaimed property. For an example of the various types of property that may go unclaimed, go to the following Web page, which is part of the state of Delaware's Web site:

http://www.state.de.us/revenue/information/Escheat.shtml.

Relativity of Title The law that finders of lost property may obtain good title to the property has a long history. The cases discussed in this chapter's *Landmark in the Law* feature on the origin of the law of finders illustrate the doctrine of *relativity of title.* Under this doctrine, if two contestants are before the court, neither of whom can claim absolute title to the property, the one who can claim prior possession will likely have established sufficient rights to the property to win the case.

LANDMARK IN THE LAW

The Law of Finders

The well-known children's adage, "Finders keepers, losers weepers," is actually written into law—provided that the loser (the rightful owner) cannot be found. A finder of lost personal property may acquire good title to the property *against everyone except the true owner.* A number of landmark cases have made this principle clear. An early English case, *Armory v. Delamirie,*[a] is considered a landmark in Anglo-American jurisprudence concerning finders' rights in property.

FINDERS' RIGHTS The plaintiff in the case was Armory, a chimney sweep who found a jewel in its setting during the course of his work. He took the jewel to a goldsmith to have it appraised. The goldsmith refused to return the jewel to Armory, claiming that Armory was not the rightful owner of the property. The court held that the finder, as prior possessor of the item, had rights to the jewel superior to those of all others except the rightful owner. The court stated, "The finder of a jewel, though he does not by such finding acquire an absolute property or ownership, yet . . . has such a property as will enable him to keep it against all but the rightful owner."

WHO HAS RIGHTS TO WRONGFULLY OBTAINED GOODS? A curious situation arises when goods wrongfully obtained by one person are in turn wrongfully obtained by another, and the two parties contest each other's rights to possession. In such a situation, does the *Armory* rule still apply—that is, does the first (illegal) possessor have more rights in the property than the second (illegal)

a. 93 Eng.Rep. 664 (K.B. [King's Bench] 1722).

Conversion of Lost Property When a finder knows who the true owner of the property is and fails to return it to that person, the finder is guilty of the tort of *conversion* (the wrongful taking of another's property—see Chapter 4). Many states require the finder to make a reasonably diligent search to locate the true owner of lost property.

ESTRAY STATUTE
A statute defining finders' rights in property when the true owners are unknown.

Estray Statutes Many states have **estray statutes,** which encourage and facilitate the return of property to its true owner and then reward a finder for honesty if the property remains unclaimed. These laws provide an incentive for finders to report their discoveries by making it possible for them, after the passage of a specified period of time, to acquire legal title to the property they have found. Such statutes usually require the county clerk to advertise the property in an attempt to help the owner recover what has been lost. Some preliminary questions must always be resolved before the estray statute can be employed. The item must be lost property, not merely mislaid property. When the circumstances indicate that the property was probably lost and not mislaid or abandoned, loss is presumed as a matter of public policy, and the estray statute applies.

LANDMARK IN THE LAW

The Law of Finders—Continued

possessor? In a case that came before the Minnesota Supreme Court in 1892, *Anderson v. Gouldberg,*[b] the court said yes.

In the *Anderson* case, the plaintiffs had trespassed on another's land and wrongfully cut timber. The defendants later took the logs from the mill site, allegedly in the name of the owner of the property on which the timber had been cut. The evidence at trial indicated that both parties had illegally acquired the property. The court instructed the jury that even if the plaintiffs were trespassers when they cut the logs, they were entitled to recover them from later possessors—except the true owner or an agent of the true owner. The jury found for the plaintiffs, a decision affirmed later by the Minnesota Supreme Court. The latter court held that the plaintiffs' possession, "though wrongfully obtained," justified an action to repossess the property from another who took it from them.

BE AWARE A finder who appropriates the personal property of another, knowing who the true owner is, can be guilty of conversion.

APPLICATION TO TODAY'S WORLD

Although the Armory *case was decided nearly three hundred years ago, the principle enunciated by the court in that case remains applicable today. Finders of lost property continue to acquire good title to the property against all but the true owner.*

RELEVANT WEB SITES

To locate information on the Web concerning Armory v. Delamirie, *go to this text's Web site at* **http://blt.westbuslaw.com**, *select "Chapter 23," and click on "URLs for Landmarks."*

b. 51 Minn. 294, 53 N.W. 636 (1892).

A man found the Super Bowl ring of a Chicago Bears football player under a couch that the player had once owned. Is the ring mislaid, lost, or abandoned property? Did the finder acquire valid title to the ring? Why or why not? What, if anything, might the finder be required to do? (AP Photo/ The Journal and Courier, Kevin Howell)

ABANDONED PROPERTY

Property that has been discarded by the true owner, with no intention of reclaiming title to it, is **abandoned property.** Someone who finds abandoned property acquires title to it, and such title is good against the whole world, *including the original owner.* The owner of lost property who eventually gives up any further attempt to find it is frequently held to have abandoned the property. If a person finds abandoned property while trespassing on the property of another, title vests in the owner of the land, not in the finder.

■ EXAMPLE 23.13 Aleka is driving with the windows down in her car. Somewhere along her route, a valuable scarf blows out the window. She retraces her route and searches for the scarf but cannot find it. She finally gives up her search and proceeds to her destination five hundred miles away. Six months later, Frye, a hitchhiker, finds the scarf. Frye has acquired title, which is good even against Aleka. By completely giving up her search, Aleka abandoned the scarf just as effectively as if she had intentionally discarded it. ■

ABANDONED PROPERTY
Property with which the owner has voluntarily parted, with no intention of recovering it.

Bailments

A **bailment** is formed by the delivery of personal property, without transfer of title, by one person, called a **bailor,** to another, called a **bailee,** usually under an agreement for a particular purpose—for example, to loan, lease, store, repair, or transport the property. On completion of the purpose, the bailee is obligated to return the bailed property in the same or better condition to the bailor or a third person or to dispose of it as directed.

BAILMENT
A situation in which the personal property of one person (a bailor) is entrusted to another (a bailee), who is obligated to return the bailed property to the bailor or dispose of it as directed.

BAILOR
One who entrusts goods to a bailee.

BAILEE
One to whom goods are entrusted by a bailor.

Bailments are usually created by agreement, but not necessarily by contract, because in many bailments not all of the elements of a contract (such as mutual assent and consideration) are present. ■ EXAMPLE 23.14 If you lend your bicycle to a friend, a bailment is created, but not by contract, because there is no consideration. Many commercial bailments, such as the delivery of clothing to the cleaners for dry cleaning, are based on contract, though. ■

The law of bailments applies to many routine personal and business transactions. When individuals deal with bailments, whether they realize it or not, they are subject to the obligations and duties that arise from the bailment relationship. The number, scope, and importance of bailments created daily in the business community and in everyday life make it desirable for every person to understand the elements necessary for the creation of a bailment and to know what rights, duties, and liabilities flow from bailments.

ELEMENTS OF A BAILMENT

Not all transactions involving the delivery of property from one person to another create a bailment. For such a transfer to become a bailment, three conditions must be met. We look here at each of these conditions.

Personal Property Only personal property is bailable; there can be no bailment of persons. Although a bailment of your luggage is created when it is transported by an airline, as a passenger you are not the subject of a bailment. Additionally, you cannot bail realty; thus, leasing your house to a tenant does not create a bailment. Although bailments commonly involve *tangible* items—jewelry, cattle, automobiles, and the like—*intangible* personal property, such as promissory notes and shares of corporate stock, may also be bailed.

Delivery of Possession *Delivery of possession* means the transfer of possession of the property to the bailee.

Requirements for Delivery of Possession. Two requirements must be met for delivery of possession to occur:

1. The bailee must be given exclusive possession and control over the property.
2. The bailee must *knowingly* accept the personal property.[8] In other words, the bailee must *intend* to exercise control over it.

If either delivery of possession or knowing acceptance is lacking, there is no bailment relationship. ■ EXAMPLE 23.15 Suppose that you take a friend out to dinner at an expensive restaurant. When you enter the restaurant, your friend checks her coat. In the pocket of the coat is a $20,000 diamond necklace. The bailee, by accepting the coat, does not knowingly also accept the necklace. Thus, a bailment of the coat exists—because the restaurant has exclusive possession and control over the coat and knowingly accepted it—but not a bailment of the necklace. ■

.on the Web For a discussion of the origins of the term *bailment* and how bailment relationships have been defined, go to **http://www.lectlaw.com/def/b005.htm**.

Physical versus Constructive Delivery. Two types of delivery—*physical* and *constructive*—will result in the bailee's exclusive possession of and control over the property. As discussed earlier, in the context of gifts, constructive delivery is a substitute, or symbolic, delivery. What is delivered to the bailee is not the actual property bailed (such as a car) but something so related to the property (such as the car keys) that the requirement of delivery is satisfied.

Involuntary Bailments. In certain unique situations, a bailment is found despite the apparent lack of the requisite elements of control and knowledge. In particular, the rental of a safe-deposit box is usually held to create a bailor-bailee relationship between the customer and the bank, despite the bank's lack of knowledge of the contents and its inability to have exclusive control of the property.[9] Another example of such a situation occurs when the bailee acquires the property accidentally or by mistake—as in finding someone else's lost or mislaid property. A bailment is created even though the bailor did not voluntarily deliver the property to the bailee. Such bailments are called *constructive* or *involuntary* bailments.

Bailment Agreement A bailment agreement, or contract, can be express or implied. Although a written agreement is not required for bailments of less than one year (that is, the Statute of Frauds does not apply—see Chapter 8), it is a good idea to have one, especially when valuable property is involved.

The bailment agreement expressly or impliedly provides for the return of the bailed property to the bailor or to a third person, or it provides for disposal by the bailee. The agreement presupposes that the bailee will return the identical goods originally given by the bailor. In certain types of bailments, though, such as bailments of fungible goods, the property returned need only be equivalent property.

8. We are dealing here with *voluntary bailments.* This does not apply to *involuntary bailments.*
9. By statute or by express contract, the rental of a safe-deposit box may be regarded as a lease of space or a license (a revocable right to use the space, for a fee—see Chapter 24) instead of a bailment.

■ **EXAMPLE 23.16** If Holman stores his grain (fungible goods) in Joe's Warehouse, a bailment is created. At the end of the storage period, however, the warehouse is not obligated to return to Holman exactly the same grain that he stored. As long as the warehouse returns goods of the same *type, grade,* and *quantity,* the warehouse—the bailee—has performed its obligation. ■

ORDINARY BAILMENTS

Bailments are either *ordinary* or *special (extraordinary)*. There are three types of ordinary bailments. They are distinguished according to *which party receives a benefit from the bailment.* This factor will dictate the rights and liabilities of the parties, and the courts may use it to determine the standard of care required of the bailee in possession of the personal property. The three types of ordinary bailments are as follows:

1. *Bailment for the sole benefit of the bailor.* This is a gratuitous bailment (a bailment without consideration) for the convenience and benefit of the bailor. ■ **EXAMPLE 23.17** Allen asks his friend, Sumi, to store his car in her garage while he is away. If Sumi agrees to do so, then it is a gratuitous bailment because the bailment of the car is for the sole benefit of the bailor (Allen). ■
2. *Bailment for the sole benefit of the bailee.* This type of bailment typically occurs when one person lends an item to another person (the bailee) solely for the bailee's convenience and benefit. ■ **EXAMPLE 23.18** Allen asks to borrow Sumi's boat so that he can go sailing over the weekend. The bailment of the boat is for Allen's (the bailee's) sole benefit. ■
3. *Bailment for the mutual benefit of the bailee and the bailor.* This is the most common kind of bailment and involves some form of compensation for storing items or holding property while it is being serviced. It is a contractual bailment and may be referred to as a bailment for hire or a commercial bailment. ■ **EXAMPLE 23.19** Allen leaves his car at a service station for an oil change. Because the service station will be paid to change Allen's oil, this is a mutual-benefit bailment. ■ Many lease arrangements in which the lease involves goods (leases were discussed in Chapters 11 through 13) also fall into this category of bailment once the lessee takes possession.

The owner of a dry cleaning shop in New York returns a customer's clothes. What type of ordinary bailment does this exemplify and why? (Shawn Baldwin/Bloomberg News/Landov)

Rights of the Bailee Certain rights are implicit in the bailment agreement. Generally, the bailee has the right to take possession, to utilize the property for accomplishing the purpose of the bailment, to receive some form of compensation, and to limit her or his liability for the bailed goods. These rights of the bailee are present (with some limitations) in varying degrees in all bailment transactions.

Right of Possession. A hallmark of the bailment agreement is that the bailee acquires the *right to control and possess the property temporarily.* The bailee's right of possession permits the bailee to recover damages from any third person for damage or loss of the property. If the property is stolen, the bailee has a legal right to regain possession of it or to obtain damages from any third person who has wrongfully interfered with the bailee's possessory rights. The bailee's right to regain possession of the property or to obtain damages is important because, as you will read shortly, a bailee is liable to the bailor for any loss or damage to bailed property resulting from the bailee's negligence.

Right to Use Bailed Property. Depending on the type of bailment and the terms of the bailment agreement, a bailee may also have a right to use the bailed property. When no provision is made, the extent of use depends on how necessary it is for the goods to be at the bailee's disposal for the ordinary purpose of the bailment to be carried out. ■ EXAMPLE 23.20 If you borrow a friend's car to drive to the airport, you, as the bailee, would obviously be expected to use the car. In a bailment involving the long-term storage of a car, however, the bailee is not expected to use the car because the ordinary purpose of a storage bailment does not include use of the property. ■

Right of Compensation. Except in a gratuitous bailment, a bailee has a right to be compensated as provided for in the bailment agreement, to be reimbursed for costs and services rendered in the keeping of the bailed property, or both. Even in a gratuitous bailment, a bailee has a right to be reimbursed or compensated for costs incurred in the keeping of the bailed property. ■ EXAMPLE 23.21 Margo loses her pet dog, and Justine finds it. Justine takes Margo's dog to her home and feeds it. Even though she takes good care of the dog, it becomes ill, and she takes it to a veterinarian. Justine pays the bill for the veterinarian's services and the medicine. Justine normally will be entitled to be reimbursed by Margo for all reasonable costs incurred in the keeping of Margo's dog. ■

To enforce the right of compensation, the bailee has a right to place a *possessory lien* (which entitles a creditor to retain possession of the debtor's goods until a debt is paid) on the specific bailed property until he or she has been fully compensated. This type of lien, sometimes referred to as an artisan's lien or a *bailee's lien,* was discussed in Chapter 16.

Right to Limit Liability. In ordinary bailments, bailees have the right to limit their liability as long as the limitations are called to the attention of the bailor and are not against public policy. It is essential that the bailor be informed of the limitation in some way. Even when the bailor knows of the limitation, certain types of disclaimers of liability have been considered to be against public policy and therefore illegal. The courts carefully scrutinize *exculpatory clauses,* or clauses that limit a person's liability for her or his own wrongful acts, and in bailments they are often held to be illegal. This is particularly true in bailments for the mutual benefit of the bailor and the bailee. ■ EXAMPLE 23.22 A receipt from a parking garage expressly disclaims liability for any damage to parked cars, regardless of the cause. Because the bailee has attempted to exclude liability for the bailee's own negligence, including the parking attendant's negligence, the clause will likely be deemed unenforceable because it is against public policy. ■

Duties of the Bailee The bailee has two basic responsibilities: (1) to take appropriate care of the property and (2) to surrender the property to the bailor or dispose of it in accordance with the bailor's instructions at the end of the bailment.

The Duty of Care. The bailee must exercise reasonable care in preserving the bailed property. What constitutes reasonable care in a bailment situation normally depends on the nature and specific circumstances of the bailment. Traditionally, the courts have determined the appropriate standard of care on the basis of the type of bailment involved. In a bailment for the sole benefit of the bailor, for example, the bailee need exercise only a slight degree of care. In a bailment for the sole benefit of the bailee, however, the bailee must exercise great care. In a mutual-benefit bailment, courts normally impose a reasonable standard of care—that is, the bailee must exercise the degree of care that a reasonable and prudent person would exercise in the same circumstances. Exhibit 23–1 illustrates these concepts. A bailee's failure to exercise appropriate care in handling the bailor's property results in tort liability.

Duty to Return Bailed Property. At the end of the bailment, the bailee normally must hand over the original property to either the bailor or someone the bailor designates or must otherwise dispose of it as directed This is usually a *contractual* duty arising from the bailment agreement (contract). Failure to give up possession at the time the bailment ends is a breach of contract and could result in the tort of conversion or an action based on bailee negligence. If the bailed property has been lost or is returned damaged, a court will presume that the bailee was negligent. The exception is when the obligation is excused because the goods or chattels have been destroyed, lost, or stolen through no fault of the bailee (or claimed by a third party with a superior claim).

Because the bailee has a duty to return the bailed goods to the bailor, a bailee may be liable if the goods being held or delivered are given to the wrong person. Hence, a bailee must be satisfied that a person (other than the bailor) to whom the goods are being delivered is the actual owner or has authority from the owner to take possession of the goods. Should the bailee deliver in error, then the bailee may be liable for conversion or misdelivery.

Duties of the Bailor It goes without saying that the duties of a bailor are essentially the same as the rights of a bailee. Obviously, a bailor has a duty to compensate the bailee either as agreed or as reimbursement for costs incurred by the bailee in keeping the bailed property. A bailor also has an all-encompassing duty to provide the bailee with goods or chattels that are free from known defects that could cause injury to the bailee.

Bailor's Duty to Reveal Defects. The bailor's duty to reveal defects to the bailee translates into two rules:

1. In a *mutual-benefit bailment,* the bailor must notify the bailee of all known defects and any hidden defects that the bailor knows of or could have discovered with reasonable diligence and proper inspection.
2. In a *bailment for the sole benefit of the bailee,* the bailor must notify the bailee of any known defects.

EXHIBIT 23–1 DEGREE OF CARE REQUIRED OF A BAILEE

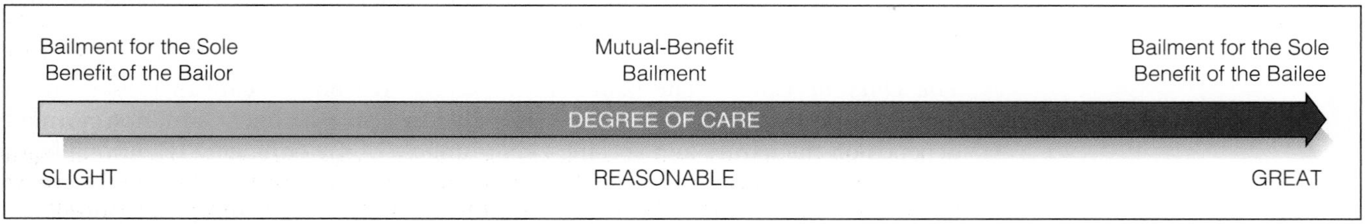

The bailor's duty to reveal defects is based on a negligence theory of tort law. A bailor who fails to give the appropriate notice is liable to the bailee and to any other person who might reasonably be expected to come into contact with the defective article.

■ EXAMPLE 23.23 Rentco (the bailor) rents a tractor to Hal Iverson. Unknown to Rentco (but *discoverable* by reasonable inspection), the brake mechanism on the tractor is defective at the time the bailment is made. Iverson uses the defective tractor without knowledge of the brake problem and is injured along with two other field workers when the tractor rolls out of control. Because this is a mutual-benefit bailment, Rentco has a *duty* to notify Iverson of the discoverable brake defect. Rentco's failure to fulfill this duty is the *proximate cause* (discussed in Chapter 4) of injuries to farm workers who might be expected to use, or have contact with, the tractor. Therefore, Rentco is liable under a negligence theory for the injuries sustained by Iverson and the two others. ■

Warranty Liability for Defective Goods. A bailor can also incur *warranty liability* based on contract law (see Chapter 13) for injuries resulting from the bailment of defective articles. Property leased by a bailor must be *fit for the intended purpose of the bailment.* Warranties of fitness arise by law in sales contracts and leases, and judges have extended these warranties to situations in which the bailees are compensated for the bailment (such as when one leaves a car with a parking attendant). Article 2A of the Uniform Commercial Code (UCC) extends the implied warranties of merchantability and fitness for a particular purpose to bailments whenever the bailments include rights to use the bailed goods.[10]

SPECIAL TYPES OF BAILMENTS

Up to this point, our discussion of bailments has been concerned with ordinary bailments—bailments in which bailees are expected to exercise ordinary care in the handling of bailed property. Some bailment transactions warrant special consideration. These include bailments in which the bailee's duty of care is *extraordinary*—that is, the bailee's liability for loss or damage to the property is absolute—as is generally true in bailments involving common carriers and innkeepers. Warehouse companies have the same duty of care as ordinary bailees; but, like carriers, they are subject to extensive regulation under federal and state laws, including Article 7 of the UCC.

COMMON CARRIER
An owner of a truck, railroad, airline, ship, or other vehicle that is licensed to offer transportation services to the public, generally in return for compensation or a payment.

Common Carriers Transportation providers that are publicly licensed to provide transportation services to the general public are referred to as **common carriers.** They are distinguished from private carriers, which operate transportation facilities for a select clientele. A private carrier is not required to provide service to every person or company making a request. A common carrier, however, must arrange carriage for all who apply, within certain limitations.[11]

The delivery of goods to a common carrier creates a bailment relationship between the shipper (bailor) and the common carrier (bailee). Unlike ordinary bailees, the common carrier is held to a standard of care based on *strict liability,* rather than reasonable care, in protecting the bailed personal property. This means

10. UCC 2A–212, 2A–213.

11. A common carrier is not required to take any and all property anywhere in all instances. Public regulatory agencies govern common carriers, and carriers can be restricted to geographic areas. They can also be limited to carrying certain kinds of goods or to providing only special types of transportation equipment.

A truck travels a highway. To what standard of care are common carriers subject? (© Peter Vadnai, Getty Images)

that the common carrier is absolutely liable, regardless of due care, for all loss or damage to goods except damage caused by one of the following common law exceptions: (1) an act of God, (2) an act of a public enemy, (3) an order of a public authority, (4) an act of the shipper, or (5) the inherent nature of the goods.

Common carriers cannot contract away their liability for damaged goods. Subject to government regulations, however, they are permitted to limit their dollar liability to an amount stated on the shipment contract or rate filing.[12]

Warehouse Companies *Warehousing* is the business of providing storage of property for compensation.[13] Like ordinary bailees, warehouse companies are liable for loss or damage to property resulting from *negligence.* A warehouse company, however, is a professional bailee and is therefore expected to exercise a high degree of care to protect and preserve the goods. A warehouse company can limit the dollar amount of its liability, but the bailor must be given the option of paying a higher rate to the bailee to increase the amount of liability.

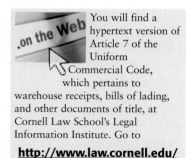

> **on the Web** You will find a hypertext version of Article 7 of the Uniform Commercial Code, which pertains to warehouse receipts, bills of lading, and other documents of title, at Cornell Law School's Legal Information Institute. Go to **http://www.law.cornell.edu/ucc/7/overview.html**.

Unlike ordinary bailees, a warehouse company can issue *documents of title*—in particular, *warehouse receipts*—and is subject to extensive government regulation, including Article 7 of the UCC.[14] A warehouse receipt describes the bailed property and the terms of the bailment contract. It can be negotiable or nonnegotiable, depending on how it is written. It is negotiable if its terms provide that the warehouse company will deliver the goods "to the bearer" of the receipt or "to the order of" a person named on the receipt.[15] The warehouse receipt represents the goods (that is, it indicates title) and hence has value and utility in financing commercial transactions.

12. Federal laws require common carriers to offer shippers the opportunity to obtain higher dollar limits for loss by paying a higher fee for the transport.

13. UCC 7–102(h) defines the person engaged in the storing of goods for hire as a "warehouseman."

14. A *document of title* is defined in UCC 1–201(15) as any "document which in the regular course of business or financing is treated as adequately evidencing that the person in possession of it is entitled to receive, hold, and dispose of the document and the goods it covers. To be a document of title, a document must purport to be issued by or addressed to a bailee and purport to cover goods in the bailee's possession." A *warehouse receipt* is a receipt issued by a person engaged in the business of storing goods for hire.

15. UCC 7–104.

INSURANCE
A contract in which, for a stipulated consideration, one party agrees to compensate the other for loss on a specific subject by a specified peril.

RISK
A prediction concerning potential loss based on known and unknown factors.

RISK MANAGEMENT
Planning that is undertaken to protect one's interest should some event threaten to undermine its security. In the context of insurance, risk management involves transferring certain risks from the insured to the insurance company.

■ EXAMPLE 23.24 Ossip delivers 6,500 cases of canned corn to Chaney, the owner of a warehouse. Chaney issues a negotiable warehouse receipt payable "to bearer" and gives it to Ossip. Ossip sells and delivers the warehouse receipt to Better Foods, Inc. Better Foods is now the owner of the corn and has the right to obtain the cases by simply presenting the warehouse receipt to Chaney. ■

Innkeepers At common law, innkeepers, hotel owners, and similar operators were held to the same strict liability as common carriers with respect to property brought into the rooms by guests. Today, only those who provide lodging to the public for compensation as a *regular* business are covered under this rule of strict liability. Moreover, the rule applies only to those who are guests, as opposed to lodgers. A lodger is a permanent resident of the hotel or inn, whereas a guest is a transient traveler.

In many states, innkeepers can avoid strict liability for loss of guests' valuables and funds by providing a safe in which to keep them. Each guest must be clearly notified of the availability of such a safe. Statutes often limit the liability of innkeepers with regard to articles that are not kept in the safe or are of such a nature that they normally are not kept in a safe. These statutes may limit the amount of monetary damages or even provide for no liability in the absence of innkeeper negligence.

Normally, the innkeeper (a motel keeper, for example) assumes no responsibility for the safety of a guest's automobile because the guest usually retains possession and control over it. If, however, the innkeeper provides parking facilities and the guest's car is entrusted to the innkeeper or to an employee, the innkeeper will be liable under the rules that pertain to parking-lot bailments (which are ordinary bailments).

A New York building was damaged by debris from the collapse of the World Trade Center in 2001. What impact has the risk of terrorist acts had on insurance? (Michael Rieger, FEMA News Photo)

Insurance

Many precautions may be taken to protect against the hazards of life. For instance, an individual may wear a seat belt to protect against injuries from automobile accidents or install smoke detectors to guard against injury from fire. Of course, no one can predict whether an accident or a fire will ever occur, but individuals and businesses must establish plans to protect their personal and financial interests should some event threaten to undermine their security.

Insurance is a contract by which the insurance company (the insurer) promises to pay a sum of money or give something of value to another (either the insured or the beneficiary) in the event that the insured is injured, dies, or sustains damage to her or his property as a result of particular, stated contingencies. Basically, insurance is an arrangement for *transferring and allocating risk*. In many cases, **risk** can be described as a prediction concerning potential loss based on known and unknown factors. Insurance, however, involves much more than a game of chance.

Risk management normally involves the transfer of certain risks from the individual to the insurance company by a contractual agreement. The insurance contract and its provisions will be examined shortly. First, however, we look at the different types of insurance that can be obtained, insurance terminology, and the concept of insurable interest.

CLASSIFICATIONS OF INSURANCE

Insurance is classified according to the nature of the risk involved. For instance, fire insurance, casualty insurance, life insurance, and title insurance apply to different types of risk. Furthermore, policies of these types protect different persons and interests. This is reasonable because the types of losses that are expected and that are foreseeable or unforeseeable vary with the nature of the activity. Exhibit 23–2 on pages 718–719 presents a list of insurance classifications. (For a discussion of insurance policies designed to cover the special kinds of risks faced by online businesses, see the *Application* feature at the end of this chapter.)

All-risk insurance is property insurance that covers damage resulting from all risks not specifically excluded. Typical exclusions are war, pollution, earthquakes, and floods. After September 11, 2001, insurance companies commonly added acts of terrorism to the list of exclusions. Separate terrorism insurance is available, though. The question in the following case was whether an agreement that required a business to carry all-risk insurance and "other reasonable insurance" included coverage against terrorism.

CASE 23.3 Omni Berkshire Corp. v. Wells Fargo Bank, N.A.

United States District Court,
Southern District of New York, 2004.
307 F.Supp.2d 534.

FACTS Omni Berkshire Corporation and its business affiliates own or operate hotels in the United States, Canada, and Mexico. In 1998, Omni borrowed $250 million from Secore Financial Corporation. The loan was secured by five of Omni's hotels, worth collectively about $349 million. The loan agreement required Omni to obtain and maintain certain insurance, including "all risk insurance" on the hotels and "such other reasonable insurance" as the lender might request. In 1998, Omni's all-risk policy provided that "damage done by terrorists * * * is insured." When Omni renewed the policy in 2002, however, it excluded coverage for acts of terrorism. Wells Fargo Bank, N.A., which collected the payments on the loan, told Omni that insurance against terrorist acts was required to comply with the agreement. Omni learned that $60 million in terrorism coverage for the five hotels for one year could be purchased for $316,000—63 percent of the cost of an all-risk policy. Omni filed a suit in a federal district court against Wells Fargo, seeking an order that it was *not* required to obtain insurance against terrorism.

ISSUE Is a business required to carry terrorism insurance under an agreement that requires "all risk insurance" and "such other reasonable insurance" as the lender might request?

DECISION Yes. The court dismissed Omni's complaint and ordered it to obtain terrorism insurance. If Omni failed to do so, the court authorized Wells Fargo to obtain a policy and charge the expense to Omni.

REASON The court concluded that Omni was not required to buy insurance against terrorist acts under the "all risk" clause, but that Wells Fargo acted reasonably in requesting the coverage under the "other reasonable insurance" clause. When the parties negotiated the loan, if they had intended to require Omni to maintain "all risk" insurance that included coverage against terrorism, "they surely would have said so." The parties did not discuss the issue at the time, and the agreement did not define "all risk" to include terrorist acts. Nevertheless, the court concluded that Wells Fargo's concern for the risk was reasonable and noted that several recent terrorist attacks had involved hotels. For example, "[i]n the World Trade Center attacks on 9/11, one hotel was destroyed and two others were damaged." Other hotel operators and commercial property owners have bought terrorism insurance. The cost appeared to be "reasonable." Also, Omni, as well as Wells Fargo, would benefit from the coverage.

WHY IS THIS CASE IMPORTANT? *The decision in this case is the first time that terrorism insurance has been classified and required as "other reasonable insurance."*

INSURANCE TERMINOLOGY

POLICY
In insurance law, a contract between the insurer and the insured in which, for a stipulated consideration, the insurer agrees to compensate the insured for loss on a specific subject by a specified peril.

PREMIUM
In insurance law, the price paid by the insured for insurance protection for a specified period of time.

UNDERWRITER
In insurance law, the insurer, or the one assuming a risk in return for the payment of a premium.

An insurance contract is called a **policy;** the consideration paid to the insurer is called a **premium;** and the insurance company is sometimes called an **underwriter.** The parties to an insurance policy are the *insurer* (the insurance company) and the *insured* (the person covered by its provisions or the holder of the policy).

Insurance contracts are usually obtained through an *agent,* who ordinarily works for the insurance company, or through a *broker,* who is ordinarily an *independent contractor.* When a broker deals with an applicant for insurance, the broker is, in effect, the applicant's agent and not an agent of the insurance company. In contrast, an insurance agent is an agent of the insurance company, not of the applicant. As a general rule, the insurance company is bound by the acts of its insurance agents when they act within the agency relationship (discussed in Chapter 17). In most situations, state law determines the status of all parties writing or obtaining insurance.

ETHICAL ISSUE 23.2

Does an insurance agent have a duty to advise insurance applicants about coverage? When a person applies for insurance coverage through an insurance company's agent, is the agent obligated to advise that person as to what coverage he or she should obtain? If the agent does not advise a client about certain types of coverage, has the agent breached a duty to the applicant? For example, suppose that a couple applies for auto insurance, and the insurance agent does not advise them that they should sign up for uninsured motorist coverage. Later, the couple is involved in an accident with an uninsured motorist, and the insurance company refuses to compensate them for their injuries and losses. The couple claims that the insurance agent was negligent in not advising them to sign up for uninsured motorist coverage. Was the agent negligent? No. As mentioned earlier, an insurance agent is an agent of the insurer, not the insured. As such, the agent owes fiduciary duties to the insurer (the insurance company), but not to the insured. The agent's only duties to the insured are contractual in nature.

While some may think that this rule is unfair to insurance applicants, who may know less about the need for certain types of insurance coverage than the agent does, a contrary rule might create even more unfairness. An insurance agent could be held liable for failure to advise a client of every possible insurance option, and the insured would be relieved of any burden to take care of his or her own financial needs and expectations. Also, as one court noted, if the state legislature does not require such coverage, why should the courts require insurance companies to offer or explain available optional coverage?[16] ■

INSURABLE INTEREST

INSURABLE INTEREST
An interest either in a person's life or well-being or in property that is sufficiently substantial that insuring against injury to (or the death of) the person or against damage to the property does not amount to a mere wagering (betting) contract.

A person can insure anything in which she or he has an **insurable interest.** Without this insurable interest, there is no enforceable contract, and a transaction to purchase insurance coverage would have to be treated as a wager. In regard to real and personal property, an insurable interest exists when the insured derives a pecuniary benefit (a benefit consisting of or relating to money) from the preservation and continued existence of the property. Put another way, one has an insurable interest in property when one would sustain a financial loss from its destruction. In regard to life insurance, a person must have a reasonable expectation of benefit from the continued life

16. *Jones v. Kennedy,* 108 S.W.3d 203 (Mo.App. 2003).

EXHIBIT 23–2 INSURANCE CLASSIFICATIONS

TYPE OF INSURANCE	COVERAGE
Accident	Covers expenses, losses, and suffering incurred by the insured because of accidents causing physical injury and any consequent disability; sometimes includes a specified payment to heirs of the insured if death results from an accident.
All-risk	Covers all losses that the insured may incur except those resulting from fraud on the part of the insured.
Automobile	May cover damage to automobiles resulting from specified hazards or occurrences (such as fire, vandalism, theft, or collision); normally provides protection against liability for personal injuries and property damage resulting from the operation of the vehicle.
Casualty	Protects against losses incurred by the insured as a result of being held liable for personal injuries or property damage sustained by others.
Credit	Pays to a creditor the balance of a debt on the disability, death, insolvency, or bankruptcy of the debtor; often offered by lending institutions.
Decreasing-term life	Provides life insurance; requires uniform payments over the life (term) of the policy, but with a decreasing face value (amount of coverage).
Employer's liability	Insures employers against liability for injuries or losses sustained by employees during the course of their employment; covers claims not covered under workers' compensation insurance.
Fidelity or guaranty	Provides indemnity against losses in trade or losses caused by the dishonesty of employees, the insolvency of debtors, or breaches of contract.
Fire	Covers losses incurred by the insured as a result of fire.
Floater	Covers movable property, as long as the property is within the territorial boundaries specified in the contract.
Group	Provides individual life, medical, or disability insurance coverage but is obtainable through a group of persons, usually employees; the policy premium is paid either entirely by the employer or partially by the employer and partially by the employee.

of another in order to have an insurable interest in that person's life. The benefit may be pecuniary (as with so-called *key-person insurance,* which insures the lives of important employees, usually in small companies), or it may be founded on the relationship between the parties (by blood or affinity).

For property insurance, the insurable interest must exist at the time the loss occurs but need not exist when the policy is purchased. In contrast, for life insurance, the insurable interest must exist at the time the policy is obtained. The existence of an insurable interest is a primary concern in determining liability under an insurance policy.

THE INSURANCE CONTRACT

NOTE The federal government has the power to regulate the insurance industry under the commerce clause of the U.S. Constitution. Instead of exercising this power itself, Congress allows the states to regulate insurance.

An insurance contract is governed by the general principles of contract law, although the insurance industry is heavily regulated by each state. Several aspects of the insurance contract will be treated here, including the application for insurance, the date when the contract takes effect, and some of the important provisions typically found in insurance contracts. In addition, we will also discuss the cancellation of an insurance policy and defenses that insurance companies can raise against payment on a policy.

EXHIBIT 23–2 INSURANCE CLASSIFICATIONS—CONTINUED

TYPE OF INSURANCE	COVERAGE
Health	Covers expenses incurred by the insured as a result of physical injury or illness and other expenses relating to health and life maintenance.
Homeowners'	Protects homeowners against some or all risks of loss to their residences and the residences' contents or liability arising from the use of the property.
Key-person	Protects a business in the event of the death or disability of a key employee.
Liability	Protects against liability imposed on the insured as a result of injuries to the person or property of another.
Life	Covers the death of the policyholder. On the death of the insured, an amount specified in the policy is paid by the insurer to the insured's beneficiary.
Major medical	Protects the insured against major hospital, medical, or surgical expenses.
Malpractice	Protects professionals (physicians, lawyers, and others) against malpractice claims brought against them by their patients or clients; a form of liability insurance.
Marine	Covers movable property (including ships, freight, and cargo) against certain perils or navigation risks during a specific voyage or time period.
Mortgage	Covers a mortgage loan; the insurer pays the balance of the mortgage to the creditor on the death or disability of the debtor.
No-fault auto	Covers personal injuries and (sometimes) property damage resulting from automobile accidents. The insured submits his or her claims to his or her own insurance company, regardless of who was at fault. A person may sue the party at fault or that party's insurer only when an accident results in serious medical injury and consequent high medical costs. Governed by state "no-fault" statutes.
Term life	Provides life insurance for a specified period of time (term) with no cash surrender value; usually renewable.
Title	Protects against any defects in title to real property and any losses incurred as a result of existing claims against or liens on the property at the time of purchase.

Application The filled-in application form for insurance is usually attached to the policy and made a part of the insurance contract. Thus, an insurance applicant is bound by any false statements that appear in the application (subject to certain exceptions). Because the insurance company evaluates the risk factors based on the information included in the insurance application, misstatements or misrepresentations can void a policy, especially if the insurance company can show that it would not have extended insurance if it had known the true facts.

Effective Date The effective date of an insurance contract—that is, the date on which the insurance coverage begins—is important. In some instances, the insurance applicant is not protected until a formal written policy is issued. In other situations, the applicant is protected between the time the application is received and the time the insurance company either accepts or rejects it. Four facts should be kept in mind:

1. A broker is merely the agent of an applicant. Therefore, until the broker obtains a policy, the applicant normally is not insured.
2. A person who seeks insurance from an insurance company's agent will usually be protected from the moment the application is made, provided that some form

BINDER
A written, temporary insurance policy.

of premium has been paid. Between the time the application is received and either rejected or accepted, the applicant is covered (possibly subject to a medical examination). Usually, the agent will write a memorandum, or **binder,** indicating that a policy is pending and stating its essential terms.

3. If the parties agree that the policy will be issued and delivered at a later time, the contract is not effective until the policy is issued and delivered or sent to the applicant, depending on the agreement. Thus, any loss sustained between the time of application and the delivery of the policy is not covered.
4. The parties may agree that a life insurance policy will be binding at the time the insured pays the first premium, or the policy may be expressly contingent on the applicant's passing a physical examination. If the applicant pays the premium and passes the examination, the policy coverage is continuously in effect. If the applicant pays the premium but dies before having the physical examination, then in order to collect, the applicant's estate must show that the applicant *would have passed* the examination had he or she not died.

Coinsurance Clauses Often, when taking out fire insurance policies, property owners insure their property for less than full value because most fires do not result in a total loss. To encourage owners to insure their property for an amount as close to full value as possible, fire insurance policies commonly include a coinsurance clause. Typically, a *coinsurance clause* provides that if the owner insures the property up to a specified percentage—usually 80 percent—of its value, she or he will recover any loss up to the face amount of the policy. If the insurance is for less than the fixed percentage, the owner is responsible for a proportionate share of the loss.

Coinsurance applies only in instances of partial loss. ■ EXAMPLE 23.25 If the owner of property valued at \$100,000 takes out a policy in the amount of \$40,000 and suffers a loss of \$30,000, the recovery will be \$15,000. The formula for calculating the recovery amount is as follows:

$$\frac{\text{amount of insurance (\$40,000)}}{\text{coinsurance percentage (80\%)} \times \text{property value (\$100,000)}} = \begin{matrix}\text{recovery percentage}\\ \text{(50\%)}\end{matrix}$$

$$\text{recovery percentage (50\%)} \times \text{amount of loss (\$30,000)} = \text{recovery amount (\$15,000)}$$

If the owner had taken out a policy in the amount of \$80,000, then, according to the same formula, the full loss would have been recovered up to the face value of the policy. ■

Other Provisions and Clauses Some other important provisions and clauses contained in insurance contracts are listed and defined in Exhibit 23–3. The courts are aware that most people do not have the special training necessary to understand the intricate terminology used in insurance policies. Thus, the words used in an insurance contract have their ordinary meanings. They are interpreted by the courts in light of the nature of the coverage involved—see, for example, this chapter's *Adapting the Law to the Online Environment* feature on page 722.

When there is an ambiguity in the policy, the provision generally is interpreted against the insurance company. Also when it is unclear whether an insurance contract actually exists because the written policy has not been delivered, the uncertainty normally is resolved against the insurance company. The court presumes that the policy is in effect unless the company can show otherwise. Similarly, an insurer must make sure that the insured is adequately notified of any change in coverage under an existing policy.

EXHIBIT 23–3 INSURANCE CONTRACT PROVISIONS AND CLAUSES

Incontestability clause	An incontestability clause provides that after a policy has been in force for a specified length of time—usually two or three years—the insurer cannot contest statements made in the application.
Appraisal clause	Insurance policies frequently provide that if the parties cannot agree on the amount of a loss covered under the policy or the value of the property lost, an appraisal, or estimate, by an impartial and qualified third party can be demanded.
Arbitration clause	Many insurance policies include clauses that call for arbitration of disputes that may arise between the insurer and the insured concerning the settlement of claims.
Antilapse clause	An antilapse clause provides that the policy will not automatically lapse if no payment is made on the date due. Ordinarily, under such a provision, the insured has a *grace period* of thirty or thirty-one days within which to pay an overdue premium before the policy is canceled.
Multiple insurance	Many insurance policies include a clause providing that if the insured has multiple insurance policies that cover the same property and the amount of coverage exceeds the loss, the loss will be shared proportionately by the insurance companies.

Cancellation The insured can cancel a policy at any time, and the insurer can cancel under certain circumstances. When an insurance company can cancel its insurance contract, the policy or a state statute usually requires that the insurer give advance written notice of the cancellation to the insured.[17] The same requirement applies when only part of a policy is canceled. Any premium paid in advance may be refundable on the policy's cancellation. The insured may also be entitled to a life insurance policy's cash surrender value.

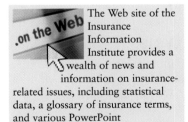

.on the Web The Web site of the Insurance Information Institute provides a wealth of news and information on insurance-related issues, including statistical data, a glossary of insurance terms, and various PowerPoint presentations. Go to **http://www.iii.org**.

The insurer may cancel an insurance policy for various reasons, depending on the type of insurance. For example, automobile insurance can be canceled for nonpayment of premiums or suspension of the insured's driver's license. Property insurance can be canceled for nonpayment of premiums or for other reasons, including the insured's fraud or misrepresentation, conviction for a crime that increases the hazard insured against, or gross negligence that increases the hazard insured against. Life and health policies can be canceled because of false statements made by the insured in the application, but cancellation can only take place before the effective date of an incontestability clause. An insurer cannot cancel—or refuse to renew—a policy for discriminatory reasons or other reasons that violate public policy, or because the insured has appeared as a witness in a case against the company.

Good Faith Obligations Both parties to an insurance contract are responsible for the obligation they assume under the contract (contract law was discussed in

17. In at least one case, the court held that a diskette containing a computerized document, which could be printed out as "hard copy," was sufficient to constitute "written notice" of cancellation. See *Clyburn v. Allstate Insurance Co.,* 826 F.Supp. 955 (D.S.C. 1993).

ADAPTING THE LAW TO THE ONLINE ENVIRONMENT

Recovering for the Loss of Computer Data

Over the past decade, hackers have spread numerous viruses that can cause computer systems to fail and stored data to be lost. When a business's computer system comes under attack, often the damage is extensive. Yet traditional business insurance policies usually do not specifically cover the risks associated with the loss of computer information. Typically, business insurance covers only "physical loss," and a number of courts have held that computer information is not physical.[a] Only in rare circumstances have courts held that general business insurance policies cover the loss of computerized information.

A COMPUTER VIRUS CAUSED SIGNIFICANT DAMAGE

In one case, the operating system of an employment agency, Lambrecht & Associates, Inc., was attacked by a computer virus. All of Lambrecht's employees were networked into a large central server that was equipped with certain prepackaged software programs, such as Microsoft Office and Norton AntiVirus™. One day when the employees came to work, they discovered the computers were having difficulty booting up and were performing strange operations. Ultimately, the entire system froze up, and all of the information that had previously been stored on the system was deleted. As a result, Lambrecht's employees were unable to use their computers to communicate with prospective employers and employees, and the business lost income. In addition, Lambrecht had to replace its server, buy a new operating system and new software, and manually reenter a large amount of data. When Lambrecht filed a claim with its insurer, State Farm Lloyd's, State Farm denied coverage. Lambrecht filed suit, but the trial court agreed with the insurer that the loss was not covered. Lambrecht appealed.

THE EXACT LANGUAGE OF THE INSURANCE POLICY

Lambrecht had a business insurance policy that provided coverage for "accidental direct physical loss to business personal property." In addition, Lambrecht had purchased $100,000 of additional coverage for replacement of valuable "papers or records, including those which exist on electronic or magnetic media," provided that the loss is not "caused by an error in programming." State Farm contended that the damage to Lambrecht's computer system was neither "accidental" nor "physical," as the insurance policy required for coverage.

THE MEANING OF "ACCIDENTAL" AND "PHYSICAL" LOSS

According to State Farm, the damage was not accidental because the hacker's act of infecting Lambrecht's computer system with a virus was voluntary and intentional. The state appellate court, however, held that the question of whether an occurrence was "accidental" should be determined by looking at the incident from the perspective of the insured. Here, there was no evidence to indicate "that Lambrecht was involved in any voluntary or intentional conduct or took any action which caused the damage Lambrecht suffered." Thus, the court held that the damage was unexpected and accidental.

The court also rejected State Farm's argument that the data loss was not "physical" because data are not tangible (capable of being touched). Although the court recognized that other judges have focused on this distinction, in this case, the plain terms of the policy expressly covered electronic records and storage media. Hence, the court held that the language of the policy dictated a finding that the data losses Lambrecht suffered were "physical" as a matter of law.[b]

FOR CRITICAL ANALYSIS

If the policy in this case had not expressly mentioned loss of electronic records, would the court have found that the loss was "physical"? Why or why not?

a. See, for example, *America Online, Inc. v. St. Paul Mercury Insurance Co.,* 207 F.Supp.2d 459 (E.D.Va. 2002).

b. *Lambrecht & Associates, Inc. v. State Farm Lloyd's,* 119 S.W.3d 16 (Tex.App. 2003).

Chapters 7 through 10). In addition, both the insured and the insurer have an implied duty to act in good faith.

Good faith requires the party who is applying for insurance to reveal everything necessary for the insurer to evaluate the risk. In other words, the applicant must disclose all material facts, including all facts that an insurer would consider in determining whether to charge a higher premium or to refuse to issue a policy altogether.

Once the insurer has accepted the risk, and some event occurs that gives rise to a claim, the insurer has a duty to investigate to determine the facts. When a policy provides insurance against third party claims, the insurer is obligated to make reasonable efforts to settle such a claim. If a settlement cannot be reached, then regardless of the claim's merit, the insurer must defend any suit against the insured. Usually, a policy provides that in this situation the insured must cooperate. A policy provision may expressly require the insured to attend hearings and trials, to help in obtaining evidence and witnesses, and to assist in reaching a settlement.

Defenses against Payment An insurance company can raise any of the defenses that would be valid in any ordinary action on a contract, as well as some defenses that do not apply in ordinary contract actions. If the insurance company can show that the policy was procured by fraud or misrepresentation, it may have a valid defense for not paying on a claim. (The insurance company may also have the right to disaffirm or rescind an insurance contract.) An absolute defense exists if the insurer can show that the insured lacked an insurable interest—thus rendering the policy void from the beginning. Improper actions, such as those that are against public policy or are otherwise illegal, can also give the insurance company a defense against the payment of a claim or allow it to rescind the contract.

An insurance company can be prevented from asserting some defenses that are normally available, however. ■ EXAMPLE 23.26 Suppose that a company tells an insured that information requested on a form is optional, and the insured provides it anyway. The company cannot use the information to avoid its contractual obligation under the insurance contract. Similarly, an insurance company normally cannot escape payment on the death of an insured on the ground that the person's age was stated incorrectly on the application. ■

APPLICATION How Can You Manage Risk in Cyberspace?*

As mentioned elsewhere, companies doing business online face many risks that are not covered by traditional types of insurance (see Exhibit 23–2). Not surprisingly, a growing number of companies are now offering policies designed to cover Web-related risks.

INSURANCE COVERAGE FOR WEB-RELATED RISKS

Consider the types of coverage that are offered by Net Secure, a venture undertaken by IBM, several insurance companies, and a New York broker. Net Secure provides insurance protection against losses resulting from programming errors; network and Web site disruptions; the theft of electronic data and assets, including intellectual property; Web-related defamation, copyright infringement, and false advertising; and the violation of users' privacy rights.

InsureTrust.com, an insurer affiliated with three leading insurance companies—American International Group, Lloyd's of London, and Reliance National—offers similar coverage. Existing insurers, such as Lloyd's of London, Hartford Insurance, and the Chubb Group of Insurance

* This *Application* is not meant to substitute for the services of an attorney who is licensed to practice law in your state.

(Continued)

APPLICATION How Can You Manage Risk in Cyberspace?—Continued

Companies, are also adding insurance for Web-related perils to their offerings. Clearly, the market for these new types of insurance coverage is rapidly evolving, and new policies will continue to appear.

CUSTOMIZED POLICIES

Unlike traditional insurance policies, which are generally drafted by insurance companies and presented to insurance applicants on a "take-it-or-leave-it" basis, Internet-particular policies are usually customized to provide protection against specific risks faced by a particular type of business. For example, an Internet service provider will face different risks than an online merchant, and a banking institution will face different risks than a law firm. The specific business-related risks are taken into consideration when determining the policy premium.

QUALIFYING CRITERIA

Many companies that offer cyberinsurance require applicants to meet high security standards. In other words, to qualify for a policy under the insurance companies' risk management processes, a business must have Web-related security measures in place. Several of the companies assess the applicant's security system before underwriting a policy. For example, Net Secure assesses the applicant's security measures and will not provide coverage unless the business scores better than 60 percent. If the business does not score that high, it can contract with Net Secure to improve its Web-related security.

CHECKLIST FOR THE BUSINESSPERSON

1. Determine the types of risks to which your Web business is exposed and try to obtain an insurance policy that protects you against those specific risks.
2. As when procuring any type of insurance coverage, read the policy carefully, including any exclusions contained in the fine print, before committing to it.
3. Do not be "penny wise and pound foolish" when it comes to insurance protection. Though insurance coverage may seem expensive, it may be much less costly than defending against a lawsuit. Often, the cost of coverage can be reduced by purchasing a policy with a high deductible.
4. Find out what the company's underwriting standards are and determine whether your Web security measures meet its standards.

KEY TERMS

CHAPTER SUMMARY Personal Property, Bailments, and Insurance

	PERSONAL PROPERTY
Definition of Personal Property (See pages 697–698.)	Personal property (personalty) includes all property not classified as real property (realty). Personal property can be tangible (such as a TV set or a car) or intangible (such as stocks or bonds). Personal property may be referred to legally as *chattel*—a term used under the common law to denote all forms of personal property.
Property Ownership (See pages 698–700.)	Having the fullest ownership rights in property is called *fee simple* ownership. There are various ways of co-owning property, including *tenancy in common, joint tenancy, tenancy by the entirety,* and *community property.*
Acquiring Ownership of Personal Property (See pages 700–705.)	The most common means of acquiring ownership in personal property is by purchasing it (see Chapters 11 through 13). Another way in which personal property is often acquired is by will or inheritance. The following are additional methods of acquiring personal property: 1. *Possession*—Ownership may be acquired by possession if no other person has ownership title (for example, capturing wild animals or finding abandoned property). 2. *Production*—Any product or item produced by an individual (with minor exceptions) becomes the property of that individual. 3. *Gift*—An effective gift exists when the following conditions exist: a. There is evidence of *intent* to make a gift of the property in question. b. The gift is *delivered* (physically or constructively) to the donee or the donee's agent. c. The gift is *accepted* by the donee or the donee's agent. 4. *Accession*—When someone adds value to an item of personal property by labor or materials, the added value generally becomes the property of the owner of the original property (includes accessions made in bad faith or wrongfully). Good faith accessions that substantially increase the property's value or change the identity of the property may cause title to pass to the improver. 5. *Confusion*—In the case of fungible goods, if a person wrongfully and willfully commingles goods with those of another in order to render them indistinguishable, the innocent party acquires title to the whole. Otherwise, the owners become tenants in common of the commingled goods.
Mislaid, Lost, and Abandoned Property (See pages 705–708.)	1. *Mislaid property*—Property that is placed somewhere voluntarily by the owner and then inadvertently forgotten. A finder of mislaid property will not acquire title to the goods, and the owner of the place where the property was mislaid becomes a caretaker of the mislaid property. 2. *Lost property*—Property that is involuntarily left and forgotten. A finder of lost property can claim title to the property against the whole world *except the true owner.* 3. *Abandoned property*—Property that has been discarded by the true owner, who has no intention of claiming title to the property in the future. A finder of abandoned property can claim title to it against the whole world, *including the original owner.*
	BAILMENTS
Elements of a Bailment (See pages 708–710.)	1. *Personal property*—Bailments involve only personal property. 2. *Delivery of possession*—For an effective bailment to exist, the bailee (the one receiving the property) must be given exclusive possession and control over the property, and in a voluntary bailment, the bailee must knowingly accept the personal property. 3. *The bailment agreement*—Expressly or impliedly provides for the return of the bailed property to the bailor or a third party, or for the disposal of the bailed property by the bailee.

(Continued)

CHAPTER SUMMARY Personal Property, Bailments, and Insurance—Continued

Ordinary Bailments (See pages 710–713.)	1. *Types of bailments*— a. Bailment for the sole benefit of the bailor—A gratuitous bailment undertaken for the sole benefit of the bailor (for example, as a favor to the bailor). b. Bailment for the sole benefit of the bailee—A gratuitous loan of an article to a person (the bailee) solely for the bailee's benefit. c. Mutual-benefit (contractual) bailment—The most common kind of bailment; involves compensation between the bailee and bailor for the service provided. 2. *Rights of a bailee (duties of a bailor)*— a. The right of possession—Allows actions against third persons who damage or convert the bailed property and allows actions against the bailor for wrongful breach of the bailment. b. The right to be compensated and reimbursed for expenses—In the event of nonpayment, the bailee has the right to place a possessory (bailee's) lien on the bailed property. c. The right to limit liability—An ordinary bailee can limit his or her liability for loss or damage, provided proper notice is given and the limitation is not against public policy. In special bailments, limitations on liability for negligence or on types of losses usually are not allowed, but limitations on the monetary amount of liability are permitted. 3. *Duties of a bailee (rights of a bailor)*— a. A bailee must exercise appropriate care over property entrusted to her or him. What constitutes appropriate care normally depends on the nature and circumstances of the bailment. b. Bailed goods in a bailee's possession must be either returned to the bailor or disposed of according to the bailor's directions. A bailee's failure to return the bailed property creates a presumption of negligence and constitutes a breach of contract or the tort of conversion of goods.
Special Types of Bailments (See pages 713–715.)	1. *Common carriers*—Carriers that are publicly licensed to provide transportation services to the general public. A common carrier is held to a standard of care based on *strict liability* unless the bailed property is lost or destroyed due to (a) an act of God, (b) an act of a public enemy, (c) an order of a public authority, (d) an act of the shipper, or (e) the inherent nature of the goods. 2. *Warehouse companies*—Professional bailees that differ from ordinary bailees in that they (a) can issue documents of title (warehouse receipts) and (b) are subject to state and federal statutes, including Article 7 of the UCC (as are common carriers). They must exercise a high degree of care over the bailed property and are liable for loss of or damage to property if they fail to do so. 3. *Innkeepers (hotel operators)*—Those who provide lodging to the public for compensation as a *regular* business. The common law strict liability standard to which innkeepers were once held is limited today by state statutes, which vary from state to state.
	INSURANCE
Classifications (See pages 715–716.)	See Exhibit 23–2 on pages 718 and 719.
Terminology (See page 717.)	1. *Policy*—The insurance contract. 2. *Premium*—The consideration paid to the insurer for a policy. 3. *Underwriter*—The insurance company. 4. *Parties*—Include the insurer (the insurance company), the insured (the person covered by insurance), an agent (a representative of the insurance company) or a broker (ordinarily an independent contractor), and a beneficiary (a person to receive proceeds under the policy).

CHAPTER SUMMARY Personal Property, Bailments, and Insurance—Continued

Insurable Interest (See pages 717–718.)	An insurable interest exists whenever an individual or entity benefits from the preservation of the health or life of the insured or the property to be insured. For life insurance, an insurable interest must exist at the time the policy is issued. For property insurance, an insurable interest must exist at the time of the loss.
The Insurance Contract (See pages 718–723.)	1. *Laws governing*—The general principles of contract law are applied; the insurance industry is also heavily regulated by the states. 2. *Application*—An insurance applicant is bound by any false statements that appear in the application (subject to certain exceptions), which is part of the insurance contract. Misstatements or misrepresentations may be grounds for voiding the policy. 3. *Effective date*—Coverage on an insurance policy can begin when a *binder* (a written memorandum indicating that a formal policy is pending and stating its essential terms) is written; when the policy is issued; at the time of contract formation; or depending on the terms of the contract, when certain conditions are met. 4. *Provisions and clauses*—See Exhibit 23–3 on page 721. Words will be given their ordinary meanings, and any ambiguity in the policy will be interpreted against the insurance company. When the written policy has not been delivered and it is unclear whether an insurance contract actually exists, the uncertainty will be resolved against the insurance company. The court will presume that the policy is in effect unless the company can show otherwise. 5. *Defenses against payment to the insured*—Defenses include misrepresentation, fraud, or violation of warranties by the applicant.

FOR REVIEW

Answers for the even-numbered questions in this For Review *section can be found in Appendix I at the end of this text.*

1. What is real property? What is personal property?
2. What are the three elements necessary for an effective gift? How else can property be acquired?
3. What are the three elements of a bailment? What are the basic rights and duties of a bailee? What are the rights and duties of a bailor?
4. What is an insurable interest? When must an insurable interest exist—at the time the insurance policy is obtained, at the time the loss occurs, or both?
5. What clauses are typically included in insurance contracts?

QUESTIONS AND CASE PROBLEMS

23–1. Duties of the Bailee. Discuss the standard of care traditionally required of the bailee for the bailed property in each of the following situations, and determine whether the bailee breached that duty.

(a) Ricardo borrows Steve's lawn mower because his own lawn mower needs repair. Ricardo mows his front yard. To mow the backyard, he needs to move some hoses and lawn furniture. He leaves the mower in front of his house while doing so. When he returns to the front yard, he discovers that the mower has been stolen.

(b) Alicia owns a valuable speedboat. She is going on vacation and asks her neighbor, Maureen, to store the boat in one stall of Maureen's double garage. Maureen consents, and the boat is moved into the garage. Maureen needs some grocery items for dinner and drives to the store. She leaves the garage door open while she is gone, as is her custom, and the speedboat is stolen during that time.

23–2. Gifts. Reineken, very old and ill, wanted to make a gift to his nephew, Gerald. He had a friend obtain $2,500 in cash for him from his bank account, placed this cash in an envelope, and wrote on the envelope, "This is for my nephew, Gerald." Reineken then placed the envelope in his dresser drawer. When Reineken died a month later, his family found the envelope, and Gerald got word of the intended gift. Gerald then demanded that Reineken's daughter, the executor of Reineken's estate (the person who was appointed by Reineken to handle his affairs after his death), turn over the gift to him. The daughter refused to do so. Discuss fully whether Gerald can successfully claim ownership rights to the $2,500.

23–3. Timing of Insurance Coverage. On October 10, Joleen Vora applied for a $50,000 life insurance policy with Magnum Life Insurance Co.; she named her husband, Jay, as the beneficiary. Joleen paid the insurance company the first year's policy premium on making the application. Two days later, before she had a chance to take the physical examination required by the insurance company and before the policy was issued, Joleen was killed in an automobile accident. Jay submitted a claim to the insurance company for the $50,000. Can Jay collect? Explain.

23–4. Insurer's Defenses. In 1990, the city of Worcester, Massachusetts, adopted an ordinance that required rooming houses to be equipped with automatic sprinkler systems no later than September 25, 1995. In Worcester, James and Mark Duffy owned a forty-eight-room lodging house with two retail stores on the first floor. In 1994, the Duffys applied with General Star Indemnity Co. for an insurance policy to cover the premises. The application indicated that the premises had a sprinkler system. General issued a policy that required, among other safety features, a sprinkler system. Within a month, the premises were inspected on behalf of General. On the inspection form forwarded to the insurer, the inspector inserted only a hyphen next to the word *sprinkler* in the list of safety systems. In July 1995, when the premises sustained over $100,000 in fire damage, General learned that there was no sprinkler system. The insurer filed a suit in a federal district court against the Duffys to rescind the policy, alleging misrepresentation in their insurance application about the presence of sprinklers. How should the court rule, and why? [*General Star Indemnity Co. v. Duffy,* 191 F.3d 55 (1st Cir. 1999)]

23–5. Interpretation of an Insurance Policy's Terms. Valley Furniture & Interiors, Inc., bought an insurance policy from Transportation Insurance Co. (TIC). The policy provided coverage of $50,000 for each occurrence of property loss caused by employee dishonesty. An "occurrence" was defined as "a single act or series of related acts." Valley allowed its employees to take pay advances and to buy discounted merchandise, with the advances and the cost of the merchandise deducted from their paychecks. The payroll manager was to notify the payroll company to make the deductions. Over a period of six years, without notifying the payroll company, the payroll manager issued advances to other employees and herself and bought merchandise for herself, in amounts totaling more than $200,000. Valley filed claims with TIC for three "occurrences" of employee theft. TIC considered the acts a "series of related acts" and paid only $50,000. Valley filed a suit in a Washington state court against TIC, alleging, in part, breach of contract. What is the standard for interpreting an insurance clause? How should this court interpret "series of related acts"? Why? [*Valley Furniture & Interiors, Inc. v. Transportation Insurance Co.,* 107 Wash.App. 104, 26 P.3d 952 (Div. 1 2001)]

CASE PROBLEM WITH SAMPLE ANSWER

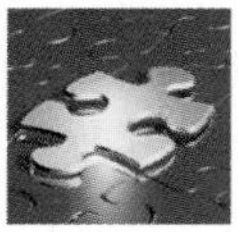

23–6. A. D. Lock owned Lock Hospitality, Inc., which in turn owned the Best Western Motel in Conway, Arkansas. Joe Terry and David Stocks were preparing the motel for renovation. As they were removing the ceiling tiles in room 118, with Lock present in the room, they noticed a dusty cardboard box near the heating and air-supply vent where it had apparently been concealed. Terry climbed a ladder to reach the box, opened it, and handed it to Stocks. The box was filled with more than $38,000 in old currency. Lock took possession of the box and its contents. Terry and Stocks filed a suit in an Arkansas state court against Lock and his corporation to obtain the money. Should the money be characterized as lost, mislaid, or abandoned property? To whom should the court award it? Explain. [*Terry v. Lock,* 37 S.W.3d 202 (Ark. 2001)]

After you have answered this problem, compare your answer with the sample answer given on the Web site that accompanies this text. Go to http://blt.westbuslaw.com, select "Chapter 23," and click on "Case Problem with Sample Answer."

23–7. Concurrent Ownership. Vincent Slavin was a partner at Cantor Fitzgerald Securities in the World Trade Center (WTC) in New York City. In 1998, Slavin and Anna Baez became engaged and began living together. They placed both of their names on three accounts at Chase Manhattan Bank according to the bank's terms, which provided that "accounts with multiple owners are joint, payable to either owner or the survivor." Slavin arranged for the direct deposit of his salary and commissions into one of the accounts. On September 11, 2001, Slavin died when two planes piloted by terrorists crashed into the WTC towers, causing their collapse. At the time, the balance in the three accounts was $656,944.36. On September 14, Cantor Fitzgerald deposited an additional $58,264.73 into the direct-deposit account. Baez soon withdrew the entire amount from all of the accounts. Mary Jelnek, Slavin's mother, filed a suit in a New York state court against Baez to determine the ownership of the funds that had been in the accounts. In what form of ownership were the accounts held? Who is entitled to which of the funds, and why? [*In re Jelnek,* 3 Misc.3d 725, 777 N.Y.S.2d 871 (Sur. 2004)]

A QUESTION OF ETHICS

23–8. George Cook stayed at a Day's Inn motel in Nashville, Tennessee, while attending a trade show. At the trade show, Cook received orders for 225 cases of his firm's product, representing $17,336.25 in profits to the company. On the third day of his stay, Cook's room was burglarized while he was gone from the room. The burglar took Cook's order lists, as well as $174 in cash and medicine worth about $10. Cook sued the owner of the motel, Columbia Sussex Corp., alleging negligence. The motel defended by stating that it had posted a notice on the door of Cook's room informing guests of the fact that the motel would not be liable for any valuable property not placed in the motel safe for safekeeping. Given these circumstances, evaluate and answer the following questions. [*Cook v. Columbia Sussex Corp.*, 807 S.W.2d 567 (Tenn.App. 1990)]

1. The relevant state statute governing the liability of innkeepers allowed motels to disclaim their liability by posting a notice such as the one posted by Day's Inn, but the statute also required that the notice be posted "in a conspicuous manner." The notice posted by Day's Inn on the inside of the door to Cook's room was six-by-three inches in size. In your opinion, is the notice sufficiently conspicuous? If you were the guest, would you have seen the disclaimer? Is it fair to guests to assume that they will notice such disclaimers? Discuss fully.
2. Should hotels or motels ever be allowed to disclaim liability by posting such notices? From a policy point of view, evaluate the implications of your answer.

FOR CRITICAL ANALYSIS

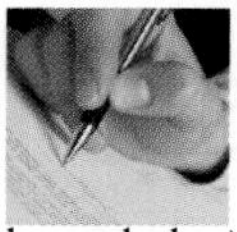

23–9. Suppose that a certificate of deposit (CD) owned by two joint tenants (with the right of survivorship) is given by one of the joint tenants as security for a loan (without the other joint tenant's knowledge). Further suppose that the joint tenant dies after defaulting on the loan. Who has superior rights in the CD, the creditor or the other surviving joint tenant?

VIDEO QUESTION

23–10. Go to this text's Web site at **http://blt.westbuslaw.com** and select "Chapter 23." Click on "Video Questions" and view the video titled *Personal Property and Bailments.* Then answer the following questions.

1. What type of bailment is discussed in the video?
2. What were Vinny's duties with regard to the rug-cleaning machine? What standard of care should apply?
3. Did Vinny exercise the appropriate degree of care? Why or why not? How would a court decide this issue?

INTERNET EXERCISES

Go to the *Business Law Today: The Essentials* home page at **http://blt.westbuslaw.com,** select "Chapter 23," and click on "Internet Exercises." There you will find the following Internet research exercises that you can perform to learn more about topics covered in this chapter.

Activity 23–1: LEGAL PERSPECTIVE—Lost Property

Activity 23–2: MANAGEMENT PERSPECTIVE—Bailments

Activity 23–3: MANAGEMENT PERSPECTIVE—Risk Management in Cyberspace

BEFORE THE TEST

Go to the *Business Law Today: The Essentials* home page at **http://blt.westbuslaw.com,** select "Chapter 23," and click on "Interactive Quizzes." You will find at least twenty interactive questions relating to this chapter.

CHAPTER 24

Real Property and Environmental Law

"The right of property is the most sacred of all the rights of citizenship."
Jean-Jacques Rousseau, 1712–1778
(French writer and philosopher)

CHAPTER OUTLINE

- THE NATURE OF REAL PROPERTY
- OWNERSHIP INTERESTS IN REAL PROPERTY
- TRANSFER OF OWNERSHIP
- LEASEHOLD ESTATES
- LANDLORD-TENANT RELATIONSHIPS
- ENVIRONMENTAL LAW

LEARNING OBJECTIVES

After reading this chapter, you should be able to answer the following questions:

1. What can a person who holds property in fee simple absolute do with the property? Can a person who holds property as a life estate do the same?
2. How can ownership rights in real property be transferred?
3. What are the respective duties of the landlord and tenant concerning the use and maintenance of leased property? Is the tenant responsible for all damages that he or she causes?
4. What is contained in an environmental impact statement, and who must file one?
5. What major federal statutes regulate air and water pollution? What is Superfund, and who is potentially liable under Superfund?

From earliest times, property has provided a means for survival. Primitive peoples lived off the fruits of the land, eating the vegetation and wildlife. Later, as the wildlife was domesticated and the vegetation cultivated, property provided pasturage and farmland. In the twelfth and thirteenth centuries in Europe, the power of feudal lords was determined by the amount of land they held; the more land, the more powerful they were. After the age of feudalism passed, property continued to be an indicator of family wealth and social position. In the Western world, an individual's right to his or her property has become, in the words of Jean-Jacques Rousseau, one of the "most sacred of all the rights of citizenship."

In this chapter, we first examine the nature of real property. We then look at the various ways in which real property can be owned and at how ownership rights in real property are transferred from one person to another. Finally, we look at some of the major statutes that help to protect our environment.

The Nature of Real Property

Real property consists of land and the buildings, plants, and trees that are on it. Real property also includes subsurface and air rights, as well as personal property that has become permanently attached to real property. Whereas personal property is movable, real property—also called *real estate* or *realty*—is immovable.

LAND

Land includes the soil on the surface of the earth and the natural or artificial structures that are attached to it. It further includes all the waters contained on or under the surface and much, but not necessarily all, of the airspace above it. The exterior boundaries of land extend down to the center of the earth and up to the farthest reaches of the atmosphere (subject to certain qualifications).

on the Web For links to numerous online legal sources relating to real property, go to **http://www.findlaw.com/01topics/index.html** and click on "Property Law & Real Estate."

AIR AND SUBSURFACE RIGHTS

The owner of real property has rights to the airspace above the land, as well as to the soil and minerals underneath it. Limitations on either air rights or subsurface rights normally have to be indicated on the document that transfers title at the time of purchase. When no such limitations, or *encumbrances,* are noted, a purchaser can normally expect to have an unlimited right to possession of the property.

Air Rights Early cases involving air rights dealt with such matters as whether a telephone wire could be run across a person's property when the wire did not touch any of the property[1] and whether a bullet shot over a person's land constituted trespass.[2] Today, disputes concerning air rights may involve the right of commercial and private planes to fly over property and the right of individuals and governments to seed clouds and produce rain artificially. Flights over private land normally do not violate the property owners' rights unless the flights are low and frequent enough to cause a direct interference with the enjoyment and use of the land.[3] Leaning walls or buildings and projecting eave spouts or roofs may also violate the air rights of an adjoining property owner.

A plane flies low over a residential area. Are the property owners' rights violated by such a low-flying plane? Why or why not? (© Jonathan Nourok, PhotoEdit)

1. *Butler v. Frontier Telephone Co.,* 186 N.Y. 486, 79 N.E. 716 (1906).
2. *Herrin v. Sutherland,* 74 Mont. 587, 241 P. 328 (1925). Shooting over a person's land constitutes trespass.
3. *United States v. Causby,* 328 U.S. 256, 66 S.Ct. 1062, 90 L.Ed. 1206 (1946).

Subsurface Rights In many states, land ownership may be separated, in that the surface of a piece of land and the subsurface may have different owners. Subsurface rights can be extremely valuable, as these rights include the ownership of minerals, oil, and natural gas. But subsurface rights would be of little value if the owner could not use the surface to exercise those rights. Hence, a subsurface owner will have a right (called a *profit,* discussed later in this chapter) to go onto the surface of the land to, for example, discover and mine minerals.

When the ownership is separated into surface and subsurface rights, each owner can pass title to what she or he owns without the consent of the other owner. Of course, conflicts can arise between a surface owner's use and the subsurface owner's need to extract minerals, oil, or natural gas. One party's interest may become subservient (secondary) to the other party's interest either by statute or case law. At common law and generally today if the owners of the subsurface rights excavate (dig), they are absolutely liable if their excavation causes the surface to collapse. Depending on the circumstances, the excavators may also be liable for any damage to structures on the land. Many states have statutes that extend excavators' liability to include damage to structures on the property. Typically, these statutes provide precise requirements for excavations of various depths.

Plant Life and Vegetation

Plant life, both natural and cultivated, is also considered to be real property. In many instances, the natural vegetation, such as trees, adds greatly to the value of the realty. When a parcel of land is sold and the land has growing crops on it, the sale includes the crops, unless otherwise specified in the sales contract. When crops are sold by themselves, however, they are considered to be personal property or goods. Consequently, the sale of crops is a sale of goods and thus is governed by the Uniform Commercial Code (UCC) rather than by real property law.[4]

Fixtures

FIXTURE
A thing that was once personal property but has become attached to real property in such a way that it takes on the characteristics of real property and becomes part of that real property.

Certain personal property can become so closely associated with the real property to which it is attached that the law views it as real property. Such property is known as a **fixture**—a thing *affixed* to realty, meaning that it is attached to the real property by roots; embedded in it; permanently situated on it; or permanently attached by means of cement, plaster, bolts, nails, or screws. The fixture can be physically attached to real property, be attached to another fixture, or even be without any actual physical attachment to the land (such as a statue). As long as the owner intends the property to be a fixture, normally it will be a fixture.

Fixtures are included in the sale of land if the sales contract does not provide otherwise. The sale of a house includes the land and the house and the garage on the land, as well as the cabinets, plumbing, and windows. Because these are permanently affixed to the property, they are considered to be a part of it. Certain items, such as drapes and window-unit air conditioners, are difficult to classify. Thus, a contract for the sale of a house or commercial realty should indicate which items of this sort are included in the sale.

At issue in the following case was whether an agricultural irrigation system qualified as a fixture.

4. See UCC 2–107(2).

CASE 24.1 In re Sand & Sage Farm & Ranch, Inc.

United States Bankruptcy Court,
District of Kansas, 2001.
266 Bankr. 507.

FACTS In 1988, Randolf and Sandra Ardery bought an eighty-acre tract in Edwards County, Kansas. On the land was an eight-tower center-pivot irrigation system. The system consisted of an underground well and pump connected to a pipe that ran to the pivot where the water line was attached to a further system of pipes and sprinklers suspended from the towers, extending over the land in a circular fashion. The system's engine and gearhead were bolted to a concrete slab above the pump and well and were attached to the pipe. To secure a loan to buy the land, the Arderys granted to Farmers State Bank a mortgage that covered "all buildings, improvements, and fixtures." In 1996, the Arderys, and their firm Sand & Sage Farm & Ranch, Inc., granted Ag Services of America a security interest in the farm's "equipment." Nothing in the security agreement or financing statement referred to fixtures.[a] In 2000, the Arderys and Sand & Sage filed for bankruptcy in a federal bankruptcy court and asked for permission to sell the land, with the irrigation system, to Bohn Enterprises, Limited Partnership. Ag Services claimed that it had priority to the proceeds covering the value of the irrigation system. The bank responded that it had priority because the system was a "fixture."

ISSUE Was this irrigation system a "fixture"?

a. Security agreements and financing statements were discussed in Chapter 16.

DECISION Yes. The court concluded that the system was a fixture. The bank was entitled to the proceeds from its sale.

REASON The court explained that whether personal property attached to land is a fixture depends on "(i) how firmly the goods are attached or the ease of their removal (annexation); (ii) the relationship of the parties involved (intent); and (iii) how operation of the goods is related to the use of the land (adaptation). Of the three factors, intent is the controlling factor and is deduced largely from the property-owner's acts and the surrounding circumstances." Here, the irrigation system was firmly attached to the realty. Disassembly and removal would be time consuming and expensive. As for intent, in each transaction all of the parties—except Ag Services, whose security agreement and financing statement did not refer to the irrigation system—"share[d] the intent that the system in question should pass with the land." Furthermore, the system "is suitably adapted to the land. There can be little dispute concerning the need for pivot irrigation in the semi-arid conditions of southwestern Kansas. * * * This alone demonstrates the relation between the operation of the goods and use of the land."

WHY IS THIS CASE IMPORTANT? *When dealing with real property, it is crucial that the parties to a contract specifically list which fixtures they intend to be subjected to a security interest or included in a sale or transfer. In the end, it is far simpler and less expensive to itemize fixtures in a contract than to engage in litigation.*

Ownership Interests in Real Property

Ownership of property is an abstract concept that cannot exist independently of the legal system. No one can actually possess or *hold* a piece of land, the air above it, the earth below it, and all the water contained on it. The legal system therefore recognizes certain rights and duties that constitute ownership interests in real property.

Recall from Chapter 23 that property ownership is often viewed as a bundle of rights. One who possesses the entire bundle of rights is said to hold the property in *fee simple*, which is the most complete form of ownership. When only some of the rights in the bundle are transferred to another person, the effect is to limit the ownership rights of both the transferor of the rights and the recipient.

Ownership in Fee Simple

FEE SIMPLE ABSOLUTE
An ownership interest in land in which the owner has the greatest possible aggregation of rights, privileges, and power. Ownership in fee simple absolute is limited absolutely to a person and her or his heirs.

In a **fee simple absolute,** the owner has the greatest aggregation of rights, privileges, and power possible. The owner can give the property away, sell the property, or transfer the property by will to another. Also, the owner has the rights of *exclusive* possession and use of the property. The fee simple is limited to a person and his or her heirs and is assigned forever without limitation or condition.

The rights that accompany a fee simple include the right to use the land for whatever purpose the owner sees fit. Of course, other laws, including laws that prevent the owner from unreasonably interfering with another person's land and applicable zoning and environmental laws, may limit the owner's ability to use the property in certain ways. A fee simple is potentially infinite in duration and can be disposed of by deed (the instrument used to transfer property, which will be discussed later in this chapter) or by will. When there is no will, the fee simple passes to the owner's legal heirs.

Life Estates

LIFE ESTATE
An interest in land that exists only for the duration of the life of some person, usually the holder of the estate.

CONVEYANCE
The transfer of a title to land from one person to another by deed; a document (such as a deed) by which an interest in land is transferred from one person to another.

A **life estate** is an estate that lasts for the life of some specified individual. A **conveyance,** or transfer of real property, "to A for his life" creates a life estate.[5] In a life estate, the life tenant's ownership rights cease to exist on the life tenant's death. The life tenant has the right to use the land, provided that he or she commits no waste (injury to the land). In other words, the life tenant cannot use the land in a manner that would adversely affect its value. The life tenant is entitled to any rents generated by the land and can harvest crops from the land. If mines and oil wells are already on the land, the life tenant is entitled to any royalties and can extract minerals and oil from it, but he or she cannot exploit the land by creating new wells or mines.

The life tenant has the right to mortgage the life estate and can create liens, *easements* (discussed below), and leases, but none can extend beyond the life of the tenant. In addition, with few exceptions, the owner of a life estate has an exclusive right to possession during her or his life.

Along with these rights, the life tenant also has some duties—to keep the property in repair and to pay property taxes. In short, the owner of the life estate has the same rights as a fee simple owner except that the life tenant must maintain the value of the property during her or his tenancy.

Nonpossessory Interests

In contrast to the types of property interests just described, some interests in land do not include any rights to possess the property. These interests, known as *nonpossessory interests,* include easements, profits, and licenses.

EASEMENT
A nonpossessory right to use another's property in a manner established by either express or implied agreement.

PROFIT
In real property law, the right to enter on and remove things from the property of another (for example, the right to enter onto a person's land and remove sand and gravel therefrom).

Easements and Profits An **easement** is the right of a person to make limited use of another person's real property without taking anything from the property. An easement, for instance, can be the right to walk or drive across another's property. In contrast, a **profit**[6] is the right to go onto land in possession of another and take away some part of the land itself or some product of the land. ■ EXAMPLE 24.1

5. A less common type of life estate is created by the conveyance "to A for the life of B." This is known as an estate *pur autre vie,* or an estate for the duration of the life of another.

6. The term *profit,* as used here, does not refer to the "profits" made by a business firm. Rather, it means a gain or an advantage.

Akmed owns Sandy View. Akmed gives Carmen the right to go there to remove all the sand and gravel that she needs for her cement business. Carmen has a profit. ■

LICENSE
A revocable right or privilege of a person to come onto another person's land.

Licenses A **license** is the revocable right of a person to come onto another person's land. It is a personal privilege that arises from the consent of the owner of the land and can be revoked by the owner. A ticket to attend a movie at a theater is an example of a license. ■ EXAMPLE 24.2 The owner of a Broadway theater issues Alena a ticket to see a play. If Alena is refused entry into the theater because she is improperly dressed, she has no right to force her way into the theater. The ticket is only a revocable license, not a conveyance of an interest in property. ■

Transfer of Ownership

Ownership of real property can pass from one person to another in several ways. Commonly, ownership interests in land are transferred by sale, and the terms of the transfer are specified in a real estate sales contract. Often, real estate brokers or agents who are licensed by the state assist the buyers and sellers during the sales transaction. (For a discussion of some issues involving online advertising by real estate professionals, see this chapter's *Adapting the Law to the Online Environment* feature on page 736). Real property ownership can also be transferred by gift, by will or inheritance, by possession, or by *eminent domain.* When ownership rights in real property are transferred, the type of interest being transferred and the conditions of the transfer normally are set forth in a *deed* executed by the person who is conveying the property.

DEEDS

DEED
A document by which title to property (usually real property) is passed.

Possession and title to land are passed from person to person by means of a **deed**—the instrument of conveyance of real property. A deed is a writing signed by an owner of real property that transfers title to another. Deeds must meet certain requirements. Unlike a contract, a deed does not have to be supported by legally sufficient consideration. Gifts of real property are common, and they require deeds even though there is no consideration for the gift. The necessary components of a valid deed are the following:

1. The names of the *grantor* (the giver or seller) and the *grantee* (donee or buyer).
2. Words evidencing an intent to convey the property (for example, "I hereby bargain, sell, grant, or give").
3. A legally sufficient description of the land.
4. The grantor's (and usually her or his spouse's) signature.
5. Delivery of the deed.

WARRANTY DEED
A deed in which the grantor assures (warrants to) the grantee that the grantor has title to the property conveyed in the deed, that there are no encumbrances on the property other than what the grantor has represented, and that the grantee will enjoy quiet possession of the property; a deed that provides the greatest amount of protection for the grantee.

Warranty Deeds Different types of deeds provide different degrees of protection against defects of title. A **warranty deed** makes the greatest number of warranties and thus provides the greatest protection against defects of title.

Creation of a Warranty Deed. In most states, special language is required to create a general warranty deed. Typically, the deed must include a written promise to protect the buyer against all claims of ownership of the property. A general warranty deed makes the grantor liable for all defects of title occurring while he or she (the grantor) and the previous titleholders held the property.

ADAPTING THE LAW TO THE ONLINE ENVIRONMENT

Potential Problems When Real Estate Is Advertised Online

The Internet has transformed the real estate business, just as it has transformed other industries. Today's real estate professionals market properties—and themselves—online. Given that the Internet knows no physical borders, what happens when an online advertisement reaches people outside the state in which the real estate professional is licensed? Is this illegal? Can the agent be sued for fraud if the ad contains misrepresentations? Such questions are likely to arise in the future as more and more people use the Internet to search for properties.

STATE LICENSING STATUTES AND ADVERTISING

Every state requires anyone who sells or offers to sell real property in that state to obtain a license. To be licensed, a person normally must pass a state examination and pay a fee and then must take a minimum number of continuing education courses periodically (every year or two) to maintain the license. The purpose of requiring real estate licenses is to protect the public and to maintain quality standards for real property transactions in that state. Usually, a person must also be licensed to list real property for sale or to negotiate the purchase, sale, lease, or exchange of real property or a business opportunity involving real property.[a] Often, a state agency, such as a real estate commission, is in charge of granting licenses and enforcing the laws and regulations governing real estate professionals.

Although some states have rules regarding the advertising of real property, these regulations usually do not specifically address Internet advertising, which necessarily reaches consumers beyond the state's borders. At least one state, California, flatly prohibits Internet advertising of real estate by individuals not licensed in the state.[b] But how can a state enforce such a law or check the credentials of Web advertisers? California's Department of Real Estate *suggests* that anyone who advertises real property online and is not licensed in California should include a disclaimer on the ad—but this is not required.

a. See, for example, Section 10131 of the Cal. Bus. & Prof. Code and Vermont's 26 V.S.A. Sections 2211–2212.
b. 9 Cal. Code of Regs. Section 2770.

ACTIONS FOR MISREPRESENTATIONS (FRAUD)

Suppose that a real estate agent, either inadvertently or intentionally, makes a misstatement online about some important aspect of real property that is for sale. Someone, relying on the statements, responds to the ad and eventually contracts to buy the property, only to discover later that the ad misrepresented it. What remedies does the buyer have? In this situation, the buyer can complain to the state authority that granted the agent's license, and the state may even revoke the license for such conduct. If the buyer wants to obtain damages or cancel the contract, however, he or she will have to sue the agent for fraud (see Chapters 4 and 8). At this point, jurisdiction problems may arise.

If the real estate agent and the buyer are located in different states and the Internet ad was the agent's only contact with the buyer's state, the buyer may have to travel to the agent's state to file the suit. Courts have reached different conclusions on the type of Internet advertising that permits a court to have jurisdiction over an out-of-state advertiser. In many states, a court will not have jurisdiction unless the Web site advertisement is *interactive*. In other states, the courts have held that a passive Web site that solicited business in the state,[c] or a passive Web site coupled with a toll-free phone number or downloadable forms,[d] provided the minimum contacts necessary for jurisdiction. Thus, people who are deceived when buying real property from an online ad and wish to sue the perpetrator of the fraud may be in a precarious position depending on the state where they live.

FOR CRITICAL ANALYSIS

Do you think that the federal government should regulate the advertising of real property on the Internet to protect consumers from potential fraud? If so, what kind of regulations would be appropriate, and how might they be enforced?

c. *Telco Communications v. An Apple A Day,* 977 F.Supp. 404 (E.D.Va. 1997); *Inset Systems, Inc. v. Instruction Set, Inc.,* 937 F.Supp. 161 (D.Conn. 1996).
d. *State by Humphrey v. Granite Gate Resorts, Inc.,* 1996 WL 767431 (Minn.Dist.Ct. 1996), aff'd, 568 N.W.2d 715 (Minn.App. 1997), aff'd again, 576 N.W.2d 747 (Minn. 1998); *Hasbro, Inc. v. Clue Computing, Inc.,* 994 F.Supp. 34 (D.Mass. 1997).

The Usual Covenants. Warranty deeds commonly include a number of *covenants,* or promises, that the grantor makes to the grantee. A *covenant of seisin*[7] and a *covenant of the right to convey* warrant that the seller has title to, and the power to convey, the property described in the deed. A *covenant against encumbrances* is a promise that the property being sold or conveyed is not subject to any outstanding rights or interests of third parties, except as explicitly stated. Examples of common encumbrances include mortgages, liens, profits, easements, and private deed restrictions on the use of the land. (For an example of how an owner's use of the land might be restricted, see this chapter's *Letter of the Law* feature.)

A *covenant of quiet enjoyment* guarantees that the buyer will not be disturbed in her or his possession of the land by the seller or any third persons. ■ EXAMPLE 24.3 Assume that Julio sells a two-acre lot and office building by warranty deed. Subsequently, a third person shows up who has better title than Julio had and forces the buyer off the property. Here, the covenant of quiet enjoyment has been breached, and the buyer can sue Julio to recover the purchase price of the land plus any other damages incurred as a result. ■

If a contract calls for a "warranty deed" without specifying the covenants to be included in the deed, or if a deed states that the seller is providing the "usual covenants," most courts will infer that all of the covenants mentioned above are included.

SPECIAL WARRANTY DEED
A deed in which the grantor only warrants that the grantor or seller held good title during his or her ownership of the property and does not warrant that there were no defects of title when the property was held by previous owners.

Special Warranty Deeds. In contrast to a warranty deed, a **special warranty deed,** which is frequently referred to as a *limited warranty deed,* warrants only that the

7. Pronounced *see*-zuhn.

LETTER OF THE LAW A Shed Is One Thing, a Garage Quite Another

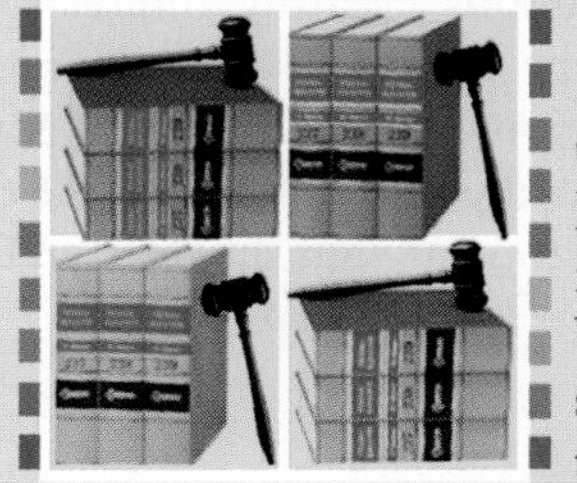

Shortly after Richard and Laura Dufrane purchased a home with an attached garage in a subdivision in Greenfield, Wisconsin, they began constructing a detached garage on the edge of their property. Their neighbor, Mary Pietrowski, told the Dufranes "multiple times" that the garage violated a restrictive covenant that prevented property owners in the subdivision from erecting any buildings other than one house and one garage on their land. After the garage had been built, Pietrowski asked a court to issue an order that the garage be razed (destroyed).

The Dufranes argued that Pietrowski herself had violated the covenant because she had built a shed on her property. Thus, by violating the covenant herself, she had waived her equitable right to enforce it. After all, a fundamental principle of equity is that a person seeking equitable relief must come to the court with clean hands. Further, claimed the Dufranes, enforcing the covenant would lead to unjust results because Pietrowski would be allowed to maintain a violation of the restrictions on her property while enforcing the restrictions on her neighbors. The Dufranes' arguments were in vain, however. The court interpreted the letter of the law in this case to mean that building a shed constituted only a "minor violation" of the covenant, whereas building a garage was a "major violation" that materially breached the covenant. According to the court, "enforcement against a major violation of the restrictive covenant by a party who committed a minor violation does not result in an injustice." The court ordered that the garage be razed.[a]

THE BOTTOM LINE

Those who purchase real estate should check carefully to determine what restrictive covenants, if any, apply to the property.

a. *Pietrowski v. Dufrane,* 634 N.W.2d 109 (Wis.App. 2001).

grantor or seller held good title during his or her ownership of the property. In other words, the grantor is not warranting that there were no defects of title when the property was held by previous owners.

If the special warranty deed discloses all liens or other encumbrances, the seller will not be liable to the buyer if a third person subsequently interferes with the buyer's ownership. If the third person's claim arises out of, or is related to, some act of the seller, however, the seller will be liable to the buyer for damages.

QUITCLAIM DEED
A deed intended to pass any title, interest, or claim that the grantor may have in the property without warranting that such title is valid. A quitclaim deed offers the least amount of protection against defects in the title.

Quitclaim Deeds A **quitclaim deed** offers the least amount of protection against defects in the title. Basically, a quitclaim deed conveys to the grantee whatever interest the grantor had; so, if the grantor had no interest, then the grantee receives no interest. Naturally, if the grantor had a defective title or no title at all, a conveyance by warranty deed or special warranty deed would not cure the defects. Such deeds, however, will give the buyer a cause of action to sue the seller.

A quitclaim deed can and often does serve as a release of the grantor's interest in a particular parcel of property. ■ EXAMPLE 24.4 Sandi and Jim were married for ten years and are now getting a divorce. During the marriage, Sandi purchased a parcel of waterfront property next to her grandparents' home in Louisiana. Jim helped make some improvements to the property, but he is not sure what ownership interests, if any, he has in the property because Sandi used her own funds to purchase the lot. Jim agrees to quitclaim the property to Sandi as part of the divorce settlement, releasing any interest he might have in that piece of property. ■

RECORDING STATUTES
Statutes that allow deeds, mortgages, and other real property transactions to be recorded so as to provide notice to future purchasers or creditors of an existing claim on the property.

Recording Statutes Every jurisdiction has **recording statutes,** which allow deeds to be recorded for a fee. The grantee normally pays this fee because he or she is the one who will be protected by recording the deed.

Recording a deed gives notice to the public that a certain person is now the owner of a particular parcel of real estate. Thus, prospective buyers can check the public records to see whether there have been earlier transactions creating interests or rights in specific parcels of real property. Placing everyone on notice as to the identity of the true owner is intended to prevent the previous owners from fraudulently conveying the land to other purchasers. Deeds are recorded in the county where the property is located. Many state statutes require that the grantor sign the deed in the presence of two witnesses before it can be recorded.

WILL OR INHERITANCE

Property that is transferred on an owner's death is passed either by will or by state inheritance laws. If the owner of land dies with a will, the land passes in accordance with the terms of the will. If the owner dies without a will, state inheritance statutes prescribe how and to whom the property will pass.

ADVERSE POSSESSION

ADVERSE POSSESSION
The acquisition of title to real property by occupying it openly, without the consent of the owner, for a period of time specified by a state statute. The occupation must be actual, open, notorious, exclusive, and in opposition to all others, including the owner.

Adverse possession is a means of obtaining title to land without delivery of a deed. Essentially, when one person possesses the property of another for a certain statutory period of time (three to thirty years, with ten years being most common), that person, called the *adverse possessor,* acquires title to the land and cannot be removed from it by the original owner. The adverse possessor may ultimately obtain a perfect title just as if there had been a conveyance by deed.

For property to be held adversely, four elements must be satisfied:

Should the government be permitted to take undeveloped coastal property from private citizens for public use without compensation? Why or why not? (©Vic Bider, PhotoEdit)

1. Possession must be actual and exclusive—that is, the possessor must take sole physical occupancy of the property.
2. The possession must be open, visible, and notorious, not secret or clandestine. The possessor must occupy the land for all the world to see.
3. Possession must be continuous and peaceable for the required period of time. This requirement means that the possessor must not be interrupted in the occupancy by the true owner or by the courts.
4. Possession must be hostile and adverse. In other words, the possessor must claim the property as against the whole world. He or she cannot be living on the property with the permission of the owner.

EMINENT DOMAIN

EMINENT DOMAIN
The power of a government to take land for public use from private citizens for just compensation.

CONDEMNATION
The process of taking private property for public use through the government's power of eminent domain.

TAKING
The taking of private property by the government for public use. The government may not take private property for public use without "just compensation."

Even ownership in real property in fee simple absolute is limited by a superior ownership. Just as in medieval England the king was the ultimate landowner, so in the United States the government has an ultimate ownership right in all land. This right is called **eminent domain,** and it allows the government to take land for public use. Eminent domain gives the government the right to acquire possession of real property in the manner directed by the U.S. Constitution and the laws of the state whenever the public interest requires it. Property may be taken only for public use, not for private benefit.

The power of eminent domain is generally invoked through **condemnation** proceedings (and the power of eminent domain is sometimes referred to as the *condemnation power* of government). When a new public highway is to be built, for instance, the government must decide where to build it and how much land to condemn. After the government determines that a particular parcel of land is necessary for public use, it will first offer to buy the property. If the owner refuses the offer, the government brings a judicial (condemnation) proceeding to obtain title to the land. Then, in another proceeding, the court determines the *fair value* of the land, which is usually approximately equal to its market value.

When the government takes land owned by a private party for public use, it is referred to as a **taking,** and the government must compensate the private party. Under the so-called *takings clause* of the Fifth Amendment to the U.S. Constitution, the government may not take private property for public use without "just compensation." State constitutions contain similar provisions.

ETHICAL ISSUE 24.1

Should eminent domain be used to promote private developments? Issues of fairness often arise when the government takes private property for public use. One issue is whether it is fair for property taken by eminent domain to then be conveyed to private developers. For example, suppose that a city government decides that it is in the public interest to have a larger parking lot for a local, privately owned sports stadium or to have a manufacturing plant locate in the city to create more jobs. The government may condemn certain tracts of existing housing or business property and then, later, convey the land to the privately owned stadium or to the owner of the manufacturing plant. The increasingly widespread use of eminent domain for such purposes has generated substantial controversy. Government officials claim that this use of eminent domain helps bring in private developers and businesses that provide jobs and increase tax revenues, thus revitalizing communities. Critics of this trend, however, contend that when eminent domain is used in this way, essentially one group of private owners simply replaces another group of private owners. In other words, the land is not being taken for "public" use, as required by the Fifth Amendment to the U.S. Constitution. Although the courts, by and large, have supported the government agencies in cases challenging such takings of private property, the tide may be turning. In recent years, some courts have held for the landowners in these cases.[8] ■

Leasehold Estates

LEASEHOLD ESTATE
An estate in realty held by a tenant under a lease. In every leasehold estate, the tenant has a qualified right to possess and/or use the land.

A **leasehold estate** is created when a real property owner or lessor (landlord) agrees to convey the right to possess and use the property to a lessee (tenant) for a certain period of time. In every leasehold estate, the tenant has a *qualified* right to exclusive possession (qualified by the right of the landlord to enter on the premises to assure that waste is not being committed). The tenant can use the land—for example, by harvesting crops—but cannot injure it by such activities as cutting down timber for sale or extracting oil.

The respective rights and duties of the landlord and tenant that arise under a lease agreement will be discussed shortly. Here we look at the types of leasehold estates, or tenancies, that can be created when real property is leased.

Tenancy for Years

TENANCY FOR YEARS
A type of tenancy under which property is leased for a specified period of time, such as a month, a year, or a period of years.

A **tenancy for years** is created by an express contract by which property is leased for a specified period of time, such as a day, a month, a year, or a period of years. Signing a one-year lease to occupy an apartment, for instance, creates a tenancy for years. At the end of the period specified in the lease, the lease ends (without notice), and possession of the apartment returns to the lessor. If the tenant dies during the period of the lease, the lease interest passes to the tenant's heirs as personal property. Often, leases include renewal or extension provisions.

Periodic Tenancy

PERIODIC TENANCY
A lease interest in land for an indefinite period involving payment of rent at fixed intervals, such as week to week, month to month, or year to year.

A **periodic tenancy** is created by a lease that does not specify how long it is to last but does specify that rent is to be paid at certain intervals. This type of tenancy is automatically renewed for another rental period unless properly terminated. ■ EXAMPLE 24.5 Kayla enters a lease with Capital Properties. The lease states, "Rent is due on the tenth day of every month." This provision creates a periodic tenancy from month to month. ■ This type of tenancy can also extend from week to week or from year to year.

8. See, for example, *Southwestern Illinois Development Authority v. National City Environmental, L.L.C.*, 199 Ill.2d 225, 798 N.E.2d 1, 263 Ill.Dec. 241 (2002); *In re Condemnation of 110 Washington St.*, 767 A.2d 1154 (Pa. Cmwlth. 2001); and *99 Cents Only Stores v. Lancaster Redevelopment Agency*, 237 F.Supp.2d 1123 (C.D.Cal. 2001).

Under the common law, to terminate a periodic tenancy, the landlord or tenant must give at least one period's notice to the other party. If the tenancy extends from month to month, for example, one month's notice must be given prior to the last month's rent payment. State statutes may require a different period for notice of termination in a periodic tenancy, however.

TENANCY AT WILL

TENANCY AT WILL
A type of tenancy that either party can terminate without notice; usually arises when a tenant who has been under a tenancy for years retains possession, with the landlord's consent, after the tenancy for years has terminated.

Suppose that a landlord rents an apartment to a tenant "for as long as both agree." In such a situation, the tenant receives a leasehold estate known as a **tenancy at will.** Under the common law, either party can terminate the tenancy without notice (that is, "at will"). This type of estate usually arises when a tenant who has been under a tenancy for years retains possession after the termination date of that tenancy with the landlord's consent. Before the tenancy has been converted into a periodic tenancy—by the periodic payment of rent—it is a tenancy at will, terminable by either party without notice. Once the tenancy is treated as a periodic tenancy, notice of termination must conform to the requirements already discussed for that type of tenancy. The death of either party or the voluntary commission of waste by the tenant will terminate a tenancy at will.

TENANCY AT SUFFERANCE

TENANCY AT SUFFERANCE
A type of tenancy under which a tenant who, after rightfully being in possession of leased premises, continues (wrongfully) to occupy the property after the lease has been terminated. The tenant has no rights to possess the property and occupies it only because the person entitled to evict the tenant has not done so.

The mere possession of land without right is called a **tenancy at sufferance.** A tenancy at sufferance is not a true tenancy because it is created when a tenant *wrongfully* retains possession of property. Whenever a tenancy for years or a periodic tenancy ends and the tenant continues to retain possession of the premises without the owner's permission, a tenancy at sufferance is created.

Landlord-Tenant Relationships

.on the Web You can find online links to most uniform laws, including the URLTA, at **http://www.lawsource.com**.

In the past several decades, landlord-tenant relationships have become much more complex, as has the law governing them. Generally, the law has come to apply contract doctrines, such as those relating to implied warranties and unconscionability, to the landlord-tenant relationship. Increasingly, landlord-tenant relationships have become subject to specific state and local statutes and ordinances as well. In 1972, in an effort to create more uniformity in the law governing landlord-tenant relationships, the National Conference of Commissioners on Uniform State Laws issued the Uniform Residential Landlord and Tenant Act (URLTA). More than one-third of the states have adopted variations of the URLTA. We look now at how a landlord-tenant relationship is created and at the respective rights and duties of landlords and tenants.

CREATING THE LANDLORD-TENANT RELATIONSHIP

A landlord-tenant relationship is established by a lease contract. As mentioned, a lease contract arises when a property owner (landlord) agrees to give another party (the tenant) the exclusive right to possess the property—usually for a price and for a specified term.

Form of the Lease A lease contract may be oral or written. Under the common law, an oral lease is valid. As with most oral contracts, however, a party who seeks to enforce an oral lease may have difficulty proving its existence. In most states, statutes mandate that leases be in writing for some tenancies (such as those exceeding one year). Therefore, to ensure the validity of a lease agreement, it should be in writing and do the following:

1. Express an intent to establish the relationship.
2. Provide for the transfer of the property's possession to the tenant at the beginning of the term.
3. Provide for the landlord's *reversionary* (future) interest, which entitles the property owner to retake possession at the end of the term.
4. Describe the property—for example, give its street address.
5. Indicate the length of the term, the amount of the rent, and how and when it is to be paid.

In drafting commercial leases, sound business practice dictates that the leases be written carefully and that the parties' rights and obligations be clearly defined in the lease agreements. (The *Application* feature at the end of this chapter provides suggestions to businesspersons on how to negotiate a favorable lease contract.)

Illegality State or local law often dictates permissible lease terms. For example, a statute or ordinance might prohibit the leasing of a structure that is in a certain physical condition or is not in compliance with local building codes. Similarly, a statute may prohibit the leasing of property for a particular purpose. For instance, a state law might prohibit gambling houses. Thus, if a landlord and tenant intend that the leased premises be used only to house an illegal betting operation, their lease is unenforceable.

A property owner cannot legally discriminate against prospective tenants on the basis of race, color, national origin, religion, gender, or disability. In addition, a tenant cannot legally promise to do something counter to laws prohibiting discrimination. A commercial tenant, for example, cannot legally promise to do business only with members of a particular race. The public policy underlying these prohibitions is to treat all people equally. In the following case, a rental housing applicant claimed that her rental application had been denied because of her live-in boyfriend's race.

CASE 24.2 Osborn v. Kellogg

Court of Appeals of Nebraska, 1996.
4 Neb.App. 594,
547 N.W.2d 504.

FACTS Kristi Kellogg, her daughter Mindy, and her boyfriend James Greene attempted to lease half of a house. The house was owned by Keith Osborn and Pam Lyman and managed, as rental property, by Keith's mother, Barbara Osborn. Kellogg was white. Greene was African American. The owners refused to rent to them, claiming, among other things, that three people were too many, Greene's income was too low, and Greene had not provided credit references. They later rented half of the house to the Li family, which had five members, and the other half to the Suggett family, which numbered three. Both the Li family and the Suggett family had less income than Kellogg and Greene. Kellogg had provided extensive credit references, but the Lis and the Suggetts had provided none. Kellogg filed a complaint with the Nebraska Equal Opportunity Commission (NEOC) against the Osborns and Lyman. The NEOC concluded that the defendants had discriminated against Kellogg in violation of state fair housing laws. A Nebraska state trial court

CASE 24.2—Continued

adopted the NEOC's conclusion. The defendants appealed to an intermediate state appellate court.

ISSUE Had the defendants discriminated against Kellogg in violation of state fair housing laws?

DECISION Yes. The intermediate state appellate court affirmed the judgment of the lower court.

REASON The appellate court reasoned that while Kellogg was not a member of a racial minority, Greene was, and Kellogg thus qualified as a person who had been injured by a discriminatory housing practice. The court stated, "The NEOC hearing examiner found that Kellogg proved by a preponderance of the evidence that the Osborns' seemingly legitimate reasons for rejecting Kellogg were, in fact, a pretext for intentional discrimination. * * * [W]e conclude that competent evidence supports the NEOC hearing examiner's factual findings."

FOR CRITICAL ANALYSIS—Ethical Consideration *What if the Osborns and Lyman discriminated against Kellogg not because her boyfriend was African American but because they disapproved of cohabitation by unmarried couples? Should this form of discrimination be permissible?*

Rights and Duties

The rights and duties of landlords and tenants generally pertain to four broad areas of concern—the possession, use, maintenance, and, of course, rent of leased property.

Possession A landlord is obligated to give a tenant possession of the property that the tenant has agreed to lease. Many states follow the "English" rule, which requires the landlord to provide actual *physical possession* to the tenant (making sure that the previous tenant has vacated). Other states follow the "American" rule, which requires the landlord to transfer only the *legal right to possession* (thus, the new tenant is responsible for removing a previous tenant). After obtaining possession, the tenant retains the property exclusively until the lease expires, unless the lease states otherwise.

.on the Web Many Web sites now provide information on laws and other information relating to landlord-tenant relationships. One of them is TenantNet™ at **http://www.tenant.net**.

The covenant of quiet enjoyment mentioned previously also applies to leased premises. Under this covenant, the landlord promises that during the lease term, neither the landlord nor anyone having a superior title to the property will disturb the tenant's use and enjoyment of the property. This covenant forms the essence of the landlord-tenant relationship, and if it is breached, the tenant can terminate the lease and sue for damages.

If the landlord deprives the tenant of possession of the leased property or interferes with the tenant's use or enjoyment of it, an **eviction** occurs. An eviction occurs, for instance, when the landlord changes the lock and refuses to give the tenant a new key. A **constructive eviction** occurs when the landlord wrongfully performs or fails to perform any of the duties the lease requires, thereby making the tenant's further use and enjoyment of the property exceedingly difficult or impossible. Examples of constructive eviction include a landlord's failure to provide heat in the winter, light, or other essential utilities.

EVICTION
A landlord's act of depriving a tenant of possession of the leased premises.

CONSTRUCTIVE EVICTION
A form of eviction that occurs when a landlord fails to perform adequately any of the undertakings (such as providing heat in the winter) required by the lease, thereby making the tenant's further use and enjoyment of the property exceedingly difficult or impossible.

Use and Maintenance of the Premises If the parties do not limit by agreement the uses to which the property may be put, the tenant may make any use of it, as long as the use is legal and reasonably relates to the purpose for which the property is adapted or ordinarily used and does not injure the landlord's interest.

The tenant is responsible for any damages to the premises that he or she causes, intentionally or negligently, and may be held liable for the cost of returning the property to the physical condition it was in at the lease's inception. Also, the tenant is not entitled to substantially interfere with others' quiet enjoyment of their property rights. Unless the parties have agreed otherwise, the tenant is not responsible for ordinary wear and tear and the property's consequent depreciation in value.

In some jurisdictions, landlords of residential property are required by statute to maintain the premises in good repair. Landlords must also comply with any applicable state statutes and city ordinances regarding maintenance and repair of buildings.

IMPLIED WARRANTY OF HABITABILITY An implied promise by a landlord that rented residential premises are fit for human habitation—that is, in a condition that is safe and suitable for people to live in.

Implied Warranty of Habitability The **implied warranty of habitability** requires a landlord who leases residential property to furnish premises that are in a habitable condition—that is, in a condition that is safe and suitable for people to live. Also, the landlord must make repairs to maintain the premises in that condition for the lease's duration. Some state legislatures have enacted this warranty into law. In other jurisdictions, courts have based the warranty on the existence of a landlord's statutory duty to keep leased premises in good repair, or they have simply applied it as a matter of public policy.

Generally, this warranty applies to major, or *substantial,* physical defects that the landlord knows or should know about and has had a reasonable time to repair—for example, a large hole in the roof. An unattractive or annoying feature, such as a crack in the wall, may be unpleasant, but unless the crack is a structural defect or affects the residence's heating capabilities, it is probably not sufficiently substantial to make the place uninhabitable.

Rent *Rent* is the tenant's payment to the landlord for the tenant's occupancy or use of the landlord's real property. Usually, the tenant must pay the rent even if she or he refuses to occupy the property or moves out, as long as the refusal or the move is unjustified and the lease is in force. Under the common law, if the leased premises were destroyed by fire or flood, the tenant still had to pay rent. Today, however, most state's statutes provide that if an apartment building burns down, tenants are not required to continue to pay rent.

NOTE Options that may be available to a tenant on a landlord's breach of the implied warranty of habitability include repairing the defect and deducting the amount from the rent, canceling the lease, and suing for damages.

In some situations, such as when a landlord breaches the implied warranty of habitability, a tenant may be allowed to withhold rent as a remedy. When rent withholding is authorized under a statute, the tenant must usually put the amount withheld into an *escrow account.* This account is held in the name of the depositor (the tenant) and an *escrow agent* (usually the court or a government agency), and the funds are returnable to the depositor if the third person (the landlord) fails to make the premises habitable. Generally, the tenant may withhold an amount equal to the amount by which the defect rendering the premises unlivable reduces the property's rental value. How much that is may be determined in different ways, and a tenant who withholds more than is legally permissible is liable to the landlord for the excessive amount withheld.

TRANSFERRING RIGHTS TO LEASED PROPERTY

Either the landlord or the tenant may wish to transfer her or his rights to the leased property during the term of the lease.

Transferring the Landlord's Interest Just as any other real property owner can sell, give away, or otherwise transfer his or her property, so can a landlord—who is, of course, the leased property's owner. If complete title to the leased property is

Under what conditions can this lessee sublease the premises? (Scott Saltzman, Bloomberg News/Landov)

transferred, the tenant becomes the tenant of the new owner. The new owner may collect subsequent rent but must abide by the terms of the existing lease agreement.

Transferring the Tenant's Interest The tenant's transfer of his or her entire interest in the leased property to a third person is an *assignment of the lease.* The tenant's transfer of all or part of the premises for a period shorter than the lease term is a *sublease.*

A lease assignment is an agreement to transfer all rights, title, and interest in the lease to the assignee. It is a complete transfer. Many leases require that the assignment have the landlord's written consent. An assignment that lacks consent can be avoided (nullified) by the landlord. State statutes may specify that the landlord may not unreasonably withhold such consent, though. Also, a landlord who knowingly accepts rent from the assignee may be held to have waived the consent requirement.

When an assignment is valid, the assignee acquires all of the tenant's rights under the lease. But an assignment does not release the assigning tenant from the obligation to pay rent should the assignee default. Also, if the assignee exercises an option under the original lease to extend the term, the assigning tenant remains liable for the rent during the extension, unless the landlord agrees otherwise.

SUBLEASE
A lease executed by the lessee of real estate to a third person, conveying the same interest that the lessee enjoys but for a shorter term than that held by the lessee.

The tenant's transfer of all or part of the premises for a period shorter than the lease term is a **sublease.** The same restrictions that apply to an assignment of the tenant's interest in leased property apply to a sublease. If the landlord's consent is required, a sublease without such permission is ineffective. Also, a sublease does not release the tenant from her or his obligations under the lease any more than an assignment does. ■ EXAMPLE 24.6 Derek, a student, leases an apartment for a two-year period. Although Derek had planned on attending summer school, he is offered a job in Europe for the summer months, and he accepts. Because he does not wish to pay three months' rent for an unoccupied apartment, Derek subleases the apartment to Adva, who becomes a sublessee. (Derek may have to obtain his landlord's consent for this sublease if the lease requires it.) Adva is bound by the same terms of the lease as Derek. As in a lease assignment, the landlord can hold Derek liable if Adva violates the lease terms. ■

Environmental Law

We now turn to a discussion of the various ways in which businesses are regulated by the government in the interest of protecting the environment. To a great extent, environmental law consists of statutes passed by federal, state, or local governments and regulations issued by administrative agencies.

STATE AND LOCAL REGULATION

Many states regulate the degree to which the environment may be polluted. Thus, for example, even when state zoning laws permit a business's proposed development, the proposal may have to be altered to lessen the development's impact on the environment. State laws may restrict a business's discharge of chemicals into the air or water or regulate its disposal of toxic wastes. States may also regulate the disposal or recycling of other wastes, including glass, metal, and plastic containers and paper. Additionally, states may restrict the emissions from motor vehicles.

City, county, and other local governments control some aspects of the environment. For instance, local zoning laws control some land use. These laws may be designed to inhibit or regulate the growth of cities and suburbs or to protect the natural environment. Other aspects of the environment may be subject to local regulation for other reasons. Methods of waste and garbage removal and disposal, for example, can have a substantial impact on a community. The appearance of buildings and other structures, including advertising signs and billboards, may affect traffic safety, property values, or local aesthetics. Noise generated by a business or its customers may be annoying, disruptive, or damaging to neighbors. The location and condition of parks, streets, and other publicly used land subject to local control affect the environment and can also affect business.

In recent years, many state and local governments have passed what are referred to as *brownfields redevelopment laws*. These laws are designed to provide incentives to buyers to purchase and clean up contaminated land ("brownfields") or old buildings containing asbestos. Incentives may be in the form of tax credits, government grants, or other assistance. In 2004, the Environmental Protection Agency gave a record $75.4 million in brownfields grants to communities in forty-two states and Puerto Rico.

Federal Regulation

Congress has enacted a number of statutes to control the impact of human activities on the environment. Some of these laws have been passed to improve the quality of air and water. Some of them specifically regulate toxic chemicals, including pesticides, herbicides, and hazardous wastes.

Environmental Regulatory Agencies Much of the body of federal law governing business activities consists of the regulations issued and enforced by administrative agencies. The most well known of the agencies regulating environmental law is, of course, the Environmental Protection Agency (EPA), which was created in 1970 to coordinate federal environmental responsibilities. Other federal agencies with authority to regulate specific environmental matters include the Department of the Interior, the Department of Defense, the Department of Labor, the Food and Drug Administration, and the Nuclear Regulatory Commission. These regulatory agencies—and all other agencies of the federal government—must take environmental factors into consideration when making significant decisions.

Most federal environmental laws provide that citizens can sue to enforce environmental regulations if government agencies fail to do so—or if agencies go too far in their enforcement actions. Typically, a threshold hurdle in such suits is meeting the requirements for standing to sue.

State and local regulatory agencies also play a significant role in implementing federal environmental legislation. Typically, the federal government relies on state and local governments to enforce federal environmental statutes and regulations such as those regulating air quality.

ENVIRONMENTAL IMPACT STATEMENT (EIS)
A statement required by the National Environmental Policy Act for any major federal action that will significantly affect the quality of the environment. The statement must analyze the action's impact on the environment and explore alternative actions that might be taken.

Environmental Impact Statements The National Environmental Policy Act (NEPA) of 1969[9] requires that an **environmental impact statement (EIS)** be pre-

9. 42 U.S.C. Sections 4321–4370d.

pared for every major federal action that significantly affects the quality of the environment. An EIS must analyze (1) the impact on the environment that the action will have, (2) any adverse effects on the environment and alternative actions that might be taken, and (3) irreversible effects the action might generate.

An action qualifies as "major" if it involves a substantial commitment of resources (monetary or otherwise). An action is "federal" if a federal agency has the power to control it. Construction by a private developer of a ski resort on federal land, for example, may require an EIS.[10] Building or operating a nuclear plant, which requires a federal permit,[11] would require an EIS, as would constructing a dam as part of a federal project.[12] If an agency decides that an EIS is unnecessary, it must issue a statement supporting this conclusion. EISs have become instruments for private citizens, consumer interest groups, businesses, and others to challenge federal agency actions on the basis that the actions improperly threaten the environment.

Air Pollution

Federal involvement with air pollution goes back to the 1950s, when Congress authorized funds for air-pollution research. In 1963, the federal government passed the Clean Air Act,[13] which focused on multistate air pollution and provided assistance to states. Various amendments, particularly in 1970, 1977, and 1990, have strengthened the government's authority to regulate the quality of air. These laws provide the basis for issuing regulations to control pollution coming primarily from mobile sources (such as automobiles) and stationary sources (such as electric utilities and industrial plants).

.on the Web For information on EPA standards, guidelines, and regulations, go to the EPA's Web site at **http://www.epa.gov**.

Mobile Sources of Pollution Regulations governing air pollution from automobiles and other mobile sources specify pollution standards and establish time schedules for meeting the standards. For example, under the 1990 amendments to the Clean Air Act, automobile manufacturers were required to cut new automobiles' exhaust emissions of nitrogen oxide by 60 percent and of other pollutants by 35 percent by 1998. Regulations that became effective beginning with 2004 model cars call for nitrogen oxide tailpipe emissions to be cut by nearly 10 percent by 2007. For the first time, sport utility vehicles (SUVs) and light trucks are required to meet the same standards as automobiles.

Service stations are also subject to environmental regulations. The 1990 amendments require service stations to sell gasoline with a higher oxygen content in forty-one cities that experience carbon monoxide pollution in the winter. Service stations are required to sell even cleaner burning gasoline in the most polluted urban areas.

The EPA attempts to update pollution-control standards when new scientific information becomes available. For example, studies conducted in the 1990s purportedly showed that very small particles (2.5 microns, or about one-thirtieth the size of a human hair) of soot affect our health as significantly as larger particles. Based on this evidence, the EPA issued new particulate standards for motor vehicle exhaust systems and other sources of pollution. The EPA also instituted a more rigorous standard for ozone (the basic ingredient of smog), which is formed when sunlight combines with pollutants from cars and other sources.

10. *Robertson v. Methow Valley Citizens' Council,* 490 U.S. 332, 109 S.Ct. 1835, 104 L.Ed.2d 351 (1989).
11. *Calvert Cliffs Coordinating Committee v. Atomic Energy Commission,* 449 F.2d 1109 (D.C. Cir. 1971).
12. *Marsh v. Oregon Natural Resources Council,* 490 U.S. 360, 109 S.Ct. 1851, 104 L.Ed.2d 377 (1989).
13. 42 U.S.C. Sections 7401 *et seq.*

ETHICAL ISSUE 24.2 ***Should the costs of EPA regulations be weighed against their prospective benefits?*** In setting standards governing air quality, traditionally the EPA has not been required to take costs into account. Rather, the emphasis is on the benefits. For example, when the EPA issued its new rules on particulate matter and ozone, the head of the EPA claimed that the new standards would save 15,000 lives a year. Given that the EPA values a human life at $5 million, the agency calculated that the lives saved and medical expenses avoided by the strict standards would amount to $100 billion a year in benefits. Nothing was said about the costs of implementing these rules, though. Environmental groups tend to downplay these costs and to value potential lives saved very highly. In contrast, business groups, particularly those that are affected adversely by strict air standards, think that the EPA should factor in these costs.

In 2001, the United States Supreme Court resolved the debate over this issue after years of litigation. A number of business groups had challenged the EPA's stricter air-quality standards, claiming that the EPA had exceeded its authority under the Clean Air Act by issuing the regulations. The groups also claimed that the EPA had to take economic costs into account when developing new regulations. The Court, however, held that the EPA had not exceeded its authority under the Clean Air Act and confirmed that the EPA does not have to take economic costs into account when creating new rules.[14] ■

Stationary Sources of Pollution The Clean Air Act authorizes the EPA to establish air-quality standards for stationary sources (such as manufacturing plants) but recognizes that the primary responsibility for preventing and controlling air pollution rests with state and local governments. The EPA sets primary and secondary levels of ambient standards—that is, the maximum levels of certain pollutants—and the states formulate plans to achieve those standards. Different standards apply depending on whether the sources of pollution are in clean areas or polluted areas and whether they are already existing sources or major new sources. Generally, major sources are required to use the *maximum achievable control technology,* or MACT, to reduce emissions. The EPA issues guidelines as to what equipment meets this standard.

Under the 1990 amendments to the Clean Air Act, 110 of the oldest coal-burning power plants in the United States had to cut their emissions by 40 percent by the year 2001 to reduce acid rain. Utilities were granted "credits" to emit certain amounts of sulfur dioxide, and those that emit less than the allowed amounts can sell their credits to other polluters. The amendments also required an end to the production of chlorofluorocarbons, carbon tetrachloride, and methyl chloroform, which are used in air-conditioning, refrigeration, and insulation and have been linked to depletion of the ozone layer. The relationship between the Clean Air Act's 1990 amendments and a New York state law was at issue in the following case.

14. *Whitman v. American Trucking Associations,* 531 U.S. 457, 121 S.Ct. 903, 149 L.Ed.2d 1 (2001).

CASE 24.3 Clean Air Markets Group v. Pataki

United States District Court,
Northern District of New York, 2002.
194 F.Supp.2d 147.

HISTORICAL AND ENVIRONMENTAL SETTING *Acid rain allegedly has negative effects on water, forests, human health, and buildings and other structures. Acid rain consists of atmospheric sulfates and nitrates, which are formed from sulfur dioxide (SO_2) and nitrogen oxides (NO_x). These substances are emitted as by-products of the combustion of fossil fuels, most notably*

CASE 24.3—Continued

during the generation of electricity. Emissions originating in fourteen midwestern, eastern, and southern states, referred to as "upwind states," contribute significantly to acid rain in New York.

FACTS By 1999, it was clear to some scientists that SO_2 emissions at the rates permitted by the Clean Air Act would not permit the environmental restoration of parts of the state of New York. Additional reductions in SO_2 emissions would be required. George Pataki, the governor of New York, ordered New York utilities to cut SO_2 emissions to half of the amount permitted by the Clean Air Act by January 2, 2007. By doing this, the New York utilities would have additional SO_2 credits to sell. In May 2000, the New York state legislature enacted the Air Pollution Mitigation Law (APML), which stipulated that most sums received for the sale or trade of SO_2 allowances to a polluter in an upwind state would be forfeited to the New York Public Service Commission (PSC), which regulates New York utilities. This effectively lowered the market value of credits originating with New York utilities. Clean Air Markets Group (CAMG) filed a suit in a federal district court against Pataki and others, claiming in part that the APML was preempted under the U.S. Constitution's supremacy clause.[a] All parties filed motions for summary judgment.

a. As explained in Chapter 1, if federal law has not supplanted a whole field of state law, state law is preempted to the extent that it actually conflicts with federal law. A conflict between state and federal law occurs when compliance with both is physically impossible or when the state law is an obstacle to accomplishing the objective of federal law.

ISSUE Is New York's Air Pollution Mitigation Law preempted, under the supremacy clause, by the federal Clean Air Act?

DECISION Yes. The court granted CAMG's motion for summary judgment, holding that New York's Air Pollution Mitigation Law is preempted by the Clean Air Act.

REASON The court held that under the supremacy clause, the Clean Air Act preempts the APML because the state law interferes with the Clean Air Act's methods for achieving air-pollution control. The court enjoined (prevented) the enforcement of the APML. The court noted that the Clean Air Act provides that SO_2 allowances "may be transferred among designated representatives of the owners or operators of covered units (utilities) and *any* other person who holds such allowances." Thus, the APML's "restriction on transferring allowances to units in the Upwind States is contrary to the federal provision that allowances be tradeable to any other person," the court reasoned. Additionally, both Congress and the EPA had considered geographically restricted allowance transfers at some time and rejected them. In the court's view, "[t]he rejection of a regionally restricted allowance trading system illustrates the Congressional objective of having a nationwide trading market for SO_2 allowances. New York's regional restriction on SO_2 allowance trading by New York units is an obstacle to the execution of that objective."

FOR CRITICAL ANALYSIS—Environmental Consideration *Suppose that the APML also provided for a subsidy to those who claimed that the value of their pollution credits had been reduced. Would this have affected the outcome of the case? Why or why not?*

Hazardous Air Pollutants Hazardous air pollutants are those likely to cause death or serious irreversible or incapacitating illness. In all, there are 189 of these pollutants, including asbestos, benzene, beryllium, cadmium, mercury, and vinyl chloride. These pollutants may cause cancer as well as neurological and reproductive damage. They are emitted from stationary sources by a variety of business activities, including smelting (melting ore to produce metal), dry cleaning, house painting, and commercial baking. Instead of establishing specific emissions standards for each hazardous air pollutant, the 1990 amendments to the Clean Air Act require industry to use pollution-control equipment that represents the maximum achievable control technology to limit emissions. The EPA issues guidelines as to what equipment meets this standard.

In 1996, the EPA issued a rule to regulate hazardous air pollutants emitted by landfills. The rule required landfills constructed after May 30, 1991, that emit more than a specified amount of pollutants to install landfill gas collection and control systems.

This worker is cleaning asbestos, a hazardous air pollutant, from the interior of an old building. Does the Clean Air Act establish specific emission standards for hazardous air pollutants? Why or why not? What is the EPA's role in controlling hazardous air pollutants? (© Corbis)

The rule also required the states to impose the same requirements on landfills constructed before May 30, 1991, if they accepted waste after November 8, 1987.[15]

Violations of the Clean Air Act For violations of emission limits under the Clean Air Act, the EPA can assess civil penalties of up to $25,000 per day. Additional fines of up to $5,000 per day can be assessed for other violations, such as failing to maintain the required records. To penalize those who find it more cost-effective to violate the act than to comply with it, the EPA is authorized to obtain a penalty equal to the violator's economic benefits from noncompliance. Persons who provide information about violators may be paid up to $10,000. Private citizens can also sue violators.

Those who knowingly violate the act may be subject to criminal penalties, including fines of up to $1 million and imprisonment for up to two years (for false statements or failures to report violations). Corporate officers are among those who may be subject to these penalties.

WATER POLLUTION

Water pollution stems mostly from industrial, municipal, and agricultural sources. Pollutants entering streams, lakes, and oceans include organic wastes, heated water, sediments from soil runoff, nutrients (including detergents, fertilizers, and human and animal wastes), and toxic chemicals and other hazardous substances. We look here at laws and regulations governing water pollution.

Navigable Waters Federal regulations governing the pollution of water can be traced back to the Rivers and Harbors Appropriations Act of 1899.[16] These regulations prohibited ships and manufacturers from discharging or depositing refuse in navigable waterways without a permit. In 1948, Congress passed the Federal Water Pollution Control Act (FWPCA),[17] but its regulatory system and enforcement powers proved to be inadequate.

In 1972, amendments to the FWPCA—known as the Clean Water Act—established the following goals: (1) make waters safe for swimming, (2) protect fish and wildlife, and (3) eliminate the discharge of pollutants into the water. The amendments set specific time schedules, which were extended by amendment in 1977 and by the Water Quality Act of 1987.[18] Under these schedules, the EPA limits the discharge of various types of pollutants based on the technology available for controlling them. The 1972 act also requires municipal and industrial polluters to apply for permits before discharging wastes into navigable waters.

Under the act, violators are subject to a variety of civil and criminal penalties. Depending on the violation, civil penalties range from $10,000 per day to as much as $25,000 per day, but not more than $25,000 per violation. Criminal penalties, which apply only if a violation was intentional, range from a fine of $2,500 per day and imprisonment for up to one year to a fine of $1 million and fifteen years' imprisonment. Injunctive relief and damages can also be imposed. The polluting party can be required to clean up the pollution or pay for the cost of doing so.

WETLANDS
Water-saturated areas of land that are designated by government agencies (such as the Army Corps of Engineers or the Environmental Protection Agency) as protected areas that support wildlife and therefore cannot be filled in or dredged by private contractors or parties without a permit.

Wetlands The Clean Water Act prohibits the filling or dredging of **wetlands** unless a permit is obtained from the Army Corps of Engineers. The EPA defines *wetlands* as

15. 40 C.F.R. Sections 60.750–759.
16. 33 U.S.C. Sections 401–418.
17. 33 U.S.C. Sections 1251–1387.
18. This act amended 33 U.S.C. Section 1251.

"those areas that are inundated or saturated by surface or ground water at a frequency and duration sufficient to support, and that under normal circumstances do support, a prevalence of vegetation typically adapted for life in saturated soil conditions." In recent years, the broad interpretation of what constitutes a wetland subject to the regulatory authority of the federal government has generated substantial controversy.

■ EXAMPLE 24.7 Perhaps one of the most controversial regulations was the "migratory-bird rule" issued by the Army Corps of Engineers. Under this rule, any bodies of water that could affect interstate commerce, including seasonal ponds or waters "used or suitable for use by migratory birds" that fly over state borders, were "navigable waters" subject to federal regulation as wetlands under the Clean Water Act. The rule was challenged in a case brought by a group of communities in the Chicago suburbs that wanted to build a landfill in a tract of land northwest of Chicago that had once been used as a strip mine. Over time, areas that were once pits in the mine became ponds used by a variety of migratory birds. The Army Corps of Engineers, claiming that the shallow ponds formed a habitat for migratory birds, refused to grant a permit for the landfill. Ultimately, the United States Supreme Court held that the Army Corps of Engineers had exceeded its authority under the Clean Water Act. The Court stated that it was not prepared to hold that isolated and seasonable ponds, puddles, and "prairie potholes" become "navigable waters of the United States" simply because they serve as a habitat for migratory birds.[19] ■

Drinking Water Another statute governing water pollution is the Safe Drinking Water Act of 1974.[20] This act requires the EPA to set maximum levels for pollutants in public water systems. Public water system operators must come as close as possible to meeting the EPA's standards by using the best available technology that is economically and technologically feasible. The EPA is particularly concerned about contamination from underground sources. Pesticides and wastes leaked from landfills or disposed of in underground injection wells are among the more than two hundred pollutants known to exist in groundwater used for drinking in at least thirty-four states. Many of these substances may be associated with cancer and may cause damage to the central nervous system, liver, and kidneys. The act was amended in 1996 to give the EPA more flexibility in setting regulatory standards.

Ocean Dumping The Marine Protection, Research, and Sanctuaries Act of 1972[21] (popularly known as the Ocean Dumping Act), as amended in 1983, regulates the transportation and dumping of material into ocean waters. It prohibits entirely the ocean dumping of radiological, chemical, and biological warfare agents and high-level radioactive waste. Each violation of any provision may result in a civil penalty of up to $50,000, and a knowing violation is a criminal offense that may result in a $50,000 fine, imprisonment for not more than a year, or both. The court may also grant an injunction to prevent an imminent or continuing violation of the Ocean Dumping Act.

Oil Spills In 1989, the supertanker *Exxon Valdez* caused the worst oil spill in North American history in the waters of Alaska's Prince William Sound. A quarter of a million barrels of crude oil—more than ten million gallons—leaked out of the ship's broken hull. In response to the *Exxon Valdez* disaster, Congress passed the Oil

19. *Solid Waste Agency of Northern Cook County v. U.S. Army Corps of Engineers,* 531 U.S. 159, 121 S.Ct. 675, 148 L.Ed.2d 576 (2001).

20. 42 U.S.C. Sections 300f to 300j-25.

21. 16 U.S.C. Sections 1401–1445.

Pollution Act of 1990.[22] Any onshore or offshore oil facility, oil shipper, vessel owner, or vessel operator that discharges oil into navigable waters or onto an adjoining shore may be liable for clean-up costs, as well as damages.

Under the act, damage to natural resources, private property, and the local economy, including the increased cost of providing public services, is compensable. The act provides for civil penalties of $1,000 per barrel spilled or $25,000 for each day of the violation. The party held responsible for the clean-up costs can bring a civil suit for contribution from other potentially liable parties. The act also decreed that by the year 2011, oil tankers using U.S. ports must be double hulled to limit the severity of accidental spills.

NOISE POLLUTION

Regulations concerning noise pollution include the Noise Control Act of 1972.[23] This act directed the EPA to establish standards for noise emissions—for example, for railroad noise emissions. The standards must be achievable by the best available technology, and they must be economically within reason. The act prohibits, among other things, distributing products manufactured in violation of the standards and tampering with noise-control devices. Violations of the Noise Control Act can result in penalties of not more than $50,000 per day and imprisonment for not more than two years.

TOXIC CHEMICALS

Originally, most environmental clean-up efforts were directed toward reducing smog and making water safe for fishing and swimming. Over time, however, control of toxic chemicals has become an important part of environmental law.

Clean-up efforts in Alaska's Prince William Sound following the Exxon Valdez *oil spill. How did this disaster change the law regarding oil spills? Who can be held responsible for clean-up costs? (Photo Courtesy of* Exxon Valdez *Oil Spill Trustee Council and National Oceanic & Atmospheric Administration)*

Pesticides and Herbicides The Federal Insecticide, Fungicide, and Rodenticide Act (FIFRA) of 1947 regulates pesticides and herbicides.[24] Under FIFRA, pesticides and herbicides must be (1) registered before they can be sold, (2) certified and used only for approved applications, and (3) used in limited quantities when applied to food crops. The EPA can cancel or suspend registration of substances that are identified as harmful and may also inspect factories where the chemicals are made. Under 1996 amendments to FIFRA, there must be no more than a one-in-a-million risk to people of developing cancer from any kind of exposure to the substance, including eating food that contains pesticide residues.[25] Also, the EPA must distribute brochures to grocery stores on the high-risk pesticides that are in or on food, and the stores must display these brochures for consumers.

It is a violation of FIFRA to sell a pesticide or herbicide that is unregistered or has had its registration canceled or suspended. It is also a violation to sell a pesticide or herbicide with a false or misleading label or to destroy or deface any labeling required under the act. Penalties for commercial dealers include imprisonment for up to one year and a fine of no more than $25,000. Farmers and

22. 33 U.S.C. Sections 2701–2761.
23. 42 U.S.C. Sections 4901–4918.
24. 7 U.S.C. Sections 135–136y.
25. 21 U.S.C. Section 346a.

other private users of pesticides or herbicides who violate the act are subject to a $1,000 fine and incarceration for up to thirty days.

Toxic Substances The first comprehensive law covering toxic substances was the Toxic Substances Control Act of 1976.[26] The act was passed to regulate chemicals and chemical compounds that are known to be toxic—such as asbestos and polychlorinated biphenyls, popularly known as PCBs—and to institute investigation of any possible harmful effects from new chemical compounds. The regulations authorize the EPA to require that manufacturers, processors, and other organizations planning to use chemicals first determine their effects on human health and the environment. The EPA can regulate substances that potentially pose an imminent hazard or an unreasonable risk of injury to health or the environment. The EPA may require special labeling, limit the use of a substance, set production quotas, or prohibit the use of a substance altogether.

Hazardous Waste Disposal

Some industrial, agricultural, and household wastes pose more serious threats than others. If not properly disposed of, these toxic chemicals may present a substantial danger to human health and the environment. If released into the environment, they may contaminate public drinking water resources.

Resource Conservation and Recovery Act In 1976, Congress passed the Resource Conservation and Recovery Act (RCRA)[27] in reaction to the growing concern over the effects of hazardous waste materials on the environment. The RCRA required the EPA to determine which forms of solid waste should be considered hazardous and to establish regulations to monitor and control hazardous waste disposal. The act also requires all producers of hazardous waste materials to label and package properly any hazardous waste to be transported. The RCRA was amended in 1984 and 1986 to decrease the use of land containment in the disposal of hazardous waste and to require smaller generators of hazardous waste to comply with the act.

Under the RCRA, a company may be assessed a civil penalty of up to $25,000 for each violation.[28] Penalties are based on the seriousness of the violation, the probability of harm, and the extent to which the violation deviates from RCRA requirements. Criminal penalties include fines of up to $50,000 for each day of violation, imprisonment for up to two years (in most instances), or both.[29] Criminal fines and the period of imprisonment can be doubled for certain repeat offenders.

A hazardous waste–disposal team cleans up toxic chemicals that spilled from a truck onto a public highway. If the substance was not properly labeled in violation of the RCRA, what civil penalty might a court impose on the company that operated the vehicle? (Courtesy of Minnesota Pollution Control Agency)

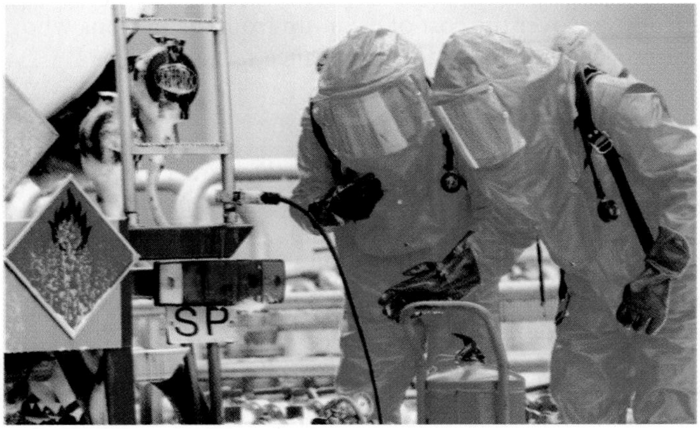

Superfund In 1980, Congress passed the Comprehensive Environmental Response, Compensation, and Liability Act (CERCLA),[30] commonly known as Superfund, to regulate the clean-up of leaking hazardous waste–disposal sites. A special federal fund was created for that purpose. Because of its impact on the business community, the act is presented as this chapter's *Landmark in the Law* feature on the following page.

26. 15 U.S.C. Sections 2601–2692.
27. 42 U.S.C. Sections 6901 *et seq.*
28. 42 U.S.C. Section 6928(a).
29. 42 U.S.C. Section 6928(d).
30. 42 U.S.C. Sections 9601–9675.

LANDMARK IN THE LAW

Superfund

The origins of the Comprehensive Environmental Response, Compensation, and Liability Act (CERCLA) of 1980, commonly referred to as Superfund, can be traced to drafts that the Environmental Protection Agency (EPA) started to circulate in 1978.

DUMP SITES CHARACTERIZED AS "TICKING TIME BOMBS" EPA officials emphasized the necessity of new legislation by pointing to what they characterized as "ticking time bombs"—dump sites around the country that were ready to explode and injure the public with toxic fumes.

The popular press was also running prominent stories about hazardous waste–dump sites at the time. The New York Love Canal disaster first made headlines in 1978 when residents in the area complained about health problems, contaminated sludge oozing into their basements, and chemical "volcanoes" erupting in their yards. These problems were the result of approximately 21,000 tons of chemicals that Hooker Chemical had dumped into the canal from 1942 to 1953. By the middle of May 1980, the Love Canal situation was making the national news virtually every day, and it remained in the headlines for a month.

CERCLA—ITS PURPOSE AND PRIMARY ELEMENTS The basic purpose of CERCLA, which was amended in 1986, is to regulate the clean-up of leaking hazardous waste–disposal sites. The act has four primary elements:

1. It established an information-gathering and analysis system that enables the government to identify chemical dump sites and determine the appropriate action.
2. It authorized the EPA to respond to hazardous substance emergencies and to arrange for the clean-up of a leaking site directly if the persons responsible for the problem fail to clean up the site.
3. It created a Hazardous Substance Response Trust Fund (Superfund) to pay for the clean-up of hazardous sites using funds obtained through taxes on certain businesses.
4. It allowed the government to recover the cost of clean-up from the persons who were (even remotely) responsible for hazardous substance releases.

APPLICATION TO TODAY'S WORLD

The provisions of CERCLA profoundly affect today's businesses. Virtually any business decision relating to the purchase and sale of property, for example, requires an analysis of previous activities on the property to determine whether they resulted in contamination. Additionally, to avoid violating CERCLA, owners and managers of manufacturing plants must be extremely careful in arranging for the removal and disposal of any hazardous waste materials. Unless Congress significantly changes CERCLA and the way that it is implemented, businesses will continue to face potentially extensive liability for violations under this act.

RELEVANT WEB SITES

To locate information on the Web concerning Superfund, go to this text's Web site at **http://blt.westbuslaw.com**, *select "Chapter 24," and click on "URLs for Landmarks."*

POTENTIALLY RESPONSIBLE PARTY (PRP) A party liable for the costs of cleaning up a hazardous waste–disposal site under the Comprehensive Environmental Response, Compensation, and Liability Act (CERCLA). Any person who generated the hazardous waste, transported it, owned or operated the waste site at the time of disposal, or currently owns or operates the site may be responsible for some or all of the clean-up costs.

Potentially Responsible Parties under Superfund. Superfund provides that when a release or a threatened release of hazardous chemicals from a site occurs, the EPA can clean up the site and recover the cost of the clean-up from the following persons: (1) the person who generated the wastes disposed of at the site, (2) the person who transported the wastes to the site, (3) the person who owned or operated the site at the time of the disposal, or (4) the current owner or operator. A person falling within one of these categories is referred to as a **potentially responsible party (PRP).**

Joint and Several Liability under Superfund. Liability under Superfund is usually joint and several (separate)—that is, a person who generated *only a fraction of the hazardous waste* disposed of at the site may nevertheless be liable for *all* of the clean-up costs. CERCLA authorizes a party who has incurred clean-up costs to bring a "contribution action" against any other person who is liable or potentially liable for a percentage of the costs.

APPLICATION How to Negotiate a Favorable Business Lease*

Generally, an entrepreneur starting a business is well advised to lease rather than buy property because the future success of the business is uncertain. By leasing instead of purchasing property, persons just starting out in business allow themselves some time to determine whether business profits will warrant the outright purchase of property.

FACTORS TO CONSIDER

One thing to keep in mind when leasing property is that lease contracts are usually form contracts that favor the landlord. Thus, as a prospective tenant, you need to think about negotiating terms more favorable to you. Before negotiating the terms of the lease, do some comparison shopping to find out the rent for other similar properties in the area. Usually, rental prices for business property are stated as so many dollars per square foot (per month or per year). In commercial leases to retail stores, part or all of the rent commonly consists of a percentage of the tenant's sales made on the premises during the term of the lease. Bear in mind, too, that the nature of your business should determine, to a great extent, the location of the leased premises. If you are involved in a mail-order business, for example, you need not pay the extra price for a prime location that might be required for a restaurant business.

NEGOTIATING LEASE TERMS

When negotiating a lease, you must also determine who will pay the property taxes, insurance premiums, and utility bills and who will be responsible for repairs to the property. These terms are generally negotiable, and depending on who takes responsibility, the rent payment may be adjusted accordingly. Generally, your success in negotiating favorable lease terms will depend on the market. If the rental market is weak (that is, if you have numerous other rental options at favorable rates), you may be able to convince the landlord to be responsible for taxes, insurance, maintenance, and the like, and possibly for improvements to the property necessary for your business. Therefore, it is important to investigate the status of the market before you begin negotiations with a potential landlord.

CHECKLIST FOR THE LESSEE OF BUSINESS PROPERTY

1. When you are starting a business, leasing can be beneficial because it reduces your liability in the event that your business is unsuccessful.
2. Realize that although lease contracts normally favor the landlord, you usually can negotiate advantageous terms for your lease of the premises.
3. Make sure that the lease clearly indicates whether the landlord or the tenant is to be responsible for taxes on the property, expenses relating to necessary maintenance and repairs, and utility costs. By comparison shopping, you should be able to judge which lease terms are favorable and which are not.
4. To protect yourself in the event your business is unsuccessful, start with a short-term initial lease, perhaps with an option to renew the lease in the future.

* This *Application* is not meant to substitute for the services of an attorney who is licensed to practice law in your state.

KEY TERMS

CHAPTER SUMMARY Real Property and Environmental Law

	REAL PROPERTY
The Nature of Real Property (See pages 731–733.)	Real property (also called real estate or realty) is immovable. It includes land, subsurface and air rights, plant life and vegetation, and fixtures.
Ownership Interests in Real Property (See pages 733–735.)	1. *Fee simple absolute*—The most complete form of ownership. 2. *Life estate*—An estate that lasts for the life of a specified individual during which time the individual is entitled to possess, use, and benefit from the estate; ownership rights in a life estate are subject to the rights of the future-interest holder. 3. *Nonpossessory interest*—An interest that involves the right to use real property but not to possess it. Easements, profits, and licenses are nonpossessory interests.
Transfer of Ownership (See pages 735–740.)	1. *By deed*—When real property is sold or transferred as a gift, title to the property is conveyed by means of a deed. A deed must meet specific legal requirements. A *warranty deed* warrants the most extensive protection against defects of title. A *quitclaim deed* conveys to the grantee only whatever interest the grantor had in the property. A deed may be recorded in the manner prescribed by *recording statutes* in the appropriate jurisdiction to give third parties notice of the owner's interest. 2. *By will or inheritance*—If the owner dies after having made a valid will, the land passes as specified in the will. If the owner dies without having made a will, the heirs inherit according to state inheritance statutes. 3. *By adverse possession*—When a person possesses the property of another for a statutory period of time (three to thirty years, with ten years being the most common), that person acquires title to the property, provided the possession is actual and exclusive, open and visible, continuous and peaceable, and hostile and adverse (without the permission of the owner). 4. *By eminent domain*—The government can take land for public use, with just compensation, when the public interest requires the taking.
Leasehold Estates (See pages 740–741.)	A leasehold estate is an interest in real property that is held for only a limited period of time, as specified in the lease agreement. Types of tenancies relating to leased property include the following:

CHAPTER SUMMARY Real Property and Environmental Law—Continued

Leasehold Estates—Continued	1. *Tenancy for years*—Tenancy for a period of time stated by express contract. 2. *Periodic tenancy*—Tenancy for a period determined by the frequency of rent payments; automatically renewed unless proper notice is given. 3. *Tenancy at will*—Tenancy for as long as both parties agree; no notice of termination is required. 4. *Tenancy at sufferance*—Possession of land without legal right.
Landlord-Tenant Relationships (See pages 741–745.)	1. *Lease agreement*—The landlord-tenant relationship is created by a lease agreement. State or local laws may dictate whether the lease must be in writing and what lease terms are permissible. 2. *Rights and duties*—The rights and duties that arise under a lease agreement generally pertain to the following areas: a. Possession—The tenant has an exclusive right to possess the leased premises, which must be available to the tenant at the agreed-on time. Under the covenant of quiet enjoyment, the landlord promises that during the lease term neither the landlord nor anyone having superior title to the property will disturb the tenant's use and enjoyment of the property. b. Use and maintenance of the premises—Unless the parties agree otherwise, the tenant may make any legal use of the property. The tenant is responsible for any damage that he or she causes. The landlord must comply with laws that set specific standards for the maintenance of real property. The implied warranty of habitability requires that a landlord furnish and maintain residential premises in a habitable condition (that is, in a condition safe and suitable for human life). c. Rent—The tenant must pay the rent as long as the lease is in force, unless the tenant justifiably refuses to occupy the property or withholds the rent because of the landlord's failure to maintain the premises properly. 3. *Transferring rights to leased property*— a. If the landlord transfers complete title to the leased property, the tenant becomes the tenant of the new owner. The new owner may then collect the rent but must abide by the existing lease. b. Generally, in the absence of an agreement to the contrary, tenants may assign their rights (but not their duties) under a lease contract to a third person. Tenants may also sublease leased property to a third person, but the original tenant is not relieved of any obligations to the landlord under the lease. In either situation, the landlord's consent may be required, but statutes may prohibit the landlord from unreasonably withholding such consent.
	ENVIRONMENTAL LAW
State and Local Regulation (See pages 745–746.)	Activities affecting the environment are controlled at the local and state levels through regulations relating to land use, the disposal and recycling of garbage and waste, and pollution-causing activities in general.
Federal Regulation (See pages 746–755.)	1. *Environmental protection agencies*—The most well known of the agencies regulating environmental law is the federal Environmental Protection Agency (EPA), which was created in 1970 to coordinate federal environmental programs. The EPA administers most federal environmental policies and statutes. 2. *Assessing environmental impact*—The National Environmental Policy Act of 1969 imposes environmental responsibilities on all federal agencies and requires the preparation of an environmental impact statement (EIS) for every major federal action. An EIS must analyze the action's impact on the environment, its adverse effects and possible alternatives, and its irreversible effects on environmental quality.

(Continued)

CHAPTER SUMMARY Real Property and Environmental Law—Continued

Federal Regulation—Continued	3. *Important areas regulated by the federal government*—Important areas regulated by the federal government include the following: a. Air pollution—Regulated under the authority of the Clean Air Act of 1963 and its amendments, particularly those of 1970, 1977, and 1990. b. Water pollution—Regulated under the authority of the Rivers and Harbors Appropriation Act of 1899, as amended, and the Federal Water Pollution Control Act of 1948, as amended by the Clean Water Act of 1972. c. Noise pollution—Regulated by the Noise Control Act of 1972. d. Toxic chemicals and hazardous waste—Pesticides and herbicides, toxic substances, and hazardous waste are regulated under the authority of the Federal Insecticide, Fungicide, and Rodenticide Act of 1947, the Toxic Substances Control Act of 1976, and the Resource Conservation and Recovery Act of 1976, respectively. The Comprehensive Environmental Response, Compensation, and Liability Act (CERCLA) of 1980, as amended, regulates the clean-up of hazardous waste–disposal sites.

FOR REVIEW

Answers for the even-numbered questions in this For Review *section can be found in Appendix I at the end of this text.*

1. What can a person who holds property in fee simple absolute do with the property? Can a person who holds property as a life estate do the same?
2. How can ownership rights in real property be transferred?
3. What are the respective duties of the landlord and tenant concerning the use and maintenance of leased property? Is the tenant responsible for all damages that he or she causes?
4. What is contained in an environmental impact statement, and who must file one?
5. What major federal statutes regulate air and water pollution? What is Superfund, and who is potentially liable under Superfund?

QUESTIONS AND CASE PROBLEMS

24–1. Clean Air Act. Current scientific knowledge indicates that there is no safe level of exposure to a cancer-causing agent. In theory, even one molecule of such a substance has the potential for causing cancer. Section 112 of the Clean Air Act requires that all cancer-causing substances be regulated to ensure a margin of safety. Some environmental groups have argued that all emissions of such substances must be eliminated if a margin of safety is to be reached. Such a total elimination would likely shut down many major U.S. industries. Should the Environmental Protection Agency totally eliminate all emissions of cancer-causing chemicals? Discuss.

24–2. Property Ownership. Twenty-two years ago Lorenz was a wanderer. At that time, he decided to settle down on an unoccupied, three-acre parcel of land that he did not own. People in the area told him that they had no idea who owned the property. Lorenz built a house on the land, got married, and raised three children while living there. He fenced in the land, installed a gate with a sign above it that read "Lorenz's Homestead," and had trespassers removed. Lorenz is now confronted by Joe Reese, who has a deed in his name as owner of the property. Reese, claiming ownership of the land, orders Lorenz and his family off the property. Discuss who has the better "title" to the property.

24–3. Deeds. Wiley and Gemma are neighbors. Wiley's lot is extremely large, and his present and future use of it will not involve the entire area. Gemma wants to build a single-car garage and driveway along the present lot boundary. Because of ordinances requiring buildings to be set back fifteen feet from an adjoining property line, and because of the placement of her existing structures, Gemma cannot build the garage. Gemma contracts to purchase ten feet of Wiley's property along their boundary line for $3,000. Wiley is willing to sell but will give Gemma only a quitclaim deed, whereas Gemma wants a warranty deed. Discuss the differences between these deeds as they would affect the rights of the parties if the title to this ten feet of land later proves to be defective.

24–4. Adverse Possession. In 1972, Ted Pafundi bought a quarry in West Pawlet, Vermont, from his neighbor, Marguerite Scott. The deed vaguely described the eastern boundary of the quarry as "the westerly boundary of the lands of" the neighboring property owners. Pafundi quarried green slate from the west wall until his death in 1979, when his son Gary began to work the east wall until *his* death in 1989. Gary's daughter Connie then took over operations. All of the Pafundis used the floor of the quarry as their base of operations. In 1992, N.A.S. Holdings, Inc., bought the neighboring property. A survey revealed that virtually the entire quarry was within the boundaries of N.A.S.'s property and that twenty years earlier, Ted had actually bought only a small strip of land on the west side. When N.A.S. attempted to begin quarrying, Connie blocked the access. N.A.S. filed a suit in a Vermont state court against Connie, seeking to establish title. Connie argued that she had title to the quarry through adverse possession under a state statute with a possessory period of fifteen years. What are the elements to acquire title by adverse possession? Are they satisfied in this case? In whose favor should the court rule, and why? [*N.A.S. Holdings, Inc. v. Pafundi,* 736 A.2d 780 (Vt. 1999)]

CASE PROBLEM WITH SAMPLE ANSWER

24–5. Jennifer Tribble leased an apartment from Spring Isle II, a limited partnership. The written lease agreement provided that if Tribble was forced to move because of a job transfer or because she accepted a new job, she could vacate on sixty days' notice and owe only an extra two months' rent plus no more than a $650 rerenting fee. The initial term was for one year, and the parties renewed the lease for a second one-year term. The security deposit was $900. State law allowed a landlord to withhold a security deposit for the nonpayment of rent but required timely notice stating valid reasons for the withholding or the tenant would be entitled to twice the amount of the deposit as damages. One month into the second term, Tribble notified Spring Isle in writing that she had accepted a new job and would move out within a week. She paid the extra rent required by the lease, but not the rerental fee, and vacated the apartment. Spring Isle wrote her a letter, stating that it was keeping the entire security deposit until the apartment was rerented or the lease term ended, whichever came first. Spring Isle later filed a suit in a Wisconsin state court against Tribble, claiming that she owed, among other things, the rest of the rent until the apartment had been rented again and the costs of rerenting. Tribble responded that withholding the security deposit was improper and that she was entitled to "any penalties." Does Tribble owe Spring Isle anything? Does Spring Isle owe Tribble anything? Explain. [*Spring Isle II v. Tribble,* 610 N.W.2d 229 (Wis.App. 2000)]

After you have answered this problem, compare your answer with the sample answer given on the Web site that accompanies this text. Go to http://blt.westbuslaw.com, select "Chapter 24," and click on "Case Problem with Sample Answer."

24–6. Commercial Lease Terms. Metropolitan Life Insurance Co. leased space in its Trail Plaza Shopping Center in Florida to Winn-Dixie Stores, Inc., to operate a supermarket. Under the lease, the landlord agreed not to permit "any [other] property located within the shopping center to be used for or occupied by any business dealing in or which shall keep in stock or sell for off-premises consumption any staple or fancy groceries" in more than "500 square feet of sales area." In 1999, Metropolitan leased 22,000 square feet of space in Trail Plaza to 99 Cent Stuff-Trail Plaza, LLC, under a lease that prohibited it from selling "groceries" in more than 500 square feet of "sales area." Shortly after 99 Cent Stuff opened, it began selling food and other products, including soap, matches, and paper napkins. Alleging that these sales violated the parties' leases, Winn-Dixie filed a suit in a Florida state court against 99 Cent Stuff and others. The defendants argued in part that the groceries provision covered only food and the 500-square-foot restriction included only shelf space, not store aisles. How should these lease terms be interpreted? Should the court grant an injunction in Winn-Dixie's favor? Explain. [*Winn-Dixie Stores, Inc. v. 99 Cent Stuff-Trail Plaza, LLC,* 811 So.2d 719 (Fla.App. 3 Dist. 2002)]

24–7. Environmental Impact Statement. Greers Ferry Lake is in Arkansas, and its shoreline is under the management of the U.S. Army Corps of Engineers, which is part of the U.S. Department of Defense (DOD). The Corps's 2000 Shoreline Management Plan (SMP) rezoned numerous areas along the lake, authorized the Corps to issue permits for the construction of new boat docks in the rezoned areas, increased by 300 percent the area around habitable structures that could be cleared of vegetation, and instituted a Wildlife Enhancement Permit to allow limited modifications of the shoreline. In relation to the SMP's adoption, the Corps issued a Finding of No Significant Impact, which declared that no environmental impact statement (EIS) was necessary. The Corps issued thirty-two boat dock construction permits under the SMP before Save Greers Ferry Lake, Inc., filed a suit in a federal district court against the DOD, asking the court to, among other things, stop the Corps from acting under the SMP and order it to prepare an EIS. What are the requirements for an EIS? Is an EIS needed in this case? Explain. [*Save Greers Ferry Lake, Inc. v. Department of Defense,* 255 F.3d 498 (8th Cir. 2001)]

24–8. CERCLA. Beginning in 1926, Marietta Dyestuffs Co. operated an industrial facility in Marietta, Ohio, to make dyes and other chemicals. In 1944, Dyestuffs became part of American Home Products Corp. (AHP), which sold the Marietta facility to American Cyanamid Co. in 1946. In 1950, AHP sold the rest of the Dyestuffs assets and all of its stock to B. F. Goodrich Co., which immediately liquidated the acquired corporation. Goodrich continued to operate the dissolved corporation's business, however. Cyanamid continued to make chemicals at the Marietta facility, and in 1993, it created Cytec Industries, Inc., which expressly assumed all environmental liabilities associated with Cyanamid's ownership and operation of the facility. Cytec spent nearly $25 million in clean-up costs and filed a suit in a federal district court against Goodrich to recover, under the Comprehensive Environmental Response, Compensation, and Liability Act (CERCLA), a portion of the costs attributable to the clean-up of hazardous wastes that may have been discarded at the site between 1926 and 1946. Cytec filed a motion for summary judgment in its favor. Should the court grant Cytec's motion? Explain. [*Cytec Industries, Inc. v. B. F. Goodrich Co.,* 196 F.Supp.2d 644 (S.D. Ohio 2002)]

A QUESTION OF ETHICS

24–9. The Endangered Species Act of 1973 makes it unlawful for any person to "take" endangered or threatened species. The act defines *take* to mean to "harass, harm, pursue," "wound," or "kill." The secretary of the interior (Bruce Babbitt) issued a regulation that further defined *harm* to include "significant habitat modification or degradation where it actually kills or injures wildlife." A group of businesses and individuals involved in the timber industry brought an action against the secretary of the interior and others. The group complained that the application of the "harm" regulation to the red-cockaded woodpecker and the northern spotted owl had injured the group economically because it prevented logging operations (habitat modification) in Pacific Northwest forests containing these species. The group challenged the regulation's validity, contending that Congress did not intend the word *take* to include habitat modification. The case ultimately reached the United States Supreme Court, which held that the secretary reasonably construed Congress's intent when he defined *harm* to include habitat modification. [*Babbitt v. Sweet Home Chapter of Communities for a Great Oregon,* 515 U.S. 687, 115 S.Ct. 2407, 132 L.Ed.2d 597 (1995)]

1. Traditionally, the term *take* has been used to refer to the capture or killing of wildlife, usually for private gain. Is the secretary's regulation prohibiting habitat modification consistent with this definition?
2. One of the issues in this case was whether Congress intended to protect existing generations of species or future generations. How do the terms *take* and *habitat modification* relate to this issue?
3. Three dissenting Supreme Court justices contended that construing the act as prohibiting habitat modification "imposes unfairness to the point of financial ruin—not just upon the rich, but upon the simplest farmer who finds his land conscripted to national zoological use." Should private parties be required to bear the burden of preserving habitats for wildlife?
4. Generally, should the economic welfare of private parties be taken into consideration when creating and applying environmental statutes and regulations?

FOR CRITICAL ANALYSIS

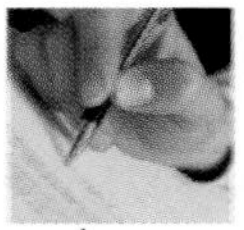

24–10. Real property law dates back hundreds of years. What changes have occurred in society, including business and technological changes, that have affected the development and application of real property law? (Hint: Was airspace an issue three hundred years ago?)

INTERNET EXERCISES

Go to the *Business Law Today: The Essentials* home page at **http://blt.westbuslaw.com**, select "Chapter 24," and click on "Internet Exercises." There you will find the following Internet research exercises that you can perform to learn more about topics covered in this chapter.

Activity 24–1: LEGAL PERSPECTIVE—Eminent Domain

Activity 24–2: MANAGEMENT PERSPECTIVE—Fair Housing

Activity 24–3: MANAGEMENT PERSPECTIVE—Complying with Environmental Regulation

BEFORE THE TEST

Go to the *Business Law Today: The Essentials* home page at **http://blt.westbuslaw.com**, select "Chapter 24," and click on "Interactive Quizzes." You will find at least twenty interactive questions relating to this chapter.

CHAPTER 25

International Law in a Global Economy

"Our interests are those of the open door—a door of friendship and mutual advantage. This is the only door we care to enter."
Woodrow Wilson, 1856–1924
(Twenty-eighth president of the United States, 1913–1921)

CHAPTER OUTLINE

- INTERNATIONAL PRINCIPLES AND DOCTRINES
- DOING BUSINESS INTERNATIONALLY
- COMMERCIAL CONTRACTS IN AN INTERNATIONAL SETTING
- MAKING PAYMENT ON INTERNATIONAL TRANSACTIONS
- REGULATION OF SPECIFIC BUSINESS ACTIVITIES
- U.S. LAWS IN A GLOBAL CONTEXT

LEARNING OBJECTIVES

After reading this chapter, you should be able to answer the following questions:

1. What is the principle of comity, and why do courts deciding disputes involving a foreign law or judicial decree apply this principle?
2. What is the act of state doctrine? In what circumstances is this doctrine applied?
3. Under the Foreign Sovereign Immunities Act of 1976, on what bases might a foreign state be considered subject to the jurisdiction of U.S. courts?
4. In what circumstances will U.S. antitrust laws be applied extraterritorially?
5. Do U.S. laws prohibiting employment discrimination apply in all circumstances to U.S. employees working for U.S. employers abroad?

International business transactions are not unique to the modern world. Indeed, as suggested by President Woodrow Wilson's statement in the opening quotation, people have always found that they can benefit from exchanging goods with others. What is new in our day is the dramatic growth in world trade and the emergence of a global business community. Because the exchange of goods, services, and ideas on a global level is now routine, students of business law should be familiar with the laws pertaining to international business transactions. In this chapter, we first examine the legal context of international business transactions. We then look at some selected areas relating to business activities in a global context, including international sales contracts, civil dispute resolution, letters of credit, and investment protection. We conclude the chapter with a discussion of the application of certain U.S. laws in a transnational setting.

International Principles and Doctrines

INTERNATIONAL LAW
The law that governs relations among nations. International customs and treaties are important sources of international law.

NATIONAL LAW
Laws that pertain to a particular nation (as opposed to international law).

International law can be defined as a body of law—formed as a result of international customs, treaties, and organizations—that governs relations among or between nations. **National law,** in contrast, is the law of a particular nation, such as the United States, Japan, Germany, or Brazil. Here, we look at some legal principles and doctrines of international law that have evolved over time and that the courts of various nations have employed—to a greater or lesser extent—to resolve or reduce conflicts that involve a foreign element. The three important legal principles and doctrines discussed in the following subsections are based primarily on courtesy and respect and are applied in the interests of maintaining harmonious relations among nations.

THE PRINCIPLE OF COMITY

COMITY
The principle by which one nation defers and gives effect to the laws and judicial decrees of another nation. This recognition is based primarily on respect.

Under what is known as the principle of **comity,** one nation will defer and give effect to the laws and judicial decrees of another country, as long as those laws and judicial decrees are consistent with the law and public policy of the accommodating nation.

■ EXAMPLE 25.1 Assume that a Swedish seller and a U.S. buyer have formed a contract, which the buyer breaches. The seller sues the buyer in a Swedish court, which awards damages. The buyer's assets, however, are in the United States and cannot be reached unless the judgment is enforced by a U.S. court of law. In this situation, if a U.S. court determines that the procedures and laws applied in the Swedish court were consistent with U.S. national law and policy, that court will likely defer to (and enforce) the foreign court's judgment. ■

One way to understand the principle of comity (and the *act of state doctrine,* which will be discussed shortly) is to consider the relationships among the states in our federal form of government. Each state honors (gives "full faith and credit" to) the contracts, property deeds, wills, and other legal obligations formed in other states, as well as judicial decisions with respect to such obligations. On a worldwide basis, nations similarly attempt to honor judgments rendered in other countries when it is feasible to do so. Of course, in the United States the states are constitutionally required to honor other states' actions, whereas, internationally, nations are not *required* to honor the actions of other nations.

Normally, the principle of comity is extended to foreign bankruptcy proceedings. The question in the following case was whether a U.S. court is required to determine the ownership of a disputed asset before a bankruptcy case goes forward in a foreign court.

CASE 25.1 JP Morgan Chase Bank v. Altos Hornos de Mexico, S.A. de C.V.

United States District Court,
Southern District of New York, 2004.
__ F.Supp.2d __.

FACTS In April 1997, Altos Hornos de Mexico, S.A. de C.V., Mexico's largest liquid steel producer, borrowed $330 million from twenty-eight banks, including JP Morgan Chase Bank (JPMCB). JPMCB was the loan's "facility agent," distributing payments among the lenders through a "collection account" set up in the loan documents. As a term of the loan, Altos Hornos told three of its customers to pay into the collection account. The loan documents contained forum-selection and choice-of-law clauses in favor of New York. In May 1999, after significant losses in the global steel market, Altos Hornos filed a petition with a Mexican court to be declared in *suspensión de pagos* (suspension of payments, or SOP, which, under Mexican

CASE 25.1—Continued

bankruptcy law, is similar to a Chapter 11 reorganization under U.S. bankruptcy law—see Chapter 16). The court granted the petition. In June and August, Altos Hornos's three customers paid $4.7 million into JPMCB's collection account. Altos Hornos asked the SOP court to order JPMCB to reimburse the funds for distribution in the SOP proceeding. Meanwhile, JPMCB filed a suit in a federal district court against Altos Hornos, seeking a declaration that these funds did not belong to the borrower. Altos Hornos filed a motion to dismiss this suit.

ISSUE Is a U.S. court required to resolve the question of the ownership of a bank account before its possible owner's bankruptcy proceeding in a Mexican court?

DECISION No. The court held that it was not required to determine the ownership of the funds in the account and dismissed JPMCB's complaint on the basis of comity.

REASON The court stated that "comity is especially appropriate for foreign bankruptcy proceedings." The court acknowledged that under Mexican law, the SOP court was not required to resolve the question of ownership. But under Mexican law, the SOP court had jurisdiction to rule on JPMCB's claim to the funds in the SOP proceedings, which, the U.S. court noted, were fundamentally fair and did not violate public policy in the United States. The U.S. court also reasoned that the loan's forum-selection and choice-of-law clauses did not proscribe comity if it was otherwise warranted. Under most contracts, "the considerations associated with comity trump [take precedence over] the parties' express wishes. * * * [T]here are important considerations that may not have concerned the parties" when they entered into their contract, but with which the court must be concerned, such as "Altos Hornos's other creditors and the importance of a unified administration rather than a piecemeal administration of its estate in the SOP proceeding."

FOR CRITICAL ANALYSIS—Social Consideration *Why might a Mexican court be better able to determine the ownership of the funds in the collection account in this case?*

The Act of State Doctrine

ACT OF STATE DOCTRINE
A doctrine providing that the judicial branch of one country will not examine the validity of public acts committed by a recognized foreign government within its own territory.

The **act of state doctrine** is a judicially created doctrine that provides that the judicial branch of one country will not examine the validity of public acts committed by a recognized foreign government within its own territory. This doctrine is premised on the theory that the judicial branch should not "pass upon the validity of foreign acts when to do so would vex the harmony of our international relations with that foreign nation."[1]

EXPROPRIATION
The seizure by a government of a privately owned business or personal property for a proper public purpose and with just compensation.

CONFISCATION
A government's taking of a privately owned business or personal property without a proper public purpose or an award of just compensation.

When a Foreign Government Takes Private Property The act of state doctrine can have important consequences for individuals and firms doing business with, and investing in, other countries. For example, this doctrine is frequently employed in situations involving expropriation or confiscation. **Expropriation** occurs when a government seizes a privately owned business or privately owned goods for a proper public purpose and awards just compensation. When a government seizes private property for an illegal purpose or without just compensation, the taking is referred to as a **confiscation.** The line between these two forms of taking is sometimes blurred because of differing interpretations of what is illegal and what constitutes just compensation.

■ EXAMPLE 25.2 Flaherty, Inc., a U.S. company, owns a mine in Brazil. The government of Brazil seizes the mine for public use and claims that the profits that Flaherty realized from the mine in preceding years constitute just compensation.

1. *Libra Bank, Ltd. v. Banco Nacional de Costa Rica, S.A.*, 570 F.Supp. 870 (S.D.N.Y. 1983).

Flaherty disagrees, but the act of state doctrine may prevent the company's recovery in a U.S. court. ■

Immunity from U.S. Jurisdiction When applicable, both the act of state doctrine and the doctrine of *sovereign immunity* (to be discussed next) tend to immunize (protect) foreign governments from the jurisdiction of U.S. courts. This means that firms or individuals who own property overseas often have diminished legal protection against government actions in the countries in which they operate.

THE DOCTRINE OF SOVEREIGN IMMUNITY

SOVEREIGN IMMUNITY
A doctrine that immunizes foreign nations from the jurisdiction of U.S. courts when certain conditions are satisfied.

When certain conditions are satisfied, the doctrine of **sovereign immunity** immunizes foreign nations from the jurisdiction of U.S. courts. In 1976, Congress codified this rule in the Foreign Sovereign Immunities Act (FSIA).[2] The FSIA exclusively governs the circumstances in which an action may be brought in the United States against a foreign nation, including attempts to attach a foreign nation's property.

Section 1605 of the FSIA sets forth the major exceptions to the jurisdictional immunity of a foreign state or country. A foreign state is not immune from the jurisdiction of U.S. courts when the state has "waived its immunity either explicitly or by implication" or when the action is taken "in connection with a commercial activity carried on in the United States by the foreign state" or having "a direct effect in the United States."[3]

on the Web FindLaw's Web site includes an extensive array of links to international doctrines, treaties, and other nations' laws. Go to

http://www.findlaw.com

and select "International Law."

The question frequently arises as to whether an entity falls within the category of a foreign state. The question of what is a commercial activity has also been the subject of dispute. Under Section 1603 of the FSIA, a *foreign state* includes both a political subdivision of a foreign state and an instrumentality of a foreign state. Section 1603 broadly defines a *commercial activity* as a commercial activity that is carried out by a foreign state within the United States, but it does not describe the particulars of what constitutes a commercial activity. Thus, the courts are left to decide whether a particular activity is governmental or commercial in nature.

Doing Business Internationally

EXPORT
To sell products to buyers located in other countries.

A U.S. domestic firm can engage in international business transactions in a number of ways. The simplest way is to seek out foreign markets for domestically produced products or services. In other words, U.S. firms can look abroad for **export** markets for their goods and services.

Alternatively, a U.S. firm can establish foreign production facilities so as to be closer to the foreign market or markets in which its products are sold. The advantages may include lower labor costs, fewer government regulations, and lower taxes and trade barriers. A domestic firm can also obtain revenues by licensing its technology to an existing foreign company. Yet another way to expand abroad is by selling franchises to overseas entities. The presence of McDonald's, Burger King, and KFC franchises throughout the world attests to the popularity of franchising.

2. 28 U.S.C. Sections 1602–1611.
3. See, for example, *Keller v. Central Bank of Nigeria,* 277 F.3d 811 (6th Cir. 2002), in which the court held that failure to pay promised funds to a Cleveland account was an action having a direct effect in the United States.

EXPORTING

If you are interested in learning more about what is involved in exporting goods to other countries, go to the state of New Mexico's Web page on "How to Export" at

http://www.edd.state.nm.us/TRADE/HOWTO/howto.html.

Most U.S. companies make their initial foray into international business through exporting. Exporting can take two forms: direct exporting and indirect exporting. In *direct exporting*, a U.S. company signs a sales contract with a foreign purchaser that provides for the conditions of shipment and payment for the goods. (How payments are made in international transactions is discussed later in this chapter.) If sufficient business develops in a foreign country, a U.S. corporation may set up a specialized marketing organization in that foreign market by appointing a foreign agent or a foreign distributor. This is called *indirect exporting*.

Foreign Agent When a U.S. firm desires to limit its involvement in an international market, it will typically establish an *agency relationship* with a foreign firm. In an agency relationship (discussed in Chapter 17), one person (the agent) agrees to act on behalf of another (the principal). The foreign agent is thereby empowered to enter into contracts in the agent's country on behalf of the U.S. principal.

DISTRIBUTION AGREEMENT
A contract between a seller and a distributor of the seller's products setting out the terms and conditions of the distributorship.

EXCLUSIVE DISTRIBUTORSHIP
A distributorship in which the seller and the distributor of the seller's products agree that the distributor has the exclusive right to distribute the seller's products in a certain geographic area.

Foreign Distributor When a substantial market exists in a foreign country, a U.S. firm may wish to appoint a distributor located in that country. The U.S. firm and the distributor enter into a **distribution agreement,** which is a contract between the seller and the distributor setting out the terms and conditions of the distributorship—for example, price, currency of payment, availability of supplies, and method of payment. The terms and conditions primarily involve contract law. Disputes concerning distribution agreements may involve jurisdictional or other issues (discussed in detail later in this chapter). In addition, some **exclusive distributorships—**in which distributors agree to distribute only the sellers' goods—have raised antitrust problems.

MANUFACTURING ABROAD

An alternative to direct or indirect exporting is the establishment of foreign manufacturing facilities. Typically, U.S. firms establish manufacturing plants abroad if they believe that doing so will reduce their costs—particularly for labor, shipping, and raw materials—and enable them to compete more effectively in foreign markets. Apple Computer, IBM, General Motors, and Ford are some of the many U.S. companies that have established manufacturing facilities abroad. Foreign firms have done the same in the United States. Sony, Nissan, and other Japanese manufacturers have established U.S. plants to avoid import duties that the U.S. Congress may impose on Japanese products entering this country.

A U.S. firm can manufacture goods in other countries in several ways. They include licensing and franchising, as well as investing in a wholly owned subsidiary or a joint venture.

Licensing A U.S. firm can obtain business from abroad by licensing a foreign manufacturing company to use its copyrighted, patented, or trademarked intellectual property or trade secrets. Like any other licensing agreement (see Chapters 5 and 10), a licensing agreement with a foreign-based firm calls for a payment of royalties on some basis—such as so many cents per unit produced or a certain percentage of profits from units sold in a particular geographic territory.

In some circumstances, even in the absence of a patent, a firm may be able to license the "know-how" associated with a particular manufacturing process—for example, a plant design or a secret formula. The foreign firm that agrees to sign the

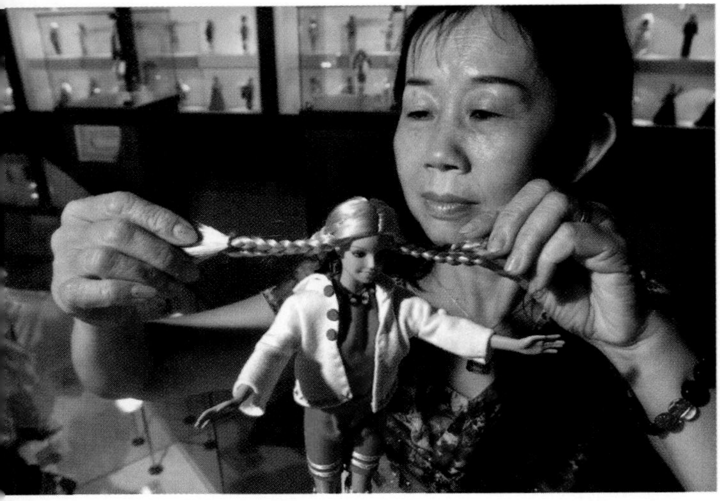

A woman in Taiwan holds a Barbie doll that was manufactured in Taiwan. Why would a U.S. corporation, such as Mattel, Inc., outsource its manufacturing jobs to a foreign firm? (AP Photo/ Wally Santana)

licensing agreement further agrees to keep the know-how confidential and to pay royalties. ■ EXAMPLE 25.3 Coca-Cola licenses firms worldwide to use (and keep confidential) its secret formula for the syrup used in its soft drink. In return, the foreign firms licensed to make the syrup pay Coca-Cola a percentage of the income earned from the sale of the soft drink. ■

The licensing of intellectual property rights benefits all parties to the transaction. The firm that receives the license can take advantage of an established reputation for quality. The firm that grants the license receives income from the foreign sales of its products and also establishes a global reputation. Additionally, once a firm's trademark is known worldwide, the firm may see increased demand for other products it manufactures or sells—obviously an important consideration.

Franchising Franchising is a well-known form of licensing. Recall from Chapter 19 that in a franchise arrangement the owner of a trademark, trade name, or copyright (the franchisor) licenses another (the franchisee) to use the trademark, trade name, or copyright under certain conditions or limitations in the selling of goods or services. In return, the franchisee pays a fee, which is usually based on a percentage of gross or net sales. Examples of international franchises include McDonald's, Holiday Inn, Avis, and Hertz.

Investing in a Wholly Owned Subsidiary or a Joint Venture Another way to expand into a foreign market is to establish a wholly owned subsidiary firm in a foreign country. In many European countries, a subsidiary would take the form of what is called in French a *société anonyme* (S.A.), which is similar to a U.S. corporation. In German-speaking nations, it would be called an *Aktiengesellschaft* (A.G.). When a wholly owned subsidiary is established, the parent company, which remains in the United States, retains complete ownership of all the facilities in the foreign country, as well as complete authority and control over all phases of the operation.

A U.S. firm can also expand into international markets through a joint venture. In a joint venture, the U.S. company owns only part of the operation; the rest is owned either by local owners in the foreign country or by another foreign entity. All of the firms involved in a joint venture share responsibilities, as well as profits and liabilities.

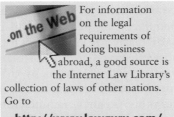

.on the Web For information on the legal requirements of doing business abroad, a good source is the Internet Law Library's collection of laws of other nations. Go to

http://www.lawguru.com/ilawlib/index.html.

Commercial Contracts in an International Setting

Like all commercial contracts, an international contract should be in writing. For an example of an actual international sales contract, see this chapter's foldout contract.

Language and legal differences among nations can create special problems for parties to international contracts when disputes arise. It is possible to avoid these problems by including in a contract special provisions designating the official language of the contract, the legal forum (court or place) in which disputes under the contract will be settled, and the substantive law that will be applied in settling any disputes. Parties to international contracts should also indicate in their contracts what acts or events will excuse the parties from performance under the contract and whether disputes under the contract will be arbitrated or litigated.

RECALL The interpretation of the words in a contract can be a matter of dispute even when both parties communicate in the same language.

CHOICE OF LANGUAGE

CHOICE-OF-LANGUAGE CLAUSE
A clause in a contract designating the official language by which the contract will be interpreted in the event of a future disagreement over the contract's terms.

A deal struck between a U.S. company and a company in another country normally involves two languages. Typically, many phrases in one language are not readily translatable into another. Consequently, the complex contractual terms involved may not be understood by one party in the other party's language. To make sure that no disputes arise out of this language problem, an international sales contract should have a **choice-of-language clause** designating the official language by which the contract will be interpreted in the event of disagreement.

CHOICE OF FORUM

FORUM-SELECTION CLAUSE
A provision in a contract designating the court, jurisdiction, or tribunal that will decide any disputes arising under the contract.

When parties from several countries are involved, litigation may be pursued in courts in different nations. There are no universally accepted rules as to which court has jurisdiction over particular subject matter or parties to a dispute. Consequently, parties to an international transaction should always include in the contract a **forum-selection clause** indicating what court, jurisdiction, or tribunal will decide any disputes arising under the contract. It is especially important to indicate the specific court that will have jurisdiction. The forum does not necessarily have to be within the geographic boundaries of the home nation of either party. The following case involved a question about the application of a forum-selection clause.

CASE 25.2 Garware Polyester, Ltd. v. Intermax Trading Corp.

United States District Court,
Southern District of New York, 2001.
__ F.Supp.2d __.

FACTS Garware Polyester, Ltd., based in Mumbai, India, develops and makes plastics and high-tech polyester film. In 1987, Intermax Trading Corporation, based in New York, became Garware's North American sales agent. Over the next decade, the parties executed four written agreements, collectively referred to as the "Agency Agreements." Each agreement provided, "The courts at Bombay [India] alone will have jurisdiction to try out suits in respect of any claim or dispute arising out of or under this agreement or in any way relating to the same." Intermax sold Garware products on a commission basis. In some transactions, Intermax arranged for customers to order products directly from Garware. In other transactions, Intermax sold Garware products through warehouse sales by which Intermax bought products from Garware, warehoused them in the United States, and resold them. When Intermax fell behind in its payments, Garware filed a suit in a U.S. district court to collect on the unpaid invoices. Garware argued that the forum-selection clause did not apply to the invoices in dispute because they involved the warehouse sales, which, Garware claimed, were not part of, and did not relate to, the Agency Agreements.

ISSUE Did the forum-selection clause require the dismissal of this suit?

DECISION Yes. The court held that each of the Agency Agreements contained a valid and enforceable forum-selection clause, which applied to this suit. The court dismissed the case for improper venue.

REASON The court recognized that forum-selection clauses "eliminate uncertainty in international commerce and insure that the parties are not unexpectedly subjected to hostile forums and laws. Moreover, international comity dictates that American courts enforce these sorts of clauses out of respect for the integrity and respect of foreign tribunals." The court stated that a forum-selection clause applies when "claims grow out of the contractual relationship, or if the gist of those claims is a breach of that relationship." Here, "the 'gist' of Garware's claim is a breach of the Agency Agreements. The warehouse sales in question were made by Intermax for the purpose of selling Garware products in the contractually defined territory. The Agency Agreements specifically relate to Intermax's role as Garware's 'selling agent * * * in the United States of America * * * .' Thus, if these sales are not squarely within the scope of the Agency

(Continued)

CASE 25.2—Continued

Agreements, they are, at the very least, related to the Agreements. Further, the parties' course of dealing supports the conclusion that the parties themselves believed the Agency Agreements included warehouse sales: as required by the Agreements, Garware paid commissions to Intermax on these sales."

WHY IS THIS CASE IMPORTANT? *As this case illustrates, when the underlying transaction is international, courts generally presume that forum-selection clauses are valid because such clauses eliminate uncertainty in international commerce. It takes a strong showing that the clause was unreasonable under the circumstances to overcome this presumptive validity.*

CHOICE OF LAW

CHOICE-OF-LAW CLAUSE
A clause in a contract designating the law (such as the law of a particular state or nation) that will govern the contract.

A contractual provision designating the applicable law—such as the law of Germany or England or California—is called a **choice-of-law clause.** Every international contract typically includes a choice-of-law clause. At common law (and in European civil law systems), parties are allowed to choose the law that will govern their contractual relationship, provided that the law chosen is the law of a jurisdiction that has a substantial relationship to the parties and to the international business transaction.

Under Section 1–105 of the Uniform Commercial Code, parties may choose the law that will govern the contract as long as the choice is "reasonable." Article 6 of the United Nations Convention on Contracts for the International Sale of Goods, however, imposes no limitation on the parties' choice of what law will govern the contract. The 1986 Hague Convention on the Law Applicable to Contracts for the International Sale of Goods—often referred to as the Choice-of-Law Convention—allows unlimited autonomy in the choice of law. The Hague Convention indicates that whenever a contract does not specify a choice of law, the governing law is that of the country in which the *seller's* place of business is located.

FORCE MAJEURE CLAUSE

***FORCE MAJEURE* CLAUSE**
A provision in a contract stipulating that certain unforeseen events–such as war, political upheavals, or acts of God–will excuse a party from liability for nonperformance of contractual obligations.

Every contract, particularly those involving international transactions, should have a ***force majeure* clause.** *Force majeure* is a French term meaning "impossible or irresistible force"—sometimes loosely identified as "an act of God." In international business contracts, *force majeure* clauses commonly stipulate that in addition to acts of God, a number of other eventualities (such as government orders or embargoes, for example) may excuse a party from liability for nonperformance.

CIVIL DISPUTE RESOLUTION

International contracts frequently include arbitration clauses. By means of such clauses, the parties agree in advance to be bound by the decision of a specified third party in the event of a dispute, as discussed in Chapter 3. The third party may be a neutral entity (such as the International Chamber of Commerce), a panel of individuals representing both parties' interests, or some other group or organization. (For an example of an arbitration clause in an international contract, refer to the foldout exhibit in this chapter.) The United Nations Convention on the Recognition and Enforcement of Foreign Arbitral Awards (often referred to as the New York Convention) assists in the enforcement of arbitration clauses, as do provisions in specific treaties among nations. The New York Convention has been implemented in nearly one hundred countries, including the United States.

If a sales contract does not include an arbitration clause, litigation may occur. If the contract contains forum-selection and choice-of-law clauses, the lawsuit will be heard by a court in the specified forum and decided according to that forum's law. If no

Workers at a manufacturing plant owned by a U.S. company in Beijing, China. What contract clauses would affect where and how these foreign workers are able to resolve disputes with their U.S. employer? (Ricky Wong, Bloomberg News/Landov)

forum and choice of law have been specified, however, legal proceedings will be more complex and attended by much more uncertainty. For instance, litigation may take place in two or more countries, with each country applying its own choice-of-law rules to determine the substantive law that will be applied to the particular transactions.

Even if a plaintiff wins a favorable judgment in a lawsuit litigated in the plaintiff's country, there is no way to predict whether courts in the defendant's country will enforce the judgment. As discussed earlier in this chapter, courts in the defendant's country may enforce the judgment under the principle of comity, particularly if the defendant's country is the United States and the foreign court's decision is consistent with U.S. national law and policy. Other nations, though, may not be as accommodating as the United States in this respect.

Making Payment on International Transactions

Currency differences between nations and the geographic distance between parties to international sales contracts add a degree of complexity to international sales that does not exist in the domestic market. Because international contracts involve greater financial risks, special care should be taken in drafting these contracts to specify both the currency in which payment is to be made and the method of payment.

MONETARY SYSTEMS

Although our national currency, the U.S. dollar, is one of the primary forms of international currency, any U.S. firm undertaking business transactions abroad must be prepared to deal with one or more other currencies. After all, just as a U.S. firm wants to be paid in U.S. dollars for goods and services sold abroad, so, too, does a Japanese firm want to be paid in Japanese yen for goods and services sold outside Japan. Both firms therefore must rely on the convertibility of currencies.

FOREIGN EXCHANGE MARKET
A worldwide system in which foreign currencies are bought and sold.

Foreign Exchange Markets Currencies are convertible when they can be freely exchanged one for the other at some specified market rate in a **foreign exchange market.** Foreign exchange markets comprise a worldwide system for the buying and selling of foreign currencies. At any point in time, the foreign exchange rate is set by the forces of supply and demand in unrestricted foreign exchange markets. The foreign exchange rate is simply the price of a unit of one country's currency in terms of another country's currency. For example, if today's exchange rate is one hundred Japanese yen for one dollar, that means that anybody with one hundred yen can obtain one dollar, and vice versa.

CORRESPONDENT BANK
A bank in which another bank has an account (and vice versa) for the purpose of facilitating fund transfers.

Correspondent Banking Frequently, a U.S. company can rely on its domestic bank to take care of all international transfers of funds. Commercial banks often transfer funds internationally through their **correspondent banks** in other countries.

■ EXAMPLE 25.4 Suppose that a customer of Citibank wishes to pay a bill in euros to a company in Paris. Citibank can draw a bank check payable in euros on its account in Crédit Lyonnais, a Paris correspondent bank, and then send the check to the French company to which its customer owes the funds. Alternatively, Citibank's customer can request a wire transfer of the funds to the French company. Citibank instructs Crédit Lyonnais by wire to pay the necessary amount in euros. ■

The Clearinghouse Interbank Payment System (CHIPS) handles about 90 percent of both national and international interbank transfers of U.S. funds. In addition, the Society for Worldwide International Financial Telecommunications (SWIFT) is a communication system that provides banks with messages concerning international transactions.

LETTERS OF CREDIT

LETTER OF CREDIT
A written instrument, usually issued by a bank on behalf of a customer or other person, in which the issuer promises to honor drafts or other demands for payment by third persons in accordance with the terms of the instrument.

Because buyers and sellers engaged in international business transactions are frequently separated by thousands of miles, special precautions are often taken to ensure performance under the contract. Sellers want to avoid delivering goods for which they might not be paid. Buyers desire the assurance that sellers will not be paid until there is evidence that the goods have been shipped. Thus, **letters of credit** are frequently used to facilitate international business transactions.

In a simple letter-of-credit transaction, the *issuer* (a bank) agrees to issue a letter of credit and to ascertain whether the *beneficiary* (seller) performs certain acts. In return, the *account party* (buyer) promises to reimburse the issuer for the amount paid to the beneficiary. The transaction may also involve an *advising bank* that transmits information and a *paying bank* that expedites payment under the letter of credit. See Exhibit 25–1 for an illustration of a letter-of-credit transaction.

Under a letter of credit, the issuer is bound to pay the beneficiary (seller) when the beneficiary has complied with the terms and conditions of the letter of credit.

EXHIBIT 25–1 A LETTER-OF-CREDIT TRANSACTION

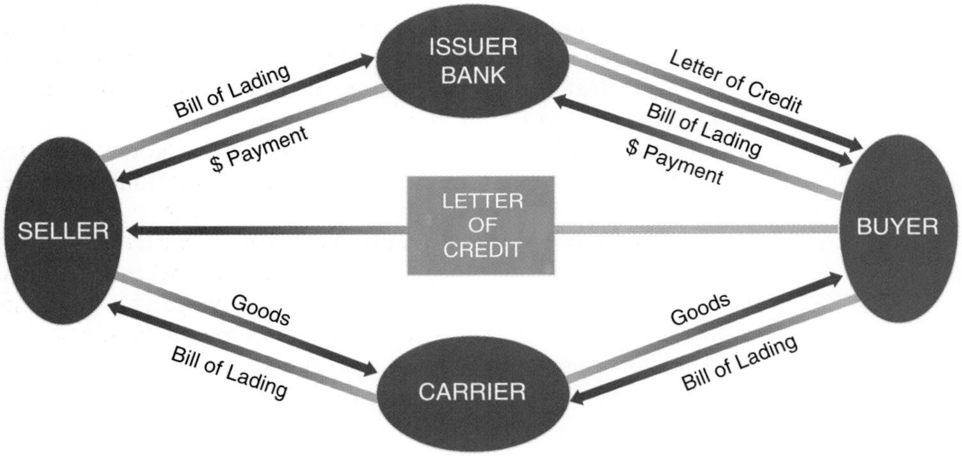

CHRONOLOGY OF EVENTS

1. Buyer contracts with issuer bank to issue a letter of credit; this sets forth the bank's obligation to pay on the letter of credit and buyer's obligation to pay the bank.
2. Letter of credit is sent to seller informing seller that on compliance with the terms of the letter of credit (such as presentment of necessary documents—in this example, a bill of lading), the bank will issue payment for the goods.
3. Seller delivers goods to carrier and receives a bill of lading.
4. Seller delivers the bill of lading to issuer bank and, if the document is proper, receives payment.
5. Issuer bank delivers the bill of lading to buyer.
6. Buyer delivers the bill of lading to carrier.
7. Carrier delivers the goods to buyer.
8. Buyer settles with issuer bank.

The beneficiary looks to the issuer, not to the account party (buyer), when it presents the documents required by the letter of credit. Typically, the letter of credit will require that the beneficiary deliver a *bill of lading* to the issuing bank to prove that shipment has been made. A letter of credit assures the beneficiary (seller) of payment and at the same time assures the account party (buyer) that payment will not be made until the beneficiary has complied with the terms and conditions of the letter of credit.

The Value of a Letter of Credit The basic principle behind letters of credit is that payment is made against the documents presented by the beneficiary and not against the facts that the documents purport to reflect. Thus, in a letter-of-credit transaction, the issuer does not police the underlying contract; a letter of credit is independent of the underlying contract between the buyer and the seller. Eliminating the need for banks (issuers) to inquire into whether actual contractual conditions have been satisfied greatly reduces the costs of letters of credit. Moreover, the use of a letter of credit protects both buyers and sellers.

DON'T FORGET A letter of credit is independent of the underlying contract between the buyer and the seller.

Compliance with a Letter of Credit A letter-of-credit transaction generally involves at least three separate and distinct contracts: the contract between the account party (buyer) and the beneficiary (seller); the contract between the issuer (bank) and the account party (buyer); and, finally, the letter of credit itself, which involves the issuer (bank) and the beneficiary (seller). These contracts are separate and distinct, and the issuer's obligations under the letter of credit do not concern the underlying contract between the buyer and the seller. Rather, it is the issuer's duty to ascertain whether the documents presented by the beneficiary (seller) comply with the terms of the letter of credit.

If the documents presented by the beneficiary comply with the terms of the letter of credit, the issuer (bank) must honor the letter of credit. If the issuing bank refuses to pay the beneficiary (seller) even though the beneficiary has complied with all the requirements, the beneficiary can bring an action to enforce payment. Sometimes, however, it can be difficult to determine exactly what a letter of credit requires. Traditionally, courts required strict compliance with the terms of a letter of credit, but in recent years, some courts have moved to a standard of *reasonable* compliance.

Regulation of Specific Business Activities

Doing business abroad can affect the economies, foreign policies, domestic policies, and other national interests of the countries involved. For this reason, nations impose laws to restrict or facilitate international business. Controls may also be imposed by international agreements. We discuss here how different types of international activities are regulated.

Investing

Firms that invest in foreign nations face the risk that the foreign government may take possession of the investment property. Expropriation, as already mentioned, occurs when property is taken and the owner is paid just compensation for what is taken. Expropriation does not violate generally observed principles of international law. Such principles are normally violated, however, when a government confiscates property without compensation (or without adequate compensation). Few remedies are available for confiscation of property by a foreign government. Claims are often resolved by lump-sum settlements after negotiations between the United States and the taking nation.

To counter the deterrent effect that the possibility of confiscation may have on potential investors, many countries guarantee that foreign investors will be compensated if their property is taken. A guaranty can take the form of national constitutional or statutory laws or provisions in international treaties. As further protection for foreign investments, some countries provide insurance for their citizens' investments abroad.

EXPORT CONTROLS

NOTE Most countries restrict exports for the same reasons: to protect national security, to further foreign policy objectives, to prevent the spread of nuclear weapons, and to preserve scarce commodities.

The U.S. Constitution provides in Article I, Section 9, that "No Tax or Duty shall be laid on Articles exported from any State." Thus, Congress cannot impose any export taxes. Congress can, however, use a variety of other devices to control exports. Congress may set export quotas on various items, such as grain being sold abroad. Under the Export Administration Act of 1979,[4] the flow of technologically advanced products and technical data can be restricted. In recent years, the U.S. Department of Commerce has made a controversial attempt to restrict the export of encryption software.

While restricting certain exports, the United States (and other nations) also use devices such as export incentives and subsidies to stimulate other exports and thereby aid domestic businesses. The Revenue Act of 1971,[5] for instance, gave tax benefits to firms marketing their products overseas through certain foreign sales corporations by exempting income produced by the exports. Under the Export Trading Company Act of 1982,[6] U.S. banks are encouraged to invest in export trading companies, which are formed when exporting firms join together to export a line of goods. The Export-Import Bank of the United States provides financial assistance, consisting primarily of credit guaranties given to commercial banks that in turn lend funds to U.S. exporting companies.

IMPORT CONTROLS

All nations have restrictions on imports, and the United States is no exception. Restrictions include strict prohibitions, quotas, and tariffs. Under the Trading with the Enemy Act of 1917,[7] for instance, no goods may be imported from nations that have been designated enemies of the United States. Other laws prohibit the importation of illegal drugs, books that urge insurrection against the United States, and agricultural products that pose dangers to domestic crops or animals.

QUOTA
A set limit on the amount of goods that can be imported.

TARIFF
A tax on imported goods.

Quotas and Tariffs Limits on the amounts of goods that can be imported are known as **quotas.** At one time, the United States had legal quotas on the number of automobiles that could be imported from Japan. Today, Japan "voluntarily" restricts the number of automobiles exported to the United States. **Tariffs** are taxes on imports. A tariff is usually a percentage of the value of the import, but it can be a flat rate per unit (for example, per barrel of oil). Tariffs raise the prices of goods, causing some consumers to purchase less expensive, domestically manufactured goods.

4. 50 U.S.C. Sections 2401–2420.
5. 26 U.S.C. Sections 991–994.
6. 15 U.S.C. Sections 4001, 4003.
7. 12 U.S.C. Section 95a.

DUMPING
The selling of goods in a foreign country at a price below the price charged for the same goods in the domestic market.

Dumping The United States has specific laws directed at what it sees as unfair international trade practices. **Dumping,** for example, is the sale of imported goods at "less than fair value." "Fair value" is usually determined by the price of those goods in the exporting country. Foreign firms that engage in dumping in the United States hope to undersell U.S. businesses to obtain a larger share of the U.S. market. To prevent this, an extra tariff—known as an *antidumping duty*—may be assessed on the imports.

NORMAL TRADE RELATIONS (NTR) STATUS
A status granted in an international treaty by a provision stating that the citizens of the contracting nations may enjoy the privileges accorded by either party to citizens of its NTR nations. Generally, this status is designed to establish equality of international treatment.

Minimizing Trade Barriers Restrictions on imports are also known as *trade barriers.* The elimination of trade barriers is sometimes seen as essential to the world's economic well-being. Most of the world's leading trading nations are members of the World Trade Organization (WTO), which was established in 1995. To minimize trade barriers among nations, each member country of the WTO is required to grant **normal trade relations (NTR) status** (formerly known as *most-favored-nation status*) to other member countries. This means each member is obligated to treat other members at least as well as it treats the country that receives its most favorable treatment with regard to imports or exports.

Various regional trade agreements and associations also help to minimize trade barriers between nations. The European Union (EU), for example, is working to minimize or remove barriers to trade among its member countries. The EU is a single integrated trading unit made up of twenty-five European nations. Another important regional trade agreement is the North American Free Trade Agreement (NAFTA). NAFTA, which became effective on January 1, 1994, created a regional trading unit consisting of Mexico, the United States, and Canada. The primary goal of NAFTA is to eliminate tariffs among these three countries on substantially all goods over a period of fifteen to twenty years.

BRIBING FOREIGN OFFICIALS

Giving cash or in-kind benefits to foreign government officials to obtain business contracts and other favors is often considered normal practice. To reduce such bribery by representatives of U.S. corporations, Congress enacted the Foreign Corrupt Practices Act in 1977.[8] This act and its implications for American businesspersons engaged in international business transactions were discussed in Chapter 2.

U.S. Laws in a Global Context

The internationalization of business raises questions about the extraterritorial application of a nation's laws—that is, the effect of the country's laws outside its boundaries. To what extent do U.S. domestic laws apply to other nations' businesses? To what extent do U.S. domestic laws apply to U.S. firms doing business abroad? Here, we discuss these questions in the context of U.S. antitrust law. We also look at the extraterritorial application of U.S. laws prohibiting employment discrimination.

U.S. ANTITRUST LAWS

U.S. antitrust laws (discussed in Chapter 22) have a wide application. They may *subject* persons in foreign nations to their provisions, as well as *protect* foreign consumers and competitors from violations committed by U.S. citizens. Consequently, *foreign persons,* a term that by definition includes foreign governments, may sue under U.S. antitrust laws in U.S. courts.

8. 15 U.S.C. Sections 78m–78ff.

Section 1 of the Sherman Act provides for the extraterritorial effect of the U.S. antitrust laws. The United States is a major proponent of free competition in the global economy. Thus, any conspiracy that has a *substantial effect* on U.S. commerce is within the reach of the Sherman Act. The law applies even if the violation occurs outside the United States, and foreign governments as well as persons can be sued for violations.

Before U.S. courts will exercise jurisdiction and apply antitrust laws, however, it must be shown that the alleged violation had a substantial effect on U.S. commerce. U.S. jurisdiction is automatically invoked when a *per se* violation occurs.[9] An example of a *per se* violation is a price-fixing contract. ■ EXAMPLE 25.5 If a domestic firm joins a foreign cartel to control the production, price, or distribution of goods, and this cartel has a *substantial restraining effect* on U.S. commerce, a *per se* violation may exist. Hence, both the domestic firm and the foreign cartel may be sued for violation of the U.S. antitrust laws. Likewise, if foreign firms doing business in the United States enter into a price-fixing or other anticompetitive agreement to control a portion of U.S. markets, a *per se* violation may exist. ■

In the following case, the court considered whether a *criminal* prosecution under the Sherman Act could be based on price-fixing activities that took place entirely outside the United States but had a substantial effect in this country.

9. Certain types of restrictive contracts, such as price-fixing agreements, are deemed inherently anticompetitive and thus in restraint of trade as a matter of law. Such a restrictive contract constitutes a *per se* violation of the antitrust laws. See Chapter 22.

CASE 25.3 United States v. Nippon Paper Industries Co.

United States Court of Appeals,
First Circuit, 1997.
109 F.3d 1.

FACTS Nippon Paper Industries Company (NPI) makes paper and paper products, including thermal fax paper for use in fax machines and medical printing equipment. A federal grand jury issued a criminal indictment against NPI and others, charging the defendants with agreeing to fix the price of thermal fax paper throughout North America. The indictment alleged that the meetings to reach the agreement had occurred entirely in Japan but that the defendants had sold the paper through subsidiaries in the United States at above-normal prices. The indictment stated that these activities had had a substantial adverse effect on commerce in the United States and had unreasonably restrained trade in violation of Section 1 of the Sherman Act. NPI filed a motion to dismiss the indictment. The court granted the motion, declaring that a criminal antitrust prosecution could not be based on wholly extraterritorial conduct. The government appealed.

ISSUE May a criminal antitrust prosecution in the United States be based on wholly extraterritorial conduct?

DECISION Yes. The U.S. Court of Appeals for the First Circuit reversed the decision of the lower court.

REASON The appellate court stated that the criminal indictment under the Sherman Act should not be dismissed simply because the actions on which it was based occurred outside the United States. The court reasoned that "in both criminal and civil cases, the claim that Section One applies extraterritorially is based on the same language in the same section of the same statute." The court noted that "civil antitrust actions predicated on wholly foreign conduct which has an intended and substantial effect in the United States come within Section One's jurisdictional reach." The court concluded that because "the text under consideration is not merely a duplicate appearing somewhere else in the statute, but is the original phrase in the original setting," Section 1 applies.

FOR CRITICAL ANALYSIS—Economic Consideration *Why should the United States apply its antitrust laws to business firms owned by citizens or the government of another nation?*

DISCRIMINATION LAWS

As explained in Chapter 18, federal laws in the United States prohibit discrimination on the basis of race, color, national origin, religion, gender, age, and disability. These laws, as they affect employment relationships, generally apply extraterritorially. Since 1984, for example, the Age Discrimination in Employment Act of 1967 has covered U.S. employees working abroad for U.S. employers. The Americans with Disabilities Act of 1990, which requires employers to accommodate the needs of workers with disabilities, also applies to U.S. nationals working abroad for U.S. firms.

For some time, it was uncertain whether the major U.S. law regulating discriminatory practices in the workplace, Title VII of the Civil Rights Act of 1964, applied extraterritorially. The Civil Rights Act of 1991 addressed this issue. The act provides that Title VII applies extraterritorially to all U.S. employees working for U.S. employers abroad. Generally, U.S. employers must abide by U.S. discrimination laws unless to do so would violate the laws of the country where their workplaces are located. This "foreign laws exception" allows employers to avoid being subjected to conflicting laws.

KEY TERMS

act of state doctrine 763
choice-of-language clause 767
choice-of-law clause 768
comity 762
confiscation 763
correspondent bank 769
distribution agreement 765
dumping 773
exclusive distributorship 765
export 764
expropriation 763
force majeure clause 768
foreign exchange market 769
forum-selection clause 767
international law 762
letter of credit 770
national law 762
normal trade relations (NTR) status 773
quota 772
sovereign immunity 764
tariff 772

CHAPTER SUMMARY International Law in a Global Economy

International Principles and Doctrines (See pages 762–764.)	1. *The principle of comity*—Under this principle, nations give effect to the laws and judicial decrees of other nations for reasons of courtesy and international harmony. 2. *The act of state doctrine*—A doctrine under which U.S. courts avoid passing judgment on the validity of public acts committed by a recognized foreign government within its own territory. 3. *The doctrine of sovereign immunity*—When certain conditions are satisfied, foreign nations are immune from U.S. jurisdiction under the Foreign Sovereign Immunities Act of 1976. Exceptions are made (a) when a foreign state has "waived its immunity either explicitly or by implication" or (b) when the action is "based upon a commercial activity carried on in the United States by the foreign state."
Doing Business Internationally (See pages 764–766.)	Ways in which U.S. domestic firms engage in international business transactions include (a) exporting, which may involve foreign agents or distributors, and (b) manufacturing abroad through licensing arrangements, franchising operations, wholly owned subsidiaries, or joint ventures.

(Continued)

CHAPTER SUMMARY International Law in a Global Economy—Continued

Commercial Contracts in an International Setting (See pages 766–769.)	International business contracts often include choice-of-language, forum-selection, and choice-of-law clauses to reduce the uncertainties associated with interpreting the language of the agreement and dealing with legal differences. Most domestic and international contracts include *force majeure* clauses. They commonly stipulate that certain events, such as floods, fires, accidents, labor strikes, and government orders, may excuse a party from liability for nonperformance of the contract. Arbitration clauses are also frequently found in international contracts.
Making Payment on International Transactions (See pages 769–771.)	1. *Currency conversion*—Because nations have different monetary systems, payment on international contracts requires currency conversion at a rate specified in a foreign exchange market. 2. *Correspondent banking*—Correspondent banks facilitate the transfer of funds from a buyer in one country to a seller in another. 3. *Letters of credit*—Letters of credit facilitate international transactions by ensuring payment to sellers and assuring buyers that payment will not be made until the sellers have complied with the terms of the letters of credit. Typically, compliance occurs when a bill of lading is delivered to the issuing bank.
Regulation of Specific Business Activities (See pages 771–773.)	In the interests of their economies, foreign policies, domestic policies, or other national priorities, nations impose laws that restrict or facilitate international business. Such laws regulate foreign investments, exporting, and importing. The World Trade Organization attempts to minimize trade barriers among nations, as do regional trade agreements and associations, including the European Union and the North American Free Trade Agreement.
U.S. Laws in a Global Context (See pages 773–775.)	1. *Antitrust laws*—U.S. antitrust laws may be applied beyond the borders of the United States. Any conspiracy that has a substantial effect on commerce within the United States may be subject to the Sherman Act, even if the violation occurs outside the United States. 2. *Discrimination laws*—The major U.S. laws prohibiting employment discrimination, including Title VII of the Civil Rights Act of 1964, the Age Discrimination in Employment Act of 1967, and the Americans with Disabilities Act of 1990, cover U.S. employees working abroad for U.S. firms—*unless* to apply the U.S. laws would violate the laws of the host country.

FOR REVIEW

Answers for the even-numbered questions in this For Review *section can be found in Appendix I at the end of this text.*

1. What is the principle of comity, and why do courts deciding disputes involving a foreign law or judicial decree apply this principle?
2. What is the act of state doctrine? In what circumstances is this doctrine applied?
3. Under the Foreign Sovereign Immunities Act of 1976, on what bases might a foreign state be considered subject to the jurisdiction of U.S. courts?
4. In what circumstances will U.S. antitrust laws be applied extraterritorially?
5. Do U.S. laws prohibiting employment discrimination apply in all circumstances to U.S. employees working for U.S. employers abroad?

QUESTIONS AND CASE PROBLEMS

25–1. Letters of Credit. The Swiss Credit Bank issued a letter of credit in favor of Antex Industries to cover the sale of 92,000 electronic integrated circuits manufactured by Electronic Arrays. The letter of credit specified that the chips would be transported to Tokyo by ship. Antex shipped the circuits by air. Payment on the letter of credit was dishonored because the shipment by air did not fulfill the precise terms of the letter of credit. Should a court compel payment? Explain.

25–2. Antitrust Claims. Billy Lamb and Carmon Willis (the plaintiffs) were tobacco growers in Kentucky. Phillip Morris, Inc., and B.A.T. Industries, PLC, routinely purchased tobacco not only from Kentucky growers but also from producers in several foreign countries. In 1982, subsidiaries of Phillip Morris and B.A.T. (the defendants) entered into an agreement with La Fundacion Del Niño (the Children's Foundation) of Caracas, Venezuela, headed by the wife of the president of Venezuela. The agreement provided that the two subsidiaries would donate a total of approximately $12.5 million to the Children's Foundation, and in exchange, the subsidiaries would obtain price controls on Venezuelan tobacco, elimination of controls on retail cigarette prices in Venezuela, tax deductions for the donations, and assurances that existing tax rates applicable to tobacco companies would not be increased. The plaintiffs brought an action, alleging that the Venezuelan arrangement was an inducement designed to restrain trade in violation of U.S. antitrust laws. Such an arrangement, the plaintiffs contended, would result in the artificial depression of tobacco prices to the detriment of domestic tobacco growers, while ensuring lucrative retail prices for tobacco products sold abroad. The trial court held that the plaintiffs' claim was barred by the act of state doctrine. What will result on appeal? Discuss. [*Lamb v. Phillip Morris, Inc.,* 915 F.2d 1024 (6th Cir. 1990)]

25–3. Discrimination Claims. Radio Free Europe and Radio Liberty (RFE/RL), a U.S. corporation doing business in Germany, employs more than three hundred U.S. citizens at its principal place of business in Munich, Germany. The concept of mandatory retirement is deeply embedded in German labor policy, and a contract formed in 1982 between RFE/RL and a German labor union contained a clause that required workers to be retired when they reach the age of sixty-five. When William Mahoney and other U.S. employees (the plaintiffs) reached the age of sixty-five, RFE/RL terminated their employment as required under its contract with the labor union. The plaintiffs sued RFE/RL for discriminating against them on the basis of age, in violation of the Age Discrimination in Employment Act of 1967. Will the plaintiffs succeed in their suit? Discuss fully. [*Mahoney v. RFE/RL, Inc.,* 47 F.3d 447 (D.C. Cir. 1995)]

25–4. Sovereign Immunity. Nuovo Pignone, Inc., is an Italian company that designs and manufactures turbine systems. Nuovo sold a turbine system to Cabinda Gulf Oil Co. (CABGOC). The system was manufactured, tested, and inspected in Italy; then it was sent to Louisiana for mounting on a platform by CABGOC's contractor. Nuovo sent a representative to consult on the mounting. The platform went to a CABGOC site off the coast of West Africa. Marcus Pere, an instrument technician at the site, was killed when a turbine within the system exploded. Pere's widow filed a suit in a U.S. district court against Nuovo and others. Nuovo claimed sovereign immunity on the ground that its majority shareholder at the time of the explosion was Ente Nazionale Idrocaburi, which was created by the government of Italy to lead its oil and gas exploration and development. Is Nuovo exempt from suit under the doctrine of sovereign immunity? Is it subject to suit under the "commercial activity" exception? Why or why not? [*Pere v. Nuovo Pignone, Inc.,* 150 F.3d 477 (5th Cir. 1998)]

25–5. Dumping. In response to a petition filed on behalf of the U.S. pineapple industry, the U.S. Commerce Department initiated an investigation of canned pineapple imported from Thailand. The investigation concerned Thai producers of the canned fruit, including the Thai Pineapple Public Co. The Thai producers also turned out products, such as pineapple juice and juice concentrate, outside the scope of the investigation. These products use separate parts of the same fresh pineapple, so they share raw material costs. To determine fair value and antidumping duties, the Commerce Department had to calculate the Thai producers' cost of production and, in so doing, had to allocate a portion of the shared fruit costs to the canned fruit. These allocations were based on the producers' own financial records, which were consistent with Thai generally accepted accounting principles. The result was a determination that more than 90 percent of the canned fruit sales were below the cost of production. The producers filed a suit in the U.S. Court of International Trade against the federal government, challenging this allocation. The producers argued that their records did not reflect actual production costs, which instead should be based on the weight of fresh fruit used to make the products. Did the Commerce Department act reasonably in determining the cost of production? Why or why not? [*Thai Pineapple Public Co. v. United States,* 187 F.3d 1362 (Fed.Cir. 1999)]

CASE PROBLEM WITH SAMPLE ANSWER

25–6. Tonoga, Ltd., doing business as Taconic Plastics, Ltd., is a manufacturer incorporated in Ireland with its principal place of business in New York. In 1997, Taconic entered into a contract with a German construction company to supply special material for a tent project designed to shelter religious pilgrims visiting holy sites in Saudi Arabia. Most of the material was made in, and shipped from, New York. The company did not pay Taconic and eventually filed for bankruptcy. Another German firm, Werner Voss Architects and Engineers, acting as an agent for the government of Saudi Arabia, guaranteed the payments due Taconic to induce it to complete the project. When it did not receive the final payment, Taconic filed a suit in a U.S. district court against the government of Saudi Arabia, claiming a breach of the guaranty and seeking to collect, in part, about $3 million. The defendant filed a motion to dismiss based, in part, on the doctrine of sovereign immunity. Under what circumstances does this doctrine apply? What are its exceptions? Should this suit be dismissed under the "commercial activity" exception? Explain. [*Tonoga, Ltd. v. Ministry of Public Works and Housing of Kingdom of Saudi Arabia,* 135 F.Supp.2d 350 (N.D.N.Y. 2001)]

After you have answered this problem, compare your answer with the sample answer given on the Web site that accompanies this text. Go to http://blt.westbuslaw.com, select "Chapter 25," and click on "Case Problem with Sample Answer."

25–7. Imports. DaimlerChrysler Corp. makes and markets motor vehicles. DaimlerChrysler assembled the 1993 and 1994 model years of its trucks at plants in Mexico. Assembly involved sheet metal components sent from the United States. DaimlerChrysler subjected some of the parts to a complicated treatment process, which included applying coats of paint to prevent corrosion, impart color, and protect the finish. Under U.S. law, goods that are assembled abroad using U.S.–made parts can be imported tariff free. A U.S. *statute* provides that painting is "incidental" to assembly and does not affect the status of the goods. A U.S. *regulation,* however, states that "painting primarily intended to enhance the appearance of an article or to impart distinctive features or characteristics" is not incidental. The U.S. Customs Service levied a tariff on the trucks. DaimlerChrysler filed a suit in the U.S. Court of International Trade, challenging the levy. Should the court rule in DaimlerChrysler's favor? Why or why not? [*DaimlerChrysler Corp. v. United States,* 361 F.3d 1378 (Fed.Cir. 2004)]

A QUESTION OF ETHICS

25–8. Ronald Riley, a U.S. citizen, and Council of Lloyd's, a British insurance corporation with its principal place of business in London, entered into an agreement in 1980 that allowed Riley to underwrite insurance through Lloyd's. The agreement provided that if any dispute arose between Lloyd's and Riley, the courts of England would have exclusive jurisdiction, and the laws of England would apply. Over the next decade, some of the parties insured under policies that Riley underwrote experienced large losses, for which they filed claims. Instead of paying his share of the claims, Riley filed a lawsuit in a U.S. district court against Lloyd's and its managers and directors (all British citizens or entities), seeking, among other things, rescission of the 1980 agreement. Riley alleged that the defendants had violated the Securities Act of 1933, the Securities Exchange Act of 1934, and Rule 10b-5. The defendants asked the court to enforce the forum-selection clause in the agreement. Riley argued that if the clause was enforced, he would be deprived of his rights under the U.S. securities laws. The court held that the parties were to resolve their dispute in England. [*Riley v. Kingsley Underwriting Agencies, Ltd.,* 969 F.2d 953 (10th Cir. 1992)]

1. Did the court's decision fairly balance the rights of the parties? How would you argue in support of the court's decision in this case? How would you argue against it?
2. Should the fact that an international transaction may be subject to laws and remedies different from or less favorable than those of the United States be a valid basis for denying enforcement of forum-selection and choice-of-law clauses?
3. All parties to this litigation other than Riley were British. Should the court consider this fact in deciding this case?

FOR CRITICAL ANALYSIS

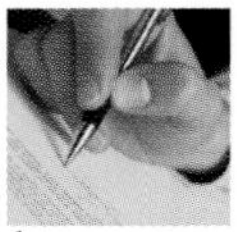

25–9. Business cartels and monopolies that are legal in some countries may engage in practices that violate U.S. antitrust laws. In view of this fact, what are some of the implications of applying U.S. antitrust laws extraterritorially?

VIDEO QUESTION

25–10. Go to this text's Web site at **http://blt.westbuslaw.com** and select "Chapter 25." Click on "Video Questions" and view the video titled *International Letter of Credit.* Then answer the following questions.

1. Do banks always require the same documents to be presented in letter-of-credit transactions? If not, who dictates what documents will be required in the letter of credit?
2. At what point does the seller receive payment in a letter-of-credit transaction?
3. What assurances does a letter of credit provide to the buyer and the seller involved in the transaction?

INTERNET EXERCISES

Go to the *Business Law Today: The Essentials* home page at **http://blt.westbuslaw.com,** select "Chapter 25," and click on "Internet Exercises." There you will find the following Internet research exercises that you can perform to learn more about topics covered in this chapter.

Activity 25–1: LEGAL PERSPECTIVE—The World Trade Organization

Activity 25–2: MANAGEMENT PERSPECTIVE—Overseas Business Opportunities

BEFORE THE TEST

Go to the *Business Law Today: The Essentials* home page at **http://blt.westbuslaw.com,** select "Chapter 25," and click on "Interactive Quizzes." You will find at least twenty interactive questions relating to this chapter.

APPENDIX A
The Constitution of the United States

Preamble

We the People of the United States, in Order to form a more perfect Union, establish Justice, insure domestic Tranquility, provide for the common defence, promote the general Welfare, and secure the Blessings of Liberty to ourselves and our Posterity, do ordain and establish this Constitution for the United States of America.

Article I

Section 1. All legislative Powers herein granted shall be vested in a Congress of the United States, which shall consist of a Senate and House of Representatives.

Section 2. The House of Representatives shall be composed of Members chosen every second Year by the People of the several States, and the Electors in each State shall have the Qualifications requisite for Electors of the most numerous Branch of the State Legislature.

No Person shall be a Representative who shall not have attained to the Age of twenty five Years, and been seven Years a Citizen of the United States, and who shall not, when elected, be an Inhabitant of that State in which he shall be chosen.

Representatives and direct Taxes shall be apportioned among the several States which may be included within this Union, according to their respective Numbers, which shall be determined by adding to the whole Number of free Persons, including those bound to Service for a Term of Years, and excluding Indians not taxed, three fifths of all other Persons. The actual Enumeration shall be made within three Years after the first Meeting of the Congress of the United States, and within every subsequent Term of ten Years, in such Manner as they shall by Law direct. The Number of Representatives shall not exceed one for every thirty Thousand, but each State shall have at Least one Representative; and until such enumeration shall be made, the State of New Hampshire shall be entitled to chuse three, Massachusetts eight, Rhode Island and Providence Plantations one, Connecticut five, New York six, New Jersey four, Pennsylvania eight, Delaware one, Maryland six, Virginia ten, North Carolina five, South Carolina five, and Georgia three.

When vacancies happen in the Representation from any State, the Executive Authority thereof shall issue Writs of Election to fill such Vacancies.

The House of Representatives shall chuse their Speaker and other Officers; and shall have the sole Power of Impeachment.

Section 3. The Senate of the United States shall be composed of two Senators from each State, chosen by the Legislature thereof, for six Years; and each Senator shall have one Vote.

Immediately after they shall be assembled in Consequence of the first Election, they shall be divided as equally as may be into three Classes. The Seats of the Senators of the first Class shall be vacated at the Expiration of the second Year, of the second Class at the Expiration of the fourth Year, and of the third Class at the Expiration of the sixth Year, so that one third may be chosen every second Year; and if Vacancies happen by Resignation, or otherwise, during the Recess of the Legislature of any State, the Executive thereof may make temporary Appointments until the next Meeting of the Legislature, which shall then fill such Vacancies.

No Person shall be a Senator who shall not have attained to the Age of thirty Years, and been nine Years a Citizen of the United States, and who shall not, when elected, be an Inhabitant of that State for which he shall be chosen.

The Vice President of the United States shall be President of the Senate, but shall have no Vote, unless they be equally divided.

The Senate shall chuse their other Officers, and also a President pro tempore, in the Absence of the Vice President, or when he shall exercise the Office of President of the United States.

The Senate shall have the sole Power to try all Impeachments. When sitting for that Purpose, they shall be on Oath or Affirmation. When the President of the United States is tried, the Chief Justice shall preside: And no Person shall be convicted without the Concurrence of two thirds of the Members present.

Judgment in Cases of Impeachment shall not extend further than to removal from Office, and disqualification to hold and enjoy any Office of honor, Trust, or Profit under the United States: but the Party convicted shall nevertheless be liable and subject to Indictment, Trial, Judgment, and Punishment, according to Law.

Section 4. The Times, Places and Manner of holding Elections for Senators and Representatives, shall be prescribed in each State by the Legislature thereof; but the Congress may at any time by Law make or alter such Regulations, except as to the Places of chusing Senators.

The Congress shall assemble at least once in every Year, and such Meeting shall be on the first Monday in December, unless they shall by Law appoint a different Day.

Section 5. Each House shall be the Judge of the Elections, Returns, and Qualifications of its own Members, and a Majority of each shall constitute a Quorum to do Business; but a smaller Number may adjourn from day to day, and may be authorized to compel the Attendance of absent Members, in such Manner, and under such Penalties as each House may provide.

Each House may determine the Rules of its Proceedings, punish its Members for disorderly Behavior, and, with the Concurrence of two thirds, expel a Member.

Each House shall keep a Journal of its Proceedings, and from time to time publish the same, excepting such Parts as may in their Judgment require Secrecy; and the Yeas and Nays of the Members of either House on any question shall, at the Desire of one fifth of those Present, be entered on the Journal.

Neither House, during the Session of Congress, shall, without the Consent of the other, adjourn for more than three days, nor to any other Place than that in which the two Houses shall be sitting.

Section 6. The Senators and Representatives shall receive a Compensation for their Services, to be ascertained by Law, and paid out of the Treasury of the United States. They shall in all Cases, except Treason, Felony and Breach of the Peace, be privileged from Arrest during their Attendance at the Session of their respective Houses, and in going to and returning from the same; and for any Speech or Debate in either House, they shall not be questioned in any other Place.

No Senator or Representative shall, during the Time for which he was elected, be appointed to any civil Office under the Authority of the United States, which shall have been created, or the Emoluments whereof shall have been increased during such time; and no Person holding any Office under the United States, shall be a Member of either House during his Continuance in Office.

Section 7. All Bills for raising Revenue shall originate in the House of Representatives; but the Senate may propose or concur with Amendments as on other Bills.

Every Bill which shall have passed the House of Representatives and the Senate, shall, before it become a Law, be presented to the President of the United States; If he approve he shall sign it, but if not he shall return it, with his Objections to the House in which it shall have originated, who shall enter the Objections at large on their Journal, and proceed to reconsider it. If after such Reconsideration two thirds of that House shall agree to pass the Bill, it shall be sent together with the Objections, to the other House, by which it shall likewise be reconsidered, and if approved by two thirds of that House, it shall become a Law. But in all such Cases the Votes of both Houses shall be determined by Yeas and Nays, and the Names of the Persons voting for and against the Bill shall be entered on the Journal of each House respectively. If any Bill shall not be returned by the President within ten Days (Sundays excepted) after it shall have been presented to him, the Same shall be a Law, in like Manner as if he had signed it, unless the Congress by their Adjournment prevent its Return in which Case it shall not be a Law.

Every Order, Resolution, or Vote, to which the Concurrence of the Senate and House of Representatives may be necessary (except on a question of Adjournment) shall be presented to the President of the United States; and before the Same shall take Effect, shall be approved by him, or being disapproved by him, shall be repassed by two thirds of the Senate and House of Representatives, according to the Rules and Limitations prescribed in the Case of a Bill.

Section 8. The Congress shall have Power To lay and collect Taxes, Duties, Imposts and Excises, to pay the Debts and provide for the common Defence and general Welfare of the United States; but all Duties, Imposts and Excises shall be uniform throughout the United States;

To borrow Money on the credit of the United States;

To regulate Commerce with foreign Nations, and among the several States, and with the Indian Tribes;

To establish an uniform Rule of Naturalization, and uniform Laws on the subject of Bankruptcies throughout the United States;

To coin Money, regulate the Value thereof, and of foreign Coin, and fix the Standard of Weights and Measures;

To provide for the Punishment of counterfeiting the Securities and current Coin of the United States;

To establish Post Offices and post Roads;

To promote the Progress of Science and useful Arts, by securing for limited Times to Authors and Inventors the exclusive Right to their respective Writings and Discoveries;

To constitute Tribunals inferior to the supreme Court;

To define and punish Piracies and Felonies committed on the high Seas, and Offenses against the Law of Nations;

To declare War, grant Letters of Marque and Reprisal, and make Rules concerning Captures on Land and Water;

To raise and support Armies, but no Appropriation of Money to that Use shall be for a longer Term than two Years;

To provide and maintain a Navy;

To make Rules for the Government and Regulation of the land and naval Forces;

To provide for calling forth the Militia to execute the Laws of the Union, suppress Insurrections and repel Invasions;

To provide for organizing, arming, and disciplining, the Militia, and for governing such Part of them as may be employed in the Service of the United States, reserving to the States respectively, the Appointment of the Officers, and the Authority of training the Militia according to the discipline prescribed by Congress;

To exercise exclusive Legislation in all Cases whatsoever, over such District (not exceeding ten Miles square) as may, by Cession of particular States, and the Acceptance of Congress, become the Seat of the Government of the United States, and to exercise like Authority over all Places purchased by the Consent of the Legislature of the State in which the Same shall be, for the Erection of Forts, Magazines, Arsenals, dock-Yards, and other needful Buildings;—And

To make all Laws which shall be necessary and proper for carrying into Execution the foregoing Powers, and all other Powers vested by this Constitution in the Government of the United States, or in any Department or Officer thereof.

Section 9. The Migration or Importation of such Persons as any of the States now existing shall think proper to admit, shall not be prohibited by the Congress prior to the Year one thousand eight hundred and eight, but a Tax or duty may be imposed on such Importation, not exceeding ten dollars for each Person.

The privilege of the Writ of Habeas Corpus shall not be suspended, unless when in Cases of Rebellion or Invasion the public Safety may require it.

No Bill of Attainder or ex post facto Law shall be passed.

No Capitation, or other direct, Tax shall be laid, unless in Proportion to the Census or Enumeration herein before directed to be taken.

No Tax or Duty shall be laid on Articles exported from any State.

No Preference shall be given by any Regulation of Commerce or Revenue to the Ports of one State over those of another: nor shall Vessels bound to, or from, one State be obliged to enter, clear, or pay Duties in another.

No Money shall be drawn from the Treasury, but in Consequence of Appropriations made by Law; and a regular Statement and Account of the Receipts and Expenditures of all public Money shall be published from time to time.

No Title of Nobility shall be granted by the United States: And no Person holding any Office of Profit or Trust under them, shall, without the Consent of the Congress, accept of any present, Emolument, Office, or Title, of any kind whatever, from any King, Prince, or foreign State.

Section 10. No State shall enter into any Treaty, Alliance, or Confederation; grant Letters of Marque and Reprisal; coin Money; emit Bills of Credit; make any Thing but gold and silver Coin a Tender in Payment of Debts; pass any Bill of Attainder, ex post facto Law, or Law impairing the Obligation of Contracts, or grant any Title of Nobility.

No State shall, without the Consent of the Congress, lay any Imposts or Duties on Imports or Exports, except what may be absolutely necessary for executing its inspection Laws: and the net Produce of all Duties and Imposts, laid by any State on Imports or Exports, shall be for the Use of the Treasury of the United States; and all such Laws shall be subject to the Revision and Controul of the Congress.

No State shall, without the Consent of Congress, lay any Duty of Tonnage, keep Troops, or Ships of War in time of Peace, enter into any Agreement or Compact with another State, or with a foreign Power, or engage in War, unless actually invaded, or in such imminent Danger as will not admit of delay.

Article II

Section 1. The executive Power shall be vested in a President of the United States of America. He shall hold his Office during the Term of four Years, and, together with the Vice President, chosen for the same Term, be elected, as follows:

Each State shall appoint, in such Manner as the Legislature thereof may direct, a Number of Electors, equal to the whole Number of Senators and Representatives to which the State may be entitled in the Congress; but no Senator or Representative, or Person holding an Office of Trust or Profit under the United States, shall be appointed an Elector.

The Electors shall meet in their respective States, and vote by Ballot for two Persons, of whom one at least shall not be an Inhabitant of the same State with themselves. And they shall make a List of all the Persons voted for, and of the Number of Votes for each; which List they shall sign and certify, and transmit sealed to the Seat of the Government of the United States, directed to the President of the Senate. The President of the Senate shall, in the Presence of the Senate and House of Representatives, open all the Certificates, and the Votes shall then be counted. The Person having the greatest Number of Votes shall be the President, if such Number be a Majority of the whole Number of Electors appointed; and if there be more than one who have such Majority, and have an equal Number of Votes, then the House of Representatives shall immediately chuse by Ballot one of them for President; and if no Person have a Majority, then from the five highest on the List the said House shall in like Manner chuse the President. But in chusing the President, the Votes shall be taken by States, the Representation from each State having one Vote; A quorum for this Purpose shall consist of a Member or Members from two thirds of the States, and a Majority of all the States shall be necessary to a Choice. In every Case, after the Choice of the President, the Person having the greater Number of Votes of the Electors shall be the Vice President. But if there should remain two or more who have equal Votes, the Senate shall chuse from them by Ballot the Vice President.

The Congress may determine the Time of chusing the Electors, and the Day on which they shall give their Votes; which Day shall be the same throughout the United States.

No person except a natural born Citizen, or a Citizen of the United States, at the time of the Adoption of this Constitution, shall be eligible to the Office of President; neither shall any Person be eligible to that Office who shall not have attained to the Age of thirty five Years, and been fourteen Years a Resident within the United States.

In Case of the Removal of the President from Office, or of his Death, Resignation or Inability to discharge the Powers and Duties of the said Office, the same shall devolve on the Vice President, and the Congress may by Law provide for the Case of Removal, Death, Resignation or Inability, both of the President and Vice President, declaring what Officer shall then act as President, and such Officer shall act accordingly, until the Disability be removed, or a President shall be elected.

The President shall, at stated Times, receive for his Services, a Compensation, which shall neither be increased nor diminished during the Period for which he shall have been elected, and he shall not receive within that Period any other Emolument from the United States, or any of them.

Before he enter on the Execution of his Office, he shall take the following Oath or Affirmation: "I do solemnly swear (or affirm) that I will faithfully execute the Office of President of the United States, and will to the best of my Ability, preserve, protect and defend the Constitution of the United States."

Section 2. The President shall be Commander in Chief of the Army and Navy of the United States, and of the Militia of the several States, when called into the actual Service of the United States; he may require the Opinion, in writing, of the principal Officer in each of the executive Departments, upon any Subject relating to the Duties of their respective Offices, and he shall have Power to grant Reprieves and Pardons for Offenses against the United States, except in Cases of Impeachment.

He shall have Power, by and with the Advice and Consent of the Senate to make Treaties, provided two thirds of the Senators present concur; and he shall nominate, and by and with the Advice and Consent of the Senate, shall appoint Ambassadors, other public Ministers and Consuls, Judges of the supreme Court, and all other Officers of the United States, whose Appointments are not herein otherwise provided for, and which shall be established by Law; but the Congress may by Law vest the Appointment of such inferior Officers, as they think proper, in the President alone, in the Courts of Law, or in the Heads of Departments.

The President shall have Power to fill up all Vacancies that may happen during the Recess of the Senate, by granting Commissions which shall expire at the End of their next Session.

Section 3. He shall from time to time give to the Congress Information of the State of the Union, and recommend to their Consideration such Measures as he shall judge necessary and expedient; he may, on extraordinary Occasions, convene both Houses, or either of them, and in Case of Disagreement between them, with Respect to the Time of Adjournment, he may adjourn them to such Time as he shall think proper; he shall receive Ambassadors and other public Ministers; he shall take Care that the Laws be faithfully executed, and shall Commission all the Officers of the United States.

Section 4. The President, Vice President and all civil Officers of the United States, shall be removed from Office on Impeachment for, and Conviction of, Treason, Bribery, or other high Crimes and Misdemeanors.

Article III

Section 1. The judicial Power of the United States, shall be vested in one supreme Court, and in such inferior Courts as the Congress may from time to time ordain and establish. The Judges, both of the supreme and inferior Courts, shall hold their Offices during good Behaviour, and shall, at stated Times, receive for their Services a Compensation, which shall not be diminished during their Continuance in Office.

Section 2. The judicial Power shall extend to all Cases, in Law and Equity, arising under this Constitution, the Laws of the United States, and Treaties made, or which shall be made, under their Authority;—to all Cases affecting Ambassadors, other public Ministers and Consuls;—to all Cases of admiralty and maritime Jurisdiction;—to Controversies to which the United States shall be a Party;—to Controversies between two or more States;—between a State and Citizens of another State;—between Citizens of different States;—between Citizens of the same State claiming Lands under Grants of different States, and between a State, or the Citizens thereof, and foreign States, Citizens or Subjects.

In all Cases affecting Ambassadors, other public Ministers and Consuls, and those in which a State shall be a Party, the supreme Court shall have original Jurisdiction. In all the other Cases before mentioned, the supreme Court shall have appellate Jurisdiction, both as to Law and Fact, with such Exceptions, and under such Regulations as the Congress shall make.

The Trial of all Crimes, except in Cases of Impeachment, shall be by Jury; and such Trial shall be held in the State where the said Crimes shall have been committed; but when not committed within any State, the Trial shall be at such Place or Places as the Congress may by Law have directed.

Section 3. Treason against the United States, shall consist only in levying War against them, or, in adhering to their Enemies, giving them Aid and Comfort. No Person shall be convicted of Treason unless on the Testimony of two Witnesses to the same overt Act, or on Confession in open Court.

The Congress shall have Power to declare the Punishment of Treason, but no Attainder of Treason shall work Corruption of Blood, or Forfeiture except during the Life of the Person attainted.

Article IV

Section 1. Full Faith and Credit shall be given in each State to the public Acts, Records, and judicial Proceedings of every other State. And the Congress may by general Laws prescribe the Manner in which such Acts, Records and Proceedings shall be proved, and the Effect thereof.

Section 2. The Citizens of each State shall be entitled to all Privileges and Immunities of Citizens in the several States.

A Person charged in any State with Treason, Felony, or other Crime, who shall flee from Justice, and be found in another State, shall on Demand of the executive Authority of the State from which he fled, be delivered up, to be removed to the State having Jurisdiction of the Crime.

No Person held to Service or Labour in one State, under the Laws thereof, escaping into another, shall, in Consequence of any Law or Regulation therein, be discharged from such Service or Labour, but shall be delivered up on Claim of the Party to whom such Service or Labour may be due.

Section 3. New States may be admitted by the Congress into this Union; but no new State shall be formed or erected within the Jurisdiction of any other State; nor any State be formed by the Junction of two or more States, or Parts of States, without the Consent of the Legislatures of the States concerned as well as of the Congress.

The Congress shall have Power to dispose of and make all needful Rules and Regulations respecting the Territory or other Property belonging to the United States; and nothing in this Constitution shall be so construed as to Prejudice any Claims of the United States, or of any particular State.

Section 4. The United States shall guarantee to every State in this Union a Republican Form of Government, and shall protect each of them against Invasion; and on Application of the Legislature, or of the Executive (when the Legislature cannot be convened) against domestic Violence.

Article V

The Congress, whenever two thirds of both Houses shall deem it necessary, shall propose Amendments to this Constitution, or, on the Application of the Legislatures of two thirds of the several States, shall call a Convention for proposing Amendments, which, in either Case, shall be valid to all Intents and Purposes, as part of this Constitution, when ratified by the Legislatures of three fourths of the several States, or by Conventions in three fourths thereof, as the one or the other Mode of Ratification may be proposed by the Congress; Provided that no Amendment which may be made prior to the Year One thousand eight hundred and eight shall in any Manner affect the first and fourth Clauses in the Ninth Section of the first Article; and that no State, without its Consent, shall be deprived of its equal Suffrage in the Senate.

Article VI

All Debts contracted and Engagements entered into, before the Adoption of this Constitution shall be as valid against the United States under this Constitution, as under the Confederation.

This Constitution, and the Laws of the United States which shall be made in Pursuance thereof; and all Treaties made, or which shall be made, under the Authority of the United States, shall be the supreme Law of the Land; and the Judges in every State shall be bound thereby, any Thing in the Constitution or Laws of any State to the Contrary notwithstanding.

The Senators and Representatives before mentioned, and the Members of the several State Legislatures, and all executive and judicial Officers, both of the United States and of the several States, shall be bound by Oath or Affirmation, to support this Constitution; but no religious Test shall ever be required as a Qualification to any Office or public Trust under the United States.

Article VII

The Ratification of the Conventions of nine States shall be sufficient for the Establishment of this Constitution between the States so ratifying the Same.

Amendment I [1791]

Congress shall make no law respecting an establishment of religion, or prohibiting the free exercise thereof; or abridging the freedom of speech, or of the press; or the right of the people peaceably to assembly, and to petition the Government for a redress of grievances.

Amendment II [1791]

A well regulated Militia, being necessary to the security of a free State, the right of the people to keep and bear Arms, shall not be infringed.

Amendment III [1791]

No Soldier shall, in time of peace be quartered in any house, without the consent of the Owner, nor in time of war, but in a manner to be prescribed by law.

Amendment IV [1791]

The right of the people to be secure in their persons, houses, papers, and effects, against unreasonable searches and seizures, shall not be violated, and no Warrants shall issue, but upon probable cause, supported by Oath or affirmation, and particularly describing the place to be searched, and the persons or things to be seized.

Amendment V [1791]

No person shall be held to answer for a capital, or otherwise infamous crime, unless on a presentment or indictment of a Grand Jury, except in cases arising in the land or naval forces, or in the Militia, when in actual service in time of War or public danger; nor shall any person be subject for the same offence to be twice put in jeopardy of life or limb; nor shall be compelled in any criminal case to be a witness against himself, nor be deprived of life, liberty, or property, without due process of law; nor shall private property be taken for public use, without just compensation.

Amendment VI [1791]

In all criminal prosecutions, the accused shall enjoy the right to a speedy and public trial, by an impartial jury of the State and district wherein the crime shall have been committed, which district shall have been previously ascertained by law, and to be informed of the nature and cause of the accusation; to be confronted with the witnesses against him; to have compulsory process for obtaining witnesses in his favor, and to have the Assistance of Counsel for his defence.

Amendment VII [1791]

In Suits at common law, where the value in controversy shall exceed twenty dollars, the right of trial by jury shall be preserved, and no fact tried by jury, shall be otherwise re-examined in any Court of the United States, than according to the rules of the common law.

Amendment VIII [1791]

Excessive bail shall not be required, nor excessive fines imposed, nor cruel and unusual punishments inflicted.

Amendment IX [1791]

The enumeration in the Constitution, of certain rights, shall not be construed to deny or disparage others retained by the people.

Amendment X [1791]

The powers not delegated to the United States by the Constitution, nor prohibited by it to the States, are reserved to the States respectively, or to the people.

Amendment XI [1798]

The Judicial power of the United States shall not be construed to extend to any suit in law or equity, commenced or prosecuted against one of the United States by Citizens of another State, or by Citizens or Subjects of any Foreign State.

Amendment XII [1804]

The Electors shall meet in their respective states, and vote by ballot for President and Vice-President, one of whom, at least, shall not be an inhabitant of the same state with themselves; they shall name in their ballots the person voted for as President, and in distinct ballots the person voted for as Vice-President, and they shall make distinct lists of all persons voted for as President, and of all persons voted for as Vice-President, and of the number of votes for each, which lists they shall sign and certify, and transmit sealed to the seat of the government of the United States, directed to the President of the Senate;—The President of the Senate shall, in the presence of the Senate and House of Representatives, open all the certificates and the votes shall then be counted;—The person having the greatest number of votes for President, shall be the President, if such number be a majority of the whole number of Electors appointed; and if no person have such majority, then from the persons having the highest numbers not exceeding three on the list of those voted for as President, the House of Representatives shall choose immediately, by ballot, the President. But in choosing the President, the votes shall be taken by states, the representation from each state having one vote; a quorum for this purpose shall consist of a member or members from two-thirds of the states, and a majority of all states shall be necessary to a choice. And if the House of Representatives shall not choose a President whenever the right of choice shall devolve upon them, before the fourth day of March next following, then the Vice-President shall act as President, as in the case of the death or other constitutional disability of the President.—The person having the greatest number of votes as Vice-President, shall be the Vice-President, if such number be a majority of the whole number of Electors appointed, and if no person have a majority, then from the two highest numbers on the list, the Senate shall choose the Vice-President; a quorum for the purpose shall consist of two-thirds of the whole number of Senators, and a majority of the whole number shall be necessary to a choice. But no person constitutionally ineligible to the office of President shall be eligible to that of Vice-President of the United States.

Amendment XIII [1865]

Section 1. Neither slavery nor involuntary servitude, except as a punishment for crime whereof the party shall have been duly convicted, shall exist within the United States, or any place subject to their jurisdiction.

Section 2. Congress shall have power to enforce this article by appropriate legislation.

Amendment XIV [1868]

Section 1. All persons born or naturalized in the United States, and subject to the jurisdiction thereof, are citizens of the United States and of the State wherein they reside. No State shall make or enforce any law which shall abridge the privileges or immunities of citizens of the United States; nor shall any State deprive any person of life, liberty, or property, without due process of law; nor deny to any person within its jurisdiction the equal protection of the laws.

Section 2. Representatives shall be apportioned among the several States according to their respective numbers, counting the whole number of persons in each State, excluding Indians not taxed. But when the right to vote at any election for the choice of electors for President and Vice President of the United States, Representatives in Congress, the Executive and Judicial officers of a State, or the members of the Legislature thereof, is denied to any of the male inhabitants of such State, being twenty-one years of age, and citizens of the United States, or in any way abridged, except for participation in rebellion, or other crime, the basis of representation therein shall be reduced in the proportion which the number of such male citizens shall bear to the whole number of male citizens twenty-one years of age in such State.

Section 3. No person shall be a Senator or Representative in Congress, or elector of President and Vice President, or hold any office, civil or military, under the United States, or under any State, who having previously taken an oath, as a member of Congress, or as an officer of the United States, or as a member of any State legislature, or as an executive or judicial officer of any State, to support the Constitution of the United States, shall have engaged in insurrection or rebellion against the same, or given aid or comfort to the enemies thereof. But Congress may by a vote of two-thirds of each House, remove such disability.

Section 4. The validity of the public debt of the United States, authorized by law, including debts incurred for payment of pensions and bounties for services in suppressing insurrection or rebellion, shall not be questioned. But neither the United States nor any State shall assume or pay any debt or obligation incurred in aid of insurrection or rebellion against the United States, or any claim for the loss or emancipation of any slave; but all such debts, obligations and claims shall be held illegal and void.

Section 5. The Congress shall have power to enforce, by appropriate legislation, the provisions of this article.

AMENDMENT XV [1870]

Section 1. The right of citizens of the United States to vote shall not be denied or abridged by the United States or by any State on account of race, color, or previous condition of servitude.

Section 2. The Congress shall have power to enforce this article by appropriate legislation.

AMENDMENT XVI [1913]

The Congress shall have power to lay and collect taxes on incomes, from whatever source derived, without apportionment among the several States, and without regard to any census or enumeration.

AMENDMENT XVII [1913]

Section 1. The Senate of the United States shall be composed of two Senators from each State, elected by the people thereof, for six years; and each Senator shall have one vote. The electors in each State shall have the qualifications requisite for electors of the most numerous branch of the State legislatures.

Section 2. When vacancies happen in the representation of any State in the Senate, the executive authority of such State shall issue writs of election to fill such vacancies: *Provided,* That the legislature of any State may empower the executive thereof to make temporary appointments until the people fill the vacancies by election as the legislature may direct.

Section 3. This amendment shall not be so construed as to affect the election or term of any Senator chosen before it becomes valid as part of the Constitution.

AMENDMENT XVIII [1919]

Section 1. After one year from the ratification of this article the manufacture, sale, or transportation of intoxicating liquors within, the importation thereof into, or the exportation thereof from the United States and all territory subject to the jurisdiction thereof for beverage purposes is hereby prohibited.

Section 2. The Congress and the several States shall have concurrent power to enforce this article by appropriate legislation.

Section 3. This article shall be inoperative unless it shall have been ratified as an amendment to the Constitution by the legislatures of the several States, as provided in the Constitution, within seven years from the date of the submission hereof to the States by the Congress.

AMENDMENT XIX [1920]

Section 1. The right of citizens of the United States to vote shall not be denied or abridged by the United States or by any State on account of sex.

Section 2. Congress shall have power to enforce this article by appropriate legislation.

AMENDMENT XX [1933]

Section 1. The terms of the President and Vice President shall end at noon on the 20th day of January, and the terms of Senators and Representatives at noon on the 3d day of January, of the years in which such terms would have ended if this article had not been ratified; and the terms of their successors shall then begin.

Section 2. The Congress shall assemble at least once in every year, and such meeting shall begin at noon on the 3d day of January, unless they shall by law appoint a different day.

Section 3. If, at the time fixed for the beginning of the term of the President, the President elect shall have died, the Vice President elect shall become President. If the President shall not have been chosen before the time fixed for the beginning of his term, or if the President elect shall have failed to qualify, then the Vice President elect shall act as President until a President shall have qualified; and the Congress may by law provide for the case wherein neither a President elect nor a Vice President elect shall have qualified, declaring who shall then act as President, or the manner in which one who is to act shall be selected, and such person shall act accordingly until a President or Vice President shall have qualified.

Section 4. The Congress may by law provide for the case of the death of any of the persons from whom the House of Representatives may choose a President whenever the right of choice shall have devolved upon them, and for the case of the death of any of the persons from whom the Senate may choose a Vice President whenever the right of choice shall have devolved upon them.

Section 5. Sections 1 and 2 shall take effect on the 15th day of October following the ratification of this article.

Section 6. This article shall be inoperative unless it shall have been ratified as an amendment to the Constitution by the legislatures of three-fourths of the several States within seven years from the date of its submission.

AMENDMENT XXI [1933]

Section 1. The eighteenth article of amendment to the Constitution of the United States is hereby repealed.

Section 2. The transportation or importation into any State, Territory, or possession of the United States for delivery or use therein of intoxicating liquors, in violation of the laws thereof, is hereby prohibited.

Section 3. This article shall be inoperative unless it shall have been ratified as an amendment to the Constitution by conventions in the several States, as provided in the Constitution, within seven years from the date of the submission hereof to the States by the Congress.

Amendment XXII [1951]

Section 1. No person shall be elected to the office of the President more than twice, and no person who has held the office of President, or acted as President, for more than two years of a term to which some other person was elected President shall be elected to the office of President more than once. But this Article shall not apply to any person holding the office of President when this Article was proposed by the Congress, and shall not prevent any person who may be holding the office of President, or acting as President, during the term within which this Article becomes operative from holding the office of President or acting as President during the remainder of such term.

Section 2. This article shall be inoperative unless it shall have been ratified as an amendment to the Constitution by the legislatures of three-fourths of the several States within seven years from the date of its submission to the States by the Congress.

Amendment XXIII [1961]

Section 1. The District constituting the seat of Government of the United States shall appoint in such manner as the Congress may direct:

A number of electors of President and Vice President equal to the whole number of Senators and Representatives in Congress to which the District would be entitled if it were a State, but in no event more than the least populous state; they shall be in addition to those appointed by the states, but they shall be considered, for the purposes of the election of President and Vice President, to be electors appointed by a state; and they shall meet in the District and perform such duties as provided by the twelfth article of amendment.

Section 2. The Congress shall have power to enforce this article by appropriate legislation.

Amendment XXIV [1964]

Section 1. The right of citizens of the United States to vote in any primary or other election for President or Vice President, for electors for President or Vice President, or for Senator or Representative in Congress, shall not be denied or abridged by the United States, or any State by reason of failure to pay any poll tax or other tax.

Section 2. The Congress shall have power to enforce this article by appropriate legislation.

Amendment XXV [1967]

Section 1. In case of the removal of the President from office or of his death or resignation, the Vice President shall become President.

Section 2. Whenever there is a vacancy in the office of the Vice President, the President shall nominate a Vice President who shall take office upon confirmation by a majority vote of both Houses of Congress.

Section 3. Whenever the President transmits to the President pro tempore of the Senate and the Speaker of the House of Representatives his written declaration that he is unable to discharge the powers and duties of his office, and until he transmits to them a written declaration to the contrary, such powers and duties shall be discharged by the Vice President as Acting President.

Section 4. Whenever the Vice President and a majority of either the principal officers of the executive departments or of such other body as Congress may by law provide, transmit to the President pro tempore of the Senate and the Speaker of the House of Representatives their written declaration that the President is unable to discharge the powers and duties of his office, the Vice President shall immediately assume the powers and duties of the office as Acting President.

Thereafter, when the President transmits to the President pro tempore of the Senate and the Speaker of the House of Representatives his written declaration that no inability exists, he shall resume the powers and duties of his office unless the Vice President and a majority of either the principal officers of the executive department or of such other body as Congress may by law provide, transmit within four days to the President pro tempore of the Senate and the Speaker of the House of Representatives their written declaration that the President is unable to discharge the powers and duties of his office. Thereupon Congress shall decide the issue, assembling within forty-eight hours for that purpose if not in session. If the Congress, within twenty-one days after receipt of the latter written declaration, or, if Congress is not in session, within twenty-one days after Congress is required to assemble, determines by two-thirds vote of both Houses that the President is unable to discharge the powers and duties of his office, the Vice President shall continue to discharge the same as Acting President; otherwise, the President shall resume the powers and duties of his office.

Amendment XXVI [1971]

Section 1. The right of citizens of the United States, who are eighteen years of age or older, to vote shall not be denied or abridged by the United States or by any State on account of age.

Section 2. The Congress shall have power to enforce this article by appropriate legislation.

Amendment XXVII [1992]

No law, varying the compensation for the services of the Senators and Representatives, shall take effect, until an election of Representatives shall have intervened.

APPENDIX B

Articles 2 and 2A of the Uniform Commercial Code

Article 2
SALES

Part 1 Short Title, General Construction and Subject Matter

§ 2–101. Short Title.

This Article shall be known and may be cited as Uniform Commercial Code—Sales.

§ 2–102. Scope; Certain Security and Other Transactions Excluded From This Article.

Unless the context otherwise requires, this Article applies to transactions in goods; it does not apply to any transaction which although in the form of an unconditional contract to sell or present sale is intended to operate only as a security transaction nor does this Article impair or repeal any statute regulating sales to consumers, farmers or other specified classes of buyers.

§ 2–103. Definitions and Index of Definitions.

(1) In this Article unless the context otherwise requires

(a) "Buyer" means a person who buys or contracts to buy goods.

(b) "Good faith" in the case of a merchant means honesty in fact and the observance of reasonable commercial standards of fair dealing in the trade.

(c) "Receipt" of goods means taking physical possession of them.

(d) "Seller" means a person who sells or contracts to sell goods.

(2) Other definitions applying to this Article or to specified Parts thereof, and the sections in which they appear are:

"Acceptance". Section 2–606.
"Banker's credit". Section 2–325.
"Between merchants". Section 2–104.
"Cancellation". Section 2–106(4).
"Commercial unit". Section 2–105.
"Confirmed credit". Section 2–325.
"Conforming to contract". Section 2–106.
"Contract for sale". Section 2–106.
"Cover". Section 2–712.
"Entrusting". Section 2–403.
"Financing agency". Section 2–104.
"Future goods". Section 2–105.
"Goods". Section 2–105.
"Identification". Section 2–501.
"Installment contract". Section 2–612.
"Letter of Credit". Section 2–325.
"Lot". Section 2–105.
"Merchant". Section 2–104.
"Overseas". Section 2–323.
"Person in position of seller". Section 2–707.
"Present sale". Section 2–106.
"Sale". Section 2–106.
"Sale on approval". Section 2–326.
"Sale or return". Section 2–326.
"Termination". Section 2–106.

(3) The following definitions in other Articles apply to this Article:

"Check". Section 3–104.

"Consignee". Section 7–102.
"Consignor". Section 7–102.
"Consumer goods". Section 9–109.
"Dishonor". Section 3–507.
"Draft". Section 3–104.

(4) In addition Article 1 contains general definitions and principles of construction and interpretation applicable throughout this Article.

As amended in 1994 and 1999.

§ 2–104. Definitions: "Merchant"; "Between Merchants"; "Financing Agency".

(1) "Merchant" means a person who deals in goods of the kind or otherwise by his occupation holds himself out as having knowledge or skill peculiar to the practices or goods involved in the transaction or to whom such knowledge or skill may be attributed by his employment of an agent or broker or other intermediary who by his occupation holds himself out as having such knowledge or skill.

(2) "Financing agency" means a bank, finance company or other person who in the ordinary course of business makes advances against goods or documents of title or who by arrangement with either the seller or the buyer intervenes in ordinary course to make or collect payment due or claimed under the contract for sale, as by purchasing or paying the seller's draft or making advances against it or by merely taking it for collection whether or not documents of title accompany the draft. "Financing agency" includes also a bank or other person who similarly intervenes between persons who are in the position of seller and buyer in respect to the goods (Section 2–707).

(3) "Between merchants" means in any transaction with respect to which both parties are chargeable with the knowledge or skill of merchants.

§ 2–105. Definitions: Transferability; "Goods"; "Future" Goods; "Lot"; "Commercial Unit".

(1) "Goods" means all things (including specially manufactured goods) which are movable at the time of identification to the contract for sale other than the money in which the price is to be paid, investment securities (Article 8) and things in action. "Goods" also includes the unborn young of animals and growing crops and other identified things attached to realty as described in the section on goods to be severed from realty (Section 2–107).

(2) Goods must be both existing and identified before any interest in them can pass. Goods which are not both existing and identified are "future" goods. A purported present sale of future goods or of any interest therein operates as a contract to sell.

(3) There may be a sale of a part interest in existing identified goods.

(4) An undivided share in an identified bulk of fungible goods is sufficiently identified to be sold although the quantity of the bulk is not determined. Any agreed proportion of such a bulk or any quantity thereof agreed upon by number, weight or other measure may to the extent of the seller's interest in the bulk be sold to the buyer who then becomes an owner in common.

(5) "Lot" means a parcel or a single article which is the subject matter of a separate sale or delivery, whether or not it is sufficient to perform the contract.

(6) "Commercial unit" means such a unit of goods as by commercial usage is a single whole for purposes of sale and division of which materially impairs its character or value on the market or in use. A commercial unit may be a single article (as a machine) or a set of articles (as a suite of furniture or an assortment of sizes) or a quantity (as a bale, gross, or carload) or any other unit treated in use or in the relevant market as a single whole.

§ 2–106. Definitions: "Contract"; "Agreement"; "Contract for Sale"; "Sale"; "Present Sale"; "Conforming" to Contract; "Termination"; "Cancellation".

(1) In this Article unless the context otherwise requires "contract" and "agreement" are limited to those relating to the present or future sale of goods. "Contract for sale" includes both a present sale of goods and a contract to sell goods at a future time. A "sale" consists in the passing of title from the seller to the buyer for a price (Section 2–401). A "present sale" means a sale which is accomplished by the making of the contract.

(2) Goods or conduct including any part of a performance are "conforming" or conform to the contract when they are in accordance with the obligations under the contract.

(3) "Termination" occurs when either party pursuant to a power created by agreement or law puts an end to the contract otherwise than for its breach. On "termination" all obligations which are still executory on both sides are discharged but any right based on prior breach or performance survives.

(4) "Cancellation" occurs when either party puts an end to the contract for breach by the other and its effect is the same as that of "termination" except that the cancelling party also retains any remedy for breach of the whole contract or any unperformed balance.

§ 2–107. Goods to Be Severed From Realty: Recording.

(1) A contract for the sale of minerals or the like (including oil and gas) or a structure or its materials to be removed from realty is a contract for the sale of goods within this Article if they are to be severed by the seller but until severance a purported present sale thereof which is not effective as a transfer of an interest in land is effective only as a contract to sell.

(2) A contract for the sale apart from the land of growing crops or other things attached to realty and capable of severance without material harm thereto but not described in subsection (1) or of timber to be cut is a contract for the sale of goods within this Article whether the subject matter is to be severed by the buyer or by the seller even though it forms part of the realty at the time of contracting, and the parties can by identification effect a present sale before severance.

(3) The provisions of this section are subject to any third party rights provided by the law relating to realty records, and the contract for sale may be executed and recorded as a document transferring an interest in land and shall then constitute notice to third parties of the buyer's rights under the contract for sale.

As amended in 1972.

Part 2 Form, Formation and Readjustment of Contract

§ 2–201. Formal Requirements; Statute of Frauds.

(1) Except as otherwise provided in this section a contract for the sale of goods for the price of $500 or more is not enforceable by way of action or defense unless there is some writing sufficient to indicate that a contract for sale has been made between the parties and signed by the party against whom enforcement is sought or by his authorized agent or broker. A writing is not insufficient because it omits or incorrectly states a term agreed upon but the contract is not enforceable under this paragraph beyond the quantity of goods shown in such writing.

(2) Between merchants if within a reasonable time a writing in confirmation of the contract and sufficient against the sender is received and the party receiving it has reason to know its contents, its satisfies the requirements of subsection (1) against such party unless written notice of objection to its contents is given within ten days after it is received.

(3) A contract which does not satisfy the requirements of subsection (1) but which is valid in other respects is enforceable

(a) if the goods are to be specially manufactured for the buyer and are not suitable for sale to others in the ordinary course of the seller's business and the seller, before notice of repudiation is received and under circumstances which reasonably indicate that the goods are for the buyer, has made either a substantial beginning of their manufacture or commitments for their procurement; or

(b) if the party against whom enforcement is sought admits in his pleading, testimony or otherwise in court that a contract for sale was made, but the contract is not enforceable under this provision beyond the quantity of goods admitted; or

(c) with respect to goods for which payment has been made and accepted or which have been received and accepted (Sec. 2–606).

§ 2–202. Final Written Expression: Parol or Extrinsic Evidence.

Terms with respect to which the confirmatory memoranda of the parties agree or which are otherwise set forth in a writing intended by the parties as a final expression of their agreement with respect to such terms as are included therein may not be contradicted by evidence of any prior agreement or of a contemporaneous oral agreement but may be explained or supplemented

(a) by course of dealing or usage of trade (Section 1–205) or by course of performance (Section 2–208); and

(b) by evidence of consistent additional terms unless the court finds the writing to have been intended also as a complete and exclusive statement of the terms of the agreement.

§ 2–203. Seals Inoperative.

The affixing of a seal to a writing evidencing a contract for sale or an offer to buy or sell goods does not constitute the writing a sealed instrument and the law with respect to sealed instruments does not apply to such a contract or offer.

§ 2–204. Formation in General.

(1) A contract for sale of goods may be made in any manner sufficient to show agreement, including conduct by both parties which recognizes the existence of such a contract.

(2) An agreement sufficient to constitute a contract for sale may be found even though the moment of its making is undetermined.

(3) Even though one or more terms are left open a contract for sale does not fail for indefiniteness if the parties have intended to make a contract and there is a reasonably certain basis for giving an appropriate remedy.

§ 2–205. Firm Offers.

An offer by a merchant to buy or sell goods in a signed writing which by its terms gives assurance that it will be held open is not revocable, for lack of consideration, during the time stated or if no time is stated for a reasonable time, but in no event may such period of irrevocability exceed three months; but any such term of assurance on a form supplied by the offeree must be separately signed by the offeror.

§ 2–206. Offer and Acceptance in Formation of Contract.

(1) Unless other unambiguously indicated by the language or circumstances

(a) an offer to make a contract shall be construed as inviting acceptance in any manner and by any medium reasonable in the circumstances;

(b) an order or other offer to buy goods for prompt or current shipment shall be construed as inviting acceptance either by a prompt promise to ship or by the prompt or current shipment of conforming or nonconforming goods, but such a shipment of non-conforming goods does not constitute an acceptance if the seller seasonably notifies the buyer that the shipment is offered only as an accommodation to the buyer.

(2) Where the beginning of a requested performance is a reasonable mode of acceptance an offeror who is not notified of acceptance within a reasonable time may treat the offer as having lapsed before acceptance.

§ 2–207. Additional Terms in Acceptance or Confirmation.

(1) A definite and seasonable expression of acceptance or a written confirmation which is sent within a reasonable time

operates as an acceptance even though it states terms additional to or different from those offered or agreed upon, unless acceptance is expressly made conditional on assent to the additional or different terms.

(2) The additional terms are to be construed as proposals for addition to the contract. Between merchants such terms become part of the contract unless:

(a) the offer expressly limits acceptance to the terms of the offer;

(b) they materially alter it; or

(c) notification of objection to them has already been given or is given within a reasonable time after notice of them is received.

(3) Conduct by both parties which recognizes the existence of a contract is sufficient to establish a contract for sale although the writings of the parties do not otherwise establish a contract. In such case the terms of the particular contract consist of those terms on which the writings of the parties agree, together with any supplementary terms incorporated under any other provisions of this Act.

§ 2–208. Course of Performance or Practical Construction.

(1) Where the contract for sale involves repeated occasions for performance by either party with knowledge of the nature of the performance and opportunity for objection to it by the other, any course of performance accepted or acquiesced in without objection shall be relevant to determine the meaning of the agreement.

(2) The express terms of the agreement and any such course of performance, as well as any course of dealing and usage of trade, shall be construed whenever reasonable as consistent with each other; but when such construction is unreasonable, express terms shall control course of performance and course of performance shall control both course of dealing and usage of trade (Section 1–205).

(3) Subject to the provisions of the next section on modification and waiver, such course of performance shall be relevant to show a waiver or modification of any term inconsistent with such course of performance.

§ 2–209. Modification, Rescission and Waiver.

(1) An agreement modifying a contract within this Article needs no consideration to be binding.

(2) A signed agreement which excludes modification or rescission except by a signed writing cannot be otherwise modified or rescinded, but except as between merchants such a requirement on a form supplied by the merchant must be separately signed by the other party.

(3) The requirements of the statute of frauds section of this Article (Section 2–201) must be satisfied if the contract as modified is within its provisions.

(4) Although an attempt at modification or rescission does not satisfy the requirements of subsection (2) or (3) it can operate as a waiver.

(5) A party who has made a waiver affecting an executory portion of the contract may retract the waiver by reasonable notification received by the other party that strict performance will be required of any term waived, unless the retraction would be unjust in view of a material change of position in reliance on the waiver.

§ 2–210. Delegation of Performance; Assignment of Rights.

(1) A party may perform his duty through a delegate unless otherwise agreed or unless the other party has a substantial interest in having his original promisor perform or control the acts required by the contract. No delegation of performance relieves the party delegating of any duty to perform or any liability for breach.

(2) Except as otherwise provided in Section 9–406, unless otherwise agreed, all rights of either seller or buyer can be assigned except where the assignment would materially change the duty of the other party, or increase materially the burden or risk imposed on him by his contract, or impair materially his chance of obtaining return performance. A right to damages for breach of the whole contract or a right arising out of the assignor's due performance of his entire obligation can be assigned despite agreement otherwise.

(3) The creation, attachment, perfection, or enforcement of a security interest in the seller's interest under a contract is not a transfer that materially changes the duty of or increases materially the burden or risk imposed on the buyer or impairs materially the buyer's chance of obtaining return performance within the purview of subsection (2) unless, and then only to the extent that, enforcement actually results in a delegation of material performance of the seller. Even in that event, the creation, attachment, perfection, and enforcement of the security interest remain effective, but (i) the seller is liable to the buyer for damages caused by the delegation to the extent that the damages could not reasonably by prevented by the buyer, and (ii) a court having jurisdiction may grant other appropriate relief, including cancellation of the contract for sale or an injunction against enforcement of the security interest or consummation of the enforcement.

(4) Unless the circumstnaces indicate the contrary a prohibition of assignment of "the contract" is to be construed as barring only the delegation to the assigness of the assignor's performance.

(5) An assignment of "the contract" or of "all my rights under the contract" or an assignment in similar general terms is an assignment of rights and unless the language or the circumstances (as in an assignment for security) indicate the contrary, it is a delegation of performance of the duties of the assignor and its acceptance by the assignee constitutes a promise by him to perform those duties. This promise is enforceable by either the assignor or the other party to the original contract.

(6) The other party may treat any assignment which delegates performance as creating reasonable grounds for insecurity and may without prejudice to his rights against the assignor demand assurances from the assignee (Section 2–609).

As amended in 1999.

Part 3 General Obligation and Construction of Contract

§ 2–301. General Obligations of Parties.

The obligation of the seller is to transfer and deliver and that of the buyer is to accept and pay in accordance with the contract.

§ 2–302. Unconscionable Contract or Clause.

(1) If the court as a matter of law finds the contract or any clause of the contract to have been unconscionable at the time it was made the court may refuse to enforce the contract, or it may enforce the remainder of the contract without the unconscionable clause, or it may so limit the application of any unconscionable clause as to avoid any unconscionable result.

(2) When it is claimed or appears to the court that the contract or any clause thereof may be unconscionable the parties shall be afforded a reasonable opportunity to present evidence as to its commercial setting, purpose and effect to aid the court in making the determination.

§ 2–303. Allocations or Division of Risks.

Where this Article allocates a risk or a burden as between the parties "unless otherwise agreed", the agreement may not only shift the allocation but may also divide the risk or burden.

§ 2–304. Price Payable in Money, Goods, Realty, or Otherwise.

(1) The price can be made payable in money or otherwise. If it is payable in whole or in part in goods each party is a seller of the goods which he is to transfer.

(2) Even though all or part of the price is payable in an interest in realty the transfer of the goods and the seller's obligations with reference to them are subject to this Article, but not the transfer of the interest in realty or the transferor's obligations in connection therewith.

§ 2–305. Open Price Term.

(1) The parties if they so intend can conclude a contract for sale even though the price is not settled. In such a case the price is a reasonable price at the time for delivery if

(a) nothing is said as to price; or

(b) the price is left to be agreed by the parties and they fail to agree; or

(c) the price is to be fixed in terms of some agreed market or other standard as set or recorded by a third person or agency and it is not so set or recorded.

(2) A price to be fixed by the seller or by the buyer means a price for him to fix in good faith.

(3) When a price left to be fixed otherwise than by agreement of the parties fails to be fixed through fault of one party the other may at his option treat the contract as cancelled or himself fix a reasonable price.

(4) Where, however, the parties intend not to be bound unless the price be fixed or agreed and it is not fixed or agreed there is no contract. In such a case the buyer must return any goods already received or if unable so to do must pay their reasonable value at the time of delivery and the seller must return any portion of the price paid on account.

§ 2–306. Output, Requirements and Exclusive Dealings.

(1) A term which measures the quantity by the output of the seller or the requirements of the buyer means such actual output or requirements as may occur in good faith, except that no quantity unreasonably disproportionate to any stated estimate or in the absence of a stated estimate to any normal or otherwise comparable prior output or requirements may be tendered or demanded.

(2) A lawful agreement by either the seller or the buyer for exclusive dealing in the kind of goods concerned imposes unless otherwise agreed an obligation by the seller to use best efforts to supply the goods and by the buyer to use best efforts to promote their sale.

§ 2–307. Delivery in Single Lot or Several Lots.

Unless otherwise agreed all goods called for by a contract for sale must be tendered in a single delivery and payment is due only on such tender but where the circumstances give either party the right to make or demand delivery in lots the price if it can be apportioned may be demanded for each lot.

§ 2–308. Absence of Specified Place for Delivery.

Unless otherwise agreed

(a) the place for delivery of goods is the seller's place of business or if he has none his residence; but

(b) in a contract for sale of identified goods which to the knowledge of the parties at the time of contracting are in some other place, that place is the place for their delivery; and

(c) documents of title may be delivered through customary banking channels.

§ 2–309. Absence of Specific Time Provisions; Notice of Termination.

(1) The time for shipment or delivery or any other action under a contract if not provided in this Article or agreed upon shall be a reasonable time.

(2) Where the contract provides for successive performances but is indefinite in duration it is valid for a reasonable time but unless otherwise agreed may be terminated at any time by either party.

(3) Termination of a contract by one party except on the happening of an agreed event requires that reasonable notification be received by the other party and an agreement dispensing with notification is invalid if its operation would be unconscionable.

§ 2–310. Open Time for Payment or Running of Credit; Authority to Ship Under Reservation.

Unless otherwise agreed

(a) payment is due at the time and place at which the buyer is to receive the goods even though the place of shipment is the place of delivery; and

(b) if the seller is authorized to send the goods he may ship them under reservation, and may tender the documents of title, but the buyer may inspect the goods after their arrival before payment is due unless such inspection is inconsistent with the terms of the contract (Section 2–513); and

(c) if delivery is authorized and made by way of documents of title otherwise than by subsection (b) then payment is due at the time and place at which the buyer is to receive the documents regardless of where the goods are to be received; and

(d) where the seller is required or authorized to ship the goods on credit the credit period runs from the time of shipment but post-dating the invoice or delaying its dispatch will correspondingly delay the starting of the credit period.

§ 2–311. Options and Cooperation Respecting Performance.

(1) An agreement for sale which is otherwise sufficiently definite (subsection (3) of Section 2–204) to be a contract is not made invalid by the fact that it leaves particulars of performance to be specified by one of the parties. Any such specification must be made in good faith and within limits set by commercial reasonableness.

(2) Unless otherwise agreed specifications relating to assortment of the goods are at the buyer's option and except as otherwise provided in subsections (1)(c) and (3) of Section 2–319 specifications or arrangements relating to shipment are at the seller's option.

(3) Where such specification would materially affect the other party's performance but is not seasonably made or where one party's cooperation is necessary to the agreed performance of the other but is not seasonably forthcoming, the other party in addition to all other remedies

(a) is excused for any resulting delay in his own performance; and

(b) may also either proceed to perform in any reasonable manner or after the time for a material part of his own performance treat the failure to specify or to cooperate as a breach by failure to deliver or accept the goods.

§ 2–312. Warranty of Title and Against Infringement; Buyer's Obligation Against Infringement.

(1) Subject to subsection (2) there is in a contract for sale a warranty by the seller that

(a) the title conveyed shall be good, and its transfer rightful; and

(b) the goods shall be delivered free from any security interest or other lien or encumbrance of which the buyer at the time of contracting has no knowledge.

(2) A warranty under subsection (1) will be excluded or modified only by specific language or by circumstances which give the buyer reason to know that the person selling does not claim title in himself or that he is purporting to sell only such right or title as he or a third person may have.

(3) Unless otherwise agreed a seller who is a merchant regularly dealing in goods of the kind warrants that the goods shall be delivered free of the rightful claim of any third person by way of infringement or the like but a buyer who furnishes specifications to the seller must hold the seller harmless against any such claim which arises out of compliance with the specifications.

§ 2–313. Express Warranties by Affirmation, Promise, Description, Sample.

(1) Express warranties by the seller are created as follows:

(a) Any affirmation of fact or promise made by the seller to the buyer which relates to the goods and becomes part of the basis of the bargain creates an express warranty that the goods shall conform to the affirmation or promise.

(b) Any description of the goods which is made part of the basis of the bargain creates an express warranty that the goods shall conform to the description.

(c) Any sample or model which is made part of the basis of the bargain creates an express warranty that the whole of the goods shall conform to the sample or model.

(2) It is not necessary to the creation of an express warranty that the seller use formal words such as "warrant" or "guarantee" or that he have a specific intention to make a warranty, but an affirmation merely of the value of the goods or a statement purporting to be merely the seller's opinion or commendation of the goods does not create a warranty.

§ 2–314. Implied Warranty: Merchantability; Usage of Trade.

(1) Unless excluded or modified (Section 2–316), a warranty that the goods shall be merchantable is implied in a contract for their sale if the seller is a merchant with respect to goods of that kind. Under this section the serving for value of food or drink to be consumed either on the premises or elsewhere is a sale.

(2) Goods to be merchantable must be at least such as

(a) pass without objection in the trade under the contract description; and

(b) in the case of fungible goods, are of fair average quality within the description; and

(c) are fit for the ordinary purposes for which such goods are used; and

(d) run, within the variations permitted by the agreement, of even kind, quality and quantity within each unit and among all units involved; and

(e) are adequately contained, packaged, and labeled as the agreement may require; and

(f) conform to the promises or affirmations of fact made on the container or label if any.

(3) Unless excluded or modified (Section 2–316) other implied warranties may arise from course of dealing or usage of trade.

§ 2–315. Implied Warranty: Fitness for Particular Purpose.

Where the seller at the time of contracting has reason to know any particular purpose for which the goods are required and that the buyer is relying on the seller's skill or judgment to select or furnish suitable goods, there is unless excluded or modified under the next section an implied warranty that the goods shall be fit for such purpose.

§ 2–316. Exclusion or Modification of Warranties.

(1) Words or conduct relevant to the creation of an express warranty and words or conduct tending to negate or limit warranty shall be construed wherever reasonable as consistent with each other; but subject to the provisions of this Article on parol or extrinsic evidence (Section 2–202) negation or limitation is inoperative to the extent that such construction is unreasonable.

(2) Subject to subsection (3), to exclude or modify the implied warranty of merchantability or any part of it the language must mention merchantability and in case of a writing must be conspicuous, and to exclude or modify any implied warranty of fitness the exclusion must be by a writing and conspicuous. Language to exclude all implied warranties of fitness is sufficient if it states, for example, that "There are no warranties which extend beyond the description on the face hereof."

(3) Notwithstanding subsection (2)

(a) unless the circumstances indicate otherwise, all implied warranties are excluded by expressions like "as is", "with all faults" or other language which in common understanding calls the buyer's attention to the exclusion of warranties and makes plain that there is no implied warranty; and

(b) when the buyer before entering into the contract has examined the goods or the sample or model as fully as he desired or has refused to examine the goods there is no implied warranty with regard to defects which an examination ought in the circumstances to have revealed to him; and

(c) an implied warranty can also be excluded or modified by course of dealing or course of performance or usage of trade.

(4) Remedies for breach of warranty can be limited in accordance with the provisions of this Article on liquidation or limitation of damages and on contractual modification of remedy (Sections 2–718 and 2–719).

§ 2–317. Cumulation and Conflict of Warranties Express or Implied.

Warranties whether express or implied shall be construed as consistent with each other and as cumulative, but if such construction is unreasonable the intention of the parties shall determine which warranty is dominant. In ascertaining that intention the following rules apply:

(a) Exact or technical specifications displace an inconsistent sample or model or general language of description.

(b) A sample from an existing bulk displaces inconsistent general language of description.

(c) Express warranties displace inconsistent implied warranties other than an implied warranty of fitness for a particular purpose.

§ 2–318. Third Party Beneficiaries of Warranties Express or Implied.

Note: If this Act is introduced in the Congress of the United States this section should be omitted. (States to select one alternative.)

Alternative A

A seller's warranty whether express or implied extends to any natural person who is in the family or household of his buyer or who is a guest in his home if it is reasonable to expect that such person may use, consume or be affected by the goods and who is injured in person by breach of the warranty. A seller may not exclude or limit the operation of this section.

Alternative B

A seller's warranty whether express or implied extends to any natural person who may reasonably be expected to use, consume or be affected by the goods and who is injured in person by breach of the warranty. A seller may not exclude or limit the operation of this section.

Alternative C

A seller's warranty whether express or implied extends to any person who may reasonably be expected to use, consume or be affected by the goods and who is injured by breach of the warranty. A seller may not exclude or limit the operation of this section with respect to injury to the person of an individual to whom the warranty extends.

As amended 1966.

§ 2–319. F.O.B. and F.A.S. Terms.

(1) Unless otherwise agreed the term F.O.B. (which means "free on board") at a named place, even though used only in connection with the stated price, is a delivery term under which

(a) when the term is F.O.B. the place of shipment, the seller must at that place ship the goods in the manner provided in this Article (Section 2–504) and bear the expense and risk of putting them into the possession of the carrier; or

(b) when the term is F.O.B. the place of destination, the seller must at his own expense and risk transport the goods to that place and there tender delivery of them in the manner provided in this Article (Section 2–503);

(c) when under either (a) or (b) the term is also F.O.B. vessel, car or other vehicle, the seller must in addition at his own expense and risk load the goods on board. If the term is F.O.B. vessel the buyer must name the vessel and in an appropriate case the seller must comply with the provisions of this Article on the form of bill of lading (Section 2–323).

(2) Unless otherwise agreed the term F.A.S. vessel (which means "free alongside") at a named port, even though used

only in connection with the stated price, is a delivery term under which the seller must

(a) at his own expense and risk deliver the goods alongside the vessel in the manner usual in that port or on a dock designated and provided by the buyer; and

(b) obtain and tender a receipt for the goods in exchange for which the carrier is under a duty to issue a bill of lading.

(3) Unless otherwise agreed in any case falling within subsection (1)(a) or (c) or subsection (2) the buyer must seasonably give any needed instructions for making delivery, including when the term is F.A.S. or F.O.B. the loading berth of the vessel and in an appropriate case its name and sailing date. The seller may treat the failure of needed instructions as a failure of cooperation under this Article (Section 2–311). He may also at his option move the goods in any reasonable manner preparatory to delivery or shipment.

(4) Under the term F.O.B. vessel or F.A.S. unless otherwise agreed the buyer must make payment against tender of the required documents and the seller may not tender nor the buyer demand delivery of the goods in substitution for the documents.

§ 2–320. C.I.F. and C. & F. Terms.

(1) The term C.I.F. means that the price includes in a lump sum the cost of the goods and the insurance and freight to the named destination. The term C. & F. or C.F. means that the price so includes cost and freight to the named destination.

(2) Unless otherwise agreed and even though used only in connection with the stated price and destination, the term C.I.F. destination or its equivalent requires the seller at his own expense and risk to

(a) put the goods into the possession of a carrier at the port for shipment and obtain a negotiable bill or bills of lading covering the entire transportation to the named destination; and

(b) load the goods and obtain a receipt from the carrier (which may be contained in the bill of lading) showing that the freight has been paid or provided for; and

(c) obtain a policy or certificate of insurance, including any war risk insurance, of a kind and on terms then current at the port of shipment in the usual amount, in the currency of the contract, shown to cover the same goods covered by the bill of lading and providing for payment of loss to the order of the buyer or for the account of whom it may concern; but the seller may add to the price the amount of the premium for any such war risk insurance; and

(d) prepare an invoice of the goods and procure any other documents required to effect shipment or to comply with the contract; and

(e) forward and tender with commercial promptness all the documents in due form and with any indorsement necessary to perfect the buyer's rights.

(3) Unless otherwise agreed the term C. & F. or its equivalent has the same effect and imposes upon the seller the same obligations and risks as a C.I.F. term except the obligation as to insurance.

(4) Under the term C.I.F. or C. & F. unless otherwise agreed the buyer must make payment against tender of the required documents and the seller may not tender nor the buyer demand delivery of the goods in substitution for the documents.

§ 2–321. C.I.F. or C. & F.: "Net Landed Weights"; "Payment on Arrival"; Warranty of Condition on Arrival.

Under a contract containing a term C.I.F. or C. & F.

(1) Where the price is based on or is to be adjusted according to "net landed weights", "delivered weights", "out turn" quantity or quality or the like, unless otherwise agreed the seller must reasonably estimate the price. The payment due on tender of the documents called for by the contract is the amount so estimated, but after final adjustment of the price a settlement must be made with commercial promptness.

(2) An agreement described in subsection (1) or any warranty of quality or condition of the goods on arrival places upon the seller the risk of ordinary deterioration, shrinkage and the like in transportation but has no effect on the place or time of identification to the contract for sale or delivery or on the passing of the risk of loss.

(3) Unless otherwise agreed where the contract provides for payment on or after arrival of the goods the seller must before payment allow such preliminary inspection as is feasible; but if the goods are lost delivery of the documents and payment are due when the goods should have arrived.

§ 2–322. Delivery "Ex-Ship".

(1) Unless otherwise agreed a term for delivery of goods "ex-ship" (which means from the carrying vessel) or in equivalent language is not restricted to a particular ship and requires delivery from a ship which has reached a place at the named port of destination where goods of the kind are usually discharged.

(2) Under such a term unless otherwise agreed

(a) the seller must discharge all liens arising out of the carriage and furnish the buyer with a direction which puts the carrier under a duty to deliver the goods; and

(b) the risk of loss does not pass to the buyer until the goods leave the ship's tackle or are otherwise properly unloaded.

§ 2–323. Form of Bill of Lading Required in Overseas Shipment; "Overseas".

(1) Where the contract contemplates overseas shipment and contains a term C.I.F. or C. & F. or F.O.B. vessel, the seller unless otherwise agreed must obtain a negotiable bill of lading stating that the goods have been loaded on board or, in the case of a term C.I.F. or C. & F., received for shipment.

(2) Where in a case within subsection (1) a bill of lading has been issued in a set of parts, unless otherwise agreed if the documents

are not to be sent from abroad the buyer may demand tender of the full set; otherwise only one part of the bill of lading need be tendered. Even if the agreement expressly requires a full set

(a) due tender of a single part is acceptable within the provisions of this Article on cure of improper delivery (subsection (1) of Section 2–508); and

(b) even though the full set is demanded, if the documents are sent from abroad the person tendering an incomplete set may nevertheless require payment upon furnishing an indemnity which the buyer in good faith deems adequate.

(3) A shipment by water or by air or a contract contemplating such shipment is "overseas" insofar as by usage of trade or agreement it is subject to the commercial, financing or shipping practices characteristic of international deep water commerce.

§ 2–324. "No Arrival, No Sale" Term.

Under a term "no arrival, no sale" or terms of like meaning, unless otherwise agreed,

(a) the seller must properly ship conforming goods and if they arrive by any means he must tender them on arrival but he assumes no obligation that the goods will arrive unless he has caused the non-arrival; and

(b) where without fault of the seller the goods are in part lost or have so deteriorated as no longer to conform to the contract or arrive after the contract time, the buyer may proceed as if there had been casualty to identified goods (Section 2–613).

§ 2–325. "Letter of Credit" Term; "Confirmed Credit".

(1) Failure of the buyer seasonably to furnish an agreed letter of credit is a breach of the contract for sale.

(2) The delivery to seller of a proper letter of credit suspends the buyer's obligation to pay. If the letter of credit is dishonored, the seller may on seasonable notification to the buyer require payment directly from him.

(3) Unless otherwise agreed the term "letter of credit" or "banker's credit" in a contract for sale means an irrevocable credit issued by a financing agency of good repute and, where the shipment is overseas, of good international repute. The term "confirmed credit" means that the credit must also carry the direct obligation of such an agency which does business in the seller's financial market.

§ 2–326. Sale on Approval and Sale or Return; Rights of Creditors.

(1) Unless otherwise agreed, if delivered goods may be returned by the buyer even though they conform to the contract, the transaction is

(a) a "sale on approval" if the goods are delivered primarily for use, and

(b) a "sale or return" if the goods are delivered primarily for resale.

(2) Goods held on approval are not subject to the claims of the buyer's creditors until acceptance; goods held on sale or return are subject to such claims while in the buyer's possession.

(3) Any "or return" term of a contract for sale is to be treated as a separate contract for sale within the statute of frauds section of this Article (Section 2–201) and as contradicting the sale aspect of the contract within the provisions of this Article or on parol or extrinsic evidence (Section 2–202).

As amended in 1999.

§ 2–327. Special Incidents of Sale on Approval and Sale or Return.

(1) Under a sale on approval unless otherwise agreed

(a) although the goods are identified to the contract the risk of loss and the title do not pass to the buyer until acceptance; and

(b) use of the goods consistent with the purpose of trial is not acceptance but failure seasonably to notify the seller of election to return the goods is acceptance, and if the goods conform to the contract acceptance of any part is acceptance of the whole; and

(c) after due notification of election to return, the return is at the seller's risk and expense but a merchant buyer must follow any reasonable instructions.

(2) Under a sale or return unless otherwise agreed

(a) the option to return extends to the whole or any commercial unit of the goods while in substantially their original condition, but must be exercised seasonably; and

(b) the return is at the buyer's risk and expense.

§ 2–328. Sale by Auction.

(1) In a sale by auction if goods are put up in lots each lot is the subject of a separate sale.

(2) A sale by auction is complete when the auctioneer so announces by the fall of the hammer or in other customary manner. Where a bid is made while the hammer is falling in acceptance of a prior bid the auctioneer may in his discretion reopen the bidding or declare the goods sold under the bid on which the hammer was falling.

(3) Such a sale is with reserve unless the goods are in explicit terms put up without reserve. In an auction with reserve the auctioneer may withdraw the goods at any time until he announces completion of the sale. In an auction without reserve, after the auctioneer calls for bids on an article or lot, that article or lot cannot be withdrawn unless no bid is made within a reasonable time. In either case a bidder may retract his bid until the auctioneer's announcement of completion of the sale, but a bidder's retraction does not revive any previous bid.

(4) If the auctioneer knowingly receives a bid on the seller's behalf or the seller makes or procures such as bid, and notice has not been given that liberty for such bidding is reserved, the buyer may at his option avoid the sale or take the goods at the

price of the last good faith bid prior to the completion of the sale. This subsection shall not apply to any bid at a forced sale.

Part 4 Title, Creditors and Good Faith Purchasers

§ 2–401. Passing of Title; Reservation for Security; Limited Application of This Section.

Each provision of this Article with regard to the rights, obligations and remedies of the seller, the buyer, purchasers or other third parties applies irrespective of title to the goods except where the provision refers to such title. Insofar as situations are not covered by the other provisions of this Article and matters concerning title became material the following rules apply:

(1) Title to goods cannot pass under a contract for sale prior to their identification to the contract (Section 2–501), and unless otherwise explicitly agreed the buyer acquires by their identification a special property as limited by this Act. Any retention or reservation by the seller of the title (property) in goods shipped or delivered to the buyer is limited in effect to a reservation of a security interest. Subject to these provisions and to the provisions of the Article on Secured Transactions (Article 9), title to goods passes from the seller to the buyer in any manner and on any conditions explicitly agreed on by the parties.

(2) Unless otherwise explicitly agreed title passes to the buyer at the time and place at which the seller completes his performance with reference to the physical delivery of the goods, despite any reservation of a security interest and even though a document of title is to be delivered at a different time or place; and in particular and despite any reservation of a security interest by the bill of lading

(a) if the contract requires or authorizes the seller to send the goods to the buyer but does not require him to deliver them at destination, title passes to the buyer at the time and place of shipment; but

(b) if the contract requires delivery at destination, title passes on tender there.

(3) Unless otherwise explicitly agreed where delivery is to be made without moving the goods,

(a) if the seller is to deliver a document of title, title passes at the time when and the place where he delivers such documents; or

(b) if the goods are at the time of contracting already identified and no documents are to be delivered, title passes at the time and place of contracting.

(4) A rejection or other refusal by the buyer to receive or retain the goods, whether or not justified, or a justified revocation of acceptance revests title to the goods in the seller. Such revesting occurs by operation of law and is not a "sale".

§ 2–402. Rights of Seller's Creditors Against Sold Goods.

(1) Except as provided in subsections (2) and (3), rights of unsecured creditors of the seller with respect to goods which have been identified to a contract for sale are subject to the buyer's rights to recover the goods under this Article (Sections 2–502 and 2–716).

(2) A creditor of the seller may treat a sale or an identification of goods to a contract for sale as void if as against him a retention of possession by the seller is fraudulent under any rule of law of the state where the goods are situated, except that retention of possession in good faith and current course of trade by a merchant-seller for a commercially reasonable time after a sale or identification is not fraudulent.

(3) Nothing in this Article shall be deemed to impair the rights of creditors of the seller

(a) under the provisions of the Article on Secured Transactions (Article 9); or

(b) where identification to the contract or delivery is made not in current course of trade but in satisfaction of or as security for a pre-existing claim for money, security or the like and is made under circumstances which under any rule of law of the state where the goods are situated would apart from this Article constitute the transaction a fraudulent transfer or voidable preference.

§ 2–403. Power to Transfer; Good Faith Purchase of Goods; "Entrusting".

(1) A purchaser of goods acquires all title which his transferor had or had power to transfer except that a purchaser of a limited interest acquires rights only to the extent of the interest purchased. A person with voidable title has power to transfer a good title to a good faith purchaser for value. When goods have been delivered under a transaction of purchase the purchaser has such power even though

(a) the transferor was deceived as to the identity of the purchaser, or

(b) the delivery was in exchange for a check which is later dishonored, or

(c) it was agreed that the transaction was to be a "cash sale", or

(d) the delivery was procured through fraud punishable as larcenous under the criminal law.

(2) Any entrusting of possession of goods to a merchant who deals in goods of that kind gives him power to transfer all rights of the entruster to a buyer in ordinary course of business.

(3) "Entrusting" includes any delivery and any acquiescence in retention of possession regardless of any condition expressed between the parties to the delivery or acquiescence and regardless of whether the procurement of the entrusting or the possessor's disposition of the goods have been such as to be larcenous under the criminal law.

(4) The rights of other purchasers of goods and of lien creditors are governed by the Articles on Secured Transactions (Article 9), Bulk Transfers (Article 6) and Documents of Title (Article 7).

As amended in 1988.

Part 5 Performance

§ 2–501. Insurable Interest in Goods; Manner of Identification of Goods.

(1) The buyer obtains a special property and an insurable interest in goods by identification of existing goods as goods to which the contract refers even though the goods so identified are non-conforming and he has an option to return or reject them. Such identification can be made at any time and in any manner explicitly agreed to by the parties. In the absence of explicit agreement identification occurs

(a) when the contract is made if it is for the sale of goods already existing and identified;

(b) if the contract is for the sale of future goods other than those described in paragraph (c), when goods are shipped, marked or otherwise designated by the seller as goods to which the contract refers;

(c) when the crops are planted or otherwise become growing crops or the young are conceived if the contract is for the sale of unborn young to be born within twelve months after contracting or for the sale of crops to be harvested within twelve months or the next normal harvest season after contracting whichever is longer.

(2) The seller retains an insurable interest in goods so long as title to or any security interest in the goods remains in him and where the identification is by the seller alone he may until default or insolvency or notification to the buyer that the identification is final substitute other goods for those identified.

(3) Nothing in this section impairs any insurable interest recognized under any other statute or rule of law.

§ 2–502. Buyer's Right to Goods on Seller's Insolvency.

(1) Subject to subsections (2) and (3) and even though the goods have not been shipped a buyer who has paid a part or all of the price of goods in which he has a special property under the provisions of the immediately preceding section may on making and keeping good a tender of any unpaid portion of their price recover them from the seller if:

(a) in the case of goods bought for personal, family, or household purposes, the seller repudiates or fails to deliver as required by the contract; or

(b) in all cases, the seller becomes insolvent within ten days after receipt of the first installment on their price.

(2) The buyer's right to recover the goods under subsection (1)(a) vests upon acquisition of a special property, even if the seller had not then repudiated or failed to deliver.

(3) If the identification creating his special property has been made by the buyer he acquires the right to recover the goods only if they conform to the contract for sale.

As amended in 1999.

§ 2–503. Manner of Seller's Tender of Delivery.

(1) Tender of delivery requires that the seller put and hold conforming goods at the buyer's disposition and give the buyer any notification reasonably necessary to enable him to take delivery. The manner, time and place for tender are determined by the agreement and this Article, and in particular

(a) tender must be at a reasonable hour, and if it is of goods they must be kept available for the period reasonably necessary to enable the buyer to take possession; but

(b) unless otherwise agreed the buyer must furnish facilities reasonably suited to the receipt of the goods.

(2) Where the case is within the next section respecting shipment tender requires that the seller comply with its provisions.

(3) Where the seller is required to deliver at a particular destination tender requires that he comply with subsection (1) and also in any appropriate case tender documents as described in subsections (4) and (5) of this section.

(4) Where goods are in the possession of a bailee and are to be delivered without being moved

(a) tender requires that the seller either tender a negotiable document of title covering such goods or procure acknowledgment by the bailee of the buyer's right to possession of the goods; but

(b) tender to the buyer of a non-negotiable document of title or of a written direction to the bailee to deliver is sufficient tender unless the buyer seasonably objects, and receipt by the bailee of notification of the buyer's rights fixes those rights as against the bailee and all third persons; but risk of loss of the goods and of any failure by the bailee to honor the non-negotiable document of title or to obey the direction remains on the seller until the buyer has had a reasonable time to present the document or direction, and a refusal by the bailee to honor the document or to obey the direction defeats the tender.

(5) Where the contract requires the seller to deliver documents

(a) he must tender all such documents in correct form, except as provided in this Article with respect to bills of lading in a set (subsection (2) of Section 2–323); and

(b) tender through customary banking channels is sufficient and dishonor of a draft accompanying the documents constitutes non-acceptance or rejection.

§ 2–504. Shipment by Seller.

Where the seller is required or authorized to send the goods to the buyer and the contract does not require him to deliver them at a particular destination, then unless otherwise agreed he must

(a) put the goods in the possession of such a carrier and make such a contract for their transportation as may be reasonable having regard to the nature of the goods and other circumstances of the case; and

(b) obtain and promptly deliver or tender in due form any document necessary to enable the buyer to obtain possession of the goods or otherwise required by the agreement or by usage of trade; and

(c) promptly notify the buyer of the shipment.

Failure to notify the buyer under paragraph (c) or to make a proper contract under paragraph (a) is a ground for rejection only if material delay or loss ensues.

§ 2–505. Seller's Shipment under Reservation.

(1) Where the seller has identified goods to the contract by or before shipment:

(a) his procurement of a negotiable bill of lading to his own order or otherwise reserves in him a security interest in the goods. His procurement of the bill to the order of a financing agency or of the buyer indicates in addition only the seller's expectation of transferring that interest to the person named.

(b) a non-negotiable bill of lading to himself or his nominee reserves possession of the goods as security but except in a case of conditional delivery (subsection (2) of Section 2–507) a non-negotiable bill of lading naming the buyer as consignee reserves no security interest even though the seller retains possession of the bill of lading.

(2) When shipment by the seller with reservation of a security interest is in violation of the contract for sale it constitutes an improper contract for transportation within the preceding section but impairs neither the rights given to the buyer by shipment and identification of the goods to the contract nor the seller's powers as a holder of a negotiable document.

§ 2–506. Rights of Financing Agency.

(1) A financing agency by paying or purchasing for value a draft which relates to a shipment of goods acquires to the extent of the payment or purchase and in addition to its own rights under the draft and any document of title securing it any rights of the shipper in the goods including the right to stop delivery and the shipper's right to have the draft honored by the buyer.

(2) The right to reimbursement of a financing agency which has in good faith honored or purchased the draft under commitment to or authority from the buyer is not impaired by subsequent discovery of defects with reference to any relevant document which was apparently regular on its face.

§ 2–507. Effect of Seller's Tender; Delivery on Condition.

(1) Tender of delivery is a condition to the buyer's duty to accept the goods and, unless otherwise agreed, to his duty to pay for them. Tender entitles the seller to acceptance of the goods and to payment according to the contract.

(2) Where payment is due and demanded on the delivery to the buyer of goods or documents of title, his right as against the seller to retain or dispose of them is conditional upon his making the payment due.

§ 2–508. Cure by Seller of Improper Tender or Delivery; Replacement.

(1) Where any tender or delivery by the seller is rejected because non-conforming and the time for performance has not yet expired, the seller may seasonably notify the buyer of his intention to cure and may then within the contract time make a conforming delivery.

(2) Where the buyer rejects a non-conforming tender which the seller had reasonable grounds to believe would be acceptable with or without money allowance the seller may if he seasonably notifies the buyer have a further reasonable time to substitute a conforming tender.

§ 2–509. Risk of Loss in the Absence of Breach.

(1) Where the contract requires or authorizes the seller to ship the goods by carrier

(a) if it does not require him to deliver them at a particular destination, the risk of loss passes to the buyer when the goods are duly delivered to the carrier even though the shipment is under reservation (Section 2–505); but

(b) if it does require him to deliver them at a particular destination and the goods are there duly tendered while in the possession of the carrier, the risk of loss passes to the buyer when the goods are there duly so tendered as to enable the buyer to take delivery.

(2) Where the goods are held by a bailee to be delivered without being moved, the risk of loss passes to the buyer

(a) on his receipt of a negotiable document of title covering the goods; or

(b) on acknowledgment by the bailee of the buyer's right to possession of the goods; or

(c) after his receipt of a non-negotiable document of title or other written direction to deliver, as provided in subsection (4)(b) of Section 2–503.

(3) In any case not within subsection (1) or (2), the risk of loss passes to the buyer on his receipt of the goods if the seller is a merchant; otherwise the risk passes to the buyer on tender of delivery.

(4) The provisions of this section are subject to contrary agreement of the parties and to the provisions of this Article on sale on approval (Section 2–327) and on effect of breach on risk of loss (Section 2–510).

§ 2–510. Effect of Breach on Risk of Loss.

(1) Where a tender or delivery of goods so fails to conform to the contract as to give a right of rejection the risk of their loss remains on the seller until cure or acceptance.

(2) Where the buyer rightfully revokes acceptance he may to the extent of any deficiency in his effective insurance coverage treat the risk of loss as having rested on the seller from the beginning.

(3) Where the buyer as to conforming goods already identified to the contract for sale repudiates or is otherwise in breach before risk of their loss has passed to him, the seller may to the extent of any deficiency in his effective insurance coverage treat the risk of loss as resting on the buyer for a commercially reasonable time.

§ 2–511. Tender of Payment by Buyer; Payment by Check.

(1) Unless otherwise agreed tender of payment is a condition to the seller's duty to tender and complete any delivery.

(2) Tender of payment is sufficient when made by any means or in any manner current in the ordinary course of business unless the seller demands payment in legal tender and gives any extension of time reasonably necessary to procure it.

(3) Subject to the provisions of this Act on the effect of an instrument on an obligation (Section 3–310), payment by check is conditional and is defeated as between the parties by dishonor of the check on due presentment.

As amended in 1994.

§ 2–512. Payment by Buyer Before Inspection.

(1) Where the contract requires payment before inspection non-conformity of the goods does not excuse the buyer from so making payment unless

(a) the non-conformity appears without inspection; or

(b) despite tender of the required documents the circumstances would justify injunction against honor under this Act (Section 5–109(b)).

(2) Payment pursuant to subsection (1) does not constitute an acceptance of goods or impair the buyer's right to inspect or any of his remedies.

As amended in 1995.

§ 2–513. Buyer's Right to Inspection of Goods.

(1) Unless otherwise agreed and subject to subsection (3), where goods are tendered or delivered or identified to the contract for sale, the buyer has a right before payment or acceptance to inspect them at any reasonable place and time and in any reasonable manner. When the seller is required or authorized to send the goods to the buyer, the inspection may be after their arrival.

(2) Expenses of inspection must be borne by the buyer but may be recovered from the seller if the goods do not conform and are rejected.

(3) Unless otherwise agreed and subject to the provisions of this Article on C.I.F. contracts (subsection (3) of Section 2–321), the buyer is not entitled to inspect the goods before payment of the price when the contract provides

(a) for delivery "C.O.D." or on other like terms; or

(b) for payment against documents of title, except where such payment is due only after the goods are to become available for inspection.

(4) A place or method of inspection fixed by the parties is presumed to be exclusive but unless otherwise expressly agreed it does not postpone identification or shift the place for delivery or for passing the risk of loss. If compliance becomes impossible, inspection shall be as provided in this section unless the place or method fixed was clearly intended as an indispensable condition failure of which avoids the contract.

§ 2–514. When Documents Deliverable on Acceptance; When on Payment.

Unless otherwise agreed documents against which a draft is drawn are to be delivered to the drawee on acceptance of the draft if it is payable more than three days after presentment; otherwise, only on payment.

§ 2–515. Preserving Evidence of Goods in Dispute.

In furtherance of the adjustment of any claim or dispute

(a) either party on reasonable notification to the other and for the purpose of ascertaining the facts and preserving evidence has the right to inspect, test and sample the goods including such of them as may be in the possession or control of the other; and

(b) the parties may agree to a third party inspection or survey to determine the conformity or condition of the goods and may agree that the findings shall be binding upon them in any subsequent litigation or adjustment.

Part 6 Breach, Repudiation and Excuse

§ 2–601. Buyer's Rights on Improper Delivery.

Subject to the provisions of this Article on breach in installment contracts (Section 2–612) and unless otherwise agreed under the sections on contractual limitations of remedy (Sections 2–718 and 2–719), if the goods or the tender of delivery fail in any respect to conform to the contract, the buyer may

(a) reject the whole; or

(b) accept the whole; or

(c) accept any commercial unit or units and reject the rest.

§ 2–602. Manner and Effect of Rightful Rejection.

(1) Rejection of goods must be within a reasonable time after their delivery or tender. It is ineffective unless the buyer seasonably notifies the seller.

(2) Subject to the provisions of the two following sections on rejected goods (Sections 2–603 and 2–604),

(a) after rejection any exercise of ownership by the buyer with respect to any commercial unit is wrongful as against the seller; and

(b) if the buyer has before rejection taken physical possession of goods in which he does not have a security interest under the provisions of this Article (subsection (3) of Section 2–711), he is under a duty after rejection to hold them with reasonable care at the seller's disposition for a time sufficient to permit the seller to remove them; but

(c) the buyer has no further obligations with regard to goods rightfully rejected.

(3) The seller's rights with respect to goods wrongfully rejected are governed by the provisions of this Article on Seller's remedies in general (Section 2–703).

§ 2–603. Merchant Buyer's Duties as to Rightfully Rejected Goods.

(1) Subject to any security interest in the buyer (subsection (3) of Section 2–711), when the seller has no agent or place of business at the market of rejection a merchant buyer is under a duty after rejection of goods in his possession or control to follow any reasonable instructions received from the seller with respect to the goods and in the absence of such instructions to make reasonable efforts to sell them for the seller's account if they are perishable or threaten to decline in value speedily. Instructions are not reasonable if on demand indemnity for expenses is not forthcoming.

(2) When the buyer sells goods under subsection (1), he is entitled to reimbursement from the seller or out of the proceeds for reasonable expenses of caring for and selling them, and if the expenses include no selling commission then to such commission as is usual in the trade or if there is none to a reasonable sum not exceeding ten per cent on the gross proceeds.

(3) In complying with this section the buyer is held only to good faith and good faith conduct hereunder is neither acceptance nor conversion nor the basis of an action for damages.

§ 2–604. Buyer's Options as to Salvage of Rightfully Rejected Goods.

Subject to the provisions of the immediately preceding section on perishables if the seller gives no instructions within a reasonable time after notification of rejection the buyer may store the rejected goods for the seller's account or reship them to him or resell them for the seller's account with reimbursement as provided in the preceding section. Such action is not acceptance or conversion.

§ 2–605. Waiver of Buyer's Objections by Failure to Particularize.

(1) The buyer's failure to state in connection with rejection a particular defect which is ascertainable by reasonable inspection precludes him from relying on the unstated defect to justify rejection or to establish breach

(a) where the seller could have cured it if stated seasonably; or

(b) between merchants when the seller has after rejection made a request in writing for a full and final written statement of all defects on which the buyer proposes to rely.

(2) Payment against documents made without reservation of rights precludes recovery of the payment for defects apparent on the face of the documents.

§ 2–606. What Constitutes Acceptance of Goods.

(1) Acceptance of goods occurs when the buyer

(a) after a reasonable opportunity to inspect the goods signifies to the seller that the goods are conforming or that he will take or retain them in spite of their nonconformity; or

(b) fails to make an effective rejection (subsection (1) of Section 2–602), but such acceptance does not occur until the buyer has had a reasonable opportunity to inspect them; or

(c) does any act inconsistent with the seller's ownership; but if such act is wrongful as against the seller it is an acceptance only if ratified by him.

(2) Acceptance of a part of any commercial unit is acceptance of that entire unit.

§ 2–607. Effect of Acceptance; Notice of Breach; Burden of Establishing Breach After Acceptance; Notice of Claim or Litigation to Person Answerable Over.

(1) The buyer must pay at the contract rate for any goods accepted.

(2) Acceptance of goods by the buyer precludes rejection of the goods accepted and if made with knowledge of a non-conformity cannot be revoked because of it unless the acceptance was on the reasonable assumption that the non-conformity would be seasonably cured but acceptance does not of itself impair any other remedy provided by this Article for non-conformity.

(3) Where a tender has been accepted

(a) the buyer must within a reasonable time after he discovers or should have discovered any breach notify the seller of breach or be barred from any remedy; and

(b) if the claim is one for infringement or the like (subsection (3) of Section 2–312) and the buyer is sued as a result of such a breach he must so notify the seller within a reasonable time after he receives notice of the litigation or be barred from any remedy over for liability established by the litigation.

(4) The burden is on the buyer to establish any breach with respect to the goods accepted.

(5) Where the buyer is sued for breach of a warranty or other obligation for which his seller is answerable over

(a) he may give his seller written notice of the litigation. If the notice states that the seller may come in and defend and that if the seller does not do so he will be bound in any action against him by his buyer by any determination of fact common to the two litigations, then unless the seller after seasonable receipt of the notice does come in and defend he is so bound.

(b) if the claim is one for infringement or the like (subsection (3) of Section 2–312) the original seller may demand in writing that his buyer turn over to him control of the litigation including settlement or else be barred from any remedy over and if he also agrees to bear all expense and to satisfy any adverse judgment, then unless the buyer after seasonable receipt of the demand does turn over control the buyer is so barred.

(6) The provisions of subsections (3), (4) and (5) apply to any obligation of a buyer to hold the seller harmless against infringement or the like (subsection (3) of Section 2–312).

§ 2–608. Revocation of Acceptance in Whole or in Part.

(1) The buyer may revoke his acceptance of a lot or commercial unit whose non-conformity substantially impairs its value to him if he has accepted it

(a) on the reasonable assumption that its nonconformity would be cured and it has not been seasonably cured; or

(b) without discovery of such non-conformity if his acceptance was reasonably induced either by the difficulty of discovery before acceptance or by the seller's assurances.

(2) Revocation of acceptance must occur within a reasonable time after the buyer discovers or should have discovered the ground for it and before any substantial change in condition of the goods which is not caused by their own defects. It is not effective until the buyer notifies the seller of it.

(3) A buyer who so revokes has the same rights and duties with regard to the goods involved as if he had rejected them.

§ 2–609. Right to Adequate Assurance of Performance.

(1) A contract for sale imposes an obligation on each party that the other's expectation of receiving due performance will not be impaired. When reasonable grounds for insecurity arise with respect to the performance of either party the other may in writing demand adequate assurance of due performance and until he receives such assurance may if commercially reasonable suspend any performance for which he has not already received the agreed return.

(2) Between merchants the reasonableness of grounds for insecurity and the adequacy of any assurance offered shall be determined according to commercial standards.

(3) Acceptance of any improper delivery or payment does not prejudice the party's right to demand adequate assurance of future performance.

(4) After receipt of a justified demand failure to provide within a reasonable time not exceeding thirty days such assurance of due performance as is adequate under the circumstances of the particular case is a repudiation of the contract.

§ 2–610. Anticipatory Repudiation.

When either party repudiates the contract with respect to a performance not yet due the loss of which will substantially impair the value of the contract to the other, the aggrieved party may

(a) for a commercially reasonable time await performance by the repudiating party; or

(b) resort to any remedy for breach (Section 2–703 or Section 2–711), even though he has notified the repudiating party that he would await the latter's performance and has urged retraction; and

(c) in either case suspend his own performance or proceed in accordance with the provisions of this Article on the seller's right to identify goods to the contract notwithstanding breach or to salvage unfinished goods (Section 2–704).

§ 2–611. Retraction of Anticipatory Repudiation.

(1) Until the repudiating party's next performance is due he can retract his repudiation unless the aggrieved party has since the repudiation cancelled or materially changed his position or otherwise indicated that he considers the repudiation final.

(2) Retraction may be by any method which clearly indicates to the aggrieved party that the repudiating party intends to perform, but must include any assurance justifiably demanded under the provisions of this Article (Section 2–609).

(3) Retraction reinstates the repudiating party's rights under the contract with due excuse and allowance to the aggrieved party for any delay occasioned by the repudiation.

§ 2–612. "Installment Contract"; Breach.

(1) An "installment contract" is one which requires or authorizes the delivery of goods in separate lots to be separately accepted, even though the contract contains a clause "each delivery is a separate contract" or its equivalent.

(2) The buyer may reject any installment which is non-conforming if the non-conformity substantially impairs the value of that installment and cannot be cured or if the non-conformity is a defect in the required documents; but if the non-conformity does not fall within subsection (3) and the seller gives adequate assurance of its cure the buyer must accept that installment.

(3) Whenever non-conformity or default with respect to one or more installments substantially impairs the value of the whole contract there is a breach of the whole. But the aggrieved party reinstates the contract if he accepts a non-conforming installment without seasonably notifying of cancellation or if he brings an action with respect only to past installments or demands performance as to future installments.

§ 2–613. Casualty to Identified Goods.

Where the contract requires for its performance goods identified when the contract is made, and the goods suffer casualty without fault of either party before the risk of loss passes to the buyer, or in a proper case under a "no arrival, no sale" term (Section 2–324) then

(a) if the loss is total the contract is avoided; and

(b) if the loss is partial or the goods have so deteriorated as no longer to conform to the contract the buyer may nevertheless demand inspection and at his option either treat the contract as voided or accept the goods with due allowance from the contract price for the deterioration or the deficiency in quantity but without further right against the seller.

§ 2–614. Substituted Performance.

(1) Where without fault of either party the agreed berthing, loading, or unloading facilities fail or an agreed type of carrier becomes unavailable or the agreed manner of delivery otherwise becomes commercially impracticable but a commercially reasonable substitute is available, such substitute performance must be tendered and accepted.

(2) If the agreed means or manner of payment fails because of domestic or foreign governmental regulation, the seller may withhold or stop delivery unless the buyer provides a means or manner of payment which is commercially a substantial equivalent. If delivery has already been taken, payment by the means or in the manner provided by the regulation discharges the buyer's obligation unless the regulation is discriminatory, oppressive or predatory.

§ 2–615. Excuse by Failure of Presupposed Conditions.

Except so far as a seller may have assumed a greater obligation and subject to the preceding section on substituted performance:

(a) Delay in delivery or non-delivery in whole or in part by a seller who complies with paragraphs (b) and (c) is not a breach of his duty under a contract for sale if performance as agreed has been made impracticable by the occurrence of a contingency the nonoccurrence of which was a basic assumption on which the contract was made or by compliance in good faith with any applicable foreign or domestic governmental regulation or order whether or not it later proves to be invalid.

(b) Where the causes mentioned in paragraph (a) affect only a part of the seller's capacity to perform, he must allocate production and deliveries among his customers but may at his option include regular customers not then under contract as well as his own requirements for further manufacture. He may so allocate in any manner which is fair and reasonable.

(c) The seller must notify the buyer seasonably that there will be delay or non-delivery and, when allocation is required under paragraph (b), of the estimated quota thus made available for the buyer.

§ 2–616. Procedure on Notice Claiming Excuse.

(1) Where the buyer receives notification of a material or indefinite delay or an allocation justified under the preceding section he may by written notification to the seller as to any delivery concerned, and where the prospective deficiency substantially impairs the value of the whole contract under the provisions of this Article relating to breach of installment contracts (Section 2–612), then also as to the whole,

(a) terminate and thereby discharge any unexecuted portion of the contract; or

(b) modify the contract by agreeing to take his available quota in substitution.

(2) If after receipt of such notification from the seller the buyer fails so to modify the contract within a reasonable time not exceeding thirty days the contract lapses with respect to any deliveries affected.

(3) The provisions of this section may not be negated by agreement except in so far as the seller has assumed a greater obligation under the preceding section.

Part 7 Remedies

§ 2–701. Remedies for Breach of Collateral Contracts Not Impaired.

Remedies for breach of any obligation or promise collateral or ancillary to a contract for sale are not impaired by the provisions of this Article.

§ 2–702. Seller's Remedies on Discovery of Buyer's Insolvency.

(1) Where the seller discovers the buyer to be insolvent he may refuse delivery except for cash including payment for all goods theretofore delivered under the contract, and stop delivery under this Article (Section 2–705).

(2) Where the seller discovers that the buyer has received goods on credit while insolvent he may reclaim the goods upon demand made within ten days after the receipt, but if misrepresentation of solvency has been made to the particular seller in writing within three months before delivery the ten day limitation does not apply. Except as provided in this subsection the seller may not base a right to reclaim goods on the buyer's fraudulent or innocent misrepresentation of solvency or of intent to pay.

(3) The seller's right to reclaim under subsection (2) is subject to the rights of a buyer in ordinary course or other good faith purchaser under this Article (Section 2–403). Successful reclamation of goods excludes all other remedies with respect to them.

§ 2–703. Seller's Remedies in General.

Where the buyer wrongfully rejects or revokes acceptance of goods or fails to make a payment due on or before delivery or repudiates with respect to a part or the whole, then with respect to any goods directly affected and, if the breach is of the whole contract (Section 2–612), then also with respect to the whole undelivered balance, the aggrieved seller may

(a) withhold delivery of such goods;

(b) stop delivery by any bailee as hereafter provided (Section 2–705);

(c) proceed under the next section respecting goods still unidentified to the contract;

(d) resell and recover damages as hereafter provided (Section 2–706);

(e) recover damages for non-acceptance (Section 2–708) or in a proper case the price (Section 2–709);

(f) cancel.

§ 2–704. Seller's Right to Identify Goods to the Contract Notwithstanding Breach or to Salvage Unfinished Goods.

(1) An aggrieved seller under the preceding section may

(a) identify to the contract conforming goods not already identified if at the time he learned of the breach they are in his possession or control;

(b) treat as the subject of resale goods which have demonstrably been intended for the particular contract even though those goods are unfinished.

(2) Where the goods are unfinished an aggrieved seller may in the exercise of reasonable commercial judgment for the purposes of avoiding loss and of effective realization either complete the manufacture and wholly identify the goods to the contract or cease manufacture and resell for scrap or salvage value or proceed in any other reasonable manner.

§ 2–705. Seller's Stoppage of Delivery in Transit or Otherwise.

(1) The seller may stop delivery of goods in the possession of a carrier or other bailee when he discovers the buyer to be insolvent (Section 2–702) and may stop delivery of carload, truckload, planeload or larger shipments of express or freight when the buyer repudiates or fails to make a payment due before delivery or if for any other reason the seller has a right to withhold or reclaim the goods.

(2) As against such buyer the seller may stop delivery until

(a) receipt of the goods by the buyer; or

(b) acknowledgment to the buyer by any bailee of the goods except a carrier that the bailee holds the goods for the buyer; or

(c) such acknowledgment to the buyer by a carrier by reshipment or as warehouseman; or

(d) negotiation to the buyer of any negotiable document of title covering the goods.

(3) (a) To stop delivery the seller must so notify as to enable the bailee by reasonable diligence to prevent delivery of the goods.

(b) After such notification the bailee must hold and deliver the goods according to the directions of the seller but the seller is liable to the bailee for any ensuing charges or damages.

(c) If a negotiable document of title has been issued for goods the bailee is not obliged to obey a notification to stop until surrender of the document.

(d) A carrier who has issued a non-negotiable bill of lading is not obliged to obey a notification to stop received from a person other than the consignor.

§ 2–706. Seller's Resale Including Contract for Resale.

(1) Under the conditions stated in Section 2–703 on seller's remedies, the seller may resell the goods concerned or the undelivered balance thereof. Where the resale is made in good faith and in a commercially reasonable manner the seller may recover the difference between the resale price and the contract price together with any incidental damages allowed under the provisions of this Article (Section 2–710), but less expenses saved in consequence of the buyer's breach.

(2) Except as otherwise provided in subsection (3) or unless otherwise agreed resale may be at public or private sale including sale by way of one or more contracts to sell or of identification to an existing contract of the seller. Sale may be as a unit or in parcels and at any time and place and on any terms but every aspect of the sale including the method, manner, time, place and terms must be commercially reasonable. The resale must be reasonably identified as referring to the broken contract, but it is not necessary that the goods be in existence or that any or all of them have been identified to the contract before the breach.

(3) Where the resale is at private sale the seller must give the buyer reasonable notification of his intention to resell.

(4) Where the resale is at public sale

(a) only identified goods can be sold except where there is a recognized market for a public sale of futures in goods of the kind; and

(b) it must be made at a usual place or market for public sale if one is reasonably available and except in the case of goods which are perishable or threaten to decline in value speedily the seller must give the buyer reasonable notice of the time and place of the resale; and

(c) if the goods are not to be within the view of those attending the sale the notification of sale must state the place where the goods are located and provide for their reasonable inspection by prospective bidders; and

(d) the seller may buy.

(5) A purchaser who buys in good faith at a resale takes the goods free of any rights of the original buyer even though the seller fails to comply with one or more of the requirements of this section.

(6) The seller is not accountable to the buyer for any profit made on any resale. A person in the position of a seller (Section 2–707) or a buyer who has rightfully rejected or justifiably revoked acceptance must account for any excess over the amount of his security interest, as hereinafter defined (subsection (3) of Section 2–711).

§ 2–707. "Person in the Position of a Seller".

(1) A "person in the position of a seller" includes as against a principal an agent who has paid or become responsible for the price of goods on behalf of his principal or anyone who otherwise holds a security interest or other right in goods similar to that of a seller.

(2) A person in the position of a seller may as provided in this Article withhold or stop delivery (Section 2–705) and resell (Section 2–706) and recover incidental damages (Section 2–710).

§ 2–708. Seller's Damages for Non-Acceptance or Repudiation.

(1) Subject to subsection (2) and to the provisions of this Article with respect to proof of market price (Section 2–723),

the measure of damages for non-acceptance or repudiation by the buyer is the difference between the market price at the time and place for tender and the unpaid contract price together with any incidental damages provided in this Article (Section 2–710), but less expenses saved in consequence of the buyer's breach.

(2) If the measure of damages provided in subsection (1) is inadequate to put the seller in as good a position as performance would have done then the measure of damages is the profit (including reasonable overhead) which the seller would have made from full performance by the buyer, together with any incidental damages provided in this Article (Section 2–710), due allowance for costs reasonably incurred and due credit for payments or proceeds of resale.

§ 2–709. **Action for the Price.**

(1) When the buyer fails to pay the price as it becomes due the seller may recover, together with any incidental damages under the next section, the price

(a) of goods accepted or of conforming goods lost or damaged within a commercially reasonable time after risk of their loss has passed to the buyer; and

(b) of goods identified to the contract if the seller is unable after reasonable effort to resell them at a reasonable price or the circumstances reasonably indicate that such effort will be unavailing.

(2) Where the seller sues for the price he must hold for the buyer any goods which have been identified to the contract and are still in his control except that if resale becomes possible he may resell them at any time prior to the collection of the judgment. The net proceeds of any such resale must be credited to the buyer and payment of the judgment entitles him to any goods not resold.

(3) After the buyer has wrongfully rejected or revoked acceptance of the goods or has failed to make a payment due or has repudiated (Section 2–610), a seller who is held not entitled to the price under this section shall nevertheless be awarded damages for non-acceptance under the preceding section.

§ 2–710. **Seller's Incidental Damages.**

Incidental damages to an aggrieved seller include any commercially reasonable charges, expenses or commissions incurred in stopping delivery, in the transportation, care and custody of goods after the buyer's breach, in connection with return or resale of the goods or otherwise resulting from the breach.

§ 2–711. **Buyer's Remedies in General; Buyer's Security Interest in Rejected Goods.**

(1) Where the seller fails to make delivery or repudiates or the buyer rightfully rejects or justifiably revokes acceptance then with respect to any goods involved, and with respect to the whole if the breach goes to the whole contract (Section 2–612), the buyer may cancel and whether or not he has done so may in addition to recovering so much of the price as has been paid

(a) "cover" and have damages under the next section as to all the goods affected whether or not they have been identified to the contract; or

(b) recover damages for non-delivery as provided in this Article (Section 2–713).

(2) Where the seller fails to deliver or repudiates the buyer may also

(a) if the goods have been identified recover them as provided in this Article (Section 2–502); or

(b) in a proper case obtain specific performance or replevy the goods as provided in this Article (Section 2–716).

(3) On rightful rejection or justifiable revocation of acceptance a buyer has a security interest in goods in his possession or control for any payments made on their price and any expenses reasonably incurred in their inspection, receipt, transportation, care and custody and may hold such goods and resell them in like manner as an aggrieved seller (Section 2–706).

§ 2–712. **"Cover"; Buyer's Procurement of Substitute Goods.**

(1) After a breach within the preceding section the buyer may "cover" by making in good faith and without unreasonable delay any reasonable purchase of or contract to purchase goods in substitution for those due from the seller.

(2) The buyer may recover from the seller as damages the difference between the cost of cover and the contract price together with any incidental or consequential damages as hereinafter defined (Section 2–715), but less expenses saved in consequence of the seller's breach.

(3) Failure of the buyer to effect cover within this section does not bar him from any other remedy.

§ 2–713. **Buyer's Damages for Non-Delivery or Repudiation.**

(1) Subject to the provisions of this Article with respect to proof of market price (Section 2–723), the measure of damages for non-delivery or repudiation by the seller is the difference between the market price at the time when the buyer learned of the breach and the contract price together with any incidental and consequential damages provided in this Article (Section 2–715), but less expenses saved in consequence of the seller's breach.

(2) Market price is to be determined as of the place for tender or, in cases of rejection after arrival or revocation of acceptance, as of the place of arrival.

§ 2–714. **Buyer's Damages for Breach in Regard to Accepted Goods.**

(1) Where the buyer has accepted goods and given notification (subsection (3) of Section 2–607) he may recover as damages for any non-conformity of tender the loss resulting in the ordinary course of events from the seller's breach as determined in any manner which is reasonable.

(2) The measure of damages for breach of warranty is the difference at the time and place of acceptance between the value of

the goods accepted and the value they would have had if they had been as warranted, unless special circumstances show proximate damages of a different amount.

(3) In a proper case any incidental and consequential damages under the next section may also be recovered.

§ 2–715. **Buyer's Incidental and Consequential Damages.**

(1) Incidental damages resulting from the seller's breach include expenses reasonably incurred in inspection, receipt, transportation and care and custody of goods rightfully rejected, any commercially reasonable charges, expenses or commissions in connection with effecting cover and any other reasonable expense incident to the delay or other breach.

(2) Consequential damages resulting from the seller's breach include

(a) any loss resulting from general or particular requirements and needs of which the seller at the time of contracting had reason to know and which could not reasonably be prevented by cover or otherwise; and

(b) injury to person or property proximately resulting from any breach of warranty.

§ 2–716. **Buyer's Right to Specific Performance or Replevin.**

(1) Specific performance may be decreed where the goods are unique or in other proper circumstances.

(2) The decree for specific performance may include such terms and conditions as to payment of the price, damages, or other relief as the court may deem just.

(3) The buyer has a right of replevin for goods identified to the contract if after reasonable effort he is unable to effect cover for such goods or the circumstances reasonably indicate that such effort will be unavailing or if the goods have been shipped under reservation and satisfaction of the security interest in them has been made or tendered. In the case of goods bought for personal, family, or household purposes, the buyer's right of replevin vests upon acquisition of a special property, even if the seller had not then repudiated or failed to deliver.

As amended in 1999.

§ 2–717. **Deduction of Damages From the Price.**

The buyer on notifying the seller of his intention to do so may deduct all or any part of the damages resulting from any breach of the contract from any part of the price still due under the same contract.

§ 2–718. **Liquidation or Limitation of Damages; Deposits.**

(1) Damages for breach by either party may be liquidated in the agreement but only at an amount which is reasonable in the light of the anticipated or actual harm caused by the breach, the difficulties of proof of loss, and the inconvenience or nonfeasibility of otherwise obtaining an adequate remedy. A term fixing unreasonably large liquidated damages is void as a penalty.

(2) Where the seller justifiably withholds delivery of goods because of the buyer's breach, the buyer is entitled to restitution of any amount by which the sum of his payments exceeds

(a) the amount to which the seller is entitled by virtue of terms liquidating the seller's damages in accordance with subsection (1), or

(b) in the absence of such terms, twenty per cent of the value of the total performance for which the buyer is obligated under the contract or $500, whichever is smaller.

(3) The buyer's right to restitution under subsection (2) is subject to offset to the extent that the seller establishes

(a) a right to recover damages under the provisions of this Article other than subsection (1), and

(b) the amount or value of any benefits received by the buyer directly or indirectly by reason of the contract.

(4) Where a seller has received payment in goods their reasonable value or the proceeds of their resale shall be treated as payments for the purposes of subsection (2); but if the seller has notice of the buyer's breach before reselling goods received in part performance, his resale is subject to the conditions laid down in this Article on resale by an aggrieved seller (Section 2–706).

§ 2–719. **Contractual Modification or Limitation of Remedy.**

(1) Subject to the provisions of subsections (2) and (3) of this section and of the preceding section on liquidation and limitation of damages,

(a) the agreement may provide for remedies in addition to or in substitution for those provided in this Article and may limit or alter the measure of damages recoverable under this Article, as by limiting the buyer's remedies to return of the goods and repayment of the price or to repair and replacement of nonconforming goods or parts; and

(b) resort to a remedy as provided is optional unless the remedy is expressly agreed to be exclusive, in which case it is the sole remedy.

(2) Where circumstances cause an exclusive or limited remedy to fail of its essential purpose, remedy may be had as provided in this Act.

(3) Consequential damages may be limited or excluded unless the limitation or exclusion is unconscionable. Limitation of consequential damages for injury to the person in the case of consumer goods is prima facie unconscionable but limitation of damages where the loss is commercial is not.

§ 2–720. **Effect of "Cancellation" or "Rescission" on Claims for Antecedent Breach.**

Unless the contrary intention clearly appears, expressions of "cancellation" or "rescission" of the contract or the like shall not be construed as a renunciation or discharge of any claim in damages for an antecedent breach.

§ 2–721. **Remedies for Fraud.**

Remedies for material misrepresentation or fraud include all remedies available under this Article for non-fraudulent breach.

Neither rescission or a claim for rescission of the contract for sale nor rejection or return of the goods shall bar or be deemed inconsistent with a claim for damages or other remedy.

§ 2–722. Who Can Sue Third Parties for Injury to Goods.

Where a third party so deals with goods which have been identified to a contract for sale as to cause actionable injury to a party to that contract

(a) a right of action against the third party is in either party to the contract for sale who has title to or a security interest or a special property or an insurable interest in the goods; and if the goods have been destroyed or converted a right of action is also in the party who either bore the risk of loss under the contract for sale or has since the injury assumed that risk as against the other;

(b) if at the time of the injury the party plaintiff did not bear the risk of loss as against the other party to the contract for sale and there is no arrangement between them for disposition of the recovery, his suit or settlement is, subject to his own interest, as a fiduciary for the other party to the contract;

(c) either party may with the consent of the other sue for the benefit of whom it may concern.

§ 2–723. Proof of Market Price: Time and Place.

(1) If an action based on anticipatory repudiation comes to trial before the time for performance with respect to some or all of the goods, any damages based on market price (Section 2–708 or Section 2–713) shall be determined according to the price of such goods prevailing at the time when the aggrieved party learned of the repudiation.

(2) If evidence of a price prevailing at the times or places described in this Article is not readily available the price prevailing within any reasonable time before or after the time described or at any other place which in commercial judgment or under usage of trade would serve as a reasonable substitute for the one described may be used, making any proper allowance for the cost of transporting the goods to or from such other place.

(3) Evidence of a relevant price prevailing at a time or place other than the one described in this Article offered by one party is not admissible unless and until he has given the other party such notice as the court finds sufficient to prevent unfair surprise.

§ 2–724. Admissibility of Market Quotations.

Whenever the prevailing price or value of any goods regularly bought and sold in any established commodity market is in issue, reports in official publications or trade journals or in newspapers or periodicals of general circulation published as the reports of such market shall be admissible in evidence. The circumstances of the preparation of such a report may be shown to affect its weight but not its admissibility.

§ 2–725. Statute of Limitations in Contracts for Sale.

(1) An action for breach of any contract for sale must be commenced within four years after the cause of action has accrued. By the original agreement the parties may reduce the period of limitation to not less than one year but may not extend it.

(2) A cause of action accrues when the breach occurs, regardless of the aggrieved party's lack of knowledge of the breach. A breach of warranty occurs when tender of delivery is made, except that where a warranty explicitly extends to future performance of the goods and discovery of the breach must await the time of such performance the cause of action accrues when the breach is or should have been discovered.

(3) Where an action commenced within the time limited by subsection (1) is so terminated as to leave available a remedy by another action for the same breach such other action may be commenced after the expiration of the time limited and within six months after the termination of the first action unless the termination resulted from voluntary discontinuance or from dismissal for failure or neglect to prosecute.

(4) This section does not alter the law on tolling of the statute of limitations nor does it apply to causes of action which have accrued before this Act becomes effective.

Article 2 Amendments (Excerpts)[1]

Part 1 Short Title, General Construction and Subject Matter

* * * *

§ 2–103. Definitions and Index of Definitions.

(1) In this article unless the context otherwise requires

* * * *

(b) "Conspicuous", with reference to a term, means so written, displayed, or presented that a reasonable person against which it is to operate ought to have noticed it. A term in an electronic record intended to evoke a response by an electronic agent is conspicuous if it is presented in a form that would enable a reasonably configured electronic agent to take it into account or react to it without review of the record by an individual. Whether a term is "conspicuous" or not is a decision for the court. Conspicuous terms include the following:

(i) for a person:

(A) a heading in capitals equal to or greater in size than the surrounding text, or in contrasting type, font, or color to the surrounding text of the same or lesser size and;

(B) language in the body of a record or display in larger type than the surrounding text, or in contrasting type, font, or color to the surrounding text of the

1. Additions and new wording are underlined. What follows represents only selected changes made by the 2003 amendments. Although the National Conference of Commissioners on Uniform State Laws and the American Law Institute approved the amendments in May of 2003, as of this writing, they have not as yet been adopted by any state.

same size, or set off from surrounding text of the same size by symbols or other marks that call attention to the language; and

(ii) for a person or an electronic agent, a term that is so placed in a record or display that the person or electronic agent cannot proceed without taking action with respect to the particular term.

(c) "Consumer" means an individual who buys or contracts to buy goods that, at the time of contracting, are intended by the individual to be used primarily for personal, family, or household purposes.

(d) "Consumer contract" means a contract between a merchant seller and a consumer.

* * * *

(j) "Good faith" means honesty in fact and the observance of reasonable commercial standards of fair dealing.

(k) "Goods" means all things that are movable at the time of identification to a contract for sale. The term includes future goods, specially manufactured goods, the unborn young of animals, growing crops, and other identified things attached to realty as described in Section 2–107. The term does not include information, the money in which the price is to be paid, investment securities under Article 8, the subject matter of foreign exchange transactions, and choses in action.

* * * *

(m) "Record" means information that is inscribed on a tangible medium or that is stored in an electronic or other medium and is retrievable in perceivable form.

(n) "Remedial promise" means a promise by the seller to repair or replace the goods or to refund all or part of the price upon the happening of a specified event.

* * * *

(p) "Sign" means, with present intent to authenticate or adopt a record,

(i) to execute or adopt a tangible symbol; or

(ii) to attach to or logically associate with the record an electronic sound, symbol, or process.

* * * *

Part 2 Form, Formation, Terms and Readjustment of Contract; Electronic Contracting

§ 2–201. Formal Requirements; Statute of Frauds.

(1) A contract for the sale of goods for the price of $5,000 or more is not enforceable by way of action or defense unless there is some record sufficient to indicate that a contract for sale has been made between the parties and signed by the party against which enforcement is sought or by the party's authorized agent or broker. A record is not insufficient because it omits or incorrectly states a term agreed upon but the contract is not enforceable under this subsection beyond the quantity of goods shown in the record.

(2) Between merchants if within a reasonable time a record in confirmation of the contract and sufficient against the sender is received and the party receiving it has reason to know its contents, it satisfies the requirements of subsection (1) against the recipient unless notice of objection to its contents is given in a record within 10 days after it is received.

(3) A contract which does not satisfy the requirements of subsection (1) but which is valid in other respects is enforceable

(a) if the goods are to be specially manufactured for the buyer and are not suitable for sale to others in the ordinary course of the seller's business and the seller, before notice of repudiation is received and under circumstances which reasonably indicate that the goods are for the buyer, has made either a substantial beginning of their manufacture or commitments for their procurement; or

(b) if the party against which enforcement is sought admits in the party's pleading, or in the party's testimony or otherwise under oath that a contract for sale was made, but the contract is not enforceable under this paragraph beyond the quantity of goods admitted; or

(c) with respect to goods for which payment has been made and accepted or which have been received and accepted (Sec. 2–606).

(4) A contract that is enforceable under this section is not rendered unenforceable merely because it is not capable of being performed within one year or any other applicable period after its making.

* * * *

§ 2–207. Terms of Contract; Effect of Confirmation.

Subject to Section 2–202, if (i) conduct by both parties recognizes the existence of a contract although their records do not otherwise establish a contract, (ii) a contract is formed by an offer and acceptance, or (iii) a contract formed in any manner is confirmed by a record that contains terms additional to or different from those in the contract being confirmed, the terms of the contract, are:

(a) terms that appear in the records of both parties;

(b) terms, whether in a record or not, to which both parties agree; and

(c) terms supplied or incorporated under any provision of this Act.

* * * *

Part 3 General Obligation and Construction of Contract

* * * *

§ 2–312. Warranty of Title and Against Infringement; Buyer's Obligation Against Infringement.

(1) Subject to subsection (3) there is in a contract for sale a warranty by the seller that

(a) the title conveyed shall be, good and its transfer rightful and shall not, unreasonably expose the buyer to litigation because of any colorable claim to or interest in the goods; and

(b) the goods shall be delivered free from any security interest or other lien or encumbrance of which the buyer at the time of contracting has no knowledge.

(2) Unless otherwise agreed a seller that is a merchant regularly dealing in goods of the kind warrants that the goods shall be delivered free of the rightful claim of any third person by way of infringement or the like but a buyer that furnishes specifications to the seller must hold the seller harmless against any such claim that arises out of compliance with the specifications.

(3) A warranty under this section may be disclaimed or modified only by specific language or by circumstances that give the buyer reason to know that the seller does not claim title, that the seller is purporting to sell only the right or title as the seller or a third person may have, or that the seller is selling subject to any claims of infringement or the like.

§ 2–313. Express Warranties by Affirmation, Promise, Description, Sample; Remedial Promise.

(1) In this section, "immediate buyer" means a buyer that enters into a contract with the seller.

* * * *

(4) Any remedial promise made by the seller to the immediate buyer creates an obligation that the promise will be performed upon the happening of the specified event.

§ 2–313A. Obligation to Remote Purchaser Created by Record Packaged with or Accompanying Goods.

(1) In this section:

(a) "Immediate buyer" means a buyer that enters into a contract with the seller.

(b) "Remote purchaser" means a person that buys or leases goods from an immediate buyer or other person in the normal chain of distribution.

(2) This section applies only to new goods and goods sold or leased as new goods in a transaction of purchase in the normal chain of distribution.

(3) If in a record packaged with or accompanying the goods the seller makes an affirmation of fact or promise that relates to the goods, provides a description that relates to the goods, or makes a remedial promise, and the seller reasonably expects the record to be, and the record is, furnished to the remote purchaser, the seller has an obligation to the remote purchaser that:

(a) the goods will conform to the affirmation of fact, promise or description unless a reasonable person in the position of the remote purchaser would not believe that the affirmation of fact, promise or description created an obligation; and

(b) the seller will perform the remedial promise.

(4) It is not necessary to the creation of an obligation under this section that the seller use formal words such as "warrant" or "guarantee" or that the seller have a specific intention to undertake an obligation, but an affirmation merely of the value of the goods or a statement purporting to be merely the seller's opinion or commendation of the goods does not create an obligation.

(5) The following rules apply to the remedies for breach of an obligation created under this section:

(a) The seller may modify or limit the remedies available to the remote purchaser if the modification or limitation is furnished to the remote purchaser no later than the time of purchase or if the modification or limitation is contained in the record that contains the affirmation of fact, promise or description.

(b) Subject to a modification or limitation of remedy, a seller in breach is liable for incidental or consequential damages under Section 2–715, but not for lost profits.

(c) The remote purchaser may recover as damages for breach of a seller's obligation arising under subsection (2) the loss resulting in the ordinary course of events as determined in any reasonable manner.

(5) An obligation that is not a remedial promise is breached if the goods did not conform to the affirmation of fact, promise or description creating the obligation when the goods left the seller's control.

§ 2–313B. Obligation to Remote Purchaser Created by Communication to the Public.

(1) In this section:

(a) "Immediate buyer" means a buyer that enters into a contract with the seller.

(b) "Remote purchaser" means a person that buys or leases goods from an immediate buyer or other person in the normal chain of distribution.

(2) This section applies only to new goods and goods sold or leased as new goods in a transaction of purchase in the normal chain of distribution.

(3) If in an advertisement or a similar communication to the public a seller makes an affirmation of fact or promise that relates to the goods, provides a description that relates to the goods, or makes a remedial promise, and the remote purchaser enters into a transaction of purchase with knowledge of and with the expectation that the goods will conform to the affirmation of fact, promise, or description, or that the seller will perform the remedial promise, the seller has an obligation to the remote purchaser that:

(a) the goods will conform to the affirmation of fact, promise or description unless a reasonable person in the position of the remote purchaser would not believe that the affirmation of fact, promise or description created an obligation; and

(b) the seller will perform the remedial promise.

(4) It is not necessary to the creation of an obligation under this section that the seller use formal words such as "warrant" or "guarantee" or that the seller have a specific intention to undertake an obligation, but an affirmation merely of the value of the goods or a statement purporting to be merely the seller's opinion or commendation of the goods does not create an obligation.

(5) The following rules apply to the remedies for breach of an obligation created under this section:

(a) The seller may modify or limit the remedies available to the remote purchaser if the modification or limitation is furnished to the remote purchaser no later than the time of purchase. The modification or limitation may be furnished as part of the communication that contains the affirmation of fact, promise or description.

(b) Subject to a modification or limitation of remedy, a seller in breach is liable for incidental or consequential damages under Section 2–715, but not for lost profits.

(c) The remote purchaser may recover as damages for breach of a seller's obligation arising under subsection (2) the loss resulting in the ordinary course of events as determined in any reasonable manner.

(6) An obligation that is not a remedial promise is breached if the goods did not conform to the affirmation of fact, promise or description creating the obligation when the goods left the seller's control.

* * * *

§ 2–316. Exclusion or Modification of Warranties.

* * * *

(2) Subject to subsection (3), to exclude or modify the implied warranty of merchantability or any part of it in a consumer contract the language must be in a record, be conspicuous, and state "The seller undertakes no responsibility for the quality of the goods except as otherwise provided in this contract," and in any other contract the language must mention merchantability and in case of a record must be conspicuous. Subject to subsection (3), to exclude or modify the implied warranty of fitness the exclusion must be in a record and be conspicuous. Language to exclude all implied warranties of fitness in a consumer contract must state "The seller assumes no responsibility that the goods will be fit for any particular purpose for which you may be buying these goods, except as otherwise provided in the contract," and in any other contract the language is sufficient if it states, for example, that "There are no warranties that extend beyond the description on the face hereof." Language that satisfies the requirements of this subsection for the exclusion and modification of a warranty in a consumer contract also satisfies the requirements for any other contract.

(3) Notwithstanding subsection (2):

(a) unless the circumstances indicate otherwise, all implied warranties are excluded by expressions like "as is", "with all faults" or other language which in common understanding calls the buyer's attention to the exclusion of warranties, makes plain that there is no implied warranty, and in a consumer contract evidenced by a record is set forth conspicuously in the record; and

(b) when the buyer before entering into the contract has examined the goods or the sample or model as fully as desired or has refused to examine the goods after a demand by the seller there is no implied warranty with regard to defects which an examination ought in the circumstances to have revealed to the buyer; and

(c) an implied warranty can also be excluded or modified by course of dealing or course of performance or usage of trade.

* * * *

§ 2–318. Third Party Beneficiaries of Warranties and Obligations.

(1) In this section:

(a) "Immediate buyer" means a buyer that enters into a contract with the seller.

(b) "Remote purchaser" means a person that buys or leases goods from an immediate buyer or other person in the normal chain of distribution.

Alternative A to subsection (2)

(2) A seller's warranty to an immediate buyer, whether express or implied, a seller's remedial promise to an immediate buyer, or a seller's obligation to a remote purchaser under Section 2–313A or 2–313B extends to any natural person who is in the family or household of the immediate buyer or the remote purchaser or who is a guest in the home of either if it is reasonable to expect that the person may use, consume or be affected by the goods and who is injured in person by breach of the warranty, remedial promise or obligation. A seller may not exclude or limit the operation of this section.

Alternative B to subsection (2)

(2) A seller's warranty to an immediate buyer, whether express or implied, a seller's remedial promise to an immediate buyer, or a seller's obligation to a remote purchaser under Section 2–313A or 2–313B extends to any natural person who may reasonably be expected to use, consume or be affected by the goods and who is injured in person by breach of the warranty, remedial promise or obligation. A seller may not exclude or limit the operation of this section.

Alternative C to subsection (2)

(2) A seller's warranty to an immediate buyer, whether express or implied, a seller's remedial promise to an immediate buyer, or a seller's obligation to a remote purchaser under Section

2–313A or 2–313B extends to any person that may reasonably be expected to use, consume or be affected by the goods and that is injured by breach of the warranty, remedial promise or obligation. A seller may not exclude or limit the operation of this section with respect to injury to the person of an individual to whom the warranty, remedial promise or obligation extends.

* * * *

Part 5 Performance

* * * *

§ 2–502. Buyer's Right to Goods on Seller's Insolvency.

(1) Subject to subsections (2) and (3) and even though the goods have not been shipped a buyer that has paid a part or all of the price of goods in which the buyer has a special property under the provisions of the immediately preceding section may on making and keeping good a tender of any unpaid portion of their price recover them from the seller if:

(a) in the case of goods bought by a consumer, the seller repudiates or fails to deliver as required by the contract; or

(b) in all cases, the seller becomes insolvent within ten days after receipt of the first installment on their price.

(2) The buyer's right to recover the goods under subsection (1) vests upon acquisition of a special property, even if the seller had not then repudiated or failed to deliver.

(3) If the identification creating the special property has been made by the buyer, the buyer acquires the right to recover the goods only if they conform to the contract for sale.

* * * *

§ 2–508. Cure by Seller of Improper Tender or Delivery; Replacement.

(1) Where the buyer rejects goods or a tender of delivery under Section 2–601 or 2–612 or, except in a consumer contract, justifiably revokes acceptance under Section 2–608(1)(b) and the agreed time for performance has not expired, a seller that has performed in good faith, upon seasonable notice to the buyer and at the seller's own expense, may cure the breach of contract by making a conforming tender of delivery within the agreed time. The seller shall compensate the buyer for all of the buyer's reasonable expenses caused by the seller's breach of contract and subsequent cure.

(2) Where the buyer rejects goods or a tender of delivery under Section 2–601 or 2–612 or except in a consumer contract justifiably revokes acceptance under Section 2–608(1)(b) and the agreed time for performance has expired, a seller that has performed in good faith, upon seasonable notice to the buyer and at the seller's own expense, may cure the breach of contract, if the cure is appropriate and timely under the circumstances, by making a tender of conforming goods. The seller shall compensate the buyer for all of the buyer's reasonable expenses caused by the seller's breach of contract and subsequent cure.

§ 2–509. Risk of Loss in the Absence of Breach.

(1) Where the contract requires or authorizes the seller to ship the goods by carrier

(a) if it does not require the seller to deliver them at a particular destination, the risk of loss passes to the buyer when the goods are delivered to the carrier even though the shipment is under reservation (Section 2–505); but

(b) if it does require the seller to deliver them at a particular destination and the goods are there tendered while in the possession of the carrier, the risk of loss passes to the buyer when the goods are there so tendered as to enable the buyer to take delivery.

(2) Where the goods are held by a bailee to be delivered without being moved, the risk of loss passes to the buyer

(a) on the buyer's receipt of a negotiable document of title covering the goods; or

(b) on acknowledgment by the bailee to the buyer of the buyer's right to possession of the goods; or

(c) after the buyer's receipt of a non-negotiable document of title or other direction to deliver in a record, as provided in subsection (4)(b) of Section 2–503.

(3) In any case not within subsection (1) or (2), the risk of loss passes to the buyer on the buyer's receipt of the goods.

(4) The provisions of this section are subject to contrary agreement of the parties and to the provisions of this Article on sale on approval (Section 2–327) and on effect of breach on risk of loss (Section 2–510).

* * * *

§ 2–513. Buyer's Right to Inspection of Goods.

* * * *

(3) Unless otherwise agreed, the buyer is not entitled to inspect the goods before payment of the price when the contract provides

(a) for delivery on terms that under applicable course of performance, course of dealing, or usage of trade are interpreted to preclude inspection before payment; or

(b) for payment against documents of title, except where such payment is due only after the goods are to become available for inspection.

* * * *

Part 6 Breach, Repudiation and Excuse

* * * *

§ 2–605. Waiver of Buyer's Objections by Failure to Particularize.

(1) The buyer's failure to state in connection with rejection a particular defect or in connection with revocation of acceptance a defect that justifies revocation precludes the buyer from relying

on the unstated defect to justify rejection or revocation of acceptance if the defect is ascertainable by reasonable inspection

(a) where the seller had a right to cure the defect and could have cured it if stated seasonably; or

(b) between merchants when the seller has after rejection made a request in a record for a full and final statement in record form of all defects on which the buyer proposes to rely.

(2) A buyer's payment against documents tendered to the buyer made without reservation of rights precludes recovery of the payment for defects apparent on the face of the documents.

* * * *

§ 2–607. Effect of Acceptance; Notice of Breach; Burden of Establishing Breach After Acceptance; Notice of Claim or Litigation to Person Answerable Over.

* * * *

(3) Where a tender has been accepted

(a) the buyer must within a reasonable time after the buyer discovers or should have discovered any breach notify the seller. However, failure to give timely notice bars the buyer from a remedy only to the extent that the seller is prejudiced by the failure and

(b) if the claim is one for infringement or the like (subsection (3) of Section 2–312) and the buyer is sued as a result of such a breach the buyer must so notify the seller within a reasonable time after the buyer receives notice of the litigation or be barred from any remedy over for liability established by the litigation.

* * * *

§ 2–608. Revocation of Acceptance in Whole or in Part.

* * * *

(4) If a buyer uses the goods after a rightful rejection or justifiable revocation of acceptance, the following rules apply:

(a) Any use by the buyer which is unreasonable under the circumstances is wrongful as against the seller and is an acceptance only if ratified by the seller.

(b) Any use of the goods which is reasonable under the circumstances is not wrongful as against the seller and is not an acceptance, but in an appropriate case the buyer shall be obligated to the seller for the value of the use to the buyer.

* * * *

§ 2–612. "Installment Contract"; Breach.

* * * *

(2) The buyer may reject any installment which is non-conforming if the non-conformity substantially impairs the value of that installment to the buyer or if the non-conformity is a defect in the required documents; but if the non-conformity does not fall within subsection (3) and the seller gives adequate assurance of its cure the buyer must accept that installment.

(3) Whenever non-conformity or default with respect to one or more installments substantially impairs the value of the whole contract there is a breach of the whole. But the aggrieved party reinstates the contract if the party accepts a non-conforming installment without seasonably notifying of cancellation or if the party brings an action with respect only to past installments or demands performance as to future installments.

* * * *

Part 7 Remedies

§ 2–702. Seller's Remedies on Discovery of Buyer's Insolvency.

* * * *

(2) Where the seller discovers that the buyer has received goods on credit while insolvent the seller may reclaim the goods upon demand made within a reasonable time after the buyer's receipt of the goods. Except as provided in this subsection the seller may not base a right to reclaim goods on the buyer's fraudulent or innocent misrepresentation of solvency or of intent to pay.

* * * *

§ 2–703. Seller's Remedies in General.

(1) A breach of contract by the buyer includes the buyer's wrongful rejection or wrongful attempt to revoke acceptance of goods, wrongful failure to perform a contractual obligation, failure to make a payment when due, and repudiation.

(2) If the buyer is in breach of contract the seller, to the extent provided for by this Act or other law, may:

(a) withhold delivery of the goods:

(b) stop delivery of the goods under Section 2–705;

(c) proceed under Section 2–704 with respect to goods unidentified to the contract or unfinished;

(d) reclaim the goods under Section 2–507(2) or 2–702(2);

(e) require payment directly from the buyer under Section 2–325(c);

(f) cancel;

(g) resell and recover damages under Section 2–706;

(h) recover damages for nonacceptance or repudiation under Section 2–708(1);

(i) recover lost profits under Section 2–708(2);

(j) recover the price under Section 2–709;

(k) obtain specific performance under Section 2–716;

(l) recover liquidated damages under Section 2–718;

(m) in other cases, recover damages in any manner that is reasonable under the circumstances.

(3) If a buyer becomes insolvent, the seller may:

(a) withhold delivery under Section 2–702(1);

(b) stop delivery of the goods under Section 2–705;

(c) reclaim the goods under Section 2–702(2).

* * * *

§ 2–705. Seller's Stoppage of Delivery in Transit or Otherwise.

(1) The seller may stop delivery of goods in the possession of a carrier or other bailee when the seller discovers the buyer to be insolvent (Section 2–702) or when the buyer repudiates or fails to make a payment due before delivery or if for any other reason the seller has a right to withhold or reclaim the goods.

* * * *

§ 2–706. Seller's Resale Including Contract for Resale.

(1) In an appropriate case involving breach by the buyer, the seller may resell the goods concerned or the undelivered balance thereof. Where the resale is made in good faith and in a commercially reasonable manner the seller may recover the difference between the contract price and the resale price together with any incidental or consequential damages allowed under the provisions of this Article (Section 2–710), but less expenses saved in consequence of the buyer's breach.

* * * *

§ 2–708. Seller's Damages for Non-Acceptance or Repudiation.

(1) Subject to subsection (2) and to the provisions of this Article with respect to proof of market price (Section 2–723)

(a) the measure of damages for non-acceptance by the buyer is the difference between the contract price and the market price at the time and place for tender together with any incidental or consequential damages provided in this Article (Section 2–710), but less expenses saved in consequence of the buyer's breach; and

(b) the measure of damages for repudiation by the buyer is the difference between the contract price and the market price at the place for tender at the expiration of a commercially reasonable time after the seller learned of the repudiation, but no later than the time stated in paragraph (a), together with any incidental or consequential damages provided in this Article (Section 2–710), but less expenses saved in consequence of the buyer's breach.

(2) If the measure of damages provided in subsection (1) or in Section 2–706 is inadequate to put the seller in as good a position as performance would have done then the measure of damages is the profit (including reasonable overhead) which the seller would have made from full performance by the buyer, together with any incidental or consequential damages provided in this Article (Section 2–710).

§ 2–709. Action for the Price.

(1) When the buyer fails to pay the price as it becomes due the seller may recover, together with any incidental or consequential damages under the next section, the price

(a) of goods accepted or of conforming goods lost or damaged within a commercially reasonable time after risk of their loss has passed to the buyer; and

(b) of goods identified to the contract if the seller is unable after reasonable effort to resell them at a reasonable price or the circumstances reasonably indicate that such effort will be unavailing.

* * * *

§ 2–710. Seller's Incidental and Consequential Damages.

(1) Incidental damages to an aggrieved seller include any commercially reasonable charges, expenses or commissions incurred in stopping delivery, in the transportation, care and custody of goods after the buyer's breach, in connection with return or resale of the goods or otherwise resulting from the breach.

(2) Consequential damages resulting from the buyer's breach include any loss resulting from general or particular requirements and needs of which the buyer at the time of contracting had reason to know and which could not reasonably be prevented by resale or otherwise.

(3) In a consumer contract, a seller may not recover consequential damages from a consumer.

* * * *

§ 2–711. Buyer's Remedies in General; Buyer's Security Interest in Rejected Goods.

(1) A breach of contract by the seller includes the seller's wrongful failure to deliver or to perform a contractual obligation, making of a nonconforming tender of delivery or performance, and repudiation.

(2) If a seller is in breach of contract under subsection (1) the buyer, to the extent provided for by this Act or other law, may:

(a) in the case of rightful cancellation, rightful rejection or justifiable revocation of acceptance recover so much of the price as has been paid;

(b) deduct damages from any part of the price still due under Section 2–717;

(c) cancel;

(d) cover and have damages under Section 2–712 as to all goods affected whether or not they have been identified to the contract;

(e) recover damages for non-delivery or repudiation under Section 2–713;

(f) recover damages for breach with regard to accepted goods or breach with regard to a remedial promise under Section 2–714;

(g) recover identified goods under Section 2–502;

(h) obtain specific performance or obtain the goods by replevin or similar remedy under Section 7–716;

(i) recover liquidated damages under Section 2–718;

(j) in other cases, recover damages in any manner that is reasonable under the circumstances.

(3) On rightful rejection or justifiable revocation of acceptance a buyer has a security interest in goods in the buyer's possession or control for any payments made on their price and any expenses reasonably incurred in their inspection, receipt, transportation, care and custody and may hold such goods and resell them in like manner as an aggrieved seller (Section 2–706).

* * * *

§ 2–713. **Buyer's Damages for Non-Delivery or Repudiation.**

(1) Subject to the provisions of this Article with respect to proof of market price (Section 2–723), if the seller wrongfully fails to deliver or repudiates or the buyer rightfully rejects or justifiably revokes acceptance

(a) the measure of damages in the case of wrongful failure to deliver by the seller or rightful rejection or justifiable revocation of acceptance by the buyer is the difference between the market price at the time for tender under the contract and the contract price together with any incidental or consequential damages provided in this Article (Section 2–715), but less expenses saved in consequence of the seller's breach; and

(b) the measure of damages for repudiation by the seller is the difference between the market price at the expiration of a commercially reasonable time after the buyer learned of the repudiation, but no later than the time stated in paragraph (a), and the contract price together with any incidental or consequential damages provided in this Article (Section 2–715), less expenses saved in consequence of the seller's breach.

* * * *

§ 2–725. **Statute of Limitations in Contracts for Sale.**

(1) Except as otherwise provided in this section, an action for breach of any contract for sale must be commenced within the later of four years after the right of action has accrued under subsection (2) or (3) or one year after the breach was or should have been discovered, but no longer than five years after the right of action accrued. By the original agreement the parties may reduce the period of limitation to not less than one year but may not extend it. However, in a consumer contract, the period of limitation may not be reduced.

(2) Except as otherwise provided in subsection (3), the following rules apply:

(a) Except as otherwise provided in this subsection, a right of action for breach of a contract accrues when the breach occurs, even if the aggrieved party did not have knowledge of the breach.

(b) For breach of a contract by repudiation, a right of action accrues at the earlier of when the aggrieved party elects to treat the repudiation as a breach or when a commercially reasonable time for awaiting performance has expired.

(c) For breach of a remedial promise, a right of action accrues when the remedial promise is not performed when performance is due.

(d) In an action by a buyer against a person that is answerable over to the buyer for a claim asserted against the buyer, the buyer's right of action against the person answerable over accrues at the time the claim was originally asserted against the buyer.

(3) If a breach of a warranty arising under Section 2–312, 2–313(2), 2–314, or 2–315, or a breach of an obligation, other than a remedial promise, arising under Section 2–313A or 2–313B, is claimed the following rules apply:

(a) Except as otherwise provided in paragraph (c), a right of action for breach of a warranty arising under Section 2–313(2), 2–314 or 2–315 accrues when the seller has tendered delivery to the immediate buyer, as defined in Section 2–313, and has completed performance of any agreed installation or assembly of the goods.

(b) Except as otherwise provided in paragraph (c), a right of action for breach of an obligation other than a remedial promise arising under Section 2–313A or 2–313B accrues when the remote purchaser, as defined in sections 2–313A and 2–313B, receives the goods.

(c) Where a warranty arising under Section 2–313(2) or an obligation, other than a remedial promise, arising under 2–313A or 2–313B explicitly extends to future performance of the goods and discovery of the breach must await the time for performance the right of action accrues when the immediate buyer as defined in Section 2–313 or the remote purchaser as defined in Sections 2–313A and 2–313B discovers or should have discovered the breach.

(d) A right of action for breach of warranty arising under Section 2–312 accrues when the aggrieved party discovers or should have discovered the breach. However, an action for breach of the warranty of non-infringement may not be commenced more than six years after tender of delivery of the goods to the aggrieved party.

* * * *

Article 2A
LEASES

Part 1 General Provisions

§ 2A–101. **Short Title.**

This Article shall be known and may be cited as the Uniform Commercial Code—Leases.

§ 2A–102. **Scope.**

This Article applies to any transaction, regardless of form, that creates a lease.

§ 2A–103. Definitions and Index of Definitions.

(1) In this Article unless the context otherwise requires:

(a) "Buyer in ordinary course of business" means a person who in good faith and without knowledge that the sale to him [or her] is in violation of the ownership rights or security interest or leasehold interest of a third party in the goods buys in ordinary course from a person in the business of selling goods of that kind but does not include a pawnbroker. "Buying" may be for cash or by exchange of other property or on secured or unsecured credit and includes receiving goods or documents of title under a pre-existing contract for sale but does not include a transfer in bulk or as security for or in total or partial satisfaction of a money debt.

(b) "Cancellation" occurs when either party puts an end to the lease contract for default by the other party.

(c) "Commercial unit" means such a unit of goods as by commercial usage is a single whole for purposes of lease and division of which materially impairs its character or value on the market or in use. A commercial unit may be a single article, as a machine, or a set of articles, as a suite of furniture or a line of machinery, or a quantity, as a gross or carload, or any other unit treated in use or in the relevant market as a single whole.

(d) "Conforming" goods or performance under a lease contract means goods or performance that are in accordance with the obligations under the lease contract.

(e) "Consumer lease" means a lease that a lessor regularly engaged in the business of leasing or selling makes to a lessee who is an individual and who takes under the lease primarily for a personal, family, or household purpose [, if the total payments to be made under the lease contract, excluding payments for options to renew or buy, do not exceed $_____].

(f) "Fault" means wrongful act, omission, breach, or default.

(g) "Finance lease" means a lease with respect to which:

(i) the lessor does not select, manufacture or supply the goods;

(ii) the lessor acquires the goods or the right to possession and use of the goods in connection with the lease; and

(iii) one of the following occurs:

(A) the lessee receives a copy of the contract by which the lessor acquired the goods or the right to possession and use of the goods before signing the lease contract;

(B) the lessee's approval of the contract by which the lessor acquired the goods or the right to possession and use of the goods is a condition to effectiveness of the lease contract;

(C) the lessee, before signing the lease contract, receives an accurate and complete statement designating the promises and warranties, and any disclaimers of warranties, limitations or modifications of remedies, or liquidated damages, including those of a third party, such as the manufacturer of the goods, provided to the lessor by the person supplying the goods in connection with or as part of the contract by which the lessor acquired the goods or the right to possession and use of the goods; or

(D) if the lease is not a consumer lease, the lessor, before the lessee signs the lease contract, informs the lessee in writing (a) of the identity of the person supplying the goods to the lessor, unless the lessee has selected that person and directed the lessor to acquire the goods or the right to possession and use of the goods from that person, (b) that the lessee is entitled under this Article to any promises and warranties, including those of any third party, provided to the lessor by the person supplying the goods in connection with or as part of the contract by which the lessor acquired the goods or the right to possession and use of the goods, and (c) that the lessee may communicate with the person supplying the goods to the lessor and receive an accurate and complete statement of those promises and warranties, including any disclaimers and limitations of them or of remedies.

(h) "Goods" means all things that are movable at the time of identification to the lease contract, or are fixtures (Section 2A–309), but the term does not include money, documents, instruments, accounts, chattel paper, general intangibles, or minerals or the like, including oil and gas, before extraction. The term also includes the unborn young of animals.

(i) "Installment lease contract" means a lease contract that authorizes or requires the delivery of goods in separate lots to be separately accepted, even though the lease contract contains a clause "each delivery is a separate lease" or its equivalent.

(j) "Lease" means a transfer of the right to possession and use of goods for a term in return for consideration, but a sale, including a sale on approval or a sale or return, or retention or creation of a security interest is not a lease. Unless the context clearly indicates otherwise, the term includes a sublease.

(k) "Lease agreement" means the bargain, with respect to the lease, of the lessor and the lessee in fact as found in their language or by implication from other circumstances including course of dealing or usage of trade or course of performance as provided in this Article. Unless the context clearly indicates otherwise, the term includes a sublease agreement.

(*l*) "Lease contract" means the total legal obligation that results from the lease agreement as affected by this Article and any other applicable rules of law. Unless the context clearly indicates otherwise, the term includes a sublease contract.

(m) "Leasehold interest" means the interest of the lessor or the lessee under a lease contract.

(n) "Lessee" means a person who acquires the right to possession and use of goods under a lease. Unless the context clearly indicates otherwise, the term includes a sublessee.

(o) "Lessee in ordinary course of business" means a person who in good faith and without knowledge that the lease to him [or her] is in violation of the ownership rights or security interest or leasehold interest of a third party in the goods, leases in ordinary course from a person in the business of selling or leasing goods of that kind but does not include a pawnbroker. "Leasing" may be for cash or by exchange of other property or on secured or unsecured credit and includes receiving goods or documents of title under a pre-existing lease contract but does not include a transfer in bulk or as security for or in total or partial satisfaction of a money debt.

(p) "Lessor" means a person who transfers the right to possession and use of goods under a lease. Unless the context clearly indicates otherwise, the term includes a sublessor.

(q) "Lessor's residual interest" means the lessor's interest in the goods after expiration, termination, or cancellation of the lease contract.

(r) "Lien" means a charge against or interest in goods to secure payment of a debt or performance of an obligation, but the term does not include a security interest.

(s) "Lot" means a parcel or a single article that is the subject matter of a separate lease or delivery, whether or not it is sufficient to perform the lease contract.

(t) "Merchant lessee" means a lessee that is a merchant with respect to goods of the kind subject to the lease.

(u) "Present value" means the amount as of a date certain of one or more sums payable in the future, discounted to the date certain. The discount is determined by the interest rate specified by the parties if the rate was not manifestly unreasonable at the time the transaction was entered into; otherwise, the discount is determined by a commercially reasonable rate that takes into account the facts and circumstances of each case at the time the transaction was entered into.

(v) "Purchase" includes taking by sale, lease, mortgage, security interest, pledge, gift, or any other voluntary transaction creating an interest in goods.

(w) "Sublease" means a lease of goods the right to possession and use of which was acquired by the lessor as a lessee under an existing lease.

(x) "Supplier" means a person from whom a lessor buys or leases goods to be leased under a finance lease.

(y) "Supply contract" means a contract under which a lessor buys or leases goods to be leased.

(z) "Termination" occurs when either party pursuant to a power created by agreement or law puts an end to the lease contract otherwise than for default.

(2) Other definitions applying to this Article and the sections in which they appear are:

"Accessions". Section 2A–310(1).
"Construction mortgage". Section 2A–309(1)(d).
"Encumbrance". Section 2A–309(1)(e).
"Fixtures". Section 2A–309(1)(a).
"Fixture filing". Section 2A–309(1)(b).
"Purchase money lease". Section 2A–309(1)(c).

(3) The following definitions in other Articles apply to this Article:

"Accounts". Section 9–106.
"Between merchants". Section 2–104(3).
"Buyer". Section 2–103(1)(a).
"Chattel paper". Section 9–105(1)(b).
"Consumer goods". Section 9–109(1).
"Document". Section 9–105(1)(f).
"Entrusting". Section 2–403(3).
"General intangibles". Section 9–106.
"Good faith". Section 2–103(1)(b).
"Instrument". Section 9–105(1)(i).
"Merchant". Section 2–104(1).
"Mortgage". Section 9–105(1)(j).
"Pursuant to commitment". Section 9–105(1)(k).
"Receipt". Section 2–103(1)(c).
"Sale". Section 2–106(1).
"Sale on approval". Section 2–326.
"Sale or return". Section 2–326.
"Seller". Section 2–103(1)(d).

(4) In addition Article 1 contains general definitions and principles of construction and interpretation applicable throughout this Article.

As amended in 1990 and 1999.

§ 2A–104. Leases Subject to Other Law.

(1) A lease, although subject to this Article, is also subject to any applicable:

(a) certificate of title statute of this State: (list any certificate of title statutes covering automobiles, trailers, mobile homes, boats, farm tractors, and the like);

(b) certificate of title statute of another jurisdiction (Section 2A–105); or

(c) consumer protection statute of this State, or final consumer protection decision of a court of this State existing on the effective date of this Article.

(2) In case of conflict between this Article, other than Sections 2A–105, 2A–304(3), and 2A–305(3), and a statute or decision referred to in subsection (1), the statute or decision controls.

(3) Failure to comply with an applicable law has only the effect specified therein.

As amended in 1990.

§ 2A–105. Territorial Application of Article to Goods Covered by Certificate of Title.

Subject to the provisions of Sections 2A–304(3) and 2A–305(3), with respect to goods covered by a certificate of title issued under a statute of this State or of another jurisdiction, compliance and the effect of compliance or noncompliance with a certificate of title statute are governed by the law (including the conflict of laws rules) of the jurisdiction issuing the certificate until the earlier of (a) surrender of the certificate, or (b) four months after the goods are removed from that jurisdiction and thereafter until a new certificate of title is issued by another jurisdiction.

§ 2A–106. Limitation on Power of Parties to Consumer Lease to Choose Applicable Law and Judicial Forum.

(1) If the law chosen by the parties to a consumer lease is that of a jurisdiction other than a jurisdiction in which the lessee resides at the time the lease agreement becomes enforceable or within 30 days thereafter or in which the goods are to be used, the choice is not enforceable.

(2) If the judicial forum chosen by the parties to a consumer lease is a forum that would not otherwise have jurisdiction over the lessee, the choice is not enforceable.

§ 2A–107. Waiver or Renunciation of Claim or Right After Default.

Any claim or right arising out of an alleged default or breach of warranty may be discharged in whole or in part without consideration by a written waiver or renunciation signed and delivered by the aggrieved party.

§ 2A–108. Unconscionability.

(1) If the court as a matter of law finds a lease contract or any clause of a lease contract to have been unconscionable at the time it was made the court may refuse to enforce the lease contract, or it may enforce the remainder of the lease contract without the unconscionable clause, or it may so limit the application of any unconscionable clause as to avoid any unconscionable result.

(2) With respect to a consumer lease, if the court as a matter of law finds that a lease contract or any clause of a lease contract has been induced by unconscionable conduct or that unconscionable conduct has occurred in the collection of a claim arising from a lease contract, the court may grant appropriate relief.

(3) Before making a finding of unconscionability under subsection (1) or (2), the court, on its own motion or that of a party, shall afford the parties a reasonable opportunity to present evidence as to the setting, purpose, and effect of the lease contract or clause thereof, or of the conduct.

(4) In an action in which the lessee claims unconscionability with respect to a consumer lease:

(a) If the court finds unconscionability under subsection (1) or (2), the court shall award reasonable attorney's fees to the lessee.

(b) If the court does not find unconscionability and the lessee claiming unconscionability has brought or maintained an action he [or she] knew to be groundless, the court shall award reasonable attorney's fees to the party against whom the claim is made.

(c) In determining attorney's fees, the amount of the recovery on behalf of the claimant under subsections (1) and (2) is not controlling.

§ 2A–109. Option to Accelerate at Will.

(1) A term providing that one party or his [or her] successor in interest may accelerate payment or performance or require collateral or additional collateral "at will" or "when he [or she] deems himself [or herself] insecure" or in words of similar import must be construed to mean that he [or she] has power to do so only if he [or she] in good faith believes that the prospect of payment or performance is impaired.

(2) With respect to a consumer lease, the burden of establishing good faith under subsection (1) is on the party who exercised the power; otherwise the burden of establishing lack of good faith is on the party against whom the power has been exercised.

Part 2 Formation and Construction of Lease Contract

§ 2A–201. Statute of Frauds.

(1) A lease contract is not enforceable by way of action or defense unless:

(a) the total payments to be made under the lease contract, excluding payments for options to renew or buy, are less than $1,000; or

(b) there is a writing, signed by the party against whom enforcement is sought or by that party's authorized agent, sufficient to indicate that a lease contract has been made between the parties and to describe the goods leased and the lease term.

(2) Any description of leased goods or of the lease term is sufficient and satisfies subsection (1)(b), whether or not it is specific, if it reasonably identifies what is described.

(3) A writing is not insufficient because it omits or incorrectly states a term agreed upon, but the lease contract is not enforceable under subsection (1)(b) beyond the lease term and the quantity of goods shown in the writing.

(4) A lease contract that does not satisfy the requirements of subsection (1), but which is valid in other respects, is enforceable:

(a) if the goods are to be specially manufactured or obtained for the lessee and are not suitable for lease or sale to others in the ordinary course of the lessor's business, and the lessor, before notice of repudiation is received and under circumstances that reasonably indicate that the goods are for the lessee, has made either a substantial beginning of their manufacture or commitments for their procurement;

(b) if the party against whom enforcement is sought admits in that party's pleading, testimony or otherwise in court that a lease contract was made, but the lease contract is not enforceable under this provision beyond the quantity of goods admitted; or

(c) with respect to goods that have been received and accepted by the lessee.

(5) The lease term under a lease contract referred to in subsection (4) is:

(a) if there is a writing signed by the party against whom enforcement is sought or by that party's authorized agent specifying the lease term, the term so specified;

(b) if the party against whom enforcement is sought admits in that party's pleading, testimony, or otherwise in court a lease term, the term so admitted; or

(c) a reasonable lease term.

§ 2A–202. Final Written Expression: Parol or Extrinsic Evidence.

Terms with respect to which the confirmatory memoranda of the parties agree or which are otherwise set forth in a writing intended by the parties as a final expression of their agreement with respect to such terms as are included therein may not be contradicted by evidence of any prior agreement or of a contemporaneous oral agreement but may be explained or supplemented:

(a) by course of dealing or usage of trade or by course of performance; and

(b) by evidence of consistent additional terms unless the court finds the writing to have been intended also as a complete and exclusive statement of the terms of the agreement.

§ 2A–203. Seals Inoperative.

The affixing of a seal to a writing evidencing a lease contract or an offer to enter into a lease contract does not render the writing a sealed instrument and the law with respect to sealed instruments does not apply to the lease contract or offer.

§ 2A–204. Formation in General.

(1) A lease contract may be made in any manner sufficient to show agreement, including conduct by both parties which recognizes the existence of a lease contract.

(2) An agreement sufficient to constitute a lease contract may be found although the moment of its making is undetermined.

(3) Although one or more terms are left open, a lease contract does not fail for indefiniteness if the parties have intended to make a lease contract and there is a reasonably certain basis for giving an appropriate remedy.

§ 2A–205. Firm Offers.

An offer by a merchant to lease goods to or from another person in a signed writing that by its terms gives assurance it will be held open is not revocable, for lack of consideration, during the time stated or, if no time is stated, for a reasonable time, but in no event may the period of irrevocability exceed 3 months. Any such term of assurance on a form supplied by the offeree must be separately signed by the offeror.

§ 2A–206. Offer and Acceptance in Formation of Lease Contract.

(1) Unless otherwise unambiguously indicated by the language or circumstances, an offer to make a lease contract must be construed as inviting acceptance in any manner and by any medium reasonable in the circumstances.

(2) If the beginning of a requested performance is a reasonable mode of acceptance, an offeror who is not notified of acceptance within a reasonable time may treat the offer as having lapsed before acceptance.

§ 2A–207. Course of Performance or Practical Construction.

(1) If a lease contract involves repeated occasions for performance by either party with knowledge of the nature of the performance and opportunity for objection to it by the other, any course of performance accepted or acquiesced in without objection is relevant to determine the meaning of the lease agreement.

(2) The express terms of a lease agreement and any course of performance, as well as any course of dealing and usage of trade, must be construed whenever reasonable as consistent with each other; but if that construction is unreasonable, express terms control course of performance, course of performance controls both course of dealing and usage of trade, and course of dealing controls usage of trade.

(3) Subject to the provisions of Section 2A–208 on modification and waiver, course of performance is relevant to show a waiver or modification of any term inconsistent with the course of performance.

§ 2A–208. Modification, Rescission and Waiver.

(1) An agreement modifying a lease contract needs no consideration to be binding.

(2) A signed lease agreement that excludes modification or rescission except by a signed writing may not be otherwise modified or rescinded, but, except as between merchants, such a requirement on a form supplied by a merchant must be separately signed by the other party.

(3) Although an attempt at modification or rescission does not satisfy the requirements of subsection (2), it may operate as a waiver.

(4) A party who has made a waiver affecting an executory portion of a lease contract may retract the waiver by reasonable notification received by the other party that strict performance will be required of any term waived, unless the retraction would be unjust in view of a material change of position in reliance on the waiver.

§ 2A–209. Lessee under Finance Lease as Beneficiary of Supply Contract.

(1) The benefit of the supplier's promises to the lessor under the supply contract and of all warranties, whether express or implied, including those of any third party provided in connection with or as part of the supply contract, extends to the lessee to the extent of the lessee's leasehold interest under a finance lease related to the supply contract, but is subject to the terms warranty and of the supply contract and all defenses or claims arising therefrom.

(2) The extension of the benefit of supplier's promises and of warranties to the lessee (Section 2A–209(1)) does not: (i) modify the rights and obligations of the parties to the supply contract, whether arising therefrom or otherwise, or (ii) impose any duty or liability under the supply contract on the lessee.

(3) Any modification or rescission of the supply contract by the supplier and the lessor is effective between the supplier and the lessee unless, before the modification or rescission, the supplier has received notice that the lessee has entered into a finance lease related to the supply contract. If the modification or rescission is effective between the supplier and the lessee, the lessor is deemed to have assumed, in addition to the obligations of the lessor to the lessee under the lease contract, promises of the supplier to the lessor and warranties that were so modified or rescinded as they existed and were available to the lessee before modification or rescission.

(4) In addition to the extension of the benefit of the supplier's promises and of warranties to the lessee under subsection (1), the lessee retains all rights that the lessee may have against the supplier which arise from an agreement between the lessee and the supplier or under other law.

As amended in 1990.

§ 2A–210. Express Warranties.

(1) Express warranties by the lessor are created as follows:

(a) Any affirmation of fact or promise made by the lessor to the lessee which relates to the goods and becomes part of the basis of the bargain creates an express warranty that the goods will conform to the affirmation or promise.

(b) Any description of the goods which is made part of the basis of the bargain creates an express warranty that the goods will conform to the description.

(c) Any sample or model that is made part of the basis of the bargain creates an express warranty that the whole of the goods will conform to the sample or model.

(2) It is not necessary to the creation of an express warranty that the lessor use formal words, such as "warrant" or "guarantee," or that the lessor have a specific intention to make a warranty, but an affirmation merely of the value of the goods or a statement purporting to be merely the lessor's opinion or commendation of the goods does not create a warranty.

§ 2A–211. Warranties Against Interference and Against Infringement; Lessee's Obligation Against Infringement.

(1) There is in a lease contract a warranty that for the lease term no person holds a claim to or interest in the goods that arose from an act or omission of the lessor, other than a claim by way of infringement or the like, which will interfere with the lessee's enjoyment of its leasehold interest.

(2) Except in a finance lease there is in a lease contract by a lessor who is a merchant regularly dealing in goods of the kind a warranty that the goods are delivered free of the rightful claim of any person by way of infringement or the like.

(3) A lessee who furnishes specifications to a lessor or a supplier shall hold the lessor and the supplier harmless against any claim by way of infringement or the like that arises out of compliance with the specifications.

§ 2A–212. Implied Warranty of Merchantability.

(1) Except in a finance lease, a warranty that the goods will be merchantable is implied in a lease contract if the lessor is a merchant with respect to goods of that kind.

(2) Goods to be merchantable must be at least such as

(a) pass without objection in the trade under the description in the lease agreement;

(b) in the case of fungible goods, are of fair average quality within the description;

(c) are fit for the ordinary purposes for which goods of that type are used;

(d) run, within the variation permitted by the lease agreement, of even kind, quality, and quantity within each unit and among all units involved;

(e) are adequately contained, packaged, and labeled as the lease agreement may require; and

(f) conform to any promises or affirmations of fact made on the container or label.

(3) Other implied warranties may arise from course of dealing or usage of trade.

§ 2A–213. Implied Warranty of Fitness for Particular Purpose.

Except in a finance of lease, if the lessor at the time the lease contract is made has reason to know of any particular purpose for which the goods are required and that the lessee is relying on the lessor's skill or judgment to select or furnish suitable goods, there is in the lease contract an implied warranty that the goods will be fit for that purpose.

§ 2A–214. Exclusion or Modification of Warranties.

(1) Words or conduct relevant to the creation of an express warranty and words or conduct tending to negate or limit a warranty must be construed wherever reasonable as consistent with each other; but, subject to the provisions of Section 2A–202 on parol or extrinsic evidence, negation or limitation is inoperative to the extent that the construction is unreasonable.

(2) Subject to subsection (3), to exclude or modify the implied warranty of merchantability or any part of it the language must mention "merchantability", be by a writing, and be conspicuous. Subject to subsection (3), to exclude or modify any implied

warranty of fitness the exclusion must be by a writing and be conspicuous. Language to exclude all implied warranties of fitness is sufficient if it is in writing, is conspicuous and states, for example, "There is no warranty that the goods will be fit for a particular purpose".

(3) Notwithstanding subsection (2), but subject to subsection (4),

(a) unless the circumstances indicate otherwise, all implied warranties are excluded by expressions like "as is" or "with all faults" or by other language that in common understanding calls the lessee's attention to the exclusion of warranties and makes plain that there is no implied warranty, if in writing and conspicuous;

(b) if the lessee before entering into the lease contract has examined the goods or the sample or model as fully as desired or has refused to examine the goods, there is no implied warranty with regard to defects that an examination ought in the circumstances to have revealed; and

(c) an implied warranty may also be excluded or modified by course of dealing, course of performance, or usage of trade.

(4) To exclude or modify a warranty against interference or against infringement (Section 2A–211) or any part of it, the language must be specific, be by a writing, and be conspicuous, unless the circumstances, including course of performance, course of dealing, or usage of trade, give the lessee reason to know that the goods are being leased subject to a claim or interest of any person.

§ 2A–215. Cumulation and Conflict of Warranties Express or Implied.

Warranties, whether express or implied, must be construed as consistent with each other and as cumulative, but if that construction is unreasonable, the intention of the parties determines which warranty is dominant. In ascertaining that intention the following rules apply:

(a) Exact or technical specifications displace an inconsistent sample or model or general language of description.

(b) A sample from an existing bulk displaces inconsistent general language of description.

(c) Express warranties displace inconsistent implied warranties other than an implied warranty of fitness for a particular purpose.

§ 2A–216. Third-Party Beneficiaries of Express and Implied Warranties.

Alternative A

A warranty to or for the benefit of a lessee under this Article, whether express or implied, extends to any natural person who is in the family or household of the lessee or who is a guest in the lessee's home if it is reasonable to expect that such person may use, consume, or be affected by the goods and who is injured in person by breach of the warranty. This section does not displace principles of law and equity that extend a warranty to or for the benefit of a lessee to other persons. The operation of this section may not be excluded, modified, or limited, but an exclusion, modification, or limitation of the warranty, including any with respect to rights and remedies, effective against the lessee is also effective against any beneficiary designated under this section.

Alternative B

A warranty to or for the benefit of a lessee under this Article, whether express or implied, extends to any natural person who may reasonably be expected to use, consume, or be affected by the goods and who is injured in person by breach of the warranty. This section does not displace principles of law and equity that extend a warranty to or for the benefit of a lessee to other persons. The operation of this section may not be excluded, modified, or limited, but an exclusion, modification, or limitation of the warranty, including any with respect to rights and remedies, effective against the lessee is also effective against the beneficiary designated under this section.

Alternative C

A warranty to or for the benefit of a lessee under this Article, whether express or implied, extends to any person who may reasonably be expected to use, consume, or be affected by the goods and who is injured by breach of the warranty. The operation of this section may not be excluded, modified, or limited with respect to injury to the person of an individual to whom the warranty extends, but an exclusion, modification, or limitation of the warranty, including any with respect to rights and remedies, effective against the lessee is also effective against the beneficiary designated under this section.

§ 2A–217. Identification.

Identification of goods as goods to which a lease contract refers may be made at any time and in any manner explicitly agreed to by the parties. In the absence of explicit agreement, identification occurs:

(a) when the lease contract is made if the lease contract is for a lease of goods that are existing and identified;

(b) when the goods are shipped, marked, or otherwise designated by the lessor as goods to which the lease contract refers, if the lease contract is for a lease of goods that are not existing and identified; or

(c) when the young are conceived, if the lease contract is for a lease of unborn young of animals.

§ 2A–218. Insurance and Proceeds.

(1) A lessee obtains an insurable interest when existing goods are identified to the lease contract even though the goods identified are nonconforming and the lessee has an option to reject them.

(2) If a lessee has an insurable interest only by reason of the lessor's identification of the goods, the lessor, until default or insolvency or notification to the lessee that identification is final, may substitute other goods for those identified.

(3) Notwithstanding a lessee's insurable interest under subsections (1) and (2), the lessor retains an insurable interest until an option to buy has been exercised by the lessee and risk of loss has passed to the lessee.

(4) Nothing in this section impairs any insurable interest recognized under any other statute or rule of law.

(5) The parties by agreement may determine that one or more parties have an obligation to obtain and pay for insurance covering the goods and by agreement may determine the beneficiary of the proceeds of the insurance.

§ 2A–219. **Risk of Loss.**

(1) Except in the case of a finance lease, risk of loss is retained by the lessor and does not pass to the lessee. In the case of a finance lease, risk of loss passes to the lessee.

(2) Subject to the provisions of this Article on the effect of default on risk of loss (Section 2A–220), if risk of loss is to pass to the lessee and the time of passage is not stated, the following rules apply:

(a) If the lease contract requires or authorizes the goods to be shipped by carrier

(i) and it does not require delivery at a particular destination, the risk of loss passes to the lessee when the goods are duly delivered to the carrier; but

(ii) if it does require delivery at a particular destination and the goods are there duly tendered while in the possession of the carrier, the risk of loss passes to the lessee when the goods are there duly so tendered as to enable the lessee to take delivery.

(b) If the goods are held by a bailee to be delivered without being moved, the risk of loss passes to the lessee on acknowledgment by the bailee of the lessee's right to possession of the goods.

(c) In any case not within subsection (a) or (b), the risk of loss passes to the lessee on the lessee's receipt of the goods if the lessor, or, in the case of a finance lease, the supplier, is a merchant; otherwise the risk passes to the lessee on tender of delivery.

§ 2A–220. **Effect of Default on Risk of Loss.**

(1) Where risk of loss is to pass to the lessee and the time of passage is not stated:

(a) If a tender or delivery of goods so fails to conform to the lease contract as to give a right of rejection, the risk of their loss remains with the lessor, or, in the case of a finance lease, the supplier, until cure or acceptance.

(b) If the lessee rightfully revokes acceptance, he [or she], to the extent of any deficiency in his [or her] effective insurance coverage, may treat the risk of loss as having remained with the lessor from the beginning.

(2) Whether or not risk of loss is to pass to the lessee, if the lessee as to conforming goods already identified to a lease contract repudiates or is otherwise in default under the lease contract, the lessor, or, in the case of a finance lease, the supplier, to the extent of any deficiency in his [or her] effective insurance coverage may treat the risk of loss as resting on the lessee for a commercially reasonable time.

§ 2A–221. **Casualty to Identified Goods.**

If a lease contract requires goods identified when the lease contract is made, and the goods suffer casualty without fault of the lessee, the lessor or the supplier before delivery, or the goods suffer casualty before risk of loss passes to the lessee pursuant to the lease agreement or Section 2A–219, then:

(a) if the loss is total, the lease contract is avoided; and

(b) if the loss is partial or the goods have so deteriorated as to no longer conform to the lease contract, the lessee may nevertheless demand inspection and at his [or her] option either treat the lease contract as avoided or, except in a finance lease that is not a consumer lease, accept the goods with due allowance from the rent payable for the balance of the lease term for the deterioration or the deficiency in quantity but without further right against the lessor.

Part 3 **Effect of Lease Contract**

§ 2A–301. **Enforceability of Lease Contract.**

Except as otherwise provided in this Article, a lease contract is effective and enforceable according to its terms between the parties, against purchasers of the goods and against creditors of the parties.

§ 2A–302. **Title to and Possession of Goods.**

Except as otherwise provided in this Article, each provision of this Article applies whether the lessor or a third party has title to the goods, and whether the lessor, the lessee, or a third party has possession of the goods, notwithstanding any statute or rule of law that possession or the absence of possession is fraudulent.

§ 2A–303. **Alienability of Party's Interest Under Lease Contract or of Lessor's Residual Interest in Goods; Delegation of Performance; Transfer of Rights.**

(1) As used in this section, "creation of a security interest" includes the sale of a lease contract that is subject to Article 9, Secured Transactions, by reason of Section 9–109(a)(3).

(2) Except as provided in subsections (3) and Section 9–407, a provision in a lease agreement which (i) prohibits the voluntary or involuntary transfer, including a transfer by sale, sublease, creation or enforcement of a security interest, or attachment, levy, or other judicial process, of an interest of a party under the lease contract or of the lessor's residual interest in the goods, or (ii) makes such a transfer an event of default, gives rise to the rights and remedies provided in subsection (4), but a transfer that is prohibited or is an event of default under the lease agreement is otherwise effective.

(3) A provision in a lease agreement which (i) prohibits a transfer of a right to damages for default with respect to the whole lease contract or of a right to payment arising out of the transferor's due performance of the transferor's entire obligation, or (ii) makes such a transfer an event of default, is not enforceable, and such a transfer is not a transfer that materially impairs the propsect of obtaining return performance by, materially changes the duty of, or materially increases the burden or risk imposed on, the other party to the lease contract within the purview of subsection (4).

(4) Subject to subsection (3) and Section 9–407:

(a) if a transfer is made which is made an event of default under a lease agreement, the party to the lease contract not making the transfer, unless that party waives the default or otherwise agrees, has the rights and remedies described in Section 2A–501(2);

(b) if paragraph (a) is not applicable and if a transfer is made that (i) is prohibited under a lease agreement or (ii) materially impairs the prospect of obtaining return performance by, materially changes the duty of, or materially increases the burden or risk imposed on, the other party to the lease contract, unless the party not making the transfer agrees at any time to the transfer in the lease contract or otherwise, then, except as limited by contract, (i) the transferor is liable to the party not making the transfer for damages caused by the transfer to the extent that the damages could not reasonably be prevented by the party not making the transfer and (ii) a court having jurisdiction may grant other appropriate relief, including cancellation of the lease contract or an injunction against the transfer.

(5) A transfer of "the lease" or of "all my rights under the lease", or a transfer in similar general terms, is a transfer of rights and, unless the language or the circumstances, as in a transfer for security, indicate the contrary, the transfer is a delegation of duties by the transferor to the transferee. Acceptance by the transferee constitutes a promise by the transferee to perform those duties. The promise is enforceable by either the transferor or the other party to the lease contract.

(6) Unless otherwise agreed by the lessor and the lessee, a delegation of performance does not relieve the transferor as against the other party of any duty to perform or of any liability for default.

(7) In a consumer lease, to prohibit the transfer of an interest of a party under the lease contract or to make a transfer an event of default, the language must be specific, by a writing, and conspicuous.

As amended in 1990 and 1999.

§ 2A–304. **Subsequent Lease of Goods by Lessor.**

(1) Subject to Section 2A–303, a subsequent lessee from a lessor of goods under an existing lease contract obtains, to the extent of the leasehold interest transferred, the leasehold interest in the goods that the lessor had or had power to transfer, and except as provided in subsection (2) and Section 2A–527(4), takes subject to the existing lease contract. A lessor with voidable title has power to transfer a good leasehold interest to a good faith subsequent lessee for value, but only to the extent set forth in the preceding sentence. If goods have been delivered under a transaction of purchase the lessor has that power even though:

(a) the lessor's transferor was deceived as to the identity of the lessor;

(b) the delivery was in exchange for a check which is later dishonored;

(c) it was agreed that the transaction was to be a "cash sale"; or

(d) the delivery was procured through fraud punishable as larcenous under the criminal law.

(2) A subsequent lessee in the ordinary course of business from a lessor who is a merchant dealing in goods of that kind to whom the goods were entrusted by the existing lessee of that lessor before the interest of the subsequent lessee became enforceable against that lessor obtains, to the extent of the leasehold interest transferred, all of that lessor's and the existing lessee's rights to the goods, and takes free of the existing lease contract.

(3) A subsequent lessee from the lessor of goods that are subject to an existing lease contract and are covered by a certificate of title issued under a statute of this State or of another jurisdiction takes no greater rights than those provided both by this section and by the certificate of title statute.

As amended in 1990.

§ 2A–305. **Sale or Sublease of Goods by Lessee.**

(1) Subject to the provisions of Section 2A–303, a buyer or sublessee from the lessee of goods under an existing lease contract obtains, to the extent of the interest transferred, the leasehold interest in the goods that the lessee had or had power to transfer, and except as provided in subsection (2) and Section 2A–511(4), takes subject to the existing lease contract. A lessee with a voidable leasehold interest has power to transfer a good leasehold interest to a good faith buyer for value or a good faith sublessee for value, but only to the extent set forth in the preceding sentence. When goods have been delivered under a transaction of lease the lessee has that power even though:

(a) the lessor was deceived as to the identity of the lessee;

(b) the delivery was in exchange for a check which is later dishonored; or

(c) the delivery was procured through fraud punishable as larcenous under the criminal law.

(2) A buyer in the ordinary course of business or a sublessee in the ordinary course of business from a lessee who is a merchant dealing in goods of that kind to whom the goods were entrusted by the lessor obtains, to the extent of the interest transferred, all of the lessor's and lessee's rights to the goods, and takes free of the existing lease contract.

(3) A buyer or sublessee from the lessee of goods that are subject to an existing lease contract and are covered by a certificate of title issued under a statute of this State or of another jurisdiction

takes no greater rights than those provided both by this section and by the certificate of title statute.

§ 2A–306. Priority of Certain Liens Arising by Operation of Law.

If a person in the ordinary course of his [or her] business furnishes services or materials with respect to goods subject to a lease contract, a lien upon those goods in the possession of that person given by statute or rule of law for those materials or services takes priority over any interest of the lessor or lessee under the lease contract or this Article unless the lien is created by statute and the statute provides otherwise or unless the lien is created by rule of law and the rule of law provides otherwise.

§ 2A–307. Priority of Liens Arising by Attachment or Levy on, Security Interests in, and Other Claims to Goods.

(1) Except as otherwise provided in Section 2A–306, a creditor of a lessee takes subject to the lease contract.

(2) Except as otherwise provided in subsection (3) and in Sections 2A–306 and 2A–308, a creditor of a lessor takes subject to the lease contract unless the creditor holds a lien that attached to the goods before the lease contract became enforceable.

(3) Except as otherwise provided in Sections 9–317, 9–321, and 9–323, a lessee takes a leasehold interest subject to a security interest held by a creditor of the lessor.

As amended in 1990 and 1999.

§ 2A–308. Special Rights of Creditors.

(1) A creditor of a lessor in possession of goods subject to a lease contract may treat the lease contract as void if as against the creditor retention of possession by the lessor is fraudulent under any statute or rule of law, but retention of possession in good faith and current course of trade by the lessor for a commercially reasonable time after the lease contract becomes enforceable is not fraudulent.

(2) Nothing in this Article impairs the rights of creditors of a lessor if the lease contract (a) becomes enforceable, not in current course of trade but in satisfaction of or as security for a pre-existing claim for money, security, or the like, and (b) is made under circumstances which under any statute or rule of law apart from this Article would constitute the transaction a fraudulent transfer or voidable preference.

(3) A creditor of a seller may treat a sale or an identification of goods to a contract for sale as void if as against the creditor retention of possession by the seller is fraudulent under any statute or rule of law, but retention of possession of the goods pursuant to a lease contract entered into by the seller as lessee and the buyer as lessor in connection with the sale or identification of the goods is not fraudulent if the buyer bought for value and in good faith.

§ 2A–309. Lessor's and Lessee's Rights When Goods Become Fixtures.

(1) In this section:

(a) goods are "fixtures" when they become so related to particular real estate that an interest in them arises under real estate law;

(b) a "fixture filing" is the filing, in the office where a mortgage on the real estate would be filed or recorded, of a financing statement covering goods that are or are to become fixtures and conforming to the requirements of Section 9–502(a) and (b);

(c) a lease is a "purchase money lease" unless the lessee has possession or use of the goods or the right to possession or use of the goods before the lease agreement is enforceable;

(d) a mortgage is a "construction mortgage" to the extent it secures an obligation incurred for the construction of an improvement on land including the acquisition cost of the land, if the recorded writing so indicates; and

(e) "encumbrance" includes real estate mortgages and other liens on real estate and all other rights in real estate that are not ownership interests.

(2) Under this Article a lease may be of goods that are fixtures or may continue in goods that become fixtures, but no lease exists under this Article of ordinary building materials incorporated into an improvement on land.

(3) This Article does not prevent creation of a lease of fixtures pursuant to real estate law.

(4) The perfected interest of a lessor of fixtures has priority over a conflicting interest of an encumbrancer or owner of the real estate if:

(a) the lease is a purchase money lease, the conflicting interest of the encumbrancer or owner arises before the goods become fixtures, the interest of the lessor is perfected by a fixture filing before the goods become fixtures or within ten days thereafter, and the lessee has an interest of record in the real estate or is in possession of the real estate; or

(b) the interest of the lessor is perfected by a fixture filing before the interest of the encumbrancer or owner is of record, the lessor's interest has priority over any conflicting interest of a predecessor in title of the encumbrancer or owner, and the lessee has an interest of record in the real estate or is in possession of the real estate.

(5) The interest of a lessor of fixtures, whether or not perfected, has priority over the conflicting interest of an encumbrancer or owner of the real estate if:

(a) the fixtures are readily removable factory or office machines, readily removable equipment that is not primarily used or leased for use in the operation of the real estate, or readily removable replacements of domestic appliances that are goods subject to a consumer lease, and before the goods become fixtures the lease contract is enforceable; or

(b) the conflicting interest is a lien on the real estate obtained by legal or equitable proceedings after the lease contract is enforceable; or

(c) the encumbrancer or owner has consented in writing to the lease or has disclaimed an interest in the goods as fixtures; or

(d) the lessee has a right to remove the goods as against the encumbrancer or owner. If the lessee's right to remove terminates, the priority of the interest of the lessor continues for a reasonable time.

(6) Notwithstanding paragraph (4)(a) but otherwise subject to subsections (4) and (5), the interest of a lessor of fixtures, including the lessor's residual interest, is subordinate to the conflicting interest of an encumbrancer of the real estate under a construction mortgage recorded before the goods become fixtures if the goods become fixtures before the completion of the construction. To the extent given to refinance a construction mortgage, the conflicting interest of an encumbrancer of the real estate under a mortgage has this priority to the same extent as the encumbrancer of the real estate under the construction mortgage.

(7) In cases not within the preceding subsections, priority between the interest of a lessor of fixtures, including the lessor's residual interest, and the conflicting interest of an encumbrancer or owner of the real estate who is not the lessee is determined by the priority rules governing conflicting interests in real estate.

(8) If the interest of a lessor of fixtures, including the lessor's residual interest, has priority over all conflicting interests of all owners and encumbrancers of the real estate, the lessor or the lessee may (i) on default, expiration, termination, or cancellation of the lease agreement but subject to the agreement and this Article, or (ii) if necessary to enforce other rights and remedies of the lessor or lessee under this Article, remove the goods from the real estate, free and clear of all conflicting interests of all owners and encumbrancers of the real estate, but the lessor or lessee must reimburse any encumbrancer or owner of the real estate who is not the lessee and who has not otherwise agreed for the cost of repair of any physical injury, but not for any diminution in value of the real estate caused by the absence of the goods removed or by any necessity of replacing them. A person entitled to reimbursement may refuse permission to remove until the party seeking removal gives adequate security for the performance of this obligation.

(9) Even though the lease agreement does not create a security interest, the interest of a lessor of fixtures, including the lessor's residual interest, is perfected by filing a financing statement as a fixture filing for leased goods that are or are to become fixtures in accordance with the relevant provisions of the Article on Secured Transactions (Article 9).

As amended in 1990 and 1999.

§ 2A–310. **Lessor's and Lessee's Rights When Goods Become Accessions.**

(1) Goods are "accessions" when they are installed in or affixed to other goods.

(2) The interest of a lessor or a lessee under a lease contract entered into before the goods became accessions is superior to all interests in the whole except as stated in subsection (4).

(3) The interest of a lessor or a lessee under a lease contract entered into at the time or after the goods became accessions is superior to all subsequently acquired interests in the whole except as stated in subsection (4) but is subordinate to interests in the whole existing at the time the lease contract was made unless the holders of such interests in the whole have in writing consented to the lease or disclaimed an interest in the goods as part of the whole.

(4) The interest of a lessor or a lessee under a lease contract described in subsection (2) or (3) is subordinate to the interest of

(a) a buyer in the ordinary course of business or a lessee in the ordinary course of business of any interest in the whole acquired after the goods became accessions; or

(b) a creditor with a security interest in the whole perfected before the lease contract was made to the extent that the creditor makes subsequent advances without knowledge of the lease contract.

(5) When under subsections (2) or (3) and (4) a lessor or a lessee of accessions holds an interest that is superior to all interests in the whole, the lessor or the lessee may (a) on default, expiration, termination, or cancellation of the lease contract by the other party but subject to the provisions of the lease contract and this Article, or (b) if necessary to enforce his [or her] other rights and remedies under this Article, remove the goods from the whole, free and clear of all interests in the whole, but he [or she] must reimburse any holder of an interest in the whole who is not the lessee and who has not otherwise agreed for the cost of repair of any physical injury but not for any diminution in value of the whole caused by the absence of the goods removed or by any necessity for replacing them. A person entitled to reimbursement may refuse permission to remove until the party seeking removal gives adequate security for the performance of this obligation.

§ 2A–311. **Priority Subject to Subordination.**

Nothing in this Article prevents subordination by agreement by any person entitled to priority.

As added in 1990.

Part 4 Performance of Lease Contract: Repudiated, Substituted and Excused

§ 2A–401. **Insecurity: Adequate Assurance of Performance.**

(1) A lease contract imposes an obligation on each party that the other's expectation of receiving due performance will not be impaired.

(2) If reasonable grounds for insecurity arise with respect to the performance of either party, the insecure party may demand in writing adequate assurance of due performance. Until the insecure party receives that assurance, if commercially reasonable the insecure party may suspend any performance for which he [or she] has not already received the agreed return.

(3) A repudiation of the lease contract occurs if assurance of due performance adequate under the circumstances of the particular case is not provided to the insecure party within a reasonable time, not to exceed 30 days after receipt of a demand by the other party.

(4) Between merchants, the reasonableness of grounds for insecurity and the adequacy of any assurance offered must be determined according to commercial standards.

(5) Acceptance of any nonconforming delivery or payment does not prejudice the aggrieved party's right to demand adequate assurance of future performance.

§ 2A–402. **Anticipatory Repudiation.**

If either party repudiates a lease contract with respect to a performance not yet due under the lease contract, the loss of which performance will substantially impair the value of the lease contract to the other, the aggrieved party may:

(a) for a commercially reasonable time, await retraction of repudiation and performance by the repudiating party;

(b) make demand pursuant to Section 2A–401 and await assurance of future performance adequate under the circumstances of the particular case; or

(c) resort to any right or remedy upon default under the lease contract or this Article, even though the aggrieved party has notified the repudiating party that the aggrieved party would await the repudiating party's performance and assurance and has urged retraction. In addition, whether or not the aggrieved party is pursuing one of the foregoing remedies, the aggrieved party may suspend performance or, if the aggrieved party is the lessor, proceed in accordance with the provisions of this Article on the lessor's right to identify goods to the lease contract notwithstanding default or to salvage unfinished goods (Section 2A–524).

§ 2A–403. **Retraction of Anticipatory Repudiation.**

(1) Until the repudiating party's next performance is due, the repudiating party can retract the repudiation unless, since the repudiation, the aggrieved party has cancelled the lease contract or materially changed the aggrieved party's position or otherwise indicated that the aggrieved party considers the repudiation final.

(2) Retraction may be by any method that clearly indicates to the aggrieved party that the repudiating party intends to perform under the lease contract and includes any assurance demanded under Section 2A–401.

(3) Retraction reinstates a repudiating party's rights under a lease contract with due excuse and allowance to the aggrieved party for any delay occasioned by the repudiation.

§ 2A–404. **Substituted Performance.**

(1) If without fault of the lessee, the lessor and the supplier, the agreed berthing, loading, or unloading facilities fail or the agreed type of carrier becomes unavailable or the agreed manner of delivery otherwise becomes commercially impracticable, but a commercially reasonable substitute is available, the substitute performance must be tendered and accepted.

(2) If the agreed means or manner of payment fails because of domestic or foreign governmental regulation:

(a) the lessor may withhold or stop delivery or cause the supplier to withhold or stop delivery unless the lessee provides a means or manner of payment that is commercially a substantial equivalent; and

(b) if delivery has already been taken, payment by the means or in the manner provided by the regulation discharges the lessee's obligation unless the regulation is discriminatory, oppressive, or predatory.

§ 2A–405. **Excused Performance.**

Subject to Section 2A–404 on substituted performance, the following rules apply:

(a) Delay in delivery or nondelivery in whole or in part by a lessor or a supplier who complies with paragraphs (b) and (c) is not a default under the lease contract if performance as agreed has been made impracticable by the occurrence of a contingency the nonoccurrence of which was a basic assumption on which the lease contract was made or by compliance in good faith with any applicable foreign or domestic governmental regulation or order, whether or not the regulation or order later proves to be invalid.

(b) If the causes mentioned in paragraph (a) affect only part of the lessor's or the supplier's capacity to perform, he [or she] shall allocate production and deliveries among his [or her] customers but at his [or her] option may include regular customers not then under contract for sale or lease as well as his [or her] own requirements for further manufacture. He [or she] may so allocate in any manner that is fair and reasonable.

(c) The lessor seasonably shall notify the lessee and in the case of a finance lease the supplier seasonably shall notify the lessor and the lessee, if known, that there will be delay or nondelivery and, if allocation is required under paragraph (b), of the estimated quota thus made available for the lessee.

§ 2A–406. **Procedure on Excused Performance.**

(1) If the lessee receives notification of a material or indefinite delay or an allocation justified under Section 2A–405, the lessee may by written notification to the lessor as to any goods involved, and with respect to all of the goods if under an installment lease contract the value of the whole lease contract is substantially impaired (Section 2A–510):

(a) terminate the lease contract (Section 2A–505(2)); or

(b) except in a finance lease that is not a consumer lease, modify the lease contract by accepting the available quota in substitution, with due allowance from the rent payable for the balance of the lease term for the deficiency but without further right against the lessor.

(2) If, after receipt of a notification from the lessor under Section 2A–405, the lessee fails so to modify the lease agreement within a reasonable time not exceeding 30 days, the lease contract lapses with respect to any deliveries affected.

§ 2A–407. **Irrevocable Promises: Finance Leases.**

(1) In the case of a finance lease that is not a consumer lease the lessee's promises under the lease contract become irrevocable and independent upon the lessee's acceptance of the goods.

(2) A promise that has become irrevocable and independent under subsection (1):

(a) is effective and enforceable between the parties, and by or against third parties including assignees of the parties, and

(b) is not subject to cancellation, termination, modification, repudiation, excuse, or substitution without the consent of the party to whom the promise runs.

(3) This section does not affect the validity under any other law of a covenant in any lease contract making the lessee's promises irrevocable and independent upon the lessee's acceptance of the goods.

As amended in 1990.

Part 5 Default

A. In General

§ 2A–501. **Default: Procedure.**

(1) Whether the lessor or the lessee is in default under a lease contract is determined by the lease agreement and this Article.

(2) If the lessor or the lessee is in default under the lease contract, the party seeking enforcement has rights and remedies as provided in this Article and, except as limited by this Article, as provided in the lease agreement.

(3) If the lessor or the lessee is in default under the lease contract, the party seeking enforcement may reduce the party's claim to judgment, or otherwise enforce the lease contract by self-help or any available judicial procedure or nonjudicial procedure, including administrative proceeding, arbitration, or the like, in accordance with this Article.

(4) Except as otherwise provided in Section 1–106(1) or this Article or the lease agreement, the rights and remedies referred to in subsections (2) and (3) are cumulative.

(5) If the lease agreement covers both real property and goods, the party seeking enforcement may proceed under this Part as to the goods, or under other applicable law as to both the real property and the goods in accordance with that party's rights and remedies in respect of the real property, in which case this Part does not apply.

As amended in 1990.

§ 2A–502. **Notice After Default.**

Except as otherwise provided in this Article or the lease agreement, the lessor or lessee in default under the lease contract is not entitled to notice of default or notice of enforcement from the other party to the lease agreement.

§ 2A–503. **Modification or Impairment of Rights and Remedies.**

(1) Except as otherwise provided in this Article, the lease agreement may include rights and remedies for default in addition to or in substitution for those provided in this Article and may limit or alter the measure of damages recoverable under this Article.

(2) Resort to a remedy provided under this Article or in the lease agreement is optional unless the remedy is expressly agreed to be exclusive. If circumstances cause an exclusive or limited remedy to fail of its essential purpose, or provision for an exclusive remedy is unconscionable, remedy may be had as provided in this Article.

(3) Consequential damages may be liquidated under Section 2A–504, or may otherwise be limited, altered, or excluded unless the limitation, alteration, or exclusion is unconscionable. Limitation, alteration, or exclusion of consequential damages for injury to the person in the case of consumer goods is prima facie unconscionable but limitation, alteration, or exclusion of damages where the loss is commercial is not prima facie unconscionable.

(4) Rights and remedies on default by the lessor or the lessee with respect to any obligation or promise collateral or ancillary to the lease contract are not impaired by this Article.

As amended in 1990.

§ 2A–504. **Liquidation of Damages.**

(1) Damages payable by either party for default, or any other act or omission, including indemnity for loss or diminution of anticipated tax benefits or loss or damage to lessor's residual interest, may be liquidated in the lease agreement but only at an amount or by a formula that is reasonable in light of the then anticipated harm caused by the default or other act or omission.

(2) If the lease agreement provides for liquidation of damages, and such provision does not comply with subsection (1), or such provision is an exclusive or limited remedy that circumstances cause to fail of its essential purpose, remedy may be had as provided in this Article.

(3) If the lessor justifiably withholds or stops delivery of goods because of the lessee's default or insolvency (Section 2A–525 or 2A–526), the lessee is entitled to restitution of any amount by which the sum of his [or her] payments exceeds:

(a) the amount to which the lessor is entitled by virtue of terms liquidating the lessor's damages in accordance with subsection (1); or

(b) in the absence of those terms, 20 percent of the then present value of the total rent the lessee was obligated to pay for the balance of the lease term, or, in the case of a consumer lease, the lesser of such amount or $500.

(4) A lessee's right to restitution under subsection (3) is subject to offset to the extent the lessor establishes:

(a) a right to recover damages under the provisions of this Article other than subsection (1); and

(b) the amount or value of any benefits received by the lessee directly or indirectly by reason of the lease contract.

§ 2A–505. **Cancellation and Termination and Effect of Cancellation, Termination, Rescission, or Fraud on Rights and Remedies.**

(1) On cancellation of the lease contract, all obligations that are still executory on both sides are discharged, but any right based on prior default or performance survives, and the cancelling party also retains any remedy for default of the whole lease contract or any unperformed balance.

(2) On termination of the lease contract, all obligations that are still executory on both sides are discharged but any right based on prior default or performance survives.

(3) Unless the contrary intention clearly appears, expressions of "cancellation," "rescission," or the like of the lease contract may not be construed as a renunciation or discharge of any claim in damages for an antecedent default.

(4) Rights and remedies for material misrepresentation or fraud include all rights and remedies available under this Article for default.

(5) Neither rescission nor a claim for rescission of the lease contract nor rejection or return of the goods may bar or be deemed inconsistent with a claim for damages or other right or remedy.

§ 2A–506. **Statute of Limitations.**

(1) An action for default under a lease contract, including breach of warranty or indemnity, must be commenced within 4 years after the cause of action accrued. By the original lease contract the parties may reduce the period of limitation to not less than one year.

(2) A cause of action for default accrues when the act or omission on which the default or breach of warranty is based is or should have been discovered by the aggrieved party, or when the default occurs, whichever is later. A cause of action for indemnity accrues when the act or omission on which the claim for indemnity is based is or should have been discovered by the indemnified party, whichever is later.

(3) If an action commenced within the time limited by subsection (1) is so terminated as to leave available a remedy by another action for the same default or breach of warranty or indemnity, the other action may be commenced after the expiration of the time limited and within 6 months after the termination of the first action unless the termination resulted from voluntary discontinuance or from dismissal for failure or neglect to prosecute.

(4) This section does not alter the law on tolling of the statute of limitations nor does it apply to causes of action that have accrued before this Article becomes effective.

§ 2A–507. **Proof of Market Rent: Time and Place.**

(1) Damages based on market rent (Section 2A–519 or 2A–528) are determined according to the rent for the use of the goods concerned for a lease term identical to the remaining lease term of the original lease agreement and prevailing at the times specified in Sections 2A–519 and 2A–528.

(2) If evidence of rent for the use of the goods concerned for a lease term identical to the remaining lease term of the original lease agreement and prevailing at the times or places described in this Article is not readily available, the rent prevailing within any reasonable time before or after the time described or at any other place or for a different lease term which in commercial judgment or under usage of trade would serve as a reasonable substitute for the one described may be used, making any proper allowance for the difference, including the cost of transporting the goods to or from the other place.

(3) Evidence of a relevant rent prevailing at a time or place or for a lease term other than the one described in this Article offered by one party is not admissible unless and until he [or she] has given the other party notice the court finds sufficient to prevent unfair surprise.

(4) If the prevailing rent or value of any goods regularly leased in any established market is in issue, reports in official publications or trade journals or in newspapers or periodicals of general circulation published as the reports of that market are admissible in evidence. The circumstances of the preparation of the report may be shown to affect its weight but not its admissibility.

As amended in 1990.

B. Default by Lessor

§ 2A–508. **Lessee's Remedies.**

(1) If a lessor fails to deliver the goods in conformity to the lease contract (Section 2A–509) or repudiates the lease contract (Section 2A–402), or a lessee rightfully rejects the goods (Section 2A–509) or justifiably revokes acceptance of the goods (Section 2A–517), then with respect to any goods involved, and with respect to all of the goods if under an installment lease contract the value of the whole lease contract is substantially impaired (Section 2A–510), the lessor is in default under the lease contract and the lessee may:

(a) cancel the lease contract (Section 2A–505(1));

(b) recover so much of the rent and security as has been paid and is just under the circumstances;

(c) cover and recover damages as to all goods affected whether or not they have been identified to the lease contract (Sections 2A–518 and 2A–520), or recover damages for nondelivery (Sections 2A–519 and 2A–520);

(d) exercise any other rights or pursue any other remedies provided in the lease contract.

(2) If a lessor fails to deliver the goods in conformity to the lease contract or repudiates the lease contract, the lessee may also:

(a) if the goods have been identified, recover them (Section 2A–522); or

(b) in a proper case, obtain specific performance or replevy the goods (Section 2A–521).

(3) If a lessor is otherwise in default under a lease contract, the lessee may exercise the rights and pursue the remedies provided in the lease contract, which may include a right to cancel the lease, and in Section 2A–519(3).

(4) If a lessor has breached a warranty, whether express or implied, the lessee may recover damages (Section 2A–519(4)).

(5) On rightful rejection or justifiable revocation of acceptance, a lessee has a security interest in goods in the lessee's possession or control for any rent and security that has been paid and any expenses reasonably incurred in their inspection, receipt, transportation, and care and custody and may hold those goods and dispose of them in good faith and in a commercially reasonable manner, subject to Section 2A–527(5).

(6) Subject to the provisions of Section 2A–407, a lessee, on notifying the lessor of the lessee's intention to do so, may deduct all or any part of the damages resulting from any default under the lease contract from any part of the rent still due under the same lease contract.

As amended in 1990.

§ 2A–509. Lessee's Rights on Improper Delivery; Rightful Rejection.

(1) Subject to the provisions of Section 2A–510 on default in installment lease contracts, if the goods or the tender or delivery fail in any respect to conform to the lease contract, the lessee may reject or accept the goods or accept any commercial unit or units and reject the rest of the goods.

(2) Rejection of goods is ineffective unless it is within a reasonable time after tender or delivery of the goods and the lessee seasonably notifies the lessor.

§ 2A–510. Installment Lease Contracts: Rejection and Default.

(1) Under an installment lease contract a lessee may reject any delivery that is nonconforming if the nonconformity substantially impairs the value of that delivery and cannot be cured or the nonconformity is a defect in the required documents; but if the nonconformity does not fall within subsection (2) and the lessor or the supplier gives adequate assurance of its cure, the lessee must accept that delivery.

(2) Whenever nonconformity or default with respect to one or more deliveries substantially impairs the value of the installment lease contract as a whole there is a default with respect to the whole. But, the aggrieved party reinstates the installment lease contract as a whole if the aggrieved party accepts a nonconforming delivery without seasonably notifying of cancellation or brings an action with respect only to past deliveries or demands performance as to future deliveries.

§ 2A–511. Merchant Lessee's Duties as to Rightfully Rejected Goods.

(1) Subject to any security interest of a lessee (Section 2A–508(5)), if a lessor or a supplier has no agent or place of business at the market of rejection, a merchant lessee, after rejection of goods in his [or her] possession or control, shall follow any reasonable instructions received from the lessor or the supplier with respect to the goods. In the absence of those instructions, a merchant lessee shall make reasonable efforts to sell, lease, or otherwise dispose of the goods for the lessor's account if they threaten to decline in value speedily. Instructions are not reasonable if on demand indemnity for expenses is not forthcoming.

(2) If a merchant lessee (subsection (1)) or any other lessee (Section 2A–512) disposes of goods, he [or she] is entitled to reimbursement either from the lessor or the supplier or out of the proceeds for reasonable expenses of caring for and disposing of the goods and, if the expenses include no disposition commission, to such commission as is usual in the trade, or if there is none, to a reasonable sum not exceeding 10 percent of the gross proceeds.

(3) In complying with this section or Section 2A–512, the lessee is held only to good faith. Good faith conduct hereunder is neither acceptance or conversion nor the basis of an action for damages.

(4) A purchaser who purchases in good faith from a lessee pursuant to this section or Section 2A–512 takes the goods free of any rights of the lessor and the supplier even though the lessee fails to comply with one or more of the requirements of this Article.

§ 2A–512. Lessee's Duties as to Rightfully Rejected Goods.

(1) Except as otherwise provided with respect to goods that threaten to decline in value speedily (Section 2A–511) and subject to any security interest of a lessee (Section 2A–508(5)):

(a) the lessee, after rejection of goods in the lessee's possession, shall hold them with reasonable care at the lessor's or the supplier's disposition for a reasonable time after the lessee's seasonable notification of rejection;

(b) if the lessor or the supplier gives no instructions within a reasonable time after notification of rejection, the lessee may store the rejected goods for the lessor's or the supplier's account or ship them to the lessor or the supplier or dispose of them for the lessor's or the supplier's account with reimbursement in the manner provided in Section 2A–511; but

(c) the lessee has no further obligations with regard to goods rightfully rejected.

(2) Action by the lessee pursuant to subsection (1) is not acceptance or conversion.

§ 2A–513. Cure by Lessor of Improper Tender or Delivery; Replacement.

(1) If any tender or delivery by the lessor or the supplier is rejected because nonconforming and the time for performance has not yet expired, the lessor or the supplier may seasonably notify the lessee of the lessor's or the supplier's intention to cure and may then make a conforming delivery within the time provided in the lease contract.

(2) If the lessee rejects a nonconforming tender that the lessor or the supplier had reasonable grounds to believe would be

acceptable with or without money allowance, the lessor or the supplier may have a further reasonable time to substitute a conforming tender if he [or she] seasonably notifies the lessee.

§ 2A–514. Waiver of Lessee's Objections.

(1) In rejecting goods, a lessee's failure to state a particular defect that is ascertainable by reasonable inspection precludes the lessee from relying on the defect to justify rejection or to establish default:

(a) if, stated seasonably, the lessor or the supplier could have cured it (Section 2A–513); or

(b) between merchants if the lessor or the supplier after rejection has made a request in writing for a full and final written statement of all defects on which the lessee proposes to rely.

(2) A lessee's failure to reserve rights when paying rent or other consideration against documents precludes recovery of the payment for defects apparent on the face of the documents.

§ 2A–515. Acceptance of Goods.

(1) Acceptance of goods occurs after the lessee has had a reasonable opportunity to inspect the goods and

(a) the lessee signifies or acts with respect to the goods in a manner that signifies to the lessor or the supplier that the goods are conforming or that the lessee will take or retain them in spite of their nonconformity; or

(b) the lessee fails to make an effective rejection of the goods (Section 2A–509(2)).

(2) Acceptance of a part of any commercial unit is acceptance of that entire unit.

§ 2A–516. Effect of Acceptance of Goods; Notice of Default; Burden of Establishing Default after Acceptance; Notice of Claim or Litigation to Person Answerable Over.

(1) A lessee must pay rent for any goods accepted in accordance with the lease contract, with due allowance for goods rightfully rejected or not delivered.

(2) A lessee's acceptance of goods precludes rejection of the goods accepted. In the case of a finance lease, if made with knowledge of a nonconformity, acceptance cannot be revoked because of it. In any other case, if made with knowledge of a nonconformity, acceptance cannot be revoked because of it unless the acceptance was on the reasonable assumption that the nonconformity would be seasonably cured. Acceptance does not of itself impair any other remedy provided by this Article or the lease agreement for nonconformity.

(3) If a tender has been accepted:

(a) within a reasonable time after the lessee discovers or should have discovered any default, the lessee shall notify the lessor and the supplier, if any, or be barred from any remedy against the party notified;

(b) except in the case of a consumer lease, within a reasonable time after the lessee receives notice of litigation for infringement or the like (Section 2A–211) the lessee shall notify the lessor or be barred from any remedy over for liability established by the litigation; and

(c) the burden is on the lessee to establish any default.

(4) If a lessee is sued for breach of a warranty or other obligation for which a lessor or a supplier is answerable over the following apply:

(a) The lessee may give the lessor or the supplier, or both, written notice of the litigation. If the notice states that the person notified may come in and defend and that if the person notified does not do so that person will be bound in any action against that person by the lessee by any determination of fact common to the two litigations, then unless the person notified after seasonable receipt of the notice does come in and defend that person is so bound.

(b) The lessor or the supplier may demand in writing that the lessee turn over control of the litigation including settlement if the claim is one for infringement or the like (Section 2A–211) or else be barred from any remedy over. If the demand states that the lessor or the supplier agrees to bear all expense and to satisfy any adverse judgment, then unless the lessee after seasonable receipt of the demand does turn over control the lessee is so barred.

(5) Subsections (3) and (4) apply to any obligation of a lessee to hold the lessor or the supplier harmless against infringement or the like (Section 2A–211).

As amended in 1990.

§ 2A–517. Revocation of Acceptance of Goods.

(1) A lessee may revoke acceptance of a lot or commercial unit whose nonconformity substantially impairs its value to the lessee if the lessee has accepted it:

(a) except in the case of a finance lease, on the reasonable assumption that its nonconformity would be cured and it has not been seasonably cured; or

(b) without discovery of the nonconformity if the lessee's acceptance was reasonably induced either by the lessor's assurances or, except in the case of a finance lease, by the difficulty of discovery before acceptance.

(2) Except in the case of a finance lease that is not a consumer lease, a lessee may revoke acceptance of a lot or commercial unit if the lessor defaults under the lease contract and the default substantially impairs the value of that lot or commercial unit to the lessee.

(3) If the lease agreement so provides, the lessee may revoke acceptance of a lot or commercial unit because of other defaults by the lessor.

(4) Revocation of acceptance must occur within a reasonable time after the lessee discovers or should have discovered the ground for it and before any substantial change in condition of the goods which is not caused by the nonconformity. Revocation is not effective until the lessee notifies the lessor.

(5) A lessee who so revokes has the same rights and duties with regard to the goods involved as if the lessee had rejected them.

As amended in 1990.

§ 2A–518. **Cover; Substitute Goods.**

(1) After a default by a lessor under the lease contract of the type described in Section 2A–508(1), or, if agreed, after other default by the lessor, the lessee may cover by making any purchase or lease of or contract to purchase or lease goods in substitution for those due from the lessor.

(2) Except as otherwise provided with respect to damages liquidated in the lease agreement (Section 2A–504) or otherwise determined pursuant to agreement of the parties (Sections 1–102(3) and 2A–503), if a lessee's cover is by lease agreement substantially similar to the original lease agreement and the new lease agreement is made in good faith and in a commercially reasonable manner, the lessee may recover from the lessor as damages (i) the present value, as of the date of the commencement of the term of the new lease agreement, of the rent under the new lease agreement applicable to that period of the new lease term which is comparable to the then remaining term of the original lease agreement minus the present value as of the same date of the total rent for the then remaining lease term of the original lease agreement, and (ii) any incidental or consequential damages, less expenses saved in consequence of the lessor's default.

(3) If a lessee's cover is by lease agreement that for any reason does not qualify for treatment under subsection (2), or is by purchase or otherwise, the lessee may recover from the lessor as if the lessee had elected not to cover and Section 2A–519 governs.

As amended in 1990.

§ 2A–519. **Lessee's Damages for Non-Delivery, Repudiation, Default, and Breach of Warranty in Regard to Accepted Goods.**

(1) Except as otherwise provided with respect to damages liquidated in the lease agreement (Section 2A–504) or otherwise determined pursuant to agreement of the parties (Sections 1–102(3) and 2A–503), if a lessee elects not to cover or a lessee elects to cover and the cover is by lease agreement that for any reason does not qualify for treatment under Section 2A–518(2), or is by purchase or otherwise, the measure of damages for non-delivery or repudiation by the lessor or for rejection or revocation of acceptance by the lessee is the present value, as of the date of the default, of the then market rent minus the present value as of the same date of the original rent, computed for the remaining lease term of the original lease agreement, together with incidental and consequential damages, less expenses saved in consequence of the lessor's default.

(2) Market rent is to be determined as of the place for tender or, in cases of rejection after arrival or revocation of acceptance, as of the place of arrival.

(3) Except as otherwise agreed, if the lessee has accepted goods and given notification (Section 2A–516(3)), the measure of damages for non-conforming tender or delivery or other default by a lessor is the loss resulting in the ordinary course of events from the lessor's default as determined in any manner that is reasonable together with incidental and consequential damages, less expenses saved in consequence of the lessor's default.

(4) Except as otherwise agreed, the measure of damages for breach of warranty is the present value at the time and place of acceptance of the difference between the value of the use of the goods accepted and the value if they had been as warranted for the lease term, unless special circumstances show proximate damages of a different amount, together with incidental and consequential damages, less expenses saved in consequence of the lessor's default or breach of warranty.

As amended in 1990.

§ 2A–520. **Lessee's Incidental and Consequential Damages.**

(1) Incidental damages resulting from a lessor's default include expenses reasonably incurred in inspection, receipt, transportation, and care and custody of goods rightfully rejected or goods the acceptance of which is justifiably revoked, any commercially reasonable charges, expenses or commissions in connection with effecting cover, and any other reasonable expense incident to the default.

(2) Consequential damages resulting from a lessor's default include:

(a) any loss resulting from general or particular requirements and needs of which the lessor at the time of contracting had reason to know and which could not reasonably be prevented by cover or otherwise; and

(b) injury to person or property proximately resulting from any breach of warranty.

§ 2A–521. **Lessee's Right to Specific Performance or Replevin.**

(1) Specific performance may be decreed if the goods are unique or in other proper circumstances.

(2) A decree for specific performance may include any terms and conditions as to payment of the rent, damages, or other relief that the court deems just.

(3) A lessee has a right of replevin, detinue, sequestration, claim and delivery, or the like for goods identified to the lease contract if after reasonable effort the lessee is unable to effect cover for those goods or the circumstances reasonably indicate that the effort will be unavailing.

§ 2A–522. **Lessee's Right to Goods on Lessor's Insolvency.**

(1) Subject to subsection (2) and even though the goods have not been shipped, a lessee who has paid a part or all of the rent and security for goods identified to a lease contract (Section 2A–217) on making and keeping good a tender of any unpaid portion of the rent and security due under the lease contract may recover the goods identified from the lessor if the lessor becomes insolvent within 10 days after receipt of the first installment of rent and security.

(2) A lessee acquires the right to recover goods identified to a lease contract only if they conform to the lease contract.

C. Default by Lessee

§ 2A–523. Lessor's Remedies.

(1) If a lessee wrongfully rejects or revokes acceptance of goods or fails to make a payment when due or repudiates with respect to a part or the whole, then, with respect to any goods involved, and with respect to all of the goods if under an installment lease contract the value of the whole lease contract is substantially impaired (Section 2A–510), the lessee is in default under the lease contract and the lessor may:

(a) cancel the lease contract (Section 2A–505(1));

(b) proceed respecting goods not identified to the lease contract (Section 2A–524);

(c) withhold delivery of the goods and take possession of goods previously delivered (Section 2A–525);

(d) stop delivery of the goods by any bailee (Section 2A–526);

(e) dispose of the goods and recover damages (Section 2A–527), or retain the goods and recover damages (Section 2A–528), or in a proper case recover rent (Section 2A–529)

(f) exercise any other rights or pursue any other remedies provided in the lease contract.

(2) If a lessor does not fully exercise a right or obtain a remedy to which the lessor is entitled under subsection (1), the lessor may recover the loss resulting in the ordinary course of events from the lessee's default as determined in any reasonable manner, together with incidental damages, less expenses saved in consequence of the lessee's default.

(3) If a lessee is otherwise in default under a lease contract, the lessor may exercise the rights and pursue the remedies provided in the lease contract, which may include a right to cancel the lease. In addition, unless otherwise provided in the lease contract:

(a) if the default substantially impairs the value of the lease contract to the lessor, the lessor may exercise the rights and pursue the remedies provided in subsections (1) or (2); or

(b) if the default does not substantially impair the value of the lease contract to the lessor, the lessor may recover as provided in subsection (2).

As amended in 1990.

§ 2A–524. Lessor's Right to Identify Goods to Lease Contract.

(1) After default by the lessee under the lease contract of the type described in Section 2A–523(1) or 2A–523(3)(a) or, if agreed, after other default by the lessee, the lessor may:

(a) identify to the lease contract conforming goods not already identified if at the time the lessor learned of the default they were in the lessor's or the supplier's possession or control; and

(b) dispose of goods (Section 2A–527(1)) that demonstrably have been intended for the particular lease contract even though those goods are unfinished.

(2) If the goods are unfinished, in the exercise of reasonable commercial judgment for the purposes of avoiding loss and of effective realization, an aggrieved lessor or the supplier may either complete manufacture and wholly identify the goods to the lease contract or cease manufacture and lease, sell, or otherwise dispose of the goods for scrap or salvage value or proceed in any other reasonable manner.

As amended in 1990.

§ 2A–525. Lessor's Right to Possession of Goods.

(1) If a lessor discovers the lessee to be insolvent, the lessor may refuse to deliver the goods.

(2) After a default by the lessee under the lease contract of the type described in Section 2A–523(1) or 2A–523(3)(a) or, if agreed, after other default by the lessee, the lessor has the right to take possession of the goods. If the lease contract so provides, the lessor may require the lessee to assemble the goods and make them available to the lessor at a place to be designated by the lessor which is reasonably convenient to both parties. Without removal, the lessor may render unusable any goods employed in trade or business, and may dispose of goods on the lessee's premises (Section 2A–527).

(3) The lessor may proceed under subsection (2) without judicial process if that can be done without breach of the peace or the lessor may proceed by action.

As amended in 1990.

§ 2A–526. Lessor's Stoppage of Delivery in Transit or Otherwise.

(1) A lessor may stop delivery of goods in the possession of a carrier or other bailee if the lessor discovers the lessee to be insolvent and may stop delivery of carload, truckload, planeload, or larger shipments of express or freight if the lessee repudiates or fails to make a payment due before delivery, whether for rent, security or otherwise under the lease contract, or for any other reason the lessor has a right to withhold or take possession of the goods.

(2) In pursuing its remedies under subsection (1), the lessor may stop delivery until

(a) receipt of the goods by the lessee;

(b) acknowledgment to the lessee by any bailee of the goods, except a carrier, that the bailee holds the goods for the lessee; or

(c) such an acknowledgment to the lessee by a carrier via reshipment or as warehouseman.

(3) (a) To stop delivery, a lessor shall so notify as to enable the bailee by reasonable diligence to prevent delivery of the goods.

(b) After notification, the bailee shall hold and deliver the goods according to the directions of the lessor, but the lessor is liable to the bailee for any ensuing charges or damages.

(c) A carrier who has issued a nonnegotiable bill of lading is not obliged to obey a notification to stop received from a person other than the consignor.

§ 2A–527. Lessor's Rights to Dispose of Goods.

(1) After a default by a lessee under the lease contract of the type described in Section 2A–523(1) or 2A–523(3)(a) or after the lessor refuses to deliver or takes possession of goods (Section 2A–525 or 2A–526), or, if agreed, after other default by a lessee, the lessor may dispose of the goods concerned or the undelivered balance thereof by lease, sale, or otherwise.

(2) Except as otherwise provided with respect to damages liquidated in the lease agreement (Section 2A–504) or otherwise determined pursuant to agreement of the parties (Sections 1–102(3) and 2A–503), if the disposition is by lease agreement substantially similar to the original lease agreement and the new lease agreement is made in good faith and in a commercially reasonable manner, the lessor may recover from the lessee as damages (i) accrued and unpaid rent as of the date of the commencement of the term of the new lease agreement, (ii) the present value, as of the same date, of the total rent for the then remaining lease term of the original lease agreement minus the present value, as of the same date, of the rent under the new lease agreement applicable to that period of the new lease term which is comparable to the then remaining term of the original lease agreement, and (iii) any incidental damages allowed under Section 2A–530, less expenses saved in consequence of the lessee's default.

(3) If the lessor's disposition is by lease agreement that for any reason does not qualify for treatment under subsection (2), or is by sale or otherwise, the lessor may recover from the lessee as if the lessor had elected not to dispose of the goods and Section 2A–528 governs.

(4) A subsequent buyer or lessee who buys or leases from the lessor in good faith for value as a result of a disposition under this section takes the goods free of the original lease contract and any rights of the original lessee even though the lessor fails to comply with one or more of the requirements of this Article.

(5) The lessor is not accountable to the lessee for any profit made on any disposition. A lessee who has rightfully rejected or justifiably revoked acceptance shall account to the lessor for any excess over the amount of the lessee's security interest (Section 2A–508(5)).

As amended in 1990.

§ 2A–528. Lessor's Damages for Non-acceptance, Failure to Pay, Repudiation, or Other Default.

(1) Except as otherwise provided with respect to damages liquidated in the lease agreement (Section 2A–504) or otherwise determined pursuant to agreement of the parties (Section 1–102(3) and 2A–503), if a lessor elects to retain the goods or a lessor elects to dispose of the goods and the disposition is by lease agreement that for any reason does not qualify for treatment under Section 2A–527(2), or is by sale or otherwise, the lessor may recover from the lessee as damages for a default of the type described in Section 2A–523(1) or 2A–523(3)(a), or if agreed, for other default of the lessee, (i) accrued and unpaid rent as of the date of the default if the lessee has never taken possession of the goods, or, if the lessee has taken possession of the goods, as of the date the lessor repossesses the goods or an earlier date on which the lessee makes a tender of the goods to the lessor, (ii) the present value as of the date determined under clause (i) of the total rent for the then remaining lease term of the original lease agreement minus the present value as of the same date of the market rent as the place where the goods are located computed for the same lease term, and (iii) any incidental damages allowed under Section 2A–530, less expenses saved in consequence of the lessee's default.

(2) If the measure of damages provided in subsection (1) is inadequate to put a lessor in as good a position as performance would have, the measure of damages is the present value of the profit, including reasonable overhead, the lessor would have made from full performance by the lessee, together with any incidental damages allowed under Section 2A–530, due allowance for costs reasonably incurred and due credit for payments or proceeds of disposition.

As amended in 1990.

§ 2A–529. Lessor's Action for the Rent.

(1) After default by the lessee under the lease contract of the type described in Section 2A–523(1) or 2A–523(3)(a) or, if agreed, after other default by the lessee, if the lessor complies with subsection (2), the lessor may recover from the lessee as damages:

(a) for goods accepted by the lessee and not repossessed by or tendered to the lessor, and for conforming goods lost or damaged within a commercially reasonable time after risk of loss passes to the lessee (Section 2A–219), (i) accrued and unpaid rent as of the date of entry of judgment in favor of the lessor (ii) the present value as of the same date of the rent for the then remaining lease term of the lease agreement, and (iii) any incidental damages allowed under Section 2A–530, less expenses saved in consequence of the lessee's default; and

(b) for goods identified to the lease contract if the lessor is unable after reasonable effort to dispose of them at a reasonable price or the circumstances reasonably indicate that effort will be unavailing, (i) accrued and unpaid rent as of the date of entry of judgment in favor of the lessor, (ii) the present value as of the same date of the rent for the then remaining lease term of the lease agreement, and (iii) any incidental damages allowed under Section 2A–530, less expenses saved in consequence of the lessee's default.

(2) Except as provided in subsection (3), the lessor shall hold for the lessee for the remaining lease term of the lease agreement any goods that have been identified to the lease contract and are in the lessor's control.

(3) The lessor may dispose of the goods at any time before collection of the judgment for damages obtained pursuant to subsection (1). If the disposition is before the end of the remaining

lease term of the lease agreement, the lessor's recovery against the lessee for damages is governed by Section 2A–527 or Section 2A–528, and the lessor will cause an appropriate credit to be provided against a judgment for damages to the extent that the amount of the judgment exceeds the recovery available pursuant to Section 2A–527 or 2A–528.

(4) Payment of the judgment for damages obtained pursuant to subsection (1) entitles the lessee to the use and possession of the goods not then disposed of for the remaining lease term of and in accordance with the lease agreement.

(5) After default by the lessee under the lease contract of the type described in Section 2A–523(1) or Section 2A–523(3)(a) or, if agreed, after other default by the lessee, a lessor who is held not entitled to rent under this section must nevertheless be awarded damages for non-acceptance under Sections 2A–527 and 2A–528.

As amended in 1990.

§ 2A–530. Lessor's Incidental Damages.

Incidental damages to an aggrieved lessor include any commercially reasonable charges, expenses, or commissions incurred in stopping delivery, in the transportation, care and custody of goods after the lessee's default, in connection with return or disposition of the goods, or otherwise resulting from the default.

§ 2A–531. Standing to Sue Third Parties for Injury to Goods.

(1) If a third party so deals with goods that have been identified to a lease contract as to cause actionable injury to a party to the lease contract (a) the lessor has a right of action against the third party, and (b) the lessee also has a right of action against the third party if the lessee:

(i) has a security interest in the goods;

(ii) has an insurable interest in the goods; or

(iii) bears the risk of loss under the lease contract or has since the injury assumed that risk as against the lessor and the goods have been converted or destroyed.

(2) If at the time of the injury the party plaintiff did not bear the risk of loss as against the other party to the lease contract and there is no arrangement between them for disposition of the recovery, his [or her] suit or settlement, subject to his [or her] own interest, is as a fiduciary for the other party to the lease contract.

(3) Either party with the consent of the other may sue for the benefit of whom it may concern.

§ 2A–532. Lessor's Rights to Residual Interest.

In addition to any other recovery permitted by this Article or other law, the lessor may recover from the lessee an amount that will fully compensate the lessor for any loss of or damage to the lessor's residual interest in the goods caused by the default of the lessee.

As added in 1990.

APPENDIX C

Securities Act of 1933 (Excerpts)

Definitions

Section 2. When used in this title, unless the context requires—

(1) The term "security" means any note, stock, treasury stock, bond, debenture, evidence of indebtedness, certificate of interest or participation in any profit-sharing agreement, collateral-trust certificate, preorganization certificate or subscription, transferable share, investment contract, voting-trust certificate, certificate of deposit for a security, fractional undivided interest in oil, gas, or other mineral rights, any put, call, straddle, option, or privilege on any security, certificate of deposit, or group or index of securities (including any interest therein or based on the value thereof), or any put, call, straddle, option, or privilege entered into on a national securities exchange relating to foreign currency, or, in general, any interest or participation in, temporary or interim certificate for, receipt for, guarantee of, or warrant or right to subscribe to or purchase, any of the foregoing.

Exempted Securities

Section 3. (a) Except as hereinafter expressly provided the provisions of this title shall not apply to any of the following classes of securities:

* * * *

(2) Any security issued or guaranteed by the United States or any territory thereof, or by the District of Columbia, or by any State of the United States, or by any political subdivision of a State or Territory, or by any public instrumentality of one or more States or Territories, or by any person controlled or supervised by and acting as an instrumentality of the Government of the United States pursuant to authority granted by the Congress of the United States; or any certificate of deposit for any of the foregoing; or any security issued or guaranteed by any bank; or any security issued by or representing an interest in or a direct obligation of a Federal Reserve Bank. * * *

(3) Any note, draft, bill of exchange, or banker's acceptance which arises out of a current transaction or the proceeds of which have been or are to be used for current transactions, and which has a maturity at the time of issuance of not exceeding nine months, exclusive of days of grace, or any renewal thereof the maturity of which is likewise limited;

(4) Any security issued by a person organized and operated exclusively for religious, educational, benevolent, fraternal, charitable, or reformatory purposes and not for pecuniary profit, and no part of the net earnings of which inures to the benefit of any person, private stockholder, or individual;

* * * *

(11) Any security which is a part of an issue offered and sold only to persons resident within a single State or Territory, where the issuer of such security is a person resident and doing business within, or, if a corporation, incorporated by and doing business within, such State or Territory.

(b) The Commission may from time to time by its rules and regulations and subject to such terms and conditions as may be described therein, add any class of securities to the securities exempted as provided in this section, if it finds that the enforcement of this title with respect to such securities is not necessary in the public interest and for the protection of investors by reason of the small amount involved or the limited character of the public offering; but no issue of securities shall be exempted under this subsection where the aggregate amount at which such issue is offered to the public exceeds $5,000,000.

Exempted Transactions

Section 4. The provisions of section 5 shall not apply to—

(1) transactions by any person other than an issuer, underwriter, or dealer.

(2) transactions by an issuer not involving any public offering.

(3) transactions by a dealer (including an underwriter no longer acting as an underwriter in respect of the security involved in such transactions), except—

(A) transactions taking place prior to the expiration of forty days after the first date upon which the security was bona fide offered to the public by the issuer or by or through an underwriter.

(B) transactions in a security as to which a registration statement has been filed taking place prior to the expiration of forty days after the effective date of such registration statement or prior to the expiration of forty days after the first date upon which the security was bona fide offered to the public by the issuer or by or through an underwriter after such effective date, whichever is later (excluding in the computation of such forty days any time during which a stop order issued under section 8 is in effect as to the security), or such shorter period as the Commission may specify by rules and regulations or order, and

(C) transactions as to the securities constituting the whole or a part of an unsold allotment to or subscription by such dealer as a participant in the distribution of such securities by the issuer or by or through an underwriter.

With respect to transactions referred to in clause (B), if securities of the issuer have not previously been sold pursuant to an earlier effective registration statement the applicable period, instead of forty days, shall be ninety days, or such shorter period as the Commission may specify by rules and regulations or order.

(4) brokers' transactions, executed upon customers' orders on any exchange or in the over-the-counter market but not the solicitation of such orders.

* * * *

(6) transactions involving offers or sales by an issuer solely to one or more accredited investors, if the aggregate offering price of an issue of securities offered in reliance on this paragraph does not exceed the amount allowed under Section 3(b) of this title, if there is no advertising or public solicitation in connection with the transaction by the issuer or anyone acting on the issuer's behalf, and if the issuer files such notice with the Commission as the Commission shall prescribe.

Prohibitions Relating to Interstate Commerce and the Mails

Section 5. (a) Unless a registration statement is in effect as to a security, it shall be unlawful for any person, directly or indirectly—

(1) to make use of any means or instruments of transportation or communication in interstate commerce or of the mails to sell such security through the use or medium of any prospectus or otherwise; or

(2) to carry or cause to be carried through the mails or in interstate commerce, by any means or instruments of transportation, any such security for the purpose of sale or for delivery after sale.

(b) It shall be unlawful for any person, directly or indirectly—

(1) to make use of any means or instruments of transportation or communication in interstate commerce or of the mails to carry or transmit any prospectus relating to any security with respect to which a registration statement has been filed under this title, unless such prospectus meets the requirements of section 10, or

(2) to carry or to cause to be carried through the mails or in interstate commerce any such security for the purpose of sale or for delivery after sale, unless accompanied or preceded by a prospectus that meets the requirements of subsection (a) of section 10.

(c) It shall be unlawful for any person, directly, or indirectly, to make use of any means or instruments of transportation or communication in interstate commerce or of the mails to offer to sell or offer to buy through the use or medium of any prospectus or otherwise any security, unless a registration statement has been filed as to such security, or while the registration statement is the subject of a refusal order or stop order or (prior to the effective date of the registration statement) any public proceeding of examination under section 8.

APPENDIX D

Securities Exchange Act of 1934 (Excerpts)

Definitions and Application of Title

Section 3. (a) When used in this title, unless the context otherwise requires—

* * * *

(4) The term "broker" means any person engaged in the business of effecting transactions in securities for the account of others, but does not include a bank.

(5) The term "dealer" means any person engaged in the business of buying and selling securities for his own account, through a broker or otherwise, but does not include a bank, or any person insofar as he buys or sells securities for his own account, either individually or in some fiduciary capacity, but not as part of a regular business.

* * * *

(7) The term "director" means any director of a corporation or any person performing similar functions with respect to any organization, whether incorporated or unincorporated.

(8) The term "issuer" means any person who issues or proposes to issue any security; except that with respect to certificates of deposit for securities, voting-trust certificates, or collateral-trust certificates, or with respect to certificates of interest or shares in an unincorporated investment trust not having a board of directors or the fixed, restricted management, or unit type, the term "issuer" means the person or persons performing the acts and assuming the duties of depositor or manager pursuant to the provisions of the trust or other agreement or instrument under which such securities are issued; and except that with respect to equipment-trust certificates or like securities, the term "issuer" means the person by whom the equipment or property is, or is to be, used.

(9) The term "person" means a natural person, company, government, or political subdivision, agency, or instrumentality of a government.

Regulation of the Use of Manipulative and Deceptive Devices

Section 10. It shall be unlawful for any person, directly or indirectly, by the use of any means or instrumentality of interstate commerce or of the mails, or of any facility of any national securities exchange—

(a) To effect a short sale, or to use or employ any stop-loss order in connection with the purchase or sale, of any security registered on a national securities exchange, in contravention of such rules and regulations as the Commission may prescribe as necessary or appropriate in the public interest or for the protection of investors.

(b) To use or employ, in connection with the purchase or sale of any security registered on a national securities exchange or any security not so registered, any manipulative or deceptive device or contrivance in contravention of such rules and regulations as the Commission may prescribe as necessary or appropriate in the public interest or for the protection of investors.

APPENDIX E

Title VII of the Civil Rights Act of 1964 (Excerpts)

Section 703. **Unlawful Employment Practices.** (a) It shall be an unlawful employment practice for an employer—

(1) to fail or refuse to hire or to discharge any individual, or otherwise to discriminate against any individual with respect to his compensation, terms, conditions, or privileges of employment, because of such individual's race, color, religion, sex, or national origin; or

(2) to limit, segregate, or classify his employees or applicants for employment in any way which would deprive or tend to deprive any individual of employment opportunities or otherwise adversely affect his status as an employee, because of such individual's race, color, religion, sex, or national origin.

(b) It shall be an unlawful employment practice for an employment agency to fail or refuse to refer for employment, or otherwise to discriminate against, any individual because of his race, color, religion, sex, or national origin, or to classify or refer for employment any individual on the basis or his race, color, religion, sex, or national origin.

(c) It shall be an unlawful employment practice for a labor organization—

(1) to exclude or to expel from its membership, or otherwise to discriminate against, any individual because of his race, color, religion, sex, or national origin;

(2) to limit, segregate, or classify its membership or applicants for membership, or to classify or fail or refuse to refer for employment any individual, in any way which would deprive or tend to deprive any individual of employment opportunities, or would limit such employment opportunities or otherwise adversely affect his status as an employee or as an applicant for employment, because of such individual's race, color, religion, sex, or national origin; or

(3) to cause or attempt to cause an employer to discriminate against an individual in violation of this section.

(d) It shall be an unlawful employment practice for any employer, labor organization, or joint labor-management committee controlling apprenticeship or other training or retraining, including on-the-job training programs to discriminate against any individual because of his race, color, religion, sex, or national origin in admission to, or employment in, any program established to provide apprenticeship or other training.

(e) Notwithstanding any other provision of this subchapter—

(1) it shall not be an unlawful employment practice for an employer to hire and employ employees, for an employment agency to classify, or refer for employment any individual, for a labor organization to classify its membership or to classify or refer for employment any individual, or for an employer, labor organization, or joint labor-management committee controlling apprenticeship or other training or retraining programs to admit or employ any individual in any such program, on the basis of his religion, sex, or national origin in those certain instances where religion, sex, or national origin is a bona fide occupational qualification reasonably necessary to the normal operation of that particular business or enterprise, and

(2) it shall not be an unlawful employment practice for a school, college, university, or other educational institution or institution of learning to hire and employ employees of a particular religion if such school, college, university, or other educational institution or institution of learning is, in whole or in substantial part,

owned, supported, controlled, or managed by a particular religion or by a particular religious corporation, association, or society, or if the curriculum of such school, college, university, or other educational institution or institution of learning is directed toward the propagation of a particular religion.

(f) As used in this subchapter, the phrase "unlawful employment practice" shall not be deemed to include any action or measure taken by an employer, labor organization, joint labor-management committee, or employment agency with respect to an individual who is a member of the Communist Party of the United States or of any other organization required to register as a Communist-action or Communist-front organization. * * *

(g) Notwithstanding any other provision of this subchapter, it shall not be an unlawful employment practice for an employer to fail or refuse to hire and employ any individual for any position, for an employer to discharge any individual from any position, or for an employment agency to fail or refuse to refer any individual for employment in any position, or for a labor organization to fail or refuse to refer any individual for employment in any position, if—

(1) the occupancy of such position, or access to the premises in or upon which any part of the duties of such position is performed or is to be performed, is subject to any requirement imposed in the interest of the national security of the United States * * * and

(2) such individual has not fulfilled or has ceased to fulfill that requirement.

(h) Notwithstanding any other provision of this subchapter, it shall not be an unlawful employment practice for an employer to apply different standards of compensation, or different terms, conditions, or privileges of employment pursuant to a bona fide seniority or merit system, or a system which measures earnings by quantity or quality of production or to employees who work in different locations, provided that such differences are not the result of an intention to discriminate because of race, color, religion, sex, or national origin, nor shall it be an unlawful employment practice for an employer to give and act upon the results of any professionally developed ability test provided that such test, its administration or action upon the results is not designed, intended or used to discriminate because of race, color, religion, sex, or national origin. * * *

(j) Nothing contained in this subchapter shall be interpreted to require any employer, employment agency, labor organization, or joint labor-management committee subject to this subchapter to grant preferential treatment to any individual or to any group because of the race, color, religion, sex, or national origin of such individual or group on account of an imbalance which may exist with respect to the total number or percentage of persons of any race, color, religion, sex, or national origin employed by any employer, referred or classified for employment by any employment agency or labor organization, or admitted to, or employed in, any apprenticeship or other training program, in comparison with the total number or percentage of persons of such race, color, religion, sex, or national origin in any community, State, section, or other area, or in the available work force in any community, State, section, or other area.

* * * *

Section 704. **Other Unlawful Employment Practices.** (a) It shall be an unlawful employment practice for an employer to discriminate against any of his employees or applicants for employment, for an employment agency, or joint labor-management committee controlling apprenticeship or other training or retraining, including on-the-job training programs, to discriminate against any individual, or for a labor organization to discriminate against any member thereof or applicant for membership, because he has opposed any practice made an unlawful employment practice by this subchapter, or because he has made a charge, testified, assisted, or participated in any manner in an investigation, proceeding, or hearing under this subchapter.

(b) It shall be an unlawful employment practice for an employer, labor organization, employment agency, or joint labor-management committee controlling apprenticeship or other training or retraining, including on-the-job training programs, to print or publish or cause to be printed or published any notice or advertisement relating to employment by such an employer or membership or any classification or referral for employment by such a labor organization, or relating to any classification or referral for employment by such an employment agency, or relating to admission to, or employment in, any program established to provide apprenticeship or other training by such a joint-labor-management committee, indicating any preference, limitation, specification, or discrimination, based on race, color, religion, sex, or national origin, except that such a notice or advertisement may indicate a preference, limitation, specification, or discrimination based on religion, sex or national origin when religion, sex, or national origin is a bona fide occupational qualification for employment.

APPENDIX F

Digital Millennium Copyright Act of 1998 (Excerpts)

Sec. 1201. Circumvention of copyright protection systems

(a) VIOLATIONS REGARDING CIRCUMVENTION OF TECHNOLOGICAL MEASURES—(1)(A) No person shall circumvent a technological measure that effectively controls access to a work protected under this title. * * *

* * * *

(b) ADDITIONAL VIOLATIONS—(1) No person shall manufacture, import, offer to the public, provide, or otherwise traffic in any technology, product, service, device, component, or part thereof, that—

(A) is primarily designed or produced for the purpose of circumventing protection afforded by a technological measure that effectively protects a right of a copyright owner under this title in a work or a portion thereof;

(B) has only limited commercially significant purpose or use other than to circumvent protection afforded by a technological measure that effectively protects a right of a copyright owner under this title in a work or a portion thereof; or

(C) is marketed by that person or another acting in concert with that person with that person's knowledge for use in circumventing protection afforded by a technological measure that effectively protects a right of a copyright owner under this title in a work or a portion thereof.

* * * *

Sec. 1202. Integrity of copyright management information

(a) FALSE COPYRIGHT MANAGEMENT INFORMATION—No person shall knowingly and with the intent to induce, enable, facilitate, or conceal infringement—

(1) provide copyright management information that is false, or

(2) distribute or import for distribution copyright management information that is false.

(b) REMOVAL OR ALTERATION OF COPYRIGHT MANAGEMENT INFORMATION—No person shall, without the authority of the copyright owner or the law—

(1) intentionally remove or alter any copyright management information,

(2) distribute or import for distribution copyright management information knowing that the copyright management information has been removed or altered without authority of the copyright owner or the law, or

(3) distribute, import for distribution, or publicly perform works, copies of works, or phonorecords, knowing that copyright management information has been removed or altered without authority of the copyright owner or the law, knowing, or, with respect to civil remedies under section 1203, having reasonable grounds to know, that it will induce, enable, facilitate, or conceal an infringement of any right under this title.

(c) DEFINITION—As used in this section, the term "copyright management information" means any of the following information conveyed in connection with copies or phonorecords of a work or performances or displays of a work, including in digital form, except that such term does not include any personally identifying information about a user of a work or of a copy, phonorecord, performance, or display of a work:

(1) The title and other information identifying the work, including the information set forth on a notice of copyright.

(2) The name of, and other identifying information about, the author of a work.
(3) The name of, and other identifying information about, the copyright owner of the work, including the information set forth in a notice of copyright.
(4) With the exception of public performances of works by radio and television broadcast stations, the name of, and other identifying information about, a performer whose performance is fixed in a work other than an audiovisual work.
(5) With the exception of public performances of works by radio and television broadcast stations, in the case of an audiovisual work, the name of, and other identifying information about, a writer, performer, or director who is credited in the audiovisual work.
(6) Terms and conditions for use of the work.
(7) Identifying numbers or symbols referring to such information or links to such information.
(8) Such other information as the Register of Copyrights may prescribe by regulation, except that the Register of Copyrights may not require the provision of any information concerning the user of a copyrighted work.

* * * *

Sec. 512. Limitations on liability relating to material online

(a) TRANSITORY DIGITAL NETWORK COMMUNICATIONS—A service provider shall not be liable for monetary relief, or, except as provided in subsection (j), for injunctive or other equitable relief, for infringement of copyright by reason of the provider's transmitting, routing, or providing connections for, material through a system or network controlled or operated by or for the service provider, or by reason of the intermediate and transient storage of that material in the course of such transmitting, routing, or providing connections, if—

(1) the transmission of the material was initiated by or at the direction of a person other than the service provider;
(2) the transmission, routing, provision of connections, or storage is carried out through an automatic technical process without selection of the material by the service provider;
(3) the service provider does not select the recipients of the material except as an automatic response to the request of another person;
(4) no copy of the material made by the service provider in the course of such intermediate or transient storage is maintained on the system or network in a manner ordinarily accessible to anyone other than anticipated recipients, and no such copy is maintained on the system or network in a manner ordinarily accessible to such anticipated recipients for a longer period than is reasonably necessary for the transmission, routing, or provision of connections; and
(5) the material is transmitted through the system or network without modification of its content.

APPENDIX G

Uniform Electronic Transactions Act (Excerpts)

* * * *

Section 5. USE OF ELECTRONIC RECORDS AND ELECTRONIC SIGNATURES; VARIATION BY AGREEMENT.

(a) This [Act] does not require a record or signature to be created, generated, sent, communicated, received, stored, or otherwise processed or used by electronic means or in electronic form.

(b) This [Act] applies only to transactions between parties each of which has agreed to conduct transactions by electronic means. Whether the parties agree to conduct a transaction by electronic means is determined from the context and surrounding circumstances, including the parties' conduct.

(c) A party that agrees to conduct a transaction by electronic means may refuse to conduct other transactions by electronic means. The right granted by this subsection may not be waived by agreement.

(d) Except as otherwise provided in this [Act], the effect of any of its provisions may be varied by agreement. The presence in certain provisions of this [Act] of the words "unless otherwise agreed," or words of similar import, does not imply that the effect of other provisions may not be varied by agreement.

(e) Whether an electronic record or electronic signature has legal consequences is determined by this [Act] and other applicable law.

Section 6. CONSTRUCTION AND APPLICATION. This [Act] must be construed and applied:

(1) to facilitate electronic transactions consistent with other applicable law;

(2) to be consistent with reasonable practices concerning electronic transactions and with the continued expansion of those practices; and

(3) to effectuate its general purpose to make uniform the law with respect to the subject of this [Act] among States enacting it.

Section 7. LEGAL RECOGNITION OF ELECTRONIC RECORDS, ELECTRONIC SIGNATURES, AND ELECTRONIC CONTRACTS.

(a) A record or signature may not be denied legal effect or enforceability solely because it is in electronic form.

(b) A contract may not be denied legal effect or enforceability solely because an electronic record was used in its formation.

(c) If a law requires a record to be in writing, an electronic record satisfies the law.

(d) If a law requires a signature, an electronic signature satisfies the law.

* * * *

Section 10. EFFECT OF CHANGE OR ERROR. If a change or error in an electronic record occurs in a transmission between parties to a transaction, the following rules apply:

(1) If the parties have agreed to use a security procedure to detect changes or errors and one party has conformed to the procedure, but the other party has not, and the nonconforming party would have detected the change or error had that party also conformed, the conforming party may avoid the effect of the changed or erroneous electronic record.

(2) In an automated transaction involving an individual, the individual may avoid the effect of an electronic record that resulted from an error made by the individual in dealing with the electronic agent of another person if the electronic agent did not provide an opportunity for the prevention or correction of the error and, at the time the individual learns of the error, the individual:

(A) promptly notifies the other person of the error and that the individual did not intend to be bound by the electronic record received by the other person;

(B) takes reasonable steps, including steps that conform to the other person's reasonable instructions, to return to the other person or, if instructed by the other person, to destroy the consideration received, if any, as a result of the erroneous electronic record; and

(C) has not used or received any benefit or value from the consideration, if any, received from the other person.

(3) If neither paragraph (1) nor paragraph (2) applies, the change or error has the effect provided by other law, including the law of mistake, and the parties' contract, if any.

(4) Paragraphs (2) and (3) may not be varied by agreement.

APPENDIX H

Electronic Signatures in Global and National Commerce Act of 2000 (Excerpts)

SEC. 101. GENERAL RULE OF VALIDITY.

(a) IN GENERAL—Notwithstanding any statute, regulation, or other rule of law (other than this title and title II), with respect to any transaction in or affecting interstate or foreign commerce—

(1) a signature, contract, or other record relating to such transaction may not be denied legal effect, validity, or enforceability solely because it is in electronic form; and

(2) a contract relating to such transaction may not be denied legal effect, validity, or enforceability solely because an electronic signature or electronic record was used in its formation.

* * * *

(d) RETENTION OF CONTRACTS AND RECORDS—

(1) ACCURACY AND ACCESSIBILITY—If a statute, regulation, or other rule of law requires that a contract or other record relating to a transaction in or affecting interstate or foreign commerce be retained, that requirement is met by retaining an electronic record of the information in the contract or other record that—

(A) accurately reflects the information set forth in the contract or other record; and

(B) remains accessible to all persons who are entitled to access by statute, regulation, or rule of law, for the period required by such statute, regulation, or rule of law, in a form that is capable of being accurately reproduced for later reference, whether by transmission, printing, or otherwise.

(2) EXCEPTION—A requirement to retain a contract or other record in accordance with paragraph (1) does not apply to any information whose sole purpose is to enable the contract or other record to be sent, communicated, or received.

(3) ORIGINALS—If a statute, regulation, or other rule of law requires a contract or other record relating to a transaction in or affecting interstate or foreign commerce to be provided, available, or retained in its original form, or provides consequences if the contract or other record is not provided, available, or retained in its original form, that statute, regulation, or rule of law is satisfied by an electronic record that complies with paragraph (1).

(4) CHECKS—If a statute, regulation, or other rule of law requires the retention of a check, that requirement is satisfied by retention of an electronic record of the information on the front and back of the check in accordance with paragraph (1).

* * * *

(g) NOTARIZATION AND ACKNOWLEDGMENT—If a statute, regulation, or other rule of law requires a signature or record relating to a transaction in or affecting interstate or foreign commerce to be notarized, acknowledged, verified, or made under oath, that requirement is satisfied if the electronic signature of the person authorized to perform those acts, together with all other information required to be included by other applicable statute, regulation, or rule of law, is attached to or logically associated with the signature or record.

(h) ELECTRONIC AGENTS—A contract or other record relating to a transaction in or affecting interstate or foreign commerce may not be denied legal effect, validity, or enforceability solely because its formation, creation, or delivery involved the action of one or more electronic agents so long as the action of any such electronic agent is legally attributable to the person to be bound.

(i) INSURANCE—It is the specific intent of the Congress that this title and title II apply to the business of insurance.

(j) INSURANCE AGENTS AND BROKERS—An insurance agent or broker acting under the direction of a party that enters into a contract by means of an electronic record or electronic signature may not be held liable for any deficiency in the electronic procedures agreed to by the parties under that contract if—

(1) the agent or broker has not engaged in negligent, reckless, or intentional tortious conduct;
(2) the agent or broker was not involved in the development or establishment of such electronic procedures; and
(3) the agent or broker did not deviate from such procedures.

* * * *

SEC. 103. SPECIFIC EXCEPTIONS.

(a) EXCEPTED REQUIREMENTS—The provisions of section 101 shall not apply to a contract or other record to the extent it is governed by—

(1) a statute, regulation, or other rule of law governing the creation and execution of wills, codicils, or testamentary trusts;
(2) a State statute, regulation, or other rule of law governing adoption, divorce, or other matters of family law; or
(3) the Uniform Commercial Code, as in effect in any State, other than sections 1–107 and 1–206 and Articles 2 and 2A.

(b) ADDITIONAL EXCEPTIONS—The provisions of section 101 shall not apply to—

(1) court orders or notices, or official court documents (including briefs, pleadings, and other writings) required to be executed in connection with court proceedings;
(2) any notice of—
    (A) the cancellation or termination of utility services (including water, heat, and power);
    (B) default, acceleration, repossession, foreclosure, or eviction, or the right to cure, under a credit agreement secured by, or a rental agreement for, a primary residence of an individual;
    (C) the cancellation or termination of health insurance or benefits or life insurance benefits (excluding annuities); or
    (D) recall of a product, or material failure of a product, that risks endangering health or safety; or
(3) any document required to accompany any transportation or handling of hazardous materials, pesticides, or other toxic or dangerous materials.

APPENDIX I

Answers to Even-Numbered *For Review* Questions

CHAPTER 1

2A. *Precedent*
Judges attempt to be consistent, and when possible, they base their decisions on the principles suggested by earlier cases. They seek to decide similar cases in a similar way and consider new cases with care, because they know that their conflicting decisions make new law. Each interpretation becomes part of the law on the subject and serves as a legal precedent—a decision that furnishes an example or authority for deciding subsequent cases involving similar legal principles or facts. A court will depart from the rule of a precedent when it decides that the rule should no longer be followed. If a court decides that a precedent is simply incorrect or that technological or social changes have rendered the precedent inapplicable, the court might rule contrary to the precedent.

4A. *Commercial activities*
To prevent states from establishing laws and regulations that would interfere with trade and commerce among the states, the Constitution expressly delegated to the national government the power to regulate interstate commerce. The commerce clause (Article I, Section 8, of the U.S. Constitution) expressly permits Congress "[t]o regulate Commerce with foreign Nations, and among the several States, and with the Indian Tribes."

CHAPTER 2

2A. *Ensuring legal and ethical behavior*
Ethical leadership is important to create and maintain an ethical workplace. Management can set standards, and apply those standards to themselves and their firm's employees.

4A. *Professionals' duties*
Generally, professionals are subject to standards of conduct established by codes of professional ethics, as well as the law. To those who rely on their services, professionals owe duties that include compliance with the standards of care, knowledge, and judgment set by these sources.

CHAPTER 3

2A. *Jurisdiction*
To hear a case, a court must have jurisdiction over the person against whom the suit is brought or over the property involved in the suit. The court must also have jurisdiction over the subject matter. Generally, courts apply a "sliding-scale" standard to determine when it is proper to exercise jurisdiction over a defendant whose only connection with the jurisdiction is the Internet.

4A. *Pleadings, discovery, and electronic filing*
The pleadings include a plaintiff's complaint and a defendant's answer (and the counterclaim and reply). The pleadings inform each party of the other's claims and specify the issues involved in a case. Discovery is the process of obtaining information and evidence about a case from the other party or third parties. Discovery entails gaining access to witnesses, documents, records, and other types of evidence. Electronic discovery differs in its subject (e-media rather than traditional sources of information). Electronic filing involves the filing of court documents in electronic media, typically over the Internet.

CHAPTER 4

2A. *Purpose and categories of torts*
Generally, the purpose of tort law is to provide remedies for the invasion of legally recognized and protected interests (personal

safety, freedom of movement, property, and some intangibles, including privacy and reputation). The two broad categories of torts are intentional and unintentional.

4A. *Strict liability*
Strict liability is liability without fault. Strict liability for damages proximately caused by an abnormally dangerous or exceptional activity, or the keeping of dangerous animals is an application of this doctrine. Another significant application of strict liability is in the area of product liability.

CHAPTER 5

2A. *Trademarks and patents*
As stated in Article I, Section 8, of the Constitution, Congress is authorized "[t]o promote the Progress of Science and useful Arts, by securing for limited Times to Authors and Inventors the exclusive Right to their respective Writings and Discoveries." Laws protecting patents and trademarks, as well copyrights, are designed to protect and reward inventive and artistic creativity.

4A. *Trade secrets*
Trade secrets are business processes and information that are not or cannot be patented, copyrighted, or trademarked. Trade secrets consist of generally anything that makes an individual company unique and that would have value to a competitor. The Uniform Trade Secrets Act, the Economic Espionage Act, and the common law offer trade secrets protection.

CHAPTER 6

2A. *Types of crime and white-collar crime*
Traditionally, crimes have been grouped into the following categories: violent crime (crimes against persons), property crime, public order crime, white-collar crime, and organized crime. White-collar crime is an illegal act or series of acts committed by an individual or business entity using some nonviolent means, usually in the course of a legitimate occupation.

4A. *Constitutional safeguards and criminal process*
Under the Fourth Amendment, before searching or seizing private property, law enforcement officers must obtain a search warrant, which requires probable cause. Under the Fifth Amendment, no one can be deprived of "life, liberty, or property without due process of law." The Fifth Amendment also protects persons against double jeopardy and self-incrimination. The Sixth Amendment guarantees the right to a speedy trial, the right to a jury trial, the right to a public trial, the right to confront witnesses, and the right to counsel. All evidence obtained in violation of the Fourth, Fifth, and Sixth Amendments must be excluded from the trial, as well as all evidence derived from the illegally obtained evidence. Individuals who are arrested must be informed of certain constitutional rights, including their Fifth Amendment right to remain silent and their Sixth Amendment right to counsel. The Eighth Amendment prohibits excessive bails and fines, and cruel and unusual punishment. The basic steps in the criminal process include an arrest, the booking, the initial appearance, a preliminary hearing, a grand jury or magistrate's review, the arraignment, a plea bargain (if any), and the trial or guilty plea.

CHAPTER 7

2A. *Types of contracts*
The various types of contracts include bilateral, unilateral, express, implied, formal, informal, quasi, valid, void, voidable, and unenforceable.

4A. *Acceptance of an offer*
An acceptance is a voluntary act on the part of the offeree that shows assent, or agreement, to the terms of an offer. The acceptance must be unequivocal and must be timely communicated to the offeror.

CHAPTER 8

2A. *Intoxication*
If a person who is sufficiently intoxicated to lack mental capacity enters into a contract, the contract is voidable at the option of that person. It must be proved that the person's reason and judgment were impaired to the extent that he or she did not comprehend the legal consequences of entering into the contract.

4A. *Elements of fraudulent misrepresentation*
Fraudulent misrepresentation has three elements: (1) misrepresentation of a material fact must occur, (2) there must be an intent to deceive, and (3) the innocent party must justifiably rely on the misrepresentation. Also, to collect damages, a party must have been injured as a result of the misrepresentation.

CHAPTER 9

2A. *Intended beneficiary*
A beneficiary will be considered an intended beneficiary if a reasonable person in the position of the beneficiary would believe that the promisee intended to confer on the beneficiary the right to bring suit to enforce the contract. Other factors include whether performance is rendered directly to the third party, whether the third party has the right to control the details of performance, and whether the third party is expressly designated as a beneficiary in the contract.

4A. *Equitable remedies*
When fraud, mistake, duress, or failure of consideration is present, rescission is available. The failure of one party to perform under a contract entitles the other party to rescind the contract. Specific performance might be granted as a remedy when damages is an inadequate remedy and the subject matter of the contract is unique. Reformation allows a contract to be rewritten to reflect the parties' true intentions. It applies most often when fraud or mutual mistake occurs.

CHAPTER 10

2A. *Shrink-wrap and click-on agreements*
A shrink-wrap agreement is an agreement whose terms are expressed inside a box in which the goods are packaged.

Generally, courts have enforced the terms of shrink-wrap agreements the same as the terms of other contracts, applying the traditional common law of contracts.

4A. *Partnering agreement*
A partnering agreement is an agreement between a seller and a buyer who often do business on the terms and conditions that apply to all of their transactions conducted electronically. Such an agreement reduces the likelihood of a dispute and provides for the resolution of any dispute that does arise.

CHAPTER 11

2A. *Additional terms*
Under the UCC, a contract can be formed even if the acceptance includes an offeree's additional or different terms. If one of the parties is a nonmerchant, the contract does not include the additional terms. If both parties are merchants, the additional terms automatically become part of the contract unless (1) the original offer expressly limits acceptance to the terms of the offer, (2) the new or changed terms *materially* alter the contract, or (3) the offeror objects to the new or changed terms within a reasonable period of time. (If the additional terms expressly require the offeror's assent, the offeree's expression is not an acceptance, but a counteroffer.) Under some circumstances, a court might strike the additional terms.

4A. *Passage of risk without movement of goods*
If the goods are held by a seller, and the seller is a merchant, the risk of loss passes to the buyer when the buyer actually takes physical possession of the goods. If the seller is not a merchant, the risk of loss to goods held by the seller passes to the buyer on tender of delivery. When a bailee is holding the goods, the risk of loss passes to the buyer when (1) the buyer receives a negotiable document of title for the goods, (2) the bailee acknowledges the buyer's right to possess the goods, or (3) the buyer receives a nonnegotiable document of title and has had a reasonable time to present the document to the bailee and demand the goods.

CHAPTER 12

2A. *Perfect tender rule*
Under the perfect tender rule, the seller or lessor has an obligation to ship or tender conforming goods, and if goods or tender of delivery fail in any respect, the buyer or lessee has the right to accept the goods, reject the entire shipment, or accept part and reject part. Exceptions to the perfect tender rule may be established by agreement. When tender is rejected because of nonconforming goods and the time for performance has not yet expired, the seller or lessor can notify the buyer or lessee promptly of the intention to cure and can then do so within the contract time for performance. Once the time for performance has expired, the seller or lessor can, for a reasonable time, exercise the right to cure if he or she had, at the time of delivery, reasonable grounds to believe that the nonconforming tender would be acceptable to the buyer or lessee. When an agreed-on manner of delivery becomes impracticable or unavailable through no fault of either party, a seller may choose a commercially reasonable substitute. In an installment contract, a buyer or lessee can reject an installment only if the nonconformity substantially impairs the value of the installment and cannot be cured. Delay in delivery or nondelivery in whole or in part is not a breach when performance is commercially impracticable. If an unexpected event totally destroys goods identified at the time the contract is formed through no fault of either party and before risk passes to the buyer or lessee, the parties are excused from performance. If a party has reasonable grounds to believe that the other party will not perform, he or she may in writing demand assurance of performance from the other party. Until such assurance is received, he or she may suspend further performance. Finally, when required cooperation is not forthcoming, the cooperative party can suspend her or his own performance without liability.

4A. *Remedies for breach*
Depending on the circumstances at the time of a buyer's breach, a seller may have the right to cancel the contract, withhold delivery, resell or dispose of the goods subject to the contract, recover the purchase price (or lease payments), recover damages, stop delivery in transit, or reclaim the goods. Similarly, on a seller's breach, a buyer may have the right to cancel the contract, recover the goods, obtain specific performance, obtain cover, replevy the goods, recover damages, reject the goods, withhold delivery, resell or dispose of the goods, stop delivery, or revoke acceptance.

CHAPTER 13

2A. *Implied warranties*
Implied warranties that arise under the UCC include the implied warranty of merchantability, the implied warranty of fitness for a particular purpose, and implied warranties that may arise from, or be excluded or modified by, course of dealing, course of performance, or usage of trade.

4A. *Defenses*
Defenses to product liability include plaintiff's assumption of risk, product misuse, and comparative negligence, as well as the attribution of injuries to commonly known dangers. Also, as in any suit, a defendant can avoid liability by showing that the elements of the cause of action have not been properly pleaded or proved.

CHAPTER 14

2A. *Requirements for negotiability*
For an instrument to be negotiable, it must (1) be in writing, (2) be signed by the maker or the drawer, (3) be an unconditional promise or order to pay, (4) state a fixed amount of money, (5) be payable on demand or at a definite time, and (6) be payable to order or to bearer, unless it is a check.

4A. *Liability*
The key to liability on a negotiable instrument is a signature. Every party, except a qualified indorser, who signs a negotiable instrument is primarily or secondarily liable for payment of that instrument when it comes due. Signature liability arises from indorsing an instrument. Warranty liability arises from transferring an instrument, whether or not the transferor also indorses it.

CHAPTER 15

2A. *Dishonor*
A bank may dishonor a customer's check without liability to the customer when the customer's account contains insufficient funds to pay the check, providing the bank did not agree to cover overdrafts. A bank may also properly dishonor a stale check, a timely check subject to a valid stop-payment order, a check drawn after the customer's death, and forged or altered checks.

4A. *EFTs and consumers*
The four most common types of EFT systems used by bank customers are automated teller machines, point-of-sale systems, systems handling direct deposits and withdrawals of funds, and pay-by-telephone systems. The EFTA provides a basic framework for the rights, liabilities, and responsibilities of users of these EFT systems. For consumers, the terms and conditions of EFTs must be disclosed in readily understandable language, a receipt must be provided at an e-terminal at the time of a transfer, periodic statements must describe transfers for each account through which an EFT system provides access, and some preauthorized payments can be stopped within three days before they are made.

CHAPTER 16

2A. *Attachment and writs of execution*
Attachment is a court-ordered seizure and taking into custody of property prior to the securing of a judgment for a past-due debt. To use attachment as a remedy, a creditor (1) files with a court an affidavit, stating that a debtor is in default and the grounds on which attachment is sought, and (2) posts a bond to cover costs, the value of the loss of use of the good by the debtor, and the value of the property. The court directs the sheriff or other officer to seize nonexempt property, which can be sold to satisfy a judgment. A *writ of execution* is a court order directing a sheriff to seize and sell any of the debtor's nonexempt real or personal property within the court's jurisdiction. This is used when a debtor will not or cannot pay a judgment.

4A. *Debtor's estate in bankruptcy and debtor in possession*
In a bankruptcy proceeding, a *debtor's estate in property* consists of all the debtor's legal and equitable interests in property currently held, wherever located, together with certain jointly owned property, property transferred in transactions voidable by the trustee, proceeds and profits from the property of the estate, and certain after-acquired property. Federal law exempts (1) up to $18,450 in equity in the debtor's residence and burial plot; (2) interest in a motor vehicle up to $2,950; (3) interest in household goods and furnishings, wearing apparel, appliances, books, animals, crops, and musical instruments up to $475 in a particular item but limited to $9,850 in total; (4) interest in jewelry up to $1,225; (5) any other property worth up to $975, plus any unused part of the $18,450 homestead exemption up to an amount of $9,250; (6) interest in any tools of the debtor's trade, up to $1,850; (7) certain life insurance contracts owned by the debtor; (8) certain interests in accrued dividends or interests under life insurance contracts owned by the debtor; (9) professionally prescribed health aids; (10) the right to receive Social Security and certain welfare benefits, alimony and support payments, and certain pension benefits; and (11) the right to receive certain personal injury and other awards, up to $18,450.

CHAPTER 17

2A. *Agency relationships*
Agency relationships normally are consensual: they arise by voluntary consent and agreement between the parties.

4A. *Liability to third parties*
A disclosed or partially disclosed principal is liable to a third party for a contract made by an agent who is acting within the scope of her or his authority. If the agent exceeds the scope of authority and the principal fails to ratify the contract, the agent may be liable (and the principal may not). When neither the fact of agency nor the identity of the principal is disclosed, the agent is liable, and if an agent has acted within the scope of his or her authority, the undisclosed principal is also liable. Each party is liable for his or her own torts and crimes. A principal may also be liable for an agent's torts committed within the course or scope of employment. A principal is liable for an agent's crime if the principal participated by conspiracy or other action.

CHAPTER 18

2A. *Hours, wages, health, and safety*
The Fair Labor Standards Act is the most significant federal statute governing working hours and wages. To protect the health and safety of workers, Congress passed the Occupational Safety and Health Act.

4A. *Federal employment discrimination acts*
Title VII of the Civil Rights Act of 1964 and its amendments prohibit job discrimination against employees, applicants, and union members on the basis of race, color, national origin, religion, and gender at any stage of employment. The Age Discrimination in Employment Act of 1967 and the Americans with Disabilities Act of 1990 prohibit discrimination on the basis of age and disability, respectively.

CHAPTER 19

2A. *Advantages and disadvantages of business forms*
Advantages of the sole proprietorship include the proprietor receiving all of the profits and the ease and inexpensiveness to start the business. Disadvantages of the sole proprietorship include the exclusive burden on the owner of any losses or liabilities incurred by the business enterprise and the limitation on capital to personal funds and the funds of those who are willing to make loans. One of the advantages of a partnership is that it can be organized fairly easily and inexpensively. Additionally, the partnership itself files only an informational tax return. The main disadvantage of the partnership form of business is that partners are subject to personal liability for partnership obligations. One of the key advantages of a corporation is that the liability of its owners is limited to their investments. A disadvantage of the corporate form is that profits are taxed twice.

4A. *Joint ventures and other business organizational forms*
A *joint venture* is an enterprise in which two or more persons or business entities combine their efforts or their property for a single transaction or project, or a related series of transactions or projects. Other special business organizational forms include a joint stock company, syndicate, and cooperative. A *joint stock company* has many characteristics of a corporation (its ownership is represented by transferable shares of stock, it is usually managed by directors and officers of the company or association, and it can have a perpetual existence), but most of its other features are more characteristic of a partnership, and it is usually treated like a partnership. A *syndicate* is a group of individuals getting together to finance a particular project, such as the building of a shopping center. A *business trust* is created by a written trust agreement that sets forth the interests of the beneficiaries, who receive the profits, and the obligations and powers of the trustees, with whom legal ownership and management of the property of the business rests. A *cooperative* is an association, which may not or may be incorporated, that is organized to provide an economic service to its members (or shareholders), who have limited liability. Cooperatives that are unincorporated are often treated like partnerships, and the members have joint liability for the cooperative's acts.

CHAPTER 20

2A. *Duties of directors and officers*
Directors and officers are fiduciaries of the corporation. The fiduciary duties of the directors and officers include the duty of care and the duty of loyalty.

4A. *Shareholders*
Shareholders have an equitable interest in the firm. They are ultimately responsible for choosing the board of directors. Shareholders must approve fundamental corporate changes before the changes can be effected. Shareholders possess numerous rights, including preemptive rights in the purchase of new stock, dividends from corporate profits, and the right to inspection of corporate books and records. Shareholders also have the right to act on behalf of the firm by filing a shareholder's derivative suit to compel the directors to act to redress a wrong suffered by the corporation.

CHAPTER 21

2A. *Major statutes and Securities and Exchange Commission*
The major statutes regulating the securities industry are the Securities Act of 1933 and the Securities Exchange Act of 1934, which created the Securities and Exchange Commission (SEC). The SEC's major functions are to (1) require the disclosure of facts concerning offerings of securities listed on national securities exchanges and of certain securities traded over the counter; (2) regulate the trade in securities on the national and regional securities exchanges and in the over-the-counter markets; (3) investigate securities fraud; (4) regulate the activities of securities brokers, dealers, and investment advisers and requiring their registration; (5) supervise the activities of mutual funds; and (6) recommend administrative sanctions, injunctive remedies, and criminal prosecution against those who violate securities laws.

4A. *State securities laws*
Typically, state laws have disclosure requirements and antifraud provisions patterned after Section 10(b) of the Securities Exchange Act of 1934 and SEC Rule 10b-5. State laws provide for the registration or qualification of securities offered or issued for sale within the state with the appropriate state official. Also, most state securities laws regulate securities brokers and dealers.

CHAPTER 22

2A. *Sherman Act*
Section 1 prohibits agreements that are anticompetitively restrictive—that is, agreements that have the wrongful purpose of restraining competition. Section 2 prohibits the misuse, and attempted misuse, of monopoly power in the marketplace.

4A. *Enforcing agencies*
The federal agencies that enforce the federal antitrust laws are the U.S. Department of Justice and the Federal Trade Commission.

CHAPTER 23

2A. *Gifts and other means of acquisition*
To make an effective gift, the donor must intend to make the gift, the gift must be delivered to the donee, and the donee must accept the gift. Property can also be acquired by purchase, possession, production, accession, and confusion.

4A. *Insurable interest*
For real and personal property, an insurable interest exists when the insured derives a pecuniary benefit from the existence of the property and would sustain a pecuniary loss from its destruction. For a life, an insurable interest exists when a person has a reasonable expectation of benefit from the continued life of another. The benefit may be pecuniary, or it may be founded on the relationship between the parties (by blood or affinity). For property insurance, the interest must exist at the time the loss occurs but need not exist when the policy is purchased. For life insurance, the interest must exist at the time the policy is obtained.

CHAPTER 24

2A. *Transfers*
Ownership of real property can pass from one person to another by sale, gift, will, inheritance laws, adverse possession, or eminent domain. In the case of sale or gift, title to the property is conveyed by means of a deed—the instrument of conveyance of real property. On an owner's death, real property can be transferred by will or by state inheritance laws. An adverse possessor can acquire title to land and cannot be removed from it by the original owner if he or she possesses the property for a certain statutory period of time. The government has the power, called eminent domain, to take land for public use.

4A. *Environmental impact statements*
An environmental impact statement (EIS) analyzes (1) the impact on the environment that an action will have, (2) any

adverse effects on the environment and alternative actions that might be taken, and (3) irreversible effects the action might generate. For every major federal action that significantly affects the quality of the environment, an EIS must be prepared. An action is "major" if it involves a substantial commitment of resources (monetary or otherwise). An action is "federal" if a federal agency has the power to control it.

CHAPTER 25

2A. ***Act of state doctrine***
The *act of state doctrine* is a judicially created doctrine that provides that the judicial branch of one country will not examine the validity of public acts committed by a recognized foreign government within its own territory. This doctrine is often employed in cases involving expropriation or confiscation.

4A. ***Antitrust laws***
U.S. courts will apply U.S. antitrust laws extraterritorially when it is shown that an alleged violation has a substantial effect on U.S. commerce.

GLOSSARY

A

ABANDONED PROPERTY ■ Property with which the owner has voluntarily parted, with no intention of recovering it.

ACCELERATION CLAUSE ■ A clause that allows a payee or other holder of a time instrument to demand payment of the entire amount due, with interest, if a certain event occurs, such as a default in the payment of an installment when due.

ACCEPTANCE ■ In contract law, a voluntary act by the offeree that shows assent, or agreement, to the terms of an offer; may consist of words or conduct. In negotiable instruments law, the drawee's signed agreement to pay a draft when presented.

ACCEPTOR ■ A drawee that is legally obligated to pay an instrument when the instrument is presented later for payment.

ACCESSION ■ Occurs when an individual adds value to personal property by either labor or materials. In some situations, a person may acquire ownership rights in another's property through accession.

ACCOMMODATION PARTY ■ A person who signs an instrument for the purpose of lending his or her name as credit to another party on the instrument.

ACCORD AND SATISFACTION ■ A common means of settling a disputed claim, in which a debtor offers to pay a lesser amount than the creditor purports to be owed. The creditor's acceptance of the offer creates an accord (agreement), and when the accord is executed, satisfaction occurs.

ACCREDITED INVESTORS ■ In the context of securities offerings, "sophisticated" investors, such as banks, insurance companies, investment companies, the issuer's executive officers and directors, and persons whose income or net worth exceeds certain limits.

ACT OF STATE DOCTRINE ■ A doctrine providing that the judicial branch of one country will not examine the validity of public acts committed by a recognized foreign government within its own territory.

ACTIONABLE ■ Capable of serving as the basis of a lawsuit. An actionable claim can be pursued in a lawsuit or other court action.

ACTUAL MALICE ■ In a defamation suit, a statement made about a public figure normally must be made with actual malice (with either knowledge of its falsity or a reckless disregard of the truth) for liability to be incurred.

ADEQUATE PROTECTION DOCTRINE ■ In bankruptcy law, a doctrine that protects secured creditors from losing the value of their security as a result of the automatic stay on legal proceedings. The bankruptcy court can provide adequate protection by requiring the debtor or trustee to make cash payments to the creditor or to provide additional collateral or replacement liens in case the stay causes the property to lose value.

ADHESION CONTRACT ■ A "standard-form" contract, such as that between a large retailer and a consumer, in which the stronger party dictates the terms.

ADJUDICATE ■ To render a judicial decision. In the administrative process, the proceeding in which an administrative law judge hears and decides issues that arise when an administrative agency charges a person or a firm with violating a law or regulation enforced by the agency.

ADMINISTRATIVE AGENCY ■ A federal or state government agency established to perform a specific function. Administrative agencies are authorized by legislative acts to make and enforce rules to administer and enforce the acts.

ADMINISTRATIVE LAW ■ The body of law created by administrative agencies (in the form of rules, regulations, orders, and decisions) in order to carry out their duties and responsibilities.

ADMINISTRATIVE LAW JUDGE (ALJ) ■ One who presides over an administrative agency hearing and has the power to administer oaths, take testimony, rule on questions of evidence, and make determinations of fact.

ADMINISTRATIVE PROCESS ■ The procedure used by administrative agencies in the administration of law.

ADMINISTRATOR ■ One who is appointed by a court to handle the probate (disposition) of a person's estate if that person dies intestate (without a valid will) or if the executor named in the will cannot serve.

ADVERSE POSSESSION ■ The acquisition of title to real property by occupying it openly, without the consent of the owner, for a period of time specified by a state statute. The occupation must be actual, open, notorious, exclusive, and in opposition to all others, including the owner.

AFFIRMATIVE ACTION ■ Job-hiring policies that give special consideration to members of protected classes in an effort to overcome present effects of past discrimination.

AFTER-ACQUIRED PROPERTY ■ Property that is acquired by the debtor after the execution of a security agreement.

AGENCY ■ A relationship between two parties in which one party (the agent) agrees to represent or act for the other (the principal).

AGENT A person who agrees to represent or act for another, called the principal.

AGREEMENT ■ A meeting of two or more minds in regard to the terms of a contract; usually broken down into two events—an offer by one party to form a contract, and an acceptance of the offer by the person to whom the offer is made.

ALIEN CORPORATION ■ A designation in the United States for a corporation formed in another country but doing business in the United States.

ALIENATION ■ The process of transferring land out of one's possession (thus "alienating" the land from oneself).

ALLONGE ■ A piece of paper firmly attached to a negotiable instrument, on which transferees can make indorsements if there is no room left on the instrument itself.

ALTERNATIVE DISPUTE RESOLUTION (ADR) ■ The resolution of disputes in ways other than those involved in the traditional judicial process. Negotiation, mediation, and arbitration are forms of ADR.

ANSWER ■ Procedurally, a defendant's response to the plaintiff's complaint.

ANTICIPATORY REPUDIATION ■ An assertion or action by a party indicating that he or she will not perform an obligation that the party is contractually obligated to perform at a future time.

ANTITRUST LAWS ■ Laws protecting commerce from unlawful restraints.

APPRAISAL RIGHT ■ The right of a dissenting shareholder, who objects to an extraordinary transaction of the corporation (such as a merger or a consolidation), to have his or her shares appraised and to be paid the fair value of those shares by the corporation.

APPROPRIATION ■ In tort law, the use by one person of another person's name, likeness, or other identifying characteristic without permission and for the benefit of the user.

ARBITRATION ■ The settling of a dispute by submitting it to a disinterested third party (other than a court), who renders a decision that is (most often) legally binding.

ARBITRATION CLAUSE ■ A clause in a contract that provides that, in the event of a dispute, the parties will submit the dispute to arbitration rather than litigate the dispute in court.

ARSON ■ The intentional burning of another's dwelling. Some statutes have expanded this to include any real property regardless of ownership and the destruction of property by other means—for example, by explosion.

ARTICLES OF INCORPORATION ■ The document filed with the appropriate governmental agency, usually the secretary of state, when a business is incorporated. State statutes usually prescribe what kind of information must be contained in the articles of incorporation.

ARTICLES OF ORGANIZATION ■ The document filed with a designated state official by which a limited liability company is formed.

ARTICLES OF PARTNERSHIP ■ A written agreement that sets forth each partner's rights and obligations with respect to the partnership.

ARTISAN'S LIEN ■ A possessory lien given to a person who has made improvements and added value to another person's personal property as security for payment for services performed.

ASSAULT ■ Any word or action intended to make another person fearful of immediate physical harm; a reasonably believable threat.

ASSIGNEE ■ A party to whom the rights under a contract are transferred, or assigned.

ASSIGNMENT ■ The act of transferring to another all or part of one's rights arising under a contract.

ASSIGNOR ■ A party who transfers (assigns) his or her rights under a contract to another party (called the assignee).

ASSUMPTION OF RISK ■ A doctrine under which a plaintiff may not recover for injuries or damages suffered from risks he or she knows of and has voluntarily assumed.

ATTACHMENT ■ In a secured transaction, the process by which a secured creditor's interest "attaches" to the property of another (collateral) and the creditor's security interest becomes enforceable. In the context of judicial liens, a court-ordered seizure and taking into custody of property prior to the securing of a judgment for a past-due debt.

ATTEMPTED MONOPOLIZATION ■ Any actions by a firm to eliminate competition and gain monopoly power.

AUTOMATIC STAY ■ In bankruptcy proceedings, the suspension of virtually all litigation and other action by creditors against the debtor or the debtor's property. The stay is effective the moment the debtor files a petition in bankruptcy.

AWARD ■ In litigation, the amount of money awarded to a plaintiff in a civil lawsuit as damages. In the context of alternative dispute resolution, the decision rendered by an arbitrator.

B

BAILEE ■ One to whom goods are entrusted by a bailor. Under the UCC, a party who, by a bill of lading, warehouse receipt, or other document of title, acknowledges possession of goods and/or contracts to deliver them.

BAILMENT ■ A situation in which the personal property of one person (a bailor) is entrusted to another (a bailee), who is obligated to return the bailed property to the bailor or dispose of it as directed.

BAILOR ■ One who entrusts goods to a bailee.

BAIT-AND-SWITCH ADVERTISING ■ Advertising a product at a very attractive price (the "bait") and then, once the consumer is in the store, saying that the advertised product is either not available or is of poor quality; the customer is then urged to purchase ("switched" to) a more expensive item.

BANKRUPTCY COURT ■ A federal court of limited jurisdiction that handles only bankruptcy proceedings. Bankruptcy proceedings are governed by federal bankruptcy law.

BATTERY ■ The unprivileged, intentional touching of another.

BEARER INSTRUMENT ■ Any instrument that is not payable to a specific person, including instruments payable to the bearer or to "cash."

BEARER ■ A person in possession of an instrument payable to bearer or indorsed in blank.

BEQUEST ■ A gift by will of personal property (from the verb *to bequeath*).

BEYOND A REASONABLE DOUBT ■ The burden of proof used in criminal cases. If there is any reasonable doubt that a criminal defendant did not commit the crime with which she or he has been charged, then the verdict must be "not guilty."

BILATERAL CONTRACT ■ A type of contract that arises when a promise is given in exchange for a return promise.

BILL OF RIGHTS ■ The first ten amendments to the U.S. Constitution.

BINDER ■ A written, temporary insurance policy.

BINDING AUTHORITY ■ Any source of law that a court must follow when deciding a case. Binding authorities include constitutions, statutes, and regulations that govern the issue being decided, as well as court decisions that are controlling precedents within the jurisdiction.

BLANK INDORSEMENT ■ An indorsement that specifies no particular indorsee and can consist of a mere signature. An order instrument that is indorsed in blank becomes a bearer instrument.

BLUE LAWS ■ State or local laws that prohibit the performance of certain types of commercial activities on Sunday.

BLUE SKY LAWS ■ State laws that regulate the offer and sale of securities.

BONA FIDE OCCUPATIONAL QUALIFICATION (BFOQ) ■ Identifiable characteristics reasonably necessary to the normal operation of a particular business. These characteristics can include gender, national origin, and religion, but not race.

BOND ■ A certificate that evidences a corporate (or government) debt. It is a security that involves no ownership interest in the issuing entity.

BOND INDENTURE ■ A contract between the issuer of a bond and the bondholder.

BOUNTY PAYMENT ■ A reward (payment) given to a person or persons who perform a certain service, such as informing legal authorities of illegal actions.

BREACH ■ The failure to perform a legal obligation.

BREACH OF CONTRACT ■ The failure, without legal excuse, of a promisor to perform the obligations of a contract.

BRIEF ■ A formal legal document submitted by the attorney for the appellant or the appellee (in answer to the appellant's brief) to an appellate court when a case is appealed. The appellant's brief outlines the facts and issues of the case, the judge's rulings or jury's findings that should be reversed or modified, the applicable law, and the arguments on the client's behalf.

BROWSE-WRAP TERMS ■ Terms and conditions of use that are presented to an Internet user at the time certain products, such as software, are being downloaded but that need not be agreed to (by clicking "I agree," for example) before the user is able to install or use the product.

BURGLARY ■ The unlawful entry or breaking into a building with the intent to commit a felony. (Some state statutes expand this to include the intent to commit any crime.)

BUSINESS ETHICS ■ Ethics in a business context; a consensus of what constitutes right or wrong behavior in the world of business and the application of moral principles to situations that arise in a business setting.

BUSINESS INVITEE ■ A person, such as a customer or a client, who is invited onto business premises by the owner of those premises for business purposes.

BUSINESS JUDGMENT RULE ■ A rule that immunizes corporate management from liability for actions that result in corporate losses or damages if the actions are undertaken in good faith and are within both the power of the corporation and the authority of management to make.

BUSINESS NECESSITY ■ A defense to allegations of employment discrimination in which the employer demonstrates that an employment practice that discriminates against members of a protected class is related to job performance.

BUSINESS TORT ■ Wrongful interference with another's business rights.

BUSINESS TRUST ■ A form of business organization in which investors (trust beneficiaries) transfer cash or property to trustees in exchange for trust certificates that represent their investment shares. The certificate holders share in the trust's profits but have limited liability.

BUYOUT PRICE ■ The amount payable to a partner on his or her dissociation from a partnership, based on the amount distributable to that partner if the firm were wound up on that date, and offset by any damages for wrongful dissociation.

BYLAWS ■ A set of governing rules adopted by a corporation or other association.

C

CASE LAW ■ The rules of law announced in court decisions. Case law includes the aggregate of reported cases that interpret judicial precedents, statutes, regulations, and constitutional provisions.

CASHIER'S CHECK ■ A check drawn by a bank on itself.

CATEGORICAL IMPERATIVE ■ A concept developed by the philosopher Immanuel Kant as an ethical guideline for behavior. In deciding whether an action is right or wrong, or desirable or undesirable, a person should evaluate the action in terms of what would happen if everybody else in the same situation, or category, acted the same way.

CAUSATION IN FACT ■ An act or omission without which an event would not have occurred.

CEASE-AND-DESIST ORDER ■ An administrative or judicial order prohibiting a person or business firm from conducting activities that an agency or court has deemed illegal.

CERTIFICATE OF DEPOSIT (CD) ■ A note of a bank in which the bank acknowledges a receipt of money from a party and promises to repay the money, with interest, to the party on a certain date.

CERTIFICATE OF INCORPORATION ■ The primary document that evidences corporate existence (often referred to as the *corporate charter*).

CERTIFICATE OF LIMITED PARTNERSHIP ■ The basic document filed with a designated state official by which a limited partnership is formed.

CERTIFIED CHECK ■ A check that has been accepted in writing by the bank on which it is drawn. Essentially, the bank, by certifying (accepting) the check, promises to pay the check at the time the check is presented.

CHARGING ORDER ■ In partnership law, an order granted by a court to a judgment creditor that entitles the creditor to attach profits or assets of a partner on the dissolution of the partnership.

CHARITABLE TRUST ■ A trust in which the property held by the trustee must be used for a charitable purpose, such as the advancement of health, education, or religion.

CHATTEL ■ All forms of personal property.

CHECK ■ A draft drawn by a drawer ordering the drawee bank or financial institution to pay a fixed amount of money to the holder on demand.

CHECKS AND BALANCES ■ The principle under which the powers of the national government are divided among three separate branches—the executive, legislative, and judicial branches—each of which exercises a check on the actions of the others.

CHOICE-OF-LANGUAGE CLAUSE ■ A clause in a contract designating the official language by which the contract will be interpreted in the event of a future disagreement over the contract's terms.

CHOICE-OF-LAW CLAUSE ■ A clause in a contract designating the law (such as the law of a particular state or nation) that will govern the contract.

CHOSE IN ACTION ■ A right that can be enforced in court to recover a debt or to obtain damages.

CITATION ■ A reference to a publication in which a legal authority—such as a statute or a court decision—or other source can be found.

CIVIL LAW ■ The branch of law dealing with the definition and enforcement of all private or public rights, as opposed to criminal matters.

CIVIL LAW SYSTEM ■ A system of law derived from that of the Roman Empire and based on a code rather than case law; the predominant system of law in the nations of continental Europe and the nations that were once their colonies. In the United States, Louisiana, because of its historical ties to France, has in part a civil law system.

CLEARINGHOUSE ■ A system or place where banks exchange checks and drafts drawn on each other and settle daily balances.

CLICK-ON AGREEMENT ■ An agreement that arises when a buyer, engaging in a transaction on a computer, indicates his or her assent to be bound by the terms of an offer by clicking on a button that says, for example, "I agree"; sometimes referred to as a *click-on license* or a *click-wrap agreement*.

CLOSE CORPORATION ■ A corporation whose shareholders are limited to a small group of persons, often including only family members. In a close corporation, the shareholders' rights to transfer shares to others are usually restricted.

CLOSED SHOP ■ A firm that requires union membership by its workers as a condition of employment. The closed shop was made illegal by the Labor-Management Relations Act of 1947.

CODICIL ■ A written supplement or modification to a will. A codicil must be executed with the same formalities as a will.

COLLATERAL ■ Under Article 9 of the UCC, the property subject to a security interest, including accounts and chattel paper that have been sold.

COLLATERAL PROMISE ■ A secondary promise that is ancillary (subsidiary) to a principal transaction or primary contractual relationship, such as a promise made by one person to pay the debts of another if the latter fails to perform. A collateral promise normally must be in writing to be enforceable.

COLLECTING BANK ■ Any bank handling an item for collection, except the payor bank.

COLLECTIVE BARGAINING ■ The process by which labor and management negotiate the terms and conditions of employment, including working hours and workplace conditions.

COMITY ■ The principle by which one nation defers and gives effect to the laws and judicial decrees of another nation. This recognition is based primarily on respect.

COMMERCE CLAUSE ■ The provision in Article I, Section 8, of the U.S. Constitution that gives Congress the power to regulate interstate commerce.

COMMINGLE ■ To mix together; to put funds or goods together into one mass so that they are so mixed that they no longer have separate identities. In corporate law, if personal and corporate interests are commingled to the extent that the corporation has no separate identity, a court may "pierce the corporate veil" and expose the shareholders to personal liability.

COMMON CARRIER ■ An owner of a truck, railroad, airline, ship, or other vehicle that is licensed to offer transportation services to the public, generally in return for compensation or a payment.

COMMON LAW ■ That body of law developed from custom or judicial decisions in English and U.S. courts, not attributable to a legislature.

COMMON STOCK ■ Shares of ownership in a corporation that give the owner of the stock a proportionate interest in the corporation with regard to control, earnings, and net assets. Shares of common stock are lowest in priority with respect to payment of dividends and distribution of the corporation's assets on dissolution.

COMMUNITY PROPERTY ■ A form of concurrent ownership of property in which each spouse technically owns an undivided one-half interest in property acquired during the marriage. This form of joint ownership occurs in only ten states and Puerto Rico.

COMPARATIVE NEGLIGENCE ■ A rule in tort law that reduces the plaintiff's recovery in proportion to the plaintiff's degree of fault, rather than barring recovery completely; used in the majority of states.

COMPENSATORY DAMAGES ■ A money award equivalent to the actual value of injuries or damages sustained by the aggrieved party.

COMPLAINT ■ The pleading made by a plaintiff alleging wrongdoing on the part of the defendant; the document that, when filed with a court, initiates a lawsuit.

COMPUTER CRIME ■ Any act that is directed against computers and computer parts, that uses computers as instruments of crime, or that involves computers and constitutes abuse.

COMPUTER INFORMATION ■ As defined by the Uniform Computer Information Transactions Act, "information in an electronic form obtained from or through use of a computer, or that is in digital or an equivalent form capable of being processed by a computer."

CONCURRENT CONDITIONS ■ Conditions that must occur or be performed at the same time; they are mutually dependent. No obligations arise until these conditions are simultaneously performed.

CONCURRENT JURISDICTION ■ Jurisdiction that exists when two different courts have the power to hear a case. For example, some cases can be heard in a federal or a state court.

CONCURRENT OWNERSHIP ■ Joint ownership.

CONDEMNATION ■ The process of taking private property for public use through the government's power of eminent domain.

CONDITION ■ A qualification, provision, or clause in a contractual agreement, the occurrence or nonoccurrence of which creates, suspends, or terminates the obligations of the contracting parties.

CONDITION PRECEDENT ■ In a contractual agreement, a condition that must be met before a party's promise becomes absolute.

CONDITION SUBSEQUENT ■ A condition in a contract that, if not fulfilled, operates to terminate a party's absolute promise to perform.

CONFESSION OF JUDGMENT ■ The act or agreement of a debtor in permitting a judgment to be entered against him or her by a creditor, for an agreed sum, without the institution of legal proceedings.

CONFISCATION ■ A government's taking of a privately owned business or personal property without a proper public purpose or an award of just compensation.

CONFUSION ■ The mixing together of goods belonging to two or more owners so that the separately owned goods cannot be identified.

CONSENT ■ The voluntary agreement to a proposition or an act of another; a concurrence of wills.

CONSEQUENTIAL DAMAGES ■ Special damages that compensate for a loss that does not directly or immediately result from the breach (for example, lost profits). For the plaintiff to collect consequential damages, they must have been reasonably foreseeable at the time the breach or injury occurred.

CONSIDERATION ■ Generally, the value given in return for a promise. The consideration must result in a detriment to the promisee (something of legally sufficient value and bargained for) or a benefit to the promisor.

CONSIGNMENT ■ A transaction in which an owner of goods (the consignor) delivers the goods to another (the consignee) for the consignee to sell. The consignee pays the consignor only for the goods that are sold by the consignee.

CONSOLIDATION ■ A contractual and statutory process in which two or more corporations join to become a completely new corporation. The original corporations cease to exist, and the new corporation acquires all their assets and liabilities.

CONSTITUTIONAL LAW ■ The body of law derived from the U.S. Constitution and the constitutions of the various states.

CONSTRUCTIVE DELIVERY ■ An act equivalent to the actual, physical delivery of property that cannot be physically delivered because of difficulty or impossibility. For example, the transfer of a key to a safe constructively delivers the contents of the safe.

CONSTRUCTIVE DISCHARGE ■ A termination of employment brought about by making the employee's working conditions so intolerable that the employee reasonably feels compelled to leave.

CONSTRUCTIVE EVICTION ■ A form of eviction that occurs when a landlord fails to perform adequately any of the undertakings (such as providing heat in the winter) required by the lease, thereby making the tenant's further use and enjoyment of the property exceedingly difficult or impossible.

CONSTRUCTIVE TRUST ■ An equitable trust that is imposed in the interests of fairness and justice when someone wrongfully holds legal title to property. A court may require the owner to hold the property in trust for the person or persons who rightfully should own the property.

CONSUMER-DEBTOR ■ An individual whose debts are primarily consumer debts (debts for purchases made primarily for personal or household use).

CONTINUATION STATEMENT ■ A statement that, if filed within six months prior to the expiration date of the original financing statement, continues the perfection of the original security interest for another five years. The perfection of a security interest can be continued in the same manner indefinitely.

CONTRACT ■ An agreement that can be enforced in court; formed by two or more competent parties who agree, for consideration, to perform or to refrain from performing some legal act now or in the future.

CONTRACTUAL CAPACITY ■ The threshold mental capacity required by law for a party who enters into a contract to be bound by that contract.

CONTRIBUTORY NEGLIGENCE ■ A rule in tort law that completely bars the plaintiff from recovering any damages if the damage suffered is partly the plaintiff's own fault; used in a minority of states.

CONVERSION ■ Wrongfully taking or retaining possession of an individual's personal property and placing it in the service of another.

CONVEYANCE ■ The transfer of a title to land from one person to another by deed; a document (such as a deed) by which an interest in land is transferred from one person to another.

"COOLING-OFF" LAWS ■ Laws that allow buyers a period of time, such as three days, in which to cancel door-to-door sales contracts.

COOPERATIVE ■ An association, which may or may not be incorporated, that is organized to provide an economic service to its members. Unincorporated cooperatives are often treated like partnerships for tax and other legal purposes. Examples of cooperatives include consumer purchasing cooperatives, credit cooperatives, and farmers' cooperatives.

COPYRIGHT ■ The exclusive right of "authors" to publish, print, or sell an intellectual production for a statutory period of time. A copyright has the same monopolistic nature as a patent or trademark, but it differs in that it applies exclusively to works of art, literature, and other works of authorship (including computer programs).

CORPORATE CHARTER ■ The document issued by a state agency or authority (usually the secretary of state) that grants a corporation legal existence and the right to function.

CORPORATION ■ A legal entity formed in compliance with statutory requirements that is distinct from its shareholder-owners.

CORRESPONDENT BANK ■ A bank in which another bank has an account (and vice versa) for the purpose of facilitating fund transfers.

COST-BENEFIT ANALYSIS ■ A decision-making technique that involves weighing the costs of a given action against the benefits of that action.

CO-SURETY ■ A joint surety; a person who assumes liability jointly with another surety for the payment of an obligation.

COUNTERADVERTISING ■ New advertising that is undertaken pursuant to a Federal Trade Commission order for the purpose of correcting earlier false claims that were made about a product.

COUNTERCLAIM ■ A claim made by a defendant in a civil lawsuit against the plaintiff. In effect, the defendant is suing the plaintiff.

COUNTEROFFER ■ An offeree's response to an offer in which the offeree rejects the original offer and at the same time makes a new offer.

COURSE OF DEALING ■ Prior conduct between the parties to a contract that establishes a common basis for their understanding.

COURSE OF PERFORMANCE ■ The conduct that occurs under the terms of a particular agreement. Such conduct indicates what the parties to an agreement intended it to mean.

COVENANT NOT TO COMPETE ■ A contractual promise of one party to refrain from conducting business similar to that of another party for a certain period of time and within a specified geographic area. Courts commonly enforce such covenants if they are reasonable in terms of time and geographic area and part of, or supplemental to, an employment contract or a contract for the sale of a business.

COVENANT NOT TO SUE ■ An agreement to substitute a contractual obligation for some other type of legal action based on a valid claim.

COVER ■ Under the UCC, a remedy that allows the buyer or lessee, on the seller's or lessor's breach, to purchase the goods, in good faith and within a reasonable time, from another seller or lessor and substitute them for the goods due under the contract. If the cost of cover exceeds the cost of the contract goods, the breaching seller or lessor will be liable to the buyer or lessee for the difference, plus incidental and consequential damages.

CRAM-DOWN PROVISION ■ A provision of the Bankruptcy Code that allows a court to confirm a debtor's Chapter 11 reorganization plan even though only one class of creditors has accepted it. To exercise the court's right under this provision, the court must demonstrate that the plan does not discriminate unfairly against any creditors and is fair and equitable.

CREDITORS' COMPOSITION AGREEMENT ■ An agreement formed between a debtor and his or her creditors in which the creditors agree to accept a lesser sum than that owed by the debtor in full satisfaction of the debt.

CRIME ■ A wrong against society proclaimed in a statute and, if committed, punishable by society through fines and/or imprisonment—and, in some cases, death.

CRIMINAL LAW ■ Law that defines and governs actions that constitute crimes. Generally, criminal law has to do with wrongful actions committed against society for which society demands redress.

CURE ■ The right of a party who tenders nonconforming performance to correct that performance within the contract period [UCC 2–508(1)].

CYBER CRIME ■ A crime that occurs online, in the virtual community of the Internet, as opposed to the physical world.

CYBER MARK ■ A trademark in cyberspace.

CYBER STALKER ■ A person who commits the crime of stalking in cyberspace. Generally, stalking consists of harassing a person and putting that person in reasonable fear for his or her safety or the safety of the person's immediate family.

CYBER TERRORIST ■ A hacker whose purpose is to exploit a target computer for a serious impact, such as corrupting a program to sabotage a business.

CYBER TORT ■ A tort committed in cyberspace.

CYBERLAW ■ An informal term used to refer to all laws governing electronic communications and transactions, particularly those conducted via the Internet.

CYBERNOTARY ■ A legally recognized authority that can certify the validity of digital signatures.

CYBERSQUATTING ■ The act of registering a domain name that is the same as, or confusingly similar to, the trademark of another and then offering to sell that domain name back to the trademark owner.

D

DAMAGES ■ Money sought as a remedy for a breach of contract or a tortious action.

DEBTOR ■ Under Article 9 of the UCC, a debtor is any party who owes payment or performance of a secured obligation, whether or not the party actually owns or has rights in the collateral.

DEBTOR IN POSSESSION (DIP) ■ In Chapter 11 bankruptcy proceedings, a debtor who is allowed to continue in possession of the estate in property (the business) and to continue business operations.

DECEPTIVE ADVERTISING ■ Advertising that misleads consumers, either by unjustified claims concerning a product's performance or by the omission of a material fact concerning the product's composition or performance.

DEED ■ A document by which title to property (usually real property) is passed.

DEFAMATION ■ Anything published or publicly spoken that causes injury to another's good name, reputation, or character.

DEFAULT ■ The failure to observe a promise or discharge an obligation. The term is commonly used to mean the failure to pay a debt when it is due.

DEFAULT JUDGMENT ■ A judgment entered by a court against a defendant who has failed to appear in court to answer or defend against the plaintiff's claim.

DEFENDANT ■ One against whom a lawsuit is brought; the accused person in a criminal proceeding.

DEFENSE ■ A reason offered and alleged by a defendant in an action or suit as to why the plaintiff should not recover or establish what she or he seeks.

DEFICIENCY JUDGMENT ■ A judgment against a debtor for the amount of a debt remaining unpaid after the collateral has been repossessed and sold.

DELEGATEE ■ A party to whom contractual obligations are transferred, or delegated.

DELEGATION OF DUTIES ■ The act of transferring to another all or part of one's duties arising under a contract.

DELEGATOR ■ A party who transfers (delegates) her or his obligations under a contract to another party (called the delegatee).

DEPOSITARY BANK ■ The first bank to receive a check for payment.

DEPOSITION ■ The testimony of a party to a lawsuit or a witness taken under oath before a trial.

DESTINATION CONTRACT ■ A contract for the sale of goods in which the seller is required or authorized to ship the goods by carrier and tender delivery of the goods at a particular destination. The seller assumes liability for any losses or damage to the goods until they are tendered at the destination specified in the contract.

DEVISE ■ To make a gift of real property by will.

DEVISEE ■ One designated in a will to receive a gift of real property.

DIGITAL CASH ■ Funds contained on computer software, in the form of secure programs stored on microchips and other computer devices.

DISAFFIRMANCE ■ The legal avoidance, or setting aside, of a contractual obligation.

DISCHARGE ■ The termination of an obligation. In bankruptcy proceedings, the extinction of the debtor's dischargeable debts. In contract law, discharge occurs when the parties have fully performed their contractual obligations or when events, conduct of the parties, or operation of law releases the parties from performance.

DISCLOSED PRINCIPAL ■ A principal whose identity is known to a third party at the time the agent makes a contract with the third party.

DISCOVERY ■ A phase in the litigation process during which the opposing parties may obtain information from each other and from third parties prior to trial.

DISPARAGEMENT OF PROPERTY ■ An economically injurious falsehood made about another's product or property. A general term for torts that are more specifically referred to as slander of quality or slander of title.

DISPARATE-IMPACT DISCRIMINATION ■ A form of employment discrimination that results from certain employer practices or procedures that, although not discriminatory on their face, have a discriminatory effect.

DISPARATE-TREATMENT DISCRIMINATION ■ A form of employment discrimination that results when an employer intentionally discriminates against employees who are members of protected classes.

DISSOCIATION ■ The severance of the relationship between a partner and a partnership when the partner ceases to be associated with the carrying on of the partnership business.

DISSOLUTION ■ The formal disbanding of a partnership or a corporation. It can take place by (1) acts of the partners or, in a corporation, of the shareholders and board of directors; (2) the subsequent illegality of the partnership business; (3) the expiration of a time period stated in a partnership agreement or a certificate of incorporation; or (4) judicial decree.

DISTRIBUTED NETWORK ■ A network that can be used by persons located (distributed) around the country or the globe to share computer files.

DISTRIBUTION AGREEMENT ■ A contract between a seller and a distributor of the seller's products setting out the terms and conditions of the distributorship.

DIVERSITY OF CITIZENSHIP ■ Under Article III, Section 2, of the Constitution, a basis for federal district court jurisdiction over a lawsuit between (1) citizens of different states, (2) a foreign country and citizens of a state or of different states, or (3) citizens of a state and citizens or subjects of a foreign country. The amount in controversy must be more than $75,000 before a federal district court can take jurisdiction in such cases.

DIVESTITURE ■ The act of selling one or more of a company's divisions or parts, such as a subsidiary or plant; often mandated by the courts in merger or monopolization cases.

DIVIDEND ■ A distribution to corporate shareholders of corporate profits or income, disbursed in proportion to the number of shares held.

DOCKET ■ The list of cases entered on a court's calendar and thus scheduled to be heard by the court.

DOCUMENT OF TITLE ■ Paper exchanged in the regular course of business that evidences the right to possession of goods (for example, a bill of lading or a warehouse receipt).

DOMAIN NAME ■ The last part of an Internet address, such as "westlaw.com." The top level (the part of the name to the right of the period) indicates the type of entity that operates the site ("com" is an abbreviation for "commercial"). The second level (the part of the name to the left of the period) is chosen by the entity.

DOMESTIC CORPORATION ■ In a given state, a corporation that does business in, and is organized under the law of, that state.

DOMINION ■ Ownership rights in property, including the right to possess and control the property.

DOUBLE JEOPARDY ■ A situation occurring when a person is tried twice for the same criminal offense; prohibited by the Fifth Amendment to the Constitution.

DRAFT ■ Any instrument drawn on a drawee that orders the drawee to pay a certain sum of money, usually to a third party (the payee), on demand or at a definite future time.

DRAM SHOP ACT ■ A state statute that imposes liability on the owners of bars and taverns, as well as those who serve alcoholic drinks to the public, for injuries resulting from accidents caused by intoxicated persons when the sellers or servers of alcoholic drinks contributed to the intoxication.

DRAWEE ■ The party that is ordered to pay a draft or check. With a check, a bank or a financial institution is always the drawee.

DRAWER ■ The party that initiates a draft (such as a check), thereby ordering the drawee to pay.

DUE PROCESS CLAUSE ■ The provisions in the Fifth and Fourteenth Amendments to the Constitution that guarantee that no person shall be deprived of life, liberty, or property without due process of law. Similar clauses are found in most state constitutions.

DUMPING ■ The selling of goods in a foreign country at a price below the price charged for the same goods in the domestic market.

DURESS ■ Unlawful pressure brought to bear on a person, causing the person to perform an act that she or he would not otherwise perform.

DUTY OF CARE ■ The duty of all persons, as established by tort law, to exercise a reasonable amount of care in their dealings with others. Failure to exercise due care, which is normally determined by the "reasonable person standard," constitutes the tort of negligence.

E

E-AGENT ■ A computer program that by electronic or other automated means can independently initiate an action or respond to electronic messages or data without review by an individual.

EARLY NEUTRAL CASE EVALUATION ■ A form of alternative dispute resolution in which a neutral third party evaluates the strengths and weaknesses of the disputing parties' positions. The evaluator's opinion then forms the basis for negotiating a settlement.

EASEMENT ■ A nonpossessory right to use another's property in a manner established by either express or implied agreement.

E-CONTRACT ■ A contract that is formed electronically.

E-EVIDENCE ■ A type of evidence that consists of computer-generated or electronically recorded information, including e-mail, voice mail, spreadsheets, word processing documents, and other data.

ELECTRONIC FUND TRANSFER (EFT) ■ A transfer of funds through the use of an electronic terminal, a telephone, a computer, or magnetic tape.

EMANCIPATION ■ In regard to minors, the act of being freed from parental control; occurs when a child's parent or legal guardian relinquishes the legal right to exercise control over the child. Normally, a minor who leaves home to support himself or herself is considered emancipated.

EMBEZZLEMENT ■ The fraudulent appropriation of funds or other property by a person to whom the funds or property has been entrusted.

EMINENT DOMAIN ■ The power of a government to take land for public use from private citizens for just compensation.

E-MONEY ■ Prepaid funds recorded on a computer or a card (such as a smart card or a stored-value card).

EMPLOYMENT AT WILL ■ A common law doctrine under which either party may terminate an employment relationship at any time for any reason, unless a contract specifies otherwise.

EMPLOYMENT CONTRACT ■ A contract between an employer and an employee in which the terms and conditions of employment are stated.

EMPLOYMENT DISCRIMINATION ■ Treating employees or job applicants unequally on the basis of race, color, national origin, religion, gender, age, or disability; prohibited by federal statutes.

ENABLING LEGISLATION ■ A statute enacted by Congress that authorizes the creation of an administrative agency and specifies the name, composition, purpose, and powers of the agency being created.

ENTRAPMENT ■ In criminal law, a defense in which the defendant claims that he or she was induced by a public official—usually an undercover agent or police officer—to commit a crime that he or she would otherwise not have committed.

ENTREPRENEUR ■ One who initiates and assumes the financial risk of a new business enterprise and undertakes to provide or control its management.

ENVIRONMENTAL IMPACT STATEMENT (EIS) ■ A statement required by the National Environmental Policy Act for any major federal action that will significantly affect the quality of the environment. The statement must analyze the action's impact on the environment and explore alternative actions that might be taken.

EQUAL DIGNITY RULE ■ In most states, a rule stating that express authority given to an agent must be in writing if the contract to be made on behalf of the principal is required to be in writing.

EQUAL PROTECTION CLAUSE ■ The provision in the Fourteenth Amendment to the Constitution that guarantees that no state will "deny to any person within its jurisdiction the equal protection of the laws." This clause mandates that the state governments treat similarly situated individuals in a similar manner.

EQUITABLE PRINCIPLES AND MAXIMS ■ General propositions or principles of law that have to do with fairness (equity).

E-SIGNATURE ■ As defined by the Uniform Electronic Transactions Act, "an electronic sound, symbol, or process attached to or logically associated with a record and executed or adopted by a person with the intent to sign the record."

ESTABLISHMENT CLAUSE ■ The provision in the First Amendment to the Constitution that prohibits the government from establishing any state-sponsored religion or enacting any law that promotes religion or favors one religion over another.

ESTATE IN PROPERTY ■ In bankruptcy proceedings, all of the debtor's interests in property currently held, wherever located, together with certain jointly owned property, property transferred in transactions voidable by the trustee, proceeds and profits from the property of the estate, and certain property interests to which the debtor becomes entitled within 180 days after filing for bankruptcy.

ESTOPPED ■ Barred, impeded, or precluded.

ESTRAY STATUTE ■ A statute defining finders' rights in property when the true owners are unknown.

ETHICAL REASONING ■ A reasoning process in which an individual links his or her moral convictions or ethical standards to the particular situation at hand.

ETHICS ■ Moral principles and values applied to social behavior.

EVICTION ■ A landlord's act of depriving a tenant of possession of the leased premises.

EXCLUSIONARY RULE ■ In criminal procedure, a rule under which any evidence that is obtained in violation of the accused's constitutional rights guaranteed by the Fourth, Fifth, and Sixth Amendments, as well as any evidence derived from illegally obtained evidence, will not be admissible in court.

EXCLUSIVE DISTRIBUTORSHIP ■ A distributorship in which the seller and the distributor of the seller's products agree that the distributor has the exclusive right to distribute the seller's products in a certain geographic area.

EXCLUSIVE JURISDICTION ■ Jurisdiction that exists when a case can be heard only in a particular court or type of court.

EXCLUSIVE-DEALING CONTRACT ■ An agreement under which a seller forbids a buyer to purchase products from the seller's competitors.

EXCULPATORY CLAUSE ■ A clause that releases a contractual party from liability in the event of monetary or physical injury, no matter who is at fault.

EXECUTED CONTRACT ■ A contract that has been completely performed by both parties.

EXECUTION ■ An action to carry into effect the directions in a court decree or judgment.

EXECUTIVE AGENCY ■ An administrative agency within the executive branch of government. At the federal level, executive agencies are those within the cabinet departments.

EXECUTOR ■ A person appointed by a testator in a will to see that her or his will is administered appropriately.

EXECUTORY CONTRACT ■ A contract that has not as yet been fully performed.

EXPORT ■ To sell products to buyers located in other countries.

EXPRESS CONTRACT ■ A contract in which the terms of the agreement are stated in words, oral or written.

EXPRESS WARRANTY ■ A seller's or lessor's oral or written promise or affirmation of fact ancillary to an underlying sales or lease agreement, as to the quality, description, or performance of the goods being sold or leased.

EXPROPRIATION ■ The seizure by a government of a privately owned business or personal property for a proper public purpose and with just compensation.

EXTENSION CLAUSE ■ A clause in a time instrument that allows the instrument's date of maturity to be extended into the future.

F

FAMILY LIMITED LIABILITY PARTNERSHIP (FLLP) ■ A type of limited liability partnership owned by family members or fiduciaries of family members.

FEDERAL FORM OF GOVERNMENT ■ A system of government in which the states form a union and the sovereign power is divided between the central government and the member states.

FEDERAL QUESTION ■ A question that pertains to the U.S. Constitution, acts of Congress, or treaties. A federal question provides a basis for federal jurisdiction.

FEDERAL RESERVE SYSTEM ■ A network of twelve district banks and related branches located around the country and headed by the Federal Reserve Board of Governors. Most banks in the United States have Federal Reserve accounts.

FEE SIMPLE ■ An absolute form of property ownership entitling the property owner to use, possess, or dispose of the property as he or she chooses during his or her lifetime. On death, the interest in the property descends to the owner's heirs.

FEE SIMPLE ABSOLUTE ■ An ownership interest in land in which the owner has the greatest possible aggregation of rights, privileges, and power. Ownership in fee simple absolute is limited absolutely to a person and her or his heirs.

FELONY ■ A crime—such as arson, murder, rape, or robbery—that carries the most severe sanctions, which range from more than one year in a state or federal prison to the death penalty.

FICTITIOUS PAYEE ■ A payee on a negotiable instrument whom the maker or drawer does not intend to have an interest in the instrument. Indorsements by fictitious payees are treated as authorized indorsements under Article 3 of the UCC.

FIDUCIARY ■ As a noun, a person having a duty created by his or her undertaking to act primarily for another's benefit in matters connected with the undertaking. As an adjective, a relationship founded on trust and confidence.

FILTERING SOFTWARE ■ A computer program that includes a pattern through which data are passed. When designed to block access to certain Web sites, the pattern blocks the retrieval of a site whose URL or key words are on a list within the program.

FINANCING STATEMENT ■ A document prepared by a secured creditor, and filed with the appropriate state or local official, to give notice to the public that the creditor has a security interest in collateral belonging to the debtor named in the statement.

FIRM OFFER ■ An offer (by a merchant) that is irrevocable without consideration for a stated period of time or, if no definite period is stated, for a reasonable time (neither period to exceed three months). A firm offer by a merchant must be in writing and must be signed by the offeror.

FIXTURE ■ A thing that was once personal property but has become attached to real property in such a way that it takes on the characteristics of real property and becomes part of that real property.

FLOATING LIEN ■ A security interest in proceeds, after-acquired property, or collateral subject to future advances by the secured party (or all three); a security interest in collateral that is retained even when the collateral changes in character, classification, or location.

FORBEARANCE ■ The act of refraining from an action that one has a legal right to undertake.

***FORCE MAJEURE* CLAUSE** ■ A provision in a contract stipulating that certain unforeseen events—such as war, political upheavals, or acts of God—will excuse a party from liability for nonperformance of contractual obligations.

FOREIGN CORPORATION ■ In a given state, a corporation that does business in the state without being incorporated therein.

FOREIGN EXCHANGE MARKET ■ A worldwide system in which foreign currencies are bought and sold.

FORGERY ■ The fraudulent making or altering of any writing in a way that changes the legal rights and liabilities of another.

FORMAL CONTRACT ■ A contract that by law requires a specific form, such as being executed under seal, for its validity.

FORUM-SELECTION CLAUSE ■ A provision in a contract designating the court, jurisdiction, or tribunal that will decide any disputes arising under the contract.

FRANCHISE ■ Any arrangement in which the owner of a trademark, trade name, or copyright licenses another to use that trademark, trade name, or copyright in the selling of goods and services.

FRANCHISEE ■ One receiving a license to use another's (the franchisor's) trademark, trade name, or copyright in the sale of goods and services.

FRANCHISOR ■ One licensing another (the franchisee) to use the owner's trademark, trade name, or copyright in the sale of goods or services.

FRAUDULENT MISREPRESENTATION ■ Any misrepresentation, either by misstatement or omission of a material fact, knowingly made with the intention of deceiving another and on which a reasonable person would and does rely to his or her detriment.

FREE EXERCISE CLAUSE ■ The provision in the First Amendment to the Constitution that prohibits the government from interfering with people's religious practices or forms of worship.

FUNGIBLE GOODS ■ Goods that are alike by physical nature, by agreement, or by trade usage. Examples of fungible goods are wheat, oil, and wine that are identical in type and quality. When owners of fungible goods hold the goods as tenants in common, title and risk can pass without actually separating the goods being sold from the mass of fungible goods.

G

GARNISHMENT ■ A legal process used by a creditor to collect a debt by seizing property of the debtor (such as wages) that is being held by a third party (such as the debtor's employer).

GENERAL PARTNER ■ In a limited partnership, a partner who assumes responsibility for the management of the partnership and liability for all partnership debts.

GENERALLY ACCEPTED ACCOUNTING PRINCIPLES (GAAP) ■ The conventions, rules, and procedures necessary to define accepted accounting practices at a particular time. The source of the principles is the Financial Accounting Standards Board (FASB).

GENERALLY ACCEPTED AUDITING STANDARDS (GAAS) ■ Standards concerning an auditor's professional qualities and the judgment exercised by him or her in the performance of an examination and report. The source of the standards is the American Institute of Certified Public Accountants.

GIFT ■ Any voluntary transfer of property made without consideration, past or present.

GIFT *CAUSA MORTIS* ■ A gift made in contemplation of death. If the donor does not die of that ailment, the gift is revoked.

GIFT *INTER VIVOS* ■ A gift made during one's lifetime and not in contemplation of imminent death, in contrast to a gift *causa mortis*.

GOOD FAITH PURCHASER ■ A purchaser who buys without notice of any circumstance that would put a person of ordinary prudence on inquiry as to whether the seller has valid title to the goods being sold.

GOOD SAMARITAN STATUTE ■ A state statute stipulating that persons who provide emergency services to, or rescue, someone in peril cannot be sued for negligence, unless they act recklessly, thereby causing further harm.

GRAND JURY ■ A group of citizens called to decide, after hearing the state's evidence, whether a reasonable basis (probable cause) exists for believing that a crime has been committed and whether a trial ought to be held.

GROUP BOYCOTT ■ The refusal by a group of competitors to deal with a particular person or firm; prohibited by the Sherman Act.

GUARANTOR ■ A person who agrees to satisfy the debt of another (the debtor) only after the principal debtor defaults. Thus, a guarantor's liability is secondary.

H

HACKER ■ A person who uses one computer to break into another. Professional computer programmers refer to such persons as "crackers."

HISTORICAL SCHOOL ■ A school of legal thought that emphasizes the evolutionary process of law and that looks to the past to discover what the principles of contemporary law should be.

HOLDER ■ Any person in possession of an instrument drawn, issued, or indorsed to him or her, to his or her order, to bearer, or in blank.

HOLDER IN DUE COURSE (HDC) ■ A holder who acquires a negotiable instrument for value; in good faith; and without notice that the instrument is overdue, that it has been dishonored, that any person has a defense against it or a claim to it, or that the instrument contains unauthorized signatures, has been altered, or is so irregular or incomplete as to call into question its authenticity.

HOLOGRAPHIC WILL ■ A will written entirely in the signer's handwriting and usually not witnessed.

HOMESTEAD EXEMPTION ■ A law permitting a debtor to retain the family home, either in its entirety or up to a specified dollar amount, free from the claims of unsecured creditors or trustees in bankruptcy.

HORIZONTAL MERGER ■ A merger between two firms that are competing in the same marketplace.

HORIZONTAL RESTRAINT ■ Any agreement that in some way restrains competition between rival firms competing in the same market.

HOT-CARGO AGREEMENT ■ An agreement in which employers voluntarily agree with unions not to handle, use, or deal in other employers' goods that were not produced by union employees; a type of secondary boycott explicitly prohibited by the Labor-Management Reporting and Disclosure Act of 1959.

I

IDENTIFICATION ■ In a sale of goods, the express designation of the goods provided for in the contract.

IDENTITY THEFT ■ The act of stealing another's identifying information—such as a name, date of birth, or Social Security number—and using that information to access the victim's financial resources.

IMPLIED-IN-FACT CONTRACT ■ A contract formed in whole or in part from the conduct of the parties (as opposed to an express contract).

IMPLIED WARRANTY ■ A warranty that arises by law because of the circumstances of a sale, rather than by the seller's express promise.

IMPLIED WARRANTY OF FITNESS FOR A PARTICULAR PURPOSE ■ A warranty that goods sold or leased are fit for a particular purpose. The warranty arises when any seller or lessor knows the particular purpose for which a buyer or lessee will use the goods and knows that the buyer or lessee is relying on the skill and judgment of the seller or lessor to select suitable goods.

IMPLIED WARRANTY OF HABITABILITY ■ An implied promise by a landlord that rented residential premises are fit for human habitation—that is, in a condition that is safe and suitable for people to live in.

IMPLIED WARRANTY OF MERCHANTABILITY ■ A warranty that goods being sold or leased are reasonably fit for the general purpose for which they are sold or leased, are properly packaged and labeled, and are of proper quality. The warranty automatically arises in every sale or lease of goods made by a merchant who deals in goods of the kind sold or leased.

IMPOSSIBILITY OF PERFORMANCE ■ A doctrine under which a party to a contract is relieved of his or her duty to perform when performance becomes objectively impossible or totally impracticable (through no fault of either party).

IMPOSTER ■ One who, by use of the mails, Internet, telephone, or personal appearance, induces a maker or drawer to issue an instrument in the name of an impersonated payee. Indorsements by imposters are treated as authorized indorsements under Article 3 of the UCC.

INCIDENTAL BENEFICIARY ■ A third party who incidentally benefits from a contract but whose benefit was not the reason the contract was formed. An incidental beneficiary has no rights in a contract and cannot sue to have the contract enforced.

INCIDENTAL DAMAGES ■ All costs resulting from a breach of contract, including all reasonable expenses incurred because of the breach.

INDEPENDENT CONTRACTOR ■ One who works for, and receives payment from, an employer but whose working conditions and methods are not controlled by the employer. An independent contractor is not an employee but may be an agent.

INDEPENDENT REGULATORY AGENCY ■ An administrative agency that is not considered part of the government's executive branch and is not subject to the authority of the president. Independent agency officials cannot be removed without cause.

INDICTMENT ■ A charge by a grand jury that a named person has committed a crime.

INDORSEE ■ The person to whom a negotiable instrument is transferred by indorsement.

INDORSEMENT ■ A signature placed on an instrument for the purpose of transferring one's ownership rights in the instrument.

INDORSER ■ A person who transfers an instrument by signing (indorsing) it and delivering it to another person.

INFORMAL CONTRACT ■ A contract that does not require a specified form or formality to be valid.

INFORMATION ■ A formal accusation or complaint (without an indictment) issued in certain types of actions (usually criminal actions involving lesser crimes) by a law officer, such as a magistrate.

INFORMATION RETURN ■ A tax return submitted by a partnership that only reports the income and losses earned by the business. The partnership as an entity does not pay taxes on the income received by the partnership. A partner's profit from the partnership (whether distributed or not) is taxed as individual income to the individual partner.

INNKEEPER'S LIEN ■ A possessory lien placed on the luggage of hotel guests for hotel charges that remain unpaid.

INSIDER TRADING ■ The purchase or sale of securities on the basis of "inside information" (information that has not been made available to the public).

INSOLVENT ■ Under the UCC, a term describing a person who ceases to pay "his [or her] debts in the ordinary course of business or cannot pay his [or her] debts as they become due or is insolvent within the meaning of federal bankruptcy law" [UCC 1–201(23)].

INSTALLMENT CONTRACT ■ Under the UCC, a contract that requires or authorizes delivery in two or more separate lots to be accepted and paid for separately.

INSURABLE INTEREST ■ An interest either in a person's life or well-being or in property that is sufficiently substantial that insuring against injury to (or the death of) the person or against damage to the property does not amount to a mere wagering (betting) contract.

INSURANCE ■ A contract in which, for a stipulated consideration, one party agrees to compensate the other for loss on a specific subject by a specified peril.

INTANGIBLE PROPERTY ■ Property that cannot be seen or touched but exists only conceptually, such as corporate stocks and bonds, patents and copyrights, and ordinary contract rights. Article 2 of the UCC does not govern intangible property.

INTEGRATED CONTRACT ■ A written contract that constitutes the final expression of the parties' agreement. If a contract is integrated, evidence extraneous to the contract that contradicts or alters the meaning of the contract in any way is inadmissible.

INTELLECTUAL PROPERTY ■ Property resulting from intellectual, creative processes.

INTENDED BENEFICIARY ■ A third party for whose benefit a contract is formed. An intended beneficiary can sue the promisor if such a contract is breached.

INTENTIONAL TORT ■ A wrongful act knowingly committed.

***INTER VIVOS* TRUST** ■ A trust created by the grantor (settlor) and effective during the grantor's lifetime; a trust not established by a will.

INTERMEDIARY BANK ■ Any bank to which an item is transferred in the course of collection, except the depositary or payor bank.

INTERNATIONAL LAW ■ The law that governs relations among nations. National laws, customs, treaties, and international conferences and organizations are generally considered to be the most important sources of international law.

INTERROGATORIES ■ A series of written questions for which written answers are prepared, usually with the assistance of the party's attorney, and then signed under oath by a party to a lawsuit.

INTESTACY LAWS ■ State statutes that specify how property will be distributed when a person dies intestate (without a valid will); also called statutes of descent and distribution.

INTESTATE ■ As a noun, one who has died without having created a valid will; as an adjective, the state of having died without a will.

INVESTMENT COMPANY ■ A company that acts on behalf of many smaller shareholders/owners by buying a large portfolio of securities and professionally managing that portfolio.

J

JOINT AND SEVERAL LIABILITY ■ In partnership law, a doctrine under which a plaintiff may sue, and collect a judgment from all of the partners together (jointly), or one or more of the partners separately (severally, or individually). This is true even if one of the partners sued did not participate in, ratify, or know about whatever it was that gave rise to the cause of action.

JOINT STOCK COMPANY ■ A hybrid form of business organization that combines characteristics of a corporation and a partnership. Usually, a joint stock company is regarded as a partnership for tax and other legal purposes.

JOINT TENANCY ■ The joint ownership of property by two or more co-owners in which each co-owner owns an undivided portion of the property. On the death of one of the joint tenants, his or her interest automatically passes to the surviving joint tenant(s).

JOINT VENTURE ■ A joint undertaking of a specific commercial enterprise by an association of persons. A joint venture normally is not a legal entity and is treated like a partnership for federal income tax purposes.

JUDICIAL REVIEW ■ The process by which a court decides on the constitutionality of legislative enactments and actions of the executive branch.

JURISDICTION ■ The authority of a court to hear and decide a specific action.

JURISPRUDENCE ■ The science or philosophy of law.

JUSTICIABLE CONTROVERSY ■ A controversy that is not hypothetical or academic but real and substantial; a requirement that must be satisfied before a court will hear a case.

L

LARCENY ■ The wrongful taking and carrying away of another person's personal property with the intent to permanently deprive the owner of the property. Some states classify larceny as either grand or petit, depending on the property's value.

LAW ■ A body of enforceable rules governing relationships among individuals and between individuals and their society.

LEASE AGREEMENT ■ In regard to the lease of goods, an agreement in which one person (the lessor) agrees to transfer the right to the possession and use of property to another person (the lessee) in exchange for rental payments.

LEASEHOLD ESTATE ■ An estate in realty held by a tenant under a lease. In every leasehold estate, the tenant has a qualified right to possess and/or use the land.

LEGACY ■ A gift of personal property under a will.

LEGAL POSITIVISM ■ A school of legal thought centered on the assumption that there is no law higher than the laws created by a national government. Laws must be obeyed, even if they are unjust, to prevent anarchy.

LEGAL REALISM ■ A school of legal thought of the 1920s and 1930s that generally advocated a less abstract and more realistic approach to the law, an approach that takes into account customary practices and the circumstances in which transactions take place. This school left a lasting imprint on American jurisprudence.

LEGATEE ■ One designated in a will to receive a gift of personal property.

LESSEE ■ A person who acquires the right to the possession and use of another's goods in exchange for rental payments.

LESSOR ■ A person who sells the right to the possession and use of goods to another in exchange for rental payments.

LETTER OF CREDIT ■ A written instrument, usually issued by a bank on behalf of a customer or other person, in which the issuer promises to honor drafts or other demands for payment by third persons in accordance with the terms of the instrument.

LEVY ■ The obtaining of money by legal process through the seizure and sale of nonsecured property, usually done after a writ of execution has been issued.

LIBEL ■ Defamation in writing or other permanent form (such as a digital recording) having the quality of permanence.

LICENSE ■ A revocable right or privilege of a person to come onto another person's land.

LIEN ■ An encumbrance on a property to satisfy a debt or protect a claim for payment of a debt.

LIFE ESTATE ■ An interest in land that exists only for the duration of the life of some person, usually the holder of the estate.

LIMITED LIABILITY COMPANY (LLC) ■ A hybrid form of business enterprise that offers the limited liability of a corporation and the tax advantages of a partnership.

LIMITED LIABILITY LIMITED PARTNERSHIP (LLLP) ■ A type of limited partnership in which the liability of all of the partners, including general partners, is limited to the amount of their investments.

LIMITED LIABILITY PARTNERSHIP (LLP) ■ A hybrid form of business organization that is used mainly by professionals who normally do business in a partnership. Like a partnership, an LLP is a pass-through entity for tax purposes, but the personal liability of the partners is limited.

LIMITED PARTNER ■ In a limited partnership, a partner who contributes capital to the partnership but has no right to participate in the management and operation of the business. The limited partner assumes no liability for partnership debts beyond the capital contributed.

LIMITED PARTNERSHIP ■ A partnership consisting of one or more general partners (who manage the business and are liable to the full extent of their personal assets for debts of the partnership) and one or more limited partners (who contribute only assets and are liable only up to the extent of their contributions).

LIQUIDATED DAMAGES ■ An amount, stipulated in a contract, that the parties to the contract believe to be a reasonable estimation of the damages that will occur in the event of a breach.

LIQUIDATION ■ In regard to corporations, the process by which corporate assets are converted into cash and distributed among creditors and shareholders according to specific rules of preference. In bankruptcy proceedings, the sale of all of the nonexempt assets of a debtor and the distribution of the proceeds to the debtor's creditors. Chapter 7 of the Bankruptcy Code provides for liquidation bankruptcy proceedings.

LITIGATION ■ The process of resolving a dispute through the court system.

LONG ARM STATUTE ■ A state statute that permits a state to obtain personal jurisdiction over nonresident defendants. A defendant must have certain "minimum contacts" with that state for the statute to apply.

LOST PROPERTY ■ Property with which the owner has involuntarily parted and then cannot find or recover.

M

MAILBOX RULE ■ A rule providing that an acceptance of an offer becomes effective on dispatch (on being placed in an official mailbox), if mail is, expressly or impliedly, an authorized means of communication of acceptance to the offeror.

MAKER ■ One who promises to pay a fixed amount of money to the holder of a promissory note or a certificate of deposit (CD).

MALPRACTICE ■ Professional misconduct or the lack of the requisite degree of skill as a professional. Negligence—the failure to exercise due care—on the part of a professional, such as a physician, is commonly referred to as malpractice.

MARKET CONCENTRATION ■ The degree to which a small number of firms control a large percentage share of a relevant market; determined by calculating the percentages held by the largest firms in that market.

MARKET POWER ■ The power of a firm to control the market price of its product. A monopoly has the greatest degree of market power.

MARKET-SHARE TEST ■ The primary measure of monopoly power. A firm's market share is the percentage of a market that the firm controls.

MECHANIC'S LIEN ■ A statutory lien on the real property of another, created to ensure payment for work performed and materials furnished in the repair or improvement of real property, such as a building.

MEDIATION ■ A method of settling disputes outside of court by using the services of a neutral third party, who acts as a communicating agent between the parties and assists them in negotiating a settlement.

MEMBER ■ The term used to designate a person who has an ownership interest in a limited liability company.

MERCHANT ■ A person who is engaged in the purchase and sale of goods. Under the UCC, a person who deals in goods of the kind involved in the sales contract or who holds herself or himself out as having skill or knowledge peculiar to the practices or use of the goods being purchased or sold. For definitions, see UCC 2–104.

MERGER ■ A contractual and statutory process in which one corporation (the surviving corporation) acquires all of the assets and liabilities of another corporation (the merged corporation). The shareholders of the merged corporation either are paid for their shares or receive shares in the surviving corporation.

META TAG ■ A key word in a document that can serve as an index reference to the document. On the Web, search engines return results based, in part, on the tags in Web documents. Words inserted into a Web site's key-word field to increase the site's inclusion in search engine results.

MINIMUM WAGE ■ The lowest wage, either by government regulation or union contract, that an employer may pay an hourly worker.

MINI-TRIAL ■ A private proceeding in which each party to a dispute argues its position before the other side and vice versa. A neutral third party may be present as an adviser and may render an opinion if the parties fail to reach an agreement.

MIRROR IMAGE RULE ■ A common law rule that requires that the terms of the offeree's acceptance adhere exactly to the terms of the offeror's offer for a valid contract to be formed.

MISDEMEANOR ■ A lesser crime than a felony, punishable by a fine or incarceration in jail for up to one year.

MISLAID PROPERTY ■ Property with which the owner has voluntarily parted and then cannot find or recover.

MITIGATION OF DAMAGES ■ A rule requiring a plaintiff to do whatever is reasonable to minimize the damages caused by the defendant.

MONEY LAUNDERING ■ Falsely reporting income that has been obtained through criminal activity as income obtained through a legitimate business enterprise—in effect, "laundering" the "dirty money."

MONOPOLIZATION ■ The possession of monopoly power in the relevant market and the willful acquisition or maintenance of that power, as distinguished from growth or development as a consequence of a superior product, business acumen, or historic accident.

MONOPOLY ■ A term generally used to describe a market in which there is a single seller or a limited number of sellers.

MONOPOLY POWER ■ The ability of a monopoly to dictate what takes place in a given market.

MORAL MINIMUM ■ The minimum degree of ethical behavior expected of a business firm, which is usually defined as compliance with the law.

MORTGAGEE ■ Under a mortgage agreement, the creditor who takes a security interest in the debtor's property.

MORTGAGOR ■ Under a mortgage agreement, the debtor who gives the creditor a security interest in the debtor's property in return for a mortgage loan.

MOTION FOR A DIRECTED VERDICT ■ In a jury trial, a motion for the judge to take the decision out of the hands of the jury and to direct a verdict for the party who filed the motion on the ground that the other party has not produced sufficient evidence to support her or his claim.

MOTION FOR A NEW TRIAL ■ A motion asserting that the trial was so fundamentally flawed (because of error, newly discovered evidence, prejudice, or other reason) that a new trial is necessary to prevent a miscarriage of justice.

MOTION FOR JUDGMENT *N.O.V.* ■ A motion requesting the court to grant judgment in favor of the party making the motion on the ground that the jury's verdict against him or her was unreasonable and erroneous.

MOTION FOR JUDGMENT ON THE PLEADINGS ■ A motion by either party to a lawsuit at the close of the pleadings requesting the court to decide the issue solely on the pleadings without proceeding to trial. The motion will be granted only if no facts are in dispute.

MOTION FOR SUMMARY JUDGMENT ■ A motion requesting the court to enter a judgment without proceeding to trial. The motion can be based on evidence outside the pleadings and will be granted only if no facts are in dispute.

MOTION TO DISMISS ■ A pleading in which a defendant asserts that the plaintiff's claim fails to state a cause of action (that is, has no basis in law) or that there are other grounds on which a suit should be dismissed.

MUTUAL FUND ■ A specific type of investment company that continually buys or sells to investors shares of ownership in a portfolio.

N

NATIONAL LAW ■ Law that pertains to a particular nation (as opposed to international law).

NATURAL LAW ■ The belief that government and the legal system should reflect universal moral and ethical principles that are inherent in human nature. The natural law school is the oldest and one of the most significant schools of legal thought.

NECESSARIES ■ Necessities required for life, such as food, shelter, clothing, and medical attention; may include whatever is believed to be necessary to maintain a person's standard of living or financial and social status.

NEGLIGENCE ■ The failure to exercise the standard of care that a reasonable person would exercise in similar circumstances.

NEGLIGENCE *PER SE* ■ An action or failure to act in violation of a statutory requirement.

NEGOTIABLE INSTRUMENT ■ A signed writing (record) that contains an unconditional promise or order to pay an exact sum of money on demand or at an exact future time to a specific person or order, or to bearer.

NEGOTIATION ■ In alternative dispute resolution, a process in which parties attempt to settle their dispute informally, with or without attorneys to represent them. In negotiable instruments law, the transfer of an instrument in such form that the transferee (the person to whom the instrument is transferred) becomes a holder.

NOMINAL DAMAGES ■ A small monetary award (often one dollar) granted to a plaintiff when no actual damage was suffered.

NO-PAR SHARES ■ Corporate shares that have no face value; that is, no specific dollar amount is printed on their face.

NORMAL TRADE RELATIONS (NTR) STATUS ■ A status granted in an international treaty by a provision stating that the citizens of the contracting nations may enjoy the privileges accorded by either party to citizens of its NTR nations. Generally, this status is designed to establish equality of international treatment.

NOTARY PUBLIC ■ A public official authorized to attest to the authenticity of signatures.

NOVATION ■ The substitution, by agreement, of a new contract for an old one, with the rights under the old one being terminated. Typically, novation involves the substitution of a new person who is responsible for the contract and the removal of the original party's rights and duties under the contract.

NUISANCE ■ A common law doctrine under which persons may be held liable for using their property in a manner that unreasonably interferes with others' rights to use or enjoy their own property.

NUNCUPATIVE WILL ■ An oral will (often called a deathbed will) made before witnesses; usually limited to transfers of personal property.

O

OBJECTIVE THEORY OF CONTRACTS ■ A theory under which the intent to form a contract will be judged by outward, objective facts (what the party said when entering into the contract, how the party acted or appeared, and the circumstances surrounding the transaction) as interpreted by a reasonable person, rather than by the party's own secret, subjective intentions.

OBLIGEE ■ One to whom an obligation is owed.

OBLIGOR ■ One who owes an obligation to another.

OFFER ■ A promise or commitment to perform or refrain from performing some specified act in the future.

OFFEREE ■ A person to whom an offer is made.

OFFEROR ■ A person who makes an offer.

ONLINE DISPUTE RESOLUTION (ODR) ■ The resolution of disputes with the assistance of organizations that offer dispute-resolution services via the Internet.

OPERATING AGREEMENT ■ In a limited liability company, an agreement in which the members set forth the details of how the business will be managed and operated. State statutes typically give the members wide latitude in deciding for themselves the rules that will govern their organization.

OPTION CONTRACT ■ A contract under which the offeror cannot revoke his or her offer for a stipulated time period, and the offeree can accept or reject the offer during this period without fear that the offer will be made to another person. The offeree must give consideration for the option (the irrevocable offer) to be enforceable.

ORDER FOR RELIEF ■ A court's grant of assistance to a complainant. In bankruptcy proceedings, the order relieves the debtor of the immediate obligation to pay the debts listed in the bankruptcy petition.

ORDER INSTRUMENT ■ A negotiable instrument that is payable "to the order of an identified person" or "to an identified person or order."

ORDINANCE ■ A regulation enacted by a city or county legislative body that becomes part of that state's statutory law.

OUTPUT CONTRACT ■ An agreement in which a seller agrees to sell and a buyer agrees to buy all or up to a stated amount of what the seller produces.

OVERDRAFT ■ A check that is paid by the bank when the checking account on which the check is written contains insufficient funds to cover the check.

P

PARENT-SUBSIDIARY MERGER ■ A merger of companies in which one company (the parent corporation) owns most of the stock of the other corporation (the subsidiary corporation). A parent-subsidiary merger (short-form merger) can use a simplified procedure when the parent corporation owns at least 90 percent of the outstanding shares of each class of stock of the subsidiary corporation.

PARTIALLY DISCLOSED PRINCIPAL ■ A principal whose identity is unknown by a third party, but the third party knows that the agent is or may be acting for a principal at the time the agent and the third party form a contract.

PARTNERING AGREEMENT ■ An agreement between a seller and a buyer who frequently do business with each other concerning the terms and conditions that will apply to all subsequently formed electronic contracts.

PARTNERSHIP ■ An agreement by two or more persons to carry on, as co-owners, a business for profit.

PAR-VALUE SHARES ■ Corporate shares that have a specific face value, or formal cash-in value, written on them, such as one dollar.

PASS-THROUGH ENTITY ■ A business entity that has no tax liability; the entity's income is passed through to the owners, and the owners pay taxes on the income.

PAST CONSIDERATION ■ An act that takes place before the contract is made and that ordinarily, by itself, cannot be consideration for a later promise to pay for the act.

PATENT ■ A government grant that gives an inventor the exclusive right or privilege to make, use, or sell his or her invention for a limited time period.

PAYEE ■ A person to whom an instrument is made payable.

PAYOR BANK ■ The bank on which a check is drawn (the drawee bank).

PEER-TO-PEER (P2P) NETWORKING ■ The sharing of resources (such as files, hard drives, and processing styles) among multiple computers without necessarily requiring a central network server.

PENALTY ■ A contractual clause that states that a certain amount of money damages will be paid in the event of a future default or breach of contract. The damages are not a measure of compensation for the contract's breach but rather a punishment for a default. The agreement as to the amount will not be enforced, and recovery will be limited to actual damages.

PER CAPITA ■ A Latin term meaning "per person." In the law governing estate distribution, a method of distributing the property of an intestate's estate so that each heir in a certain class (such as grandchildren) receives an equal share.

***PER SE* VIOLATION** ■ A type of anticompetitive agreement that is considered to be so injurious to the public that there is no need to determine whether it actually injures market competition; rather, it is in itself *(per se)* a violation of the Sherman Act.

PER STIRPES ■ A Latin term meaning "by the roots." In the law governing estate distribution, a method of distributing an intestate's estate so that each heir in a certain class (such as grandchildren) takes the share to which her or his deceased ancestor (such as a mother or father) would have been entitled.

PERFECTION ■ The legal process by which secured parties protect themselves against the claims of third parties who may wish to have their debts satisfied out of the same collateral; usually accomplished by filing a financing statement with the appropriate government official.

PERFORMANCE ■ In contract law, the fulfillment of one's duties arising under a contract with another; the normal way of discharging one's contractual obligations.

PERIODIC TENANCY ■ A lease interest in land for an indefinite period involving payment of rent at fixed intervals, such as week to week, month to month, or year to year.

PERSONAL DEFENSES ■ Defenses that can be used to avoid payment to an ordinary holder of a negotiable instrument but not a holder in due course (HDC) or a holder with the rights of an HDC.

PERSONAL PROPERTY ■ Property that is movable; any property that is not real property.

PERSUASIVE AUTHORITY ■ Any legal authority or source of law that a court may look to for guidance but on which it need not rely in making its decision. Persuasive authorities include cases from other jurisdictions and secondary sources of law.

PETITION IN BANKRUPTCY ■ The document that is filed with a bankruptcy court to initiate bankruptcy proceedings. The official forms required for a petition in bankruptcy must be completed accurately, sworn to under oath, and signed by the debtor.

PETTY OFFENSE ■ In criminal law, the least serious kind of criminal offense, such as a traffic or building-code violation.

PIERCING THE CORPORATE VEIL ■ An action in which a court disregards the corporate entity and holds the shareholders personally liable for corporate debts and obligations.

PLAINTIFF ■ One who initiates a lawsuit.

PLEA BARGAINING ■ The process by which a defendant and the prosecutor in a criminal case work out a mutually satisfactory disposition of the case, subject to court approval; usually involves the defendant's pleading guilty to a lesser offense in return for a lighter sentence.

PLEADINGS ■ Statements made by the plaintiff and the defendant in a lawsuit that detail the facts, charges, and defenses involved in the litigation. The complaint and answer are part of the pleadings.

PLEDGE ■ A common law security device (retained in Article 9 of the UCC) in which personal property is transferred into the possession of the creditor as security for the payment of a debt and retained by the creditor until the debt is paid.

POLICE POWERS ■ Powers possessed by the states as part of their inherent sovereignty. These powers may be exercised to protect or promote the public order, health, safety, morals, and general welfare.

POLICY ■ In insurance law, a contract between the insurer and the insured in which, for a stipulated consideration, the insurer agrees to compensate the insured for loss on a specific subject by a specified peril.

POSITIVE LAW ■ The body of conventional, or written, law of a particular society at a particular point in time.

POTENTIALLY RESPONSIBLE PARTY (PRP) ■ A party liable for the costs of cleaning up a hazardous waste–disposal site under the Comprehensive Environmental Response, Compensation, and Liability Act (CERCLA). Any person who generated the hazardous waste, transported it, owned or operated the waste site at the time of disposal, or currently owns or operates the site may be responsible for some or all of the clean-up costs.

POWER OF ATTORNEY ■ A written document, which is usually notarized, authorizing another to act as one's agent; can be special (permitting the agent to do specified acts only) or general (permitting the agent to transact all business for the principal).

PRECEDENT ■ A court decision that furnishes an example or authority for deciding subsequent cases involving identical or similar facts.

PREDATORY BEHAVIOR ■ Business behavior that is undertaken with the intention of unlawfully driving competitors out of the market.

PREDATORY PRICING ■ The pricing of a product below cost with the intent to drive competitors out of the market.

PREDOMINANT-FACTOR TEST ■ A test courts use to determine whether a contract is primarily for the sale of goods or for the sale of services.

PREEMPTION ■ A doctrine under which certain federal laws preempt, or take precedence over, conflicting state or local laws.

PREEMPTIVE RIGHTS ■ Rights held by shareholders that entitle them to purchase newly issued shares of a corporation's stock, equal in percentage to shares currently held, before the stock is offered to any outside buyers. Preemptive rights enable shareholders to maintain their proportionate ownership and voice in the corporation.

PREFERENCE ■ In bankruptcy proceedings, property transfers or payments made by the debtor that favor (give preference to) one creditor over others. The bankruptcy trustee is allowed to recover payments made both voluntarily and involuntarily to one creditor in preference over another.

PREFERRED STOCK ■ Classes of stock that have priority over common stock as to both payment of dividends and distribution of assets on the corporation's dissolution.

PREMIUM ■ In insurance law, the price paid by the insured for insurance protection for a specified period of time.

PRENUPTIAL AGREEMENT ■ An agreement made before marriage that defines each partner's ownership rights in the other partner's property. Prenuptial agreements must be in writing to be enforceable.

PRESENTMENT ■ The act of presenting an instrument to the party liable on the instrument to collect payment. Presentment also occurs when a person presents an instrument to a drawee for a required acceptance.

PRESENTMENT WARRANTIES ■ Implied warranties, made by any person who presents an instrument for payment or acceptance, that (1) the person obtaining payment or acceptance is entitled to enforce the instrument or is authorized to obtain payment or acceptance on behalf of a person who is entitled to enforce the instrument, (2) the instrument has not been altered, and (3) the person obtaining payment or acceptance has no knowledge that the signature of the drawer of the instrument is unauthorized.

PRICE DISCRIMINATION ■ Setting prices in such a way that two competing buyers pay two different prices for an identical product or service.

PRICE-FIXING AGREEMENT ■ An agreement between competitors to fix the prices of products or services at a certain level.

***PRIMA FACIE* CASE** ■ A case in which the plaintiff has produced sufficient evidence of his or her conclusion that the case can go to a jury; a case in which the evidence compels the plaintiff's conclusion if the defendant produces no affirmative defense or evidence to disprove it.

PRIMARY SOURCE OF LAW ■ A document that establishes the law on a particular issue, such as a constitution, a statute, an administrative rule, or a court decision.

PRINCIPAL ■ In agency law, a person who agrees to have another, called the agent, act on her or his behalf.

PRINCIPLE OF RIGHTS ■ The principle that human beings have certain fundamental rights (to life, freedom, and the pursuit of happiness, for example). Those who adhere to this "rights theory" believe that a key factor in determining whether a business decision is ethical is how that decision affects the rights of various groups. These groups include the firm's owners, its employees, the consumers of its products or services, its suppliers, the community in which it does business, and society as a whole.

PRIVILEGE ■ A legal right, exemption, or immunity granted to a person or a class of persons. In the context of defamation, an absolute privilege immunizes the actor from suit, regardless of whether the actor's statements were malicious. A qualified privilege immunizes an actor from suit only when the privilege is properly exercised in the performance of a legal or moral duty.

PRIVITY OF CONTRACT ■ The relationship that exists between the promisor and the promisee of a contract.

PROBABLE CAUSE ■ Reasonable grounds for believing that a person should be arrested or searched.

PROBATE ■ The process of proving and validating a will and settling all matters pertaining to an estate.

PROBATE COURT ■ A state court of limited jurisdiction that conducts proceedings relating to the settlement of a deceased person's estate.

PROCEDURAL LAW ■ Law that establishes the methods of enforcing the rights established by substantive law.

PROCEEDS ■ Under Article 9 of the UCC, whatever is received when the collateral is sold or otherwise disposed of, such as by exchange.

PRODUCT LIABILITY ■ The legal liability of manufacturers, sellers, and lessors of goods to consumers, users, and bystanders for injuries or damages that are caused by the goods.

PROFIT ■ In real property law, the right to enter upon and remove things from the property of another (for example, the right to enter onto a person's land and remove sand and gravel therefrom).

PROMISE ■ An assertion that something either will or will not happen in the future.

PROMISEE ■ A person to whom a promise is made.

PROMISOR ■ A person who makes a promise.

PROMISSORY ESTOPPEL ■ A doctrine that applies when a promisor makes a clear and definite promise on which the promisee justifiably relies; such a promise is binding if justice will be better served by the enforcement of the promise.

PROMISSORY NOTE ■ A written promise made by one person (the maker) to pay a fixed amount of money to another person (the payee or a subsequent holder) on demand or on a specified date.

PROMOTER ■ A person who takes the preliminary steps in organizing a corporation, including (usually) issuing a prospectus, procuring stock subscriptions, making contracts for necessary purchases and services, securing a corporate charter, and the like.

PROPERTY ■ Legally protected rights and interests in anything with an ascertainable value that is subject to ownership.

PROSPECTUS ■ A document required by federal or state securities laws that describes the financial operations of the corporation, thus allowing investors to make informed decisions.

PROTECTED CLASS ■ A group of persons protected by specific laws because of the group's defining characteristics. Under laws prohibiting employment discrimination, these characteristics include race, color, religion, national origin, gender, age, and disability.

PROXIMATE CAUSE ■ Legal cause; exists when the connection between an act and an injury is strong enough to justify imposing liability.

PROXY ■ In corporation law, a written agreement between a stockholder and another party under which the stockholder authorizes the other party to vote the stockholder's shares in a certain manner.

PUFFERY ■ A salesperson's often exaggerated claims concerning the quality of property offered for sale. Such claims involve opinions rather than facts and are not considered to be legally binding promises or warranties.

PUNITIVE DAMAGES ■ Money damages that may be awarded to a plaintiff to punish the defendant and deter future similar conduct.

PURCHASE-MONEY SECURITY INTEREST (PMSI) ■ A security interest that arises when a seller or lender extends credit for part or all of the purchase price of goods purchased by a buyer.

Q

QUALIFIED INDORSEMENT ■ An indorsement on a negotiable instrument in which the indorser disclaims any contract liability on the instrument. The notation "without recourse" is commonly used to create a qualified indorsement.

QUASI CONTRACT ■ A fictional contract imposed on parties by a court in the interests of fairness and justice; usually imposed to avoid the unjust enrichment of one party at the expense of another.

QUITCLAIM DEED ■ A deed intended to pass any title, interest, or claim that the grantor may have in the property without warranting that such title is valid. A quitclaim deed offers the least amount of protection against defects in the title.

QUORUM ■ The number of members of a decision-making body that must be present before business may be transacted.

QUOTA ■ A set limit on the amount of goods that can be imported.

R

RATIFICATION ■ The act of accepting and giving legal force to an obligation that previously was not enforceable.

REAFFIRMATION AGREEMENT ■ An agreement between a debtor and a creditor in which the debtor voluntarily agrees to pay, or reaffirm, a debt dischargeable in bankruptcy. To be enforceable, the agreement must be made before the debtor is granted a discharge.

REAL PROPERTY ■ Land and everything attached to it, such as trees and buildings.

REASONABLE PERSON STANDARD ■ The standard of behavior expected of a hypothetical "reasonable person"; the standard against which negligence is measured and that must be observed to avoid liability for negligence.

RECEIVER ■ In a corporate dissolution, a court-appointed person who winds up corporate affairs and liquidates corporate assets.

RECORD ■ According to the Uniform Electronic Transactions Act, information that is either inscribed on a tangible medium or stored in an electronic or other medium and that is retrievable. The Uniform Computer Information Transactions Act also uses the term *record* instead of *writing*.

RECORDING STATUTES ■ Statutes that allow deeds, mortgages, and other real property transactions to be recorded so as to provide notice to future purchasers or creditors of an existing claim on the property.

RED HERRING ■ A preliminary prospectus that can be distributed to potential investors after the registration statement (for a securities offering) has been filed with the Securities and Exchange Commission. The name derives from the red legend printed across the prospectus stating that the registration has been filed but has not become effective.

REFORMATION ■ A court-ordered correction of a written contract so that it reflects the true intentions of the parties.

REGULATION E ■ A set of rules issued by the Federal Reserve System's Board of Governors to protect users of elecronic fund transfer systems.

REGULATION Z ■ A set of rules promulgated by the Federal Reserve Board of Governors to implement the provisions of the Truth-in-Lending Act.

RELEASE ■ A contract in which one party forfeits the right to pursue a legal claim against the other party.

REMEDY ■ The relief given to an innocent party to enforce a right or compensate for the violation of a right.

REPLEVIN ■ An action to recover identified goods in the hands of a party who is wrongfully withholding them from the other party. Under the UCC, this remedy is usually available only if the buyer or lessee is unable to cover.

REPLY ■ Procedurally, a plaintiff's response to a defendant's answer.

REQUIREMENTS CONTRACT ■ An agreement in which a buyer agrees to purchase and the seller agrees to sell all or up to a stated amount of what the buyer needs or requires.

RES IPSA LOQUITUR ■ A doctrine under which negligence may be inferred simply because an event occurred, if it is the type of event that would never occur in the absence of negligence. Literally, the term means "the facts speak for themselves."

RESALE PRICE MAINTENANCE AGREEMENT ■ An agreement between a manufacturer and a retailer in which the manufacturer specifies what the retail prices of its products must be.

RESCISSION ■ A remedy whereby a contract is canceled and the parties are returned to the positions they occupied before the contract was made; may be effected through the mutual consent of the parties, by the parties' conduct, or by court decree.

RESPONDEAT SUPERIOR ■ Latin for "let the master respond." A doctrine under which a principal or an employer is held liable for the wrongful acts committed by agents or employees while acting within the course and scope of their agency or employment.

RESTITUTION ■ An equitable remedy under which a person is restored to his or her original position prior to loss or injury, or placed in the position he or she would have been in had the breach not occurred.

RESTRICTIVE INDORSEMENT ■ Any indorsement on a negotiable instrument that requires the indorsee to comply with certain instructions regarding the funds involved. A restrictive indorsement does not prohibit the further negotiation of the instrument.

RESULTING TRUST ■ An implied trust arising from the conduct of the parties. A trust in which a party holds the actual legal title to another's property but only for that person's benefit.

RETAINED EARNINGS ■ The portion of a corporation's profits that has not been paid out as dividends to shareholders.

REVOCATION ■ In contract law, the withdrawal of an offer by an offeror. Unless the offer is irrevocable, it can be revoked at any time prior to acceptance without liability.

RIGHT OF CONTRIBUTION ■ The right of a co-surety who pays more than his or her proportionate share on a debtor's default to recover the excess paid from other co-sureties.

RIGHT OF FIRST REFUSAL ■ The right to purchase personal or real property—such as corporate shares or real estate—before the property is offered for sale to others.

RIGHT OF REIMBURSEMENT ■ The legal right of a person to be restored, repaid, or indemnified for costs, expenses, or losses incurred or expended on behalf of another.

RIGHT OF SUBROGATION ■ The right of a person to stand in the place of (be substituted for) another, giving the substituted party the same legal rights that the original party had.

RIGHT-TO-WORK LAW ■ A state law providing that employees may not be required to join a union as a condition of retaining employment.

RISK ■ A prediction concerning potential loss based on known and unknown factors.

RISK MANAGEMENT ■ Planning that is undertaken to protect one's interest should some event threaten to undermine its security. In the context of insurance, risk management involves transferring certain risks from the insured to the insurance company.

ROBBERY ■ The act of forcefully and unlawfully taking personal property of any value from another. Force or intimidation is usually necessary for an act of theft to be considered a robbery.

RULE OF FOUR ■ A rule of the United States Supreme Court under which the Court will not issue a *writ of certiorari* unless at least four justices approve of the decision to issue the writ.

RULE OF REASON ■ A test by which a court balances the positive effects (such as economic efficiency) of an agreement against its potentially anticompetitive effects. In antitrust litigation, many practices are analyzed under the rule of reason.

RULEMAKING ■ The process undertaken by an administrative agency when formally adopting a new regulation or amending an old one. Rulemaking involves notifying the public of a proposed rule or change and receiving and considering the public's comments.

S

S CORPORATION ■ A close business corporation that has met certain requirements set out in the Internal Revenue Code and thus qualifies for special income tax treatment. Essentially, an S corporation is taxed the same as a partnership, but its owners enjoy the privilege of limited liability.

SALE ■ The passing of title to property from the seller to the buyer for a price.

SALE ON APPROVAL ■ A type of conditional sale in which the buyer may take the goods on a trial basis. The sale becomes absolute only when the buyer approves of (or is satisfied with) the goods being sold.

SALE OR RETURN ■ A type of conditional sale in which title and possession pass from the seller to the buyer, but the buyer retains the option to return the goods during a specified period even though the goods conform to the contract.

SALES CONTRACT ■ A contract for the sale of goods under which the ownership of goods is transferred from a seller to a buyer for a price.

SCIENTER ■ Knowledge by the misrepresenting party that material facts have been falsely represented or omitted with an intent to deceive.

SEARCH WARRANT ■ An order granted by a public authority, such as a judge, that authorizes law enforcement personnel to search particular premises or property.

SEASONABLY ■ Within a specified time period or, if no period is specified, within a reasonable time.

SEC RULE 10b-5 ■ A rule of the Securities and Exchange Commission (SEC) that makes it unlawful, in connection with the purchase or sale of any security, to make any untrue statement of a material fact or to omit a material fact if such omission causes the statement to be misleading.

SECONDARY BOYCOTT ■ A union's refusal to work for, purchase from, or handle the products of a secondary employer, with whom the union has no dispute, in order to force that employer to stop doing business with the primary employer, with whom the union has a labor dispute.

SECONDARY SOURCE OF LAW ■ A publication that summarizes or interprets the law, such as a legal encyclopedia, a legal treatise, or an article in a law review.

SECURED PARTY ■ A lender, seller, or any other person in whose favor there is a security interest, including a person to whom accounts or chattel paper has been sold.

SECURED TRANSACTION ■ Any transaction in which the payment of a debt is guaranteed, or secured, by personal property owned by the debtor or in which the debtor has a legal interest.

SECURITIES ■ Generally, stock certificates, bonds, notes, debentures, warrants, or other documents given as evidence of an ownership interest in a corporation or as a promise of repayment by a corporation.

SECURITY ■ Generally, a stock certificate, bond, note, debenture, warrant, or other document given as evidence of an ownership interest in a corporation or as a promise of repayment by a corporation.

SECURITY AGREEMENT ■ An agreement that creates or provides for a security interest between the debtor and a secured party.

SECURITY INTEREST ■ Any interest in personal property or fixtures that secures payment or performance of an obligation.

SELF-DEFENSE ■ The legally recognized privilege to protect oneself or one's property against injury by another. The privilege of self-defense protects only acts that are reasonably necessary to protect oneself, one's property, or another person.

SELF-INCRIMINATION ■ The giving of testimony that may subject the testifier to criminal prosecution. The Fifth Amendment to the Constitution protects against self-incrimination by providing that no person "shall be compelled in any criminal case to be a witness against himself."

SENIORITY SYSTEM ■ In regard to employment relationships, a system in which those who have worked longest for the company are first in line for promotions, salary increases, and other benefits; they are also the last to be laid off if the work force must be reduced.

SERVICE MARK ■ A mark used in the sale or the advertising of services to distinguish the services of one person from those of others. Titles, character names, and other distinctive features of radio and television programs may be registered as service marks.

SEXUAL HARASSMENT ■ In the employment context, the demanding of sexual favors in return for job promotions or other benefits, or language or conduct that is so sexually offensive that it creates a hostile working environment.

SHAREHOLDER'S DERIVATIVE SUIT ■ A suit brought by a shareholder to enforce a corporate cause of action against a third person.

SHELTER PRINCIPLE ■ The principle that the holder of a negotiable instrument who cannot qualify as a holder in due course (HDC), but who derives his or her title through an HDC, acquires the rights of an HDC.

SHIPMENT CONTRACT ■ A contract for the sale of goods in which the seller is required or authorized to ship the goods by carrier. The seller assumes liability for any losses or damage to the goods until they are delivered to the carrier.

SHORT-FORM MERGER ■ A merger between a subsidiary corporation and a parent corporation that owns at least 90 percent of the outstanding shares of each class of stock issued by the subsidiary corporation. Short-form mergers can be accomplished without the approval of the shareholders of either corporation.

SHRINK-WRAP AGREEMENT ■ An agreement whose terms are expressed in a document located inside a box in which goods (usually software) are packaged; sometimes called a *shrink-wrap license*.

SIGNATURE ■ Under the UCC, "any symbol executed or adopted by a party with a present intention to authenticate a writing."

SLANDER ■ Defamation in oral form.

SLANDER OF QUALITY (TRADE LIBEL) ■ The publication of false information about another's product, alleging that it is not what its seller claims.

SLANDER OF TITLE ■ The publication of a statement that denies or casts doubt on another's legal ownership of any property, causing financial loss to that property's owner.

SMALL CLAIMS COURT ■ A special court in which parties may litigate small claims (such as $5,000 or less). Attorneys are not required in small claims courts and, in some states, are not allowed to represent the parties.

SMART CARD ■ A card containing a microprocessor that permits storage of funds via security programming, can communicate with other computers, and does not require online authorization for fund transfers.

SOCIOLOGICAL SCHOOL ■ A school of legal thought that views the law as a tool for promoting justice in society.

SOLE PROPRIETORSHIP ■ The simplest form of business organization, in which the owner is the business. The owner reports business income on his or her personal income tax return and is legally responsible for all debts and obligations incurred by the business.

SOVEREIGN IMMUNITY ■ A doctrine that immunizes foreign nations from the jurisdiction of U.S. courts when certain conditions are satisfied.

SPAM ■ Bulk, unsolicited ("junk") e-mail.

SPECIAL INDORSEMENT ■ An indorsement on an instrument that indicates the specific person to whom the indorser intends to make the instrument payable; that is, it names the indorsee.

SPECIAL WARRANTY DEED ■ A deed in which the grantor only warrants that the grantor or seller held good title during his or her ownership of the property and does not warrant that there were no defects of title when the property was held by previous owners.

SPECIFIC PERFORMANCE ■ An equitable remedy requiring exactly the performance that was specified in a contract; usually granted only when money damages would be an inadequate remedy and the subject matter of the contract is unique (for example, real property).

SPENDTHRIFT TRUST ■ A trust created to protect the beneficiary from spending all the funds to which she or he is entitled. Only a certain portion of the total amount is given to the beneficiary at any one time, and most states prohibit creditors from attaching assets of the trust.

STALE CHECK ■ A check, other than a certified check, that is presented for payment more than six months after its date.

STANDING TO SUE ■ The requirement that an individual must have a sufficient stake in a controversy before he or she can bring a lawsuit. The plaintiff must demonstrate that he or she has been either injured or threatened with injury.

STARE DECISIS ■ A common law doctrine under which judges are obligated to follow the precedents established in prior decisions.

STATUTE OF FRAUDS ■ A state statute under which certain types of contracts must be in writing to be enforceable.

STATUTE OF LIMITATIONS ■ A federal or state statute setting the maximum time period during which a certain action can be brought or certain rights enforced.

STATUTE OF REPOSE ■ Basically, a statute of limitations that is not dependent on the happening of a cause of action. Statutes of repose generally begin to run at an earlier date and run for a longer period of time than statutes of limitations.

STATUTORY LAW ■ The body of law enacted by legislative bodies (as opposed to constitutional law, administrative law, or case law).

STOCK ■ An equity (ownership) interest in a corporation, measured in units of shares.

STOCK CERTIFICATE ■ A certificate issued by a corporation evidencing the ownership of a specified number of shares in the corporation.

STOCK WARRANT ■ A certificate that grants the owner the option to buy a given number of shares of stock, usually within a set time period.

STOP-PAYMENT ORDER ■ An order by a bank customer to his or her bank not to pay or certify a certain check.

STORED-VALUE CARD ■ A card bearing magnetic strips that hold magnetically encoded data, providing access to stored funds.

STRICT LIABILITY ■ Liability regardless of fault. In tort law, strict liability is imposed on a manufacturer or seller that introduces into commerce a good that is unreasonably dangerous when in a defective condition.

STRIKE ■ An action undertaken by unionized workers when collective bargaining fails; the workers leave their jobs, refuse to work, and (typically) picket the employer's workplace.

SUBLEASE ■ A lease executed by the lessee of real estate to a third person, conveying the same interest that the lessee enjoys but for a shorter term than that held by the lessee.

SUBSTANTIVE LAW ■ Law that defines, describes, regulates, and creates legal rights and obligations.

SUMMARY JURY TRIAL (SJT) ■ A method of settling disputes, used in many federal courts, in which a trial is held, but the jury's verdict is not binding. The verdict acts only as a guide to both sides in reaching an agreement during the mandatory negotiations that immediately follow the summary jury trial.

SUMMONS ■ A document informing a defendant that a legal action has been commenced against him or her and that the defendant must appear in court on a certain date to answer the plaintiff's complaint. The document is delivered by a sheriff or any other person so authorized.

SUPREMACY CLAUSE ■ The provision in Article VI of the Constitution that provides that the Constitution, laws, and treaties of the United States are "the supreme Law of the Land." Under this clause, state and local laws that directly conflict with federal law will be rendered invalid.

SURETY ■ A person, such as a cosigner on a note, who agrees to be primarily responsible for the debt of another.

SURETYSHIP ■ An express contract in which a third party to a debtor-creditor relationship (the surety) promises to be primarily responsible for the debtor's obligation.

SYMBOLIC SPEECH ■ Nonverbal expressions of beliefs. Symbolic speech, which includes gestures, movements, and articles of clothing, is given substantial protection by the courts.

SYNDICATE ■ An investment group of persons or firms brought together for the purpose of financing a project that they would not or could not undertake independently.

T

TAKEOVER ■ The acquisition of control over a corporation through the purchase of a substantial number of the voting shares of the corporation.

TAKING ■ The taking of private property by the government for public use. The government may not take private property for public use without "just compensation."

TANGIBLE PROPERTY ■ Property that has physical existence and can be distinguished by the senses of touch, sight, and so on. A car is tangible property; a patent right is intangible property.

TARGET CORPORATION ■ The corporation to be acquired in a corporate takeover; a corporation to whose shareholders a tender offer is submitted.

TARIFF ■ A tax on imported goods.

TENANCY AT SUFFERANCE ■ A type of tenancy under which a tenant who, after rightfully being in possession of leased premises, continues (wrongfully) to occupy the property after the lease has been terminated. The tenant has no rights to possess the property and occupies it only because the person entitled to evict the tenant has not done so.

TENANCY AT WILL ■ A type of tenancy that either party can terminate without notice; usually arises when a tenant who has been under a tenancy for years retains possession, with the landlord's consent, after the tenancy for years has terminated.

TENANCY BY THE ENTIRETY ■ The joint ownership of property by a husband and wife. Neither party can transfer her or his interest in the property without the consent of the other.

TENANCY FOR YEARS ■ A type of tenancy under which property is leased for a specified period of time, such as a month, a year, or a period of years.

TENANCY IN COMMON ■ Co-ownership of property in which each party owns an undivided interest that passes to her or his heirs at death.

TENDER ■ An unconditional offer to perform an obligation by a person who is ready, willing, and able to do so.

TENDER OFFER ■ An offer to purchase shares made by one company directly to the shareholders of another (target) company; often referred to as a "takeover bid."

TESTAMENTARY TRUST ■ A trust that is created by will and therefore does not take effect until the death of the testator.

TESTATE ■ Having left a will at death.

TESTATOR ■ One who makes and executes a will.

THIRD PARTY BENEFICIARY ■ One for whose benefit a promise is made in a contract but who is not a party to the contract.

TIPPEE ■ A person who receives inside information.

TOMBSTONE AD ■ An advertisement, historically in a format resembling a tombstone, of a securities offering. The ad tells potential investors where and how they may obtain a prospectus.

TORT ■ A civil wrong not arising from a breach of contract. A breach of a legal duty that proximately causes harm or injury to another.

TORTFEASOR ■ One who commits a tort.

TOTTEN TRUST ■ A trust created by the deposit of a person's own funds in his or her own name as a trustee for another. It is a tentative trust, revocable at will until the depositor dies or completes the gift in his or her lifetime by some unequivocal act or declaration.

TOXIC TORT ■ A civil wrong arising from exposure to a toxic substance, such as asbestos, radiation, or hazardous waste.

TRADE ACCEPTANCE ■ A draft that is drawn by a seller of goods ordering the buyer to pay a specified sum of money to the seller, usually at a stated time in the future. The buyer accepts the draft by signing the face of the draft, thus creating an enforceable obligation to pay the draft when it comes due. On a trade acceptance, the seller is both the drawer and the payee.

TRADE DRESS ■ The image and overall appearance of a product—for example, the distinctive decor, menu, layout, and style of service of a particular restaurant. Basically, trade dress is subject to the same protection as trademarks.

TRADE NAME ■ A term that is used to indicate part or all of a business's name and that is directly related to the business's reputation and goodwill. Trade names are protected under the common law (and under trademark law, if the name is the same as the firm's trademarked property).

TRADE SECRETS ■ Information or processes that give a business an advantage over competitors that do not know the information or processes.

TRADEMARK ■ A distinctive mark, motto, device, or emblem that a manufacturer stamps, prints, or otherwise affixes to the goods it produces so that they may be identified on the market and their origins made known. Once a trademark is established (under the common law or through registration), the owner is entitled to its exclusive use.

TRANSFER WARRANTIES ■ Implied warranties, made by any person who transfers an instrument for consideration to subsequent transferees and holders who take the instrument in good faith, that (1) the transferor is entitled to enforce the instrument; (2) all signatures are authentic and authorized; (3) the instrument has not been altered; (4) the instrument is not subject to a defense or claim of any party that can be asserted against the transferor; and (5) the transferor has no knowledge of any insolvency proceedings against the maker, the acceptor, or the drawer of the instrument.

TRAVELER'S CHECK ■ A check that is payable on demand, drawn on or payable through a financial institution (bank), and designated as a traveler's check.

TREBLE DAMAGES ■ Damages that, by statute, are three times the amount that the fact finder determines is owed.

TRESPASS TO LAND ■ The entry onto, above, or below the surface of land owned by another without the owner's permission or legal authorization.

TRESPASS TO PERSONAL PROPERTY ■ The unlawful taking or harming of another's personal property; interference with another's right to the exclusive possession of his or her personal property.

TRUST ■ An arrangement in which title to property is held by one person (a trustee) for the benefit of another (a beneficiary).

TRUST INDORSEMENT ■ An indorsement for the benefit of the indorser or a third person; also known as an agency indorsement. The indorsement results in legal title vesting in the original indorsee.

TYING ARRANGEMENT ■ An agreement between a buyer and a seller in which the buyer of a specific product or service becomes obligated to purchase additional products or services from the seller.

U

U.S. TRUSTEE ■ A government official who performs certain administrative tasks that a bankruptcy judge would otherwise have to perform.

ULTRA VIRES ■ A Latin term meaning "beyond the powers"; in corporate law, acts of a corporation that are beyond its express and implied powers to undertake.

UNCONSCIONABLE CONTRACT (OR UNCONSCIONABLE CLAUSE) ■ A contract or clause that is void on the basis of public policy because one party, as a result of disproportionate bargaining power, is forced to accept terms that are unfairly burdensome and that unfairly benefit the dominating party.

UNDERWRITER ■ In insurance law, the insurer, or the one assuming a risk in return for the payment of a premium.

UNDISCLOSED PRINCIPAL ■ A principal whose identity is unknown by a third person, and the third person has no knowledge that the agent is acting for a principal at the time the agent and the third person form a contract.

UNENFORCEABLE CONTRACT ■ A valid contract rendered unenforceable by some statute or law.

UNILATERAL CONTRACT ■ A contract that results when an offer can be accepted only by the offeree's performance.

UNION SHOP ■ A place of employment where all workers, once employed, must become union members within a specified period of time as a condition of their continued employment.

UNIVERSAL DEFENSES ■ Defenses that are valid against all holders of a negotiable instrument, including holders in due course (HDCs) and holders with the rights of HDCs.

UNREASONABLY DANGEROUS PRODUCT ■ In product liability, a product that is defective to the point of threatening a consumer's health and safety. A product will be considered unreasonably dangerous if it is dangerous beyond the expectation of the ordinary consumer or if a less dangerous alternative was economically feasible for the manufacturer, but the manufacturer failed to produce it.

USAGE OF TRADE ■ Any practice or method of dealing having such regularity of observance in a place, vocation, or trade as to justify an expectation that it will be observed with respect to the transaction in question.

USURY ■ Charging an illegal rate of interest.

UTILITARIANISM ■ An approach to ethical reasoning that evaluates behavior not on the basis of any absolute ethical or moral values but on the consequences of that behavior for those who will be affected by it. In utilitarian reasoning, a "good" decision is one that results in the greatest good for the greatest number of people affected by the decision.

V

VALID CONTRACT ■ A contract that results when the elements necessary for contract formation (agreement, consideration, legal purpose, and contractual capacity) are present.

VENUE ■ The geographic district in which an action is tried and from which the jury is selected.

VERTICAL MERGER ■ The acquisition by a company at one level in a marketing chain of a company at a higher or lower level in the chain (such as a company merging with one of its suppliers or retailers).

VERTICAL RESTRAINT ■ Any restraint on trade created by agreements between firms at different levels in the manufacturing and distribution process.

VERTICALLY INTEGRATED FIRM ■ A firm that carries out two or more functional phases (manufacture, distribution, and retailing, for example) of the chain of production.

VESTING ■ The creation of an absolute or unconditional right or power.

VICARIOUS LIABILITY ■ Legal responsibility placed on one person for the acts of another; indirect liability imposed on a supervisory party (such as an employer) for the actions of a subordinate (such as an employee) because of the relationship between the two parties.

VOID CONTRACT ■ A contract having no legal force or binding effect.

VOIDABLE CONTRACT ■ A contract that may be legally avoided (canceled, or annulled) at the option of one or both of the parties.

VOIR DIRE ■ An old French phrase meaning "to speak the truth." In legal language, the phrase refers to the process in which the attorneys question prospective jurors to learn about their backgrounds, attitudes, biases, and other characteristics that may affect their ability to serve as impartial jurors.

VOTING TRUST ■ An agreement (trust contract) under which legal title to shares of corporate stock is transferred to a trustee who is authorized by the shareholders to vote the shares on their behalf.

W

WARRANTY DEED ■ A deed in which the grantor assures (warrants to) the grantee that the grantor has title to the property conveyed in the deed, that there are no encumbrances on the property other than what the grantor has represented, and that the grantee will enjoy quiet possession of the property; a deed that provides the greatest amount of protection for the grantee.

WATERED STOCK ■ Shares of stock issued by a corporation for which the corporation receives, as payment, less than the stated value of the shares.

WETLANDS ■ Water-saturated areas of land that are designated by government agencies (such as the Army Corps of Engineers or the Environmental Protection Agency) as protected areas that support wildlife and therefore cannot be filled in or dredged by private contractors or parties without a permit.

WHISTLEBLOWING ■ An employee's disclosure to government authorities, upper-level managers, or the press that the employer is engaged in unsafe or illegal activities.

WHITE-COLLAR CRIME ■ Nonviolent crime committed by individuals or corporations to obtain a personal or business advantage.

WILL ■ An instrument directing what is to be done with the testator's property on his or her death, made by the testator and revocable during his or her lifetime. No interests in the testator's property pass until the testator dies.

WILL SUBSTITUTES ■ Various documents that attempt to dispose of an estate in the same or similar manner as a will, such as trusts or life insurance plans.

WINDING UP ■ The second of two stages in the termination of a partnership or corporation. Once the firm is dissolved, it continues to exist legally until the process of winding up all business affairs (collecting and distributing the firm's assets) is complete.

WORKERS' COMPENSATION LAWS ■ State statutes establishing an administrative procedure for compensating workers' injuries that arise out of—or in the course of—their employment, regardless of fault.

WORKOUT ■ An out-of-court agreement between a debtor and creditors in which the parties work out a payment plan or schedule under which the debtor's debts can be discharged.

WRIT OF ATTACHMENT ■ A court's order, issued prior to a trial to collect a debt, directing the sheriff or other officer to seize nonexempt property of the debtor. If the creditor prevails at trial, the seized property can be sold to satisfy the judgment.

WRIT OF CERTIORARI ■ A writ from a higher court asking the lower court for the record of a case.

WRIT OF EXECUTION ■ A court's order, issued after a judgment has been entered against the debtor, directing the sheriff to seize (levy) and sell any of the debtor's nonexempt real or personal property. The proceeds of the sale are used to pay off the judgment, accrued interest, and costs of the sale; any surplus is paid to the debtor.

WRONGFUL DISCHARGE ■ An employer's termination of an employee's employment in violation of the law.

TABLE OF CASES

U

V

W

Y

Z

INDEX

E

F

G

H

M

N

S

U